The Dreyfus Affair

A Chronological History

In this impressive work, George Whyte has assembled in unprecedented detail the evidence surrounding one of the most bitterly contested moments in modern European history. It will become a standard reference work for those interested in this fascinating case.
Professor Sir Jonathan Sacks
Chief Rabbi of the United Kingdom and Commonwealth

The sad history of the Dreyfus Affair is as relevant in today's battle against racism as it was in the days so uniquely and remarkably set out in George Whyte's new book. It is important both for its meticulous historical accuracy and for the mirror that it holds up to the past, reflecting the grim and growing dangers both for the present and of the future.
Lord Janner of Braunstone, QC, Chairman, Holocaust Educational Trust, London

George Whyte takes his distinguished place in the continuity of the great works on the Dreyfus Affair. He has placed at the disposal of the English speaking public a remarkable resource of study and reflection on the immortal Affair. We thank him profoundly and wish the book all the success it merits.
Dr Jean-Louis Levy (Dreyfus), Grandson of Captain Dreyfus, Paris

The author, Chairman of the Dreyfus Society for Human Rights, has produced a work of first-rate scholarship.
The Contemporary Review, Oxford

A comprehensive account of the Dreyfus Affair, this work chronicles the drama that destabilized French society (1894-1906) and reverberated across the world. Meticulous research, new translations of key documents, a wealth of primary sources and illustrations, and a select bibliography.
Jewish Book World, New York City

Whyte has, without doubt, created the best reference book on the Affair and has written a book that is eminently suited to being used in relevant University studies.
Dr Andreas Fahrmeier, *Sehepunkte*, Munich

George R. Whyte's exemplary new publication must rank as the single most forensic account ever compiled of this sour chapter in French military, political and judicial history. What is so remarkable about this book, is the breadth and depth of the material assembled. The reader can follow, in minute detail, the day-by-day unfolding of an event which would have consequences beyond France's borders.
P. Anderson, *Quadrant*, Sydney

In his wide-ranging book George Whyte provides us not only with the most authoritative and detailed study of the Dreyfus Affair, but a historical periscope through which we see the evolution and consequences of European antisemitism.
Shalom Magazine, Rome

This remarkable work of erudition will serve as an authoritative reference book for any serious student of l'Affaire Dreyfus and the evolution of European antisemitism.
Dr Frederick Rosner, *South African Jewish Observer*

The Dreyfus Affair finally brought alive with urgency and relevance to the current crisis of proliferating global antisemitism. How antisemitism can, and does, engulf both its perpetrators and the object of their hatred is both the compelling question and response that fuels Whyte's analysis of the Affair.
Dr George Halasz, *Australian Jewish News*, Melbourne

The style of this book is unique. At virtually every step, the reader is prompted to question the responsibility of the protagonists and, more generally, the responsibility of the citizens.
L'Arche Magazine, Paris

George R. Whyte

The Dreyfus Affair

A Chronological History

Foreword by Sir Martin Gilbert

First published in hardback 2005

First published in paperback 2008 by
PALGRAVE MACMILLAN
Houndmills, Basingstoke, Hampshire RG21 6XS and
175 Fifth Avenue, New York, N.Y. 10010
Companies and representatives throughout the world

PALGRAVE MACMILLAN is the global academic imprint of the Palgrave
Macmillan division of St. Martin's Press, LLC and of Palgrave Macmillan Ltd.
Macmillan® is a registered trademark in the United States, United Kingdom
and other countries. Palgrave is a registered trademark in the European
Union and other countries.

ISBN-13: 978-1-4039-3829-9 hardback
ISBN-10: 1-4039-3829-6 hardback
ISBN-13: 978-0-230-20285-6 paperback
ISBN-10: 0-230-20285-3 paperback

This book is printed on paper suitable for recycling and made from fully
managed and sustained forest sources. Logging, pulping and manufacturing
processes are expected to conform to the environmental regulations of the
country of origin.

A catalogue record for this book is available from the British Library.

A catalogue record for this book is available from the Library of Congress.

10   9   8   7   6   5   4   3   2   1
17 16 15 14 13 12 11 10 09 08

Printed and bound in Great Britain by
CPI Antony Rowe, Chippenham and Eastbourne

For

Sally

Caroline and David

Gaby, Alix, Aimée and their children to be

Be quick and courageous
to confront any sign of injustice,
lest it grows to engulf you

Le Petit Journal

Le Petit Journal
CHAQUE JOUR 5 CENTIMES
Le Supplément illustré
CHAQUE SEMAINE 5 CENTIMES

SUPPLÉMENT ILLUSTRÉ
Huit pages : CINQ centimes

ABONNEMENTS

	TROIS MOIS	SIX MOIS	UN AN
PARIS	1 fr.	2 fr.	3 fr. 50
DÉPARTEMENTS	1 fr.	2 fr.	4 fr.
ÉTRANGER	1 50	2 50	5 fr.

Cinquième année · DIMANCHE 23 DÉCEMBRE 1894 · Numéro 214

Le capitaine Dreyfus devant le conseil de guerre

Captain Dreyfus at his court martial in Paris, 1894

CONTENTS

Part 1: Politics and Protagonists: 1789–July 1894   1

French Revolution – Franco-Prussian War – Establishment of the Third
Republic – The Section de Statistique – Antisemitism in France –
Boulangism – La *'voie ordinaire'* – La Libre Parole – Panama scandal
– *Ce canaille de D.*

Part 2: Arrest and Court Martial: July–December 1894   23

Genesis of the Affair – Discovery of the *bordereau* – Arrest of Dreyfus
– Du Paty's Investigation – Press coverage – Pannizardi's telegram
of 2 November – D'Ormescheville's preliminary investigation – The
Secret Dossier – Du Paty's commentary – Court martial of Dreyfus
– Henry's false testimony – Conviction of Dreyfus

Part 3: Degradation and Devil's Island: January 1895–January 1896   57

Public degradation – Rumours of an alleged confession – Mathieu's
researches – Journey to Devil's Island – Picquart's appointment as
head of the Section de Statistique

Part 4: Treachery: March 1896–16 October 1897   73

The *petit bleu* – Picquart's secret investigation of Esterhazy – *'Pour les
Juifs'* – Picquart's discovery of Esterhazy's involvement – Revelations
by L'Eclair – The Gonse–Picquart conflict – Lucie's supplication to
the Pope – Conspiracy against Picquart – The *faux Henry* – Bernard
Lazare's *Une erreur judiciare* – Facsimile of the *bordereau* published
– The transfer of Picquart – The Speranza letter – Schemes against
Picquart – The intervention of Scheurer-Kestner – Compilation of a
second Secret Dossier

Part 5: Collusion: 16 October–December 1897   109

The collusion of the military – The Espérance letter – Meeting at the
parc Montsouris – Esterhazy's approach to the President – Scheurer-
Kestner's campaign for a revision – The *document libérateur* and *la
dame voilée* – Speranza and Blanche telegrams – Mathieu's public
denunciation of Esterhazy – Pellieux's first investigation of Esterhazy
– La *note aux deux écritures* – Pellieux's second investigation – The
faux Otto – The Boulancy letters – 'Le Syndicat' – *'Il n'y a pas d'affaire
Dreyfus'* – Ravary's judicial investigation – The *'bordereau annoté'*

Part 9: Exoneration: 1901–July 1906   **303**

Cinq années de ma vie – The Government of Emile Combes – Death of Zola – Jaurès' interpellation in the Chamber – General André's investigation – The appeal of Dreyfus for a revision – Second revision: Criminal Chamber's hearing – Second revision investigation: Criminal Chamber – Law of separation of Church and State – Second revision: Combined Chambers' hearing – Proclamation of the innocence of Dreyfus – Exoneration of Dreyfus

Part 10: Legacies, Memories and Repercussions: 1907–2006   **319**

Transfer of Zola's ashes to the Pantheon/Assassination attempt on Dreyfus – The Camelots du roi – Outbreak of World War I – The Dreyfus family during World War I – Esterhazy–Waverly–Smith articles – Theatre riots – L'Affaire Stavisky – Assault on the Palais Bourbon – Death of Dreyfus – Government of Léon Blum – Outbreak of World War II – Fall of the Third Republic: Foundation of Vichy France – La rafle du Vélodrome d'hiver – Conviction of Maurras – Declaration of the State of Israel – 50th anniversary of Zola's death/Cause of Zola's death questioned – The Dreyfus statue – The Dreyfus centenary – Centenary of Zola's 'J'Accuse'

LIST OF ILLUSTRATIONS

ABBREVIATIONS AND CONVENTION USED IN THE NOTES

AD	Leblois, Louis, *L'Affair Dreyfus, L'Iniquité, la réparation. Les principaux faits et les principaux documents* (Paris: Quillet, 1929).
ATQV	Dreyfus, Mathieu, *L'Affaire telle que je l'ai vécue* (Paris: Grasset, 1978).
ASD	Thomas, Marcel, *L'Affaire sans Dreyfus* (Paris: Fayard, 1961).
DFA	Burns, Michael, *Dreyfus, a Family Affair* (New York: HarperCollins, 1991).
DC	Charpentier, Armand, *The Dreyfus Case*. Translated from French by J. Lewis May (London: Geoffrey Bles, 1935).
DT	Chapman, Guy, *The Dreyfus Trials* (London: Batsford, 1972).
HAD	Reinach, Joseph, *Histoire de l'Affaire Dreyfus* (Paris: Edition de la Revue Blanche & Fasquelle, 1901–1911) 7 vols.
Déb. Cass., 1898	*La révision du procès Dreyfus à la cour de cassation (27–29 octobre 1898)* compte-rendu sténographique 'in extenso' (Paris: Stock, 1898).
Cass.	*Enquête de la cour de cassation* (Paris: Stock, 1899) 2 vols (*Instruction de la chambre criminelle* – vol. I; *Instruction des chambres réunies* – vol. II).
Déb. Cass., 1899	*La révision du procès Dreyfus. Débats de la cour de cassation (Rapport de M. Ballot-Beaupré; conclusion de M. le procureur général Manau; mémoire et plaidoirie de Maître Mornard; arrêt de la cour)* (Paris: Stock, 1899).
Déb. Cass., 1904	*La révision du procès Dreyfus. Débats de la cour de cassation (3–5 mars 1904)* (Paris: Ligue française pour la défense des droits de l'Homme et du citoyen, 1904).
3ème Cass.,	*Enquête de la chambre criminelle (5 mars–19 novembre 1904)* (Paris: Ligues des droits de l'Homme, 1908–1909), 3 vols.
Déb. Cass., 1906	*La révision du procès Dreyfus. Débats de la cour de cassation. Chambres réunies. (15 juin–12 juillet 1906)* (Paris: Ligue des droits de l'Homme, 1906) 2 vols.
Fabre	*L'Instruction Fabre et les décision judiciaires ultérieures [Le procès du colonel Picquart et de Me Leblois]* (Paris: Le Siècle, 1901).

Pro. Zola　　　*Le Procès Zola devant la cour d'assisses de la Seine et la cour de Cassation (7–23 février et 31 mars–2 avril 1898)* compte rendu sténographique 'in extenso et documents annexes (Paris: Stock, 1898) 2 vols.

Rennes　　　*Le Procès Dreyfus devant le conseil de guerre de Rennes (7 août–9 septembre)* compte rendu sténographique 'in extenso' (Paris: Stock, 1900) 3 vols.

Répertoire　　　Desachy, Paul, *Répertoire de l'Affaire Dreyfus* (1894–1899), (n.p., n.d. [privately printed] [1905]).

Révision　　　Guyot, Yves, *La Révision du procès Dreyfus, faits et documents juridiques* (Paris: Stock, 1898).

CREDITS and ACKNOWLEDGEMENTS

Livia Parnes principal researcher

On completion of *The Dreyfus Affair: A Chronological History,* the author would like to record the outstanding contributions of

Elisabeth Maxwell-Meynard (senior adviser)
Elizabeth Stone (editorial adviser)
Sarah Nathan-Whyte (pictorial history)
Eva Foley-Comer (co-ordination)
The Dreyfus Society for Human Rights.

On completion of two intensive periods of research on the Dreyfus Affair – 1984–94 for the preparation of *The Dreyfus Trilogy* and 2002–05 for the preparation of *The Dreyfus Affair: A Chronological History* – the author expresses his gratitude to

Jean-Louis Lévy

France Beck; Charles Dreyfus; Simone Perl

Françoise Basch; Jean-Denis Bredin; Michael Burns; Norman Kleeblatt

Barthold C. Witte

Dieter W. Benecke; Horst Dahlhaus; Udi Eichler; Götz Friedrich

Patricia Benecke; Agnes Bruma; Caroline Buchler-Whyte;
Diane Buckingham; Adina Eshelmen; Isabelle Fessaguet;
Ray Foley-Comer; Ulrich Josten, Dorothée Koehler;
Doris Langer; Sophie Rosenfeld; Karen Sanig

Alliance Israélite Universelle, Paris; Archives Municipales de Rixheim; Archivio Segreto Vaticano; Leo Baeck Library, London; Leo Baeck Institute, New York; Bibliothèque Cantonale et Universitaire, Lausanne; Bibliothèque du Haut Plateau, Crans-sur-Sierre; Bibliothèque Historique de la Ville de Paris; Bibliothèque Municipale de Mulhouse; the Bodleian Library, Oxford; the British Library, London; Zentrale Bibliothek der Freien Universität, Berlin; Centre de Documentation Juive Contemporaine, Paris; French Embassy, London; Fondation Bellanger, Martigny; Jewish Museum, New York; the Hebrew University, Jerusalem; the Houghton Library, Harvard University, Massachusetts; the Jewish Chronicle Library, London; Kunstbibliothek und Staatsbibliothek der Stiftung Preußischer Kulturbesitz, Berlin; the Knesset Archives, Jerusalem; Musée de Bretagne, Rennes; the Public Library, New York; Österreichische Nationalbibliothek, Vienna; Staatsbibliothek, Vienna; Zentrum für Antisemitismusforschung, Technische Universität Berlin; the Sourasky Central Library, Tel Aviv; Wiener Library Institute of Contemporary History, London; Yale University Library, Connecticut and the many other private and public sources.

Picture Credits

The genealogical tree (page xxxii) incorporates information from *Dreyfus, A Family Affair 1789-1945* (New York: HarperCollins, 1991), courtesy of the author Michael Burns and from the Rixheim Municipal Archives by courtesy of Benoît Meyer; the Ketubbah (page 12) is reproduced by courtesy of the National Library of the Hebrew University, Jerusalem. Maps drawn by Bow Watkinson on information supplied by the author. All other illustrations are from The Whyte Archives of French, English and German contemporary images, periodicals and publications, in particular *Le Petit Journal* (Paris), pages vi, 58, 164, 187 (left) ; *L'Illustration* (Paris), pages 24, 65 (bottom), 131, 160, 190, 202, 222, 234, 235, 241, 260, 311; *The Graphic* (London), pages 35, 40, 68, 183, 263, 276, 277, 285; F.W. Esterhazy, *Les dessous de l'affaire Dreyfus* (Paris: Fayard, 1898), pages 45, 48, 77, 110, 115, 146, 175, 179, 193, 197, 304; and the illustrations on pages 83 and 97 have appeared in various French and German contemporary editions of A. Dreyfus, *Cinq années de ma vie, 1894-1899.* Despite every effort it has not been possible to trace the original sources of some images. Any information which may come to light will be incorporated in any future edition.

Author's special acknowledgements

The modest credits and acknowledgements pay inadequate tribute to the friendship, counsel and encouragement received over two decades from so many individuals and institutions. I am grateful to them all. For this volume I owe a particular debt of gratitude to Elisabeth Maxwell-Meynard, who cared and advised; Livia Parnes, whose devoted and meticulous research informs all of the chronology; the great historian Martin Gilbert for his far-seeing introduction; Eva Foley-Comer, who was a mainstay throughout all the phases of this undertaking, and my wife Sally, who stood staunchly by my side during an arduous journey as a Dreyfusard and whose forbearance has earned her a place among the just.

FOREWORD

Winston Churchill was in Paris when the Dreyfus case was at its height. He was 18 years old. 'Bravo Zola!' he wrote to his mother. 'I am delighted to witness the complete debacle of this monstrous conspiracy.'

Familiar though the outlines of the Dreyfus Case may be, the detail is vast and complex, deserving the treatment it is given in these pages. One thing struck me as I read the material that George Whyte and his principal researcher have so patiently and thoroughly pieced together: that even the 'familiar' outlines are often misunderstood or misrepresented.

George Whyte sets the record straight, and in doing so, shows what a landmark and turning point this scandalous episode in French – and European – history was, and how much it needs to be studied today, in the light of all the evidence that he has assembled with such diligence.

Dreyfus, an assimilated Jew, had become a captain on the French General Staff in 1892, and the only Jew in this central part of the French military establishment. Two years later, aged 35, he was tried in secret by a French military court and found guilty of treason. Sentenced to life imprisonment, he was publicly demoted in a degrading ceremony, at which a well-coached crowd fulminated against him and against all Jews. He was then sent to Devil's Island, in French Guyana, off the coast of South America, a harsh, evil place, where he languished for over four grim years. But in France the campaign for justice was growing. In 1899 a second court martial was held. He was still found guilty of treason, but his sentence was reduced from life to ten years (five of which he had already served).

The campaign to assert Dreyfus' innocence and to secure his release continued. Finally, in 1906, a Court of Appeal declared that the evidence against him had no basis in fact. Dreyfus was reinstated in the army and received the Legion of Honour.

George Whyte has done a great service in publishing an annotated, day-by-day, documentary account of that 'monstrous conspiracy', the conviction of a French Jewish officer, Captain Alfred Dreyfus, on trumped-up charges of espionage for Germany.

The significance of the Dreyfus case spans both Jewish and European history. For Europe, it was a stark revelation of how vicious antisemitism could be, at the highest reaches of civilized Christian society. For Jewish history it showed how essential it was to challenge every manifestation of antisemitic behaviour.

One result of the long struggle to clear Dreyfus' name was the successful defence of Mendel Beilis in the Blood Libel trial in Russia 15 years later. Another was the court case in Switzerland in 1934 at which the forgery of the *Protocols of the Learned Elders of Zion* was exposed.

An important aspect of this book is the 55 appendices. These begin, rightly and wisely, with the full text of the Declaration of the Rights of Man and the Citizen, issued on 26 August 1789, a pivotal document of the French Revolution at its most humanitarian moment. The appendices include the interrogations of Dreyfus, the verdict of the first court martial, the letter from Dreyfus to the President of the French Republic, sent from the degraded Captain's incarceration on Devil's Island, extracts of Dreyfus' letters to his wife from the island, the official report of his incarceration, extracts from Emile Zola's trial, and the text of two antisemitic songs.

There are many villains in this book, and several heroes. Standing out as a persistent champion of justice is Zola, whose article 'J'Accuse' – an open letter to the French President – first appeared in a special edition of the newspaper *L'Aurore* in 300,000 copies. 'When the truth is buried underground,' Zola wrote, 'it builds up there, it gains the force of an explosion such that, on the day it erupts, it blows up everything with it.'

Zola recognized that in setting out a list of those whom he accused of a miscarriage of justice in the Dreyfus case, he was making himself liable to prosecution. This did not deter him, he explained to the President. 'The action I am taking here,' he noted in his letter, 'is simply a revolutionary way of hastening the explosion of truth and justice. I have only one passion, that of enlightenment, in the name of humanity, which has suffered so much and has a right to happiness. My impassioned protest is only the cry of my soul.'

Zola was tried and sent to prison for this 'cry' of his soul, one more miscarriage of justice along the stony road to fair play. This book shows just how stony – and stormy – that road to justice became.

The shadow of antisemitism hangs over these pages, as it hung over the whole, long evolution of the Dreyfus Case. George Whyte notes how, in three of the Departments of France, directories were in print that listed all Jewish people in the regions and giving their business addresses. Similar lists were to be published four decades later by the Vichy Government of Marshal Pétain. During the antisemitic riots that broke out in France in January 1898 – the very month of Zola's protest – women were urged to boycott Jewish shops.

The Dreyfus case marked a dramatic high-point in the struggle of the soul of the French people. It was a struggle that was to re-emerge in all its fury after the German defeat of France in 1940: between those who found solace in right-wing and fascist values, and those for whom such values were a terrible negation of the French championing of liberty, equality and fraternity.

The case was also a dramatic turning point in the Jewish struggle for fair treatment as a people. Among those who reported on the case from Paris was a Jewish journalist from Vienna, Theodor Herzl. He was shocked by the antisemitic outbursts in France at the time of the trials. If a country as liberal and as cultured as France could spew out hatred of the Jews, might not the Jewish people be better served by a country of their own?

Dreyfus went on to serve in the French Army in World War I, responsible for the preparation of armaments being sent to the front. His son Pierre fought on the Marne, at Verdun and on the Somme. His nephew Emile was killed by a German shell on the Western Front.

Alfred Dreyfus died in 1935, with the rank of lieutenant-colonel, and was spared the sight of the renewed, German-fuelled persecutions of French Jewry, and of his own family. His widow was saved from deportation by Catholic nuns who gave her shelter. Several relatives fought in the French Resistance (one, his brother's grandson, was killed while parachuting back into France: the local Pétainist officials refused to bury him). Dreyfus' granddaughter, Madeleine Dreyfus Lévy, was deported to Auschwitz two days after her 25th birthday. She died there a month later.

The story of Dreyfus is both central, and a microcosm, of the story of French Jews. In these pages one can follow that story at its most anguished and intense, crafted by a mastercraftsman.

Martin Gilbert

Other works by the Author on the Dreyfus Affair

LITERARY

1994   *The Dreyfus Centenary Bulletin*
        (London/Bonn: The Dreyfus Centenary Committee)

1994   *L'Affaire en chanson*
        (Paris: Bibliothèque de documentation internationale
        contemporaine BDIC; Paris; Flammarion)

1994   *Unrecht – und kein Ende*
        (Berlin, Bonn, Basel: Programme Books)

1995   *Le Prix d'illusion*
        (Geneva: Revue Juive)

1995   *Un bilan du centenaire de l'Affaire Dreyfus*
        (Paris: Cahiers Jean Jaurès, No 136)

1996   *The Accused – The Dreyfus Trilogy*
        (Bonn: Inter Nationes)

1996   *Die Affäre Dreyfus als Rorschach-Test*
        (Berlin, Die Welt)

STAGE

1988   *AJIOM*
        (London: Artial)

1992   *Dreyfus Die Affäre*
        (Berlin, Basel and New York:London Coda Editions)

2002   *Dreyfus fragments*
        (London: Coda Editions)

2003   *Intimate letters*
        (London: Coda Editions)

TELEVISION & RADIO

1994   *Rage et Outrage*
        (France, ARTE)

1994   *Zorn und Schande*
        (Germany, ARTE)

1994   *Rage and Outrage*
        (UK, Channel 4)

1996   *Dreyfus – J'Accuse*
        (Germany WDR; Sweden STV1, Slovenia RTV/SLO, Finland YLE)

1998   *J'Accuse*
        (Canada, CBS)

AUTHOR'S PREFACE

From Dreyfus to Drancy – The Power of Prejudice

The chronological format in which this work is presented has been designed to enable the reader to follow, on a day-by-day basis, the evolution of a singular act of injustice into a world affair, its diverse ramifications and, within a broad historical context, gain an insight into its roots, consequences and issues of universal significance. Its aim is to provide an accurate and impartial account of the facts as they are known, the theories and suppositions put forward by historians and commentators, yet leaving the reader to form his or her own conclusions. The appendices serve to illuminate the main issues.

A deliberate miscarriage of justice, masterminded by the army, condoned by its judiciary, fuelled by racial prejudice, political skulduggery and a nascent press combined to create the Dreyfus Affair. Variously classified as a French affair, a Military affair, a Family affair, a Jewish affair – it was all of these and more.

The Dreyfus Affair went far beyond the confines of France at the turn of the 20th century, beyond too, the story of the innocent Captain Alfred Dreyfus, an unwanted Jew on the French General Staff. It was a series of events that brought into the spotlight a host of political, social and moral issues. It split France in two, saw the emergence of the intellectual and the engagement of the citizen and paved the way for new forms of civic and political expression. Its repercussions were and remain worldwide. Further afield, the Affair became a crucible for a host of human rights issues such as racism and the rights of the individual against the organs of State. Today, the Affair remains a touchstone for issues of primary importance for our societies.

An injustice becomes an affair when social passions and conflicting ideologies are aroused. France was torn by conflict – friends and relatives clashed, every dinner party and street corner became a battleground. The country was in turmoil. Society was divided, families were split. Dreyfusards clashed with anti-dreyfusards. Violence was in the air. Antisemitic riots ravaged the cities of France. An emerging media, flexing its muscles for the battles of the 20th century, propelled the fate of one soldier into history and the Affair shed its light and cast its shadow into every home in France and eventually abroad.

'Death to the Jews' drowned the protests of Alfred Dreyfus during his public degradation as he was stripped of his rank, his honour and ironically, the emblems of the very ideals which had guided his life, love of the army and devotion to the Patrie. His calvary was to last 12 years and the Affair it precipitated was to become one of the most troubled periods in the history of France, recording for future generations the far seeing testimony of the social turbulence of the times and its implications for the century to follow. The scene of this drama was set by two historical events many centuries apart: the humiliating defeat of France in the Franco-Prussian War of 1870–71 and the appearance of the Gospels 1800 years earlier.

The defeat of France in the Franco-Prussian War dealt a grievous blow to the pride of the nation. The army became the sacred instrument of revenge. It would recapture the lost territories of Alsace-Lorraine and regain France's honour. The army was revered, it was beyond reproach. It was the hallowed institution whose General Staff Alfred Dreyfus joined as a probationary officer in 1893.

The influx of foreigners and Jews into France in the second half of the 19th century met with mounting antagonism from the populace and in an atmosphere of growing xenophobia the slogan 'France for the French' became paramount. Antisemitism gathered pace when the writer Edouard Drumont, who was to become known as the 'Pope of Antisemitism', arrived on the scene. The Catholic Church and the Assumptionist daily *La Croix* had long maintained an anti-Jewish stance and the venom of Drumont would drive their bigotry to fever pitch. 'To be French was to be Catholic'. All others, especially Jews, were suspect. These undercurrents – France's defeat by Germany, reverence for the army and mistrust of the Jew – were to converge in the Affair and burst the dams of all social restraint, creating a torrent of hate and abuse on an unprecedented scale.

The Affair's galaxy of dramatis personae – as Pierre Dreyfus (the son of Alfred) described its main protagonists – exhibited the whole gamut of human virtues and failings. General Mercier, the intransigent Minister of War who, for reasons never discovered, continued to affirm the guilt of Dreyfus long after he was declared innocent; the courageous Lieutenant-Colonel Picquart, not without his own prejudices, whose devotion to truth, 'the greatest service I can render my country', took precedence over his obedience as an army officer; Emile Zola, who turned the tide of history with his audacious 'J'Accuse', the first mediatic response to an injustice and history's most famous plea for human rights; Edouard Drumont, whose ranting antisemitism became a rallying cry of hatred; Major Henry whose devotion to the army was rooted in dishonesty and the dissolute Major Esterhazy who proudly asserted that he 'only lied on orders' and whose pliable morality made him the ideal servant of a morally corrupt General Staff. And then, Lucie Dreyfus, a paragon of loyalty striving to survive as the reviled wife of a traitor; Mathieu Dreyfus, the 'good' and devoted brother, steadfast in his mission to exonerate Alfred. And the central character, exiled from his Affair on Devil's Island, in solitary confinement, stoically enduring his mental and physical torture, unaware of the passions his fate had unleashed which were tearing his country apart – a victim of his own illusions, never understanding that he was the unwanted Jewish officer, the unwelcome intruder. Paradoxically, his world contracted as the Affair expanded and, as perceived by Hannah Arendt, the dramas of 20th-century France went into rehearsal.

In the world beyond Devil's Island an anxious Europe was awaiting the day of reckoning. Alliances were being forged but trust was at a low ebb; espionage and counter-espionage were rife. The reader, when embarking on a study of the Affair, is well advised to remember Esterhazy's dictum: 'in espionage and counter-espionage nothing is as it seems to be'. Therein lie the fascination and frustrations of the Affair. Information collides with misinformation; the absence of information is compensated by a plethora of credible and incredible theories. Lies, forgeries, duplicity and cover-ups were the rule of the day in a 'kaleidoscopic' affair whose shifting elements allow any number of configurations.

However the reader navigates this quagmire of contradictions – whose evaluation becomes a personal choice – he will reach the unresolved questions which lurk at the heart of the Affair. Who wrote the *bordereau* and why? What did Henry know that necessitated his death, and who was the person he indicated in his letter to his wife Berthe just before he died, 'you know in whose interest I acted'? What was the 'terrible secret' that Esterhazy recalled on his death bed and which guaranteed his protection by the General Staff, whatever the circumstance, but demanded his exile, never to set foot in France again? Were the two men guardians of the same secret? Was there a high-ranking 'officer X', as suggested by Paléologue, who was a spy and whose identity had to be kept secret at all cost? These are unfinished chapters which will no doubt continue to attract further investigation. Meticulous research in Russian, Italian and German archives may yield some clues.

The Affair was not without its visionaries. Zola, horrified by the eruption of antisemitism addressed his letters to France and to France's youth:

> *France, you have allowed the rage of hatred to lash the face of your people, poisoned and fanatic they scream in the streets 'Down with the Jews', 'Death to the Jews'.*
>
> *What sorrow, what anxiety at the dawn of the 20th century.*

George Clemenceau, foreseeing the emergence of the totalitarian state, warned:

> *when the right of a single individual is injured, the right of all is in peril, the right of the nation itself.*

But Drumont had preceded them. Planting the signpost which would eventually lead to Drancy, he predicted with spine-chilling accuracy:

> *the Jews must be eternally blind as they have always been not to realise what is awaiting them. They will be taken away as scrap ... The leader who will suddenly emerge will have the right of life and death ... he will be able to employ any means that suit his purpose. The great organiser will achieve a result which will resound throughout this universe.*

The appearance of the Gospels, which led to the accusation of deicide against the Jewish people, marked the genesis of the longest libel in history. Enriched by groundless accusations and calumnies over the centuries, poisoning of wells, Satanic practices, taking the blood of Christian children for Passover, a Jewish stereotype emerged, a Judas figure, increasingly despised and increasingly embedded into the culture of Christian Europe. The Jews, a defenceless minority, were never in a position to challenge these allegations and unchallenged allegations harden into fact. The Jews became, by definition, guilty. As in the case of Alfred Dreyfus, evidence never reached the scales of justice but was moulded to corroborate the prejudice.

Dreyfus was doubly betrayed. Firstly, the collective conscience of his judges responded more to Jesuit indoctrination and unquestioning obedience to army discipline than the call of justice; secondly, after the callous Rennes verdict, an ignoble pardon was followed by a hurried amnesty bill in 1900 to close the unfinished chapters and stifle the embarrassing course of justice.

Nevertheless, the Dreyfus Affair was a turning point in French and European history and triggered many major developments: the strengthening of the Republic; the separation of Church and State; the power of the media and its manipulation of public opinion; Herzl's vision of a Jewish State and his manifesto *Judenstadt*. It paved the way for the publication of the fraudulent *Protocols of the Learned Elders of Zion*, consolidated anti-Jewish sentiments and laid the groundwork for the excesses of Vichy France.

Above all, the Affair was a warning signal highlighting the fragility of human rights in our most 'developed' societies. Although it is arguable whether antisemitism was the most significant aspect of the Affair, it was this aspect whose significance became paramount in the century that followed, when human rights were desecrated to the point of annihilating a whole people. It is therefore vital to examine the power of prejudice and its mechanism, as revealed in the Dreyfus Affair.

Dreyfus recalls in his diary how, as a young boy, he cried with sadness as he watched the German Army march into his home town Mulhouse during the Franco-Prussian War. He swore to become a soldier and drive the enemy from his country. He kept his promise and began the hazardous march of an assimilationist Jew to become a successful French officer, trespassing the threshold of tolerance in a bigoted terrain which was to lead him to his calvary. At the age of 35 he was a captain in the French Army and posted to the General Staff. For him, his Judaism was unimportant – for his adversaries it was all important. He did not or would not recognize that admission was not acceptance and thereby became an accomplice to his own martyrdom.

How often did Dreyfus experience expressions of antisemitism and how often did he ignore its warnings? Did he really not realize that he was living in a society in which antisemitism had become part of its fabric? Did he not read Drumont's rantings which perpetuated the calumnies levelled at Jews since the dawn of Christianity? Was he not aware of the editorials in *La Libre Parole* warning against their admission into the army? Dreyfus tried to ignore these impediments and paid for his illusions with degradation, imprisonment and exile. And although, in a unique moment of history, the injustice to one Jew became a world affair, its lessons in the vast arena of human rights have remained unlearned.

Rumblings of the Affair continued and do so to this day. The first war passed with its horrors, to be surpassed by the second with its atrocities. Members of the Dreyfus family fought valiantly, served in the Resistance and died, other family members were deported in the transports from Drancy to Auschwitz where they perished. The venomous 'Death to the Jews' was transformed into reality.

History and the passage of time have made the Dreyfus Affair a Rorschach test for all those who come into contact with it. It exposes bigotry, hypocrisy and guilt with unnerving clarity. Set in a drama where prejudice prevailed over reason, the victory of justice was finally achieved at the price of great personal suffering and national shame. In its struggle for human rights the Affair reached heroic proportions, and in the writings of Charles Péguy, a mystical dimension.

Dreyfus was exonerated of all the charges against him except that of being a Jew, and in 20 years of research and reflection on the Affair, its most penetrating summary came from a Parisian taxi driver whom I asked what he knew about the Dreyfus Affair: 'Ah, Monsieur,' he explained, 'a strange story. It was all about a French officer who was accused of being Jewish.'

George R. Whyte
Chairman – The Dreyfus Society for Human Rights
April 2005

GUIDE TO THE CHRONOLOGY

The Chronology has been structured to help the reader around a complex web of information. Part 1 is intended primarily for those unfamiliar with the history of the late nineteenth century or who are coming to the Affair for the first time. It introduces some of the main political and cultural events from the French Revolution of 1789 to the Affair proper. Its aim is to outline some of the themes crucial to the development of the Affair – the increase in Franco–German rivalry, the development of espionage and counter-espionage, the fragile hold of the Third Republic, France's stance vis-à-vis her Jewish population – and places the history of the Dreyfus family, and to some extent the other protagonists of the Affair, within the context of these historical strands.

The main focus of this volume, however, is the historical period between 1894 and 1906 that saw the arrest, conviction, deportation and eventual rehabilitation of Captain Alfred Dreyfus. This period is covered in Parts 2 – 9 of the Chronology. Inevitably, these sections bear the weight of the book, and cover events in far more detail than the first and last sections.

The final part, Part 10, deals with the aftermath, memories and perceptions of the Affair up to the present day. It covers the fate of the Dreyfus family during World Wars I and II, the expansion of nationalist movements in France, which had their origins in the Dreyfus Affair, the authoritarian regime of Vichy France (1940–44). Also emphasized is the fate of Jews in France during World War II, as well as an ongoing debate over the role of religious minorities, racism, xenophobia and antisemitism.

The chronological text and the section endnotes play different roles in this work. The intention has been to allow the main body of the Chronology to relate contemporary events as they unfold, without comment; the notes, on the other hand, offer interpretation, comment and supplementary information either not available at the time or developed since; they also point to historical debates, past and present, provide source references and suggest further reading.

The appendices have been selected with the aim of either elucidating or developing points described, mentioned or alluded to in the main body of the Chronology. Many are taken from sources previously unpublished in English.

To present the events of this complex Affair as they happened day by day has demanded some compromises; sometimes it was necessary to deviate from a strict chronological approach and group events sequentially into a series of parallel events. The various trials and investigations, for example, fall into this category. To maintain a rigidly chronological approach would have meant that the reader could not have followed the progress of a given thread. One series of parallel events inevitably overlaps with others, and also with events taking place simultaneously but outside the series of 'parallel' events.

Various visual devices have been used to help the reader distinguish the interlocking elements of the Chronology. Events relating to Dreyfus' sojourn on Devil's Island, as distinct from the development of the Affair elsewhere, are presented as tinted text areas. Events that unfold simultaneously and in parallel to events documented earlier or subsequently are indicated by sets of parallel rules. Other events, movements or developments that influenced or created a political or cultural situation are set within the Chronology and are slightly separated from the running text by additional spacing.

In the main body of the Chronology, extracts quoted in English from the original French are the author's own translations unless otherwise stated. Bibliographical references are to the original French in such cases. When the historical information in the main body of the Chronology does not involve a translation, the notes refer to the English editions of books translated from foreign languages. The translations given here retain the spirit of the original sources, but are also faithful and accurate renderings of the sources: the balance is often difficult to strike, especially as the literary styles and the formalities of behaviour are unfamiliar to readers of the 21st century.

There are slight variations in the spelling and presentation of proper names at the time of the Affair and later. In the Chronology itself, spellings have been standardized for the sake of clarity; in quotations from original sources however, and in the Appendices, the original spelling and punctuation have been retained. Titles and their translation follow the sources of documentation.

Wherever possible, the notes direct the reader to the original source; but a reference is also given where this source is reproduced in Louis Leblois, *L'Affair Dreyfus, L'Iniquité, la réparation. Les principaux faits et les principaux documents* (Paris: Quillet, 1929), to direct the reader to this significant compilation of sources, accessible in various libraries around the world.

The following secondary sources were consulted frequently. Specific mention is made to them where opinions among historians are divided (concerning dates, events, interpretations), where they are referred to as first sources (i.e. when they provide specific information or indicate archive sources).

Bredin, Jean-Denis, *The Affair*. Translated from French by Jeffrey Mehlman (New York: George Braziller, 1986).

Desachy, Paul, *Répertoire de l'Affaire Dreyfus* (1894–99), (n.p., n.d. [privately printed] [1905]).

Reinach, Joseph, *Histoire de l'Affaire Dreyfus*, (Paris: Edition de la Revue Blanche (vol. 1) Fasquelles (vols 2–7), 1901–11).

Thomas, Marcel, *L'Affaire sans Dreyfus* (Paris: Fayard, 1961).

Extracts of Dreyfus' and Lucie's letters are taken from:

Dreyfus, A., *Cinq années de ma vie 1894–1899* ([1901] (Paris: La Découverte, 1994).

Dreyfus, A., *Lettres d'un Innocent* (Paris: Stock, 1898).

Dreyfus, A., Capitaine, *Souvenirs et Correspondance publiés par son fils* (Paris: Grasset, 1936).

No bibliography of the Dreyfus Affair can claim to be comprehensive – and indeed there is no need to be comprehensive given the accessibility of online catalogues in the main national libraries around the world. The bibliography presented here is selective in several respects. One of the aims of the Chronology has been to expand the field of Dreyfus studies to English-speaking readers worldwide: this is why many primary sources not previously published in English have been included in the appendices and in quoted extracts in the main text. The Affair was not only a French but also a German Affair, with repercussions worldwide; the issues it raises are ongoing and debated across the world. The bibliography therefore includes key works in English, French and German, as well as a section devoted to works in other languages.

GENEALOGY OF ALFRED DREYFUS

Recent studies of Jewish life in Alsace-Lorraine have traced the ancestry of the family of Alfred Dreyfus to Rixheim, as far back as the 17th century.[1] The medieval form of the family name was Trèves, or Trier; both of which came from the Latin Treveris, a Roman camp near Rixheim. The later name of 'Dreyfus', in the different spellings (Dreÿfuess, Dreÿfuss) used by Jewish families, shows Germanic linguistic influence in the region as it derived from two Germanic words, *drei* (three) and *fuss* (foot).[2] In the 1770s Abraham Dreÿfuss (Alfred's great-grandfather) was a butcher, providing kosher meat for the 40 practising Jewish families in the village of Rixheim but also selling to Gentiles, in accordance with strict royal commercial regulations for dealings between Jews and Gentiles. He was also a *Mohel* (a person authorized to practise circumcision). In 1781 Abraham married Brändel Meyer, from the German village of Mülheim. They spoke together a Judeo-Alsatian dialect that combined Hebrew, Aramaic, German and a few words of French.[3] From an early age, their son Jacob (Jacques – Jacques, being the French equivalent of Jacob) attended Rixheim's *heder* (Jewish elementary school), where he learned Hebrew. He later became a dealer in second-hand goods and occasional money lender. Although Jewish leaders insisted that French should be the mother tongue for Jews in France, the Dreyfus family, like most citizens in Rixheim, rarely had the opportunity to speak or learn French. However, there was a trend towards Gallicization well before Gallic names were adopted by individual families: e.g., in some French civic documents, 'Jacob Dreÿfuss' was referred to as 'Jacques Dreyfus'.[4] In 1813 Jacob married Rachel Katz. Their two first children died in infancy. Only their third child, Raphael, survived. In 1835 Jacob settled with his family in the rue de la Justice, Mülhausen.[5] He and Raphael are recorded as tradesmen. In 1841 Raphael married Jeannette Libmann, a seamstress from the French village of Ribeauvillé. In 1844 the couple's first child was born; they named him Jacques after Raphael's father.[6] Between 1848 and 1854, Jeannette gave birth to four daughters, Henriette, Berthe, Ernestine and Louise[7] and one son, Léon, born on 28 October 1854. Raphael was engaged in the textile industry. On the birth certificate of their sixth child, Rachel (5 March 1856) Raphaël for the first time spelled the family name as 'Dreyfus'. On 2 July 1857 the couple's seventh child, Mathieu, was born. On 9 October 1859, their eighth child, Alfred, was born. In the 1860s, Alfred's brothers, Jacques and Léon, were employed by their father in the textile industry. The Dreyfus family followed the liberal religious guidelines set out by the rabbi of Mulhouse,[8] Samuel Dreyfus, whose aim was to integrate the Jewish community into French society. The mother tongue of the two youngest boys, Mathieu and Alfred was, French. The children's religious instruction in Mulhouse was probably limited.

See over for Notes and Genealogical Tree

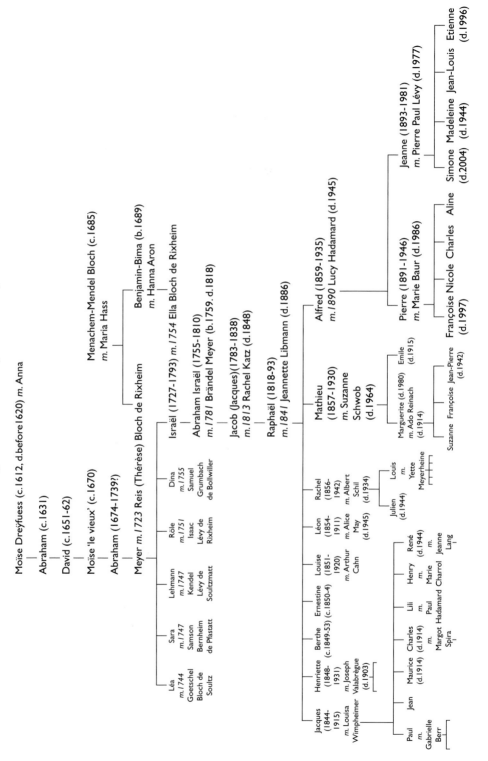

Genealogical Tree of the family of Alfred Dreyfus

NOTES

[1] O. Jurbert, 'Généalogie de la Famille Dreyfus', in *Dreyfus avant Dreyfus. Une Famille juive de Mulhouse. Catalogue de l'exposition tenue du 1er au 23 Octobre 1994 à la Filature, Mulhouse*, ed. O. Jurbert and M.C. Waille, pp. 10–14; G. Dreyfus and H.C. Mars, 'La Famille du capitaine Dreyfus', *Revue du Cercle de Généalogie Juive*, 36 (Paris, winter 1993), pp. 18–24 ; G. Boll and D. Ingold, 'Les ancêtres du capitaine Alfred Dreyfus', *Bulletin de la Société d'histoire de Rixheim*, 16 (2000), 15–20.

[2] In Alsatian documents names were usually written in German, although spellings varied from village to village. Jewish names were even more varied, changing according to pronunciation, with increasing Gallicization over time. P. Katz, 'La recherche généalogique juive en Alsace', *Revue du Cercle de Généalogie Juive*, No. 36 (Paris, winter 1993), 8–12.

[3] *DFA*, pp. 6, 17. All marriages of the Dreyfuses in this period were with members of their own faith.

[4] *DFA*, pp. 19–20.

[5] Though Mülhausen had granted temporary asylum to Jews in times of crisis, Jews were only allowed to reside there permanently from 1798, when the town became part of France.

[6] Over time the Dreyfus family's use of ancient Jewish and biblical names gradually gave way to more socially acceptable French versions. While the family continued to observe some Jewish religious practices, it leaned towards assimilation.

[7] A cholera epidemic claimed Berthe (1853) and Ernestine (1854).

[8] On the change of spelling of the town, see 1848, p. 4.

Map of France indicating locations mentioned in the Chronology

Part 1

POLITICS and PROTAGONISTS

1789–July 1894

А. ДРЕЙФУСЪ   א. דרייפוס   A. DREJFUS

Captain Alfred Dreyfus in 1894 at the age of 35

The French Revolution

1789
July 14   The storming of the Bastille marks the beginning of the French Revolution,[1] a pivotal event in European history.

July   During la Grande Peur (the Great Fear),[2] Jewish homes are pillaged in Alsace (Rixheim, Uffoltz, Durmenach, Sierentz, Blotzheim and all the villages of the Sundgau region). Nearly a thousand Jews take refuge in Basel (Switzerland) and the small town of Mülhausen.[3]

Aug 4   Representatives of the Nobility and Clergy relinquish their privileges in France's new governing body, the Assemblée nationale (the National Assembly).[4] Feudalism is consequently abolished.

Aug 26   As part of the process of drafting a new constitution, the National Constituent Assembly draws up the Declaration of the Rights of Man and the Citizen, a basic charter of human liberties.[5] It outlines principles of equality and the sovereignty of the nation. Article 10 declares: 'No one shall be disquieted on account of his opinions, including his religious views, provided their manifestation does not disturb the public order established by law'.[6] (*v.* Appendix 1)

Sept 28   Following the summer's anti-Jewish riots, the National Constituent Assembly passes a bill for the protection of Jews in Alsace.

1790
Jan 28   The Sephardic[7] Jews of south-western France and the Jews of Avignon[8] are granted French citizenship.

1791
Sept 27   All French Jews are granted full legal equality and citizenship. Consequently, a peasant uprising in Rixheim forces the town's Jews to take refuge in Mülhausen and Basel.

1793/94   During the Terror,[9] anti-Jewish violence occurs again in the villages attacked in 1789. Synagogues and Jewish cemeteries are vandalized. More Jews flee to Mülhausen and Basel.

1804   Napoleon Bonaparte declares himself Emperor of France. In addition to waging war in Europe, he initiates a vast programme of administrative, educational and cultural reform. One of the main objectives of his Jewish policy is to promote assimilation through intermarriage.

1806
July–Aug   Napoleon convenes l'Assemblée des notables (an assembly of prominent citizens) consisting of 111 Jewish representatives from all the departments of France and Northern Italy, to confer on matters relating to equal citizenship. The Assembly states that Jewish law is compatible with French civil law, but the question of intermarriage remains controversial and unresolved.

1807
Feb–Mar   Napoleon summons le Grand Sanhédrin (the Jewish council of elders)[10] to ratify the resolutions of 1806. The Sanhédrin agrees on reforms in order to facilitate citizenship. It upholds French civil law on marriage.

1808
Mar 17
Napoleon issues a decree introducing the consistorial system. Every department with a population of 2000 Jews must establish a *consistoire* (a representative body) to enforce resolutions passed by the Sanhédrin in 1807:[11] decorum must be maintained in the synagogue; Jews must participate in industrial trades; military service must not be evaded. The decree also prohibits further Jewish immigration into Alsace and comes to be known among the Jewish community as the *décret 'infâme'* (infamous decree) since it embraces Jews within French common law. Effective for ten years, by 1811 all restrictions stipulated by the decree are abolished.

1817
The *décret 'infâme'* lapses under the rule of Louis XVIII.

1819
Anti-Jewish 'hep hep' riots in Germany spread to Alsace.[12]

1820-30
Sporadic conflicts break out between the peasantry and Jewish money lenders.

1845
French socialist Alphonse Toussenel publishes *Les Juifs Rois de l'époque* 'The Jews, Kings of the Time', an antisemitic text on the economic role of Jews.

1847 Dec 26
Birth of Marie-Charles Ferdinand Walsin-Esterhazy in Paris.[13]

1847-48
Anti-Jewish violence breaks out in the villages surrounding Mülhausen. The authorities issue an order for the protection of French Jewish citizens and the Municipal Council of Mülhausen acts to limit the impact of the disturbances.

1848
Mülhausen Council abandons the German spelling 'Mülhausen' and adopts the French 'Mulhouse'.

1859 Oct 9
Birth of Alfred Dreyfus in Mulhouse.[14]

1866
Esterhazy fails the entrance examination to Saint-Cyr military academy.

1868 Jan 31
Esterhazy joins the Roman Legion, known as the Papal Zouaves, and leaves for Rome.

1869 May 22
Esterhazy is promoted to second lieutenant.

1870
Esterhazy joins the French Foreign Legion. On the outbreak of the Franco-Prussian War, he is sent to serve in Algeria. Thereafter he is granted permission to serve in the French Army, joining the Second Zouave Regiment, which meets the Prussians in battle on the Loire.

Oct 24
The Crémieux Decree grants French citizenship to Algerian Jews.

The Franco-Prussian War

1870–71
The rise of German military power and imperialism, combined with Bismarck's policy of unification of the German Empire, sparks antagonism between France and Prussia, the largest and most important of the German states.

1870

July 19 France declares war on Prussia.[15]

Aug 4 Prussian soldiers cross the border into Alsace and march towards Paris.

Sep 1 Emperor Napoleon III capitulates after he and nearly 100,000 of his men are captured at the decisive battle of Sedan.

Sep 4 When news of the defeat at Sedan reaches Paris, the city rises in protest. Léon Gambetta announces the dissolution of the Second Empire, and proclaims the Third Republic. A provisional Government of National Defence is formed. (*v.* 1870–75)

Sep 16 Prussian troops march through Mulhouse.[16]

Sept 19 The Prussians besiege Paris; the siege is to last for six months.

1871

Jan 28 A three-week ceasefire is signed. The siege of Paris is lifted.

Feb 8 National elections are held, mainly with a view to forming a new government to conclude a peace treaty with the Prussians.

Feb 17 The new National Assembly, with monarchists in the majority, names the conservative elder statesman Louis-Adolphe Thiers as head of the executive power of the Third Republic.

Mar 1 Thiers and the National Assembly accept the preliminary Prussian peace terms (confirmed on 10 May) including the occupation of Paris. Triumphal march of Prussian troops through a still-besieged Paris. The population of Paris and the National Guard (a 300,000-strong citizen militia) resent the provisional government and refuse to accept a Prussian victory. They declare themselves ready to defend the city.

Mar 18 Thiers orders French troops to enter Paris and to seize all arms within the city. The National Guard refuses to give up their weapons. Thiers and the Government take refuge in Versailles, where he is to gather force to overwhelm the rebellious city. The National Guard reorganizes itself. A supreme Central Committee is elected and assumes power in Paris.

Mar 26 Elections are held in Paris: a revolutionary 'Commune' is proclaimed. The members of the Commune are mainly Blanquists and Proudhonists.[17]

Mar 28– May 28 Thiers' troops lay siege to Paris. The fighting, intensifying over five weeks culminates in 'Bloody Week' (21–28 May), a harsh suppression of the communard revolt.[18]

May 10 The Treaty of Frankfurt marks the end of the Franco-Prussian War. France cedes to Germany Alsace (with the exception of Belfort) and a large part of Lorraine. Citizens of Alsace have to choose between French or German nationality. Those opting for French nationality have to leave Alsace by October 1872.

Sept Esterhazy is recalled to his regiment in Oran (Algeria).[19]

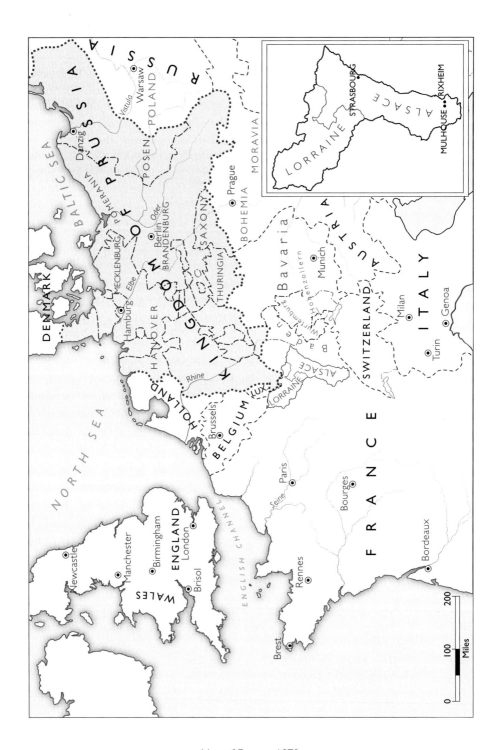

Map of Europe, 1870

Establishment of the Third Republic 1870-1875

Although the Third Republic is proclaimed in 1870 during the Franco-Prussian War the majority in the National Assembly expects a rapid restoration of the constitutional monarchy. The monarchical and Republican systems of government are frequently the subject of public debate. France's defeat in the Franco-Prussian War has far-reaching effects: a strong desire for retaliation, fear and hatred of foreign powers, especially Germany; the sanctity of the army; and the rise of nationalism. It was not until January 1875, following five years of provisional government, that the Third Republic is legally constituted by a series of constitutional laws carried by one single vote (353 to 352).

The constitution establishes a bicameral parliamentary system (the Chamber of Deputies and the Senate) under a President of the Republic, whose executive powers are limited. During its early years the Republic is in constant danger, governments lasting only a few months.

The Section de Statistique 1872-76

As part of the overall restructuring of the French Army following its defeat in the Franco-Prussian War, the Ministry of War creates four *bureaux* (departments), the first to deal with administration, the second (the Deuxième Bureau) with Intelligence, the third with warfare and training, the fourth with communications and transport. To gain experience in all four departments, officers on probation are to work for six months in each of the bureaux consecutively. In response to concerns about the European arms race and German military superiority, as well as the apprehension over a new invasion, a special Intelligence service (*service des renseignements*) is created devoted to espionage and counter-espionage. The secrecy and importance of its work is such that it does not formally acknowledge its links with the Deuxième Bureau (formal branch of Intelligence) and is given the deliberately misleading title of the Section de Statistique; the officers of the Section are not listed at the Ministry of War; the section functions under the direct control of the Chief of the General Staff. It is located in the rue Saint Dominique in Paris, near the German Embassy in the rue de Lille; this gives opportunity for surveillance.

1872

May 13   After the Treaty of Frankfurt, Raphael Dreyfus, the father of Alfred, opts for French citizenship, giving Carpentras (Provence) as the family's official domicile.[20]

Oct 1   Raphael and his family move temporarily to Basel. From there Raphael can continue to supervise his factory in Mulhouse.

Oct   At the age of 13 Alfred celebrates his bar mitzvah ceremony.

Nov 21   Alfred enters the *Realschule* in Basel.

1873   Alfred and his brother Mathieu leave for Paris to board at the Collège Sainte-Barbe.

1874 Feb 11   Esterhazy is promoted to full lieutenant.

1874–76	Alfred matriculates from the Collège Chaptal. He returns to Carpentras to prepare for his *baccalauréat*, which he takes and passes in the autumn of 1876.
	Esterhazy is appointed aide-de-camp to General François Grenier. This is the start of Esterhazy's easygoing life in Paris. He frequents aristocratic circles and exclusive clubs such as L'Union artistique, Le Cercle impérial and the Jockey Club. He also speculates on the stock market and takes mistresses.
1876–78	Dreyfus prepares for the entrance examinations to the Ecole polytechnique, France's rigorous military academy.[21]
1876 June	When General Grenier retires, Esterhazy is appointed librarian at the Réunion des Officiers, a semi-private association near the Ministry of War.
1877–79	Taking advantage of his connections in aristocratic society, Esterhazy, a polyglot, is appointed as a German translator to the Section de Statistique. His colleagues there include Captain Joseph Hubert Henry and Maurice Weil.[22]
1878	Dreyfus is awarded a place at the Ecole polytechnique, ranked 182 of the 236 students accepted.
1880	Dreyfus passes out from the Ecole polytechnique, ranked 128 of 235, and is commissioned as a second lieutenant.
1880–82	Dreyfus enrols in the Ecole d'application de l'artillerie, an artillery training school, at Fontainebleau.
1881–82	Recalled to his regiment, Esterhazy, promoted to captain, takes part in expeditions in Tunisia.[23] He continues to correspond with Madame Gabrielle de Boulancy, one of his lovers in Paris, who sends him money. She also acts unsuccessfully on his behalf, asking General Félix Gustave Saussier to transfer him back to France. Furious at her failure, Esterhazy violently criticizes the French Army in his letters to her.[24]
1882 **July**	Esterhazy is finally accepted into the Legion of Honour, after being proposed to the Council five times, for his role in the Tunisian expeditions.
Oct	Dreyfus leaves the Ecole d'application de l'artillerie, ranked 32 out of 97, as a lieutenant in the 31st Artillery Regiment garrisoned at Le Mans in north-western France.
End 1883	Dreyfus is transferred to the 11th Cavalry Regiment in Paris.
1885	Dreyfus is promoted to first lieutenant.

Antisemitism in France 1881–86

(End 1881) Crash of the Union Générale, a Catholic bank founded by Paul Bontox in 1878 to rival Protestant and Jewish banks. The Catholic press claims that the crash is the result of machinations by the Rothschild bank and other prominent Jewish financiers. The accusation is false but fuels the antisemitic press. Jewish financiers are blamed for the public, political and economic disaster caused by the crash of the bank.

(1882 May) At the instigation of Gambetta, the poet and playwright Paul Déroulède founds La Ligue des patriotes (the League of Patriots), which becomes the nucleus of the French Nationalist movement. The nature of the patriotism promoted by Déroulède's league expresses itself in feelings of revenge against Germany.[25] (*v.* 25 Sept, 1898)

(1881–84) Several short-lived antisemitic weeklies appear. In December 1881, three issues of *L'Anti-Juif, organe de défense nationale* ('The Anti-Jew: Document of National Defence') are published by Father Chabauty in Montdidier.[26] In 1882 *L'Antisémitisme: Le Juif voilà l'Ennemi!* ('Antisemitism: The Jew is the Enemy!') is published, followed in 1883 over a ten-week period by *L'Anti-Sémitique*. Further issues of the latter are published in 1884 after a change of name to *Le Péril social* ('The Social Danger').[27]

(1883) The magazine *La Croix,* founded by Father Bailly in 1880 and sponsored by the Assumptionists, develops into a popular anti-democratic and antisemitic daily newspaper.[28]

(1886) Edouard Drumont publishes *La France juive*, a keystone in modern antisemitic literature.[29] Popularly known as the 'pope of antisemitism', Drumont combines in this book antisemitic arguments on religious, national, social, political and economic grounds with racist theories.[30] Drumont's confessor at this time is the influential Jesuit priest Stanislas Du Lac.[31] (*v.* 14 May, 1898, n. 136; 22 June, 1899, n. 126)

Publication of the second edition of *Le Juif, le judaïsme et la judaïsation des peuples chrétiens* by Gougenot des Mousseaux (first published in 1869). The book presents the Catholic Church as a victim of the pernicious forces of Freemasons and Jews.

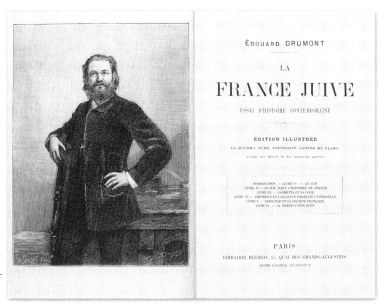

Edouard Drumont and the title page of *La France juive*

Boulangism 1886–89

(Jan 1886) General Georges Boulanger, decorated for his military achievements, is elected Minister of War. Boulanger reforms the army for the benefit of both soldiers and officers, and is regarded by the public as the man destined to avenge France for the disasters of 1870.[32]

(31 May 1887) A new government is formed by Maurice Rouvier. It excludes Boulanger.

(1888) Boulanger defies army rules preventing a soldier standing for election and mounts a series of campaigns advocating revision of the constitution, dissolution of the Chamber of Deputies and revenge against Germany. His slogan is 'Dissolve, Revise, Reconstitute'. Bonapartists, and Orleanists, both Royalist parties, rally behind Boulanger, giving birth to the movement known as Boulangism. Boulanger becomes the idol of Paris and is urged to stand for the presidency.

(27 Jan 1889) Boulanger is elected to the Chamber of Deputies by an overwhelming majority as Deputy for Paris. His supporters urge him to march on the Elysée, the presidential palace, but he wavers, giving the Government time to regroup. In August Boulanger flees to Brussels under the threat of arrest issued by the Senate for plotting a *coup d'état.*[33]

1886
Jan　　　　Esterhazy marries Anne-Marie de Nettancourt, daughter of the marquis de Nettancourt Vaubecourt, a member of a noble and wealthy family from Lorraine.[34]

1887　　　Colonel Jean Sandherr, a virulent antisemite, is appointed chef du service des renseignements (head of the Section de Statistique), which consists of five or six officers working in the rue Saint-Dominique employing agents and correspondents across France and Europe. Within this established network of espionage and counter-espionage, Sandherr introduces the tactic of drawing up false documents and providing an enemy with misinformation through double agents.[35]

1889
Sept　　　As Boulangism reaches its peak, Drumont, the marquis Antoine Amédée de Morès[36] and Jacques de Biez[37] found the Ligue nationale antisémitique de France (National Antisemitic League of France). They claim it as 'an instrument of national resurrection', aiming to 'fight the pernicious influence of the financial hold of the Jews, whose clandestine and merciless conspiracy jeopardizes the welfare, honour and security of France'[38] (*v.* Feb 1897) (*v.* Appendix 2).

Sept 12　　Dreyfus is promoted to captain of the 21st Artillery Regiment and sent to the Ecole centrale de pyrotechnie militaire, the army's special artillery training school in Bourges. He prepares for the entrance examinations to the Ecole supérieure de guerre.[39] By now his military file contains some good reports:

A very active officer, bold rider, good section lieutenant; Educated and intelligent officer; Very intelligent, very skilful, commands well despite his poor intonation; The best lieutenant of the group of batteries; Knows a lot and always learns; Excellent lieutenant; Leads his staff very well.[40]

La 'voie ordinaire' (the 'normal route')

The German Embassy engages Madame Bastian (née Marie Caudron), a cleaner. Unknown to the embassy, she also works for the Section de Statistique under the agent name Auguste. One of her duties is to collect any papers or documents from wastepaper baskets in the German Embassy and to filch documents from embassy pigeon-holes. She hands over her findings to an agent from the Section de Statistique, usually Henry,[41] at secret meeting-places, often in the churches of Sainte-Clotilde and Saint-François-Xavier. This method of transmitting information is referred to as *la 'voie ordinaire'* or the 'normal route'.

1889–92   Appointed to the 18th Infantry Regiment, Esterhazy takes up residence in Courbevoie, a northern suburb of Paris. His financial situation is increasingly strained, largely because of his frivolous way of life and speculations on the stock market.

1890

Apr 20   Dreyfus receives confirmation of his acceptance by the Ecole supérieure de guerre. He is ranked 67 out of 81 officers.

Apr 21   Dreyfus marries Lucie Hadamard, from Metz. Her devout Jewish father is a wealthy diamond dealer. Zadoc Kahn, Chief Rabbi of

Lucie Dreyfus in 1892

France, presides at the wedding, which takes place in the main synagogue of Paris, part of the complex of buildings that housed the Consistoire Israélite in the rue de la Victoire.[42]

Ketubbah – Jewish marriage certificate of Lucie and Alfred Dreyfus

Aug 30	Léon-Pierre Boutonnet, archivist at the Ministry of War's Technical Artillery Section, is sentenced to five years' imprisonment for espionage.
1891	Major Alessandro Panizzardi is appointed military attaché to the Italian Embassy in Paris.
	Five issues of a new antisemitic newspaper, *L'Anti-Youtre* ('The Anti-Yid') are published in Paris.
Apr 5	Birth of the first child of Alfred and Lucie Dreyfus, Pierre-Léon.
Dec 10	Lieutenant-Colonel Maximilien von Schwartzkoppen is appointed military attaché to the German Embassy in Paris.
1892	
Apr 17	Esterhazy writes a letter (to M. Rieu, a tailor) on *papier pelure* (India squared paper) similar to that of the *bordereau*. (*v.* 26 Sept, 1894 & early Nov 1898, First revision investigation: Criminal Chamber)

La Libre Parole and its antisemitic campaign

Apr	Drumont launches *La Libre Parole* ('Free Speech'), a newspaper with extreme views, aiming to establish the existence of the dangers of Jewish influence in France and across the world.[43]
May 2 & 21	*La Libre Parole* publishes two articles alleging that the Jewish officer Maurice Weil is a gambler and German spy.[44]
May 23	*La Libre Parole* begins a systematic attack on Jewish officers. It launches a series of articles entitled 'Les juifs dans l'armée' ('The Jews in the army'). (*v.* Appendix 3) The 300 Jewish officers serving in the French Army are accused of impeding the careers of Catholic officers and of subversion and treason. *La Croix* supports these accusations.
June 1	Captain André Crémieu-Foa, a Jewish officer, responds to the paper's accusations by challenging Drumont to a duel on behalf of the army's Jewish officers. Both Drumont and Crémieu-Foa are slightly wounded. Crémieu-Foa appoints Major Esterhazy as one of his seconds.[45]
June 20	Crémieu-Foa fights a second duel with Pradel de Lamase, another of Drumont's colleagues at *La Libre Parole*. Neither is hurt.[46]
June 23	Captain Armand Mayer, another Jewish officer, is killed in a duel with the marquis de Morès.
June 26	Mayer's funeral is attended by thousands of people, including military officers and members of the Jewish community. Mayer is buried with full military honours.
	The tragic consequences of the duel prompt the Government into action. The Chamber of Deputies adopts a motion proposed by Charles Freycinet, Minister of War, to prohibit religious discrimination in the army.[47]

July 10   Esterhazy is promoted to the rank of major.

The Panama scandal

Sept 6   *La Libre Parole* issues a series of articles on the financial dealings,
                    fraud and corruption involved in the collapse of the Panama Company
                    in 1889, which had ruined thousands of shareholders. The company
                    was mandated by the Government in 1879 to build a canal across
                    the Isthmus of Panama. Facing bankruptcy in 1888, the company's
                    agents bribed journalists and more than a hundred politicians in
                    a desperate effort to secure funds to remain solvent. Drumont's
                    successive revelations force the Government to open an inquiry.
                    As the scandal unfolds in the press, Drumont in particular attributes
                    blame to three Jewish financiers, Baron Jacques de Reinach, Emile
                    Léopold Arton and Cornélius Herz, who had only been involved
                    in the company's transactions long after the major fraud had been
                    committed. Drumont uses the scandal as his weapon for berating
                    Jewish involvement in the financial world in general. The disclosure
                    of corruption among Deputies and Senators plays a decisive role in
                    the rise of anti-parliamentary, anti-capitalist and antisemitic sentiments
                    in France and a dramatic step forward for the Socialist movement.[48]

Oct–Nov   Esterhazy asks Maurice Weil and Gaston Grenier to help him find a
                    posting near Paris.[52]

Nov   Dreyfus leaves the Ecole supérieure de guerre, coming 9th out of
                    81 officers. He is eligible for a position as a *stagiaire* (officer on
                    probation) with the General Staff. Only one of the tutors, Major
                    Georges Picquart, gives Dreyfus low marks (for cartography and
                    field manoeuvres).[49] Dreyfus complains to the commanding officer
                    about General Pierre Bonnefond, a member of the examining jury
                    who lowered the overall marks of two Jewish candidates, himself
                    and Ernest Picard, by presenting a negative assessment of their
                    personal characters. Dreyfus demands an explanation but is satisfied
                    on learning of his superiors' respect for his accomplishments.[50]

                    A report on Dreyfus written by the school principal, General Lebelin
                    de Dionne, reads:

                    > *Physique: quite good. Health: quite good; short-sighted. Character:*
                    > *easy-going. Education: good. Open-minded intelligence. Conduct:*
                    > *very good. Turn-out: very good. General knowledge: very wide-*
                    > *ranging. Knowledge of military theory: very good; practical*
                    > *knowledge: very good; administrative knowledge, very good;*
                    > *very good knowledge of German; very good rider; serves well...*
                    > *Awarded the General Staff diploma with distinction. Very good*
                    > *officer, lively mind, quick grasp of issues, ready and used to work.*
                    > *Very suitable for service on the General Staff.[51]*

1893
Jan   Dreyfus is appointed to the Ministry of War's Premier Bureau as the
                    first of his six-month probationary periods.

Esterhazy is appointed to the 74th Infantry Regiment at Rouen as a result of Weil's intervention with General Saussier, now Gouverneur militaire de Paris (Military Governor of Paris).

Feb 22   Birth of Jeanne, second child of Alfred and Lucie Dreyfus.

July   Dreyfus is transferred to the Quatrième Bureau.

Oct   Marie Forêt (known as Millescamps) denounces her former lover, Martin Brücker, to the German Embassy as an agent of the Section de Statistique. Mme Millescamps claims that the German Embassy personnel are monitored by the Deuxième Bureau in various ways. She is not taken seriously by the embassy.[53] (*v.* 4 Jan 1894)

Dec 3   General Auguste Mercier is appointed Minister of War.

Dec 25[54] Schwartzkoppen receives a laconic telegram from Berlin referring to the agent who was passing information on French defence 'master plans' to the German Army.[55]

Dec 31   At the end of Dreyfus' training period with the Quatrième Bureau, Colonel Pierre Fabre, head of this bureau, files a negative report on him:[56]

> *An incomplete officer, very intelligent and very gifted, but pretentious, and from the point of view of character, conscience and manner of service, not fulfilling the qualities necessary for employment on the General Staff of the army.*[57]

1894
Jan   Dreyfus begins his service with the Deuxième Bureau.

Jan 4   Mme Millescamps, denounced in turn by Brücker to the French authorities for stealing documents for Germany, is sentenced to five years' imprisonment for espionage by the 8th criminal division of the

Lucie Dreyfus with her children Pierre and Jeanne

Seine. The daily *Le Temps* publishes an article about this 'very curious affair of espionage'.[58] (*v.* July 1899, L'Affaire Bastian)

Feb 16 A letter from Panizzardi to his close friend and colleague Schwartzkoppen is intercepted through the 'normal route':[59]

> *I have written to Colonel Davignon again, and that is why, if you have the opportunity to broach this question with your friend, I ask you to do so in such a way that Davignon doesn't come to hear of it. Besides, he did not reply, for it must never be revealed that one [attaché] has dealings with another.*[60]

This letter is included in *Bulletin de renseignements* No. 19.[61]

Mar Grenier introduces Esterhazy to Deputy Jules Roche, President of the Chamber of Deputy's Commission de l'Armée (the Army Commission), as a potential adviser on military affairs.[62]

According to Henry, in this month another letter from Panizzardi to Schwartzkoppen is intercepted via the 'normal route':[63]

> *My very dear friend,*
> *Yesterday evening I ended up by calling the doctor, who has forbidden me to go out. Since I cannot go to your house tomorrow, please do come to mine in the morning because P... has brought me many very interesting matters, and we need to share the work as we only have ten days. We shall have to try to tell the ambassador that you cannot attend.*
> *All yours,*
> *Alexandrine*

The marquis del Val Carlos supplies information to François Guénée, former police official who at present is working for the Section de Statistique. He reports on dealings between Panizzardi and Colonel de Mendigorria, the Italian and Spanish military attachés, and Schwartzkoppen, their German colleague.[64] Val Carlos accuses Mendigorria of being a Germanophile and of acting suspiciously. (*v.* 28 & 30 March 1894)

Mar 14 The *Projet de Manuel de tir d'artillerie de campagne*, a new draft Field Artillery Firing Manual, is circulated to artillery officers.

Mar 28 & 30 Guénée produces two reports based on information from Val Carlos.[65]

Apr 7 300 copies of the draft Field Artillery Firing Manual, relating to tests of the 120mm short cannon, are distributed to artillery training schools, including Châlons.

Ce canaille de D. (That scoundrel D.)

Apr 16 An undated letter from Schwartzkoppen to Panizzardi is intercepted by the Section de Statistique and dated by them '16 April'. It reveals that someone designated by the letter 'D' has given Schwartzkoppen the master plans for Nice: [66]

I am truly sorry not to have seen you before I left. Besides, I will be back in eight days. I am enclosing 12 master plans for Nice which that scoundrel D gave me for you. I told him that you did not intend to resume relations. He claims there was a misunderstanding and that he would do his utmost to satisfy you. He says that he had insisted you would not hold it against him. I replied that he was mad and that I did not think you would resume relations with him. Do as you wish. Goodbye. I am in a hurry. Alexandrine. Don't bugger too much! [60]

Apr　　　Drumont, Morès and a group of law students establish the Groupe des étudiants antisémites (Antisemitic Student Group). The chairman is the future lawyer and Nationalist, Camille Jarre.[68]

May 17　　Officers on probation with the General Staff including Alfred Dreyfus receive an order not to take part in manoeuvres scheduled between July and October. (*v.* 6 Oct 1894)

End June　Bernard Lazare, a Jewish writer, publishes *L'antisémitisme, son histoire et ses causes* (Paris: L. Chailley).[69]

　　　　　　Pressed for money, Esterhazy seeks help from Jewish financiers through Weil. Zadoc Kahn raises money on his behalf from the community's wealthy members; Baron Edmond de Rothschild donates 2000 francs.[70]

June 27–　Dreyfus accompanies General Raoul Le Mouton de Boisdeffre, Chief
July 4　　of the General Staff, on a visit to Charmes in eastern France. Impressed by Dreyfus' analysis of the modernization of the artillery, Boisdeffre discusses military matters with him.

July　　　Dreyfus joins the Troisième Bureau.[71]

Bernard Lazare

NOTES

1   The period in French history between 1789 and 1799 that saw the end of the old regime. The monarchy was overthrown by Republicans. King Louis XVI and his wife Marie Antoinette were executed (21 January and 16 October 1793 respectively). Feudalism was abolished and the Roman Catholic Church radically restructured. While historians disagree about the causes of the Revolution, most agree that France's economic and social difficulties and the intellectual phenomena of the Enlightenment, which attacked the Church and absolutism, all played a major part.

2   The name given to spontaneous outbreaks of panic and mass hysteria that swept across France in July 1789 as a result of the power vacuum caused by the collapse of the monarchy. Most of these took the form of peasant revolts against feudalism, in which noble châteaux and records of feudal dues were burned.

3   Alsace was at that time under French control. Mülhausen remained independent until it elected to become part of France on 4 January 1798.

4   To underline its revolutionary tendencies, the National Assembly renamed itself on 9 July 1789 the Assemblée nationale constituante (the National Constituent Assembly).

5   This fundamental document of French constitutional history was embodied in the constitution of 1791. It was inspired by the American Declaration of Independence and the philosophers of the Enlightenment. The French declaration listed the 'inalienable rights' of the individual to liberty, property, security, resistance to oppression, freedom of speech and of the press.

6   The Avalon Project at Yale Law School. <www.yale.edu/lawweb/avalon/rightsof.htm>

7   The term 'Sephardic' originally referred to Jewish communities in the Iberian Peninsula ('Sephardi' is Hebrew for 'Spanish'). After the expulsion of the Jews from Spain (1492–96) and their forced conversion in Portugal, *Sephardic* refers to all Jews of Spanish or Portuguese origin. The term 'Ashkenazic' ('Ashkenaz' is Hebrew for 'Germany') refers to Jews who from the Middle Ages had settled in France and Germany and who subsequently spread to Central and Eastern Europe. 'Sephardic' is also commonly used to designate Jews from Southern and Mediterranean countries.

8   The Jewish community of Avignon (known as '*les juifs du pape*') was under the authority of the pope, not the king of France. After the French Revolution Avignon was reunited with France.

9   A nine-month period from November 1793 to July 1794 during the ascendancy of Robespierre when success in war was counterbalanced by butchery at home, with 2600 people guillotined in Paris alone and many other 'Terrors' elsewhere in France.

10 The Grand Sanhédrin was originally the supreme assembly of the Jewish nation, which governed Israel from 170 BC to AD 70. It had not met for 18 centuries.

11 Each *consistoire* consisted of a chief rabbi and three lay members, two of whom had to be residents of the town where the *consistoire* sat. The central *consistoire* consisted of three chief rabbis and two lay members.

12 These riots (named after the rallying cry, 'Hep! Hep!') broke out in Germany in 1819 in reaction to Jewish emancipation. The origin of the cry is unknown. Some scholars believe that it was an acronym for '*Hierosolyma est perdita*' (Jerusalem is Destroyed), one of the rallying cries of early Crusaders. Others think that it was simply a shepherd's call used by Jew-baiters.

13 Esterhazy's father, General Ferdinand Walsin-Esterhazy, was an illegitimate descendant of an illustrious Austro-Hungarian family. General Esterhazy was decorated for his part in the victory over Russian troops at the battle of Eupatoria during the Crimean War in 1855. On 1 September 1857 Esterhazy's father died of war wounds, leaving behind him the ten-year old Esterhazy and his sister. Esterhazy assumed the title of Count, to which he had no right, and dropped the Walsin part of his name; henceforth he was called simply Esterhazy. The biographical details in this section are taken from M. Thomas, *Esterhazy ou l'envers de l'affaire Dreyfus* (Paris: Vernal/Lebaud, 1989), pp. 14–163.

14 For the origins of the Dreyfus family, see Genealogy of Alfred Dreyfus, pp. xxxii..

15 The emergence of Prussia as the leading German power and the increasing unification of the German states were viewed with apprehension by Napoleon III after the Prussian victory in the Austro-Prussian War of 1866. The immediate pretext for war presented itself when the throne of Spain was offered to Prince Leopold of Hohenzollern-Sigmaringen, a relative of King Wilhelm of Prussia, who, in 1871, was crowned Emperor of Germany and became known as Kaiser Wilhelm I. The offer, at first accepted by Leopold on the advice of Otto von Bismarck, Prime Minister of Prussia and later Chancellor, was rejected (12 July 1870) after the French Government made a strong protest. The French Foreign Secretary, the duc de Gramont, insisted on further Prussian assurances that Leopold's candidacy would never be renewed. King Wilhelm refused to give this assurance. Bismarck provocatively made the King's refusal public (in the famous Ems despatch of 13 July 1870), which led to the declaration of war on Prussia.

16 Alfred Dreyfus watched the soldiers from his window. This scene played a decisive role in his desire to become a French officer. A. Dreyfus, *Souvenirs et correspondance publiés par son fils* (Paris: Grasset, 1936), p. 41.

17 During April the Commune decreed the separation of Church and State; the guillotine was publicly burnt in Paris; all religious symbols excluded from schools in Paris.

18 One of Thiers' generals was Gaston de Galliffet. His participation in the cruel suppression of the Commune won him the enduring enmity of the political Left. He was to become Minister of War during the last phase of the Dreyfus Affair (*v.* 22 June 1899), restoring calm to the army.

19 Esterhazy's courage won him a temporary promotion to captain. But the Commission de révision de grade (a newly established committee for review of rank) informed him that he is to resume his previous rank of second lieutenant. This decision infuriated and embittered him towards the French Army. (*v.* 1881–82)

20 Raphael gave Carpentras as his official domicile since his daughter Henriette had been living there since her marriage in 1870 into one of the town's most prominent Jewish families. *DFA*, p. 60.

21 Founded in 1794, the Ecole polytechnique aimed to give students a strong academic background, especially in mathematics, physics and chemistry, and to prepare them for the elite state postgraduate universities.

22 Esterhazy's friendships with Weil and Henry date from this period. According to Reinach, Esterhazy's friendship with Henry played a crucial role in the Dreyfus Affair. Reinach's theory is that of Esterhazy's and Henry's complicity from the beginning of the Affair, i.e. from the moment Henry discovered the document which originated the Dreyfus Affair, the *bordereau* (*v.* 26 Sept 1894). According to Reinach, Herny recognized Esterhazy's writing (*v.* 25 Oct 1898). *HAD*, 1, pp. 46–50; 2, pp. 26, 74–6. Thomas, on the other hand, believes that Esterhazy's relationship with Henry was not close, even though Henry had lent him money, whereas the Jewish officer Weil became his devoted friend. Thomas, *Esterhazy*, pp. 62, 122–5. Herzog says that Henry became 'Esterhazy's debtor' at this time, a description probably suggested by Esterhazy's own writings. (*v.* 27 Jan 1897). W. Herzog, *Der Kampf einer Republik. Die Affäre Dreyfus*. Dokumente und Tatsachen (Zürich/Vienna/Prag: Büchergilde Gutenberg, 1933), p. 352.

23 Tunisia became a French protectorate under the Treaty of Bardo on 12 May 1881.

24 When Mme de Boulancy discovered that Esterhazy was having an affair with Marie Monchanin on his return to France (Marseille) in 1885, she put an end to their relationship and entrusted all his letters to her lawyer. They were published in *Le Figaro* in 1897. (*v.* 28 Nov 1897)

25 Déroulède was the author of 'Les chants du Soldat', a collection of patriotic songs published immediately after the defeat of France in the Franco-Prussian War (1872). In 1882 Jules Ferry, Minister of Education, distributed 20,000 issues of 'Les chants du Soldat' to primary schools throughout France. From 1883 the league's publicity organ was the newspaper *Le Drapeau*. The first members of the league included politicians and intellectuals such as Victor Hugo, Félix Faure, Léon Gambetta and René Waldeck-Rousseau. Sixteen years later Waldeck-Rousseau was responsible for arraigning Déroulède in court for conspiracy against the Republic. (*v.* 9 Nov 1899–4 Jan 1900) In the 1880s Déroulède directed his league against the parliamentary system established in 1875 and developed it into a movement combining Nationalism with mass agitation, populism and militarism. It was at its height during the Boulangist years (*v.* 1886–89), but was dissolved shortly after the fall of Boulanger in March 1889. It was later re-formed under Déroulède and became increasingly active towards the end of 1898. Z. Sternhell, *La droite révolutionnaire, les origines françaises du fascisme 1885–1914* (Paris: Seuil [1978] 1984), pp. 77–99. (*v.* 1903, n. 13)

26 Father Chabauty was a Catholic priest from Poitiers and author of several antisemitic books (*Les Francs-Maçons et les juifs* (Paris, 1881), and notably *Les juifs, nos maîtres* (Paris, 1882)). In the latter, he stated that Jewish leaders were secretly guiding the Jewish nation and certain secret societies against Christianity, in order to rule the world. Chabauty's thesis contained the basic outline of one of the most famous antisemitic frauds of the 20th century, the *Protocols of the Learned Elders of Zion*. See N. Cohn, *Warrant for Genocide, the myth of the Jewish world-conspiracy and the Protocols of the Elders of Zion* (London: Eyre & Spottiswoode, 1967).

27 S. Wilson, *Ideology and Experience, Anti-Semitism in France at the Time of the Dreyfus Affair* (London/ Toronto: Association University Press, Littman Library of Jewish Civilization, 1982), pp. 205–8.

28 The Congregation of the Augustans of the Assumption was created by Emmanuel d'Alzon in 1845 and recognized by Pope Pius IX in 1864. Its principal aim was to propagate a highly conservative Catholic doctrine. To this end, Father Bailly founded a publishing house *La Bonne presse* which financed several journals, papers and other publications. Between 1892 and 1895 the daily circulation of *La Croix* rose to 170,000. Comparable figures for *Le Figaro* at this time were 30,000. P. Sorlin. *La Croix et les juifs (1880–1899)* (Paris: Grasset, 1967), pp. 15–55; 254.

29 Drumont's book became a bestseller. Within two months over 100,000 copies were sold. By 1941 it had run to 200 reprints. M. Winock, *Edouard Drumont et Cie. Antisémitisme et fascisme en France* (Paris: Seuil, 1982), p. 37.

30 The emergence of racial antisemitism in 19th-century France was related to the development of general racist theories at the time. In 1855 Ernest Renan published his *Histoire générale et système comparé des langues sémitiques*. In 1867 Gobineau published his *Essai sur l'inégalité des races humaines*, which

was to influence the development of racial theories in the Third Reich. For more on this aspect, see Wilson, *Ideology and experience*, pp. 456–508.

31 M. Winock, *La France et les juifs de 1789 à nos jours* (Paris: Seuil, 2004), pp. 62–3. In preparing this book, Drumont consulted with Père Du Lac who, although trying to soften Drumont's extreme theories, provided him with the anti-Jewish articles of the Jesuit magazine *La Civiltà Cattolica*. Founded in 1849, the magazine enjoyed unique authority since, while not an official mouthpiece of the Vatican, all its articles were approved in advance by the Vatican.

32 Boulanger was particularly anxious to reform military espionage and counter-espionage.

33 Although Boulangism collapsed after Boulanger's arrest, the movement continued to play a crucial role in the transformation of the French Right in the years leading up to the Dreyfus Affair. On 30 September 1891 Boulanger committed suicide by the grave of his mistress, who had died in the preceding July. Boulangism and antisemitism openly joined forces in January 1890, shortly after the foundation of the Ligue nationale antisémitique de France. (*v.* Sept 1889) R. Byrnes, *Antisemitism in Modern France, vol. 1 The Prologue to the Dreyfus Affair* (New Brunswick, NJ: Rutgers University Press, 1950), pp. 232–7.

34 Looking for a marriage of convenience, Esterhazy put several advertisements in the newspapers, but in vain. He was introduced to de Nettancourt by chance, through Father Castelli in Marseille. In 1888, with money from his wife, Esterhazy purchases a château for his retirement at Dommartin-la-Planchette, in the Marne. Thomas, *Esterhazy*, pp. 86–8; 162–3.

35 A. Mitchell, 'The Xenophobic Style: French Counter-Espionage and the Emergence of the Dreyfus Affair', *Journal of Modern History* (September 1980), University of Chicago, pp. 420–5.

36 The Marquis de Morès (1858–1896), an ex-army officer and aristocrat of Spanish descent, had married the daughter of a rich American banker. After adventuring in the USA and Far East, he returned to France where he plunged into Parisian social life. His encounter with Drumont was decisive. He was henceforth to devote himself and his fortune to antisemitic activities. R. Byrnes, *Antisemitism in Modern France*, pp. 225–50; S.S. Schwarzschild, 'The Marquis de Morès, the story of a failure', *Jewish Social Studies* 22, 1 (January 1960), pp. 3–26.

37 Born into a poor but aristocratic family in Normandy, Biez came to Paris in the late 1870s to pursue his career as a playwright. After failing in the theatre and as a novelist he turned to journalism, becoming a professional art and music critic. A fervent Republican and Catholic, Biez was one of Drumont's first disciples, devoting himself to antisemitism. In 1886 he helped found the new, but unsuccessful Alliance Anti-Israélite Universelle in Bucharest. (in opposition to the Alliance Israélite Universelle created in Paris in 1860). Biez wrote several anti-Jewish pamphlets. Byrnes, *Antisemitism in Modern France*, pp. 273–4.

38 Herzog, from *Dreyfus to Pétain: 'The Struggle of a Republic'*, trans. W. Sorell (New York: Creative Age Press, 1947), p. 30. The activities of the league ceased soon after its foundation. It was succeeded in March 1890 by Les amis de Morès (The Friends of Morès) created by Morès with a group of supporters. Over the following years this group attracted the main antisemitic and nationalist leaders: Jules Guérin, Paul Déroulède, Lucien Millevoye and many other aristocratic figures. The league was re-formed by Guérin in 1897. Byrnes, *Antisemitism in Modern France*, pp. 242–6; P. Pierrard, *Juifs et catholiques français (1886–1945)* (Paris: Fayard, 1970), pp. 139–40.

39 Founded in 1876, the school sought to create an elite cadre of military administrators. Top graduates were to be assigned to the General Staff.

40 *Rennes*, II, 58–9.

41 Henry was appointed to the Section de Statistique in 1877 by Chief of Staff General Joseph de Miribel. (*v.* 1877–9, n. 22) He left the service in 1886 to take part in military expeditions to Tunisia and Tonkin (Vietnam). He only resumed work with the Section de Statistique in 1893.

42 Alfred and Lucie's civil marriage took place on 18 April at the *mairie* of the 9th arrondissement.

43 *La Libre Parole* was to become the leading and most popular antisemitic paper in France, reaching its height around the turn of the century. In 1894 its daily circulation reached 200,000. Wilson, *Ideology and Experience*, pp. 173–4; 200–6.

44 Weil was decorated for his valour in the Franco-Prussian War. Devoted to the army and deeply interested in military matters, he was engaged by the Section de Statistique in 1875, where he was put in charge of certain missions to Berlin. In 1880 he left the service for reasons unknown. This, as well as his dubious financial dealings and close relationship with Saussier (Weil's wife was said to be Saussier's mistress) tarnished Weil's reputation and made him a perfect target for Drumont's antisemitic campaign. His close friendship with Esterhazy (*v.* 1877–9, n. 22) led, inevitably, to his involvement in the 'Dreyfus-Esterhazy Affair'. Thomas, *Esterhazy*, pp. 122–8.

45 André Crémieu-Foa was the brother-in-law of Prefect Gaston Grenier, son of General François Grenier, for whom Esterhazy had served as aide-de-camp between 1874 and 1876. In 1892, after General Grenier's death, Esterhazy and Gaston became close friends. (*v.* Mar 1897) Crémieu-Foa introduced Esterhazy to members of the Jewish community in Paris, whom Esterhazy befriended. On the day

after the duel Esterhazy paid a courtesy visit to Drumont and Morès at the offices of *La Libre Parole* to establish cordial relations with the object of collaboration. (*v.* Jan 1895)

46 One of Crémieu-Foa's seconds in this duel was Captain Armand Mayer. In spite of what had been agreed, Cremieu-Foa's young brother, Ernest, made public the report of this duel. Learning of this, Morès challenged Mayer to a duel the following day, 23 June 1892.

47 The marquis de Morès was tried before the Court of Assizes on 29 August 1892. The lawyer defending him was Edgar Demange, a devout Catholic and strong supporter of the French Army, who, two years later, defended Dreyfus at his court martial (1894). The president of the court was Albert Delegorgue, who, four years later, presided at Zola's trial (Feb 1898). It was confirmed that Morès had flouted duelling conventions by using a heavy battle sword. Esterhazy, called to testify despite not having been present at the duel, confirmed that the weight of de Morès' weapons had placed Mayer at a considerable disadvantage. Morès was nevertheless acquitted. Thomas, *Esterhazy*, pp. 135–7. M.R. Marrus, *The Politics of Assimilation: the Jewish Community in France at the Time of the Dreyfus Affair* (Oxford: Clarendon Press, 1971), pp. 196–8.

48 The involvement of numerous politicians in the scandal led to a ministerial crisis. Deputy Georges Clemenceau, accused of irregular conduct, was defeated in the 1893 elections. He was eclipsed from the political scene until his reappearance during the Dreyfus Affair. Jean Jaurès, Socialist Deputy, was unanimously elected head of a parliamentary commission of inquiry into the scandal. Arton and Herz fled from France. Drumont denounced Herz as a parasite who owed his position only to Clemenceau. Reinach, after his failure to appear before the commission of inquiry, was found dead, suspected of having committed suicide. The final result of the inquiry held in March 1893 against the company directorate and numerous politicians was largely a whitewash.

49 *Rennes*, I, 372, Picquart.

50 J.D. Bredin, *The Affair. The Case of Alfred Dreyfus*, trans from French by J. Mehlman (New York: George Braziller, 1986), p. 22.

51 *Rennes*, II, 60.

52 At this time he renewed his friendship with Weil (*v.* 1877–79), mainly with a view to using Weil's contacts. Weil approached General Saussier on Esterhazy's behalf, as did Grenier, who approached Deputy Joseph Reinach and Lagrange de Langre, secretary to Charles de Freycinet, Minister of War.

53 Brücker, charged by the Section de Statistique with observing foreign diplomats, recruited domestic embassy staff to work for him in stealing documents. Mme Millescamps did not mention Mme Bastian, one of Brücker's recruits. (*v.* July 1899) M. Baumont, *Aux sources de l'affaire. L'Affaire Dreyfus d'après les archives diplomatiques* (Paris: Les productions de Paris, 1959), pp. 27–8.

54 27 December according to Roget, 29 December according to Cuignet. *Répertoire*, p. 5.

55 The master plans were topographical maps of French fortifications. They were of great interest to the military attachés. Trafficking in them began in 1892 and continued throughout 1894.

56 In 1899 at the Rennes court martial, Fabre explained that he wrote this negative report on the basis of the assessments by Major Albert-Léon Bertin-Mourot and Lieutenant-Colonel Gaudéron Roget, who were directly responsible for probationary officers. Fabre noted at the time that Dreyfus was pretentious, unfriendly towards his colleagues and superiors; moreover, he was over-solicitous in obtaining information on a variety of issues. According to Roget, Dreyfus always wanted to do better and do more than was asked for; according to Bertin-Mourot, Dreyfus' nonchalance was his most worrying trait. *Cass.*, I, Roget; II, Bertin-Mourot; *Rennes*, I, 573, Fabre. Reinach remarked that Bertin-Mourot, of Jewish origin on his mother's side, was an antisemite who tried to forget his origin and held a particular dislike for Dreyfus. *HAD*, 1, p. 58.

57 *Rennes*, I, 569, Fabre. All Dreyfus' army reports from 1884 to 1894 were read at the Rennes court martial (on 22 Aug 1899). All but two were favourable to him. *Rennes*, II, 58–60. See also *AD*, pp. 115–17.

58 Mme Millescamps was released from prison in November 1898. She tried in vain to approach the Deuxième Bureau to complain about her misfortune, claiming she had been victimized by Brücker. See the German report on this affair in Baumont, *Aux sources de l'affaire*, pp. 24–31.

59 The two military attachés saw each other almost daily. The terms of endearment ('my darling'; 'my little red dog'; 'my dear little war dog') used in their many intimate letters suggest a homosexual relationship. Schwartzkoppen would sometimes sign himself 'Maximilienne', and Panizzardi 'Alexandrine': they often used pseudonyms, which makes it difficult to identify authorship. Bredin, *The Affair*, pp. 49–50; *ASD*, pp. 63–4.

60 The Deuxième Bureau was not initially worried by this letter as it only suggested the usual working relationship between military attachés, the head of the Deuxième Bureau, Colonel Sancy, and his deputy Lieutenant-Colonel Davignon. It appeared to be trivial. The Deuxième Bureau concluded that Panizzardi's 'friend' was quite clearly Sancy himself and not a secret agent. The final part of the letter was to be incorporated into the Secret Dossier compiled as evidence against Dreyfus. (*v.* Nov–Dec 1894) A. Ehrhardt, *A travers l'affaire Dreyfus Henry et Val Carlos* (Paris: Klincksieck, 1977), pp. 15–18.

61 *Bulletins de renseignements* were compilations of documents used by the Section de Statistique to report to the Minister of War. They consisted of typed or handwritten copies of intercepted documents, résumés of information from agents posted abroad and reports composed by the head of the Section de Statistique or his juniors. *ASD*, p. 118.

62 Esterhazy willingly accepted this position as a means of allying himself with the man he saw as a future Minister of War. He believed that Roche would soon replace Mercier in this post. Esterhazy had promised Grenier that he could provide Roche with military information that would earn Mercier's favour. Roche was easily satisfied by Esterhazy's information and introduced him to several, mainly left-wing Deputies. Esterhazy tried to create the new post of deputy secretary to the General Staff for which he considered his own qualifications perfect. He was also writing technical articles for the military review *La France militaire*. Thomas, *Esterhazy*, pp, 155–7.

63 Henry later altered this letter. He erased the letter 'P' and replaced it with 'D'. (*v.* Sept 1896) It was quoted by Godefroy Cavaignac, Minister of War, in the Chamber of Deputies on 7 July, 1898, as a document incriminating Dreyfus.

64 The Marquis del Val Carlos, Raimundo Guell y Borbon, was a retired honorary military attaché at the Spanish Embassy in Paris. Throughout the Dreyfus Affair, the Section de Statistique denied the fact that Val Carlos was on their payroll between 1894 and 1898. Fraudulent manoeuvres were to be used to hide the dealings with Val Carlos. (*v.* Sept 1897 & 4 June–19 Oct 1903, André's investigation)

65 These reports were included in *Bulletins de renseignements* 35 and 36, issued on 30 March and 2 April respectively. In October 1894 (after the arrest of Dreyfus) they were falsified by Guénée and inserted into the Secret Dossier. (*v.* Nov–Dec 1894)

66 This document was later included in the Secret Dossier. (*v.* Nov–Dec 1894) The date put forward by Section de Statistique officers for the arrival of this document ranged from 1892 to May 1894. The Section de Statistique had not yet adopted the system of noting date of receipt. The date of April 1894 is considered to be accurate. *HAD*, 1, pp. 32–3, 577–82; *ASD*, pp. 554–5, n. 16. When the letter was intercepted the Section de Statistique assumed that the initial 'D' did not designate an officer and probably referred to an informer whom the Italian and German military attachés had deliberately named Jacques Dubois in their previous correspondence. The Section de Statistique was unsuccessful in attempts to determine the person's real identity. It was later discovered that the military attachés regularly changed the initials of their informers to conceal their identities.

67 This is probably a play on words as this can also mean 'don't strain yourself'. However, erotic phrases such as 'bugger', 'kiss me on the mouth', etc. were frequently used in their correspondence.

68 The first manifestation of this group was a banquet in honour of Morès and Guérin, held in Lyon in February. During 1894–95 the group's activities mainly consisted of distributing antisemitic material and organizing a few public meetings and street demonstrations. It did not expand significantly until it was revitalized by the young and aggressive Edouard Dubuc at the end of 1896. The name of the group changed several times. In 1897 it became the Jeunesse antisémitique de France (Antisemitic Youth of France) (*v.* 21 Nov 1897); then in 1898 or in 1899 the Jeunesse antisémitique et nationale (Antisemitic and Nationalist Youth) (JAN). B. Joly, 'The Jeunesse antisémite et nationaliste 1894–1904', in R. Tombs (ed.) *Nationhood and Nationalism in France from Boulangism to the Great War 1899–1918* (London: HarperCollins, 1991), pp. 47–8; Pierrad, *Juifs et catholiques*, pp. 140–1; Byrnes, *Antisemitism in Modern France,* pp. 270–2.

69 On the strength of some of his previous articles and especially this book (a collection of his previously published articles) Lazare was – wrongly – accused of being antisemitic; Drumont, for instance, praised Lazare's book as 'remarkable'. Lazare was attracted by anarchism and socialism and these works developed his theory on the use of antisemitism in the rise of socialism and the fight against capitalism. The book's opening pages explain that the work should not be considered an apology nor a denunciation but an impartial historical and sociological study. Lazare was one of the first and principal dreyfusards. His view on the Jewish question was substantially transformed by the Affair and he became an ardent spokesman for the Jewish cause and later Zionism. (*v.* 6 Nov 1896; 6 Nov 1897) As early as 1896 and also explicitly in his will he affirmed that his 1894 book on antisemitism should be revised and even rewritten on many points. See N. Wilson, *Bernard-Lazare: Antisemitism and the Problem of Jewish Identity in Late Nineteenth-century France* (Cambridge, London, New York: Cambridge University Press, 1978), pp. 205–21; J.D. Bredin, *Bernard Lazare* (Paris: de Fallois, 1992), pp. 116–31; P. Oriol, *Bernard Lazare* (Paris: Stock, 2003), pp. 33–42.

70 Weil considered Esterhazy's requests for help justified, believing that the Jewish community was indebted to him for his support at the Crémieu-Foa duel against Drumont. By involving himself in this duel Esterhazy had damaged his military career, social standing and relationship with his family: his wife's family, the Nettancourts, did not approve of his contact with the Jewish community.

71 This final probationary period was terminated by his arrest before the allotted six months' training.

Part 2
ARREST and COURT MARTIAL

July–December 1894

Major Esterhazy

The genesis of the Affair[1]

July 20   Esterhazy pays his first visit to the German Embassy in Paris dressed in civilian clothes and wearing the red stripe of the Legion of Honour.[2] He asks to see Schwartzkoppen and introduces himself, without revealing his name or rank, as an officer on active duty with the French General Staff. He says he is compelled to offer his services to the German General Staff in order to save his family from destitution.[3]

July 21   Schwartzkoppen receives a letter from Esterhazy stating that he is about to leave for manoeuvres near Châlon. Esterhazy also mentions that his family connections will enable him to provide information on Russia.

July 22   Schwartzkoppen reports his meeting with Esterhazy to German Intelligence in Berlin but does not mention the meeting to Count Georges von Münster, German ambassador to Paris.

Schwartzkoppen also drafts a memorandum, presumably for his superiors in Berlin. Instead of sending it, he tears it up, throwing the pieces into his wastepaper basket. Mme Bastian (*v.* Sept 1889) finds them and delivers them in due course to the Section de Statistique.[4] The memorandum alludes to the 'dangerous' dealings Schwartzkoppen is about to enter into with a French officer. The Section de Statistique translates the pieces, originally in German, as: 'Doubt ... Proof ... letter of service[5] ... a dangerous situation for myself with a French officer ... Must not conduct negotiations personally ... Bring what he has ... *Absolute Ge*[6] ... Information Bureau ... No relation ... Regiment ... An importance only ... Leaving the Ministry ... Already elsewhere ...'[7]

July 26   German Intelligence in Berlin orders Schwartzkoppen to continue negotiations with the French officer [Esterhazy].

July 27   Esterhazy visits Schwartzkoppen at the German Embassy. On this occasion he identifies himself as a major in the 74th Infantry Regiment, showing his *journal de mobilisation* (regimental papers) which, however, do not contain information of any significance. Esterhazy leaves these papers behind and asks for a monthly retainer of 2000 francs for his services. Schwartzkoppen rejects his proposal.

Aug 3   Schwartzkoppen discusses Esterhazy's proposal with Major Müller, head of German Intelligence in Berlin.

Aug 4   Müller instructs Schwartzkoppen to pursue the contact with Esterhazy on condition that it leads to valuable information. Schwartzkoppen is not to set a monthly retainer but to scale payments according to the quality of the information.

Aug 5–9   Esterhazy attends artillery exercises near Châlons.

Aug 6   On his return from Berlin, Schwartzkoppen finds a letter from Esterhazy giving his contact addresses for the immediate future.

Aug 13   Esterhazy visits the German Embassy for the third time. Schwartzkoppen returns Esterhazy's regimental papers. (*v.* 27 July 1894) Esterhazy offers to provide the recently revised mobilization plan of the French artillery.[8]

Aug 15　　　Esterhazy gives Schwartzkoppen the mobilization plan and is paid 1000 francs.[9] At the same time Esterhazy uses the opportunity to mention the 120mm short cannon, which is of great interest to the German General Staff.[10]

Aug 17　　　Schwartzkoppen sends one of his agents, Alex, alias R.B., a double agent working also for the Section de Statistique, as an observer of the artillery exercises in Châlons furnishing him with a list of information he hopes to obtain on the 120mm short cannon. Alex sends the list to the Section de Statistique where he is provided with fabricated answers which are delivered to Schwartzkoppen.[11]

Esterhazy writes a letter (to M. Callé, a bailiff) on India squared paper identical to that on which the *bordereau* would later be written. (*v.* 26 Sept 1894; early Nov 1898, First revision investigation: Criminal Chamber)

Aug 27　　　Last-minute orders from Mercier to officers of the 74th Artillery Regiment in Rouen state that reservist officers (which includes Esterhazy) are not to leave for the main manoeuvres in Vaujours as originally planned.

Aug 28　　　Esterhazy is assigned to minor manoeuvres near Rouen.

Madame Bastian

Aug 29   Dreyfus realizes that in accordance with the order of 17 May 1894, he will not be taking part in the main manoeuvres in Vaujours.

Sept 1   Esterhazy delivers three secret military documents to Schwartzkoppen.[12]

Sept 5   Esterhazy supplies Schwartzkoppen with a report on artillery manoeuvres at Sissonne.[13]

Sept 6   Schwartzkoppen receives a letter from Esterhazy, reporting on the projected French expedition to Madagascar.[14]

Sept 15   Schwartzkoppen leaves Paris to observe manoeuvres in Beauce.

Sept 25   Schwartzkoppen goes on leave.

Discovery of the *bordereau*

Sept 26[15]   Mme Bastian gives Henry a package containing all the papers she has gathered from the German Embassy over the previous month.[16] Among them is a document written on India squared paper, almost but not completely torn into six fragments. This document, a *bordereau*, is an unsigned, undated memorandum to Schwartzkoppen listing the military documents offered by the sender:[17]

> *Without news indicating that you wish to see me, Sir, I am nevertheless forwarding you some interesting information:*
>
> *1. A note on the hydraulic brake of the 120 and how that piece performed;*[18]
>
> *2. A note on the covering troops (some modifications will be introduced by the new plan);*[19]
>
> *3. A note on a change to artillery formations;*[20]
>
> *4. A note concerning Madagascar; (v. 6 Sep 1894)*
>
> *5. The draft Field Artillery Firing Manual (14 March 1894).*
>
> *The latter document is extremely difficult to obtain and I am only able to have it at my disposal for a very few days. The Ministry of War has sent a fixed number of copies to the regiments, who are responsible for them. Each officer holding a copy is to return it after the manoeuvres.*[21] *So if you want to take from it what is of interest to you and leave it at my disposal afterwards, I will collect it unless you want me to have it copied* in extenso *and send you the copy.*
>
> *I am leaving on manoeuvres.*[22]

Original French text of the bordereau

> 'Sans nouvelles m'indiquant que vous désirez me voir, je vous adresse cependant, Monsieur, quelques renseignements intéressants :
>
> 1. Une note sur le frein hydraulique du 120, et la manière dont s'est conduite cette pièce;

> 2. *Une note sur les troupes de couverture (quelques modifications seront apportées par le nouveau plan);*
>
> 3. *Une note sur une modification aux formations de l'artillerie;*
>
> 4. *Une note relative à Madagascar;*
>
> 5. *Le projet de Manuel de tir de l'artillerie de campagne (14 mars 1894);*
>
> *Ce dernier document est extrêmement difficile à se procurer et je ne puis l'avoir à ma disposition que très peu de jours. Le Ministère de la Guerre en a envoyé un nombre fixe dans les corps, et ces corps en sont responsables. Chaque officier détenteur doit remettre le sien après les manoeuvres. Si donc vous voulez y prendre ce qui vous intéresse et le tenir à ma disposition après, je le prendrai. A moins que vous ne vouliez que je le fasse copier in extenso et ne vous en adresse la copie.*
>
> *Je vais partir en manoeuvres.'*

Sept 27   Henry shows the *bordereau* to his colleagues in the Section de Statistique, Captains Jules Lauth and Pierre-Ernest Matton, as well as Gribelin and Sandherr. From its content they conclude that the traitor is probably an artillery officer on the General Staff.[23]

The *bordereau* – or a copy of it – is appended to a first report on it written by Sandherr and included in *Bulletin de renseignements* No. 109.[24] (*v.* 16 Feb 1894, n. 6) In the absence of Boisdeffre, Chief of the General Staff, Sandherr hands the *bordereau* to Boisdeffre's deputy, General Edmond Renouard. Renouard informs Mercier, who orders an immediate investigation.

End Sept   The *bordereau* is shown to the heads of the four bureaux of the General Staff. They fail to identify the handwriting as that of any member of their own staff.

The Section de Statistique's 'normal route' intercepts a list of questions concerning the 120mm short cannon, sent by Schwartzkoppen to Esterhazy between the end of July and beginning of September 1894. The documents mentioned in the *bordereau* provide some answers. One of the unanswered questions concerns the *réglette de correspondence,* which is a component part of the 120mm cannon mechanism. (*v.* 13 Oct 1894)

Oct 4   Sandherr asks Louis Tomps, a police official seconded to the Section de Statistique, to make copies of the *bordereau*. These are sent to the heads of the four bureaux and to General Denis-François-Félix Deloye, Chief of Artillery. There is still no indication of authorship.

Oct 6   On his return from leave Lieutenant-Colonel Henri d'Aboville, deputy head of the Quatrième Bureau, is shown the *bordereau* by his superior officer, Fabre. D'Aboville is confident he can easily identify the author since he must be an artillery officer who has passed through all four bureaux.[25]

The bordereau (text on verso visible through transparent paper)

Fabre and d'Aboville consult the relevant officer lists. They come to the name of Alfred Dreyfus. Fabre had already written a negative report on Dreyfus when he served with the Quatrième Bureau. (*v.* 31 Dec 1893) They compare the handwriting on official forms completed by Dreyfus to the *bordereau* and find 'striking similarities'.[26] Fabre reports this to General Charles Gonse, Deputy Chief of the General Staff, who in turn alerts Boisdeffre and Sandherr.[27] Boisdeffre informs Mercier.

Without mentioning the name of Dreyfus, Gonse asks Major Armand Du Paty de Clam of the Troisième Bureau, known to be interested in graphology, to compare the handwriting of the *bordereau* with that of Dreyfus. Du Paty concludes that the handwriting is identical; Gonse then reveals to Du Paty the name of Dreyfus and the *bordereau*'s significance as potential evidence in a case of treason. Gonse instructs Du Paty to initiate a more thorough examination.

Oct 6–9   Mercier consults the highest military authority, General Gustave Saussier, Military Governor of Paris. Saussier advises Mercier not to pursue the matter as for the army anything is preferable to denouncing one of its officers as a German spy.[28]

Oct 7   Du Paty reports that there is enough similarity between the handwriting of Dreyfus and that of the *bordereau* to justify a full investigation. Sandherr suggests that Gonse should conduct a search of the suspect's house, but in Boisdeffre's absence neither is willing to sanction it.

Oct 9   At a meeting of the Conseil des Ministres (the Cabinet), Mercier asks Eugène Guérin, Minister of Justice, to recommend a handwriting expert. Guérin suggests Alfred Gobert, a specialist employed by the Banque de France.

Oct 10   Mercier informs President Jean Casimir-Périer and Prime Minister Charles Dupuy about the discovery of the *bordereau* and the ongoing investigation.

Mercier instructs Louis Lépine, Préfet de police (Chief of Police), to appoint a civil police officer from the Sûreté (the judicial police) to assist the military in the investigation and possible arrest. Lépine appoints Commissaire (Superintendent) Armand Cochefert.

Oct 11   Dupuy holds a petit conseil (meeting of a select Cabinet group) at the Ministry of the Interior. Present are Mercier (Minister of War), Gabriel Hanotaux (Foreign Secretary) and Guérin (Minister of Justice). Mercier shows his colleagues the *bordereau* telling them that a suspect has been identified but does not reveal his name. Despite an objection from Hanotaux, who advises against exposing a French officer and Germany's military attaché, the Ministers decide to proceed with an investigation on condition that more evidence is found. A discreet search of the suspect's house is again suggested but not carried out.

Mercier sends Sandherr, Henry and Du Paty to police headquarters to confirm Cochefert's involvement and summons Gobert to the Ministry of War: Gonse instructs Gobert to compare the *bordereau* with the handwriting of Dreyfus and to advise whether a judicial inquiry is warranted.[29]

Mercier briefs Cochefert, and tells him to work closely with Sandherr, Henry and Du Paty.

In the evening Hanotaux visits Mercier at home, pressing him – unsuccessfully – not to pursue the investigation of Dreyfus before further evidence is found.[30]

Oct 12   Without revealing the identity of Dreyfus, Gonse gives Gobert the documents for the handwriting comparison and visits Gobert twice to speed up the work.[31] Fearing that Gobert is about to report differences in the handwriting samples, Mercier asks Lépine to suggest another graphologist. Lépine recommends Alphonse Bertillon, criminologist from the judicial police.[32]

Du Paty explains to Cochefert his plan for the arrest of Dreyfus.

In the evening Boisdeffre charges Du Paty with the foreseen arrest. In accordance with military judicial procedure, he invests him with the authority of a judicial police officer.

Oct 13   Gobert presents his report to Gonse stating someone other than the suspect could have written the *bordereau*.

Bertillon is given samples of Dreyfus' handwriting and the *bordereau* for comparison. He is instructed to present his conclusions on the same day. He reports that Dreyfus wrote the *bordereau*.

In the afternoon Dreyfus receives a letter signed by Gonse:

> *Paris, 13 October 1894.*
>
> *Summons. The Division General, Chief of the Army General Staff, will conduct an inspection of the probationary officers on Monday 15 October. Captain Dreyfus, currently with the 39th Infantry Regiment in Paris, is invited to present himself on that date at 9 a.m. to the office of the Chief of the Army General Staff. Civilian Dress.*[33]

Mercier and Du Paty examine the procedure for Dreyfus' arrest.[34]

Du Paty tells Cochefert that in Bertillon's opinion the handwriting of the *bordereau* and that of Dreyfus are similar.

Esterhazy delivers to Schwartzkoppen the *réglette de correspondence.*[35]

Oct 14   Du Paty visits Mercier at the Ministry of War and is asked to return later that evening.[36]

At 6 p.m. Mercier, Boisdeffre, Sandherr, Gonse, Cochefert and Du Paty meet at the Ministry of War. Mercier approves all the details of Du Paty's plan for the arrest of Dreyfus, including a contrived dictation of a letter. (*v.* 15 October 1894)

Without informing Saussier, Mercier notifies Ferdinand Forzinetti, Governor of Cherche-Midi military prison, that he should expect a confidential letter the following day to be delivered by a high-ranking officer (d'Aboville). Mercier then signs warrants for the arrest of Dreyfus on charges of high treason and a search of his home.[37]

Du Paty and Cochefert rehearse their roles in the impending arrest.

Oct 15   D'Aboville delivers the confidential letter to Forzinetti signed by Mercier the previous day. It informs Forzinetti that Dreyfus is accused of high treason and will be escorted to prison in the morning. Forzinetti will be personally responsible for the prisoner, who is to be held in strict confinement without knife, paper, pen or ink. The imprisonment is to be a matter of complete secrecy – not even Saussier is to be informed of the arrest. D'Aboville then chooses the actual cell in which Dreyfus is to be imprisoned and warns Forzinetti of the potential reaction of *la haute juiverie* (the Jewish establishment).[38]

The arrest of Dreyfus

At 9 a.m. Dreyfus presents himself at the Ministry of War, as instructed. Picquart directs him to Boisdeffre's office, where he finds Du Paty, but the Chief of Staff is not present. Unknown to Dreyfus, three other persons in civilian clothes are also present in the room – Gribelin, Cochefert and his secretary Henri-François Boussard. All three can see the face of Dreyfus reflected in a mirror. Henry is hidden behind

Major Du Paty
de Clam

a curtain. Du Paty asks Dreyfus to enter his personal details on an inspection form. Du Paty wears a black glove on the pretence that he has hurt his right hand. He asks Dreyfus to write a letter for him that he must present to Boisdeffre. Du Paty dictates extracts from the *bordereau* to Dreyfus including the phrases 'a note on the hydraulic brake of the 120mm and how that piece performed', 'a note on covering troops' and 'a note on Madagascar'. All those present watch carefully. If Dreyfus is nervous or his hand shakes, his guilt is proven. If he does not tremble, he can be accused of concealing his guilt. Dreyfus writes a few sentences. Du Paty, interrupting suddenly, asks Dreyfus why is he shaking. Dreyfus replies that he is not shaking but his fingers are cold.[39] The dictation continues. After a few minutes Du Paty places his hand on the shoulder of Dreyfus: 'Captain Dreyfus, I arrest you in the name of the law. You are charged with the crime of high treason.' Du Paty reads out aloud Article 76 of the Penal Code: 'Whosoever contrives plots or maintains relations with foreign powers or their agents, in order to urge them to commit hostilities or undertake war against France, or to procure them the means to do so, will be punished by death.'[40] As he reads, Du Paty reveals a revolver (loaded with a single bullet), hidden beneath a folder on the table. Dreyfus exclaims, 'I am innocent. Kill me if you wish.'[41] Du Paty says, 'It is not for us to do so.' Dreyfus replies that he wants to live to establish his innocence – not to kill himself. Cochefert and his secretary seize Dreyfus and search him. Dreyfus offers no resistance: 'Take my keys, search everything in my house, I am innocent.'[42] 'At least show me the evidence,' he adds, 'of the infamy you claim I have committed.' Cochefert, Gribelin and Du Paty continue to question him but do not show him the *bordereau*. Dreyfus continues to protest his innocence. He swears that nothing in his life could give him reason to commit treason: he is from Alsace, happily married and adores his children – he is financially independent, loves his country and his profession.[43] (*v.* Appendix 4)

Accompanied by a police officer, Henry conducts Dreyfus to Cherche-Midi prison.[44] Although Henry has witnessed the handwriting text, he asks Dreyfus what he is accused of. Dreyfus replies that according to Du Paty, he is accused of handing confidential documents to a foreign power. He adds that Du Paty did not specify the documents.[45] He enters the prison about midday.

While Dreyfus is being driven to the prison, Du Paty and Cochefert go to Dreyfus' home. Du Paty announces to Lucie in a theatrical manner: 'Madame, I have a very sad mission to fulfil.' – Lucie: 'My husband is dead? – 'No, worse than that.' – 'A fall from the horse?' – 'No, Madame, he is in prison.' Du Paty and Cochefert search the house but find nothing. Du Paty refuses to give Lucie any information about her husband and forbids her – in her husband's interest – to tell anyone about the arrest, not even members of the family. He warns, 'One word from you would ruin him for ever … The only way of saving him is – silence.'[46]

Guérin, Minister of Justice, asks for Gobert's assessment of the handwriting samples. Gobert states that his examination is far from conclusive and he regrets the haste with which the matter has been conducted. As he leaves, he tells Guérin, 'At this very moment, the suspected officer is being arrested. I fear it is a mistake.'[47]

Oct 15–18   Dreyfus remains in solitary confinement for three days. Unable to sleep, haunted by nightmares, he is overwrought and repeatedly proclaims his innocence, and beating his head against the cell walls … Until 24 October he takes no solid food, only soup and sweet wine.

Oct 18   Contrary to Mercier's instructions, Forzinetti informs Saussier that a *prisonnier d'état* (a state prisoner) has been admitted. Saussier replies, 'If you were not my friend, I would put you in prison for two months for having admitted a prisoner without an order from me.' In defence, Forzinetti replies that he was acting on Mercier's orders.[48]

Du Paty's investigation

Du Paty repeatedly searches Dreyfus' home. He questions Lucie and reminds her to remain absolutely silent about her husband's arrest: 'Your husband is a coward, a wretch … [He is] guilty, I am absolutely convinced of it.'[49]

Oct 16–17   Du Paty and Cochefert examine the 22 bundles of papers taken from his home.

They find nothing suspicious.

Oct 18–30   Du Paty, assisted by his clerk, Gribelin, begins to interrogate Dreyfus in prison. Before he starts, he asks Forzinetti if he can use brutal tactics, such as entering his cell unannounced while the prisoner is asleep and shining a powerful light on him. Forzinetti refuses.[50] For the first session, Du Paty dictates passages selected from the *bordereau* and orders Dreyfus to write in various awkward and undignified positions – seated, standing, wearing a glove, and so on.[51] (*v.* Appendix 5) Altogether there are seven such interrogations, yet no helpful information is generated for the investigators.[52] Du Paty uses no other witnesses. Instead, he instructs Guénée to enquire into Dreyfus' private life. (*v.* 4 Nov 1894)

Oct 15–20   Bertillon prepares his second report confirming his initial conclusion that Dreyfus had written the *bordereau*. He elaborates a complex theory that the *bordereau* was a 'self-forgery', i.e. that Dreyfus had forged his own handwriting so that he could claim either that the document had been forged by another or deny the resemblance to his own hand.[53]

Oct 21   On Mercier's orders Lépine appoints three more graphologists, Eugène Pelletier, Pierre Teyssonnières and Etienne Charavay.[54]

Oct 25   Pelletier's report refutes that of Bertillon and clears Dreyfus.[55]

Oct 27   Forzinetti writes to Mercier informing him that Dreyfus' mental state is causing concern: 'He cries then laughs and repeats that he feels he is losing his mind. He constantly protests his innocence and shouts that he will go mad before that innocence is recognized. There is reason to fear that he will commit some desperate act, despite all the precautions taken, or that madness will take hold of him.'[56] Mercier summons Forzinetti, who is instead questioned by Boisdeffre about his opinion of Dreyfus. Forzinetti replies: 'I think you are on the wrong track. Dreyfus is as innocent as I am.' Having obtained Mercier's orders, Boisdeffre instructs Forzinetti to allow the prison doctor, Dr Defos de Rau, to visit Dreyfus 'secretly'.[57]

Boisdeffre asks Du Paty for up-to-date information and angrily points out, in the presence of Sandherr and Henry, that all that has been produced so far as evidence against Dreyfus amounts to nothing: ' … you are getting nowhere with Dreyfus … you must obtain a good confession and if you have nothing more than your scrap of paper [the *bordereau*] General Saussier is perfectly capable of refusing to sign an order for a court martial.'[58] Du Paty replies that if there is insufficient evidence they should drop the case. (*v.* 29 Oct 1894)

Oct 28   Dr de Rau visits the prisoner, prescribes sedatives and suggests close monitoring in view of his poor health.

Oct 29   Graphologists Teyssonnières and Charavay submit their reports. Teyssonnières concludes that the handwriting of Dreyfus is similar to that of the *bordereau*. Charavay is less certain but concedes that the similarity between the two is sufficiently striking for the *bordereau* to be attributed to Dreyfus.[59]

Ferdinand Forzinetti,
Governor of
Cherche-Midi prison

In the evening, Du Paty shows Dreyfus a copy of the *bordereau* for the first time. He tells him that it was intercepted abroad and asks whether he recognizes it as his own handwriting. Exhausted and weak, Dreyfus feels a 'sense of relief' at being faced with the document that is the sole basis of the charge against him, knowing that he has not written it. He states, 'I confirm that I have never written this infamous letter.' Dreyfus acknowledges that a few words therein may appear similar to his own handwriting but adds that the document is not by him and as a whole does not resemble his handwriting.[60] Du Paty asks Dreyfus to copy the *bordereau* in his own hand.[61] Dreyfus discusses the document's content and explains, point by point, why he could not have written it.

Du Paty gives Boisdeffre his first report on the interrogations. He states: 'The weakness of the material proof which will serve as the basis for the charge [against Dreyfus] could quite easily lead to his acquittal.'[62] Du Paty suggests abandoning the case, but at the same time taking all necessary measures to prevent Dreyfus from communicating with foreign agents. Boisdeffre is furious. He calls for Du Paty: 'What is this diatribe? We are too far advanced to turn back. Dreyfus is a scoundrel who deserves to be executed. Carry on with your work without thinking about the consequences and stop being difficult.'[63]

Oct 30   Du Paty interrogates Dreyfus one last time. He shows him the graphologists' reports which conclude the *bordereau* was in his handwriting. Dreyfus continues to deny this. Du Paty tries to extort a confession, telling him: 'The Minister [of War] is ready to receive you if you want to embark on the path of confession.' Dreyfus declares that it is impossible for him, while locked in prison, to try to explain this 'appalling enigma'. Asking to be put under the surveillance of the Sûreté, he exclaims: 'all my fortune, all my life, will be devoted to unravelling this affair'.[64]

Oct 31   Du Paty informs Dreyfus that he has completed his investigation.[65] His final report describes Dreyfus as presumptuous, ambitious and rich; it hints at relationships with certain high society women and implies that he was in a position to secure secret documents for Germany. Unable to reach a firm conclusion, however, Du Paty invites Mercier to judge for himself what further steps should be taken.[66]

Du Paty allows Lucie Dreyfus to break the news of the arrest to other members of the family. By telegram, Lucy implores Alfred's brother Mathieu in Mulhouse to return to Paris.

Oct 28   A letter addressed to *Libre Parole* journalist Adrien Papillaud discloses that Captain Dreyfus has been imprisoned in Cherche-Midi on espionage charges: 'They say that he [Captain Dreyfus] is travelling, but it is a lie because they want to stifle the matter. All Jewry is on the move.' The letter is signed 'Henry'.[67]

Oct 29   *La Libre Parole* publishes a short article, 'Une Question', signed Ad. P. [Adrien Papillaud]: 'Is it true that a very important arrest was made by order of the military authority recently? And the person arrested accused of espionage? If this report is true, why are the military authorities keeping it absolutely quiet? A response is called for.'

Schwartzkoppen sends a letter to the German Minister of War, enclosing French military documents regarding manoeuvres in Paris and Toul. Schwartzkoppen demands that the documents also be transmitted to General von Schlieffen, Chief of the German General Staff.[68]

Press coverage

Oct 31

The daily *L'Eclair* reports that an officer has been arrested. Another daily, *La Patrie*,[69] announces the arrest of 'a Jewish officer in the Ministry of War'. *Le Soir* reveals the name of Dreyfus, his age and rank, and that he is serving at the Ministry of War.

Paul Grenier de Cassagnac,[70] owner and editor of the daily *L'Autorité*, writes: 'To arrest a French officer for high treason without clear proof would be a crime as abominable as treason itself.'

A Ministry of War communiqué published by Havas[71] confirms the arrest of an unnamed officer 'suspected of having delivered some confidential – but not very important – documents to a foreigner'.

Nov 1

La Libre Parole announces 'the arrest of Jewish officer, A. Dreyfus, for high treason'.

An emergency Cabinet meeting is held.[72] Mercier shows the Ministers a copy of the *bordereau*, which he claims is undoubtedly written by Dreyfus. The Ministers agree to initiate a judicial investigation of Dreyfus and the case is referred to Saussier. (*v.* 3 Nov 1894)

Panizzardi reports to General Marselli, Deputy Chief of the Italian General Staff, that he has never had any dealings with Dreyfus.

Mathieu Dreyfus arrives in Paris. He sends his nephew Paul to Du Paty with an urgent message asking for a meeting. Du Paty tells Paul that his uncle is a scoundrel who should have killed himself, but he agrees to the meeting. At the Dreyfus home Du Paty tells the family that the charges against Alfred are overwhelming, that he has betrayed his wife and has already made a partial confession. Mathieu suggests that Du Paty should allow him to question his brother in the presence of hidden witnesses. He promises that if Dreyfus confesses he will provide him with a weapon so that he can commit suicide. Du Paty firmly refuses: 'One word, one single word and there will be war in Europe.'[73]

Panizzardi's telegram of 2 November

Nov 2

Following his denial of having any relation with Dreyfus, Panizzardi, suspecting that Dreyfus may have been in direct contact with Italian Army headquarters, sends a coded telegram to Marselli in Rome. He advises an official denial of any involvement. Marselli telegraphs Panizzardi denying any contact between Dreyfus and the Italian General Staff.

Panizzardi's telegram is intercepted by the postal authorities and delivered to the translation service of the Foreign Ministry for decoding since it consists of a series of numbers. A first deciphered version is handed to Sandherr: 'Arrested. Captain Dreyfus who has had no relations with Germany.' Shortly afterwards the Foreign Office hands Sandherr a second version, whose decoding is more accurate but still considered provisional, especially its last phrase: 'If Captain Dreyfus has had no dealings with you, it would be appropriate to instruct the ambassador to publish an official denial. Our emissary has been alerted.' Sandherr informs Gonse, Boisdeffre and Mercier.[74] (*v.* 11 Nov 1894)

The German military attachés in Rome, Berne and Brussels inform Berlin that the named arrested French officer is unknown to them.

Nov 3 Saussier instructs Major Bexon d'Ormescheville, *rapporteur* (reporting judge)[75] at the Premier conseil de guerre (Paris) to open the preliminary investigation on Dreyfus. (*v.* 7 Nov–3 Dec 1894, d'Ormescheville's preliminary investigation)

According to Schwartzkoppen, Esterhazy again visits him at the German Embassy and supplies him with more information. They mention the arrest of Dreyfus. Schwartzkoppen points out the risk in Esterhazy's visits. Esterhazy reassures him that he has taken measures to avoid suspicion, even if he were discovered.[76]

Nov 4 Guénée delivers his report on the private life of Dreyfus to Du Paty, including false statements that Dreyfus associates with women of the *demi-monde* and gambles in disreputable circles. Since Du Paty's investigation has already closed, he hands the report to d'Ormescheville.[77] (*v.* 7 Nov–3 Dec 1894, d'Ormescheville's preliminary investigation)

Nov 9 A report by Lépine undertaken on Mercier's instructions is submitted to Henry. It contradicts Guénée's findings, indicating the confusion of identities and affirming that Dreyfus has never gambled in Paris. This report is not shown to d'Ormescheville, who has just started his own investigation.[78] (*v.* 7 Nov–3 Dec, d'Ormescheville's preliminary investigation)

Nov 10 German Ambassador von Münster publishes a statement in *Le Figaro* that there has never been any contact between Dreyfus and Schwartzkoppen.[79]

Nov 11 Sandherr receives a definitive and accurate decoding of Panizzardi's telegram of 2 November from the Foreign Office: 'If Captain Dreyfus has had no dealings with you it would be appropriate to instruct the ambassador to publish an official denial in order to avoid comments by the press.' Sandherr makes a copy and returns the original to the Foreign Office, where it is filed. A falsified version, probably on the same day, is substituted for the copy of the original in the Ministry of War files. It reads: 'Captain Dreyfus has been arrested. The Ministry of War has evidence of his dealings with Germany. We have taken all necessary precautions.'[80]

Nov 17   In the midst of the press campaign against him Mercier breaks his silence in *Le Journal* to declare that the Dreyfus investigation will be over within ten days and that Dreyfus only had documents of secondary importance.

Nov 22   Mercier's statement in *Le Journal* provokes Drumont in *La Libre Parole* to publish a vicious attack accusing Mercier of suppressing the affair. He writes: 'Either General Mercier had Captain Dreyfus arrested without proof, and in that case his irresponsibility is a crime; or, he allowed the documents establishing treason to be stolen from him, and in that case his carelessness is an act of stupidity. In both instances General Mercier is unworthy of the position he holds. In any event, one is just as guilty in being stupid as being a criminal.'

Nov 28   According to the interview with journalist Charles Leser published in *Le Figaro,* Mercier declares that he has certain and absolute proof of Dreyfus' treason. The article further suggests that Germany is the foreign government with which Dreyfus was allegedly in contact. Worried about the devastating implications of Mercier's statement, Mathieu Dreyfus seeks advice from the lawyer René Waldeck-Rousseau, who in turn asks Dupuy to persuade Mercier to deny the statement.[81] *Le Temps* publishes a denial by Mercier.

Von Münster complains by telegram to Hanotaux about allegations that his Government has been involved in the arrest of Dreyfus. He asks him to avoid provoking further allegations.

Nov 29   Havas publishes an ambiguous unofficial statement that the previous day's interview in *Le Figaro* contained some errors. Leser, however, reaffirms its accuracy.

Nov 30   Von Münster complains repeatedly to the Foreign Office about the 'weakness' and 'inadequacy' of the French Government's official denials of German involvement in the arrest of Dreyfus. A second official denial released to Havas is published in *Le Matin*: 'In various articles on the subject of military espionage, certain newspapers persist in calling into question the foreign embassies and legations in Paris. We are authorized to declare that the allegations concerning them are entirely without foundation.'[82]

Nov   Mathieu Dreyfus seeks a lawyer to defend his brother. Waldeck-Rousseau declines the brief because for several years he has dealt only with civil cases. He recommends Edgar Demange, a highly regarded criminal lawyer.[83] Demange accepts on condition that he first studies the case thoroughly: 'I will be the first to judge your brother. If I find a single charge in the file that could make me doubt his innocence, I will refuse to defend him.' But since d'Ormescheville's investigation remains secret, Demange is only able to study the file on 5 December 1894.[84]

La Libre Parole, L'Intransigeant, Le Petit Journal and *L'Eclair* openly attack the Government, accusing Ministers of keeping the arrest of

Dreyfus secret in order to stifle the affair because the officer involved is Jewish. They attack Mercier in particular: 'There are nearly 40,000 officers in the army ... He [General Mercier] chooses to confide the secret of our national defence to a born *cosmopolite*.[85] Is this Mercier not contemptible?'[86] Attacks on Jewish officers and Jews in general intensify: 'He [Dreyfus] entered the army with the intention of betrayal. As a Jew and a German, he detests Frenchmen';[87] 'Jews are a terrible cancer ... Jews are vampires ... They lead France to slavery.'[88] Various papers repeat that Dreyfus not only sold the mobilization plans but also schedules of trains, and names of officers sent abroad on secret missions by the Ministry of War, that he was a gambler, spent considerable sums of money on women and betrayed for financial gain. *La Libre Parole* accuses him of being protected by the politician Joseph Reinach.[89] Punishments are also suggested: 'he should be shot';[90] 'put in a cage like a wild beast ... paraded in front of the troops before being shot'.[91]

Mathieu Dreyfus in 1890

Mathieu Dreyfus at the time of the Affair

D'Ormescheville's preliminary investigation

Nov 7   D'Ormescheville opens his preliminary investigation. Guided by Du Paty, he hears evidence both from the graphologists and 20 fellow-officers of Dreyfus, but who are unsympathetic towards him. None of them is confronted with the accused.[92]

Nov 14–29   D'Ormescheville interrogates Dreyfus 12 times, repeating questions that Du Paty had already put to him, but does not uncover any fresh information.[93]

Nov 19   Guénée's second report on the private life of Dreyfus is handed to d'Ormescheville. It contradicts the police report.[94] (*v.* 9 Nov 1894)

Dec 3   D'Ormescheville submits his report, written in collaboration with Du Paty, to Saussier. It recommends that Dreyfus should be court-martialled on the following grounds: the *bordereau*, 'an unsigned and undated letter' which indicates that confidential military documents were delivered to a foreign agent; the negative evidence of Dreyfus' fellow officers; his knowledge of several languages, especially German.

D'Ormescheville ignores the reports of graphologists Gobert and Pelletier, which are favourable to Dreyfus, and insists on using Bertillon's unfavourable report.[95]

The Secret Dossier (November–December 1894)

Since d'Ormescheville's investigation is proceeding slowly, Sandherr instructs his officers at the Section de Statistique to collect any espionage-related documents from their archives that could be used against Dreyfus. He eventually selects four:

(a) Schwartzkoppen's fragmented memorandum to the General Staff in Berlin, 'Doubt ... Proof' (*v.* 22 July 1894), about a French officer offering his services as an agent.

(b) Schwartzkoppen's letter to Panizzardi, *Ce canaille de D.* (*v.* 16 Apr 1894)

(c) The Davignon letter, known also as *la lettre des appels*, sent to Schwartzkoppen by Panizzardi. (*v.* 16 Feb 1894)

(d) Two reports fabricated by Guénée: in October 1894 Guénée inserted two falsified passages into his existing reports on information received from Val Carlos regarding the German, Italian and Spanish military attachés. (*v.* 28 & 30 March 1894) These interpolations are fabricated statements attributed to Val Carlos. They relate to the existence of a treacherous officer at the Ministry of War. They read:

> *Be sure to tell Major Henry on my behalf (and he may repeat it to the Colonel [Sandherr]) that there is reason to intensify surveillance at the Ministry of War, since it emerges from my last conversation with Captain von Süßkind*[96] *that the German attachés have an officer on the General Staff who is keeping them admirably well informed. Find him, Guénée; if I knew his name, I would tell you ...*

> *... And yet someone in the Ministry of War, quite certainly an attaché, has warned the German military attachés ... So that is further proof that you have one or several wolves in your sheep pen ... Find him, I cannot repeat it often enough for I am certain of the fact ...* [97]

Du Paty's commentary

In early December Sandherr gives three of the Secret Dossier documents (a, b and c above) to Du Paty.[98] He replaces Guénée's fabricated material (d) with a note that Val Carlos has recently confirmed to an officer [Henry] in the Section de Statistique – repeating his warnings of spring 1894 concerning a French officer who is Schwartzkoppen's agent. Sandherr asks Du Paty to prepare a commentary on the Secret Dossier to demonstrate its connection to Dreyfus. Sandherr submits the commentary to Mercier.[99] (*v.* 17 Jan 1895)

Early Dec Esterhazy tells Weil that he believes Dreyfus to be innocent but that his innocence will not prevent him from being convicted. He adds that the reason for his view is France's antisemitism.[100]

Dec 4 Saussier issues the order for Dreyfus to be court-martialled.

Dreyfus is permitted to contact his family for the first time since his arrest.

Dec 5 Dreyfus is given permission to write to his wife, also for the first time:

> *I will not describe for you all that I have suffered ... But I place my hope in God and in justice. The truth is bound to come to light in the end. My conscience is quiet and at peace; without reproach ... I have been devastated, totally crushed in my dark prison, alone with my thoughts. I have had moments of utter madness, even raving, but my conscience guided me, saying 'Hold your head high and look the world in the face ...' I embrace you a thousand times ... my darling Lucie. A thousand kisses to the children. I dare not say more: tears come to my eyes when I think of them.*[101]

Demange familiarizes himself with the Dreyfus file.[102] Surprised by the weakness of the charges, he tells Mathieu: 'If Captain Dreyfus were not a Jew, he would not be in Cherche-Midi ... It is an abomination. Never have I seen such a file ... If justice is done, your brother will be acquitted.' Demange visits the prisoner and agrees to defend him.[103]

Dec 11–19 The national press is impatient with the manner in which Mercier is handling the Dreyfus case. On 13 December Cassagnac writes in *L'Autorité*: 'If Dreyfus is acquitted, the Minister falls ... But if Dreyfus is convicted ... Mercier will benefit from the trial, a great man and the saviour of the country.' On 19 December, the opening day of the court martial, an article in *Le Figaro* claims: 'If through some extraordinary circumstances he [Mercier] has been deceived, he will forthwith become a wretch, a traitor, a man of infamy deserving of prison.'

Dec 13   In response to von Münster's complaints about continuing press attacks on the German Embassy and its military attaché, Hanotaux publishes a third official denial of the embassy's involvement through Havas.[104] (*v.* 30 Nov 1894; 9 Jan 1895)

Dec 14   Alfred's brothers Léon and Mathieu Dreyfus visit Sandherr at his home to question him on the accusation against their brother. Sandherr pities their feelings of disgrace, saying that he is aware of their 'French sentiments'. They reply that they are convinced of their brother's innocence, and that other than the *bordereau* there in no justification for his arrest or court martial. Mathieu insists that it is a 'plot' against his brother because he is a Jew by those who want to force him out of the army. Sandherr denies 'such ideas', and Mathieu ends the conversation, realizing that he is making no progress with Sandherr: 'Whether my brother is convicted or acquitted, I will devote my entire life and all our fortune to discovering the truth.'[105]

Dec 14–15   Bertillon explains his convoluted 'self-forgery' theory (*v.* 15–20 Oct 1894) to President Casimir-Périer and assures him that Dreyfus is guilty. Casimir-Périer finds Bertillon 'not only odd, but mad, and mad in an extraordinary, cabalistic way … I thought I had a lunatic in front of me who had escaped from the Salpêtrière or Villejuif.'[106]

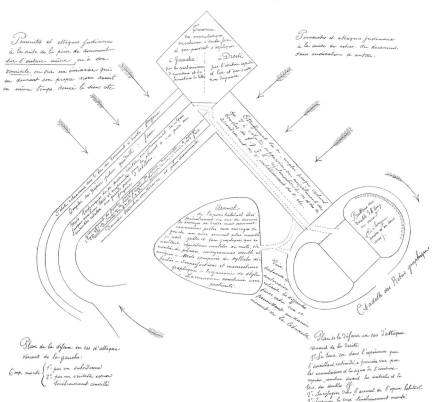

Bertillon's analytical diagram demonstrating his 'system'

Dec 18   Dreyfus writes to Lucie:

> *I am coming to the end of my suffering at last, to the end of my martyrdom. Tomorrow, I shall appear before my judges, with my head held high, my soul at peace … I shall return to you better than I was before … I am ready to appear before soldiers as a soldier who has nothing for which to reproach himself. They will see it in my face, they will read it in my soul, they will become convinced of my innocence, like all those who know me. Dedicated to my country, to which I have devoted all my strength and my whole mind, I have nothing to fear.*[107]

The court martial of Dreyfus[108]

Dec 19   **The court martial of Dreyfus, Day 1.** The Court comprises seven officers, including the president Colonel Emilien Maurel.[109] The *rapporteur* is d'Ormescheville. (*v.* 3 Nov 1894, n. 75) His report is read out in lieu of an *acte d'accusation* (indictment). Commissaire du gouvernement (Government Commissioner)[110] André Brisset calls for a closed session. Demange protests and argues for a public hearing.[111] When he points out that the accusation rests only on a single piece of evidence (the *bordereau*), he is interrupted by Maurel and told he is not to refer to any of the relevant documents. Demange tries to continue, but Maurel orders him to stop and adjourns the Court for deliberation.[112] Returning after 15 minutes, the Court announces its unanimous decision to proceed in closed session. Only two witnesses, Picquart and Lépine, remain in the courtroom, charged by Mercier and Boisdeffre to report on the trial.

Dreyfus is questioned and protests against the charge of treason. Witnesses for the prosecution are heard. Gonse discredits Gobert, whose report was favourable to Dreyfus, and concludes that Dreyfus could have had access to information on covering troops. Fabre and d'Aboville explain their [erroneous] theory that the author of the *bordereau* must be an artillery officer. Nominated by Mercier to testify for the Deuxième Bureau, Henry recounts the arrival of the *bordereau* at the Section de Statistique and the arrest of Dreyfus. He states that he is convinced of his guilt. Du Paty describes the dictation scene, testifying that Dreyfus trembled at the words 'hydraulic brake'. Demange exhibits the dictated script and asks Du Paty to point out where the handwriting shows signs of agitation.[113] Unable to do so, Du Paty becomes confused and contradicts himself. He argues that in the circumstances even an innocent man would have been flustered and therefore if Dreyfus was not, he must have been forewarned, but Du Paty could not suggest by whom. In an exchange with Du Paty, Dreyfus explains that he could not have written the *bordereau* in April or May because he was unaware of the artillery regulations until July. When Du Paty suggests that the *bordereau* might date from August, Dreyfus retorts that in that case he could not have written the phrase 'I am leaving on manoeuvres.'[114] Gribelin repeats what his superiors have already said and describes in detail 'unsavoury' character and habits of Dreyfus. Cochefert gives his version of the dictation, describing the nervousness of Dreyfus and the fruitless search he and Du Paty carried out at the family home.[115]

Dec 20   **The court martial, Day 2.** Statements are given by more of Dreyfus' fellow officers. Some give negative testimonies about his behaviour and character;[116] others consider him a loyal soldier and refuse to believe him capable of treason.[117]

Henry's false testimony

Henry asks to be heard for a second time. He gives false evidence by stating that in both February and March an 'honourable person'[118] warned the Section de Statistique about a treacherous officer. He points to Dreyfus, saying, 'There is the traitor!' Dreyfus and Demange demand that this 'honourable person' be called. Henry replies, 'There are secrets in an officer's head that even his kepi must not know.' Demange and Dreyfus insist that Henry reveal his informant's name.

Maître Demange

Maurel states that it will suffice if Henry gives his word of honour as an officer that the name of Dreyfus was given by this person. Dramatically, Henry raises his hand to the painting of Christ hanging on the wall and still looking at Dreyfus exclaims: 'He is the one. I know it, I swear it!' Graphologists Gobert, Pelletier, Teysonnières and Charavay repeat their conclusions. (*v.* 13, 28, 29 Oct 1894)

At the end of the second day Picquart reports to Boisdeffre, Mercier and Casimir-Périer that the obvious lack of evidence and flimsiness of the charges make acquittal likely and that he will not be content unless use is made of the Secret Dossier.[119]

Dec 21   **The court martial, Day 3.** Bertillon presents his convoluted theory on the handwriting of the *bordereau*.[120] The defence witnesses are heard briefly and their only supporting evidence is of the moral calibre of Dreyfus. The witnesses Koechlin and Jeanmaire, both from Alsace, testify to the integrity and patriotism of Dreyfus. Rabbi Dreyfuss (unrelated) from Paris, Professor Lucien Lévy-Brühl (a relative of Lucie), the physician Vaucaire and the prominent industrialist Arthur Amson testify that he leads a sober and honest life, and is devoted to his profession. Six other officers affirm their comradeship and respect for the accused.[121]

During the adjournment, unknown to Dreyfus or Demange, Du Paty passes a sealed envelope containing the Secret Dossier to Maurel. On Mercier's behalf, Du Paty asks Maurel to hand it to the judges during their deliberations the next day. Not a single member of the Government, even the President or Prime Minister, is informed of this.

In the prosecution's closing speech, Brisset recapitulates the charges made in d'Ormescheville's report.

Dec 22   **The court martial, Day 4.** Dreyfus leaves his prison cell still confident of acquittal. He tells Forzinetti, 'Today I will embrace my family.'[122]

The conviction of Dreyfus

Demange speaks three hours for the defence. The Government Commissioner concludes that even if no motive or moral proof of Dreyfus' treason can be found, the material evidence of the *bordereau* remains overwhelming: 'Take your magnifying glass, and you will be certain that Dreyfus has written it.'[123]

The Court withdraws to deliberate.

Maurel submits the Secret Dossier to the judges.[124] After one hour's deliberation, the verdict is read in public session and, in accordance with military law, in the absence of the accused:

> *In the name of the French people, on this day, 24 December 1894, the first permanent court martial of the military government of Paris … delivered the following verdict: A single question was put to the judges: 'Was Alfred Dreyfus, Captain of the 14th Artillery Regiment … probationer on the army's General Staff, guilty of*

having delivered to a foreign power or to its agents, in Paris in 1894, a certain number of secret or confidential documents concerning national defence ... in order to obtain for that power the means to commit hostilities or undertake war against France? ... [To which question] the Court declares unanimously, "Yes, the accused is guilty." ... The Court unanimously sentences Dreyfus to the penalty of deportation to a fortified enclosure ... The Court pronounces the discharge of Captain Alfred Dreyfus and orders his military degradation ... It declares him stripped of his decorations and privileges and of the right ever to bear arms ... It sentences him to pay costs to the State.[125] *(v. Appendix 7)*

Maurel gives the Secret Dossier back to Du Paty, who returns it to Sandherr, who passes it to Mercier.

Accompanied by Demange, Dreyfus is called into a vestibule near the courtroom, where Brisset reads the verdict and sentence to him by candlelight.

In Dreyfus' cell in Cherche-Midi prison, Demange tells the prisoner, 'Mon Capitaine, your conviction is the greatest crime of the century.' Dreyfus cries out to Forzinetti, 'My sole crime is to have been born a Jew!' In despair, he asks him for a pistol. Forzinetti calms him down to prevent him from considering suicide.[126]

Dec 23   Dreyfus asks to see Chief Rabbi Zadoc Kahn, but the request is denied.[127] He signs an appeal for a revision of his sentence.

Dec 24   Mercier proposes a bill in the Chamber of Deputies reinstating the death penalty for crimes of treason.[128] Socialist Deputy Jean Jaurès forcefully argues for equality in military law. Jaurès explains that the Military Code still allows soldiers to be shot in certain circumstances, such as insubordination or mutiny, but not in the case of treason, which is classified as a political crime. Moreover, Jaurès argues that Dreyfus could – and should – have been sentenced to death, and that if he was not, it is because the 'Republic did not want it', i.e. that there is a '*raison d'état*' embodied in the army.[129] His speech is greeted with uproar. The Chamber decides by a show of hands to impose a temporary ban on Jaurès.

Dec 25   Following press criticism of Germany, von Münster publishes another uncompromising statement in *Le Figaro*: the German Embassy has never had direct or indirect contact with Captain Dreyfus; no documentation relating to him has been stolen from the embassy; no request for a closed court martial has been issued by the embassy.

Dec 31   Dreyfus' appeal for revision is rejected.[130]

Mercier sends Du Paty to visit Dreyfus in a last attempt to make him confess. Du Paty offers him mitigation of his punishment if he admits having committed the crime out of imprudence or if he reveals his espionage contacts. But the prisoner continues to assert his innocence. In answer to Du Paty's statement, 'If you are truly innocent, you are the greatest martyr of all time', Dreyfus replies, 'I am that martyr, and

I hope that the future will prove it to you … I am innocent and your duty is to pursue your investigation.'[131]

In the evening Du Paty hands Mercier a letter in which he rephrases the words of Dreyfus: 'He [Dreyfus] hopes that five or six years on, things will sort themselves out, and that the key to this inexplicable enigma will be found … He says he is the victim of a turn of fate.'[132]

Du Paty gives Mercier a detailed report of this conversation.[133]

Dreyfus writes to Demange giving a full account of Du Paty's visit. He also writes to Mercier:

On your order, I had a visit from Major Du Paty de Clam, to whom I declared that I am innocent and that I have never committed the slightest indiscretion. I have been convicted, I ask for no favour. But in the name of my honour, which I hope will be returned to me one day, I have a duty to ask you to pursue your investigation. Once I have left, continue the search, that is the only favour I ask.[134]

General Mercier

NOTES

1 The use of the term 'the Affair' to mean the Dreyfus Affair began after the publication of Zola's 'J'Accuse'. (*v.* 13 Jan 1898) Many observers date the Dreyfus Affair from then.

2 There was nothing unusual in Esterhazy calling at the German Embassy: French officers wishing to visit Alsace and Lorraine to visit their families, after Germany's annexation of these territories, had to obtain a temporary visa from the German authorities in Strasbourg and the German military attaché could facilitate this. Both Esterhazy, in his various accounts, depositions and interviews, as well as Schwartzkoppen, in his diary, confirm that they first met in July 1894. Reinach however dates their first meeting to June 1893. (*HAD*, 2, pp. 72–4.) Details about Schwartzkoppen's relationship with Esterhazy in July-September 1894 appear in his diary edited by B. Schwertfeger: *Die Wahrheit über Dreyfus* (Berlin: Verlag für Kulturpolitik, 1930); English edition: *The Truth About Dreyfus from the Schwartzkoppen Papers* (London & New York: Putman, 1931), pp. 3–10. This personal account is at times contested by historians. (*v.* 26 Sept 1894, n. 17). These details however have been confirmed (e.g. Baumont, *Aux sources de l'affaire*; 63–4; Thomas, *Esterhazy*, 173–9).

3 Esterhazy informed Schwartzkoppen of his contacts, claiming to be close to Sandherr and to have worked for him. Esterhazy also referred to his familiarity with Roche, whom he declared would soon replace Mercier as Minister of War and engage Esterhazy as his secretary.

4 The exact date is unknown.

5 The original German word was *Brevet*.

6 The meaning of these two German words posed a problem for the Section de Statistique officers, since part of the second word was missing; they therefore left these words in German. Major Armand Du Paty de Clam, serving with the Troisième Bureau, and Sandherr translated them as 'absolute power' (in French *puissance*) and force (*Absolute Gewalt*). This indicated to them that Schwartzkoppen feared the 'absolute power' of the Section de Statistique to discover his dealings with a French officer. Later, Major Georges Picquart, who was to become head of the Section de Statistique, interpreted these words as meaning 'absolute certainty' (*Absolute Gewissheit*). This indicated to Picquart that Schwartzkoppen was convinced that Esterhazy was in contact with the Deuxième Bureau. *Rennes*, I, 401–4, Picquart. This interpretation is more likely. (*v.* 3 Nov 1894, n. 76)

7 Since the memorandum was written in German and arrived in torn pieces it was difficult to collate accurately. It is also unlikely that all the pieces were found. The memorandum was included in the Secret Dossier. (*v.* Nov–Dec 1894)

8 This plan, which was constantly modified, consisted of tactical information relating to the 1st Artillery Corps in the event of hostilities. In early 1895 the top-secret mobilization Plan XII was about to be replaced by Plan XIII.

9 Equivalent of approximately 20,000 French francs (J.F. Deniau, *Le bureau des secrets perdus* (Paris: Odile Jacob, 1998), p. 30), approximately US $4000.

10 The development of large-recoil cannons and oleopneumatic brakes was a matter of the utmost secrecy in both the French and German armies. Schwartzkoppen already had documents relating to the 120mm cannon, but he was eager to know how it worked in practice. *ASD*, p. 86 (*v.* end Sept 1894).

11 *3ème Cass.*, III, 69, Lauth.

12 Three of these documents were listed in the *bordereau* (*v.* 26 Sept 1894): 'List of covering troops'; 'Description of the 120mm short cannon'; 'draft Field Artillery Firing Manual'.

13 On the same day Esterhazy sent another four-page note to Schwartzkoppen attempting to convince him how his family connections could provide secret information on the naval situation in China. Apart from the *bordereau*, this is the only document in Esterhazy's handwriting in the German archives of information he delivered to Schwartzkoppen. Thomas discovered this manuscript and published it in the second edition (1971) of *ASD*. Also see Thomas, *Esterhazy*, pp. 184–5.

14 Although Madagascar became a French colony only in 1896, it was already likely in 1894 that the French would mount an expedition to Madagascar. Details of the expedition had already been discussed by the Army Commission and published in the press. Esterhazy may have procured information about it through his close friend Roche, then President of the Commission. Furthermore, Colonel de Torcy, the principal strategist behind the expedition was stationed at Châlons in 1894, which could have provided an opportunity for Esterhazy, who was there in August that year, to gather information about the expedition. *ASD*, p. 99.

15 During the course of the Dreyfus Affair numerous dates were given for the arrival of the *bordereau* at the Section de Statistique. They varied according to the differing testimonies from early September 1894 to the end of the month. The date of 26 September is, however, considered the most accurate. *ASD*, pp. 93–102. (*v.* following two notes)

16 Further indication that the documents were delivered on 26 September is the fact that on 27 September archivist Félix Gribelin recorded in the Section de Statistique account books the sum of 100 francs paid for 'Auguste's monthly retainer'. *ASD*, p. 108.

17   Throughout and after the Dreyfus Affair, the *bordereau*, the original basis for the accusation of Dreyfus, was the most highly discussed and analysed document. However, since 1906 the original of this crucial document has been missing from the French military archives, where only copies exist. Although it has become established that the *bordereau* was written by Esterhazy (between 27 August and 1 September) and reached the Section de Statistique by the 'normal route' (*ASD*, pp. 104–15), exactly when it was written and how it reached both the German Embassy and the Section de Statistique has been a source of controversy for those involved in and historians of the Affair. The General Staff carefully concealed the means by which the *bordereau* reached the Section de Statistique, until, at the Rennes court martial (1899) the mechanism of the 'normal route' was revealed. Similarly, they also maintained that the *bordereau* was written in April or May 1894, until, at Zola's trial (1898), they acknowledged it was written in August. (*v.* 12–17 Feb 1898, Zola's trial)

By contrast, in his diary Schwartzkoppen firmly denies that the *bordereau* ever passed through his hands, affirming that he only learned of its existence in 1896 when it was published in *Le Matin*. (*v.* 10 Nov 1896) He claims that Esterhazy must have given the document to the German Embassy porter between 16 August and 1 September; Mme Bastian or another secret agent must have found it in his pigeon-hole in the *conciergerie*, torn it into pieces and handed it over to the Section de Statistique (Schwartzkoppen, *The Truth About Dreyfus*, pp. 12–15). Schwartzkoppen's denial of having seen the *bordereau* in September 1894 has certainly troubled historians, but could be explained as an attempt on his part to protect his government and conceal his own carelessness in throwing the fragments into his waste paper basket and not destroying the *bordereau* completely. *ASD*, pp. 114–15.

Joseph Reinach, a prominent protagonist and the first to write a history of the Affair also refused to accept the 'official' version of how the *bordereau* reached the Section de Statistique. He believed that it was mailed to the German Embassy then stolen from Schwartzkoppen's pigeon-hole by one of the Section de Statistique's agents, Brücker (*v.* Oct 1893), who read it before handing it over to Henry. Reinach's theory assumes complicity between Esterhazy and Henry from the moment Henry received the *bordereau* and recognized his former colleague's handwriting. (*v.* 25 Oct 1898) Unable simply to destroy the letter (since Brücker was already aware of its existence), Henry had supposedly torn the *bordereau* into pieces to make it look as if it had come by the 'normal route' (*HAD*, 1, pp. 45–8).

Esterhazy (*Les dessous de l'Affaire Dreyfus* (Paris: Fayard, 1898), p. 136) shared Reinach's view of this issue: he said several times that the *bordereau* did not reach the Section de Statistique by the 'normal route', and that it was torn up at the Section de Statistique. Esterhazy repeatedly claimed that he had written the *bordereau* under the orders, or at the dictation of, Sandherr.

Pierre Dreyfus (A. Dreyfus, *Souvenirs et correspondence publiés par son fils*, p. 68) follows Reinach and Schwartzkoppen, stating that the *bordereau* did not reach its destination and that Schwartzkoppen only became aware of it in November 1896 after it was printed in *Le Matin*.

Maurice Beaumont (*Aux sources de l'affaire*, p. 35) also asserts that the *bordereau* did not reach the Section de Statistique by the 'normal route'. He believes it was put in the concierge's office at the Ministry of War during Schwartzkoppen's absence from Paris.

The generally accepted thesis presented in the chronology has been further challenged by many historians and other abstruse theories have been suggested:

Siegfried Thalheimer (*Macht und Gerechtigkeit, ein Beitrag zur Geschichte des Falles Dreyfus* (München: C.H. Beck'sche Verlagsbuchhandlung, 1958) suggests that the *bordereau* was a forgery fabricated in order to discredit Captain Dreyfus, the unwanted Jewish officer of the General Staff. Michel de Lombarès (*L'Affaire Dreyfus, la clef du mystère* (Paris: Robert Laffont, 1972)) argues that the *bordereau* was devised by the German Intelligence, imitating Esterhazy's handwriting and using previous information from French informants. Henri Giscard d'Estaing (*D'Esterhazy à Dreyfus* (Paris: Plon, 1960)); Jean Doise (*Un secret bien gardé, histoire militaire de l'affaire Dreyfus* (Paris: Seuil, 1994)) and Jean François Deniau (*Le Bureau des secrets perdus* (Paris: Odile Jacob, 1998)) present the *bordereau* as part of a plot masterminded by the Deuxième Bureau. Henri Mazel (*Histoire et psychologie de l'Affaire Dreyfus* (Paris: Boivin & Cie, 1934)) sees the *bordereau* as a fabrication by Schwartzkoppen himself to confuse the General Staff. He argues that it is not a letter from a spy as it does not mention a fee and because it would be unusual for a spy to offer five documents simultaneously. He stresses that the language and content of the *bordereau* reveal that it was not written by an artillery officer or a Frenchman. In his *La Psychologie du Kaiser* (Paris: la Renaissance du livre, 1919), Mazel even suggests that the *bordereau* was the work of Kaiser Wilhelm II. George Barlow (*A History of the Dreyfus Case. From the arrest of Captain Dreyfus in October 1894 up to the Flight of Esterhazy in September 1898* (London: Simpkin, Marshall, Hamilton Kent & Co. Ltd, 1899, p. 23)) also points out the technical errors in the *bordereau* and totally refutes the 'official' theory of the *bordereau* being found in a waste paper basket. Armand Charpentier (*Les côtés mystérieux de l'Affaire Dreyfus* (Paris: Rieder, 1937)) refers to the existence of secret documents known to Henry and Sandher, which implied that there was a spy in the Deuxième Bureau. Suspecting Dreyfus, they 'created' the *bordereau* to trap him. Charpentier suggests that it was either dictated by Sandherr to Esterhazy or written by Henry himself. He also refers (pp. 208–10) to the novel *Les Deux Frères* by Louis Létang serialised in *Le Petit Journal* (23 April–20 July 1894) which recounts the downfall of a brilliant Captain in the Ministry of War, accused of treason to Germany, due to the intrigues of his colleagues. Charpentier, as other historians (e.g. Baumont, *Aux sources de l'affaire*, pp. 286–7), sees in the novel a possible inspiration for the creation of the *bordereau* by Henry/Sandherr. Charles Dupuy, Prime Minister at the time of Dreyfus court martial (December 1894), admitted he was struck and 'haunted' by the extraordinary similarity between the novel and the later events related to Dreyfus arrest.

18   The 120mm short cannon had already received some field tests in 1893–94. In May 1894 it was tested at Châlons, and some artillery subalterns already possessed descriptions of its hydraulic brake. However, there was a newer 120mm cannon with a hydro-pneumatic brake, and the French were already developing another cannon, the famous .75mm, which was to ensure French victory in the battle of the Marne in September 1914.

19   Troops held as a back-up to those making the initial attack at the start of hostilities. Relevant tactics – the subject matter of the constantly modified mobilization plan – were obviously strictly secret.

20   This note probably concerned recent artillery manoeuvres, which were still being discussed and studied before being defined in the *Règlement sur les manœuvres des batteries attelées* prepared by the Ministry of War.

21   This is the only original document that Esterhazy proposed to procure. However, the General Staff later admitted that officers were not instructed to return their copies after manoeuvres, and that extracts had already been published by the Société de tir au canon in March 1894 and distributed to its members in July 1894. This, in addition to the 300 copies distributed to the artillery officers. (*v.* 7 April 1894) *Rennes*, III, 147–50, Bruyère.

22   In French: '*Je vais partir en manoeuvre.*' As with each phrase of the *bordereau*, this particular phrase was the source of countless discussions and controversies: in 1894 it could have been decisive in preventing the error of ascribing the *bordereau* to an artillery officer on probation. (*v.* 6 Oct 1894, n. 25) Later, when Esterhazy was suspected of being the author of the *bordereau*, it continued to be problematic because there was proof that Esterhazy did not participate in the main September manoeuvres but remained with the Rouen garrison. Thomas' explanation was that in the *bordereau* Esterhazy was probably referring to the minor manoeuvres near Rouen. (*v.* 28 Aug 1894) *ASD*, pp. 101–2. This phrase also supported the theories that the *bordereau* could not have been written by an artillery officer or a French officer because it was grammatically wrong. The correct formulation would have been '*Je vais partir aux manoeuvres*'. Charpentier, *Les côtés mystérieux de l'Affaire Dreyfus*, p. 13. (*v.* 7 Mar–19 Nov 1904, Second revision investigation: Criminal Chamber)

23   This reduced the possible suspects to the 86 artillery officers serving on the General Staff. Deniau, *Le Bureau des secrets perdus*, p. 36. Thomas remarks that to officers used to writing and receiving 'notes', the very word 'note' might have suggested that the author was working for the Ministry of War. *ASD*, p. 121.

24   This report was lost. *ASD*, p. 119.

25   This reduced the number of suspects to eight, being the number of artillery officers on probation in 1894 (Deniau, *Le Bureau de secrets perdus*, p. 37). D'Aboville believed that the information about the 120mm short cannon identified the traitor as a well-informed artillery officer in contact with the Premier Bureau since he had information about new artillery manoeuvres, with the Troisième Bureau since he had acquired the Firing Manual, with the Deuxième and Troisième Bureaux since he had information on the Madagascar campaign, and with the Troisième and Quatrième Bureaux since he had information on covering troops. *Rennes*, I, 575–6, d'Aboville.

26   *Rennes*, I, 577, d'Aboville. They should have recognized that the last sentence of the *bordereau*, 'I am leaving on manoeuvres', made their allegations about Dreyfus unverifiable, since as an officer on probation serving with the General Staff, Dreyfus was prevented from going on manoeuvres by the order of 17 May 1894. However, Fabre and d'Aboville preferred to interpret this phrase as referring to Dreyfus' expedition to the east in June 1894. A secret memorandum prepared in 1898 by the Deuxième Bureau, concluded that it was Fabre and not the Deuxième Bureau who promoted the first suspicions of Dreyfus' guilt. Bredin, *The Affair*, p. 561, n. 19.

As a Jew from Alsace, Dreyfus aroused special suspicion. Picquart, who was himself an antisemite, confirmed during the Rennes trial that antisemitic prejudice was rife in the army at this time (1894). *Rennes*, I, 373, Picquart. See also *AD*, p. 109. Historians continue to debate this point. See for example *DT*, pp. 20–1; *ASD*, pp. 128–31; P. Vidal-Naquet, *Les Juifs, la Mémoire et le présent* (Paris: La Découverte, 1991), vol. 2, p.11.

27   Sandherr, who was a passionate antisemite, originated from Mulhouse, like Dreyfus. He exclaimed to Gonse, slapping his forehead, 'I should have known.' *Rennes*, I, 578, d'Aboville.

28   Saussier opposed the arrest of Dreyfus on the grounds that it rested on assumptions and that clear evidence was lacking: Saussier believed that Dreyfus should be put secretly under surveillance; if there was proof that he had acted treasonably, he should be sent to Africa for execution so as not to 'stir up the country'. And he added, 'because I know my country'. *Cass.*, I, 318, Forzinetti. (*v.* 11 Oct 1894, n. 30).

29 On first sight of the *bordereau*, Gobert found it illegible and asked Gonse to have it photographically enlarged. Gonse refused, saying that if a photograph were taken, 'Tomorrow all Paris will know about the *bordereau*.' In accordance with Gobert's suggestion, a photograph was taken by Alphonse Bertillon, whose first job was as a photographer at the Chef du service de l'identité judiciaire à la préfecture de police (head of the judicial identity department (anthropometric) for the identification of criminals at police headquarters). *Rennes*, II, 300–2, Gobert.

30 Mercier admitted to Hanotaux that Saussier was against his plan and had suggested sending Dreyfus to the colonies on condition that 'he doesn't come back'. Mercier rejected this suggestion arguing that the name of Dreyfus was already too widely known at the Ministry of War, that the story would undoubtedly leak out, and that the Cabinet would be accused of doing a deal with spies. *Rennes*, I, 220, Hanotaux.

31 Gobert was, however, able to identify Dreyfus by comparing the information in the documents he was given with army directory biographies. *Rennes*, II, 304, Gobert.

32 Bertillon in fact was not a graphologist. It was in his capacity as a photographer that Gobert had already used his services. (*v.* 11 Oct 1894, n. 29)

33 *HAD*, 1, p. 100, n. 1.

34 Reinach notes that Mercier did not disclose in any of his statements his absence from Paris on 12 and 13 October but described the sequence of events as if he had not left the capital. *HAD*, 1, p. 87 n. 2.

35 Esterhazy obtained the *réglette* from his colleague Lieutenant Fernand Bernheim. *Rennes*, III, 142, Bernheim. Esterhazy continued to provide Schwartzkoppen with answers to his list of questions about the 120mm cannon. (*v.* end Sept 1894)

36 According to Du Paty, Mercier also met Dupuy and Casimir-Périer that day. Both approved of the arrest of Dreyfus. These meetings were not mentioned at any other time during the Affair. *ASD*, p. 146.

37 By signing the warrant for the arrest of Dreyfus before the result of the handwriting test, it was clear that Mercier had already decided that Dreyfus was to be arrested. Signing such a warrant without notifying the government was illegal. *HAD*, 1, p. 103. Du Paty later stated that Mercier had instructed him to arrest Dreyfus after the handwriting test, whatever its results. *Rennes*, III, 506, Du Paty's statement, read at the Rennes court martial.

38 *Rennes*, III, 103, Forzinetti.

39 Cochefert, in his second deposition at Rennes, finally admitted that he did not notice any shaking by Dreyfus when writing (*v.* 7 Sept 1899, Rennes court martial) *Rennes*, III, 520, Cochefert.

40 By reading Article 76 of the Penal Code, Du Paty increased the drama of the scene, although this article was no longer applicable. Article 5 of the constitution of 1848 had abolished the death penalty for political crimes and since the revision of the Penal Code in 1830, espionage and treason were classified as political crimes. (*v.* 22 Dec 1894, n. 125).

41 According to Cochefert, this part of the plan had also been agreed the day before in the event that Dreyfus chose to 'do justice to himself'. *Rennes*, III, 520–1, Cochefert. Also see *AD*, 211–13.

42 A. Dreyfus, *Cinq années de ma vie* (Paris: Maspero, 1982), p. 61.

43 These proceedings are published in *3ème Cass.*, III, 601–7. In his final report on the investigation he conducted on Dreyfus (*v.* 31 Oct 1894) Du Paty described Dreyfus' outburst as 'a bit theatrical, which did not leave a good impression on those present'.

44 The site of the former Cherche-Midi prison, at 38 rue Cherche-Midi in the 6th arrondissement, is now the location of the Ecole des hautes études en sciences sociales, established in 1975.

45 Reporting on 16 October his conversation with Dreyfus, Henry stated that Dreyfus had deliberately misinformed him, as he [Henry] had heard Du Paty mention three of the documents in the *bordereau*. (Henry may have been referring to the dictation, when Du Paty mentioned these documents but without telling Dreyfus that these were the documents he was accused of passing to a foreign power.) Henry's report was given to Major Bexon d'Ormescheville (who was to lead the judicial investigation on Dreyfus. (*v.* 7 Nov–3 Dec 1894) *Déb. Cass.*, 1898, 105–6.

46 *ATQV*, p. 20; A. Dreyfus, *Souvenirs et correspondance, publiés par son fils*, p. 29.

47 According to Gobert, Guérin told him at this meeting that he was responsible for civil justice, and, as this was a soldier's affair, it did not concern him. *Cass.*, I, 273; *Rennes*, II, 305, Gobert.

48 *Cass.*, I, 318, Forzinetti.

49 *ATQV*, p. 20.

50 *Cass.*, I, 318–19, Forzinetti. Du Paty always denied that he had ever made this request. Forzinetti refuted his denial. *Rennes*, III, 509; *3ème Cass* I, 273, Du Paty.

51 Du Paty later stated: 'What did we gain from all this? That I made Dreyfus write some pages in prison, standing up, seated, wearing a glove and not wearing it. I was ordered to do so and this order was given to me at the request of a graphologist, Mr Bertillon, I think.' *Cass.*, I, 440, Du

Paty. However, it was the graphologist Gobert who suggested that the handwriting of Dreyfus should be tested by writing in these positions. *Cass.*, I, 271, Gobert.

52 Du Paty's interrogation sessions are reproduced in *3ème Cass.*, III, 607–24. See extracts in *AD*, pp. 223–7.

53 The report was filed with d'Ormescheville on 23 October. See the conclusions of Bertillon's report (dated 20 October) in *AD*, pp. 123–4.

54 On the involvement of the graphologists in the Affair see B. Joly, 'La Bataille des experts en écriture', *Histoire 173*, special issue, 'L'Affaire Dreyfus: vérités et mensonges' (January 1994), pp. 36–41. See also Lazare's second edition of his pamphlet *Une erreur judiciaire* published on 12 November 1897, which included the handwriting analysis of a number of experts from around the world.

55 *Cass.*, I, 500, Pelletier; II, 79 (in d'Ormeschville's report).

56 Quoted in M. Burns, *France and the Dreyfus Affair, A documentary History* (Boston/New York: Bedford/St Martin's, 1999) p. 29.

57 *Rennes*, III, 105, Forzinetti. With his belief in the innocence of Dreyfus Forzinetti can be considered to be the first 'dreyfusard'. From 1896 the term '*dreyfusard*' was applied to those people who believed that a miscarriage of justice had occurred and were prepared to fight for a revision of the case. Another French term, similar but with a slightly different meaning, was also coined: '*dreyfusiste*'. This was used, after the Affair, to refer to new political theories and ideologies. See V. Duclert, *L'Affaire Dreyfus* (Paris: La Découverte, 1994), pp. 82–840. The behaviour of Dreyfus in prison had convinced Forzinetti of his innocence. Pierre-Victor Stock, who was to be the leading dreyfusard publisher, recalled that Forzinetti openly expressed his belief in the innocence of Dreyfus before journalists, politicians and diplomats as early as the time of his imprisonment at Cherche-Midi and before his court martial. P.-V. Stock, *L'Affaire Dreyfus, Mémorandum d'un éditeur* (Paris: Stock, [1938] 1994), p. 31.

58 Quoted in *ASD*, p. 150. The order had to come from Saussier, the Military Governor.

59 *Cass.*, II, 79 (in d'Ormescheville's report). Charavay later changed his mind. (*v.* April–May 1899, First revision investigation: Combined Chambers)

60 *3ème Cass.*, III, 622.

61 The graphological difference between the original and the *bordereau* copied by Dreyfus was so great that Du Paty decided not to show the copy to graphologists Charavay and Teyssonnières. *HAD*, 1, p. 195; *DT*, p. 31.

62 Du Paty's original report was lost, but he supplied a copy for the Rennes trial. *3ème Cass.*, I, 273. See also *AD*, p. 227.

63 Quoted in *ASD*, p. 153. Boisdeffre's use of the word *canaille* (scoundrel) may suggest that he was already aware of one of the documents intercepted by the 'normal route', *Ce canaille de D.* (*v.* 16 Apr 1894), later included in the Secret Dossier. (*v.* Nov–Dec 1894)

64 *3ème Cass*, III, 624. Mathieu Dreyfus expressed the same intention. (*v.* 14 Dec 1894)

65 Du Paty had to close his investigation in a hurry because of media disclosures. (*v.* 28 Oct 1894)

66 After annotating the draft report, Boisdeffre asked Du Paty to shorten it. The final report came to light only in 1898 during the investigation by the Criminal Division of the Supreme Court of Appeal. (*v.* 27–29 Oct 1898) *Déb. Cass., 1898*, 23–8. It is also reproduced in Leblois, although he omitted the phrases about Dreyfus' relationships with women before his marriage. *AD*, pp. 228–32.

67 Reinach believes that Major Henry wrote this letter: his aim would have been to prevent a retraction by Mercier. In *Le Siècle* of 2 April 1899, Reinach published a copy of the letter which he possessed. *HAD*, 1, pp. 191–3. Thomas refutes Reinach's assumption and attributes the letter to one of *La Libre Parole*'s regular sources. According to Thomas the letter's handwriting did not resemble Henry's and he rejects the possibility that Henry would have been party to such an indiscretion. *ASD*, pp. 154–6.

68 This letter, as well as other documents intercepted by the Section de Statistique in 1895, proved that leaks of information continued after the arrest of Dreyfus. This letter was submitted to the members of the Court at the Rennes court martial by one of Dreyfus' defence lawyers, Fernand Labori, to prove that Dreyfus could not have been Schwartzkoppen's source. *Rennes*, III, 558. (*v.* 7 Sept 1899, The Rennes court martial) Esterhazy, on the other hand, was still supplying Schwartzkoppen with information towards the end of 1894 and during 1895. (*v.* Jan 1895, n. 29)

69 The editor of *La Patrie* was Lucine Millevoye, who was to give the paper a clear nationalistic direction. *La Patrie* was to become one of the main anti-dreyfusard papers. (*v.* 15 Feb 1898)

70 A writer of the extreme Right, a Boulangist and Bonapartist.

71 Agence Havas was founded by Charles-Louis Havas in 1832 as a foreign newspaper translation agency. It became the first worldwide news agency in 1835.

72 As this was held on All Saints' Day, a public holiday, only eight Ministers attended.

73 After this first meeting Mathieu concluded, 'That man [Du Paty] is mad. It frightened me to know my brother was in the hands of that man.' *ATQV*, pp. 21–4.

74 *HAD*, 1, pp 246–7. According to Boisdeffre, Sandherr when showing this version said: 'Well, General, here is another proof of Dreyfus' guilt.' *Cass.*, I, 566, Boisdeffre.

75 The function of a *rapporteur* (reporting judge) in military jurisdiction is equivalent to that of *juge d'instruction* (examining magistrate) in civil trials.

76 Schwartzkoppen stated in his diary that he believed Esterhazy's visits were known to Henry (i.e. to the Section de Statistique) although Esterhazy never mentioned this to him. Schwartzkoppen, *The Truth About Dreyfus*, p. 74.

77 Guénée had carelessly confused Alfred Dreyfus with Maxime Dreyfus, a gambler in the Franco-American Club and a womanizer known to some journalists, and whose financial affairs had brought him to the attention of the judicial police. Guénée's report is reproduced in *Cass.*, II, 294–6. See also Stock, *Mémorandum d'un éditeur*, pp. 33–4.

78 D'Ormescheville saw only two reports by Guénée, dated 4 and 19 November. The police report was confiscated or destroyed, either by Henry or Mercier, but a copy was kept at police headquarters. Both the report and the fact that it had not reached d'Ormescheville were brought to light during the investigation by the Combined Chambers of the Supreme Court of Appeal in 1899. (*v.* April–May 1899, First revision investigation, Combined Chambers) The report is reproduced in *Cass.*, II, 349–50.

79 Baumont, *Aux sources de l'affaire*, p. 95.

80 *HAD*, 1, p. 248. This falsified version filed at the Ministry of War was the cause of many conflicts during the various investigations and trials of the Affair (e.g. *v.* 17 Nov 1897, end Apr–end May 1898; 24 Dec 1898; Jan–Feb 1899; April–May 1899; Aug–Sept 1899, The Rennes court martial).

81 Dreyfus' defence lawyer Edgar Demange appointed earlier this month (*v.* Nov 1894) commented on Mercier's iniquity in giving a press interview while the investigation was in progress and pointed to the risk it could entail – that the court martial would have to choose between the Minister of War and Captain Dreyfus.

82 Baumont, *Aux sources de l'affaire*, pp. 100–1.

83 Demange defended Morès following his duel with Mayer. (*v.* 23 June 1892)

84 *ATQV*, p. 25.

85 A contemporary word with pejorative connotations, denoting a rootless person of mixed loyalties.

86 'Les Juifs dans l'armée', an article by Drumont in *La Libre Parole*, 6 November 1894.

87 *Libre Parole*, 14 November 1894.

88 *La Croix*, 14 November 1894.

89 *Libre Parole*, 2, 6, 8, November 1894. Reinach was elected Deputy for Digne in 1889, the year he waged a campaign against Boulanger in the journal founded by Gambetta, *La République française*. His name suffered as a result of the involvement of his uncle, Baron de Reinach, in the Panama scandal.

90 *Libre Parole* 2 November 1894.

91 *Petit Journal*, 10 November 1894.

92 The records of the evidence given to d'Ormescheville are published in *Cass.*, II, 39–73. In 1898 Judge Alphonse Bard, the *rapporteur* of Lucie's appeal for the revision of Dreyfus' court martial (*v.* 27 Sept 1898) emphasized before the Criminal Chamber the tendentious and fraudulent nature of d'Ormescheville's investigation. *Déb. Cass., 1898*, 53–6.

93 The interrogation sessions are published in *3ème Cass.*, III, 625–68.

94 *Cass.*, II, 289–94.

95 D'Ormescheville's report was first published in *Le Siècle* (*v.* 7 January 1898), and soon after in Y. Guyot, *Révision*, 87–99. It can also be found in *Déb. Cass. 1898*, 37–50; *Cass.*, II, 73–86; *Rennes*, I, 10–20; *AD*, pp. 262–74; *Pro Zola [1898]*, II, 521–31. *Pro Zola*: The full proceedings of the trial were first published by Stock in 1898 as *Le procès Zola devant la cour d'Assises de la Seine et la cour de cassation (7 février-23 février – 31 mars-2 avril 1898), compte rendu sténographique 'in extenso' et documents annexes*, 2 vols. A new, one-volume edition appeared in 1998 (Paris: Stock), but without the annexed documents. Annotated extracts from the trial were also published in *Le Procès Zola (7-23 février 1898. Extraits choisis, présentés et commentés* par Thomas (Geneva: Idegraf, 1980). In the following we refer to the 1998 edition unless otherwise stated. See also Abbreviations and Conventions.

96 Schwartzkoppen's deputy, who was to replace him as military attaché in 1897.

97 *ASD*, pp. 164–8. This forged document, the first of many in the Affair, could not have been thought up by Guénée alone: it must have been approved or jointly agreed with Sandherr, Henry and probably Mercier. Val Carlos repeatedly denied having made these statements. Guénée's original reports were only discovered in Ministry of War archives in 1902 and confirm his denials: they contain only information about the conduct of the Spanish military attaché and his dealings with his German colleagues. They do not mention any leaks of information from an officer at the Ministry of War. For more on these reports see Ehrhardt, *A travers l'affaire Dreyfus*, pp. 179–203.

98 Because of the secret and fraudulent aspect of this dossier, Sandherr handed it *not* to d'Ormescheville, who was then leading the legal investigation, but to Du Paty, who was already involved in its compilation (as judicial police officer), and could thus be compromised. (Du Paty was later to be used again as a scapegoat by his superiors.) (*v.* 16–18 Oct 1897)

99 Du Paty's commentary (or *notice biographique*) is one of the most enigmatic documents of the Affair. It was repeatedly altered as it moved from hand to hand, several copies were made, some of which were destroyed, others reappeared. (*v.* 17 Jan 1895; end Dec 1897) Although attributed to Du Paty, the commentary was written in close collaboration with Sandherr. Du Paty stated, 'I was no more than a conduit. The commentary was written by me but dictated by Colonel Sandherr.' *Cass.*, II, 36, Du Paty; *3ème Cass.*, I, 238–40, Du Paty. Du Paty's commentary originally contained the statement that Dreyfus began his career as a spy in 1890 at the Ecole centrale de pyrotechnique militaire of Bourges, as well as comments on how each document in the dossier could be related to Dreyfus. The original documents were appended to the commentary. Both Du Paty and Sandherr kept copies of the commentary for themselves. Mercier inserted the texts of the original Secret Dossier documents into the text of his copy of the commentary rather than attaching them to it. Sandherr's note on the statement of Val Carlos was replaced with the complete text of Guénée's falsified reports.

100 It is possible that at this time and even during the court martial Esterhazy had not yet realized that Dreyfus had been condemned in his stead. Thomas, *Esterhazy*, p. 189.

101 A. Dreyfus, *Lettres d'un innocent* (Paris: Stock, 1898), pp. 21–2.

102 The file contained a copy of the *bordereau*, the graphologists' reports, reports and witness statements by Du Paty and d'Ormescheville.

103 *ATQV*, pp. 31–3.

104 Baumont, *Aux sources de l'affaire*, p. 102. Negotiations over this communiqué between Hanotaux and von Münster were protracted and difficult. Mercier later described the tense night as 'historic', alleging that Germany might declare war on France. (*v.* 7–8 Jan 1895) Both Schwartzkoppen and Casimir-Périer firmly denied that any such threat featured in these discussions. Schwartzkoppen, *The Truth About Dreyfus*, pp. 24–5. *Rennes*, I, 62–4; 153–9, Casimir-Périer.

105 *ATQV*, p. 38. Sandherr's friends later accused Léon and Mathieu of attempting to bribe Sandherr at this time. (*v.* 29 Dec 1897)

106 Psychiatric hospitals in Paris. M. Paléologue, *Journal de l'Affaire Dreyfus 1894–1899. L'affaire Dreyfus et le Quai d'Orsay* (Paris: Librairie Plon, 1955), p. 28.

107 A. Dreyfus, *Lettres d'un innocent*, p. 33.

108 The court martial took place in the Hôtel des conseils de guerre at 37 rue du Cherche-Midi, in front of Cherche-Midi prison. The building was demolished in 1907. E. Cahm, *L'Affaire Dreyfus, Histoire, politique et société* (Paris: LGF, 1994), p. 46. Documentation relating to Dreyfus' court martial, however incomplete, including the Secret Dossier, can be consulted at the Archives of the Service historique de l'armée de terre (SHAT) at Vincennes. There is no publication of the full transcript of the 1894 court martial.

109 There were no artillery officers among them. They were Lieutenant-Colonel Armand-Pierre-André Echermann, Major Nicolas-Théodore Florentin, Majors Benjamin-René-Pierre Patron and Marie-Alexandre Gallet, Captains Alfred Roche and Martin Freystætter.

110 A magistrate representing public authority in several jurisdictions – state councils, administrative tribunals, courts martial. In military courts, also known as the military prosecutor.

111 From the middle of November 1894 the question of whether the court martial of Dreyfus should be held in open or closed session was much debated in the French press. Some days before the opening of the court martial, Demange tried to convince Government members that a public trial would be in the interests of both the army and the accused. Through his friends Waldeck-Rousseau and Reinach, Demange appealed to the President of the Republic, but without success. For extracts of newspaper articles see *HAD*, 1, pp. 367–73.

112 See Demange's arguments for an open trial in *HAD*, 1, pp. 611–12 (Appendix XII).

113 As evidence of his guilt Du Paty also referred to Dreyfus' nervous behaviour during the first interrogation in prison, when, sitting with his legs crossed, he kept fidgeting with his foot.

114 Dreyfus insisted that the president of the Court exhibit the order of 17 May 1894 according to which all officers on probation serving with the General Staff were not to leave on manoeuvres. His request was denied. The following day, Du Paty stated again that the *bordereau* dated from April. (*v.* 12–17 February 1898, Zola's trial)

115 At the Rennes trial Cochefert gave a different version of the dictation. (*v.* 7 Sept 1899, Rennes court martial)

116 Including Bertin-Mourot, Boullenger and Gendron.

117 Among those who gave less negative evidence were Colard, Brault, Sibile, Roy, Bretaud, Mercier-Milon and Tocanne.

118 He was referring to Val Carlos. (*v.* Mar & Nov–Dec 1894)

119 Picquart did not know the content of the Secret Dossier at this time, but believed his superiors' assertion that it contained absolute proof of the guilt of Dreyfus. *Rennes*, I, 381, Picquart.

120 Many officers, as well as Picquart and Brisset, claimed that Bertillon's theory was incomprehensible. Dreyfus attached no importance to Bertillon's statement: it seemed to him to emanate from a madman. A. Dreyfus, *Cinq années de ma vie* (1982), p. 69; For more on Bertillon's theory, see *AD*, pp. 126–39.

121 Clément, de Barbarin, Ruffey, Leblond, Meyer and Devaux.

122 *Cass.*, I, 321, Forzinetti.

123 *Déb. Cass.*, 1899, 606, Demange.

124 Transmitting information secretly to the judges was strictly illegal. In so doing Maurel was acting according to the *ordre moral* (moral order) Mercier had imposed on him (as conveyed by Du Paty). (*Rennes*, II, 197, Mercier). The judges had different recollections of the items constituting the Secret Dossier and how they were presented. Some remembered that they were all read out aloud and commented on by Maurel. Others recalled that once one item had been read, the rest were handed over to them to read. In the Rennes trial, Freystaetter claimed he remembered that the dossier included the (falsified) version of Panizzardi's telegram of 2 November 1894. (*v.* 26 Aug 1899) However, they all testified that *Ce canaille de D.* had had a decisive influence on their judgment.

125 For the full text of the verdict, see *AD*, p. 327. The court martial decided on its verdict in accordance with Article 76 of the Penal Code, Article 5 of the constitution of 4 November 1848, Article 1 of the Law of 8 June 1850 and Articles 189 and 267 of the Military Code of Justice. The death penalty stipulated in Article 76 of the Penal Code had been abolished by Article 5 of the constitution of 4 November 1848 and was replaced by deportation. The sentence the Court pronounced was the heaviest sentence permissible and implied deportation for life to a fortified enclosure outside the Republic. The laws concerning the punishment for treason and espionage were some of the most confused pieces of legislation in 19th-century French penal law. The verdict against Dreyfus was to initiate future legislation on espionage and treason. (*v.* 24 Dec 1894) On this aspect see F. Hirt, *Du délit d'espionnage: étude de droit français et de législation comparée* (Paris: Librairie du Recueil Sirey, 1937) pp. 65 ff, 128–34.

126 *Rennes*, III, 106–7, Forzinetti; *Cass.*, I, 321, Forzinetti.

127 *DFA*, p. 142.

128 Since the Franco-Prussian War espionage had increased to such an extent that the deficiency in the existing laws became obvious. From 1891 various relevant bills were debated in the Chamber of Deputies. The case of Dreyfus highlighted the contradictions in and confusion of the existing legislation. Further bills were examined by the Government in 1895 and in 1898, but the rehabilitation of Dreyfus in 1906 curtailed discussion by reviving new arguments about the death penalty. Hirt, *Du délit d'espionnage: étude de droit français et de législation comparée*, pp. 81–95. France finally abolished the death penalty in 1981.

129 For the speech, see *Le Parlement et l'Affaire Dreyfus (1894–1906), douze années pour la vérité* (Paris: Assemblée nationale, 1998), pp. 20–7. See also M. Rebérioux, 'Aux origines, la justice', *Jean Jaurès cahiers trimestriels*, 137 (July–Sept 1995), p. 30.

130 The appeal could have been granted if the commission had become aware of irregularities committed during the court martial (e.g. the secret communication of documents). Boivin-Champeaux, the lawyer at the Supreme Court of Appeal who had discovered certain irregularities, intended to support the revision; but, informed by his colleagues of the Government Commissioner's strong opposition to the revision, he suppressed his personal beliefs. *ATQV*, p. 45.

131 *Cass.*, I, 321, Forzinetti.

132 *Rennes*, I, 100, Mercier.

133 *Cass.*, I, 440–1; *3ème Cass.*, I, 268, Du Paty. This report supposedly filed in the Deuxième Bureau archives was never found and thus never presented as evidence at any of the Supreme Court of Appeal investigations. (1898–99 and 1903–04) It was probably destroyed. Du Paty was asked by Gonse to reproduce it from memory. (*v.* Sept 1897)

134 A. Dreyfus, *Cinq années de ma vie* (1982), p. 76.

Part 3

DEGRADATION and DEVIL'S ISLAND

January 1895–January 1896

Le Petit Journal

Le Petit Journal	**SUPPLÉMENT ILLUSTRÉ**	ABONNEMENTS
CHAQUE JOUR 5 CENTIMES		
Le Supplément illustré	Huit pages : CINQ centimes	PARIS .... 1 fr. 2 fr. 3 fr. 50
CHAQUE SEMAINE 5 CENTIMES		DÉPARTEMENTS 1 fr. 2 fr. 4 fr.
		ÉTRANGER ...... 1 50 2 50 5 fr.

| Sixième année | DIMANCHE 13 JANVIER 1895 | Numéro 217 |

LE TRAITRE
Dégradation d'Alfred Dreyfus

The degradation ceremony of Captain Dreyfus, in the courtyard of the Ecole militaire in Paris, 1895

1895

Jan 2 Lucie Dreyfus is permitted to visit her husband for the first time since his arrest on 15 October 1894. The meeting takes place at Cherche-Midi prison, through double bars. Afterwards she writes to Saussier, requesting improved conditions for their meeting. Saussier passes the responsibility to Forzinetti. Future meetings take place in Forzinetti's private office and in his presence.[1]

Public degradation

Jan 5 The degradation ceremony takes place in the Cour Morland, the main
(Saturday)[2] courtyard of the Ecole militaire. Each regiment of the Paris garrison has been ordered to send two detachments. Nearly 4000 troops are lined up around the courtyard.

At 7.20 a.m. a Republican Guard, Captain Lebrun-Renault, arrives at Cherche-Midi prison to escort Dreyfus to the Ecole militaire.[3] The prisoner is searched, handcuffed and put into a prison van. By 7.45 the van has departed, escorted by two units of the Republican Guard. Dreyfus is taken to the office of one of the garrison adjutants, guarded by Captain Lebrun-Renault. He talks to the Captain as they wait for the ceremony to commence.[4]

Outside the courtyard gates a crowd of many thousands (estimated at 20,000) gather. Diplomats, journalists[5] and prominent personalities are admitted inside.[6] At 8.45, a drum roll accompanies the arrival of Captain Dreyfus. Wearing full dress uniform, his head held high, Dreyfus is escorted to the Ecole militaire courtyard by an officer and four artillerymen. He halts a few metres from General Paul Darras, who is mounted on horseback. The escort withdraws. Darras orders the ceremony to begin. A clerk reads out the Court's verdict. With his sword held high, Darras declares, 'Alfred Dreyfus, you are unworthy of bearing arms. In the name of the French people, we degrade you.' Dreyfus cries out, 'Soldiers, an innocent man is being degraded. Long live France! Long live the Army!' Sergeant-Major Bouxin, a Republican Guard, strips Dreyfus of his insignia, badges, buttons and stripes, then draws Dreyfus' sabre from its scabbard and shatters it over his knee.[7] The prisoner is forced to march alone in front of the troops and the whole gathering. As he approaches the courtyard gates, his protestations of innocence are drowned by the crowd's hysterical shouts, 'Death to Judas', 'Traitor', 'Death to the Jews'. Finally, in an atmosphere of jubilation, the band plays 'La Sambre-et-Meuse'.[8] The ordeal lasts ten minutes. (*v.* Appendix 8) When Dreyfus arrives at the far end of the courtyard, two gendarmes pull him into a horse-drawn prison van with a barred window, for transfer to La Santé prison. There he is searched, photographed and measured.

Von Münster gives Prime Minister Dupuy the translation of a telegram from Chlodwig von Hohenlohe, German Chancellor, sent on behalf of Kaiser Wilhelm II. The telegram demands that the French Government declare the German Embassy has not been involved in any way in the Dreyfus case. Dupuy is alarmed and asks Casimir-Périer to see von Münster.[9]

Rumours of an alleged confession

In the afternoon, the rumour of an alleged confession by Dreyfus begins to circulate at the Ministry of War. Mercier does not react.[10]

At the Moulin Rouge cabaret that evening, Lebrun-Renault recounts to journalists his conversation with Dreyfus, claiming that Dreyfus told him that he was innocent but also that 'the Minister [of War] knows that if I delivered documents to a foreign power, it was to set the process in motion and receive others of greater importance. The truth will be known within three years, and the Minister himself will take up my case again.'[11]

Jan 6   Lebrun-Renault's notebook entry for 6 January reads:

> ... *He [Dreyfus] was very despondent, and said to me that in three years his innocence would be acknowledged. About half past eight, without my questioning him, he told me: 'The Minister is well aware that if I was delivering documents to Germany, they were without value, and in order to procure others of greater importance.*[12]

Various versions of Dreyfus' alleged confession begin to circulate in the press (*La Cocarde*,[13] *Le Jour*, *Le Temps*).

Troubled by press stories of the confession, Mercier summons Lebrun-Renault.[14] Lebrun-Renault recounts his conversation with Dreyfus, including the mention of Du Paty's visit to his cell on Mercier's behalf. (*v.* 31 Dec 1894) He does not claim that Dreyfus confessed. Mercier instructs Lebrun-Renault to keep silent, also about Du Paty's visit.

Le Figaro publishes another version of Lebrun-Renault's conversations at the Moulin Rouge.[15] The article does not mention the confession but refers to Dreyfus' repeated claims of innocence. It also mentions that the main item of evidence for his conviction was 'a paper stolen from an embassy wastepaper basket'.[16]

This article angers President Casimir-Périer who informs Mercier of it. On Mercier's instructions, Lebrun-Renault is taken to the Elysée Palace. In the presence of Prime Minister Dupuy, Casimir-Périer reproaches Lebrun-Renault for spreading information damaging to Germany. Lebrun-Renault apologizes. He makes no reference to the alleged confession of Dreyfus, and is not asked about it.[17] Havas publishes an official denial of the story in *Le Figaro*.

Le Matin publishes the text of the *état signalétique* of Dreyfus (the official report of a prisoner's conduct). It states: 'Dreyfus expressed no regret at all, made no confession, despite the indisputable proof of his treason. In consequence, he should be treated as a hardened criminal completely unworthy of any pity.'[18]

Casimir-Périer receives von Münster, who repeats the complaints of the German Emperor Kaiser Wilhelm II, about the press allegations. The President tells the Ambassador that the *bordereau* was found in the German Embassy but that France cannot consider the German

Embassy responsible for the papers it receives any more than it can consider the imperial government responsible for the papers France receives. This explanation pleases von Münster, but he asks for a further government communiqué to end the matter.[19]

Jan 7–8 The French Government discusses the text of the communiqué with the German Foreign Office in Berlin.[20] (*v.* 9 Jan 1895)

Jan 8 In an unusual move, Mercier instructs Saussier to store the court martial documents at the Ministry of War rather than in the municipal offices.[21]

Jan 9 Havas publishes the latest governmental denial of German involvement in the Dreyfus case, a repeat of the statement issued on 30 November 1894.

c. Jan 10 Forzinetti hands Mathieu Dreyfus copies of the report by d'Ormescheville (the indictment), telling him it might prove useful when he decides to wage a press campaign on behalf of his brother. (*v.* 7 Jan 1898)

Jan 15 Casimir-Périer resigns following a series of political scandals and a ministerial crisis.[22]

Jan 17 Félix Faure is elected President of the Republic. A new Cabinet is formed, including Alexandre Ribot (Prime Minister), General Emile Zurlinden (Minister of War), Hanotaux (who remains Foreign Secretary) and Ludovic Trarieux[23] (Minister of Justice). Although he had not stood as a candidate, posters showing Mercier's portrait are distributed in the Chamber of Deputies supporting his candidature for the presidency as 'the patriot General [Mercier] who delivered the Jewish traitor Dreyfus to the court martial'.[24]

Before leaving the Ministry of War following the Cabinet reshuffle, Mercier burns Du Paty's commentary on the Secret Dossier in the presence of Sandherr.[25] (*v.* Nov–Dec 1894) He then orders Sandherr to separate the various component papers and return each one to its original place at the Ministry. Instead, Sandherr puts the documents into a sealed envelope adding his own copy of Du Paty's commentary and copies of the *bordereau.* He then passes the dossier to Henry, who writes 'Secret Dossier D' on the envelope and adds his own initials, 'J.H.' He locks it in the safe of the Section de Statistique at the Ministry of War.[26] (*v.* 30–31 Aug 1896)

Jan 18 At Cherche-Midi, Dreyfus is awoken during the night of 17/18 January. In extremely cold weather, with his wrists and ankles shackled, he is taken in secret to La Rochelle by special security, and held on a train throughout the afternoon of 18 January. His presence there, under heavy police guard, becomes known and attracts a growing crowd. When he is taken out of the train under cover of darkness he is knocked to the ground by the mob in spite of the guards' attempts to protect him. The launch *Nénuphar* transports him to the île de Ré; he is then transferred to the fortress of Saint-Martin de Ré where he is searched. The text of the *bordereau*, which he had managed to scribble down during his trial, is found in his pockets. It is sent immediately to Paris. Dreyfus is locked in a cell.

Censored letter to Lucie from Dreyfus on the île de Ré

Document bears the stamp

Jan 26   Dreyfus writes to Dupuy, Prime Minister and Minister of the Interior:

> *Minister, I have been convicted for the most infamous crime a soldier can commit, and I am innocent.*
>
> *After my sentence I resolved to kill myself … I ask you, Minister, not for pardon or pity, only justice … I beg you to continue the investigation to find the real culprit.* [The letter is unanswered.][27] (*v.* Appendix 9)

Jan 31   Without discussion, the Government adopts a bill proposed by Mercier to include Devil's Island, one of the îles du Salut in French Guyana, as a location of deportation.[28] (*v.* 9 Feb 1895)

Jan   Esterhazy moves with his regiment from Rouen to Paris, taking lodgings at 27 rue de la Bienfaisance. He continues to pass military secrets to Schwartzkoppen and from now on uses his connections with Weil to contribute to several military journals. He also becomes the close friend and main source of information to Major Octave Biot, military affairs correspondent of *La Libre Parole,* who writes under the pseudonym Cdt. [commandant] Z.[29]

Mathieu's researches

Jan   Soon after his appointment as Minister of Justice, Ludovic Trarieux, concerned by the disquiet provoked by the Dreyfus case combined with mounting antisemtism in France, asks Hanotaux for details of the conviction. Hanotaux says that he had opposed Mercier's decision to try Dreyfus, although, when Mercier showed him *Ce Canaille de D.* he became convinced of his guilt. Hanotaux does not tell Trarieux that the document was secretly communicated to the judges.[30]

Feb   Mathieu learns that Dr Gibert, President Faure's close friend and doctor, believes in his brother's innocence. Gibert introduces Mathieu to Léonie, one of his patients known for her gifts as a clairvoyant (Gibert had already experimented with hypnosis).[31] At their first meeting, in Le Havre, Leonie's visions astound Mathieu: she 'sees' Alfred wearing spectacles. Mathieu corrects her, saying that his brother wears a pince-nez but Léonie insists on spectacles. A few days later Mathieu learns (through Lucie) that Dreyfus had broken his pince-nez and was wearing spectacles.[32] Léonie's most startling revelation relates to the transmission of the Secret Dossier to the Court at the court martial when she asks Mathieu: 'What are these documents that are shown secretly to the judges? … If Alfred and Maître Demange saw them, their purpose would be ruined. They are documents you do not know about, which were shown to the judges. You will see later.'[33] (*v.* 21 Feb 1895)

Feb 9   The Chamber of Deputies passes the law establishing the îles du Salut as a place of detention for political prisoners sentenced to deportation. It also recommends that it should be applied specifically to the Dreyfus case. (The law is registered in the *Journal Officiel* on 12 February 1895.)

Feb 13   Lucie visits her husband on the île de Ré for the first time, having finally received permission from Georges Leygues, Minister of the Interior.[34]

Feb 18   Lucie writes to Emile Chautemps, Colonial Secretary, asking permission to join her husband in exile, in accordance with the law of 23 March 1872.[35]

Feb 21   Lucie visits Dreyfus for a second time. Picqué, the Prison Governor, allows a 45-minute meeting, but refuses Lucie's request to hold her husband's hands and to kiss him. The next visit is arranged before Lucie returns to Paris, but she is not informed that Alfred is to sail that very night for the îles du Salut.

Alerted by the news of Dreyfus' deportation to Devil's Island, and fearing that the terrible conditions there would result in his death, Gibert seeks an audience with President Faure. The President reveals that the conviction of Dreyfus was not based on the *bordereau* but on documents submitted secretly to the judges. In an attempt to influence Faure and interest him in the cause, Gibert shows him one of Dreyfus' letters to Lucie (given to him by Mathieu), in which her husband relates the disturbing incident at La Rochelle on 18 January 1895. Though moved, Faure refuses to act, but permits Gibert to tell Mathieu about their conversation. Gibert tries to convince Faure that Dreyfus had no motive to commit treason with Germany. Faure disagrees but states he cannot disclose the reason. He adds: 'The heart of man is full of mystery.' Gibert pleads with Faure to postpone the deportation. Faure refuses. Gibert warns: 'Beware this crime does not rebound on you.'[36] (*v.* 23 Nov 1897 & 7 Feb 1898, Zola's trial)

Journey to Devil's Island

Feb 21   Dreyfus is transferred to the île d'Aix by launch and boards the steamship *Ville de Saint Nazaire* in the middle of the night. By order of the Colonial Secretary the guards are forbidden to speak to him. The ship weighs anchor 24 hours later (on 22 February), commencing a voyage that is to last 15 days. Dreyfus is put in an open barred cell under the bridge. During the first few days it is bitterly cold (the temperature reaches 14 degrees below zero). From the eighth day the temperature turns torrid. Dreyfus realizes he is approaching the equator but without knowing where he is being transported to. At night he is watched by two guards. From the fifth day, he is allowed on deck once a day, for an hour, escorted by an armed guard.[37]

End Feb   Mathieu is introduced by his brother-in-law Joseph Valabrègue to journalist and writer Bernard Lazare (*v.* end June 1894) and briefs him on his brother's conviction.[38] He shows him d'Ormescheville's report and the notes taken by Dreyfus during the court martial. (*v.* June 1895)

Mar 12   Dreyfus arrives on île Royale. He is detained for 30 days in the prison complex in a small guardroom temporarily adapted as a cell.[39] Orders from Paris insist that the cell shutters must be kept closed and only Pouly, the head warder, may speak to him. During his one-month detention Dreyfus suffers from intestinal parasites, fever and dysentery.[40]

Devil's Island

Apr 14   Dreyfus is transferred to Devil's Island.[41] He is detained in solitary confinement in a stone cabin measuring 4 x 4 metres, located by the sea, with one small barred window and a metal roof. The cabin door is reinforced with steel bars and padlocked. It opens on to a smaller hut 2 x 3 metres in front of the stone cabin, where five sentries keep guard in two-hour shifts. At night, the lantern

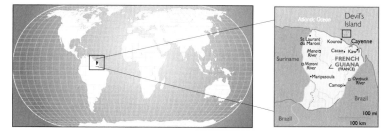

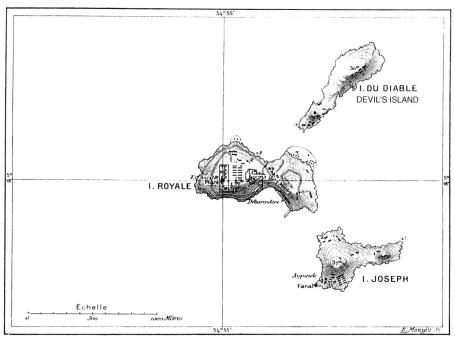

Maps of the îles du Salut, showing the location of Devil's Island

floodlights the cabin. The door of the hut is securely locked. The jangling of keys, the clatter of wooden clogs (*sabots*) and change of guard make sleep impossible. During the day he is allowed to walk within the confines of a 200-metre stretch of land between the jetty and the valley, always accompanied by an armed guard. The limits of this area are marked by wooden posts.[42]

Dreyfus starts his diary. The pages of the writing paper he receives are individually numbered and initialled.[43]

April   Demange is informed by one of his colleagues, Maître Frédéric Reitlinger, that a document mentioning *Ce canaille de D.* was secretly transmitted to the judges during the court martial. He demands an audience with Trarieux.[44] Trarieux confirms the existence of such a document, but refuses to believe it was passed secretly to the Court. Suggestion of a Secret Dossier, originating from three judges – Echemann, Freystaetter and Florentin – reaches journalists. At the Ministry of War, several officers get to know of the illegality committed at the court martial.[45]

Mathieu learns about the transmission of the Secret Dossier from Demange. He informs journalists and politicians, including Auguste Scheurer-Kestner, Vice-President of the Senate and Senator for life.[46] Scheurer-Kestner questions his colleagues about the dossier. Charles Freycinet, former Minister of War and Prime Minister, informs him about the secret transmission of a document to the judges mentioning the name of Dreyfus. His friend and colleague Senator General Jean-Baptiste Billot, advises him not to pursue the matter any further. Scheurer-Kestner tells Mathieu he is unable to assist him at the moment, but will endeavour to do so, if possible, in the future.

Henry receives information from one of the agents of the Section de Statistique that Schwartzkoppen is apprised by a French officer on artillery matters. The agent describes the officer, who is about 45 years old and frequently visits Schwartzkoppen at the German Embassy wearing the red stripe of the Legion of Honour.[47] (*v.* 10 July 1895) (*v.* Appendix 10)

May   Devil's Island: Lebars, to be Dreyfus' head warder, is sent from Paris to increase surveillance on the prisoner.[48]

May 2   Alfred receives his wife Lucy's first letter, dated 18 February, written before his departure to Devil's Island.[49]

June   Mathieu informs Lazare about the transmission of a secret document at the court martial and asks him to write on the case to incite public opinion. Lazare completes a first draft by summer 1895, but on Demange's advice Mathieu defers publication until an opportune moment.[50] (*v.* 6 Nov 1896)

Picquart's appointment as head of the Section de Statistique

July 1   Major Georges Picquart is appointed Chef du service des renseignements (head of the Intelligence Service, i.e. the Section de Statistique) replacing Sandherr, who is ill, suffering from multiple sclerosis. Henry becomes Picquart's deputy, replacing Lieutenant-Colonel Albert Cordier.[51]

July 10 Section de Statistique agent Edmond Lajoux reports to Henry in Paris about his recent meeting with German agent Richard Cuers in Luxembourg. Cuers confirmed that Germany never had any dealings with Dreyfus and that it had begun to doubt the importance and accuracy of the reports it was receiving from the French officer (*le 'décoré'*).[52] (*v.* June 1896)

July Sandherr briefs Picquart on Boisdeffre's preoccupation with the 'Dreyfus question'. He advises him to consult Henry about the Secret Dossier for further proof. He informs him of the location of the dossier at the Ministry of War, but does not mention Mercier's order to disperse its contents. Some days later Boisdeffre warns Picquart: 'The Dreyfus Affair is not over, but just beginning ... A new Jewish offensive is to be feared.'[53] He advises Picquart to add to the dossier.

Picquart instructs Guénée to renew inquiries into Dreyfus' private life. Recognizing Guénée's incompetence, Picquart pursues his own investigation: he instructs the Sûreté to place Mathieu Dreyfus under surveillance. He studies family correspondence and letters from Devil's Island. These inquiries yield no significant result.[54]

Oct A German document in Schwartzkoppen's hand reaches the Ministry of War by the 'normal route'. The name of Dreyfus and the first four letters of Boisdeffre appear on it. The document becomes known as the 'Dreyfus Bois ...' Picquart and his superiors consider it insignificant.[55]

Devil's Island: Dreyfus receives a letter signed 'Your cousin L. Blenheim'. He does not recognize the name and ignores it.[56]

Lucie renews her request to join her husband, but again receives no reply.

Oct 5 Devil's Island: Dreyfus writes to President Faure:

> *Accused and then convicted on the evidence of handwriting for the most infamous crime a soldier can commit, I have declared and declare once again that I did not write the letter attributed to me, that I have never forfeited my honour. For a year, alone with my conscience, I have been struggling against the most terrible fate that can befall a man. I do not speak of physical suffering ... but to feel the suffering of all those one loves is dreadful ... I do not seek pardon or favours; I ask, I beg that the light of complete truth be shed upon this conspiracy, of which my family and I are victims ... In the name of my honour, torn from me by a terrible blunder, in the name of my wife and my children, I ask for justice; and this justice which I seek with all my soul, with all the strength of my heart, with my hands clasped in supreme prayer, is that you should cast light on this tragedy and thus put an end to the terrible martyrdom of a soldier and a family for whom honour is everything.[57]*

Nov 1 A new Cabinet is formed with Léon Bourgeois (Prime Minister), Godefroy Cavaignac (Minister of War), Marcelin Berthelot (Foreign Secretary) and Louis Ricard (Minister of Justice).

Dec Picquart reorganizes the Section de Statistique's working procedures. He instructs Henry to bring to him personally any papers he receives from Mme Bastian for initial examination. After this procedure Picquart is to pass the documents to Lauth to collate them. Picquart also decides to increase surveillance on the Italian and German military attachés and to refer all contentious espionage matters to his old friend, lawyer Louis Leblois (originally from Strasbourg), now settled in Paris.[58]

1896

Jan 1 In financial ruin, Esterhazy lodges with his mistress, Marie-Hortense Pays, at 49 rue Douai in Paris.[59]

Jan 3 Lucie Dreyfus writes to Paul Guieysse, the new Colonial Secretary, requesting again to be allowed to join her husband on Devil's Island.[60]

Jan 12 Devil's Island: Dreyfus receives a reply to his letter of appeal dated 5 October to the President: 'Rejected without comment.'

Jan 23 Lucie learns from Guieysse that her request to join her husband has been refused.

View of the îles du Salut painted in 1898 with Devil's Island in the background

NOTES

1 *Cass.*, I, 321, Forzinetti.

2 Saussier had originally chosen 4 January as the date for the degradation, but, without explanation, the military authorities changed this to 5 January, the Jewish Sabbath. *HAD*, 1, p. 489; D.L. Lewis, *Prisoners of Honor: The Dreyfus Affair* (New York: W. Morrow and Cie, 1973), p. 56; *DFA*, p. 149.

3 Mercier wanted the degradation ceremony to take place in the parc de Vincennes or at Longchamps (the horse-racing stadium in the bois de Boulogne) to allow as many people as possible to view it. But fearing mob demonstrations, the Cabinet decided on the courtyard at the Ecole militaire. *DT*, p. 51.

4 Drefyus told Lebrun-Renault about Du Paty's visit to his cell on 31 December 1894 seeking his confession. Dreyfus had continued to assert his innocence. Nevertheless, this conversation inspired the unfounded rumour of a confession by Dreyfus which was circulated by the press in January 1895 and which was greatly supported by the General Staff between 1897 and 1899 as evidence against Dreyfus. (*v.* 5–6 Jan 1895, rumours of an alleged confession)

5 Among the journalists was Theodor Herzl, an Austrian Jew, born in Hungary, who at the time was correspondent for the Austrian newspaper *Neue Freie Presse* (New Free Press). Herzl later became the founder of modern political Zionism. He stated that it was the Affair, and especially the crowd's antisemitic behaviour during the degradation ceremony, that made him realize that antisemitism was a permanent feature of society, assimilation an impossible ideal and that only emigration to a Jewish homeland could solve the Jewish problem. In February 1896 Herzl published *Der Judenstaat: Versuch einer modernen Lösung der Judenfrage* ('The Jewish State: An Attempt at a Modern Solution to the Jewish Question'). Herzl organized the first Zionist congress held in Basel in 1897 (29–31 August) during which the World Zionist Organization was established. (*v.* Appendix 20) See T. Herzl, *L'Affaire Dreyfus. Reportages et reflexions*, traduits par Léon Vogel (Paris: Fédération sioniste de France, 1958); A. Dieckhoff, 'Le jour où Théodor Herzl devint sioniste,' *Histoire* 173, special issue, 'L'Affaire Dreyfus: vérités ou mensonges' (January 1994), pp. 106–11. See also S. Zweig, *The World of Yesterday* (London: Cassell, 1943), pp. 102–3.

6 Including the actress Sarah Bernhardt, who later became a vociferous supporter of the Dreyfus cause. See L. Verneuil, *The Fabulous Life of Sarah Bernhardt* (New York: Harper & Bross, 1942).

7 Reinach mentions Picquart's response during the ceremony to a neighbour who commented on Dreyfus' rigidity while the gold braid was stripped from his arms: 'He's a Jew, don't forget that. He's thinking of the weight of the braid and how much it's worth.' *HAD*, 4, p. 248.

8 A famous military march often played at times of celebration. Named after a regiment.

9 The translation softened the tone of the original telegram from Berlin, which had ended threateningly. Beaumont, *Aux sources de l'affaire*, pp. 111–12.

10 The rumour was circulated by Lebrun-Renault's colleagues (Colonel Aurèle Guérin, Lieutenant Pierre-Henri Philippe, Major Marie-Antoine Henry de Mitry and Captain François-Paul Anthoine) to whom he spoke after his conversation with Dreyfus before the beginning of the degradation ceremony. He had told them that Dreyfus had confessed. Picquart had heard about the alleged confession from Colonel Guérin and informed Boisdeffre and Mercier. *Cass.*, I, 142, Picquart. Despite what Lebrun-Renault had told his colleagues, in his duty report on the degradation ceremony, he wrote 'Nothing to report.' Guérin, in a telegram to Saussier dated 5 January 1895, also reported that Dreyfus has protested his innocence and that there was 'No other incident.' *3ème Cass.*, I, 70. (*v.* 14 February 1898) Nevertheless, on 5 January 1895 Ulric Civry, editor of *L'Echo de l'Armée*, wrote to his friend Sandherr asking whether Dreyfus had confessed. Sandherr wrote in reply that Dreyfus had not confessed, and urged Civry not to publish anything on this matter, to avoid protests from the family and supporters of Dreyfus. This letter was not published in the press until 1899. (*v.* 31 July 1899)

11 *Répertoire*, pp. 36–7.

12 *Répertoire*, p. 38. (*v.* 4 July 1898)

13 A newspaper founded in 1894 by Maurice Barrès.

14 Mercier knew that Dreyfus had not confessed to Du Paty. He was worried that Dreyfus might have mentioned Du Paty's visit to Lebrun-Renault revealing the fact that the *bordereau* reached the Deuxième Bureau by the 'normal route' (i.e. that it had been taken from the German Embassy). Mercier had already asked Gonse to look for Lebrun-Renault the previous night (Saturday), after he had read the evening papers. Gonse finally found Lebrun-Renault early on Sunday morning, and escorted him to Mercier.

15 This was 'Récit d'un témoin', by Eugène Clisson, pseudonym of journalist Hérisson. See article in *AD*, pp. 363–5.

16 Although the article did not specify the embassy concerned, the German Embassy was implicit because of the various rumours and repeated denials recently published in the press.

17 Casimir-Périer had not seen the article in *Le Temps*, which mentioned the alleged confession. He was only concerned by the *Figaro* article, which mentioned the theft of a document from a foreign embassy.

18 *Répertoire*, pp. 37–8.

19 Beaumont, *Aux sources de l'affaire*, pp. 114–17.

20 Later, Mercier also suggested this date as the 'historic night', on which the French government was alleged to await with concern Germany's declaration of war on France. (*v.* 12 Sep 1899, Rennes court martial)

21 Mercier's letter to Saussier was highly confidential: he had in fact already ordered the military prosecutor to transmit the file to Mercier's aide-de-camp. Bredin, *The Affair*, p. 113.

22 For the events leading to Casimir-Périer's resignation see Bredin, *The Affair*, pp. 110–11; *HAD*, 1, pp. 553–58.

23 In 1898 Trarieux established the Ligue des Droits de l'Homme et du Citoyen. (*v.* 1 April 1898)

24 *HAD*, 1, p. 560.

25 The commentary was one of the most disturbing documents for the General Staff, as it was clear proof of the infringement of the law committed in Dreyfus' court martial of 1894. Mercier later destroyed another copy. (*v.* Dec 1897) When questioned about its destruction Mercier claimed that he considered it a 'personal document', 'his property', no longer needed and not belonging in the Ministry archives. *Cass.*, II, 339, Mercier's letter to Billot. For Mercier's different statements see *AD*, pp. 322–6. However, in 1904 Du Paty finally produced a copy as well as the original of his own draft of the commentary, accompanied by a written declaration stating that the differences between his draft and the copy which was submitted to the judges (and destroyed in 1897) are minor, and mainly concern the form, not the content. *3ème Cass.*, I, 366–76, Du Paty.

26 According to Thomas, Mercier had also asked his subordinates Boisdeffre, Gonse, Sandherr, Du Paty and Henry, on their word of honour, never to reveal what had happened during the court martial of Dreyfus (the Secret Dossier). *ASD*, p.183.

27 A. Dreyfus, *Cinq années de ma vie* (1982), pp. 231–3.

28 Dreyfus was supposed to be transferred to the Ducos Peninsula in New Caledonia. The îles du Salut are an archipelago of three islands, île Royale, île Saint-Joseph and, the smallest, île du Diable (Devil's Island), situated in the Atlantic Ocean, 44 kilometres north-east of the coastal town of Cayenne in French Guyana and five degrees north of the equator. The climate is unbearable, temperatures high, disease, including malaria, rife. Political prisoners and other criminals had been deported to these islands ever since their colonization by the French in 1763. Although the Third Republic preferred to deport convicts to the Ducos Peninsula in New Caledonia, the îles du Salut remained a penal colony. Dangerous convicts were sent to île Royale, anarchists to Saint-Joseph and lepers to Devil's Island.

29 Thomas demonstrates the similarity between the articles of 'Cdt. Z', mainly from March and April 1895, and the information Esterhazy provided to Schwartzkoppen at that time, most of which was intercepted by the Section de Statistique. (Schwartzkoppen described his agent 'agent W'). *ASD*, pp. 188–95, 207 and Thomas, *Esterhazy*, pp. 195–7.

30 Trarieux later claimed that as Hanotaux confirmed the guilt of Dreyfus he 'forgot' about the Dreyfus case. It was only towards the end of 1896, when rumours were rife about the secret transmission of documents at the court martial of Dreyfus, that his attention was again drawn to the case and that he was troubled by so serious an illegality. (*v.* Mar–June 1897, n. 106) *Rennes*, III, 412, Trarieux.

31 Hypnosis, magnetism and clairvoyance were extremely fashionable at the end of the 19th century. Clairvoyants, like Léonie herself, were consulted by the police.

32 M. Dreyfus, '*Dreyfusards!' Souvenirs de Mathieu Dreyfus et autres inédits* edited by R. Gauthier (Paris: Gallimard/Julliard, 1978), p. 59.

33 On Léonie's meetings with Mathieu, see *ATQV*, pp. 47–52; 64–8.

34 Lucie was allowed to visit twice a week; on consecutive days. Each visit must not last more than 30 minutes, the couple was never to remain alone, no foreign language was to be used, they were not to speak of the Affair, no physical contact was allowed. *HAD*, 1, pp. 571–3; A. Dreyfus, *Cinq année de ma vie* (1982), pp. 102–3.

35 Receiving no reply, Lucie addressed a second letter (at the end of February) to the President of the Republic. This also remained unanswered.

36 *HAD*, 2, pp. 174–5.

37 Dreyfus, *Cinq années de ma vie*, (1982), pp. 104–6.

38 As early as 1894 Lazare had written two articles denouncing the antisemitic aspects of the Dreyfus case ('Le nouveau ghetto', *La Justice*, 17 November; 'Antisémitisme et antisémites', *L'Echo de Paris*, 31 December). But, as the publisher P.-V. Stock recalled, when he suggested to Lazare that he should become involved in the case, Lazare refused on the grounds that he did not know the Dreyfus family and that they were able to get along without him. P.-V. Stock, *Mémorandum d'un éditeur*, p. 18. It

was Patin, Governor of La Santé prison during Dreyfus' detention there, who suggested that the family should contact a writer or a journalist to focus public opinion on his brother. Patin named Drumont and Lazare. Mathieu opted for the latter. On Mathieu's first meeting with Lazare, see M. Dreyfus, '*Dreyfusards!*', pp. 82–5.

39   Locking Dreyfus in prison was contrary to legislation regarding deportation. In the cases of both simple deportation and deportation to a fortified place, prisoners were to enjoy liberty of movement as far as was compatible with their protection and the maintenance of order. On the legislation concerning deportation, see M.A. Menier, 'La détention du Capitaine Dreyfus à l'Ile du Diable, d'après les archives de l'administration pénitentiaire', *Revue française d'histoire d'Outre-Mer 44* (1977), pp. 460–1.

40   Pouly and Dr Debrieu, charged with looking after Dreyfus, were sympathetic and tried to build up his health but they were dependent on Bouchet, Commandant supérieur des îles du Salut (officer in command of the islands) *DFA*, pp. 164–6.

41   While Dreyfus waited on the île Royale the lepers' hospital on Devil's Island was evacuated and its 15 contaminated cabins burnt.

42   Dreyfus was confined in this first cabin until 26 August 1897. Due to the hasty preparations, neither toilets nor kitchen were ready. Dreyfus had to prepare his own food without utensils of any sort; he used paper for plates, old cans for pans and old pieces of metal for grilling meat. To make a fire he gathered wood himself and relied on borrowing matches from his guards. At no time was he allowed to speak to them. The head warder had standing instructions to shoot the prisoner on the slightest suspicion of an attempted escape. For Dreyfus' detention on Devil's island, see Menier, 'La détention du Capitaine Dreyfus', pp. 456–75; G.R. Whyte, *The Accused, The Dreyfus Trilogy* (Bonn: Inter Nationales, 1996), pp. 87–9. See also the diary of Dreyfus included in his book *Cinq années de ma vie* (*v.* different editions in bibliography); and the chapter 'Banquo's ghost' in *DFA*, pp. 195–217.

43   All drafts of unfinished letters and those he decided not to send were burned or sent to the Commandant supérieur. Dreyfus was to incorporate this diary into his book *Cinq années de ma vie*, first published in 1901.

44   Reitlinger heard about the existence of a secret document from Trarieux himself, who had learned about it from Hanotaux (*v.* Jan 1895).

45   The editor of *Le Gaulois*, Arthur Meyer (a Jew converted to Catholicism and who became an avid antisemite and anti-dreyfusard) heard about the Secret Dossier from one of his journalists, who obtained the information from Echemann. The Jewish officer Picard, one of Dreyfus' former colleagues at the Ecole de guerre, heard about it from Freystaetter. Besides Du Paty and Picquart, all the officers of the Deuxième Bureau were also aware of it. *HAD*, 2, p. 176.

46   Yves Guyot, editor of *Le Siècle*, told Mathieu that public hostility towards his brother would only change if the true culprit were found. Mathieu continued to pursue his investigations despite continuous police surveillance. (The police were under orders from the General Staff; even Mathieu's concierge was put on the police pay roll, and his correspondence opened.) Ernest Judet, editor of *Le Petit Journal*, an illustrated weekly and one of the papers most hostile to Dreyfus, agreed to meet Mathieu. Following their discussion, Judet promised his paper's neutrality. M. Dreyfus, '*Dreyfusards!*', pp. 54–6.

47   *3ème Cass.*, I, 19. Henry wrote a note on this information. This note was found only in 1904 (Investigation of March–Nov). The information came from one of the Section de Statistique's agents in Brussels, Edmond Lajoux, who from 1890 had been dealing with an agent from the German Intelligence Service, Richard Cuers. For several years the information Lajoux obtained from Cuers was satisfactory and enabled the Deuxième Bureau to arrest a number of German spies. From 1893 the Deuxième Bureau realized that Lajoux was acting as a double agent. Cuers informed Lajoux as early as 1895 that a '*décoré*' (a decorated officer) was informing Schwartzkoppen, without divulging his name. Cuers claimed he did not know his identity. *3ème Cass.*, II, 767–79, Targe.

48   As a deportee subject to penal administration, Dreyfus was placed under the authority of the Governor of Guyana, since the administration (a branch of the Colonial Office) was based there. Like other penal establishments, the îles du Salut had their own hierarchy: the Director of Penal Administration, the Commandant supérieur, the head warder and the military guards. Menier, 'La détention du capitaine Dreyfus', pp. 462–3.

49   The delay was the result of regulations concerning Dreyfus' correspondence. All letters addressed to him had to be vetted by the Colonial Office and his own outgoing letters were sent by the head warder to the Commandant supérieur. This meant that delivery of his and Lucy's letters suffered a delay of more than two months and that the letters were heavily censored. Menier, 'La détention du capitaine Dreyfus', pp. 467–8.

50   On Demange's advice Mathieu had already refused two other suggestions. Arthur Lévy, a writer haunted by the possibility that a miscarriage of justice had occurred, had offered to publish Lucie's protest, inviting her to explain that her husband had been convicted merely on the basis of one document and a similarity of handwriting. Salomon Reinach (Joseph's young brother) had previously submitted some ideas along the same lines to Lucien Lévy-Brühl, philosopher and Professor of History and Modern Philosophy at the Sorbonne. *IIAD*, 2, p. 164.

51   Captains Lauth, Junck, Valdant and archivist Gribelin served under Picquart and Henry at the Section de Statistique. Jean Desvernine and Louis Tomps, police officials from the Sûreté, also worked with the Intelligence.

52   According to Lajoux, Henry immediately changed his attitude when Lajoux mentioned the Dreyfus case. Soon after this meeting Picquart dismissed Lajoux, probably following Henry's suggestion. The official report of the Ministry of War stated that Lajoux was dismissed on grounds of his ill-temper and role as a double agent. The report mentions threats by Lajoux to publish his disclosures on the 'décoré' in the press. In 1896 Lajoux left for Brussels and eventually fled to Brazil. Before leaving he tried to meet Boisdeffre to ensure that Henry and Gribelin had passed on the information he had provided. But, he was arrested by Henry before he could do so and sent to the psychiatric hospital of Saint Anne in Paris. In the Rennes court martial it has also been discovered that the Section de Statistique continued to grant Lajoux a monthly payment of 200 francs. *Rennes*, II, 14–19, Rollin; *3ème Cass*, II, 768–9, Targe.

53   *Cass.*, II, 209, Picquart.

54   *Cass.*, I, 142–3; II, 263; *Rennes*, I, 384, Picquart.

55   It was not to play an important role in the Affair. For the complete text, see *HAD*, 2, p. 221.

56   This seemingly harmless letter contained several sentences written in invisible ink that could only be seen after exposure to light. Those phrases, if intercepted, could have given the impression that an accomplice to the treason was trying to maintain contact with the deportee. The invisible texts read: 'Connection broken. Try to renew. Our two attempts have failed. We must be very careful. Everything was nearly discovered. Let [me] know where was 2249. We know about the Jura affair 34.' Like all Dreyfus' correspondence, the letter was opened and first read by Guéguen, Director of Penal Administration. It was not considered suspicious as the insufficient light did not expose the texts written in invisible ink. Dreyfus only became aware of the trap years later when he returned to France and he reopened all the letters he had received on Devil's Island. Historians have not identified the author of this letter, but it was probably concocted by Henry. *HAD*, 2, pp. 217–20; *DT*, p. 82.

57   A. Dreyfus, *Cinq années de ma vie* (1982), p. 145.

58   On his death in 1928 Leblois left a significant manuscript of more than 1000 pages, containing numerous texts from the various trials and investigations relating to the Affair (from 1894 to 1906). His widow published the manuscript in 1929 as *L'Affaire Dreyfus. L'Iniquité. La Réparation. Les principaux faits et les principaux documents* (Paris: Libraire Aristide Quillet).

59   Marie was the daughter of a calvados distiller and a weaver from a small village near Rouen and began working in a spinning factory at a young age. Her working-class background and her attraction to the life of the *demi-mondaine* led her to work as a prostitute on the streets of Paris. She adopted the name of Marguerite, and was known professionally as Marie. In 1893, at the age of 24, she was already known in Montmartre as an '*horizontale*'. Her room was in the rue Victor-Massé, near the Pigalle nightclubs. It is either there, in the Moulin Rouge, or on a train to Paris, that Esterhazy met Marie in 1895. In addition to her other clients, who included journalists and senators, Marie became intimately involved with Esterhazy. Their relationship became permanent and Esterhazy settled her in an apartment at rue Douai. Marie furnished it but the lease was in Esterhazy's name. (*v.* 20 Oct 1897) Thomas, *Esterhazy*, pp. 217–21.

60   Guieysse agreed to a visit by Lucie but, not being able to dissuade her, passed on her request to the Cabinet.

Part 4

TREACHERY

March 1896–16 October 1897

Colonel von Schwartzkoppen

The *petit bleu* [1]

Early Mar   The Section de Statistique receives via the 'normal route' 32 torn fragments of a *petit bleu* (an express letter on blue paper, issued by the Paris post office).[2] The *petit bleu* is addressed to 'Monsieur le Commandant Esterhazy, 27 rue de la Bienfaisance'. It reads:

> *Sir, Above all I await a more detailed explanation on the outstanding question than the one you gave me the other day. Consequently, I ask you to send it to me in writing so that I may know whether or not I can continue my relations with House R. or not.*[3]

The *petit bleu* is not in Schwartzkoppen's handwriting but signed 'C', one of his signatures.[4]

Lauth pieces the torn fragments together and hands them to Picquart, commenting, 'This is terrible. Have we another one [traitor]?'[5]

Another letter is discovered via the 'normal route' contained in the same packet of papers as the *petit bleu*. This becomes known as the *lettre portée par le concierge* ('letter to be delivered by the concierge'). The letter is also signed 'C', in a handwriting similar to that of the *petit bleu*.[6]

> *Sir, I regret not speaking personally [to you] about a matter which [will annoy you] a great deal. My father has just [refused] the necessary funds to continue [the tour] in the conditions stipulated [between us]. I will explain his reasons, but [let me begin] by saying that already today [he considers] your conditions are too harsh for me, and [fears greatly] the results that [might ensue from the prolongation] of this trip. He proposes [another] trip, about which we could [agree. He considers] that the transactions I have [made] for him so far are not in proportion [to the amount] I have spent on the trips. [I have] to speak to you as soon as possible. I am returning the sketches which you gave me the other day; they are not the last. C.*[7]

End Mar   Leblois is seen arriving at the Ministry of War for meetings with Picquart.[8]

Apr 6   Picquart is promoted to lieutenant-colonel.

***c*. Apr 7**   Henry returns to the Section de Statistique after his mother's funeral and Lauth informs him about the discovery of the *petit bleu*.[9]

Picquart's secret investigation of Esterhazy

Early Apr   Picquart and Henry discuss the discovery of the *petit bleu*. Henry admits having known Esterhazy at the Ministry of War more than 15 years ago (*v.* 1877–79) but claims he has not seen him since. He also mentions another former colleague of theirs from the Ministry of War, the Jewish officer Maurice Weil. He does not disclose that Weil and Esterhazy have remained in contact.[10]

Without informing either Gonse or Boisdeffre, Picquart entrusts Desvernine with the discreet investigation and surveillance of Esterhazy.[11]

Apr 17   Desvernine's first report on Esterhazy reveals his financial problems and that he is keeping Marie Pays as his mistress in Paris on a monthly allowance. She is now registered as a prostitute known as 'Four-Fingered Marguerite'.[12] The report also refers to his friendship with Weil and his contact with Drumont. Nothing suspicious regarding national security is uncovered.

End Apr   Picquart instructs Lauth to photograph the *petit bleu* in a manner which conceals that it has been torn and pieced together to give the impression that it arrived by post rather than by the 'normal route'. Lauth unsuccessfully seeks the assistance of Captain Junck.[13]

Picquart calls in Major Curé, a former colleague from the Académie de Saint-Cyr, to question him about Esterhazy. Curé, serving with the 74th Regiment, to which Esterhazy belongs, expresses little respect for that '*rastaquouère*' ('rascal'), but warns Picquart that he is shrewd. Curé mentions Esterhazy's recurrent financial problems, his particular interest in artillery and the fact that he was in the habit of employing soldiers to copy documents for him. However, he refuses to help Picquart obtain a specimen of Esterhazy's handwriting.

Desvernine informs Picquart that Esterhazy has twice visited the German Embassy in broad daylight.

Apr 29   A new Cabinet is formed, with Jules Méline (Prime Minister), General Billot (Minister of War), Hanotaux (Foreign Secretary), Jean-Baptiste Darlan (Minister of Justice) and André Lebon (Colonial Secretary).

May 7   Devil's Island: Late at night armed guards enter Dreyfus' cabin, cut up his mattress, laundry, shoes and books. With no warning, they conduct a full-scale search of his possessions.[14]

'Pour les Juifs'

May 16   The celebrated writer Emile Zola publishes in *Le Figaro* his first article on antisemitism in France, entitled 'Pour les Juifs' ('In Support of the Jews'):

> *For some years I have been following, with increasing disgust and surprise, the attempted campaign in France against the Jews. To me it seems monstrous, and by that I mean something beyond all common sense, all truth and justice, a stupid, blind thing which would take us back several centuries, an event that would eventually lead to the worst possible abomination, religious persecution, causing bloodshed for all parties. There are a handful of madmen, imbeciles and clever men alike, who call out each morning, 'Let's kill the Jews, let's eat them, massacre and exterminate them ...'*

> *Let us abandon these evil lunatics who imagine they can bring justice with the blades of their knives, and bid them return to the barbarity of the forests.*[15]

May–June   Picquart's investigation of Esterhazy draws to a close. Desvernine's reports merely confirm Esterhazy's financial problems. They only provide Picquart with a few additional details of his seedy private life.

June   German agent Cuers (*v.* 10 July 1895), recently dismissed from German Intelligence, informs the French military attaché in Berlin, Lieutenant-Colonel Foucault, that a French infantry major has been delivering information on artillery to Schwartzkoppen for the last two to three years.

June–July   Devil's Island: Dreyfus suffers a serious attack of malaria.[16]

Early July   Foucault gives Picquart a complete account of the information received from Cuers. The German General staff have reaffirmed

General Billot

that Dreyfus was not working for them; the traitorous infantry major is aged between 40 and 50; he has already given Schwartzkoppen substantial information on French artillery. (*v.* 7 Aug 1896)

Picquart instructs Desvernine to obtain specimens of Esterhazy's handwriting and intercept his mail.

End July   Picquart requests an urgent meeting with Boisdeffre on an 'important matter' [i.e. his discoveries concerning Esterhazy].

Aug 5   In his meeting with Boisdeffre, Picquart names Esterhazy as another traitor. Boisdeffre tells Picquart to continue his investigation cautiously and that for the present only Billot should be informed, not Gonse, his deputy.[17]

Aug 6   Billot also recommends that Picquart should pursue the investigation with prudence. He does not permit him to ask Esterhazy's superior for a handwriting specimen.[18]

Picquart sends Lauth and Henry to interview Cuers in Basel. They are accompanied by two police officials (Louis Tomps and Paul-Léon Vuillecard). The interview lasts from 11 a.m. to 6 p.m. but according to Lauth and Henry they could obtain no further information from Cuers.[19] Lauth's report to Picquart nevertheless includes some significant facts: details of the information on French artillery delivered to Schwartzkoppen; Cuers' claim that Schwartzkoppen's contact was a major whose name Cuers refused to reveal and that for unknown reasons, dealings between Schwartzkoppen and his informer had ceased in October 1895.[20] (*v.* 19 Jan 1897)

August   Esterhazy takes steps to secure his own appointment to the Ministry of War. He first approaches Deputies Roche and Adrien de Montebello and his friend Maurice Weil requesting them to intervene on his behalf. Weil writes a personal letter of recommendation to Robert Calmon-Maison, Billot's secretary. As there is no reply, Esterhazy writes directly to Calmon-Maison.

Desvernine reports to Picquart on the frequent meetings and correspondence between Weil and Esterhazy, which leads Picquart to believe that they are accomplices. Picquart informs his superiors that he is suspicious of Weil.

Picquart's discovery of Esterhazy's involvement

Aug 26–28   Billot authorizes Calmon-Maison to hand Picquart two of Esterhazy's letters soliciting support.[21] Picquart thinks he recognizes the handwriting. Comparing the letters with one of the copies of the *bordereau*, he becomes convinced that they are identical.[22] He asks Lauth to copy Esterhazy's letters in such a way as to hide the signature and any other detail suggesting the writer's identity. He shows the copies to Du Paty and Bertillon, placing them next to the *bordereau*. Du Paty says that he recognizes the handwriting of Mathieu; Bertillon that it is in the same hand as the *bordereau*, adding, 'So the Jews have been training someone for a year to imitate the writing.'[23]

Aug 30–31 Picquart asks Gribelin for the Secret Dossier passed to the judges at the court martial in 1894.[24] Examining it, he realizes that none of the documents sustain evidence for the conviction of Dreyfus.

Sept 1 Picquart submits the first full report to Boisdeffre on the charges against Esterhazy, four pages in length, and attaches to it the *petit bleu*, samples of Esterhazy's handwriting, documents from the Secret Dossier and his request for an inquiry on Esterhazy.[25] (*v.* Appendix 11) When Picquart explains why the documents in the dossier cannot apply to Dreyfus, Boisdeffre exclaims: 'Why was the file not burnt as agreed?'[26] Without further comment, and to Picquart's astonishment, Boisdeffre tells him to see his deputy Gonse (who is on holiday), since it is he who is in charge of the Section de Statistique.

Sept 3 Picquart visits Gonse at his country house in Cormeilles-en-Paisis, Seine-Oise, and submits his report of 1 September. Gonse remarks 'it looks as if we made a mistake' and firmly instructs Picquart to 'separate the two cases, the Dreyfus affair and the Esterhazy affair'.[27]

Picquart reports Gonse's reply to Boisdeffre. Boisdeffre approves it and instruct Picquart not to inform Billot just yet. (*v.* 10 Sept 1896)

The English newspaper the *Daily Chronicle* reports that Dreyfus has escaped from Devil's Island. The story is repeated in French newspapers (*L'Eclair, La Libre Parole, L'Intransigeant*).[28]

Sept 4 On receipt of a telegram from the îles du Salut refuting the escape, the French Government publishes an official denial. Colonial Secretary Lebon gives orders that Dreyfus is to be double shackled to his bed at night – two U-shaped irons joined to a metal bar – creating severe pain, discomfort and immobility.[29]

Devil's Island: On being informed about this measure Dreyfus petitions Jules Bravard, officer in command of the îles du Salut:

> *Sir, I have just been warned that I am to be placed in iron shackles every night. I would be very grateful if you could tell me what wrong I have committed. Since I have been here, I believe I had conformed strictly to all regulations and orders: everything I was instructed to do, I have carried out fully. This is why I take the liberty of asking you what I must undertake to avoid such an appalling punishment.*
>
> *Yours respectfully, A Dreyfus.*[30]

Governor of Guyana, Henri-Eloi Danel, telegraphs the petition to Lebon, asking if the order is to be upheld. The answer is affirmative.

The Colonial Office intercepts a letter to Dreyfus dated 31 August 1896 apparently from a distant relative. The signature is unclear and could be Weill, Weiss, Weiré or Weiler. The document becomes known as the *faux Weyler*.[31]

Picquart asks Colonel Léon Abria, who serves in Esterhazy's regiment, for more samples of Esterhazy's writing.

Sept 5   The *faux Weyler* is withheld from Picquart by Billot. Gribelin is sent to examine the letter at the Colonial Office. Lebon sends it to Bertillon who shows it to Picquart.

Sept 5–15   Picquart and Gonse correspond. Picquart repeatedly seeks Gonse's approval for legal action against Esterhazy. Gonse, who is absent from Paris, insists on 'patience and prudence' until his return on 15 September. Boisdeffre and Billot support Gonse's approach.[32]

Sept 6   Devil's Island: Head warder Lebars tells the prisoner that he is no longer permitted to walk outside his cabin. First night on which Dreyfus is subjected to the double shackles.[33]

Sept 7   Devil's Island: Dreyfus is barred from receiving any letters or food packages from his family.[34] He falls seriously ill.

Sept 8   The appalling conditions on Devil's Island are exposed for the first time in an article in *Le Figaro* by Gaston Calmette, provoking a vicious press campaign against Dreyfus, led mainly by *La Libre Parole*, *L'Intransigeant* and *L'Eclair*.[35] (*v.* 14 Sept 1896 Revelations by *L'Eclair*)

Devil's Island: Dreyfus writes in his diary:

These nights in shackles! I do not speak of the physical torture, but what moral torture! And without explanation, without knowing why! What a horrible and atrocious nightmare have I been living for nearly two years? And yet it is my duty to go to the limits of my strength; I will ...[36]

Sept 9   Bravard informs Dreyfus that the double shackles are not a punishment but a 'safety measure' imposed according to instructions from Paris.

Sept 10   Dreyfus writes that he is so broken in body and spirit that he is abandoning his diary. It ends with a plea addressed to President Faure:

Mr President, I take the liberty of requesting that this diary, written on a daily basis, should be given to my wife.

Perhaps, Mr President, within its pages will be found cries of anger, of horror at the most appalling sentence ever to befall a human being, and a human being who has never forfeited his honour. I no longer have the strength to reread it ... Today I have no recriminations: all involved believed they acted according to their rights and their conscience. I simply declare once again that I am innocent of this abominable crime, and all I ask is one thing, always the same: that the search should continue for the real culprit, the perpetrator of this hideous crime. And on the day when light is finally shed, I ask that all the compassion inspired by so great a misfortune should be directed towards my dear wife and my dear children.[37]

L'Eclair publishes 'Le traître', an anonymous article that, although hostile to Dreyfus, alleges illegal proceedings at the court martial and calls on the Ministry of War to make some evidence public. (*v.* 14 Sept 1896, Revelations by *L'Eclair*)

Picquart finally obtains Boisdeffre's permission to submit his findings on Esterhazy to Billot. Billot recommends that Picquart continue his investigation to obtain more substantial evidence but should not inform Prime Minister Jules Méline or the Cabinet.[38]

Sept 11   Deputy André Castelin publicly announces his intention to question Méline in the Chamber on the Government's attitude towards the Dreyfus case.[39] (*v.* 13 and 18 Nov 1896)

Sept 14   Cassagnac, editor of *L'Autorité*, publishes his article entitled 'Le doute' ('Doubt'), calling into question the guilt of Dreyfus and the infallibility of military courts. It suggests that a judicial error may have been committed: '[We must ask ourselves] If despite all the precautions that were put in place, despite the honour and patriotism of the judges, is there is not on Devil's Island an innocent man suffering an agony of superhuman moral torture. This doubt alone is terrifying.'[40]

Revelations by *L'Eclair*

L'Eclair publishes a second anonymous article, 'Le traître; la culpabilité de Dreyfus démontrée par le dossier' ('The Traitor; The Guilt of Dreyfus demonstrated by the Dossier').[41] The generally well-informed article is hostile; it gives detailed information, some false, concerning the *bordereau* and his arrest and investigation. For the first time a reference is made publicly to the secret transmission of *Ce canaille de D.* to the Court. Significantly, the phrase '*Ce canaille de D.*' ('This scoundrel D.') was altered to 'this animal Dreyfus', either deliberately or in error.[42]

The Gonse–Picquart conflict

Sept 15   Gonse returns to Paris and receives Picquart, who suggests taking steps against *L'Eclair*. Gonse disagrees: this is not his responsibility, but that of Billot or Boisdeffre (both of whom are on manoeuvres in the Charente). The meeting becomes tense. Gonse exclaims: 'What does it matter to you if this Jew is on Devil's Island?' When Picquart insists that Dreyfus may be innocent, Gonse remarks: 'If you say nothing, no one will know about it.' Appalled, Picquart ends the conversation, exclaiming: 'General, what you are saying is abominable; I do not know what I will do but I shall not take this secret to my grave.'[43]

Sept 16   Gonse asks Picquart how he proposes to deal with Esterhazy. He rejects Picquart's suggestion that Esterhazy be called into the Ministry of War for questioning, believing there is insufficient evidence against him. (In his opinion the *petit bleu* was not significant as it was not sent through the post.) However, subject to Boisdeffre's approval, Gonse accepts a plan to put Esterhazy to the test by sending him a telegram, allegedly from Schwartzkoppen, calling him to a meeting.[44] Boisdeffre agrees to this, but insists that Picquart obtain Billot's approval. Billot refuses.[45]

Sept 18   Lucie Dreyfus addresses a petition to the President of the Chamber of Deputies, drafted by Demange.[46] (*v.* 3 Dec 1896) (*v.* Appendix 12)

Sept 21   Devil's Island: A first palisade, 2.5 metres high, is built surrounding the cabin of Dreyfus, limiting his exercise area.[47] (*v.* 12 Nov 1896) Although Dreyfus is now allowed to receive letters, they are censored and only copies of them are handed to him. Some letters are withheld and where the meaning is unclear, whole passages are deleted.

Sept 24   Roche again recommends to Billot that the Ministry of War engage the services of Esterhazy. (*v.* Aug 1896)

Lucie's supplication to the Pope

Sept   Lucie Dreyfus sends a written supplication in Latin to Pope Leo XIII appealing to the 'pity and compassion of the Father of the Catholic Church'. She mentions that Christians were beginning to express their great concern that antisemitic prejudice has had much to do with this affair.[48] (*v.* 8 Dec, 1897) (*v.* Appendix 13)

Early Oct   Boisdeffre approves Picquart's investigation of Esterhazy but still advises caution. Picquart interviews Captain Henri Le Rond (in charge of artillery practice at Châlons in 1894), and continues to read Esterhazy's correspondence.[49] He sends Desvernine to search Esterhazy's rooms in the rue de la Bienfaisance (he had already returned to his regiment in Rouen). Nothing is found apart from some visiting cards belonging to Drumont and a few insignificant letters.[50]

Dreyfus' prison enclosure on Devil's Island, with fortified watch tower

Picquart confides in Henry: he has doubts about Dreyfus' guilt and believes that the Dreyfus and Esterhazy cases are connected. Henry replies with a pointed anecdote, a last warning to Picquart: 'When I was a Zouave, the son of a colonel, a simple soldier, was found guilty of theft. The officer under whom he served wanted him charged, but his superiors disagreed. It was the officer who was broken and the culprit who was left [unscathed].' Picquart replies, 'Golden words! But this is a matter of conscience. I cannot say the opposite of what I think.'[51]

Oct   Picquart realizes that the *faux Weyler* is a forgery.[52] He seeks the help of Bertillon, who reproduces a letter identical to the original but without the phrases written in invisible ink. Picquart sends this letter to Dreyfus to test his reaction. Dreyfus puts the letter in a drawer without paying any attention to it, as he had previously done with the letter signed 'Your cousin L. Blenheim'. (*v.* Oct 1895)

Esterhazy's first cousin, Paul Esterhazy, dies suddenly in Bordeaux. Esterhazy persuades Christian, Paul's 20-year-old son and only remaining heir, to let him invest the family fortune in Paris. He promises to place the money with the Rothschild bank.[53] (*v.* April–May & 4 July 1898)

Esterhazy's wife and daughters remain at Dommartin-la-Planchette. Esterhazy moves to the rue Douai apartment with his mistress Marie-Hortense Pays. For family correspondence he continues to give his rue de Bienfaisance address.

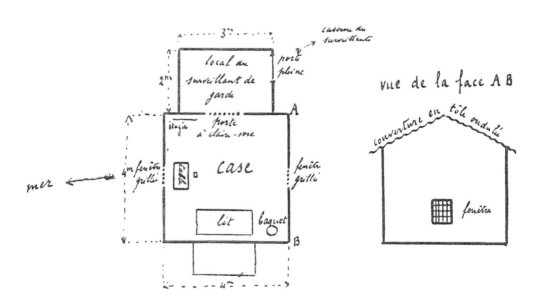

Dreyfus' sketch of his prison quarters

[Handwritten letter in Latin — Supplication of Lucie Dreyfus to Pope Leo XIII]

Supplication of Lucie Dreyfus to Pope Leo XIII (in Latin)

The conspiracy against Picquart

Henry and Gonse regularly report to Boisdeffre that Picquart's preoccupation with the investigation of Esterhazy has led him to neglect the work of the Section de Statistique. Lauth, Gribelin and Guénée agree. They become suspicious of Picquart and are reluctant to execute his orders.[54] With Gonse's approval, Henry places Picquart under secret surveillance. In mid-October Boisdeffre indicates to Picquart that he is dissatisfied with his handling of the Dreyfus-Esterhazy affair, insinuating that he is responsible for the disclosures to the press (the article in *L'Eclair* of 14 September).[55]

Boisdeffre and Gonse decide that Picquart is to be distanced discreetly from the Dreyfus-Esterhazy affair. Boisdeffre suggests he be sent to Tonkin (Vietnam), but Billot proposes instead a special mission to organize Intelligence on the eastern border of France.[56]

Oct 27   Billot accordingly signs the suggested order, but Picquart's departure date is left undecided. Picquart is not informed. (*v.* 14 Nov 1896)

Oct 29   Maître Emile Salles informs his colleague Demange that the conviction of Dreyfus was based on documents secretly transmitted to the judges at the court martial.[57]

Devil's Island: Artaut, a visiting inspector, examines the living conditions of the prisoner and specifies measures to be taken in the event of his death. One such measure requires the prisoner's face to be photographed before the body is sent to France.[58]

Oct 30   Guénée sends Gonse a confidential report on the investigation ordered by Picquart in the *Eclair* article. Guénée's report contains a false account of his conversation with Picquart held around 19 September. Picquart allegedly told Guénée of his doubts concerning Dreyfus' guilt. The report also states that during his investigation, Picquart had particularly paid attention to two items included in the Secret Dossier: Du Paty's commentary, and the two reports by Guénée, which included false passages (*v.* Nov–Dec 1894; Sept 1897).[59]

Following Henry's suggestion, Gonse retrieves the Secret Dossier from Picquart.[60]

The *faux Henry*

Nov 1   Henry fabricates a letter that is to become known as the *faux Henry*. He uses letters intercepted by the Section de Statistique via the 'normal route'. The first is a letter written in blue pencil on graph paper, sent by Panizzardi to Schwartzkoppen in the second half of June 1896. It reads: 'My Dear Friend. Here is the manual, for which I paid (180 [francs]), as agreed. It is expected on Wednesday at 8 p.m. at Laurent's. I have invited three men from the embassy, one is a Jew. Don't fail to appear. Alexandrine.'[61] Henry predates this letter to 14 June 1894 to enable it to be related to Dreyfus who was arrested in

October 1894. He then takes a fresh sheet of graph paper, similar to that normally used by Panizzardi, and tears it in order to appear as though it had arrived via the 'normal route'. On it, he writes in a blue pencil, imitating Panizzardi's handwriting and style: 'I have read that a deputy intends to raise the Dreyfus case in the Chamber.[62] If Rome is asked for new explanations, I will say that I have never had dealings with this Jew. It is agreed. If they ask you, say the same thing, for

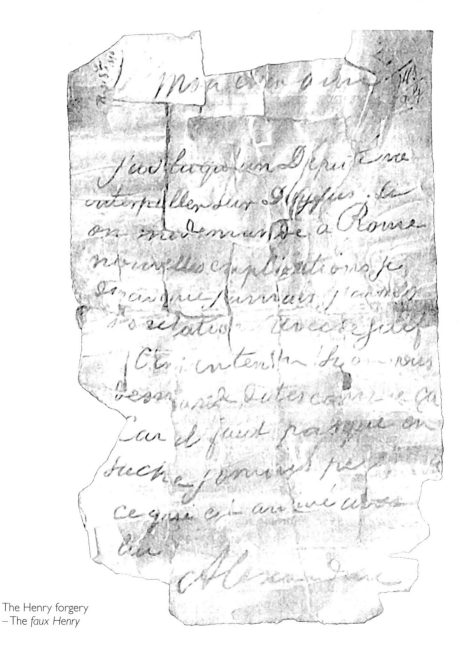

The Henry forgery
– The *faux Henry*

no one must ever know what happened with him.'[63] Henry removes from the first letter the heading 'My Dear Friend' and the signature 'Alexandrine' and attaches them to the top and bottom of the forged letter with transparent adhesive tape. He dates this September 1896. Finally, to reconstitute the first letter, he replaces the top and bottom sections which he had cut out with yet another heading and signature probably taken from a third and unimportant letter of Panizzardi which he had in his files. He destroys the rest of this third letter.[64]

Nov 2–3   Henry shows the forged document to Gonse and Boisdeffre, implying it had come by the 'normal route'. Gonse and Boisdeffre then take it to Billot. All three agree not to tell Picquart of the document's existence. Following customary procedure, a copy is made of the original. Unusually, the document is again recopied in full by Gribelin as the first copy was not clear.[65] (*v. c.* 12 Nov 1896)

Bernard Lazare's *Une erreur judiciare* [66]

Nov 6   Bernard Lazare's first pamphlet *Une erreur judiciaire: La vérité sur l'affaire Dreyfus* ('A Judicial Error: The Truth about the Dreyfus Affair') is secretly printed in Brussels by imprimerie Veuve Monnom. Copies are distributed to Deputies, journalists and various public figures in France in sealed envelopes, for fear they might be seized by the postal service in France before reaching their destination.[67] The copies are received on 7 and 8 November.[68] In this first public statement of confidence in Dreyfus' innocence, Lazare demolishes the articles published in *L'Eclair* (10 and 14 September 1896). Lazare mentions for the first time that the document referred to as *Ce canaille de D.* includes only the initial 'D', not the name Dreyfus. The pamphlet contains the complete text of the *bordereau* and a first analysis of its content. Lazare comments on the absurdity of Bertillon's report and concludes that Bertillon's methods are not worthy of an expert or of any respectable person; rather, they prove his theory is the product of a 'dangerous maniac'. Lazare recounts Dreyfus' arrest, and the fruitlessness of the two investigations of him. He emphasizes the illegalities committed in the 1894 court martial and finally calls for a revision:[69]

> *There is still time to redeem the situation so that it will not be possible to say that in dealing with a Jew justice has been forgotten … Captain Dreyfus is innocent and his conviction was achieved by illegal means. I demand a revision of his trial … Will I remain the only one to speak in the name of the law? I do not think so.*[70]

Nov 6 & 8   Esterhazy writes two letters to Maurice Weil, asking him again to approach Saussier to help him to gain promotion and obtain further financial help from Jewish sources. He reiterates the Jewish community's indebtedness to him for his role in Crémieu-Foa's duel. (*v.* 1 June 1892) Esterhazy threatens to publish articles in Drumont's *Libre Parole*, if help is not forthcoming.[71]

Publication of the facsimile of the *bordereau*

Nov 10   The Parisian daily *Le Matin* publishes a facsimile of the *bordereau*. Mathieu has posters printed showing the *bordereau* alongside letters in his brother's handwriting. The posters are displayed throughout Paris and distributed widely among friends.[72]

Seeing the facsimile in *Le Matin*, Schwartzkoppen recognizes Esterhazy's handwriting and realizes that Dreyfus has been convicted in the place of Esterhazy. He confides in Panizzardi and reveals to him the name and rank of his contact [Esterhazy].[73]

Nov 11   Suspecting Picquart is the source of the disclosures by *Le Matin* (the publication of the facsimile of the *bordereau*), Gonse asks Picquart if he has kept the original of the *bordereau*. Picquart replies that he has not, but states in error that he did not even have copies (although a few weeks earlier he compared the handwriting on the *bordereau* with that of Esterhazy). When Gribelin and Henry find a copy of the *bordereau* in the Section de Statistique, Picquart acknowledges his mistake. Gonse makes a note of Picquart's answers, which add to his mistrust.

***c*. Nov 12**   Billot describes to Picquart the content of the *faux Henry* but does not show him the actual document. Picquart doubts its authenticity, since it has not passed through the Section de Statistique but he has not yet had a chance to discuss the matter with Billot. He conveys his misgivings to Gonse and Boisdeffre.[74]

Nov 12   Devil's Island: a second wooden palisade, 2.5 metres high with vertical stakes sharpened at the top, is erected 1.5 metres from the front of the cabin, now blocking out a view of the sea. Dreyfus is only permitted to exercise in the area between the two palisades.[75]

Nov 13   Weil receives an anonymous letter (signed 'Pierre') warning that Deputy Castelin intends to accuse him and Esterhazy of being the accomplices of Dreyfus. After showing the letter to Esterhazy, Weil remains worried and delivers the letter to Deputy Montebello, who in turn forwards it to Billot. Billot also finds it disturbing, as it confirms further disclosures from the Ministry of War.[76]

The transfer of Picquart

Nov 14   Billot summons Picquart, Gonse and Boisdeffre to his office. Referring to the recent disclosures and Picquart's investigation of Esterhazy, Billot tells Picquart that the indiscretions could only come from one of those present or from the Section de Statistique. He reprimands Picquart for intercepting Esterhazy's correspondence without permission. He informs Picquart that he is to leave on a mission to eastern France within the next 48 hours.[77]

Nov 15–16   Picquart hands all his files to Gonse and gives Henry the original *petit bleu*.

Nov 16   After Picquart's departure Henry becomes the effective head of the Section de Statistique. He issues a confidential order that all correspondence addressed to Picquart is to be opened, even though Picquart remains nominal head of the Section de Statistique. The correspondence, once opened and copied, is to be forwarded to him. Henry opens a file for potentially incriminating documents, for future use against Picquart.

c. Nov 16　　Lazare's pamphlet *Une erreur judiciaire* is reprinted in Paris by P.-V. Stock. This edition includes the facsimile of the *bordereau* and the interview with Bertillon recently published in *Le Matin*. It also contains a transcript of the conversation between Dreyfus and Du Paty and Dreyfus' letter to Mercier of 31 December 1894.[78] (*v.* 12 Nov 1897)

Nov 18　　Gonse tells Desverine to continue the investigation into Esterhazy as instructed by Picquart. He is, however, to operate with the utmost discretion and to report to him.[79]

In the Chamber of Deputies, Castelin makes his interpellation. The session opens with Billot's firm statement that everything concerning the investigation and trial of Dreyfus has been carried out in accordance with military justice and that the case is therefore *res judicata* (i.e. it cannot be reopened).[80] Contrary to all expectations, Castelin does not mention Esterhazy or Weil. Instead, he demands legal action against Lazare and attacks all the defenders of Dreyfus. The Chamber passes a vote of confidence in the Government authorizing it to investigate and penalize anyone who publicly defends the 'traitor Dreyfus'.

Tomps, the police official entrusted by Henry to investigate the disclosures by *Le Matin*, informs Henry that according to his first inquiries the *bordereau* had been delivered to the newspaper by a

Louis Leblois

woman. He claimed that she had stolen it from 'someone who was instructed to keep it secret but who probably allowed it to be taken from him'.[81]

Nov 21   In a second report, Tomps informs Henry that it was graphologist Teyssonnière who had sold the facsimile of the *bordereau* to *Le Matin*.[82]

Gonse writes to Picquart that he is to continue with a second mission in eastern France immediately.

In a second confidential report, Guénée renews his accusations against Picquart (*v.* 30 Oct 1896) adding that Picquart had admitted disclosing the content of the Secret Dossier to 'an old lawyer friend' [Leblois].

Nov 22   A report from Schwartzkoppen to the Ministry of War in Berlin concludes:

> *As far as the Dreyfus case itself is concerned, it remains as much of a mystery as ever … If Dreyfus' conviction has really resulted from an alleged document emanating from him and stolen from the German Embassy [the* bordereau*], the conviction is a mistake, and after the declaration made by the German Ambassador to the French Foreign Minister, that the embassy had no dealings whatsoever with Dreyfus [November 1894], the French Government must bear the heavy responsibility for this miscarriage of justice.*[83]

Nov 27   Henry intercepts a coded letter sent to Picquart in Spanish by one of his former officers Germain Ducasse:[84]

> *Most Honourable Sir, I would never have believed it had I not seen it with my own eyes. As of today, the masterpiece is finished.*[85] *we are to call it Cagliostro Robert Houdin.*[86] *The comtesse speaks of you all the time and tells me every day that the demi-god asks when it will be possible to see you.*
>
> *Her devoted servant who kisses your hand. J.*[87]

After making a copy of the letter Henry forwards it to Picquart.[88]

Dec 3   Lucie's petition for a review of the conviction of Dreyfus is rejected by the Government' Commission of Petition on the grounds of *res judicata*.[89]

Dec 7   Roche sends Billot another letter recommending Esterhazy's promotion.[90]

Dec 11   Esterhazy thanks Roche for approaching Billot on his behalf, but begs desperately for his continued help.

The Speranza letter

Dec 15   A letter to Picquart, signed Speranza, is received at the Ministry of War. It is opened and shown to Billot. It reads:

> *I am leaving the house, our friends are dismayed, your unfortunate departure has upset everything. Hasten your return, hurry …! As the holiday time is very favourable for the cause, we are counting*

on you for the 20th. She is ready, but cannot and will not act until
she has talked to you. Once the demi-god has spoken, we will act.
Speranza [91]

Henry appropriates the letter and adds it to Picquart's file held at the
Section de Statistique. (*v.* 16 Nov 1896) No copy is sent to Picquart.[92]
This letter, based on Ducasse's letter (*v.* 27 Nov 1896), is a forgery.

Dec 22–29   Gonse continues to write cordial letters to Picquart informing him that
he is to continue on special missions to Lyon, Marseille, Tunisia and
Algeria.

Dec   On his own initiative, Du Paty compiles a report on the comparison
between the handwriting of Esterhazy's letter shown to him by
Picquart (*v.* 26–28 Aug 1896) and the *bordereau*. He concludes that
they are absolutely identical, but that the letters of Esterhazy were
written by someone else, 'a third man' who imitated the writing of the
bordereau to incriminate Esterhazy and who was either a member of
the Dreyfus family or engaged by them.[93] (*v.* 16–18 Oct 1897)

1897
Jan 6   Billot signs a temporary order for Picquart's appointment to the 4th
Rifle Brigade in Sousse (Tunisia).[94]

Jan 16   Picquart arrives in Tunis.

Jan 19   Lauth and Junck interview Cuers for the second time in Luxembourg.
According to their report dated 20 January they elicit no new
information.[95] (*v.* 6 Aug 1896)

***c.* Jan 20**   Picquart writes to Gonse asking to be redeployed to his regiment.
Gonse replies that Billot's instruction is to complete his mission in
Tunisia first.[96]

Jan 27   In a letter to Roche Esterhazy complains about his married life. He
strongly criticizes Billot for not appointing him to the Ministry of War
and Henry, whom he refers to as his 'debtor'.[97] (*v.* 1877–79)

Schemes against Picquart

Jan   Henry continues to build up the file against Picquart. He introduces
a newspaper announcement of the death of Esterhazy's father-in-law,
the marquis de Nettancourt, predating it 5 January 1896 to give the
impression that Picquart had begun his investigation two months
before receipt of the *petit bleu* (March 1896).

Picquart writes to General Ferdinand Millet, Chief of Infantry, that he
is the subject of scheming. Millet writes back to placate him. (*v.* 2–10
March 1897)

Feb   The Royalist Jules Guérin re-establishes the Ligue nationale
antisémitique de France, originally founded by Drumont and Morès
in 1889, with financial support of Philippe duc d'Orléans, pretender
to the throne.[98] (*v.* Aug 1898)

Feb 1   Picquart arrives in Sousse.

Feb 14   Devil's Island: Dreyfus begins to draft a letter to the President but tears it up without finishing it:

> *Mr President*
>
> *I am taking the liberty of appealing to you once again for justice. For more than two years I have been suffering the most terrible moral martyrdom that it is possible to imagine, innocent of an abominable crime, the very thought of which revolts one's whole being … My heart alone knows all that I have suffered; it would need the pen of another writer, not myself, to describe such tortures … But alas! I have gone through too much, my heart is at breaking point, I cannot bear any more … In the profound anguish of my whole being, in this slow death (of all my strength), I come to you, Mr President, and to the Government of my country, with an ultimate cry of appeal, certain that it will be heard …[99]*

March   Esterhazy requests General Ange-Laurent Giovaninelli, Commander-in-Chief of the 3rd Army Corps and an influential politician, to recommend him to Billot. Billot rejects the approach angrily. He shows Giovaninelli the reports made by Desvernine on Esterhazy's dishonourable private life (*v.* 17 April 1896), and advises him to watch his officers closely. Giovaninelli orders Colonel Abria to keep Esterhazy under surveillance and to file a report on him as soon as Esterhazy returns from sick leave.[100] Esterhazy also asks his friend Grenier to recommend him to the Ministry of War. Grenier first speaks to Henry about Esterhazy,[101] and then approaches Billot. This time Billot explodes: 'So you have all agreed to let me be deceived by that scoundrel, that rascal, that villain … now you, and many others are getting caught up with that unpleasant man!' In retaliation, Esterhazy urges his journalist friends Drumont and Cassagnac to attack Billot, Henry and Boisdeffre in *La Libre Parole* and *L'Autorité*.[102]

The intervention of Scheurer-Kestner

Scheurer-Kestner discovers that an army officer has falsely accused Dreyfus of secretly buying a 200,000-franc apartment in Paris. This false accusation leads him to begin to have serious doubts about his guilt:

> *If Dreyfus is guilty, I will know it; if he is not, I will save him. It is unacceptable that in the 19th century, in the Republic, with a free and democratic government, iniquities should occur worthy of a despotic regime reminiscent of centuries past!*[103]

Mar 2–10   On an eight-day leave in Paris, Picquart endeavours to obtain an interview with General Millet. (*v.* Jan 1897) Before leaving Paris he confides in his old friend Lieutenant-Colonel Mercier-Milon that there has been an error in the Dreyfus trial of 1894 and that he believes the true culprit is Esterhazy.[104]

Mar–June   Scheurer-Kestner renews his investigations concerning the conviction. (*v.* April 1895) Among others he interviews Teyssonnières, Demange, Lazare[105] and Lieutenant-Colonel Bertin-Mourot of the Quatrième Bureau who testified against Dreyfus at the 1894 court martial.

Trarieux declares that an error has been made in the case;[106] Billot that he now has clear evidence of Dreyfus' guilt – meaning the *faux Henry* but does not specifically mention it. Joseph Reinach and Senator Arthur Ranc try to convince Scheurer-Kestner of Dreyfus' innocence and persuade him to seek a judicial review. Scheurer-Kestner remains open-minded. (*v.* 13 July 1897)

Mar–Aug   Mathieu engages independent graphologists from France, Belgium, Switzerland, England and the United States to study the handwriting of the *bordereau*. All conclude that it cannot be the work of Dreyfus.[107]

Apr 2   Picquart is now convinced that his posting outside France is linked to the Dreyfus-Esterhazy affair. He prepares a codicil to his will explaining how he became involved in investigating Esterhazy, his discovery of the Secret Dossier, the disclosures to the press about his investigation of Esterhazy and why he was sent soon after to Africa by Billot. Picquart concludes that Esterhazy, perhaps helped by Weil, is the agent of Schwartzkoppen; the treasonable acts attributed to Dreyfus were committed by Esterhazy; the court martial disregarded legal formalities and was conducted with the preconceived notion of Dreyfus' guilt. Picquart places the codicil in a sealed envelope marked with the instruction, 'In the event of the death of the undersigned, this letter should be delivered to the President of the Republic, who alone should have knowledge of it.'[108] (*v.* Appendix 14)

May 18   Picquart protests to Henry: 'Let it be announced publicly once and for all that I have been relieved of my duties or that I am no longer fulfilling them. I have no reason to be ashamed; what does make me ashamed are the lies and mysteries that my true situation has provoked over the last six months.'[109] (*v.* 31 May 1897)

May 24   Sandherr dies in Montauban, France, having been infirm for at least two years.

May 26   Devil's Island: The doctor attending Dreyfus reports that the prisoner is sure to die if he remains incarcerated in his cabin. The doctor demands a new cabin to be erected. (*v.* 25 Aug 1897)

May 31   With the consent of Gonse and Boisdeffre, Henry responds to Picquart's protest (18 May) with a threatening letter. For the first time serious charges are levelled against Picquart:[110]

> *I have the honour to inform you that following receipt of your note of 18 May our investigation has revealed that the word 'mystery' can be applied to the facts related below, which took place at the S[ection] [de] S[tatistique] during 1896:*
>
> i   *The opening of correspondence unconnected to the Service [Section de Statistique], for reasons that no one here has ever understood.*
>
> ii   *Proposals made to two members of staff of the S[ection] [de] S[tatistique], asking them to testify, should the need arise, that a classified document from the Service had been seized at the post office and came from a known individual.*[111]

 iii The opening of a secret dossier and examination of its contents, leading to certain indiscretions taking place with a purpose unrelated to the Service.[112]

The material proofs of these facts exist here [Ministry of War].[113]

As for the word 'lies', also included in your note of 18 May, the investigation was not yet able to determine where, how and to whom this word should be applied.[114]

End May Hanotaux confesses to historians Gabriel Monod and Albert Sorel[115] that the Affair has become the great misfortune of his life. He tells Monod: 'You know what fictitious means General Mercier used to demonstrate the guilt of Dreyfus. I went on my knees to prevent the trial. I was unable to persuade him.'[116]

June 10 Picquart replies to Henry's letter: 'I protest in the most formal manner possible at the insinuations it contains and the way in which the facts are presented.'[117] He asks his superior officer General Jérôme Leclerc, Divisional Commander for Tunisia, for leave to Paris.

Jun 20–29 In Paris, Picquart confides to Leblois that he is convinced of the innocence of Dreyfus. He shows him documents, including his correspondence with Gonse (Nov 1896–Mar 1897) but does not mention the *petit bleu*. Picquart rejects Leblois' suggestion to inform the Government, as this is incompatible with his duty as an officer. Picquart entrusts Leblois with the most relevant documents, including the codicil to his will. (*v.* 2 Apr 1897) He gives Leblois power of attorney but forbids him to contact Dreyfus' lawyer or brother. Picquart authorizes Leblois to inform the Government if he considers it necessary. Leblois promises confidentiality.[118]

End June Esterhazy moves to his château at Dommartin-la-Planchette.

 Lebrun-Renault admits to Forzinetti that Dreyfus did not make any confession to him.[119] (*v.* 5 and 6 Jan 1895, Rumours of an alleged confession)

July 8 Devil's Island: Dreyfus writes a further letter of appeal to the President of the Republic.[120] (*v.* Appendix 15)

July 13 Leblois introduces Scheurer-Kestner to Picquart's situation by showing him some of the documents confidentially entrusted to him. He asks Scheurer-Kestner to swear not to make use of this information without consulting him. Scheurer-Kestner heads his memorandum of this meeting: 'Here is the Truth about the Dreyfus Affair'. For the first time, it explicitly accuses Esterhazy of the crime attributed to Dreyfus. Scheurer-Kestner mistakenly believes that Weil is an accomplice of Esterhazy. (*v.* Aug 1896) He emphasizes the major difficulties of the situation, especially the need to keep Picquart's name secret.[121]

July 14 During the traditional Bastille Day military parade, Scheurer-Kestner announces his belief in Dreyfus' innocence and his readiness to support his cause. He invites colleagues to circulate his views in Government circles.

In Algiers, Max Régis, a young and fiercely antisemitic student, launches the first issue of *L'Antijuif d'Alger*.[122] (*v.* Mar 1898)

July 17   Leblois encourages Scheurer-Kestner to appeal to Darlan, Minister of Justice, for an annulment of the verdict of Dreyfus' court martial on the grounds of a mistrial. Scheurer-Kestner postpones the appeal for lack of evidence but allows Reinach to write to Lucie that he is willing to help her husband.[123]

July 18   Lucie receives Reinach's letter (delivered by Lazare) indicating that Scheurer-Kestner claims to have proof of Alfred's innocence and will try to rehabilitate him as soon as the Chambers resume after the summer recess. Scheurer-Kestner insists on keeping his involvement secret.[124]

July 19   At an Elysée Palace dinner Scheurer-Kestner confides in Lucie Faure, daughter of the President: 'For three days my heart has been heavy, my conscience racked. Why? It is an atrocious story. Captain Dreyfus is innocent. Do not say anything to your father for I am not yet able to tell him more …'[125] (*v.* 23 Oct 1897)

July 20   Scheurer-Kestner leaves Paris to spend the summer at Thann in Alsace.

July 27   Scheurer-Kestner obtains specimens of Esterhazy's handwriting, via Paul-Fortuné Jaume, a retired detective he has hired, in order to uncover Esterhazy's guilt. He compares them to a copy of the facsimile of the *bordereau*. He writes to Reinach: still prudent and without naming Esterhazy, he informs Reinach that he has just made an 'interesting' comparison of handwriting.[126]

Aug 11   Scheurer-Kestner tries to persuade Leblois to break the promise of confidentiality and to reveal Picquart's situation:

> *It seems to me that there is someone [Picquart] who should be feeling his immense moral responsibility more strongly … It is impossible to accept that an honest man should keep such a terrible secret to himself, and abandon an unfortunate man to the undeserved torture of Devil's Island even for a limited time.*[127]

Aug 15   Leblois refuses to break his promise of confidentiality and calls for discretion:

> *I continue to think that the best and most logical way to proceed would be to refer such a serious breach of the rights of the defence to the Minister of Justice … On the day this affair is resolved, a whole world will collapse. Not only your colleague [Billot] but his principal collaborator [Boisdeffre] will be deeply affected, not to mention gentlemen of lesser importance. All these people will defend themselves and we know that they are without scruples. One cannot make an omelette without breaking eggs; this one is going to break very many!*[128]

Aug 17   Esterhazy is suspended from active duty after a long period of sick leave and put on half-pay on account of 'temporary infirmity'.[129] (*v.* March 1897)

Aug 25   Devil's Island: Although Dreyfus is transferred to a new and marginally more spacious cabin, he exclaims to Deniel, the officer now in command of the islands: 'Ah, they're going to bury me here!'[130] Extracts of the general conditions pertaining to deportees to Devil's Island are posted on the cabin wall:

ARTICLE 22. The deported convict attends the cleanliness of his cabin and the surrounding area allotted to him and prepares his own food.

Guyane Française

République Française
Liberté   Egalité   Fraternité

Ministère des Colonies

Administration Pénitentiaire

1896/1897

Consigne pour le Service de la Déportation à l'Île du Diable

Accès de l'Île   *Article 1:*

L'accès de l'Île du Diable est rigoureusement interdit à toute personne, quelle qu'elle soit, non accompagnée par le Commandant Supérieur, et non munie d'une autorisation spéciale du Gouverneur ou du Directeur de l'Administration pénitentiaire.

A peine de nullité, l'autorisation devra toujours être revêtue du cachet du signataire et visée par le Commandant Supérieur

Article 2:

Toutefois le Commandant Supérieur pourra, sous sa responsabilité, autoriser le Médecin Major à se rendre à l'Île du diable en cas de maladie, soit des surveillants soit du déporté.

Regulations pertaining to deportees on Devil's Island

ARTICLE 24. The deportee must hand over all letters and papers written by him to the head warder.

ARTICLE 26. Any requests or complaints which the deportee may wish to make can only be received by the head warder.

ARTICLE 27. During the day the doors of the cabin of the deportee are open and until night he is free to move about inside the palisaded area.

All external communications are forbidden to him.

ARTICLE 28. During the night the area allotted to the deportee is lit inside and, as during the day, occupied by a guard.[131]

Sept

Billot sends Bertin-Mourot to discover what evidence Scheurer-Kestner has in the Dreyfus case. (*v.* Mar–June 1897) Scheurer-Kestner tells Bertin-Mourot he 'knows everything', that he is convinced of the innocence of Dreyfus and determined to prove it. (*v.* 16 Oct 1897) Billot sends officer Léonard Martinie to see David Hadamard, the father-in-law of Dreyfus, and Mathieu Dreyfus, for the same purpose.[132] The family is still unaware of the nature of Scheurer-Kestner's evidence and can give Martinie only a few details about the 1894 court martial.

Reinach informs Darlan of Scheurer-Kestner's revelations and shows him some of Dreyfus' recent letters to Lucie. Darlan promises to investigate further. Both President Faure and Prime Minister Méline refuse to discuss the matter with Darlan.

Sept 10

Scheurer-Kestner and Leblois meet in Fribourg, Switzerland. Leblois suggests that Scheurer-Kestner speak to the President, the Minister of War, the Prime Minister and the Minister of Justice.[133]

Drawing by Dreyfus of his prison enclosure on Devil's Island

c. **Sept 10**   Scheurer-Kestner writes to Esterhazy under a false name to obtain another specimen of his handwriting and invites him to engage in a business transaction. Esterhazy asks for more information before he can consider the offer and mentions that he plans to leave shortly for Italy.[134]

Sept 15   Reinach shows Lebon a letter he wishes to send Dreyfus. The letter announces Sheurer-Kestner's belief in the innocence of Dreyfus and his willingness to strive for a revision of his verdict. Lebon objects, pointing to the fact that Dreyfus' correspondence is read by the penal administration: Lebon suggests that making Reinach's letter public in this way may bring Reinach, 'a Semite [*sic*] a source of trouble'. Reinach tells Lebon that he is prepared to accept the consequences. Lebon repeats his refusal, and states that if Scheurer-Kestner insists on writing to Dreyfus, he (Lebon) will not take the responsibility of forwarding the letter but will submit it before the Cabinet for them to decide. Reinach also learns that in 1896, following the rumour of Dreyfus' escape from Devil's Island, he has been double shackled at night.

Reinach writes to Scheurer-Kestner informing him of his meeting with Lebon.

Sept 17   Lebon writes to Scheurer-Kestner that he is 'amazed' by Reinach's request. He asks Scheurer-Kestner to take no more action in the matter without consulting members of the Government. Scheurer-Kestner's intended reply to Lebon is not sent, on the advice of Leblois.[135]

Compilation of a second Secret Dossier

Sept–Oct   Billot instructs Gonse to collect documents that might serve as evidence against Dreyfus. A new Secret Dossier is compiled in the Section de Statistique. This is an extension of the original 1894 dossier, which still contains the four documents exhibited to the Court in secret during the court martial. Henry and other officers in the Section de Statistique continually add fresh documents to this new dossier, most of which are fabricated or not genuine. Within a few months the dossier contains over 300 documents, including some relating to the alleged confession of Dreyfus; a quantity of letters intercepted via the 'normal route' after his arrest (including intimate letters unrelated to the Affair, i.e. 45 letters sent to Schwartzkoppen by one of his mistresses, Mme Weede, wife of the Chief Adviser to the Netherlands' Delegation). Included in the forgeries are the *faux Henry*, an unimportant letter from Panizzardi to Schwartzkoppen on which Henry erased the initial 'P' and substituted 'D' (*v.* Mar 1894); a fabricated note known as the *billet des quatorze armées* supposedly exchanged between the German and Italian military attachés, containing vulgar allusions to their homosexuality;[136] another note sent by Panizzardi to Schwartzkoppen on 28 March 1895 about railway organization, which Henry altered by changing the date to April 1894.[137] (*v.* end April – end May, 1898 Consolidation of the Secret Dossier)

c. Sept   Henry fabricates the most notorious forgery or forgeries of the Dreyfus Affair, a copy or copies of letters allegedly written by the Kaiser to von Münster mentioning the name of Dreyfus. (*v.* 3 Nov & 12 Dec 1897, the *bordereau annoté*)

The Section de Statistique account books are falsified. Henry is warned by Gonse that Picquart has noticed the two false passages in Guénée's reports mentioning Val Carlos (*v.* 30 Oct 1896): Henry orders Gribelin to replace the initials 'VC' with 'HG' on the payment records to Val Carlos. Val Carlos's code name – Vésigneul – is also changed, to Juana.[138] (*v.* 7 Mar–19 Nov 1904, Second revision investigation: Criminal Chamber)

Gonse asks Du Paty to write a memorandum from memory on his report of 31 December 1894 describing his visit to Dreyfus' cell at Cherche-Midi prison. This account of Du Paty's conversation with Dreyfus suggests that he made an indirect confession. The memorandum is dated 24 September 1897.[139]

Oct 2   Gribelin writes a note about the disappearance of a document containing information on artillery. The document was allegedly written in March 1893 by Major Bayle of the Premier Bureau, and kept in his office; the officer on probation with Bayle at that time was Dreyfus.[140]

Oct 2–3   Scheurer-Kestner sends Leblois copies of Esterhazy's letters (*v.* 27 July 1897) to compare the writing with that of the *bordereau*. Leblois agrees that there is a resemblance but asks Scheurer-Kestner not to consult Darlan before speaking to Picquart.

Oct 7   Devil's Island: Deniel includes the words of Dreyfus in his monthly report:

If I have asked for medicine (which was refused), it is because I believe I have the right, at the time of my choice, to put an end to an agony which seems prolonged at will. I am losing my mind and fear madness … If culprits exist, they are in the Ministry of War, which has chosen me as a victim in order to hide the infamous crimes committed there.[141]

Oct 15   Gonse submits a secret report on the Affair to Billot, hoping to convince him of the guilt of Dreyfus. The report refers to the failure of Esterhazy's investigations and to several documents, such as the letter discovered on 1 November 1896 (the *faux Henry*) and other letters intercepted via the 'normal route'; a letter from von Münster to Schwarztkoppen;[142] the disappearance of Bayle's note (*v.* 2 Oct 1897); the alleged confession of Dreyfus; and the *faux Weyler* (*v.* 4 Sept 1896).

Oct 16   Billot sends a message to Scheurer-Kestner via Bertin-Mourot, not to take any action before they meet in two weeks' time. Scheurer-Kestner agrees.

NOTES

1   This document became known as the *petit bleu* and enabled Picquart to recognize Esterhazy's treason and thus to reopen the Affair. There has been much dispute over the date on which it was discovered by the Section de Statistique. The dating is crucial in defining Picquart's attitude and the eventual accusations against him formulated both by his superiors and subalterns, claiming he had falsified and even fabricated the document. (*v.* 23 Nov–3 Dec 1897; 12 July & 14 Sept 1898) Varying dates were given by Lauth, Schwartzkoppen and even by Picquart himself. In his depositions Picquart dated the arrival of the *petit bleu* to May, April and March. He stated that these errors in dating had been given in good faith. However, it has been established that it was most probably on 7 or 8 March that Henry received from Mme Bastian the parcel of papers containing the *petit bleu*. Due to his various missions and visits to his dying mother, Henry did not examine the parcel personally but handed it to Picquart, who gave it to Lauth to reconstruct the fragments. *ASD,* pp. 226–8.

2   Controversy arose as to how the *petit bleu* arrived at the Ministry of War. In his diary Schwartzkoppen admitted responsibility for the *petit bleu* but claimed that it had not reached the Ministry of War by the 'normal route'. He declared that he had posted it to Esterhazy and that it must have been intercepted by the postal service on the instruction of the Section de Statistique (Schwartzkoppen, *The Truth About Dreyfus*, pp. 79–80.) Schwartzkoppen gave another version to Austrian military attaché Colonel Schneider stating that he dictated the *petit bleu* to one of his mistresses but decided not to send it and threw it in his wastepaper basket. (*v.* 12 Aug 1899, Rennes court martial, n. 11). As there was no postage stamp on the *petit bleu* it could not have reached its addressee, which makes Schwartzkoppen's formal version unlikely. *ASD,* pp. 224–5. (*v.* following notes)

3   Written in the concise style typical of the communication between the German military attaché and his agents, the *petit bleu* revealed Schwartzkoppen's dissatisfaction with the information provided by his informer, Esterhazy. The initial 'R' is probably a reference to the city of Rouen where Esterhazy was garrisoned in 1894. *ASD,* p. 558 n. 15.

4   The handwriting of the *petit bleu* was another mystery. Hypotheses on this subject are copious. They mostly suggest that the document was written by a woman, implying one or another of Schwartzkoppen's mistresses. The writer's identity remains unknown. *ASD,* pp. 217–23.

5   *Cass.*, I, 144, Picquart. At the time, neither Lauth nor Picquart connected the *petit bleu* with the Dreyfus Affair.

6   A vertical tear destroyed a large number of words. Thomas has pieced together the text of this letter; the words in parenthesis are hypothetical. *ASD,* pp. 215–17.

7   Until publication of Thomas's *L'Affaire sans Dreyfus* in 1961, this document remained less well known than the *petit bleu* although of equal importance. Thomas suggests that the *petit bleu* was merely a draft of this severe letter. The letter not only confirms Esterhazy's role as an agent but reveals that Schwartzkoppen and his superiors were no longer satisfied with his services. In his diary Schwartzkoppen admits that when Esterhazy visited him on 20 February 1896 he told him of this. But it was only in March 1896 that Schwartzkoppen actually broke off the relationship, having come to the conclusion that Esterhazy's information was not useful. Schwartzkoppen, *The Truth About Dreyfus*, pp. 76, 79. *ASD,* pp. 204–14.

8   Picquart asked Leblois to examine some documents on the use of carrier-pigeons in espionage, one of the main issues on which he sought his advice. Picquart was later accused of revealing to Leblois documents included in the Secret Dossier. (*v.* 23 Nov–3 Dec 1897, Pellieux's Second investigation; 1 Feb & 12 July 1898)

9   Henry's reaction when he discovered the name of Esterhazy, whom he had known at the Ministry of War more than 15 years earlier (*v.* 1877–79), remains unknown. Along with Mathieu Dreyfus several historians believe that Henry had been protecting Esterhazy since that date. Reinach goes as far as suggesting that from April Henry warned Esterhazy that he was compromised and was about to be put under surveillance. *HAD,* 2, p. 251. Thomas rejects this thesis; but suggests that once Henry saw Esterhazy's handwritings, he connected the affair to that of Dreyfus, and realized earlier than Picquart that an error had been made in 1894. *ASD,* pp. 231–2.

10   Weil, with connections to Sandherr and Saussier, was wrongly denounced by *La Libre Parole* as a traitor. (*v.* 2 & 21 May 1892)

11   Picquart's superiors later reproached him for his secrecy. Desvernine confirmed that Picquart asked him to conduct an investigation into Esterhazy's private life between 1 and 10 April 1896. He stated that Picquart made no mention of Esterhazy being suspected of treason or of having any link with the Dreyfus Affair. *Cass.*, I, 729, Desvernine.

12   Marie lost a finger in an accident, probably when she was working in a factory before she moved to Paris. Thomas, *Esterhazy*, p. 218.

13   Picquart dated this operation to the end of April or May. *Cass.*, I, 158, Picquart. Thomas dated it to March, before the 26th, when Lauth went on leave. *ASD,* p. 229. As the *petit bleu* had no stamp on it and did not reach its addressee, Picquart could not immediately incriminate Esterhazy. Picquart's request for the specific photographic procedure led Lauth, Henry and Gribelin to accuse him of

fabricating the document. The accusation was first formulated during Pellieux's investigation of him. (*v.* 23 Nov–3 Dec 1897 Pellieux's second investigation; 7–23 Feb 1848, n. 70, Zola's trial)

14 Dreyfus had been studying English. The order to search his possessions came when a rumour spread in Paris that his dictionaries and exercise books might be coded, allowing him, his family and foreign conspirators to plan his escape. Bredin, *The Affair*, p. 131; *DFA,* p. 207.

15 This article provoked a vicious response from Drumont in *La Libre Parole*, attacking both Zola and Bernard Lazare. In the newspaper *Le Voltaire* (May–June) Lazare responded with a series of articles attacking Drumont and his antisemitic supporters. Drumont rebutted these attacks, and this war of words led to a duel between Drumont and Lazare on 18 June. There was no injury to either party. The same year the editor Stock published all Lazare's articles during this four-week conflict in *Contre l'antisémitisme, histoire d'une polémique* ('Against Antisemitism, the History of a Controversy'). A new edition of this booklet was published in 1983 (Paris: La Différence), which included Lazare's testamentary will and Charles Péguy's 'Portrait of Bernard Lazare'. Zola's article was later published in his book of collected articles on the Dreyfus Affair: *La vérité en marche.* See, in the 1969 edition, pp. 55–62. See English in Emile Zola. *The Dreyfus Affair, J'Accuse and Other Writings*, ed., A. Pagès, (ed.), trans. E. Levieux (Newhaven and London: Yale University Press, 1994), pp. 2–7.

16 The determination and strong constitution of Dreyfus helped him survive the many diseases and unhealthy conditions current on Devil's Island. His guards often fell ill and had to leave. *DFA,* p. 199.

17 Neither Picquart nor Boisdeffre informed Gonse. Whether it was Picquart's idea or not, once this conspiracy of silence was discovered it added to the antagonism between Gonse and his subordinate Picquart.

18 Desvernine confirmed that he had already told Picquart on 25 July that he had obtained a specimen of Esterhazy's handwriting. *Cass.*, I, 730, Desvernine.

19 It was Lauth who requested to be accompanied by Henry, despite the fact that Henry did not speak German. They went to Basel hoping to identify the '*decoré*' whom Cuers had already mentioned to Lajoux and Foucault. On the list of questions Lauth had prepared to ask Cuers, he had written the initials V.E. (Valsin Esterhazy). *Cass.*, I, 420; *3ème Cass.*, III, 76, Lauth.

20 Their report conflicts with Cuers' own report and with depositions given in 1898 before the Criminal Chamber and later at the Rennes trial by Picquart, Tomps and Roget. In October 1896 Foucault, the French military attaché in Berlin, had told Picquart that Cuers had come to the French Embassy to complain about the officers sent to interview him. He had reported being particularly puzzled by one of them ('a corpulent and ruddy man') [Henry], who tried to pass himself off as a policeman and interrupted Cuers every time he tried to speak. Tomps suggested plying Cuers with absinthe to 'make him talk', but Henry rejected the suggestion. Cuers later claimed that during the Basel meeting he had told Lauth and Henry that Dreyfus had never worked for the German Embassy and that Schwartzkoppen's contact was a major from an Austrian family who had begun his espionage activities in 1893 but had been dismissed by Schwartzkoppen in October 1895 (letter of Cuers to *Le Figaro*, 15 July 1899). As Thomas comments, it is 'impossible to distinguish truth from falsehood in the testimonies of people whose intentions were to dilute the truth with lies'. *ASD*, pp. 244–7.

21 Letters of Esterhazy to Calmon-Maison and to Frédéric Thévenet, Billot's aide-de-camp, both dated 25 August.

22 Picquart later admitted: 'I was aghast.' He had thought for a moment that Esterhazy might have been the accomplice of Dreyfus, with the help of Weil, who seemed to him suspect. However, he admitted that he had become convinced that the '*bordereau* does not cast suspicion on Dreyfus'. *Rennes*, I, 430–1, Picquart.

23 *Cass.*, I, 155; *Rennes*, I, 431, Picquart. There was in fact a definite resemblance between the handwriting of Alfred and Mathieu. Bertillon's reaction on the other hand implied that the Dreyfus family may have used Esterhazy as a scapegoat. (*v.* Dec 1896)

24 This request was also used against Picquart later on. Henry advanced the preposterous claim that before leaving the Section de Statistique Sandherr instructed him personally that the Secret Dossier was only to be exposed in the presence of the Chief of Staff. Picquart knew about the existence of the Secret Dossier and that it was kept in the Section de Statistique, but he was still unaware of its content. *Cass.*, I, 133, Picquart. He assumed it contained absolute proof of the guilt of Dreyfus. *ASD*, p. 265.

25 This first report, which Picquart also called *Mémoire*, was an extremely precise and clear analysis of the case. Picquart committed one significant mistake in claiming that the *petit bleu* reached the Section de Statistique at the end of April 1896; it arrived in early March. Lauth, Gribelin and Henry later used this error as evidence when accusing Picquart of falsifying the *petit bleu*. *ASD*, pp. 268–71. The report is included in *Cass.*, II, 87–89; *Fabre*, 257–9. Also see *AD*, pp. 465–7.

26 *Déb., Cass. 1898*, 121. Picquart remarked later that when he mentioned the Secret Dossier to Boisdeffre he obviously recognized it. (Picquart's letter to the Minister of Justice, 15 September 1898) Boisdeffre's outburst probably referred to Mercier's order of 17 January 1895 which was to disperse the contents of the dossier after he had burnt Du Paty's commentary. Boisdeffre now realized from the existence of

the dossier that Sandherr had not obeyed Mercier's order to disperse it and, from the contents of the dossier that Picquart now showed him, that another copy of Du Paty's commentary had been kept.

27   *Cass.*, I, 140; *Rennes*, I, 432, Picquart. Gonse denied saying this. *Rennes*, I, 557, Gonse. Gonse had probably already been briefed by Boisdeffre and advised how to respond to Picquart. (*HAD*, 2, pp. 298–9; *ASD*, p. 273). Picquart found Gonse's response absurd since the *bordereau* obviously pertained to both affairs. *Cass.*, I, 161, Picquart.

28   Mathieu Dreyfus, increasingly worried about his brother's condition, orchestrated this false report as a way of renewing interest in the fate of his brother. Clifford Millage, Paris correspondent of the *Daily Chronicle*, who believed in the innocence of Dreyfus, agreed to write a false report about Dreyfus' escape for *The Wales Argus*, a Newport paper, which was published on 2 September. Mathieu rewarded him generously. The following day the *Daily Chronicle* repeated the article. *DFA*, pp. 179–80.

29   The same day Lebon secretly ordered a double palisade to be built around the cabin of Dreyfus. (*v.* 12 Nov. 1896) See detailed description of the shackles in Whyte, *The Accused*, p. 88. See also Dreyfus' own description, A. Dreyfus, *Cinq années de ma vie* (1982), pp. 167, 171.

30   *Répertoire*, p. 56.

31   This seemed to be an ordinary letter, in which the sender tells Dreyfus of his daughter's forthcoming marriage in Basel to a Jewish man. But the Colonial Secretary became alarmed when he discovered that there was writing in invisible ink between the lines which, possibly purposely, had become visible: 'Impossible to decipher last communication. Return to the former procedure in your answer. Indicate precisely where the documents are and how the cupboard can be unlocked. Actor ready to move immediately.' (*Répertoire*, p. 54). Intercepted, the letter would thus strengthen the evidence against Dreyfus, which was probably its purpose. A clear forgery, the *faux Weyler* presents another of the Affair's many mysteries. The writer has never been identified, though the consensus is that he belonged to the General Staff and was most probably Henry, or possibly Bertillon, who kept suggesting the letter was the work of the Dreyfus family. *ASD*, pp. 288–92.

32   See correspondence in *Répertoire*, pp. 57–60; *AD*, pp. 467–70.

33   This measure remained in force until 20 October 1896. *Rennes*, I, 250, Official report on Dreyfus' stay on Devil's Island. In spite of attempts to ease his pain by wrapping cloths around his legs, the shackles cut into his flesh. According to Pierre Dreyfus, 'The feet of the prisoner were placed in these shackles which were held securely to the bed by the bar in such a way that it was impossible for the body itself to move. Riveted to his bed by chains stained with blood, tortured by vermin and torrid heat, racked by spiritual torment, Dreyfus felt that his suffering had passed the limits of human endurance and that he should die.' A. and P. Dreyfus, *The Dreyfus Case, The Man Alfred Dreyfus and his son Pierre Dreyfus*, trans. D.C. McKay (New Haven: Yale University Press, 1937), p. 74.

34   This restriction remained in force until the middle of January 1897.

35   Calmette received the information regarding the conditions of Dreyfus' detention from Guégun, former head of Penal Administration in Guyana. M. Dreyfus, '*Dreyfusards!*', p. 73.

36   A. Dreyfus, *Cinq années de ma vie* (1982), p. 164.

37   A. Dreyfus, *Cinq années de ma vie* (1982), pp. 166–7.

38   There are various accounts of this interview: Picquart testified that Billot initially believed Dreyfus innocent but he then changed his mind, suggesting that both Esterhazy and Dreyfus were guilty. Billot testified that he warned Picquart that Esterhazy's guilt would not absolve Dreyfus. He even insinuated that others such as Weil might be involved. *HAD*, 2, 334–5.

39   General Staff officers were worried about Castelin's impending interpellation. They thought that despite being a Nationalist Deputy he was in the pay of the Dreyfus family. These fears were exacerbated after the publication, three days later, of the second article in *L'Eclair*. (*v.* 14 Sept 1896)

40   Cassagnac, a friend of Demange, was on the extreme political Right, but in spite of his attacks on dreyfusards and Jews in general, he intervened several times in Dreyfus' favour. (*v.* 11–19 Dec 1894)

41   The article appeared in the issue dated 15 September.

42   Various hypotheses were put forward regarding the authorship of the two articles in *L'Eclair* (10 and 14 September). Mathieu Dreyfus saw them as a reply from the General Staff to Calmette's article (8 September); Picquart and the General Staff thought they were by the Dreyfus family, or by Deputy André Castelin, a friend of *L'Eclair's* editor, Sabatier, thought to be in contact with the Dreyfus family. This reinforced Picquart's fear that Castelin's interpellation (*v.* 11 Sept 1896) would be damaging to the Ministry of War. That same day he wrote to Gonse, in a further attempt to persuade him to initiate legal action against Esterhazy: 'I told you that we [the Ministry of War] were going to be in deep trouble if we did not take the initiative.' Picquart opened an investigation to discover the author of the article. Conducted by Gribelin, it concluded that only three officers in the Section de Statistique were sufficiently informed to provide *L'Eclair* with the published information – Henry, Picquart and Gribelin. In fact the source was subsequently revealed to be a *Petit Journal* journalist called Lissajoux,

but he admitted help from a General Staff officer. *ASD*, pp. 312–20. See entire article in *AD*, pp. 470–5.

43 *Cass.*, I, 167, Picquart. Gonse denied Picquart had said this. Picquart insisted he did and also reported the conversation in a letter he addressed in 1898 to the Minister of Justice (*Deb. Cass., 1898*, p. 114). This exchange emphasized the enmity between Gonse and Picquart. In July 1906 Gonse again denied this conversation. Picquart reaffirmed it, adding 'his [Gonse's] word is worthless'. As a result of this provocation Gonse challenged Picquart to a duel. (*v.* 9 July 1906) *Déb. Cass., 1906*, II, 682–4.

44 The text of the telegram suggested by Picquart was: 'Important and urgent matter concerning the House R. Come to Paris immediately. You will be met at the station. [Signed] C'. *Fabre*, p. 225.

45 The versions of Billot's refusal differ: according to Picquart, Billot neither accepted nor rejected the idea of a bogus telegram, but refused to give Picquart a written order (*Cass.*, I, 168–9, Picquart). Billot attested that he told Picquart, 'one should not do such things … As Chief of Staff it would be incorrect of me to allow an officer to do so …'. *Rennes*, I, 171, Billot.

46 The petition is published in several papers, including *L'Eclair*, *Le Figaro* and *L'Intransigeant*.

47 The palisade measured 16.30 x 12 metres. The palisade and the hut were separated by 5 metres to the north and south, and 2.5 metre to the east and west. Rennes, I, 250. Official report on Dreyfus' stay on Devil's Island.

48 *DFA*, pp. 182–3. There is no record of a reply to Lucie's supplication. Clifford Millage. (*v.* 3 Sept 1896, n. 28) helped Lucie to draft the letter. For a facsimile of Lucie's supplication in Latin see Whyte, *The Accused*, p. 105. Whyte was unable to gain access to this correspondence in the Vatican's secret archives since Leo XIII's private papers have not yet been examined by Vatican personnel.

49 This procedure was illegal without official permission but it was common practice for the postal authorities to submit letters to the Ministry of War in response to an unofficial request from the head of the Section de Statistique.

50 Drumont's visiting card simply attested to Esterhazy's relationship with *La Libre Parole*. (*v.* Jan 1895, n. 29) Picquart later obtained more substantial proof of Esterhazy's relationship with the paper. (*v.* 6–8 Nov 1896)

51 *Rennes*, I, 447–8, Picquart.

52 Like Bertillon, Picquart first believed the letter was the work of the Dreyfus family. It was René Cavard, head of the Sûreté, who sensed from the start that it was a fake. *ASD*, pp. 288–92.

53 Esterhazy received 40,000 francs from Christian in 1897. He placed the money in his own account at the Crédit Lyonnais. He lost it all in speculative dealings on the stock market. Thomas, *Esterhazy*, pp. 235–9; 252–3; 262.

54 The complaints against Picquart were numerous: he should not have involved Bertillon in his investigations since this meant confiding in an unreliable person; he should not have consulted Leblois. These and other complaints made the following year (October 1897) formed the subject of a draft of a letter by Henry addressed to Picquart and signed by Boisdeffre and Gonse. The letter was never sent. For extracts of this little-known document, see *ASD*, pp. 409–10.

55 *Cass.*, I, 157–60, Picquart.

56 *Cass.*, I, 263, Boisdeffre.

57 Salles had learnt about the secret transmission from a judge whom he refused to name (Demange was convinced it was Florentin). *HAD*, 2, pp. 425–6.

58 *HAD*, 2, p. 553.

59 This confidential report, along with Guénée's second report (*v.* 21 Nov 1896) – proving the plot against Picquart within the Section de Statistique – were only made known to Picquart in 1898, during Tavernier's investigation of him (23 Sept–19 Nov 1898). *Cass*, I, 173, Picquart.

60 The exact date, sometime between the end of October and 14 November, was disputed by the various investigations. See *ASD*, pp. 567–8, n. 7.

61 The letter related to the Draft Field Artillery Manual prepared in 1896 and which had been handed to Panizzardi by a Section de Statistique agent. *ASD*, p. 568, n. 12.

62 Henry was referring to the impending interpellation of Deputy André Castelin. (*v.* 11 Sept 1896)

63 Reinach believed the technical aspects of the *faux Henry* were the work of renowned master-forger Lemercier-Picard, a former butcher known under various names. *HAD*, 2, pp. 412–13. Thomas rejected this theory. *ASD*, pp. 337, 569–70. Historians now agree that Henry and his wife worked on this forgery at home. Although Lemercier-Picard was never employed by the Section de Statistique, he was directly responsible for the forgery of the *faux Otto* (*v.* 25 Nov 1897), and probably involved in other manoeuvres (*v.* 2 Nov 1897, n. 37). The mysterious circumstances of the death of Lemercier-Picard in 1898 inspired various theories on his involvement in the Affair. (*v.* 3 March 1898, n. 112)

64 Henry committed three fatal mistakes in these forgeries. He had not noticed (1) that the colouring of the graph paper of the first letter (from 1896) was different from the colouring of the fresh graph paper he used for the forgery; (2) that the size of the squares was not the same on the two graph

papers; (3) that at the time of the first letter (1896), three Jewish employees were working at the Italian Embassy, but there were none on the date that he attributed to the letter (June 1894). All this was only discovered two years later. (*v.* 13 Aug 1898)

65 Even more unusual was the fact that with Gribelin's copy was a description of the sealed envelope in which it allegedly arrived. This was accompanied by a note signed by Gonse, Henry, Lauth and Gribelin attesting to its authenticity. This copy replaced the original *faux Henry* inserted into the Secret Dossier compiled as evidence against Dreyfus (*v.* Sept 1897). None of the officers asked Henry for further explanations concerning the document's date of arrival, which he claimed to be 31 October. Mme Bastian, however, made no deliveries between 8 August and 7 November. *ASD*, pp. 325–45, 571.

66 The pamphlet had been ready for some time. (*v.* June 1895) After the articles in *L'Eclair* (*v.* 10 & 14 September 1896) Mathieu considered it was necessary, and indeed essential, to publish Lazare's pamphlet, which Lazare continued to revise up to day of publication, largely to refute the *Eclair* articles.

67 Mathieu suggested to Lazare that the pamphlet should be printed in Brussels (October 1896), believing that no French publisher would accept it for fear of legal action. On his return from Brussels Mathieu went to see several newspapers, fearing that they would not review the publication. Antonin Périvier and Fernand de Rodays, editor and owner respectively of *Le Figaro*, though sympathetic and promising not to obstruct the pamphlet, said they would not be the first to mention it. Mathieu also went with Forzinetti to see Henri Rochefort, editor of *L'Intransigeant*, and tried to convince him of the innocence of Dreyfus. Rochefort agreed to hear Forzinetti's full account of the arrest of Dreyfus, promising Mathieu he would remain neutral and keep Forzinetti's visit secret. But the day after the pamphlet arrived in France, *L'Intransigeant* published a virulent article on it entitled 'Vaine tentative de réhabilitation d'un traître' ('A Vain Attempt to Rehabilitate a Traitor'). The French press followed Rochefort's example almost without exception. Lazare recalled, 'I became a pariah overnight.' Rochefort did not keep his promise and divulged Forzinetti's visit, as a result of which he lost his position as Governor of Cherche-Midi prison. (*v.* 16 Nov 1897) See Lazare's account: 'Mémoire de Bernard Lazare sur ses activités pendant l'affaire Dreyfus', in *Bernard Lazare, anarchiste et nationaliste juif*, texts compiled by Philippe Oriol (Paris: Campion, 1999), pp. 241–68, and *ATQV*, pp. 85–7.

68 According to Reinach 3500 copies were distributed. From a study of the costs involved mentioned by Lazare, it may be concluded that Reinach's estimate was far higher. Moreover, two print runs of this first pamphlet were made, identical in text – one more luxurious, containing 66 pages; another of lesser quality, containing only 24 pages (the text was thus much denser). B. Lazare, *Une erreur judiciaire l'Affaire Dreyfus*, ed. P. Oriol (Paris: Allia, 1993), pp. 75–6. (*v.* 16 Nov 1896)

69 A revision is taken here to mean a judicial review of an original case, trial or verdict, which may lead to a retrial, a confirmation of the original verdict or an annulment and a declaration of not guilty. The French term is '*révision*', and those in support of such were called '*révisionnistes*'. The word 'revision' rather than the legal term 'review' has been used throughout the *Chonological History*, partly to reflect contemporary usage and partly to avoid confusion when using related terms such as 'revisionists' and 'anti-revisionists'.

70 Emphasis as in the original. B. Lazare, *Une erreur judiciaire: La vérité sur l'Affaire Dreyfus* (Bruxelles: Imprimerie Veuve Monnom, 1896), p. 24.

71 These letters were intercepted and copied by Picquart, whose investigation of Esterhazy had already revealed his dealings with Weil and Weil's efforts to introduce Esterhazy to the Minister of War. The letters also confirmed Esterhazy's relationship with *La Libre Parole*, as well as his desperate straits: '[Saussier] can get me to clean the stairs if he wants, but let him take me on.' The tone foreshadowed his threatening letters of October–November 1897.

72 *ATQV*, p. 88.

73 Schwartzkoppen explains in his diary that after much thought, he decided to remain silent rather than reveal the truth publicly. Schwartzkoppen, *The Truth About Dreyfus*, pp. 90–1.

74 Picquart admitted later that Gonse told him: 'When a Minister tells me something, I always believe it.' *Cass.*, I, 173, Picquart.

75 *Rennes*, I, 250. Bravard appears to have protested against this measure to the Governor of Guyana, who approached Colonial Secretary Lebon, but without success. Shortly after this, Lebon sent Deniel, a cruel warder, to replace Bravard as officer in command of the islands. Deniel's first concern was to intensify security measures appertaining to Dreyfus, increasing the number of guards from five to eleven and constructing a large Mirador (observation tower), about 15 metres high, with its guard constantly on duty. Whyte, *The Accused*, p. 88; Menier, 'La détention du Capitaine Dreyfus', p. 472.

76 The author of this letter remains unknown. Esterhazy did not tell Weil about his dealings with Schwartzkoppen. It is probable that Weil knew about them, since henceforth Weil kept his distance and they met less frequently. *ASD*, p. 362.

77 Picquart later stated that he immediately understood that this was meant to keep him at a distance but that he did not express this thought to anyone. He also regretted that Billot had not told him openly

that he was no longer satisfied with his performance as head of the Section de Statistique. *Cass.*, I, 171; II, 165, Picquart. Billot always denied that Picquart was sent on mission in order to be kept at distance. *Cass.*, I, 549–52, Billot; *Pro. Zola*, 155, Billot.

78 Before his pamphlet was printed in Brussels Lazare had explained to Stock his reasons for not publishing in Paris first. Lazare had already offered Stock the rights to the first reprint, which Stock had accepted. As Stock's usual printer was afraid he would be sued, Stock's name appeared on this edition as publisher and printer. Stock, *Mémorandum d'un éditeur*, pp. 15–20. This publication marked Stock's entry into the dreyfusard camp. (*v.* Bibliography, works published by Stock).

79 Before leaving Paris, Picquart had ordered Desvernine to suspend the investigation during his absence, indicating that it should be renewed when he returned. *Cass.*, I, 733, Desvernine.

80 Billot took a copy of the *faux Henry* with him intending to read it in the Chamber in case he was strongly provoked by Castelin.

81 *ASD*, p. 368.

82 Henry however, wanted Picquart to be identified as the person responsible for delivering the *bordereau* to *Le Matin*. He therefore preferred Tomps's first hypothesis. (*v.* 18 Nov 1896) Henry asked Tomps to produce a report demonstrating Picquart's guilt but he refused. Henry also sent Gribelin to *Le Matin*, who returned with another story, similar to Tomps's first hypothesis. Tomps became indignant and was reprimanded by Lauth, in Henry's name, and was threatened with dismissal. Tomps had incurred the enmity of the Section de Statistique. *Rennes*, III, 363–5, Tomps.

83 Schwartzkoppen, *Die Wahrheit über Dreyfus*, pp. 201–2.

84 Ducasse was employed by Picquart for a time in the Section de Statistique. He was subsequently appointed secretary to comtesse Blanche de Commings, Picquart's cousin, a middle-aged spinster whose salon was frequented by Picquart and many General Staff officers. Ducasse remained grateful and loyal to Picquart, sending him two reports (24 and 26 November) written in the enigmatic style they used in their correspondence. Both reports were intercepted by Henry.

85 In French: '*Le chef-d'oeuvre est accompli*'. (*v.* 10 Nov 1897, n. 54)

86 This name refers to Desvernine.

87 *ASD*, p. 376. The first part of Ducasse's letter referred to a professional matter: the Section de Statistique was renting an apartment for Schwartzkoppen and his colleagues opposite the German Embassy, located above the officers' mess. French agents could thus watch the embassy and listen to the German officers' mealtime conversations. Picquart's personal 'improvement' to this system was to insert acoustic tubes in the chimney flues of both apartments. In 1896 Desvernine frequently reported to Picquart what he had overheard. But when chimney sweeps were due to arrive, Picquart asked Desvernine to remove the tubes. The second paragraph concerned a conversation in the salon of the comtesse.

88 Henry later made use of this letter in the Speranza forgery. (*v.* 15 Dec 1896, the Speranza Letter)

89 The Government rejected Lucie's petition since it did not meet the criteria for review stipulated by Article 445 of the Criminal Code. This article listed the grounds on which a review could be considered as follows: if, after a murder conviction, there was clear evidence that the alleged victim was still alive; if another defendant was judged guilty of the same crime, and the two verdicts were irreconcilable; if a witness for the prosecution had been convicted of false testimony against the accused. However, a fourth condition added to Article 445 on 8 June 1895 stipulated that a review could also be considered if after a conviction a new fact or facts were established or documents unknown at the time of the conviction were discovered, proving the innocence of the person convicted. In rejecting Lucie's petition the Government decided that even if the amendment was applicable to the Dreyfus case, it could not be invoked retrospectively to a verdict issued before the date of the amendment. (*v.* 12 July 1906, n. 58) On this aspect see B. Martin, 'The Dreyfus Affair and the Corruption of the French Legal System', in N.L. Kleeblatt (ed.) *The Dreyfus Affair: Art, Truth and Justice* (Berkeley and Los Angeles: University of California Press, 1987), pp. 37–49.

90 Roche obtained an interview with Billot. He was told that there were serious allegations against Esterhazy in addition to those relating to his disreputable private life (Billot described him as a womanizer). Unable to say more, Billot asked Roche to stop recommending Esterhazy.

91 The letter suggests that Picquart was working for the alleged 'Jewish Syndicate': i.e. the few people who supported Mathieu Dreyfus in his search for new evidence to obtain a reopening of his brother's case. (*v.* 16 Nov & 1 Dec 1897).

92 Picquart only became aware of this letter in 1897 during Pellieux's second investigation of Esterhazy. (23 November–3, December 1897).

93 Du Paty's little-known report was discovered by Thomas. *ASD*, pp. 260–1, 535–40.

94 Picquart was notified of this order on 15 January 1897. The letter was signed by Gonse, a normal procedure.

95 Picquart had arranged this interview before his posting abroad. *Cass.*, I, 419, Lauth.

96 Gonse continued to send Picquart polite letters throughout February and March 1897 (his last letter was dated 23 March), in an attempt to reassure him. The letters were published by Stock in February 1899 as *Gonse-Pilate and Other Stories.* See also *AD,* pp. 477–86. In February 1897 Picquart also received cordial letters from Henry.

97 *Cass.,* I, 706–10, Esterhazy's letters to Jules Roche.

98 Within a matter of weeks the new league had gained 450 supporters in Paris and the surrounding region. Its Paris committee included some of *La Libre Parole*'s principal antisemitic collaborators – Octave Biot, Adrien Papillaud, Raphaël Viau, André de Boisandré – as well as the antisemitic publisher Hayard. Branches were soon formed in various arrondissements of Paris as well as in the provinces (Bordeaux, Marseille, Toulouse, Rouen). By May 1897 the League numbered some 8000 members. S. Wilson, 'The Ligue Antisémitique Française', *Wiener Library Bulletin* 25 (London, 1972), pp. 33–9; Pierrard, *Juifs et catholiques français,* pp. 143–9.

99 *Répertoire,* pp. 73–4. This draft letter was included in the monthly report dated 1 May 1897 sent by the Governor of Guyana, Henri-Eloi Danel, to the Colonial Secretary. All drafts of the letters of Dreyfus, including those he decided not to send, and censored letters, were retained by the penal administration. Menier, 'La détention du Capitaine Dreyfus', pp. 467–8.

100 When Esterhazy returned from sick leave, Giovaninelli reprimanded him for soliciting his superiors (including himself) to approach Billot and for giving false information about his private life. Giovaninelli encouraged Esterhazy to leave the army voluntarily. Esterhazy refused, taking advantage of his poor health to reapply several times for sick leave. Giovaninelli told him that after six months, being the maximum period permitted for sick leave, he would automatically be suspended from duty on account of 'temporary infirmity'. (*v.* 17 Aug 1897) Thomas, *Esterhazy,* p. 248.

101 In spite of promising Grenier that he would help Esterhazy, Henry did nothing. This episode contradicts Reinach's view that the collaboration between Esterhazy and Henry was already active at the beginning of the Affair and also Esterhazy's future statements that he was one of Sandherr's agents, working with Henry. Thomas, *Esterhazy,* pp. 246–7.

102 Thomas, *Esterhazy,* p. 250.

103 Extract from Scheurer-Kestner's *Mémoires.* The manuscript was bequeathed to the Bibliothèque Nationale and is quoted in M. Dreyfus, *Dreyfusards!,* p. 99.

104 *Cass.,* I, 194, Picquart. The real reasons for Picquart's absence from the Section de Statistique (of which he was still officially head) were kept secret. Picquart's friends, including Mercier-Milon and Curé, tried to find out from Du Paty whether Picquart was in disgrace. Gonse assured Du Paty that Picquart was on an important mission.

105 Scheurer-Kestner wrote to Lazare in July 1897 that 'in the interest of the Dreyfus cause' he would not see him again, since the Affair should not appear to be a Jewish cause. M. Dreyfus, *Dreyfusards!,* p. 94.

106 In 1896, as Trarieux's doubts about the conviction of Dreyfus and its illegality grew stronger, he discussed the matter with graphologist Teyssonnières. Teyssonnières tried to convince Trarieux that Dreyfus is guilty (letter of 2 January 1897), and provided him with his report on the handwriting of Dreyfus and the *bordereau.* This report convinced Trarieux that the *bordereau* was not by Dreyfus. Teyssonnières was asked by Trarieux to see Scheurer-Kestner. *Pro. Zola,* 498–504; *Rennes,* III, 412–16, Trarieux.

107 Among the experts were historian Gabriel Monod, graphologists Crémieux-Jamin from Rouen, Albert de Rougemont and Ed. de Maneffe from Belgium, David Nunes Carvalho and Thomas Henry Gurrin. Lazare published their findings in the second edition of his pamphlet *L'erreur judiciaire* (*v.* 6 Nov 1897). Mathieu's costs for these additional examinations mounted to 7000 francs. Some of the graphologists refused the fee. *DFA,* p. 190.

108 See complete text in *HAD,* 2, pp. 701–04. This document was found intact in Picquart's house in 1898. *v.* 12 July 1898. *Fabre,* pp. 5, 54–5.

109 *Fabre,* 238. As Picquart was still officially head of the Section de Statistique, agents continued to send him letters at the Ministry of War. From the time Picquart was removed from Paris (November 1896) Henry continued to forward these letters to him, having first opened and read them himself. Picquart appended this letter to one he was returning to Henry. Billot did not want to remove Picquart without appointing a replacement. Although Henry was acting head during Picquart's six-month absence, Billot had no intention of appointing him permanently to this post. *ASD,* pp. 388–9.

110 The letter, dated 31 May, was sent on 3 or 4 June which led Picquart to suspect that it had been shown to Henry's superiors. Henry told Gonse that he considered this a 'personal' matter (*Fabre,* p. 141) and was replying immediately. Gonse warned Henry not to be offensive to Picquart, his superior officer. Henry maintained that he had written the letter on his own initiative, with prior consent of Gonse and Boisdeffre. *Cass.,* I, 257, Gonse.

111 This is the first reference to the various accusations later formulated against Picquart regarding his alleged falsification or even fabrication of the *petit bleu* (e.g. *v.* 23 Nov–3 Dec, Pellieux's second

investigation of Esterhazy; 7–31 Dec, Ravary's judicial investigation; 10, 14, 16 September 1898; 23 Sept–16 Nov 1898, Tavernier's investigation of Picquart).

112 This refers to Picquart's consultations with Leblois, alleging the transmission of the Secret Dossier (by Picquart) to Leblois (e.g. *v.* 23 Nov– 3 Dec, Pellieux's second investigation; 7–31 Dec, Ravary's judicial investigation; 12 Feb 1898, Zola's trial; 11 July 1898).

113 This phrase convinced Picquart that he was the subject of machinations. He realized not only that all Henry's accusations against him were false but that the so-called 'material proofs' of his alleged wrongdoing, held in the Section de Statistique, were either irrelevant or fabricated. *Cass.*, I, 196, Picquart.

114 *Fabre*, p. 239.

115 Monod was a member of the Institut, Sorel a member of the Académie française. The Institut was created in 1795 as the 'parliament of the learned world', to promote the arts and sciences according to multidisciplinary principles. It consisted of five separate academies: L'Académie française; L'Académie des inscriptions et belles lettres; L'Académie des sciences; L'Académie des beaux-arts; L'Académie des sciences morales et politiques.

116 *Cass.*, I, 458, Monod. Having studied the *bordereau* Monod was convinced it was not written by Dreyfus and that the 1894 trial was flawed. Hanotaux's statement made him realize why he had received no response to his letter to Billot in March 1897, in which he questioned Billot whether he had been convinced Dreyfus was guilty. Monod added that if Billot had answered affirmatively, 'I would perhaps have been able to catch up on the sleep I have lost these last two years and force myself not to think of it any more.'

117 *Fabre*, p. 239.

118 *Cass.*, I, 196–7, Picquart.

119 *Cass.*, I, 323, Forzinetti.

120 This letter was one of those read by the principal State Prosecutor Jean-Pierre Manau before the Supreme Court of Appeal in 1899. *Déb. Cass.*, 1899, 322–33. Between 8 July 1897 and 7 June 1898 Dreyfus addressed 13 appeals to the President.

121 This led to the failure of Scheurer-Kestner's diplomatic campaign for a judicial review of October– November 1897. See text of the memorandum in *ASD*, pp. 396–7; See English version in Bredin, *The Affair*, pp. 184–5.

122 Régis was arrested towards the end of 1897 and held for eight days on charges of insult and defamation. Despite this, the paper enjoyed immense success. Initially it had two editions a week, then three, as well as an illustrated supplement. By 1898 its circulation had reached 20,000. Wilson, *Ideology and Experience*, p. 230; P. Hebey, *Alger 1898, La grande vague antijuive* (Paris: Nil, 1996), p. 98.

123 The documents Picquart entrusted to Leblois could have served as proof, but Leblois refused to have them disclosed publicly. *ASD*, p. 398.

124 The rumour that Scheurer-Kestner was about to involve himself in the Affair had already begun to circulate among politicians and men of letters by the end of July. Reinach discussed it with Darlan and with such eminent scholars as Anatole Leroy-Beaulieu, Henri Monot, Emile Strauss, Albert Sorel and others. *ATQV*, p. 95.

125 Scheurer-Kestner's *Mémoires*, quoted in *HAD*, 2, p. 530.

126 *HAD*, 2, p. 536. Sheurer-Kestner was not yet convinced the handwriting was identical. It seemed as if Esterhazy had changed his handwriting after publication of the *bordereau*. *ASD*, p. 398.

127 AD, p. 500. The correspondence between Leblois and Scheurer-Kestner during August–October 1897 was published in 1901. See also *AD*, pp. 500–6; 509–12.

128 AD, p. 503. Leblois was trying to cautiously manoeuvre between his loyalty to Picquart and his wish to promote a judicial review. In the middle of August he sent Picquart a copy of the specimens of Esterhazy's handwriting that Jaume had given to Scheurer-Kestner (*v.* 27 July 1897), although he pretended he had obtained them by his own means. Although Picquart seemed to recognize the handwriting as Esterhazy's, he noticed several differences from the handwriting of the *bordereau*. Leblois continued his search. *ASD*, pp. 398–9.

129 Exceptionally, the announcement of Esterhazy's suspension did not appear in the *Journal officiel* or in the *Bulletin officiel du ministère de la guerre*. The decision to suspend him had been made by the Minister of War. It is likely that he also made the decision not to announce it. *ASD*, p. 414.

130 *Rennes*, I, 250, Official report on Dreyfus' detention on Devil's Island. The new cabin was divided in two by an iron fence. Dreyfus occupied one part of the cabin, the guard on duty the other, so that the prisoner was under constant observation. There were two high barred windows which let in a little light and air. A fine wire mesh was later added to the iron window bars: this prevented proper ventilation. The cabin was surrounded by a wooden palisade 3 metres high, made of pointed posts.

131 A. Dreyfus, *Cinq années de ma vie* (1982), pp. 191–2. The complete regulations on the detention of Dreyfus are also published in *3ème Cass.* III, 881–90. Also see *Cinq années de ma vie* (Paris: La Découverte, 1994), pp. 259 ff.

132 On 16 or 28 September according to *Répertoire*, p. 88, and *ATQV,* pp. 96–7 respectively.

133 Scheurer-Kestner took Leblois's advice and respected this sequence when meeting Government members. (*v.* 9 Oct to 5 Nov 1897)

134 Charpentier, who supports Reinach's theory of the complicity between Esterhazy and Henry, suggests that Esterhazy was already in contact with Henry and that Henry dissuaded Esterhazy from living abroad, promising to protect him. DC, p. 107. Thomas considers Esterhazy's answer to this letter a spontaneous act since he never mentioned it that time or later. Thomas, *Esterhazy*, pp. 254–5

135 See Scheurer-Kestner's letter to Lebon and Leblois's reply in *Répertoire*, pp. 89–90.

136 This note might have been fabricated by Lemercier-Picard, a forger whose services Henry had used from time to time. *ASD*, p. 578, n. 2. (*v.* 2 Nov 1897, n. 37 & 25 Dec 1897, n. 142).

137 This particular falsification was intended to incriminate Dreyfus, who in March 1894 was attached to the office in charge of military rail transport.

138 The Section de Statistique had secret funds supervised by Henry for remunerating its secret agents. Gribelin later stated that Henry had embezzled from secret funds, using fictitious payments to Val Carlos as a cover and that the total amount of money concealed by Henry and found after his death in August 1898 was 25,000 or 26,000 francs. Ehrhardt, *A travers l'affaire Dreyfus Henry et Val Carlos*, pp. 65–72. Rumours of such questionable financial practices are mentioned by Herzl (October 1898), to whom the Kaiser related that the King of Romania had told him that embezzlement was at the heart of the Dreyfus Affair; that money had been stolen from General Staff's secret funds; Dreyfus had been offered a share of 20,000 francs but since he refused it he had to be removed. T. Herzl, *The Complete Diaries of Theodor Herzl*, ed. R. Patai, trans. H. Zohn, 5 vols (New York and London: Herzl Press & Thomas Toseloff, 1960), p. 731.

139 Du Paty stated that he had been asked to write this memorandum 'for a purpose he did not remember'. *Cass.*, I, 442, Du Paty. He may have been told that the original had been lost; Boisdeffre or Gonse may have given orders for it to be destroyed in September or October 1897. The date of 24 September was probably false. As Reinach suggests (*HAD,* 3 pp. 287–9), it is likely that Du Paty was asked to write this memorandum in 1898, after Cavaignac's intervention in the Chamber (*v.* 14 Jan 1898), although in *HAD*, 1, Reinach gave the September 1897 date as authentic. *HAD*, 1, pp. 620–6. Du Paty's memorandum, without a date, appears in *Cass.*, II, p. 147. See also *AD*, pp. 336–7.

140 A search was made for this document at the Section de Statistique as it was supposed to be the basis of information found in a note from Schwarztkoppen intercepted on 28 December 1895 via the 'normal route'. Gribelin's secret note is reproduced in *ASD*, pp. 406–7. In 1904 it became clear that the document had been found at the Ministry. *3ème Cass*, III, 742.

141 *HAD*, 3, p. 336.

142 The letter dated 17 January 1895 reads: 'concerning Dreyfus, we are relieved, and we realize at last that I acted well [by officially affirming that the German Government had had no dealings with Dreyfus]'. *ASD*, pp. 420–1, 575, n. 12.

Part 5

COLLUSION

16 October–December 1897

Lieutenant-Colonel Picquart

The collusion of the military

Oct 16–18[1]   Gonse and Henry hold a secret meeting at the Ministry of War. They invite Du Paty informing him of the plot to 'substitute' Esterhazy for Dreyfus instigated by the Dreyfus family and their supporters.[2] They explain to him that although Esterhazy's life is disreputable and wild, the results of an 18-month investigation demonstrate that he is not guilty of delivering documents to a foreign power.[3] Esterhazy must be warned to prevent his committing 'a regrettable act [suicide or flight], which could bring disaster to the country and to some of its military leaders'. Gonse is careful not to mention the *petit bleu*.[4] Du Paty suggests Esterhazy be summoned to the Ministry, but Gonse considers this too dangerous.

An anonymous letter signed 'P.D.C.', addressed to Billot at the Ministry of War, states that the Dreyfus family is seeking to incriminate another officer [Esterhazy] in place of Dreyfus. The letter goes on to claim that two such substitutes have been found, that one of them is soon to be publicly denounced and that the family expects that his first reaction will be to kill himself or to desert. As either action could provide a fresh motive for a judicial revision, the anonymous author asks how the officer should be warned.[5]

Gonse, Henry and Du Paty agree to warn Esterhazy by an anonymous letter. Du Paty writes an almost exact copy of the anonymous letter just received. Henry shortens it, shows it to Gonse, who submits it to Billot.[6] Gonse informs Henry and Du Paty that Billot disapproves despite the grave consequences (due to irregularities) for the Section de Statistique if a revision of the Dreyfus verdict takes place. Before leaving the room Gonse twice says to Du Paty, 'You see? This is where we are.' When alone with Du Paty, Henry interprets Gonse's cryptic words as an appeal to Du Paty, as being an officer outside the Deuxième Bureau, he can act without risk. Du Paty, convinced that Esterhazy is innocent and the victim of an 'abominable plot', agrees to co-operate.[7]

The Espérance letter

Oct 18 or 19[8]   Esterhazy receives an anonymous letter at his address in Dommartin-la-Planchette:

> *Your name is to become the focus of a great scandal. The Dreffus [sic] family is going to accuse you publicly of being the author of the document which served as the basis for the Dreffus trial. The family has numerous samples of your handwriting which will serve as evidence. It was a colonel who was at the ministry last year, a certain M. Picart [sic], who gave the papers to the Dreffus family. This M. Picart is now in Tonkin, I believe.*

> *The family is counting on making you panic by publishing your handwriting in the newspapers, hoping that you will flee to your relatives in Hungary.*

That will indicate that you are the culprit and they will take advantage then to demand a revision of the case and proclaim the innocence of Dreffus. It was M. Picart who gave all this information to the family.

This M. Picart bought [samples of] your handwriting from non-commissioned officers of your regiment in Rouen last year. I learned all this from a sergeant in your regiment who was given money in exchange for your handwriting.

This is to warn you of what these scoundrels want to do to destroy you. Now it is up to you to defend your name and the honour of your children.

Act quickly, for the family is about to bring about your doom.

Your devoted friend, Espérance[9]

P.S. Never show this letter to anyone. It is for you alone, to save you from the grave dangers that surround you.[10]

On receipt of this letter Esterhazy rushes, panic-stricken, to his Paris apartment in the rue Douai, where he had settled his mistress Marie Pays. He shows her the Espérance letter, saying that he is dishonoured and must disappear immediately. Depressed, he does not leave the apartment for two days.[11]

Oct 19   First issue of *L'Aurore*, the daily founded by Ernest Vaughan,[12] managed by Alexandre Perrenx and edited by Georges Clemenceau.

Gonse, Henry, Du Paty and Lauth hold a further meeting to discuss how to warn Esterhazy. Henry hands Gribelin another anonymous letter to Esterhazy, inviting him to a meeting in the parc Monsouris. (*v.* 23 Oct 1897) Gribelin delivers the letter to the rue Douai apartment while Esterhazy is absent.

Oct 20   Esterhazy writes to the managing agent of the apartment, Autant, asking for the lease to be transferred to Marie Pays.[13] (*v.* 22 Oct & 30 Nov 1897)

Gonse calls Lebrun-Renault to his office to certify in writing, in the presence of Gonse and Henry, that Dreyfus confessed to him on the day of his degradation. (*v.* 5 Jan 1895) To strengthen its authenticity, Gonse and Henry sign an appended note that the statement was made in their presence.

Oct 22   In a fit of temper Esterhazy writes anonymously to Dreyfus' father-in-law threatening him and Mathieu:

'*One more step and it is death for you both.*'[14]

Marie Pays pleads with Autant in person to transfer Esterhazy's lease into her name within 48 hours.[15]

Scheurer-Kestner returns to Paris.

Oct 23   Esterhazy informs Schwartzkoppen at the German Embassy that their relationship has been discovered and asks him to tell Mme

Dreyfus that her husband is the real culprit. Schwartzkoppen firmly refuses, saying: 'I think you are mad, Major', and shows Esterhazy the door.[16]

Meeting at the parc Montsouris

Du Paty, Gribelin and Henry drive to the park in a carriage. Du Paty and Gribelin wear civilian dress. Du Paty is disguised with a false beard, Gribelin wearing blue spectacles. They leave the carriage while Henry watches through its rear window.[17] Du Paty approaches Esterhazy: 'Major, you know why we are here.' Esterhazy: 'Gentlemen I do not know who you are, but I declare that I am the victim of a frightful plot.' The officers reply: 'If we were not convinced of that we would not be here.'[18] Esterhazy shows them the Espérance letter. Du Paty shows Esterhazy the facsimile of the *bordereau*. Esterhazy expresses surprise at the similarity of the handwriting to his own. He then mentions that he used to work for Sandherr. Gribelin contradicts this.[19] Esterhazy talks of suicide, of killing Picquart and approaching Schwartzkoppen. He avoids mentioning that he has just seen him. The officers calm him down and assure him that the General Staff will protect him on condition that he co-operates and does nothing without consulting them first. He is to follow their instructions day by day.

Esterhazy returns to the German Embassy and informs Schwartzkoppen that General Staff officers have just promised him the protection of the French Government. Schwartzkoppen reports to General Schlieffen, Chief of the German General Staff in Berlin that a major scandal is about to break out.[20] (*v.* 2 Nov 1897)

Scheurer-Kestner requests Lucie Faure to arrange a meeting with her father, the President. (*v.* 29 Oct 1897)

Billot orders General Leclerc, Picquart's commanding officer, to extend his mission abroad by sending him to the Libyan front, which was a dangerous area.[21] Leclerc is surprised but calls in Picquart to inform him. Picquart tells Leclerc of his disgrace. Leclerc does not execute the order immediately and instructs Picquart not to go further south than Gabès in southern Tunisia.[22]

Oct 24   Du Paty and Esterhazy meet for a second time in the cemetery of Montmartre. On Du Paty's instruction Esterhazy writes to Billot requesting a meeting.[23]

Billot invites Scheurer-Kestner to lunch to ascertain his views on Dreyfus. Scheurer-Kestner declines the invitation and tells Billot that he is about to discuss the matter with President Faure.

Oct 25   Billot refuses to see Esterhazy but orders General Millet to receive him. Esterhazy explains to Millet that he is the victim of a terrible plot instigated by the Dreyfus family and a certain Lieutenant-Colonel Picquart. He admits the similarity between his own handwriting and that of the *bordereau* but invents a convoluted story to explain how

Dreyfus could have imitated his handwriting.[24] Esterhazy also admits that he has visited Schwartzkoppen, to obtain a passport for Alsace for his commanding officer. Confused, Millet suggests that Esterhazy write to Billot.

That same evening Esterhazy composes a long letter to Billot recapitulating his interview with Millet and requesting that his [Esterhazy's] honour be defended should his name be mentioned publicly; 'if driven to it', he threatens he would approach the Kaiser to obtain official denials that Germany has had any dealings with him.[25] Billot does not reply and makes no mention of it to Boisdeffre.

c. Oct 25   Esterhazy receives from Henry or Du Paty a *plaquette* (booklet), which summarizes Picquart's investigation of him in 1896 and Picquart's disputes with his commanding officers.[26] (*v.* 15 Nov 1897)

Oct 25/27   Desvernine, the police official seconded to the Ministry of War, files two reports on Esterhazy's visit to the German Embassy on 23 October.

Oct 26–27   Henry and Du Paty are surprised that Billot has not yet told Boisdeffre about Esterhazy's letter of 25 October. They instruct Esterhazy to write a similar letter directly to Boisdeffre, describing his meeting with Millet, summarizing his alibi and asking for protection. (*v.* end Oct 1897)

Oct 28   Henry tells Esterhazy: 'Méline, Billot and all the Government are occupied with the forthcoming elections and the support that Scheurer-Kestner, Reinach, etc will have ... If we don't stab all these people in the back, they will sacrifice the whole French army for their seat in the Senate or the Chamber of Deputies. Sword in hand, we will charge.'[27]

Scheurer-Kestner informs a journalist from *L'Agence Nationale:*[28] 'I am firmly convinced of Captain Dreyfus' innocence and I will do anything to prove it, not only by obtaining a verdict of acquittal at the revision of his trial, but by doing him full justice and rehabilitating him completely.' However, he refuses to give further details before discussing the matter with the Government. His statements are circulated widely in the press.

Esterhazy's approach to the President

Oct 29   Esterhazy writes to President Faure, enclosing the anonymous Espérance letter:

> ... I addressed myself to my superior and natural protector, the Minister of War ... The Minister has not replied ... I am therefore appealing to you for justice against the infamous instigator of this conspiracy, who has handed over confidential details concerning myself to the plotters, in an attempt to substitute me for a scoundrel. If I have the misfortune not to be heard by the supreme head of my country, I will take steps to ensure that my appeal reaches the head and suzerain of the Esterhazy family, the Kaiser. He is a

*soldier and will know how to put the honour of a soldier, even an
enemy soldier, above the petty and shady intrigues of politics ... It
is for you, Mr President, to decide whether you force me to move
the matter into such territory. An Esterhazy fears nothing and no
one, except God. If I am to be sacrificed to some miserable political
plan ... nothing and no one will prevent me from acting as I have
described ...*[29]

Scheurer-Kestner's campaign for a revision

Scheurer-Kestner is received by President Faure. (The President was
already in possession of Esterhazy's letter.) Scheurer-Kestner mentions
the name of Esterhazy but does not refer to Picquart, since he
does not have authorization from Leblois. The President cites his
constitutional neutrality in refusing Scheurer-Kestner's confidences
and says that the matter should be dealt with by the Minister of War.
He does, however, grant Scheurer-Kestner his *neutralité bienveillante*
(benevolent neutrality).

Auguste Scheurer-Kestner

Von Münster reports to Hohenlohe, the German Chancellor, about the rumours in the French press of an imminent attempt to retry Dreyfus. He declares he has never believed that the conviction of Dreyfus was just. The Kaiser makes a marginal note, 'Neither do I.'[30]

Du Paty shows Billot several of the documents collected by the Section de Statistique as alleged proof of Dreyfus' guilt. He also shows him a report by Gonse stating that Picquart was in Paris in June and had probably met Scheurer-Kestner and the Dreyfus family.

Oct 30   Scheurer-Kestner is received by Billot a longstanding friend from Alsace. In their discussion Scheurer-Kestner tells him that Esterhazy is guilty of the crime attributed to Dreyfus. He again refrains from naming Picquart. Billot replies that he has evidence supplied to him by Gonse which demonstrate guilt and quotes the *faux Henry* from memory. Scheurer-Kestner rejects the validity of this evidence (thereby casting doubt on certain officers, especially Gonse). Billot, however, repeats that he has proof of Dreyfus' guilt and confession.[31] Scheurer-Kestner holds his ground. After four hours of discussion he pleads with Billot to initiate an investigation. Billot finally promises to do so with the proviso that Scheurer-Kestner keeps silent on the matter for two weeks.[32]

Esterhazy is soon informed of this meeting in a note from either Du Paty or Henry: 'The Minister of [War] has just left after lunch with Scheurer-Kestner; a lengthy confidential discussion. Everything is going quite well. The enemy has been restrained.'[33]

Oct 31   The press becomes aware of Scheurer-Kestner's meeting with Billot. *Le Matin* prints a detailed account of their discussion. Esterhazy is not named but the account is clearly based on inside information from someone at the Ministry of War. *La Libre Parole* announces that 'an important person at the Ministry has handed over documents to Scheurer-Kestner'. (*v.* 9 Nov 1897)

The *document libérateur* and *la dame voilée*

Esterhazy sends a second letter to the President. He regrets that he has received no answer or word of support either from the Head of State or the Chief of Staff. He invents the implausible story of Espérance, now described as the generous lady who has already warned him of the plot hatched against him by the friends of Dreyfus: she has given him a copy of a document supposedly stolen by Picquart from a foreign legation and which is highly compromising for certain diplomatic personnel. Esterhazy threatens to publish it if he does not obtain support or justice.[34]

This letter becomes the basis of two of the most famous myths of the Dreyfus Affair, *le document libérateur* ('the liberating document') and *la dame voilée* ('the veiled lady', originally described as 'the generous lady'). The concept of the *document libérateur* can probably be attributed entirely to Henry, who may have taken the idea from Tomps' investigation into how the facsimile of the *bordereau* reached *Le Matin*. (*v.* 18 Nov 1896) Henry conceived this document to be merely a photograph of *Ce canaille de D.* The 'generous lady' was probably Esterhazy's invention, and was soon elaborated upon. Within days, in his third letter to the President (*v.* 5 Nov 1897), he stated that one night on Pont Alexandre III 'the generous lady' gave him the *document libérateur* and continued to keep him informed, always at night, at odd places in Paris. Esterhazy variously described her as 'very elegant ...', or 'a low-class woman, perfumed like a woman of dubious reputation'. Esterhazy even showed Du Paty 'her' letters inviting him to these assignations. This story intrigued officers of the General Staff, who were unable to identify this mysterious lady. According to Esterhazy's cousin Christian the lady was none other than Du Paty himself. Once Esterhazy's name was made public (*v.* 15 Nov 1897) she became known as '*la dame voilée*'. The story fascinated journalists and the public and inspired numerous drawings and images. The story of the *document libérateur*, however, was not made public at the time.

The President takes these improbable stories seriously and discusses them with Billot. (*v.* 1 Nov 1897)

End Oct   On receiving Esterhazy's letter (28 October), Boisdeffre summons Gonse and Henry. They consider it safer to deal with Esterhazy through an intermediary rather than directly. Several persons are recruited: Jacques de Nettancourt, Esterhazy's brother-in-law; Marie Pays, and Christian Esterhazy. From now on, Du Paty communicates through these intermediaries but Henry continues to meet Esterhazy without telling Du Paty and makes the decisions on most of Esterhazy's actions.[35]

Early Nov   The right-wing press (including *La Libre Parole, Le Gaulois, L'Echo de Paris, Le Petit Journal, La Croix*) mocks Scheurer-Kestner for failing to convince Billot of Dreyfus' innocence. He is described as 'Prussian', 'traitor', 'scoundrel', 'madman'. On the other hand Clemenceau (in *L'Aurore*) and Cassagnac (in *L'Autorité*) already advocate a revision of the trial.

Nov 1   Scheurer-Kestner writes to Billot complaining about the disclosures to the press concerning their private conversation and once again asks him to initiate the promised investigation:

> *Who committed the indiscretion? You have been very badly served ... I promised you my silence, you pledged yours ... I have not told you all that I know, but I pointed you in the right direction. Seek, seek and you shall find ... In what way would the army be affected if the generals themselves recognize that perhaps there has been a miscarriage of justice?*[36]

Alarmed by Esterhazy's letter to the President (of 31 October) Billot telegraphs Leclerc, asking him to question Picquart about the alleged photograph of a document stolen from him by a woman. Picquart protests against this allegation. Leclerc asks Billot for further instructions. (*v.* 9 Nov 1897)

Nov 2   Schwartzkoppen is appointed officer in command of the 2nd Grenadier Regiment of the Imperial Guard in Berlin. Baron von Süßkind is to replace him as military attaché in Paris.[37] (*v.* 11 Nov 1897)

Scheurer-Kestner is received by Prime Minister Méline. He shows Méline specimens of the handwriting of Esterhazy and Dreyfus for comparison with the *bordereau.* Méline points out that he is no expert and that other documents exist which prove the guilt of Dreyfus.[38]

Nov 3   At a second meeting with Méline Scheurer-Kestner suggests that Leblois, waiting outside, be allowed to show him Gonse's letters to Picquart. He thus names Picquart for the first time. Méline refuses and refers Scheurer-Kestner to Billot.

Maurice Paléologue, head of the secret Foreign Office department liaising with the Deuxième Bureau, meets Henry by chance on the quai d'Orsay. When Paléologue expresses doubts about the conviction, Henry assures him: 'Dreyfus was justly convicted. Since he has been shark-fishing off his island, we have found the most damning, the most significant evidence against him; I have a cabinet full of it.'[39] Paléologue asks what sort of evidence this is. Henry mentions letters between the Italian and German military attachés and an 'ultra-secret' document, which he describes as a 'master-stroke'. Paléologue insists on knowing more; Henry finally reveals that it is a letter from the Kaiser to von Münster specifically naming Dreyfus. Paléologue is incredulous.[40] (*v.* 12 Dec 1897, the *bordereau annoté*)

Nov 4   In a long open letter to *Le Siècle* (also published in *Le Temps* on 6 November) Monod (*v.* end May 1897, n. 115) states that as an expert graphologist he can assert that the *bordereau* was not written by Dreyfus. He is convinced of Dreyfus' innocence and calls for a revision of the conviction of Dreyfus:

> *I may be wrong, I would even say, I would like to be proved wrong, for I would thus escape from the torture of thinking that my country has sentenced an innocent man to such a penalty. But I do not believe I am wrong ... As for those who claim that the revision of the case would be an insult to the army, I do not know what they mean. No shame could be attached to an error made in good faith, and conscientiously rectified. On the contrary, the army would surely rejoice in seeing our impeccable corps of artillery officers cleansed of the stain that the supposed treason of Captain Dreyfus brought upon it.*[41]

Nov 5   Continuing his campaign, Scheurer-Kestner is received by Darlan, Minister of Justice, Darlan refuses to believe Scheurer-Kestner's findings and explains that if an appeal for a revision were requested, as Minister of Justice he would have to process it. He therefore wishes to remain impartial.

Le Figaro publishes Scheurer-Kestner's statement that he has given the Government concrete reasons for his belief in the innocence of Dreyfus and that he leaves it to them to take 'the necessary measures'.

Esterhazy sends his third threatening letter to the President:

> ... *The lady who warned me of the horrible plot hatched against me has given me a document that proves the villainy of Dreyfus and offers me protection. This is also a danger for my country because if it is published together with the facsimile of handwriting, France will either be forced into humiliation or war ... I appeal to you in the words of the old French cry, 'Haro, my Prince, come to my rescue!' ... Defend me and I will return the document to the Minister of War without anyone in the world having seen it. But defend me quickly for I can wait no longer and I will stop at nothing to defend or avenge my honour, which has been worthlessly sacrificed.*[42] (*v.* Appendix 16)

Nov 6 Billot informs Saussier about Esterhazy's threatening letters to the President and instructs him to remind Esterhazy of 'his duty as an officer'.[43]

Just before the Cabinet convenes Scheurer-Kestner meets Méline for a third time. He offers to acquaint him with the correspondence between Gonse and Picquart he has finally obtained from Leblois. Méline declines, commenting that Leblois has committed a breach of trust by disclosing the letters. He adds that Scheurer-Kestner in his statement in *Le Figaro* (*v.* 5 Nov 1897) has projected the Affair into the Government arena.

The Cabinet ratifies Méline's refusal to reconsider the case for a revision. As Scheurer-Kestner has produced no new evidence, the case can only be reopened by appealing to the Minister of Justice (*v.* 3 Dec 1896, n. 89). An unofficial statement to this effect is published in the evening edition of *Le Temps*. (*v.* 9 Nov 1897)

Nov 7 Summoned by Saussier, Esterhazy apologizes for the tone of his letters to the President. He refuses to reveal the content of the *document libérateur*, claiming that he has sent it to England for safekeeping.[44] (*v.* 9, 10 & 14 Nov 1897)

Esterhazy sends an insulting and threatening letter to Picquart. He accuses him of manipulating his substitution for Dreyfus; bribing non-commissioned officers to obtain specimens of his [Esterhazy's] handwriting; stealing documents from the Ministry of War and delivering them to the friends of Dreyfus. Esterhazy sends a copy of his lettter to Boisdeffre.

Boisdeffre gives orders that Picquart's correspondence arriving at the Deuxième Bureau is no longer to be forwarded to him in Tunisia.

From one of the posters displayed in Paris by Mathieu (*v.* 10 Nov 1896) Jacques de Castro, a stockbroker, recognizes the handwriting of the *bordereau* as that of Esterhazy, one of his clients.[45] De Castro contacts Mathieu Dreyfus, who informs Scheurer-Kestner. Relieved that Mathieu has learned about Esterhazy from someone other than himself (because of his promise of confidentiality to Leblois), Scheurer-Kestner confirms (to Mathieu) that his investigations also point to Esterhazy. Mathieu passes on this information to Demange, who also has samples of Esterhazy's handwriting.[46] He and Mathieu agree that the handwriting of the letters and the *bordereau* are identical.

Nov 9   Saussier summons Esterhazy again on Billot's orders. He reprimands him for writing to the President and orders him to return the *document libérateur* to the Ministry of War. Saussier reports to Billot that Esterhazy only intends to return the document if he has Billot's protection. Saussier did not discuss this matter with Esterhazy since it could have been construed as bargaining. He concludes that Esterhazy's letters to the President are not sufficient grounds for Esterhazy's court martial: the Government must decide whether to take further action.

Billot demands verification from Leclerc of Gonse's report that Picquart was seen in Paris in early July 1897: Leclerc confirms that he was.[47]

Scheurer-Kestner presses Leblois to break his silence and reveal the whole affair to Billot. Leblois agrees, and Scheurer-Kestner informs Méline. Méline refuses to receive Leblois' confidences or allow him to see Billot, as the Government has already issued its official statement to the press. (*v.* 6 Nov 1897) He reiterates to Scheurer-Kester that the only course is for him to appeal to the Minister of Justice for a revision.

The Cabinet again discusses the Dreyfus Affair. The Government issues an official communiqué stating that 'Dreyfus has been correctly and justly convicted.'[48]

Scheurer-Kestner receives an anonymous *petit bleu* (i.e. an express letter) written in capital letters: 'Picquart is a scoundrel. You will soon get proof of this by the second ship from Tunisia.'[49]

Nov 10   Esterhazy sends an impertinent letter to Saussier pressing him to exercise his influence in government circles 'for some official or unofficial action, ... to clear the character of a man they know to be perfectly innocent ...'[50] He further reassures Saussier that he is looking for the quickest way to return the *document libérateur*. Saussier forwards Esterhazy's letter to Billot.

Speranza and Blanche telegrams[51]

An unidentified individual [Esterhazy] delivers a telegram to the rue La Fayette post office addressed to Picquart in Tunis:

> *'Stop the demigod. Everything is discovered. Extremely serious matter. Speranza*[52]

A second telegram is sent from the Bourse post office to Picquart in Sousse:

> *'We have proof that the* bleu *was forged by Georges. Blanche.*[53]

Esterhazy sends Picquart an anonymous letter, in capital letters:

> '*Beware; the whole undertaking is discovered; withdraw quietly; write nothing.*[54]

Nov 11   Both telegrams (Speranza and Blanche) are seized by the Sûreté and submitted to Henry, Gonse and Billot. Cavard, head of the Sûreté, also informs Louis Barthou, Minister of the Interior, who considers the matter highly significant. He immediately notifies his colleagues during a Cabinet meeting.[55] The original telegrams are submitted to Bertillon at police headquarters. That evening, without official authorization, the head of postal services (PTT) sends copies of all Picquart's telegrams and his private correspondence since 5 November, to the Minister of the Interior.[56]

Picquart receives Esterhazy's threatening letter of 7 November and the Blanche telegram.

Schwartzkoppen takes leave of President Faure. He tells him again that he has never been in contact with Dreyfus.[57]

Nov 12   Billot issues an order for a secret judicial investigation of Picquart. He appoints Gonse as the judicial police officer. In order to protect Cavard and the PTT Billot deliberately predates the order to 11 November to rectify the unofficial transmission of copies of Picquart's correspondence the previous day.

Picquart receives the Speranza telegram.

Henry is promoted to lieutenant colonel, the same rank as Picquart.

Lazare publishes a second, revised edition of his pamphlet *Une erreur judiciaire. L'Affaire Dreyfus* to prove his innocence. (*v.* 6 Nov 1896) He prefaces this new edition with his own 64-page introduction, followed by a facsimile of the *bordereau*. It contains the independent graphologists' reports with detailed handwriting analyses concluding that the *bordereau* was not written by Dreyfus.[58] (*v.* Mar–Aug 1897)

Nov 14   Esterhazy writes to Billot that he is ready to return the *document libérateur*. The letter and the document are delivered to the Ministry of War in a sealed envelope.[59]

Under the pseudonym Vidi, senator Emmanuel Arène, a colleague and friend of Scheurer-Kestner, publishes in *Le Figaro* an article entitled 'Le dossier de M. Scheurer-Kestner'. It reveals certain essential details: that the *bordereau* was not written by Dreyfus and cannot be attributed to him; that the real traitor (unnamed) is 'an officer, who is quite well-known in Paris … married … well-connected … not attached to the Ministry of War but to a garrison near Paris'; that a 'new document' mentioned by Billot to Scheurer-Kestner (the *faux Henry*) citing the name of Dreyfus is a forgery.[60]

Picquart reports to Leclerc on Esterhazy's threatening letter (dated 7 November), as well as the Blanche and Speranza telegrams. He asks for these documents to be sent to Billot and for an end to Esterhazy's intrigues against him.[61] Leclerc telegraphs this report to Billot.

Nov 15   Billot telegraphs Leclerc instructing him to send Picquart to Tunis. Leclerc is also to question him in secrecy about the telegrams shown to the Cabinet, which imply that Picquart has given secret information to persons outside the army.

Dreyfus   *Bordereau*

Example of handwriting comparison from the second edition of Bernard Lazare's
Une erreur judiciaire

On being interrogated Picquart denies the accusation. He lodges a complaint against Esterhazy with Billot.

Le Temps publishes an open letter from Scheurer-Kestner to Senator Ranc dated 14 November stating that new facts have emerged which prove the innocence of Dreyfus and have convinced him that a judicial error has been committed: 'I shall no longer be able to live at peace with this ever-present thought that a convicted man is doing penance for another's crime.'[62]

In *La Libre Parole,* using the pseudonym Dixi, Henry, Du Paty and Esterhazy reply to the Vidi article of 14 November in *Le Figaro,* stating that an officer X.Y. [Picquart] at the Ministry of War, supported by the family and friends of Dreyfus, has taken steps to incriminate another officer [Esterhazy] for Dreyfus' alleged crime. The article describes documents and the purchase of handwriting samples for the purpose of faking another document [the *petit bleu*].[63] The article claims that the *bordereau* is only one of numerous documents on which the conviction of Dreyfus was based.[64]

Mathieu's public denunciation of Esterhazy

Nov 16   An open letter from Mathieu to Billot denouncing Esterhazy as the author of the *bordereau* is published in *Le Figaro:*[65]

> *The only basis for the accusation of 1894 against my unfortunate brother is an unsigned, undated letter establishing that confidential military documents have been delivered to an agent of a foreign power. I have the honour to inform you that the author of that document is M le Comte Walsin-Esterhazy, an Infantry Major, suspended from active service since last spring for reasons of temporary ill health. The handwriting of Major Esterhazy is identical to that of the document in question. It will be very easy for you, Minister, to obtain a sample of this officer's handwriting. Moreover, I am prepared to indicate where you can find letters of his, of unquestionable authenticity and dated before my brother's arrest. I cannot doubt, Minister, that once you know the perpetrator of the treason for which my brother has been convicted, you will act swiftly to see that justice is done.*[66]

In the days following the publication of this letter Esterhazy gives numerous press interviews (mainly to *La Libre Parole, Le Matin, L'Echo de Paris, Le Figaro* and *Le Temps*). He speaks openly of his friendly relationship with Schwartzkoppen in order to explain his visits to the German Embassy. He repeatedly presents himself as the victim of 'a Jewish syndicate' or 'a Dreyfus syndicate', whose members have 'bought' Scheurer-Kestner and Picquart in order to ruin him. He threatens to lodge a suit for libel against Mathieu and Scheurer-Kestner. Various newspapers accuse the Government of collusion with the 'Syndicate'.[67]

Billot declares in the Chamber of Deputies that Mathieu will have to produce evidence in court to justify his open denunciation of Esterhazy.

Esterhazy challenges Billot to investigate him, stating that he is 'ready to answer all accusations'.

Billot orders Saussier to open a military investigation of Esterhazy but does not have him arrested. Saussier appoints General Georges Gabriel de Pellieux to conduct the investigation. (*v.* 17–20 Nov 1897, Pellieux's first investigation of Esterhazy)

Boisdeffre orders Du Paty to stop meeting Esterhazy.[68]

Boisdeffre's aide-de-camp, Major Pauffin de Saint-Morel, visits Henry Rochefort, editor of *L'Intransigeant*, and informs him that the Ministry of War has evidence of Dreyfus' guilt which is as yet unknown to his supporters. Rochefort publishes this information.[69] (*v.* 19 Nov 1897)

Billot relieves Forzinetti of his duties at Cherche-Midi prison on the grounds that he visited Rochefort the previous year. (*v.* 6 Nov 1896) In retaliation, Forzinetti publishes an account in *Le Figaro* of Dreyfus' imprisonment at Cherche-Midi (21 November) and reiterates his belief in his innocence. (*v.* Appendix 6)

Nov 17   Von Münster assures Hanotaux that Schwartzkoppen had declared to him on his honour that he has never had any contact with Dreyfus.[70] Paléologue informs Henry and Gonse of this statement. They had never asserted that Dreyfus had direct dealings with Germany, but only through the intermediary Panizzardi. Paléologue asks Henry how he can reconcile this information with Panizzardi's telegram of 2 November 1894, which, when correctly decoded (i.e. according to the version of the Foreign Ministry, *v.* 11 Nov 1894), cleared the Italian Government of dealings with Dreyfus. Henry stammers, changes the subject and shows Paléologue other documents which he claims are evidence of Dreyfus' guilt.[71]

The Italian Ambassador in Paris, Count Giuseppe Brusati di Vergano Tornielli, writes to his Foreign Secretary, Visconti-Venosta:

> *About two months ago, our military attaché learned of indiscretions directly from his German colleague that Dreyfus is not guilty; he is blamed for the work of Walsin-Esterhazy. I beg Your Excellency not to allow this information to be spread by word of mouth* ...[72]

Nov 19   Picquart lodges a second complaint with Billot on Esterhazy's recent attacks on him in the daily press.[73]

Billot orders Leclerc to question Picquart on his alleged communication of secret documents (to Leblois).

Billot orders Boisdeffre to arrest Saint-Morel for his visit to Rochefort. (*v.* 16 Nov 1897)

Nov 20   Von Münster writes to Schwartzkoppen:

> *I am surprised but by no means worried about the fact that the French newspapers connect your transfer [to Germany] with Dreyfus. We both know that as far as we are concerned, poor Dreyfus is absolutely innocent. Therefore, the newspaper clamour leaves me completely unmoved and should leave you equally*

unmoved. Esterhazy's defence is very poor, he does indeed seem a man of shady character ...[74]

Tornielli is irritated by allusions in the French press to an alleged letter from Panizzardi to Schwartzkoppen referring to Dreyfus as a secret agent for Italy (the *Ce canaille de D*). He sends *Le Temps* a categorical but unsigned denial of any contact between Panizzardi and Dreyfus. He refutes the authenticity of the letter attributed to Panizzardi.[75] (*v.* 28 Nov 1897)

Pellieux's first investigation of Esterhazy (17–20 November)[76]

Pellieux first hears Mathieu (17 Nov) to ascertain the grounds for his accusation of Esterhazy. Mathieu explains that it is based on the similarity of handwriting and shows Pellieux a facsimile of the *bordereau* and examples of Esterhazy's letters. Mathieu demands that a new handwriting examination of the *bordereau* be undertaken and that Pellieux listens to Scheurer-Kestner. Pellieux then questions Esterhazy (18 Nov), who confirms the details of the Dixi article (*v.* 15 Nov 1897) and his letters to Billot, Boisdeffre and the President. In order to prove his theory that Dreyfus imitated his handwriting (*v.* 25 Oct 1897), Esterhazy asks to meet Gribelin and 'the officer who conducted the investigation on Dreyfus', face to face. He is careful not to mention Du Paty's name. (*v. c.* 20 Nov 1897)

Pellieux summons Scheurer-Kestner (18 Nov), who explains how he became convinced of the innocence of Dreyfus and the guilt of Esterhazy. He states that having procured letters in Esterhazy's handwriting he compared them to the *bordereau* and found the writing identical. He mentions that he does not possess any further documents, but that Leblois does. He insists that Leblois should be heard. Questioned by Pellieux about Picquart, Scheurer-Kestner declares that he does not know him and has never had any direct or indirect contact with him. He remarks: 'If Colonel Picquart is not brought in, the inquiry could never be serious, genuine or complete.'[77]

Pellieux finally questions Leblois (19 Nov) who admits that Picquart had consulted him on several espionage cases at the Ministry of War. He states that Picquart informed him about the existence of a document which is highly compromising for Esterhazy (the *petit bleu*).[78] Leblois shows Pellieux some of the documents in his dossier. Besides the *bordereau* and letters of Esterhazy, these include some of Gonse's letters to Picquart and the express letter sent to Scheurer-Kestner ('Picquart is a scoundrel') (*v.* 9 Nov 1897). Leblois suggests that the provenance of this express letter is the same as of that of the letter Esterhazy claimed to have received from *la dame voilée*,[79] (*v.* 5 Nov 1897) and demands a graphological examination. Pellieux tells Leblois that he should call for the immediate arrest and court-martial of Esterhazy for treason. This would prove the innocence of Dreyfus and ensure a revision. Leblois replies that he is not qualified to do this.[80] The hearing lasts three hours.

Pellieux reports to Gonse and Saussier. To help Pellieux make the 'right' decision, Boisdeffre calls him to the Ministry of War. There, together with Gonse, he shows him the dossier Henry has prepared on Picquart, the *petit bleu,* the Blanche and Esperanza telegrams sent to Picquart, and Esterhazy's letters since October to Billot and Boisdeffre.[81]

Pellieux files his report (20 November). He concludes that: Esterhazy must be cleared of all suspicion of treason since there is no conclusive evidence against him; no further examination of the *bordereau* is required since it was attributed to Dreyfus in 1894; the document, which Leblois considers so important and so decisive [the *petit bleu*], does not seem plausible or authentic.[82] Regarding Picquart, he enumerates a series of actions committed by him against the interests of his superior officers and Government Ministers, and concludes that he seems guilty. (*v.* Appendix 18)

Pellieux raises the question whether and how to continue the investigation: 'If Picquart is questioned in Tunis, it will be said that we were afraid to bring him here. Here, it will be difficult to isolate him from his advisers.' He finally recommends that Picquart face a commission of inquiry and be questioned in the utmost secrecy.[83]

La note aux deux écritures ('The note in two hands')

c. Nov 20   Du Paty sends Esterhazy a note outlining his argument to Pellieux if called in for questioning. The note becomes known as '*la note aux deux écritures*' (the 'note in two hands'). It is written in two styles, with some sections using only capital letters. It also tells Esterhazy to keep completely silent about their relationship.[84] (*v.* Appendix 17)

Nov 21   Following Pellieux's report, the Cabinet decides that his investigation is 'to be completed and granted the extra-judicial status invoked in articles 84, 85 and 86 of the Code of Military Justice'.[85] Accordingly, Pellieux is instructed to open an official and second judicial investigation of Esterhazy. Esterhazy engages Maurice Tézenas as his defence lawyer. Billot instructs Saussier to recall Picquart to Paris for the investigation.[86]

Furious at the Government's decision to open a second investigation Esterhazy sends an anonymous letter to Méline: 'Thanks to the colossal stupidity of your Minister Billot, the Picquart affair is going to explode with all its consequences. It is impossible to imagine such ineptitude.'[87]

The Groupe des étudiants antisémites created by Drumont in April 1894 and revived by Edouard Dubuc in 1896 changes its name to the Jeunesse antisémitique de France (Antisemitic Youth of France). Drumont is appointed Honorary President. At one of the first public meetings it calls on the Government to expel Jews from the army and all public institutions. Among the speakers are Lucien Millevoye, Jules Guérin and Edouard Dubuc.[88] (*v.* 20 Oct 1898)

Nov 22   Esterhazy writes to Pellieux before his second investigation demanding that the *chambre de bonne* rented by Picquart at 3 rue Yvon-Villarceaux should be searched. Esterhazy claims that *la dame voilée* had told him that the papers held by Picquart allegedly proving Esterhazy's innocence were there.

An anonymous letter warns Pellieux that his 'feeble approach' to the investigation will be denounced in the press.[89]

Pellieux's second investigation (23 November–3 December)

Pellieux asks the Ministry of War for the original *bordereau*, Picquart's dossier on Esterhazy and the file on Picquart collated at the Ministry of War. Boisdeffre and Gonse ask Pellieux to explain the purpose of a new examination of the *bordereau*. They are anxious that this may cast doubt on the conviction of Dreyfus. Pellieux reassures them in writing (24 November) that he does not intend to order a further examination of the document: he wants merely to verify that Esterhazy did not change his style of handwriting after the publication of the *bordereau*; and that the published facsimiles of the *bordereau* are accurate.[90]

Pellieux authorizes a search of Picquart's lodgings (23 November). Nothing important is found.

Esterhazy, interrogated twice, reveals no further details but shows two more notes he claimed were written by '*la dame voilée*' (24–25 November).[91]

Pellieux recalls Scheurer-Kestner and Mathieu for questioning (23–25 November).[92]

Picquart is then questioned (26–27 November). Arriving from Tunisia on 25 November he is unaware of the accusations against him.[93] On the first day he recounts his discoveries of Esterhazy in 1896, his investigation, his disagreements with Boisdeffre and Gonse and the background to his confidential discussions with Leblois. Picquart attributes the anonymous telegrams he has received in Tunisia to Esterhazy. Pellieux shows him the *petit bleu*. Picquart comments that as far as he can recall its handwriting was clearer and more uniform.[94] Pellieux becomes convinced that Picquart had falsified the *petit bleu* and passed it to Leblois. He reprimands Picquart for committing serious misdemeanours and forbids him to communicate with Leblois.[95] On the second day, Pellieux again questions Picquart, who mentions the *bordereau*. Pellieux interrupts him, saying that he may not discuss a closed case. Pellieux shows Picquart the forged Speranza letter of 1896. He has not seen it before, as it was kept at the Ministry of War. (*v.* 15 December 1896) Picquart realizes that it is meant to trap him. Since the letter implies that he was in league with the 'Syndicate', Pellieux questions him about his relationship with members of the Jewish community.[96] Picquart, still unaware of all the charges against him, is shown *Ce canaille de D.* Pellieux asks him whether he gave it to Leblois on a stated date. Picquart affirms that Leblois was not in Paris on that date. He is not confronted with his accusers and is eventually allowed to speak to Leblois.

Pellieux questions Henry (28 November). Henry states that he saw Leblois in Picquart's office in October 1896 and accuses Picquart of handing Leblois *Ce canaille de D.* from the Secret Dossier. Pellieux shows the *petit bleu* to Henry, who says he does not remember it arriving by the 'normal route'. In making this statement he intends to strengthen the falsification accusation against Picquart.

Pellieux questions Lieutenant Bernheim (26 November). Bernheim confirms that in 1894 he provided Esterhazy with a confidential document on artillery and the *réglette de correspondence.*[97] (*v.* 13 Oct 1894, n. 35)

After publication of the Uhlan letter (*v.* 28 November 1897, the Boulancy letters) Pellieux recalls Esterhazy for questioning (29 November) in the presence of Mme de Boulancy and his cousin Christian. Esterhazy acknowledges that with the exception of the Uhlan letter the published letters are his. In response to Esterhazy's denial and the violent press reaction caused by the publication of Esterhazy's letters, Pellieux orders a graphological examination of the Uhlan letter. He is aware of the risk that this may lead to an examination of the original *bordereau.*[98] The impossibility of locating independent graphologists prevented the examination of the Uhlan letter before the close of Pellieux's investigation. On 1 December Pellieux finally submits Esterhazy's letter to three graphologists: Belhomme, Varinard and Charavay. (*v.* 12 Jan 1898)

Pellieux questions Lauth, Gribelin and Gonse (29 Nov–2 Dec). They all support Henry's testimony and accuse Picquart of fabricating the *petit bleu* and disclosing the *Ce canaille de D.* to Leblois.

On the advice of his lawyer Tézenas and with the agreement of Boisdeffre and Billot, Esterhazy writes to Pellieux asking to be court-martialled:[99]

> *I am innocent and the torture I have been suffering for fifteen days is inhuman. I believe you have in hand all the evidence of the infamous conspiracy invented in order to destroy me … As an officer accused of high treason, I have the right to be brought before a court martial … Only a verdict emanating from that body will have the power to dishonour, by acquitting me before public opinion, which the most cowardly of slanderers dared to address.*[100]

Pellieux's final report (3 Dec) recommends that Esterhazy be tried by court martial although there is no evidence to support any of Mathieu's or Picquart's accusations against him. Pellieux further demands that Esterhazy remain at liberty during the further investigation, at least until the results of the graphological examination are known. Pellieux declares that the *petit bleu*, the basis of Picquart's accusation against Esterhazy, is not authentic. He accuses Picquart of disclosing secret documents to a person outside the Ministry of War (Leblois). He concludes that Picquart should be brought immediately before a board of inquiry to decide whether there are grounds for him to be discharged from the army for 'infringement of honour' or at least 'grave errors committed on service'.[101] (*v.* 4 Dec 1897) (*v.* Appendix 18)

Nov 23   In a letter to Monod, Dr Gibert discloses his conversation of 21 February 1895 with President Faure, his close friend and patient. The President stated that Dreyfus had been convicted on the basis of documents submitted secretly to the Court. (*v.* 24 March 1899)

Nov 25   *Le Figaro* publishes Emile Zola's first pro-Dreyfus article, 'M. Scheurer-Kestner':

> *What a poignant drama and what magnificent people! My novelist's heart leaps with passionate admiration when faced with documents of such tragic beauty, which life brings us. I know of no higher psychology … The truth is on the march and nothing will stop it.*[102]

The *faux Otto*

Lemercier-Picard, a renowned forger (*v.* 1 Nov 1896, n. 63), hands a letter incriminating Esterhazy to Fernand de Rodays, owner of *Le Figaro*. The letter is signed Otto, the name of an attaché at the German Embassy, and dated 17 December 1893. It is addressed to a woman who was supposedly with Esterhazy at the Grand Hotel in Brussels. The letter implies that Esterhazy is a contact man for Germany.[103] (*v.* 25 Dec 1897)

Devil's Island: Dreyfus sends another appeal to the President.[104]

Nov 26   Philippe duc d'Orléans, exiled in London, writes a letter to one of his agents, Colonel Fernand de Parseval, expressing his indignation and dismay at the scandals in France. He prays to God that the crown will be restored to him, since only the power of the monarchy knows how to protect the honour of the army.[105] (*v.* 7 Dec 1897)

Nov 28   Tornielli writes to Hanotaux that his military attaché has never had any contact with Dreyfus. He adds that Panizzardi will be forced to issue a public statement if the press persists in attributing to him letters in which the name of Dreyfus is mentioned (reference to *Ce canaille de D.*).[106] Tornielli requests that Panizzardi be heard as a witness in Pellieux's investigation of Esterhazy (*v.* 23 Nov–3 Dec 1897). Hanotaux replies that the decision is one of military judicial procedure. He consults Boisdeffre and decides to bring the matter before the Cabinet on 30 November.[107]

Hanotaux apologizes to von Münster for the attitude of the press, but he has no means to have influence.[108]

Von Münster writes to the Kaiser: 'My attitude was always that this affair does not concern us and does not affect us.' The Kaiser notes in the margin: 'Right'.[109]

The Boulancy letters

Le Figaro publishes extracts from letters Esterhazy wrote 13 years previously to Mme de Boulancy, his cousin and former mistress. (*v.* 1881–82) The letters express hatred and contempt for France and the French Army. The most contentious of these is the 'Uhlan letter':

> *If this evening I were told that I am to be killed tomorrow, like an Uhlan Captain running my sword through the French, I should certainly be perfectly happy ... I would not harm a little dog, but I would have a hundred thousand Frenchmen killed with pleasure ...*[110]

Nov 28–29 Havas issues an official statement:

> *General de Pellieux's investigation of the Esterhazy-Dreyfus affair was nearing its end when the incident of letters published in a morning paper occurred. General de Pellieux certifies the authenticity of these documents. As soon as his work ... is complete, he will take or entrust to the [Military] Governor of Paris... all measures required by the situation. Satisfaction will be given to the honour of the army, to justice and to truth ... Although the letters published yesterday by a morning paper have no immediate connection with the Dreyfus Affair, General de Pellieux believes it is useful to submit them to expert analysis.*[111]

Nov 28–30 Many pro-Esterhazy articles in the press claim that the *bordereau* has been copied in his handwriting and the Boulancy letters have been forged and bought by the 'Syndicate'. Conversely, Georges Clemenceau asks in *L'Aurore:* 'Who then is protecting Major Esterhazy against the judge's legitimate curiosity? What does that signify? Which of our great leaders had relations with this man? ... If indiscretions have been committed, the worst evil today would be the desire for concealment.'

Nov 30 Boisdeffre sends a secret urgent communiqué to the Cabinet, vigorously protesting against Tornielli's request that Panizzardi be heard as a witness in Pellieux's investigation. Boisdeffre argues that, as a suspect in this case, Panizzardi cannot be heard as a witness. He states that the General Staff has three of Panizzardi's letters to Schwartzkoppen which mention Dreyfus, either by his initials or his full name. These letters (including the *faux Henry* and *Ce canaille de D.*) are attached to the communiqué.[112] The Cabinet accepts Boisdeffre's arguments and refuses Tornielli's request.

Le Figaro publishes Esterhazy's letter to Autant (dated 20 October), in which he asked to transfer the lease of his apartment to Marie Pays.[113]

Le Syndicat (The 'Syndicate')

Dec 1 In response to mounting hostility towards the so-called Dreyfus 'Syndicate', *Le Figaro* publishes Zola's article 'Le Syndicat'. Zola defends the concept of a group supporting a revision of Dreyfus' conviction and declares that he wishes to belong to it. The word 'Syndicate' henceforth acquires a double meaning: to the supporters of Dreyfus it carries heroic overtones; for the adversaries, it is derogatory.

The whole story of the Syndicate is there: men of good will, truth and integrity, coming from the four corners of the earth ... not knowing each other, but all marching by different paths towards the same goal, advancing in silence ... and one fine day meeting at the same spot. They all, inevitably, found themselves hand in hand at the crossroads of truth, at this momentous rendezvous of justice ...[114]

Reinach accidentally leaves his briefcase on the Paris-Meaux train. It contains several letters relating to the Affair including a facsimile of the *bordereau* and letters from Dreyfus and Esterhazy.[115] (*v.* 15 and 18 Dec 1897)

Dec 3   Senator Victor Milliard replaces Darlan as Minister of Justice.[116]

Joseph Reinach

'Il n'y a pas d'affaire Dreyfus' ('There is no Dreyfus Affair')

Dec 4   Provocative speeches are made in the Chamber of Deputies. Deputy
               Castelin insists that Méline make a statement to reassure the army.
               Méline stresses that the accusation against an army officer (Esterhazy)
               is not related to the Dreyfus case. He claims that *'Il n'y a pas d'affaire
               Dreyfus'* ('There is no Dreyfus Affair'). Albert de Mun declares himself
               the protector of the army and of the country. He denounces the Jewish
               'Syndicate', which 'has put itself in Germany's pay'. De Mun calls upon
               Billot to avenge the army. His speech is applauded by a majority of
               the Chamber. Billot declares in his 'soul and conscience' that Dreyfus
               is guilty and that the verdict was true and just. He asks the Chamber
               to stop attacking the honour of the nation and the army. After a
               long debate, with seven different motions, the Chamber confirms its
               confidence in the Government by an overwhelming majority (490
               votes to 18) and acknowledges *'l'autorité de la chose jugée'* (the *res
               judicata*). (*v.* Appendix 19) During this dramatic session the Socialist
               Alexandre Millerand accuses the Government of being in favour of the
               campaign led by Reinach and Scheurer-Kestner for a revision. Millerand
               denounces Reinach 'who, instead of trying to rehabilitate a new Calas,
               may perhaps have other rehabilitations to pursue in his own family'.[117]

               In agreement with Boisdeffre and Billot, Saussier signs the order to
               initiate proceedings against Esterhazy. Saussier appoints Alexandre-
               Alfred Ravary, a retired major, to open a new judicial investigation of
               Esterhazy. As recommended by Pellieux, Ravary orders that Esterhazy is
               to remain at liberty. (*v.* 7–31 Dec 1897, Ravary's judicial investigation)

               Von Münster writes to the German Foreign Office: 'The Jews have
               declared war on the antisemites whom they hold responsible
               – perhaps not wrongly – for the conviction [of Dreyfus]. Hence the
               great financial resources. *Le Figaro* has apparently received 200,000
               francs on account.' The Kaiser makes a marginal note: 'The Affair has
               not advanced at all and remains obscure. It is accepted that Dreyfus
               was essentially convicted only on the basis of the *bordereau.* Now
               it appears that this *bordereau* was probably falsified, doubtless by
               Esterhazy. If this is true, it is indisputable that Dreyfus was wrongly
               convicted.'[118]

Dec 7   In the Senate, Scheurer-Kestner questions the Government about the
               Esterhazy–Dreyfus affair. He states that Dreyfus was not properly tried
               since secret documents were transmitted to the Court. He appeals for
               'justice and reason'.[119] Billot responds that Scheurer-Kestner cannot
               prove that the *bordereau* was the only basis for the accusation against
               Dreyfus. He says nothing about the Secret Dossier, and reaffirms that
               Dreyfus is guilty. Trarieux is the only Senator to support Scheurer-
               Kestner. He explains that if serious errors had been committed, a
               demand for their rectification is not an attack on the army or the *chose
               jugée.* To leave them unrectified would be a crime.[120] Interrupting,
               Méline reiterates that 'there is no Dreyfus Affair'. The Senate votes
               unanimously for the Government.

The duc d'Orléans's letter of 26 November 1897 is displayed in the streets of Paris.

Ravary's judicial investigation[121]

Dec 7–31

The Ravary investigation covers ground already dealt with by Pellieux and hears the same witnesses. Henry and Gonse are informed daily about its progress. The main new element is the examination of the handwriting of the *bordereau* and the Uhlan letter by three graphologists, Emile Couard, Edme-Etienne Belhomme and Pierre Varinard. Ravary does not ask them to examine the *petit bleu* or the handwriting of Dreyfus. However, examining magistrate Paul Bertulus strongly recommends he should do so.[122]

Gonse shows Ravary the *faux Henry.*

The three graphologists report to Ravary (26 Dec) that the *bordereau* was not written by Esterhazy; as with the Boulancy letters, it is probably the work of someone forging Esterhazy's handwriting.[123]

Ravary signs his report (31 Dec). Despite the various accusations against Esterhazy there is no proof of his guilt. Ravary concludes that the charges should be dropped for lack of evidence; and that Picquart has committed serious offences in showing *Ce canaille de D.* to Leblois and forging the *petit bleu.*[124] (*v.* Appendix 18)

On Saussier's advice Esterhazy repeats his request to be court-martialled.

Dec 8

La Libre Parole publishes a French translation of Lucie's supplication to Pope Leo XIII, originally sent in Latin in September 1896.[125]

Dec 9

First issue of *La Fronde*, France's first feminist newspaper, founded by Marguerite Durand. One of the main contributors is Caroline Rémy, known by the pseudonym Séverine. The paper is pro-Dreyfus.[126]

Panizzardi writes from Paris to Schwartzkoppen in Berlin, describing the situation:

> *The Scheurer-Kestner 'Syndicate' has circulated information in every direction, and many people know about what happened between you and E. [Esterhazy] But since they are all eager to see Dreyfus' condemnation confirmed, they say nothing.*

Panizzardi regrets the numerous publications in the French press about his dealings with Schwartzkoppen, which implicates him in the Dreyfus Affair and lays the blame on Schwartzkoppen's concierge who had taken letters from his pockets. Panizzardi remarks that these letters were later falsified, and reiterates that these forgeries [e.g. the *faux Henry*] have helped to condemn an innocent man.[127] (*v.* 21 Dec 1897)

Dec 10

In the Latin Quarter (Paris) students demonstrate against Scheurer-Kestner and Zola.

Dec 11

Devil's Island: Not receiving any letters for over a month, Dreyfus, in a high fever, exclaims: 'they want to kill me'. He asks to see Dr Debrieu:

I have been here three years ... My strength is exhausted... I would rather die than lose my mind... I ask you for the means to sustain myself for one more month. If, by then, I have no news of my family, it will be the end... Besides, I do not fear death... Relieve me of my pain.[128]

The *'bordereau annoté'* (the 'annotated *bordereau*')

Dec 12   Henri Rochefort publishes a long article in *L'Intransigeant* entitled 'La pièce secrète, la vérité sur le traître' ('The Secret Item, the Truth about the Traitor'). It accuses Dreyfus of having direct dealings with Kaiser Wilhelm. The article alleges that Dreyfus wrote to the Kaiser after the Franco-Prussian war offering his allegiance and asking to be enrolled in the German Army. The Kaiser replied that it is preferable he serves Germany while remaining in the French Army. The article claims that one of the famous secret items in the Dreyfus Affair is a letter from the Kaiser to von Münster referring to Dreyfus. In this, the Kaiser asks von Münster to communicate with Dreyfus in order to obtain information for the German General Staff. Rochefort declares that this information was received some time ago from a highly placed military official[129] and that it has been verified by previous military attachés, including Schwartzkoppen. He goes on to give further details: a few days before Dreyfus was arrested, von Münster told Prime Minister Dupuy that various documents, including eight letters addressed to him, had been stolen from the German Embassy. Dupuy asked that they be returned immediately. They were, after being photographed, and it is these photographs, the article claims, that were shown at the court martial of Dreyfus.[130]

Havas publishes the French Government's official denial of Rochefort's article.

Following von Münster's request, Hanotaux receives the German Ambassador on a Sunday and promises that he and Prime Minister Méline are ready to intervene in order to 'put an end to the scandal' and even to consider a bill restraining the press. Von Münster reports his conversation to the Kaiser. Where mentioning Hanotaux's suggestion of a bill, the Kaiser notes, 'Words?' Von Münster concludes: 'I base my attitude on the fact that Dreyfus is of no concern to us at all; but if our venerable sovereign is implicated in the proceedings, I will show with utmost energy that I am not prepared to tolerate it.'[131]

In a letter in *L'Eclair* Lucie Dreyfus protests against the paper's allegations that she had pleaded extenuating circumstances to Du Paty on behalf of her husband before his trial in 1894. She states that between 15 and 30 October 1894 her husband was intimidated by Du Paty.[132]

Dec 13   Eugène Fasquelle publishes Zola's pamphlet *Lettre à la jeunesse* ('Letter to Youth'), which calls upon young intellectuals to rally to the Dreyfus cause, against antisemitism and to Justice:

> ... *One hundred years after the Declaration of the Rights of Man, one hundred years after the supreme act of tolerance, and*

emancipation, we are returning to the wars of religion, to the most hideous and absurd fanaticism! ... Oh youth! Youth! I beg you consider the great task which awaits you. ... You are the ones who will lay the foundations of the century to come which we profoundly believe will resolve the problems of the past ... Youth! Youth! Remain always on the side of justice ... Youth! Youth! Be human. Be generous. Even if we are wrong, stay with us when we say that an innocent is suffering unbearable pain and that our outraged and anguished hearts are breaking ... Who, if not you, will undertake the sublime task of launching himself into this dangerous and superb cause and take the lead in the name of justice.? ... Where are you heading, young people? Where are you heading you students fighting in the streets, demonstrating, casting the passions and hopes of your twenty years into the midst of our troubles? We are heading towards humanity, truth and justice.[133]

Dec 13–14 Despite the Government's denial, Rochefort reconfirms the statements in his article of 12 December. On 14 December Havas publishes the second official denial of the article, claiming that:

... the Government is concerned about the campaign of fabrications and imaginary accounts that certain newspapers are systematically pursuing. If this campaign continues, the Government is determined to take the necessary measures, with the assistance of Parliament, to put an end to it.[134]

Méline's newspaper, *La République française*, describes the article as 'a guilt-ridden novel'; in Germany the *Berliner Tageblatt* refers to it as a 'stupid fable invented by hotheads'.[135]

Dec 15 *Le Petit Journal* describes Reinach's lost briefcase as a 'scoop' and presents Reinach as a forger. Ravary orders Reinach's briefcase to be seized and brought to him.

Dec 16 Von Münster writes to the Kaiser describing the mood in Paris:

Rochefort's lies would be recognized as such in any other reasonable country, in any other capital and no importance would be attached to them. But in everything relating to politics, and especially to Germany, Parisians totally lack judgement. Their levity and passionate character do not allow them time for reflection ... However incredible it may seem, I have noted on several occasions that reasonable Frenchmen, (that is those who should pass as such), put their faith in Rochefort's revelations.[136]

Dec 18 Reinach takes his briefcase to Ravary for examination. Ravary complains to him about the rumours in the press and apologizes.[137]

At the request of Leblois, Trarieux questions Minister of Justice Milliard about the false Speranza and Blanche telegrams.

Dec 19 Pressurized by public opinion, *Le Figaro* abandons its revisionist stance. Rodays hands over control to his associate, the Royalist Antonin Périvier.[138]

Dec 20	Yves Guyot, editor of *Le Siècle*, requests an interview with Méline to obtain a copy of d'Ormescheville's report, which was the indictment in the court martial. Méline refuses to do so.[139] (*v.* 7 Jan 1898)

Devil's Island: Dreyfus sends another appeal to President Faure.[140]

Dec 21	Panizzardi writes to Schwartzkoppen apologizing for having given possible cause for offence in his previous letter. (*v.* 11 Dec 1897) He continues:

> At the moment all is calm, but in a few days' time the affair will flare up more hotly than ever, when the court martial [of Esterhazy] opens. They [the General Staff] have decided to have E. proved innocent at all costs, and that is a good thing for you. They will say that the bordereau was not his work.

Panizzardi also recounts that the 'Syndicate' has tried to blackmail him, telling him they knew he possessed receipts of the money Schwartzkoppen gave Esterhazy. He believes Schwartzkoppen will be approached as well.[141] (*v.* 20 May 1898)

Dec 23	Milliard informs Trarieux that Billot had promised to examine the handwriting of the false telegrams sent to Picquart.
Dec 25	Rochefort publishes the *faux Otto* in *L'Intransigeant*.[142] (*v.* 25 Nov 1897)

Reinach publishes the *faux Otto* in *Le Temps*, declaring it a forgery.

Devil's Island: The head warder on Devil's Island remarks: 'He [Dreyfus] seems to be ageing rapidly.'[143]

Dec 26–27	Rochefort accuses Reinach of having forged the *faux Otto*.
Dec 29	Milliard orders Bertulus to lead an inquiry into the alleged attempt by Mathieu and Léon Dreyfus to bribe Sandherr on 14 December 1894.[144] (*v.* 15 March 1898)
Dec 31	Panizzardi writes to Schwartzkoppen:

> Everybody believes the affair you know of will come to an end in the first week of 1898 with an acquittal of E[sterhazy] on the charge of espionage! The Government is too keen on this result to act differently, and it is to be hoped that the 'Syndicate' will leave you in peace.[145]

Reinach initiates a libel suit against Rochefort for accusing him of forging the *faux Otto*. (*v.* 9 Feb 1898)

Dec	Italian journalist Enrico Casella interviews Panizzardi on the Dreyfus Affair. According to Casella, Panizzardi again denies having had any dealings with Dreyfus but refuses Casella's suggestion to intervene publicly. He agrees with Casella that Schwartzkoppen is the one person who knows the truth. Casella decides to interview Schwartzkoppen.[146] (*v.* 1 Jan 1898)
End Dec	On Boisdeffre's orders Gonse gives Mercier the copy of Du Paty's commentary on the Secret Dossier, which Sandherr had kept despite Mercier's instruction. (*v.* 17 Jan 1895) Mercier burns it in the presence of Gonse.[147]

Dec 1897–	The dreyfusard campaign gathers momentum, strengthened by
Jan 1898	many scientists and intellectuals. New recruits include members of

Dec 1897– Jan 1898   The dreyfusard campaign gathers momentum, strengthened by many scientists and intellectuals. New recruits include members of the Institut (Louis Havet, Gabriel Monod, Salomon Reinach, Emile Duclaux), academics and men of letters (including Anatole France, Ferdinand Buisson, Paul-Emile Appell, Octave Mirbeau, Lucien Herr, Charles Péguy, Edmond Fleg, Léon Blum). (*v.* Appendices 48 and 49)

NOTES

1   Historians of the Affair disagree about the exact sequence of events in this period, partly because of the deliberately contradictory evidence given by those involved.

2   Gonse and Henry needed a collaborator as a scapegoat. Gonse's choice of Du Paty can be explained by several contradictory factors: Du Paty was not a Section de Statistique officer (he belonged to the Troisième Bureau) and was not well informed about Esterhazy; his earlier role in the Affair meant that he was well acquainted with it. Gonse also probably believed that he could rely on Du Paty's loyalty and patriotism. *ASD*, pp. 421–2.

3   An account published in the German newspaper *Deutsche Rundschau* in June 1898 stated that at the time France was seeking the Russian alliance the French military, under Boisdeffre's direction needed to transmit false figures of the strength of the French forces to Russia. It further reported that Dreyfus refused to do so and Esterhazy was employed for this purpose which would explain the need of the General Staff to protect Esterhhazy but to dispose of Dreyfus. Barlow, *The Dreyfus Case*, p. 243.

4   The document might have aroused Du Paty's doubts about Esterhazy's innocence, since in his own report on Esterhazy's letters (dated December 1896) Du Paty acknowledged the similarity of its handwriting to that of the *bordereau*.

5   This letter was the subject of intrigue and remained the subject of debate. It is not clear whether it was a forgery drawn up by Henry to compromise Du Paty de Clam (as it is signed 'P.D.C.'). Thomas believes that although the coincidence of dates is perplexing, Henry would not have compromised his colleague Du Paty since he was about to work closely with him in warning Esterhazy. Thomas suggests that the letter was sent by someone opposed to a revision of Dreyfus' verdict and who was already aware of Scheurer-Kestner's interest in Dreyfus. *ASD*, pp. 423–4. When Du Paty was asked in 1898 by the Supreme Court of Appeal about the anonymous letter, he testified that he had never heard of it. *Cass.*, I, 445, Du Paty. The letter finally kept at the Ministry of War was given the later date of 21 October. *3ème Cass.*, I, 120–1, Targe. This was probably in order to make it seem as if it had arrived after Esterhazy has been already warned. (*v.* 18–19 Oct 1897)

6   The short version of this letter was kept in the archives of the Ministry of War. Gonse noted on it: 'letter prepared to be sent to Esterhazy. Not sent. By order of the Minister.' *3ème Cass.*, I, 120, Targe.

7   *Cass.*, II, 32, 201, Du Paty. Gonse later firmly denied that he had tried to encourage Du Paty to act against Billot's will. *Rennes*, II, 165, Gonse.

8   Esterhazy never produced the envelope of this letter, claiming it had been accidentally burnt. The exact date of the letter's arrival was the subject of controversy. *Répertoire*, pp. 93–4.

9   The misspelling of the names of Dreyfus and Picquart was deliberate. The signature 'Espérance' is reminiscent of Henry's 'Speranza' forgery sent to Picquart in 1896. (*v.* 15 Dec 1896)

10   *Répertoire*, p. 93. This letter must have been invented by Henry – with or without Du Paty's assistance. It appeared to be written in a female hand. Du Paty always denied he was responsible for this letter or having written it. In his private notes he comments that it was written by Mme Henry and dictated by her husband. Du Paty further affirmed that he recognized her writing paper. *ASD*, pp. 426–7.

11   Thomas, *Esterhazy*, p. 264.

12   Ernest Vaughan (1841–1929) was a fervent admirer of the French Socialist and anarchist philospher Proudhon and a supporter of the International in 1867. He was arrested for his involvement in the Paris Commune (1871). After several weeks in prison he fled to Brussels, where he established a branch of the International. There he contributed to several newspapers. In 1881, a year after his return to France, he became manager of *L'Intransigeant*, a paper edited by Henri Rochefort. In 1888, after disagreements with Rochefort, he became editor-in-chief of the *Petit Lyonnais*.

13   Alexander Autant and his son Edouard were the managing agents of 49 rue Douai. On 22 October Marie came in person to Autant, to plead with him to make the changes within 48 hours because of Esterhazy's intention to commit suicide. *Cass.*, II, 229, Autant.

14   The letter was sent through the Alibi Office, a special postal service in Paris, used mainly by unfaithful husbands, which allowed the place of posting to be falsified. The manager of the agency, concerned by Esterhazy's behaviour, broke the confidentiality rules and sent a copy of the letter to police headquarters. *DC*, p. 111.

15 According to Autant, Marie claimed that Esterhazy intended to commit suicide and had told her: 'I must disappear quickly.' *Cass.*, II, 229, Autant; *Pro. Zola*, 775, Stock. Esterhazy's concern for Marie explained his request to transfer the lease: if the apartment remained in his name, in the event of his death it would be sealed off by the police with all Marie's furniture and belongings inside. Marie denied having said this. *Révision*, 159–60. After a second letter from Esterhazy (26 October) to Autant, the transfer was signed on 8 November. Stock, *Memorandum*, p. 53.

16 Schwartzkoppen, *The Truth About Dreyfus*, pp. 76, 117. Esterhazy and Schwartzkoppen had not met since March 1896. Although Schwartzkoppen did not leave a detailed account in his unfinished diary of his last meeting with Esterhazy, he described it later to the Italian Ambassador Tornielli, who confided the details to Trarieux. This description, published by the Italian journalist Casella (*v.* 1 Jan 1898), and repeated by Reinach, contained other details of their dramatic meeting such as Esterhazy collapsing then pulling out a gun and threatening to kill them both. *HAD*, 2, pp. 591–3. In 1900 Esterhazy dismissed this account as ridiculous. *3ème Cass.*, III, 765; see also *AD* p. 572.

17 Henry explained to Gribelin that someone must accompany Du Paty, who 'talks too much', but that he cannot do so since Esterhazy knows him (*v.* 1877–79) and would recognize him immediately. Du Paty stated that the disguise was contrived to shield the General Staff if Esterhazy was placed under surveillance.

18 *ASD*, p. 431. It is highly likely that Esterhazy recognized them from the start. *HAD*, 2, 594.

19 Esterhazy clearly knew at this point that he was dealing with Section de Statistique officers. He was probably already considering how to defend himself – by claiming that he had acted on Sandherr's orders. Esterhazy reserved this defence for later, when it was recognized that the *bordereau* was in his writing. (*v.* 3 June 1899) *ASD*, pp. 431–2.

20 According to Reinach, Schwartzkoppen reported the same day to von Münster that his dealings with Esterhazy have been discovered. *HAD*, 2, p. 598. Von Münster had always denied this. (*v.* 20 Nov 1897 & 4 April 1898)

21 Leclerc had alerted Billot earlier in October to the massing of enemy cavalry there.

22 Leclerc reported to Billot on 3 November that the situation along the Libyan frontier had become less alarming. Billot, however, did not rescind his order. Picquart left Sousse on 8 November. *ASD*, p. 440.

23 Esterhazy acted henceforth on instructions either from Du Paty or Henry.

24 This was invented by Henry. Esterhazy claimed that in 1893 he had sent a letter to Captain Brô at the Ministry of War about the battle of Eupatoria in the Crimean War, in which Esterhazy's father had participated. The name Brô was not chosen by accident. Henry remembered that when Dreyfus was first shown the *bordereau* in 1894 he had the impression that the writing was similar to that of a certain Captain Brô on the General Staff. (Dreyfus withdrew this remark and the incident was not included in d'Ormescheville's report.) For Esterhazy's statements on the Brô story, see *AD*, pp. 563–5; 576–9. (*see following note*).

25 This letter is further evidence of the collusion: the text was given to Esterhazy by Du Paty. It was probably written or dictated by Gonse. Esterhazy published a facsimile of this original text in his book *Les dessous de l'affaire Dreyfus*, published in 1898 (p. 179). (*v.* 19 Nov 1898). This original document was not reproduced in any of the future investigations. It has since disappeared but photographs still exist. *ASD*, pp. 436, 576. Esterhazy's letter figures in *Déb. Cass., 1898*, 70.

26 This document provided the basis for the article published by Drumont, signed Dixi. (*v.* 15 Nov 1897) *Répertoire*, p. 98.

27 *Cass.*, I, 582, Esterhazy.

28 A news agency like Havas.

29 *AD*, pp. 579–80. Du Paty admitted he had given Esterhazy the outline of this letter but denied Esterhazy's claim that it was dictated by him. *Cass.*, I, 582, Estehazy; II, 192, Du Paty.

30 Beaumont, *Aux sources de l'affaire*, p. 155.

31 A reference to documents already included in the Secret Dossier. (*v.* Sept–Oct 1897)

32 Scheurer-Kestner's detailed description of this long conversation in his *Mémoires* is reproduced in Reinach. *HAD*, 2, pp. 627–30.

33 *3ème Cass.*, III, 749. See also *AD*, p. 556.

34 *AD*, pp. 580–1.

35 Although there is no record of exactly who was instructing Esterhazy, it is evident that Henry continued to provide him with information. He was far better informed on plots at the Ministry of War than Du Paty. In order to continue meeting Esterhazy in secret Henry took the precaution of ordering Desvernine to stop the surveillance on him (*v.* 16 Nov 1897, n. 68). According to Esterhazy, it was at this time that Du Paty explained to him the procedure for communicating secretly with Henry. *Cass.*, I, 584, Esterhazy.

36 Billot denied responsibility for these disclosures. He questioned Du Paty who firmly denied he had offered any information to the press. Billot promised Scheurer-Kestner he would investigate the matter

but did not do so. It is highly probable that the source of this disclosure had been Boisdeffre or Henry. *ASD*, pp. 444–6.

37 The official reason for Schwartzkoppen's departure from Paris was his appointment as head of this prestigious regiment. The coincidence with the 'revival' of the Dreyfus Affair did not go unnoticed. (*v.* 17 Nov 1897) It is possible that Henry attempted to blackmail Schwartzkoppen. He sent Lemercier-Picard to him with some forged letters allegedly in Schwartzkoppen's handwriting. (*v.* 1 Nov 1896 n. 63) They included the *billet des quatorze armées*. (*v.* Sept–Oct 1897, Compilation of a second Secret Dossier) *ASD*, pp. 63, 578 n. 2. Reinach also mentions this episode but gives a slightly different account. *HAD*, 2, pp. 598–9.

38 Méline was convinced of the authenticity of the *faux Henry*, which Billot had mentioned to him. *HAD*, 2, pp. 650–1.

39 Paléologue, *Journal de l'affaire Dreyfus*, pp. 57–60.

40 Rumours of the existence of this letter from the Kaiser began to spread from early November, both in the Nationalist press and in certain illustrious Parisian salons frequented by the higher echelons of the General Staff. The Princess Mathilde (daughter of Jerôme Bonaparte who held a famous salon) and Baron Stoffel (former French military attaché in Berlin) heard about it from Boisdeffre.

41 This letter was quoted fully by Labori, to be Zola's defence lawyer. *Pro. Zola*, 925–7, closing speech of Labori.

42 *AD*, p. 571.

43 An officer risked arrest for writing to the President in this manner.

44 Since this document probably never existed, Esterhazy could not have seen it nor known what it was supposed to contain. *ASD*, p. 471.

45 De Castro had had financial dealings with Esterhazy and possessed letters written by him.

46 Demange defended Morès following his duel with Mayer. Esterhazy was one of the witnesses. (*v.* 23 June 1892) *ATQV*, pp. 98–100.

47 This information, along with the article in *La Libre Parole* (of 31 October 1897), strengthened Billot's suspicion that Picquart was Scheurer-Kestner's informant.

48 This phrase, confirming that for the Government the conviction of Dreyfus remained *res judicata*, was frequently repeated. (*v.* 4 Dec 1897) On this occasion the Government took into consideration the 8 June 1895 amendment to Article 445 of the Code of Criminal Instruction (*v.* 3 Dec 1896, n. 89), but it concluded that no new evidence had been discovered. It was decided that Darlan would examine the court martial files to ensure that Dreyfus had been correctly and legally convicted. A few days later Billot decided with Méline's support that it was better for Ministers not to know the origins of the case. This made Darlan suspicious. He was soon replaced as Minister of Justice by Victor Milliard. (*v.* 3 Dec 1897)

49 The telegram was sent by Esterhazy. Leblois was to show it to Pellieux during his first investigation of Esterhazy. (*v.* 17–20 November 1897)

50 *ASD*, p. 459.

51 These two telegrams and the letter sent to Picquart on the same day were devised by Henry and Esterhazy, who were assisted by Du Paty and Marie Pays. Their objective was to prove that Picquart had been assisting the dreyfusards for a long time and also to invalidiate his investigations of Esterhazy. It insinuated that Picquart had access to forgeries and falsifications (see following notes). This was the commencement of a series of accusations against Picquart.

52 The telegram was sent, perhaps intentionally, to the wrong address: Picquart was in Sousse, not Tunis. Henry's involvement in this is evident. He had already used the name 'Speranza' the previous year in fabricating the Speranza letter retained at the Ministry of War. (*v.* 15 Dec 1896) The word 'demigod' had been taken from an authentic letter from Ducasse to Picquart. (*v.* 27 Nov 1896) Speranza also relates to the Espérance letter of 18 Oct 1897. *Speranza* is the Italian word for *espérance* (French). They both mean 'hope'. Encouraged by Henry, Esterhazy dictated the telegram to Marie Pays, who wrote it in her handwriting. (*v.* 15–16 July 1898, The revelations of Christian Esterhazy)

53 Blanche was the Christian name of the comtesse de Comminges, Picquart's cousin and close friend. This telegram refers to the *petit bleu*. It was created as an attempt by Picquart's friends to warn him that his alleged falsification of the *petit bleu* had been discovered. Although Henry and Esterhazy conceived this telegram, it was actually written by Du Paty. (*v.* 9 July 1898) Henry was one of the few people who knew about Picquart's discovery of the *petit bleu* and from November 1896 he was in charge of it. (*ASD*, p. 577, n. 17) It is probable that when the Blanche telegram was sent the *petit bleu* had already been further falsified, most likely by Henry. This falsification consisted of erasing the name Esterhazy and then rewriting it in the same place. The aim was to suggest that Picquart had falsified the document by erasing the original name and replacing it with that of Esterhazy. Subsequently Picquart was officially accused of erasing the 'original' name on the *petit bleu* (*v.* 14 Sept 1898) The date of this falsification and the person responsible for it remain the subject of debate. Thomas believes Henry made the alterations between December 1896 and November 1897. *ASD*, p. 462. Reinach dated them to September 1896. *HAD*, 2, pp. 460–3.

54 Henry's involvement is again clear: '*toute l'oeuvre découverte*' ('the whole undertaking is discovered') virtually repeats the phrase '*le chef-d'oeuvre est accompli*' ('the masterpiece is finished') of the Ducasse telegram of 27 November 1896.

55 It is likely that Henry unofficially asked Cavard to intercept all correspondence addressed to Picquart. *ASD*, p. 463.

56 The PTT had probably been instructed to do so by the Minister of Interior. In addition to the false telegrams, Picquart also received two authentic ones from one of his mistresses, Mme Monnier. The wife of a Foreign Office official, Mme Monnier had tried to conceal her love affair by using a *poste restante* address. (*v.* 23 Nov–3 Dec 1897, Pelliux's second investigation, n. 91). Mlle Blanche de Comminges also collaborated to shield her identity. These telegrams were sent with the forgeries to the Minister of Interior. They alarmed the Sûreté and the Minister, who believed Picquart was involved with the 'Syndicate': The word 'demigod' was thought to refer to Scheurer-Kestner, 'Georges' to Picquart, and 'Blanche' to Mlle de Comminges. Bredin, *The Affair*, pp. 208–9.

57 *HAD*, 3, pp. 42–3.

58 Lazare, *Une erreur judiciaire. L'affaire Dreyfus* (deuxième mémoire, avec des expertises d'écritures de MM. Crépieux-Jamin, Gustave Bridier, de Rougemont, Paul Moriaud, E. de Marneffe, de Gray Birch, Th. Gurrin, J.-H. Schooling, D. Carvalho, etc.) (Paris: Stock, 1897). The pamphlet was reissued without the experts' reports by Philippe Oriol: B. Lazare, *Une erreur judiciaire, l'affaire Dreyfus* (Paris: Allia, 1993).

59 Just as the original conception of this document (merely a photograph of *Ce canaille de D.*) was devised by Henry), so was its 'restitution'. Henry dictated to Esterhazy the letter addressed to Billot. He then put it into the envelope with the pretended *document libérateur* and sealed it. It was delivered to Ministry of War, probably by one of Henry's agents. *ASD*, p. 471.

60 This article mentions for the first time the French word *révisionnistes* (revisionists), to mean those in favour of a revision against the verdict against Dreyfus. Scheurer-Kestner, Mathieu, Leblois, Demange and Emmanuel Arène had agreed on 12 November to mount a publicity campaign to prepare public opinion for a revision. Scheurer-Kestner disapproved of Arène's article, which accelerated events and proved disadvantageous to the dreyfusard camp. *ASD*, pp. 468–9.

61 Picquart understood that the telegrams also came from Esterhazy, and that Henry was involved. *Cass.*, I, 196, Picquart. Although Picquart did not mention names, he believed – as Henry wished him to – that the Blanche telegram was the work of Du Paty, who had private reasons to discredit Mlle de Comminges: his proposal in 1892 to one of the Comminges daughters had been refused. *ASD*, p. 462; Bredin, *The Affair*, p. 204.

62 For the full text of the letter see *AD*, pp. 530–1.

63 Picquart was later officially accused of fabricating and falsifying the *petit bleu*. (*v.* 14 Sept 1898)

64 Esterhazy first took the article to R.P. Bailly, editor of the Catholic *La Croix*, but Bailly refused to publish it. He then submitted it to Drumont. It was based on the '*plaquette*' he had received from Henry at the end of October 1897 (summarizing Henry's complaints against Picquart). *ASD*, p. 470. Two further articles, also signed Dixi, were published in *La Libre Parole* on 16 and 17 November.

65 Mathieu copied his letter to *L'Agence Nationale*, *Le Figaro* and *Le Radical*.

66 Leblois and Demange helped Mathieu to write this letter. It was Scheurer-Kestner who asked Mathieu to denounce Esterhazy publicly when his own situation became difficult. Scheurer-Kestner had already named Esterhazy as author of the *bordereau* to the Minister of War and Prime Minister. On 14 November *La Liberté* named Denis-Louis de Rougemont as the officer Scheurer-Kestner suspected of being the author of the *bordereau*. *ATQV*, p. 100.

67 During the second half of November Drumont and Rochefort revived the myth of a corrupt and greedy Jewish 'Syndicate'. This was one of the famous allegations of 19th-century antisemitic theory. They initially used the term to describe the inner circle of Mathieu Dreyfus – Lazare, Scheurer-Kestner, Reinach – but later extended it to include all the dreyfusards. From that time the term was also used by the dreyfusards themselves. (*v.* 1 Dec 1897)

68 Boisdeffre and Gonse were worried by the possible outcome of an investigation of Esterhazy since it could reveal their collusion with him. The order to cease meetings between Du Paty and Esterhazy came as a result of a police report stating that a meeting between Esterhazy and Du Paty had been observed at the Passage Landrieu in Paris. To protect Esterhazy, especially at the beginning of Pellieux's second investigation (23 November–3 December 1897), Du Paty communicated with him through Mlle Pays, Esterhazy's lawyer Maurice Tézenas and his cousin Christian. Du Paty still met Esterhazy clandestinely (although no longer disguised with a false beard) – on bridges, on the banks of the Seine, in public squares or urinals. Du Paty was only partially informed about Esterhazy. Christian believed that Esterhazy was still looking after his financial interests (*v.* Oct 1896) and that he was a victim of a terrible plot, so he agreed to help him. *DT*, pp. 100–1, 114–15.

69 During this meeting Saint-Morel also mentioned the *bordereau annoté* to Rochefort. (*v.* 12 Dec 1897)

70 According to Paléologue, von Münster assured Hanotaux that Schwartzkoppen also gave his word of honour that the *bordereau* had not been found in his waste paper basket in the embassy. Paléologue, *Journal de l'affaire Dreyfus,* pp. 63–5.

71 *Cass.*, I, 390–2, Paléologue. On 24 November, von Münster repeated the denial to Hanotaux.

72 Baumont, *Aux sources de l'affaire*, p. 174. This information contradicted Schwartzkoppen's statement in his diary that he only revealed Esterhazy's name to his Italian colleague after the publication of the facsimile of the *bordereau* (*v.* 10 Sept 1896).

73 On the following day, and as a matter of formality, Billot requested that Pellieux reprimand Esterhazy for these articles.

74 Schwartzkoppen, *Die Wahrheit über Dreyfus*, p. 106.

75 Baumont, *Aux sources de l'affaire*, p. 174.

76 Pellieux's first investigation was informal. Its purpose was to advise the Ministry of War whether an official judicial inquiry would be appropriate. Pellieux's function in the second investigation (23 November–3 December) was to be equivalent to that of an examining magistrate in civil law, a role for which he was not qualified. This partly explains the weakness of his investigations. Pellieux wished to consult a magistrate on procedure. Henry recommended Paul Bertulus who was regularly consulted by the Section de Statistique in espionage matters. Bertulus agreed after he consulted the Minister of Justice, who only permitted him to advise Pellieux on procedure. (Bredin, *The Affair*, pp. 222–3). No full record of Pellieux's first investigation was published.

77 *3ème Cass.*, III, 395, Pellieux's final report. This was the first time Scheurer-Kestner had acknowledged he knew about Picquart.

78 Leblois could not give precise details of the *petit bleu* since Picquart had never shown it to him. Leblois only learnt of the content of the *petit bleu* from the press release during Esterhazy's court martial on 10–11 January 1898. Nevertheless, by the time Pellieux reached the end of his investigation he was convinced that Picquart had disclosed it to Leblois, and probably also to Scheurer-Kestner. *3ème Cass.*, III , 395–7, Pellieux's final report.

79 By this Leblois implied that it was Esterhazy who sent this express telegram to Scheurer-Kestner and that Esterhazy's '*dame voilée*' was a sham.

80 Pellieux's eventual report stated that it was Leblois who made this suggestion. In 1898 Pellieux and Leblois were confronted with each other concerning this interrogation. *Fabre,* 135–9. (*v.* 13 July–25 Aug 1898, Fabre's investigation of Picquart and Leblois)

81 The decision to show Pellieux the secret documents held in the Ministry of War came from the Government. (*3ème Cass.*, I, 100–1). The President issued a last-minute order to remove Esterhazy's letters to him from the dossier. *ASD*, p. 481.

82 As previously stated, the *petit bleu* has already been falsified, probably by Henry (*v.* 10 Nov 1897).

83 *3ème Cass.*, III, 392–7. See also *AD*, pp. 587–91.

84 Esterhazy was shrewd enough not to destroy this note. In 1898 Du Paty admitted having written it. *Cass.*, I, 453; II, 194, Du Paty.

85 The decision as to how to act on Pellieux's report rested not only with the Ministry of War but with the whole Government.

86 Boisdeffre and Gonse had hoped the Affair would come to an end after Pellieux's initial investigation. They sensed the danger in pursuing it further in view of the potential discovery of the collusion with the General Staff and the forgeries involved. Their decision to recall Picquart to Paris may have reflected their intention to open legal proceedings against him. Bredin, *The Affair*, pp. 218–19.

87 *ASD*, p. 483. According to Du Paty, Boisdeffre was angered when he heard that Billot forbade Du Paty from meeting Esterhazy or his cousin Christian: 'Oh, but it's not that at all! We have to move forward … Let's use all our weapons and not allow ourselves to be eaten alive.' Bredin, *The Affair*, p. 483.

88 The group's main offices were at 3 rue de Cluny (Paris). Constituted as a federation, the group welcomed supporters from provincial Nationalist and Royalist groups (Toulouse, Bordeaux, Dijon, Lille, etc.). The federation participated in the anti-dreyfusard campaign from 1898, the year in which Dubuc distributed across France the anti-dreyfusard placard 'To the Nation'. This was reproduced in the press, especially in the provincial issues of *La Croix*. Pierrard, *Juifs et catholiques*, pp. 140–1; B. Joly, 'The Jeunesse antisémite et nationaliste, 1894–1904'.

89 According to Reinach this letter was written by one of Henry's agents. *HAD*, 3, p. 93.

90 *ASD*, p. 485. The original *bordereau* was passed to Pellieux a few days later. (*v.* 20 Nov–3 Dec 1897, Pellieux's first investigation of Esterhazy)

91 The notes were actually written by Christian (*v.* 11 July 1898). The interrogations of Esterhazy are published in *Cass.*, II, 90–105. Pellieux was given misleading hints during his investigation by both Gonse and Henry as to the identity of the '*la dame voilée*'. One of them was Madame Monnier, one of Picquart's mistresses. (*v.* 11 Nov 1897, n. 56) Annoyed by the rumours in the press connecting her to the

story of *la dame voilée,* Monnier complained to Pellieux. Pellieux followed this lead. He first informed her husband. But the resulting searches were fruitless. After closing his investigation Pellieux informed Bertulus about Mme Monnier, accusing her of being *la dame voilée.* (*v.* 14 May 1898, n. 136)

92 Mathieu confirmed that both he and Scheurer-Kestner found Pellieux's attitude completely changed: 'He asked questions in a dry voice, his secretary wrote the answers; no other word was exchanged between the general and me.' *ATQV,* p. 102.

93 On arriving in Paris Picquart was met by his friend Mercier-Milon, who brought him an order from Boisdeffre that he was not to communicate with anyone before his hearing with Pellieux. Picquart gave his word of honour. He did not know what Leblois had already revealed, and as a precaution he even burnt a letter from Leblois explaining the situation. *ASD,* p. 487.

94 Picquart's comments might suggest that the *petit bleu* had already been falsified. (*v.* 10 Nov 1897, n. 53)

95 Picquart was thereafter put under strict surveillance. *Cass.,* I, 202, Picquart.

96 On 16 November 1897 the daily *Le Jour* referred to Picquart as 'of Jewish origin' and the colonel who was 'the soul of the [Dreyfus] intrigue'. On the following day *Le Figaro* claimed this information was nonsense. Pellieux then started fruitless inquiries about Picquart's alleged Jewish origin. Boussel, *L'Affaire Dreyfus et la presse,* p. 130.

97 If Pellieux had known that Schwartzkoppen showed interest in this item (*v.* end Sept 1894), he may have suspected Esterhazy but the Section de Statistique did not deem it appropriate to tell him of this. *ASD,* p. 487.

98 By that time Pellieux had received the original *bordereau.* There was a danger that Pellieux's investigation would be extended to include examination of the Secret Dossier at present collated at the Ministry of War. This was a great danger for the General Staff as the various forgeries in the dossier may have been exposed.

99 Several considerations led to this request. Tézenas suggested Esterhazy should ask for a court martial because he knew how damaging the Boulancy letter could be for him if there was a civil court action as a result of Esterhazy's threat to lodge a suit against Mathieu and Scheurer-Kestner. The General Staff officers saw no risk in bringing Esterhazy before a court martial as Pellieux's final report (3 Dec) exonerated him. Esterhazy's acquittal from the charge of treason would redeem his honour. It would also be considered a second condemnation of Dreyfus and prevent the Dreyfus case from being opened in a civil court. *DT,* pp. 112–13; Bredin, *The Affair,* p. 227.

100 *Répertoire,* pp. 124–5. Esterhazy showed a draft of the letter to Pellieux, who amended it. Disclosures about this letter reached the press.

101 Pellieux's investigation was not supposed to be directed at Picquart. Mathieu Dreyfus remarked: 'Pellieux's investigation of Esterhazy turned into an investigation of Picquart.' *ATQV,* pp. 103–4. Pellieux's report is included in *3ème Cass.,* I, 101–3. See also *AD,* pp. 591–4.

102 This last phrase of the article became a famous dreyfusard motto. It was later used as the title of Zola's book of collected articles on the Dreyfus Affair *La vérité en marche.* (*v.* 16 Feb 1901) See in the 1969 edition, pp. 65–71. See English text in *Zola, The Dreyfus Affair: 'J'Accuse' and Other Writings,* pp. 10–14.

103 Rodays did not publish the letter but informed Reinach of it. He realized it was a trap. The word *bordereau* mentioned in it was the main clue as it was very unlikely that the word would have been used in 1893, before the start of the Affair. Had the letter been published, the Dreyfus family could have been accused of forging it, as Esterhazy could prove that he was in Rouen on 17 December 1893, the date on the letter. This was just one of the many traps set for the Dreyfus family in the second half of November. *ATQV,* pp. 109–15.

104 *Déb. Cass., 1899,* 325–6. This letter can also be found in the first edition of Dreyfus *Cinq années de ma vie* (Paris: Fasquelles, 1901), pp. 346–7.

105 *Répertoire,* p. 119. Von Münster considered this letter showed an 'absolute lack of tact'. Baumont, *Aux sources de l'affaire,* p. 156.

106 Hanotaux already knew that Panizzardi had issued a statement of this kind on 24 November (printed in the Italian paper *Escrito italiano*). Hanotaux had received a letter from Monod (21 November 1897) mentioning that during his stay in Italy (November–December 1897) he had heard from various generals and politicians that there had been not been any contact between the Italian Army and Dreyfus. It was Esterhazy from whom secret documents emanated. Monod asked Hanotaux to 'shed light on the Affair'. *Cass.,* I, 458–60, Monod; Baumont, *Aux sources de l'affaire,* pp. 174–5.

107 Tornielli indicated that there had already been a precedent for such a request: in 1893 Panizzadi had given evidence in a French court regarding a fraud case. Hanotaux submitted Torniell's request to the jurisconsult Louis Renault, who on 5 December 1897 rejected the request on the grounds that French law only permits testimonies requested by judicial proceedings. Baumont, *Aux source de l'affaire,* pp. 175–6.

108 Baumont, *Aux sources de l'affaire,* p. 155.

109 Baumont, *Aux sources de l'affaire,* pp. 155–6.

110 Boulancy had entrusted Esterhazy's letters to her lawyer Lucien Jullemier, who transmitted them to Scheurer-Kestner. The latter showed them to Pellieux, who tried to laugh off their content and had no intention of taking them into consideration. Scheurer-Kestner demanded that Pellieux seize all letters from Esterhazy at Boulancy's home and summon her for questioning. After consulting Judge Bertulus, Pellieux agreed. The seizure was secret. To influence public opinion, which was pro-Esterhazy, Mathieu Dreyfus and Reinach had the letters published in *Le Figaro*. *ASD*, p. 488. When Esterhazy first saw the letters in print he was on the point of fleeing to Belgium in panic. At 2 a.m. on 26 November the Minister of the Interior issued an order for Esterhazy's arrest at all the border stations. The Government feared that his escape might be interpreted as a confession. Esterhazy was probably warned of this by Henry. *HAD*, 3, pp. 114–15.

111 *Répertoire*, p. 121.

112 Boisdeffre thus prevented Pellieux from hearing a significant witness and examining these documents. By this communiqué Boisdeffre also vouched for the authenticity of a document he (as well as Du Paty and even Billot) strongly suspected was false. ASD, pp. 491–2.

113 *Le Figaro* received Esterhazy's letter from Stock, a friend of the Autants. A few days after Mathieu's public denunciation of Esterhazy, Edouard Autant informed Stock that Esterhazy was one of his tenants. He also mentioned the letters requesting the transfer of his lease (20 & 26 October 1897) and the personal visit of his mistress (22 October). Autant gave Stock the letters, which he then copied and showed to Scheurer-Kestner, Lazare, Mathieu and Pellieux. Pellieux, however, did not take the letters into consideration. Stock and Autant were not called to testify. Stock's decision to have the letters published caused Autant problems. Marie Pays accused him of falsifying the letters. The letters were later submitted as evidence in Ravary's investigation of Esterhazy. Both Autant and Stock were called to testify in this investigation; Autant was also called to testify in Esterhazy's court martial. Both again testified at the Zola trial. In all instances the letters were rejected as proof against Esterhazy. Stock, *Mémorandum d'un éditeur*, pp. 52–7; 82–5.

114 Included in Zola's *La vérité en marche* (1969), pp. 73–80. See English text in *Zola, The Dreyfus Affair: 'J'Accuse' and Other Writings*, pp. 14–19.

115 The letters from Esterhazy in Reinach's possession were copies of Esterhazy's letters to Autant. Stock, *Memorandum*, p. 50.

116 The Senate forced Darlan to resign over an administrative irregularity, most likely using the opportunity to dismiss the only Minister in favour of a revision. *HAD*, 3, p. 126.

117 Jean Calas was a Huguenot cloth merchant whose execution in 1762 caused the philosopher Voltaire to lead a campaign for religious tolerance and reform of the French criminal code. Millerand was alluding to the involvement of Baron Reinach, Joseph Reinach's uncle, in the Panama scandal. (*v.* 6 Sept 1892) This speech provoked Reinach to challenge Millerand to a duel: the duel took place on 5 December, without injury to either party. *HAD*, 3, pp. 142–5.

118 Baumont, *Aux sources de l'affaire*, pp. 182–3.

119 Scheurer-Kestner could not table any supporting documents since Picquart had not allowed Leblois to hand over his correspondence with Gonse or mention Picquart's name in the Senate. For the complete transcription of Scheurer-Kestner's intervention in the Senate, see *AD*, pp. 517–28.

120 Trarieux later regretted that Scheurer-Kestner could not reveal more facts before the Senate. After this session Trarieux asked Scheurer-Kestner to share with him all that he knew. Scheurer-Kestner did so. Although Trarieux was then convinced that the *bordereau* was written by Esterhazy and that documents had been secretly transmitted to the judges at Dreyfus' court martial, he confided in Scheurer-Kestner: 'If, however, these secret documents showed with certainty that Dreyfus is a traitor, would it be possible to linger over questions of procedure? I myself would not have the courage.' *Pro. Zola*, 196–7, Trarieux.

121 Records of some of the evidence given during the Ravary investigation are published in *Cass.*, II, 299–305. The interrogations of Esterhazy are published in *Cass.*, II, 106–20.

122 Bertulus told Ravary: 'Your dossier has a flaw in it which causes everything to collapse. I am referring to the *petit bleu*.Until you establish that the *petit bleu* is a forgery … by Picquart, nothing holds together.' *Cass.*, I, 220, Bertulus.

123 See *AD*, pp. 145–7.

124 Despite Ravary's statement regarding the lack of evidence, his report was to become the indictment at Esterhazy's court martial. (*v.* 10–11 Jan 1898) It is published in *Révision*, 115–22. See also *Pro. Zola*, II [1898], 532–8; *AD*, pp. 597–602. An analysis of Ravary's report is published in *Révision*, 57–71.

125 A French translation appeared on 18 December in the weekly *Questions actuelles;* an English translation on 5 December 1897 in the *Sunday Special*.

126 For Séverine and her involvement in the Affair see H. Rodney, 'Séverine. Caroline Rémy, la grande prêtresse du dreyfusisme (1855–1919)' in M. Drouin (ed.) *L'Affaire Dreyfus de A à Z* (Paris: Flammarion, 1994), pp. 282–7.

127 Schwartzkoppen, *Die Wahrheit über Dreyfus*, p. 108. The two former colleagues continued to correspond after Schwartzkoppen's departure from Paris. Their relationship had changed and their letters became recriminatory. Schwartzkoppen's replies to Panizzardi's letters have not been found.

128 Menier, 'La détention du Capitaine Dreyfus', p. 473; *HAD*, 3, pp. 336–7.

129 Probably a reference to Saint-Morel, who visited Rochefort on 16 November 1897. Boisdeffre punished Saint-Maurel for this visit. (*v.* 19 Nov 1897) He later presented this punishment as proof that there was no deliberate campaign by the General Staff to circulate this myth. *Pro. Zola*, 159, Boisdeffre.

130 This untrue story soon appeared in various permutations. It was circulated by the Nationalist press and the General Staff, mainly in 1898–99, and transformed into the myth of the *bordereau annoté*, which was to play an important role in the final phase of the Affair. (*v.* 6–7 April 1903) This supposed that the *bordereau annoté* was the original *bordereau*, written on heavy paper, on which Dreyfus had written the price he wanted for each piece of information and which Schwartzkoppen had sent to the Kaiser. The Kaiser was supposed to have returned the document with annotations in his own writing, one of which read: 'This rascal Dreyfus is very demanding. Nevertheless, we have to hasten the delivery of the documents mentioned.' The rumours continued that the document was intercepted by Intelligence and that Casimir-Périer, keeping a copy, returned it to von Münster at their meeting on 6 January 1894 in order to avoid war. The true *bordereau*, on India squared paper, on which the conviction of Dreyfus was, according to this article, based, was merely a copy of the original.

131 Baumont, *Aux sources de l'affaire*, pp. 167–8.

132 *Répertoire*, p. 127.

133 Included in Zola's *La vérité en marche* (1969), pp. 89–98. Quoted in Whyte, *The Accused*, pp. 52–3. See full text in English, Zola, *The Dreyfus Affair: 'J'Accuse' and Other Writings*, pp. 29–35.

134 *Répertoire*, p. 129. Von Münster informed the Kaiser of this second denial. The Kaiser made a marginal note: 'For the moment, it is a pure and simple repetition of the first denial. Since then, the incitements … have not ceased. The Government has not intervened, and will not, despite all the assurances given.' Baumont, *Aux sources de l'affaire*, p. 169.

135 Baumont, *Aux sources de l'affaire*, p. 166.

136 Baumont, *Aux sources de l'affaire*, p. 169.

137 According to Reinach, Ravary confessed that he knew about the transmission of secret documents to the Court at the court martial of Dreyfus and that he believed the *bordereau* was not an original document but had been copied or photocopied. Despite this, he claimed that Dreyfus should remain convicted since the Ministry of War had affirmed that 'the Jew was justly tried'. *HAD*, 3, pp. 174-6.

138 Within a month of its vigorous campaign for the Dreyfus cause (following Mathieu's open denunciation of Esterhazy), *Le Figaro* came under attack from several newspapers, personal enemies and the General Staff. In January it had good reason to fear a reduction in its readership. The dreyfusards were disappointed by the paper's momentary cowardice. Following the publication of Zola's 'J'Accuse', *Le Figaro* soon rejoined the dreyfusard camp. Boussel, *L'affaire Dreyfus et la presse*, p. 159; M. Dreyfus, *Dreyfusards!* pp. 116–20.

139 Mathieu had had this report since 1895. (*v.* 10 Jan 1895)

140 *Déb. Cass.*, 1899, 326; A. Dreyfus, *Cinq années de ma vie* (1901), pp. 347–8.

141 Schwartzkoppen, *Die Wahrheit über Dreyfus*, pp. 112.

142 Lemercier-Picard sold the letter to Rochefort for 500 francs after trying unsuccessfully to publish it in *Le Figaro*, *L'Aurore* and *Le Radical*. (*v.* 3 Mar 1898)

143 Menier, 'La détention du Capitaine Dreyfus', p. 473.

144 The rumour of this attempt to bribe Sandherr was circulated largely by Father Gayraud, a Deputy, Sandherr's friend Denis-Henri Penot and Madame Sandherr. Two days after Mathieu announced he would lodge a suit against his slanderers, Milliard decided to open an inquiry to prevent the matter becoming a public issue. Penot and Sandherr's widow had already testified before Ravary that they had 'heard' from Sandherr about a bribery attempt. Sandherr had left a detailed record of his conversation with the Dreyfus brothers, written and signed on the day of their visit to him (13 December 1894). It was clear from Sandherr's record that there had been no attempt at bribery. The record was shown to Ravary. *Cass.*, II, 280–6.

145 Schwartzkoppen, *Die Wahrheit über Dreyfus*, p. 114.

146 Mathieu Dreyfus was informed by a friend about Casella's interviews with Panizzardi. According to Mathieu, Casella told him that he had learned from Panizzardi of the relationship between Schwartzkoppen and Esterhazy. Mathieu persuaded Casella to try to induce Panizzardi to announce this publicly. Following Panizzardi's refusal and at Mathieu's expense Casella went to Berlin to interview Schwartzkoppen himself. *ATQV*, pp. 118–21. See also Casella's account in *Pro. Zola*, II [1898], pp. 512-16. (*v.* 7 April 1898)

147 *Cass.*, I, 568, Gonse; II, 339–40, letters of Mercier, Freycinet and Gonse.

Part 6

ACQUITTAL and CONSEQUENCES

January–29 October 1898

Emile Zola

1898
Fabrication of evidence against Dreyfus

Jan	Gonse extends the Secret Dossier by adding material on the alleged confession of Dreyfus. One of the supplementary documents is a forgery, dated 6 January 1895. This is a letter by Gonse to Boisdeffre reporting that on that day Lebrun-Renault, summoned by Mercier and President Faure, told them that Dreyfus made 'admissions, or half admissions' to him.[1] Gonse shows the forgery to Billot as if it has just been found, and to Cavaignac, future Minister of War. (*v.* 22 Jan 1898)

Jan 1 Interviewed in Berlin by Casella, Schwartzkoppen states that the *bordereau* is not written by Dreyfus. He affirms that he knows him to be innocent and believes Esterhazy capable of anything. He also states that if Dreyfus was convicted on the basis of documents delivered in secret to the judges, those documents must have been forged. The French Government cannot, he claims, ask him or the German Government to declare officially that Esterhazy is guilty; they can only maintain their previous statements that they have not had any dealings with Dreyfus. Subsequently (5 January), Schwartzkoppen gives Casella a letter for Panizzardi.[2] (*v.* 7 Jan 1898)

Jan 2 Saussier signs the order for Esterhazy's court martial.[3]

Jan 4 Leblois files a complaint on behalf of Picquart, accusing the anonymous authors of the Speranza and Blanche telegrams and their accomplices of forgery and fraud. (*v.* 28 Jan 1898)

Jan 6 Trarieux, worried that Esterhazy's court martial may be held in closed session in order to facilitate his acquittal, writes an open letter to Billot in *Le Temps* in protest. He demands that Billot specify the reasons for Picquart's posting to Tunis, which he suspects was related to Picquart's investigation of Esterhazy. Trarieux draws attention to the fact that no attempt has been made to investigate the origin of the false telegrams sent to Picquart, nor to identify the authors of the *document libérateur* that Esterhazy claimed had been stolen from the Ministry of War.[4]

Devil's Island: Dreyfus asks the Governor of the îles du Salût to telegraph this appeal to President Faure: 'Having received no letters from those I love for two months, I am demented and write to you to declare again that I have never been, am not and never could be the culprit.'[5]

Jan 7 Returning to Paris from Berlin, Casella gives Panizzardi a letter from Schwartzkoppen. According to Casella, Panizzardi reads out loud from the letter: 'How will that scoundrel Esterhazy get himself out of this chaos? How will he be able to continue living in France even if he is acquitted?'[6] (*v.* 13 Jan 1898)

Fasquelle publishes Zola's 'Lettre à la France':

Every morning as I read in the newspapers what you seem to think of this lamentable Dreyfus Affair, my reason is increasingly

*appalled. And why? Can it be you, France, who has come to this, to
be convinced of the truth of the most obvious lies, allying yourself
with the rabble of criminals against a few honest men, losing your
head on the idiotic pretext that your army is insulted and that
there is a plot to sell you to the enemy, when on the contrary the
desire of your wisest and most loyal children is that you should
remain in the eyes of a vigilant Europe, the nation of honour, my
nation of humanity, of truth and justice?... I entreat you, France,
become the noble France again, get a grip on yourself, find your
way again...*[7]

Le Siècle publishes d'Ormescheville's report of 1894.[8]

c. Jan 8   Stock publishes Lazare's third pamphlet on the Dreyfus case,
'Comment on condamne un innocent' ('How to Condemn the
Innocent').[9] It contains his annotated version of d'Ormescheville's
report. Lazare's preface directly accuses Du Paty, 'who plotted this
abominable drama; who lied, who corrupted, who tortured'. It also
accuses General Staff officers of fabricating documents and evidence
to convict Dreyfus. Lazare writes: 'If this famous secret dossier
contains letters of Captain Dreyfus which establish his guilt... I accuse
Major Esterhazy of fabricating them and I accuse Colonel Du Paty de
Clam of having been his accomplice...'[10]

Jan 9   Esterhazy enters Cherche-Midi prison voluntarily.

First issue of the dreyfusard daily *Les droits de l'Homme*; the editor is
journalist Henri Deloncle.

The court martial of Esterhazy[11]

Jan 10–11 The court martial opens. General Charles de Luxer is President of the
Court of seven officers. The floor is largely filled by army officers.[12]
Esterhazy is represented by Tézenas; Mathieu and Lucie, who have
filed a civil suit in the matter,[13] by Maîtres Demange and Fernand Labori
respectively.[14] Demange's request to speak on behalf of Mathieu and
Lucie is unanimously rejected on the grounds that the case does not
concern Dreyfus, who was 'justly and legally convicted'. The Court
decides by five votes to two that the proceedings will be conducted
in public unless this jeopardizes national security. Consequently,
Esterhazy and all civilian witnesses except Leblois are to be heard
in public session. Military witnesses and the graphologists are to be
heard in closed session.[15] Ravary's report, the indictment of Esterhazy,
is read in court. (*v.* 31 Dec 1897)

Esterhazy recounts the story of '*la dame voilée*', whose identity he
claims to have sworn to protect. At several mysterious rendezvous he
had been informed by the lady about the plot mounted against him.
She also gave him the *document libérateur*, which, he affirms, he
returned to the Ministry of War. He refuses to reveal its contents. (*v.*
31 Oct 1897, The *document libérateur* and '*la dame voilée*') Esterhazy
protests his innocence, claiming that the *petit bleu* has been falsified

by Picquart. He agrees that the handwriting of the *bordereau* resembles his own but says it is the work of a forger. He denies writing the Uhlan letter, the most vitriolic of the Boulancy letters.[16] There are contradictions in his testimony but he is not questioned further and the public is favourably disposed towards him.

Mathieu's evidence aims to prove that Esterhazy wrote the *bordereau*. He is frequently interrupted, both by Esterhazy's lawyer and by bursts of laughter and catcalls from the body of the Court. Mathieu quotes from a letter to Weil from Esterhazy in June 1894 complaining that he can only prevent the fate which awaits his poor daughters by committing a crime.

Scheurer-Kestner, Stock and his son, Edouard Autant with his son Alexandre, Mlle Pays and Weil are called to testify.[17]

When Picquart is called to testify the session is pronounced closed. Picquart relates what he knows but Pellieux interrupts him when he mentions Billot, Boisdeffre and Mercier and contests their involvement. Luxer's constant interruptions of Picquart prompt one of the judges to remark that Picquart seems to be 'the real accused in this case' and requests that Picquart be allowed to explain fully. He completes his evidence.

On 11 January Picquart is astonished to learn during the proceedings that his subordinates Lauth, Gribelin and Henry, along with Gonse, have accused him of showing the Secret Dossier to Leblois.[18] Picquart and Leblois firmly deny the accusation and demand to be confronted with the appropriate witnesses. Picquart asks Henry to give the exact date on which he had allegedly seen him handing the Secret Dossier to Leblois. Picquart proves that Leblois was not in Paris on the date specified. Henry becomes confused.

Still in closed session, only one of the three graphologists, Belhomme, is heard. He confirms that the *bordereau* was not written by Esterhazy. Pellieux communicates to the Court the graphologists' report (*v*. 26 Dec 1897) concluding that both the *bordereau* and the Boulancy letters were probably the work of a forger imitating Esterhazy's writing.

Bertillon and Du Paty are heard, who, together with a number of officers, confirm the testimonies of Lauth and Henry against Picquart.

Government Commissioner Major Edmond Hervieu presents his conclusions. In a five-hour speech Tézenas makes his *requisitoire* (final speech). After three minutes' deliberation Luxer announces the Court's verdict: Esterhazy is unanimously acquitted.[19] Applause breaks out. Picquart and Mathieu are insulted and threatened as they leave. Esterhazy is acclaimed with shouts of 'Hats off to the martyr of the Jews!', 'Long live the Army!', 'Long live France!', 'Down with the Syndicate!' 'Death to the Jews!' A crowd of more than one thousand people waits for Esterhazy at Cherche-Midi prison as he returns for official release.

Jan 12   Devil's Island: Dreyfus addresses another appeal to President
                     Faure.[20]

                     Pellieux gives Esterhazy permission to publish the graphologists'
                     report on the Uhlan letter.[21] It concludes that it was not written by
                     him. Esterhazy writes to Pellieux of 'his profound gratitude'.[22]

                     The Nationalist press praises Esterhazy's acquittal. The headline in *La
                     Libre Parole* reads, 'A Masterstroke! Long live the Army! Down with
                     the Jews'. *L'Intransigeant* announces 'The Downfall of the Syndicate
                     of Treason'.

The arrest of Picquart

Jan 13   On Billot's orders Picquart is arrested and sent to Mont-Valérien
                     prison.[23] In an official statement Billot confirms that Picquart is to
                     remain under arrest until a board of military inquiry decides on what
                     grounds he can be dismissed. (*v.* 3 Dec 1897)

'J'Accuse'

                     L'Aurore publishes 'J'Accuse', Zola's open letter to President Faure, in
                     a special edition of 300,000 copies.[24] The letter details the whole range
                     of dreyfusard allegations of errors, aberrations, crimes, irregularities
                     and conspiracies committed in the Affair from 1894 up to Esterhazy's
                     recent acquittal.[25] The letter ends:

                     > *When the truth is buried underground, it builds up there, it gains
                     > the force of an explosion such that on the day it erupts, it blows
                     > everything up with it. We will see if we have not just prepared for
                     > later on the most resounding disaster...*

                     > *...But this is a long letter, Mr President, and it is time to
                     > conclude.*

                     > *I accuse Lieutenant-Colonel Du Paty de Clam of having been the
                     > devilish craftsman of this miscarriage of justice – unwittingly,
                     > I want to believe – and of then having defended his nefarious
                     > work for three years, with the most preposterous and culpable
                     > machinations.*

                     > *I accuse General Mercier of having been complicit, at the very
                     > least out of mental weakness, in one of the greatest iniquities of
                     > the century.*

                     > *I accuse General Billot of having had in his own hands absolute
                     > proof of the innocence of Dreyfus and of having concealed it; and
                     > of rendering himself guilty of this crime against humanity and
                     > justice, for political ends and to save the General Staff which was
                     > compromised.*

                     > *I accuse General de Boisdeffre and General Gonse of complicity in
                     > the same crime, the former, no doubt, out of clerical passion, the
                     > latter perhaps out of that sense of solidarity that has made the War
                     > Office an unassailable holy ark.*

I accuse General de Pellieux and Major Ravary of having conducted a villainous inquiry, by which I mean an enquiry of the most monstrous partiality, as seen in the report of Ravary that is a permanent monument to naïve audacity. I accuse the three handwriting experts, Mr Belhomme, Mr Varinard and Mr Couard, of having written dishonest and fraudulent reports, unless a medical examination should show them to be suffering from impaired eyesight and judgement. I accuse the War Office of having carried out an abominable press campaign, especially in L'Éclair *and* L'Écho de Paris, *to mislead public opinion and conceal their own wrongs.*

Finally, I accuse the first court martial of having contravened the law by convicting the accused on the basis of a document which remained secret, and I accuse the second court martial of having, on orders, concealed this illegality, and in its turn committing the judicial crime of knowingly acquitting a guilty party.

In making these accusations, I am not unaware that I render myself liable to articles 30 and 31 of the law of July 29 1881 on the press, which makes libel a punishable offence. I run that risk voluntarily. As for the people I am accusing, I do not know them, I have never seen them, I feel no resentment or hatred against them. For me they are merely entities, spirits of social malfeasance. The action I am taking here is simply a revolutionary way of hastening the explosion of truth and justice I have only one passion, that of enlightenment, in the name of humanity which has suffered so much and has a right to happiness. My impassioned protest is only the cry of my soul. Let them dare, then, to summon me before an assize court and may the investigation take place in the full light of day!

I am waiting.

Be assured, Mr President, of my deepest respect.[26]

The publication of 'J'Accuse' comes as a thunderbolt to all – to the General Staff, who think that with Esterhazy's acquittal they have successfully put an end to the Affair; to the Government, who are uncertain how to react to this direct accusation; to dreyfusards and anti-dreyfusards, whose opposing views are now crystallized; to all those ready to launch campaigns for justice, human rights and Republican principles; to Nationalist and antisemitic groups who are to stir up the whole of France in the coming months. What until then had been known as the 'Dreyfus question', the 'Dreyfus case' or the 'Dreyfus Affair' becomes from that moment simply 'the Affair'. 'J'Accuse' draws international attention to France and to the Affair, catapulting it into the political sphere. For many, Zola is now to become one of the great leaders of the valiant fight for justice and truth. He will receive some 30,000 telegrams and letters from around the world congratulating him on his heroic act. For others, he is a target of violent criticism, popular hatred and vehement denunciation.[27]

Lettre à M. Félix Faure
[Président de la République]

Monsieur le Président,

Me permettez-vous, dans ma gratitude pour le bienveillant accueil que vous m'avez fait un jour, d'avoir le soin de votre juste gloire et de vous dire que votre étoile, si heureuse jusqu'ici, est menacée de la plus honteuse, de la plus ineffaçable des taches?

Vous êtes sorti sain et sauf des basses calomnies, vous avez conquis les cœurs. ~~Vous apparaissez rayonnant~~ dans l'apothéose de cette ~~grande~~ fête patriotique que l'alliance russe a été pour la France et vous vous préparez à présider au solennel triomphe de notre Exposition

'J Accuse', facsimile of the manuscript

'J Accuse', as published in *L'Aurore*

Deputy de Mun questions Billot in the Chamber on the measures he intends to take following the publication of 'J'Accuse'. Cavaignac declares that the Government has 'contemporary evidence' of the confession of Dreyfus and calls on Prime Minister Méline to disclose it.[28] Méline does not deny the existence of this evidence. He refuses to disclose it because it will distract the Government from the pressing issue, how to reprimand Zola.[29] The Socialist Jean Jaurès warns that the Government is handing the Republic over to the generals. Both Méline and Billot declare that legal action will be taken against Zola. (*v.* 18 Jan 1898) The Chamber passes a vote of confidence in the Government by 312 to 122, but with 100 abstentions.

Scheurer-Kestner fails to be re-elected as Vice-President of the Senate.

Casella claims that during a visit to Panizzardi he finds him writing to Schwartzkoppen suggesting that Schwartzkoppen should speak out about his relationship with Esterhazy. Panizzardi apparently added: 'My God... so many victims... Yesterday Dreyfus, today Picquart, tomorrow Zola. How monstrous!' Regarding Zola's article in *L'Aurore* ('J'Accuse'), he says: 'Zola speaks the truth.'[30]

Jan 14   Lucie Dreyfus makes public a letter she wrote to Cavaignac protesting against his statement concerning contemporary evidence relating to the confession. (*v.* 13 Jan 1898) She quotes Dreyfus' letter to Mercier, written after Du Paty's visit to his cell.).[31] (*v.* 31 Dec 1894; 15 Jan 1898)

Jules Andrade, Professor at Rennes University, writes to Mercier explaining the need for a revision of Dreyfus' verdict. (*v.* 21 Jan 1898, Antisemitic riots)

The petition of the intellectuals

Jan 14–15   A first petition for a revision is launched by Zola and Emile Duclaux, Director of the Pasteur Institute. The signatories protest against 'the violation of legal norms in the 1894 trial and the improprieties surrounding the Esterhazy affair'.

A second signed petition to the Chamber of Deputies requests 'the preservation of legal guarantees for ordinary citizens'. The signatories are mostly scholars from the Institute as well as the Sorbonne plus writers and artists.[32] In *L'Aurore* Georges Clemenceau begins to publish the names of the signatories under the title of the 'Manifesto of the Intellectuals'.[33]

Jan 15   Cavaignac replies to Lucie that she is wrong to contest the existence of Lebrun-Renault's statement on the confession of Dreyfus. Cavaignac confirms that Billot possesses written evidence contemporaneous with the degradation attesting this statement.[34] The letter is published in *La Libre Parole* and *L'Intransigeant* on 16 and 17 January respectively.

General Emile Zurlinden replaces Saussier as Military Governor of Paris.

Tornielli writes to Hanotaux stating again that Panizzardi had no direct or indirect dealings with Dreyfus. He also states that Panizzardi's alleged letter to Schwartzkoppen mentioning Dreyfus by name or abbreviation (*Ce canaille de D.*) is a forgery. Tornielli again proposes that Panizzardi should testify under oath. (*v.* 28 Nov 1897 and 28 Jan 1898)

Jan 16   Devil's Island: Dreyfus addresses another appeal to President Faure:

> *I renew the supreme appeal I address to the Head of State, to the Government and to the Minister of War, finally to demand my honour and justice at last, if it is not the wish that an innocent man, at the end of his strength, should succumb to such torture every hour and every minute, with the appalling sorrow of leaving behind him his dishonoured children.*[35]

Lucie writes again to Cavaignac, pleading with him to clarify whether the 'evidence' he quotes is written by Lebrun-Renault who has told both Forzinetti and *Le Figaro* journalist Clisson that Dreyfus had not made any confession to him.[36]

L'Aurore publishes Forzinetti's statement that he was told by Lebrun-Renault that Dreyfus had never confessed to him. (*v.* end June 1897)

Le Siècle publishes Clisson's statement that Lebrun-Renault never told him that Dreyfus had confessed.

Jan 17   The Government issues an official statement confirming the validity of the Dreyfus verdict (*la chose jugée*). In the Chamber of Deputies Méline accuses the supporters of Dreyfus 'of reopening a new Boulangist uprising'. The Chamber passes a vote of confidence in the Government by 310 to 252.

Antisemitic riots (mid January–mid February)

A wave of antisemitic demonstrations – about 70 in three weeks – breaks out in 55 locations across France.[37] They vary from small groups shouting 'Death to Dreyfus!', 'Death to Zola!', 'Death to the Jews!', to full-scale riots lasting several days, in which Jewish shops and private homes are attacked, synagogues besieged and Jews physically assaulted. The police are called in to protect Jewish districts and there are many arrests. The demonstrations are largely instigated by political or semi-political groups, Catholic and Royalist organizations and Guérin's Ligue antisémitique. (*v.* Feb 1897) They are often supported by the local press and represent a new dimension of antisemitism, calling for the boycott of department stores and Jewish businesses by the means of posters, stickers, press articles and other forms of propaganda.[38]

Jan 17   In Paris, Drumont, Rochefort and Guérin gather some 4000 people at the Tivoli-Vauxhall to protest against the 'offenders against the army', and the 'Jewish Syndicate'. Scuffles occur between the supporters of these antisemitic demonstrators and anarchist groups.

Jan 21   In Rennes, 2000 people led by three Christian preachers attack the homes of Jules Andrade (*v.* 14 Jan 1898) and the Jewish Professor Victor Basch for their support of Zola and Dreyfus.

Jan 23–25 In several towns effigies of Dreyfus and Zola are publicly burned (Alais, 23 January; Saint-Malo, 25 January).

Jan 18–25 Violent antisemitic riots break out in Algeria.[39] In Algiers, Oran and Constantine, and in smaller towns, hundreds of Jewish shops are ransacked and pillaged. Zola's effigy is burned. Jews are physically assaulted. Many Jews and several policemen are seriously hurt. Some 500 arrests are made; one of the rioters, Cayrol, is killed. During his funeral service Jews are stoned and one is murdered. On 22 January the principal agitator, Max Régis, whose popularity is ever-increasing, exhorts a crowd of 6000 to 'water the tree of liberty with Jewish blood'.[40] (*v.* 20 Feb 1898)

Jan 18   The Cabinet deliberates on the form of legal action to be taken against Zola and Alexandre Perrenx, manager of *L'Aurore*. It decides that Billot is to file the suit *ad personam*. Billot cites only three passages (15 lines in total) from Zola's lengthy letter which contain the accusation that Esterhazy was acquitted 'by order' despite knowledge of his guilt. Perrenx is charged with libel for publishing these passages, Zola with complicity.[41] (*v.* Appendix 21)

A 'Manifesto on the Dreyfus Affair is signed by 32 Socialist Deputies, including René Viviani, Jules Guesde, Jean Jaurès and Alexandre Millerand. They declare their impartiality in regard to the Affair because 'Dreyfus belongs to the capitalist class, to the enemy class… The Dreyfus Affair has become the battlefield of two rival factions of the bourgeoisie – the opportunists and the supporters of the Church.'[42]

Jan 19   On Reinach's advice Lucie releases Dreyfus' letters from Devil's Island to the newspapers. *Le Siècle* begins their serialization as *Letters of an Innocent*.[43]

Jan 21   The three graphologists accused by Zola (Belhomme, Varinard and Couard) institute proceedings against him for libel. (*v.* 6 & 9 July & 10 Aug 1898)

Jan 22   A rowdy session takes place in the Chamber of Deputies. In an attempt to overthrow Méline, Cavaignac again presses the Government to publish the documents in its possession that prove Dreyfus had confessed.[44] Realizing the danger of losing the Government's confidence, Méline resorts to lying. He states that he did receive Lebrun-Renault's report on the evening of Dreyfus' degradation, reaffirming that Dreyfus had confessed, but he refuses to publish it. Méline is applauded. Cavaignac withdraws his demand but Jaurès intervenes, bitterly accusing the Government of 'half-measures, reticence, equivocations, lies and cowardice'. The right-wing Comte de Bernis calls Jaurès a member of the 'Syndicate'. Jaurès retaliates that Bernis is 'a miserable coward'. Bernis mounts the tribune, is hit by a Socialist Deputy and in turn strikes Jaurès on the head.

Jaurès stumbled down, then, picking himself up, throws a knotted handkerchief at Bernis. A Socialist Deputy, throws an inkstand at Bernis, but misses his aim. Loud altercation and disorder breaks out. The ushers and the military guard clears the Chamber. (*v.* Appendix 22)

Jan 23   Gaston Paris, philologist and administrator at the Collège de France,[45] writes to Hanotaux on behalf of the dreyfusards, whom he labels '*la France intellectuelle*'. He accuses Hanotaux of solidarity with the Government over the Affair and of betraying his academic past; as a former professor he should be responsive to arguments of justice, reason and truth:

> *We are living in a continuous nightmare, each day bringing new errors and new dangers... for all the people of France bear responsibility for the iniquity committed... The facts, moreover, are so obvious that one would have to be blind or close one's eyes not to see them... The only solution that should be desired by both partisans and adversaries of the first verdict is a revision, and a revision in the full light of day!*[46]

Jan 24   In the next session Jaurès continues to question Méline:

> *Yes or no, were the judges of the first court martial in possession of the secret documents without their having been communicated to the accused? Yes or no, were the legal guarantees, the common heritage all citizens must defend, respected or violated, even for the benefit of a Jew...*[47] *Why do you systematically take refuge behind a hearing in closed session?... What do you fear except to acknowledge that the General Staff itself formed doubts about the culpability of one and the innocence of the other?... The Government does not wish to take the place of the justice of the country.*[48]

Méline refuses to reply, merely declaring: 'All the Republicans are with us.' The Chamber passes a vote of confidence in the Government by 375 to 133.

Official denials by Germany and Italy

Count von Bülow, German Secretary of State, declares in the Reichstag, the German Chamber of Deputies:

> *I restrict myself to stating categorically that there have never been any relations or contacts of any description between the French former Captain Dreyfus, who is now on Devil's Island, and any German institution. The names Walsin Esterhazy and Picquart I heard for the first time in my life three weeks ago.*[49] *The story of a mysterious spy's letter supposedly found in a wastepaper basket is of course only imaginary and in reality never occurred.*[50] (*v.* 29 Jan 1898)

Jan 28   In response to Picquart's formal complaint (*v.* 4 Jan 1898), Billot asks examining magistrate Paul Bertulus to open an investigation into the Speranza and Blanche telegrams.[51] (*v.* 12 July 1898)

Hanotaux tells Tornielli that the French Government refuses to receive an official testimony from Panizzardi. (*v.* 15 Jan 1898) Such a testimony would deny dealings with Dreyfus and the authenticity of a Panizzardi letter to Schwartzkoppen allegedly referring to Dreyfus (*Ce canaille de D.*).[52]

Jan 29   The Kaiser repeats to the Marquis de Noailles, French Ambassador in Berlin, von Bülow's statement of 24 January 1898. Von Münster communicates the statement orally to Hanotaux.

Panizzardi writes to Schwartzkoppen explaining that when the 'Syndicate' learnt about Esterhazy the Ministry of War protected him and determined to acquit him in order to avoid a reopening of the Dreyfus trial – 'all this is horrible, but true'. When Picquart had learnt of this he informed the 'Syndicate', which is how 'all Paris now knows what you imagined you alone knew'. Tornielli learnt from Scheurer-Kestner and Reinach that the 'Syndicate' even has the list of documents Esterhazy supplied to Schwartzkoppen and proofs of the sums of money Esterhazy had collected for them; that the only reason this has not been announced publicly is to protect Picquart, who is about to be investigated for his indiscretions. (*v.* 1 Feb 1898) Panizzardi mentions he is in receipt of threatening anonymous letters urging him to reveal all he knows about the Affair.[53]

Feb 1   Count Longare Bonin, the Italian Under-Secretary of State for Foreign Affairs, makes an official declaration in the Italian Chamber of Deputies: 'We can affirm in the most explicit fashion that neither our military attaché, nor any other agent or representative of the Italian Government has ever had any relations, direct or indirect, with the former Captain Dreyfus.'[54]

In Mont Valérien prison, Picquart appears before a military board of inquiry.[55] General Gaston de Galliffet,[56] Leblois, Lauth, Junck, Griblin, Henry, and Gonse are called as witnesses. Picquart is accused of disclosing secret documents and Gonse's letters to Leblois. He refutes the allegations. Leblois also rebuts them. Picquart's request to be confronted with his accusers is refused. Only Galliffet protests at the accusations against Picquart. The Court rules by a majority of four to one that Picquart is to be cashiered 'for serious irregularities while on service'.[57] Instead of being released, Picquart is retained in Mont-Valérien. Billot postpones the decision whether to accept the board's conclusion until after Zola's trial.[58] (*v.* 26 Feb 1898)

Devil's Island: Dreyfus appeals again to President Faure:

I renew, with all the strength of my being, the appeal that I have already made to the Head of State, to the Government, to the Minister of War. I am not guilty. I could not be.[59]

Feb 2   Second audience (the first was held on January 25) of the trial of Rochefort, following Reinach's suit against him. (*v.* 31 Dec 1897) Rochefort admits having paid a forger to fake the *faux Otto*. The public applauds Rochefort and boos Reinach. There are shouts on the street outside, 'Death to the Jews!' 'Down with the traitors!' 'Down with Reinach!' (*v.* 9 Feb 1898)

Feb 5   The antisemitic artists Jean-Louis Forain[60] and Caran d'Ache[61] establish
                 the satirical anti-dreyfusard journal *Psst...!* A few days later, Henri-
                 Gabriel Ibels, a personal friend of Zola, founds the rival *Le Sifflet.*[62]

Feb 6   *La Libre Parole* publishes a vicious article 'Aux Français' ('[Appeal]
                 to the French'), signed by Drumont and Guérin. It denounces the
                 'outrageous pressures of foreign Jews' and threatens the jury at Zola's
                 trial: 'The honest and patriotic population of Paris would not tolerate
                 such provocations. IT WILL ESTABLISH ITS OWN POLICE [*sic*]. France will
                 never be subjected to the outrageous pressures of foreign Jews...'
                 The article is also published in *L'Intransigeant* on 7 February.

The trial of Zola (7–23 February)[63]

The trial opens before the Assize Court of the Seine (Palais de Justice,
Paris). Albert Delegorgue is Presiding Judge for the trial, Edmond
Van Cassel Counsel for the Prosecution. The 12 civilian jurors are
mostly small tradesmen.[64] Maître Fernand Labori defends Zola;
Albert Clemenceau, Georges Clemenceau's brother, defends Perrenx.
Although not a witness, Georges Clemenceau, editor of *L'Aurore*,
is authorized to appear for *L'Aurore*. A group of advisers to Zola
include Trarieux, Leblois, Reinach, Blum, and Mathieu Dreyfus.[65] The
defence seeks to raise all the accusations made in 'J'Accuse' and
so take advantage of the trial to prove the innocence of Dreyfus.
Their list of about 200 witnesses includes Mercier, Billot, officers of
the General Staff and the Deuxième Bureau, Cabinet Ministers of
1894, former President Casimir-Périer, Scheurer-Kestner, Esterhazy's
judges, Esterhazy himself, Picquart, Leblois, Demange, Lebrun-
Renault, Forzinetti, Panizzardi and Schwartzkoppen, as well as other
politicians, many journalists, intellectuals and foreign diplomats.[66]
Most of the military witnesses, including Boisdeffre, Lebrun-Renault,
Du Paty, Casimir-Périer, Mme Boulancy and judges from Dreyfus'
court martial decline their summons to appear. Their letters of excuse
are read in court. Sickness is one of the main reasons given. Some
mention that they knew 'too many details' about the Affair, others that
they know nothing. Billot objects to the appearance of military witnesses
other than those related to the Esterhazy case, which he cites as Gribelin,
Lauth, Gonse and Pellieux. The Court rules that the military witnesses
are to be called. Billot instructs Boisdeffre to order the officers to remain
silent. Esterhazy and Henry are compelled to appear.

The courtroom is crowded with excited journalists, lawyers, uniformed
officers and high-society ladies. For the following two weeks newspapers
publish detailed, daily accounts of the progress of the trial, each one
presenting the facts selectively and according to its own viewpoint.
The 'Zola–Dreyfus Affair' becomes a main subject of conversation in
society and the cause of heated discussion and controversy between
families, friends and colleagues throughout France and abroad. Outside
the Palais de Justice Guérin directs his antisemitic gangs.

Feb 7   **The Trial, Day 1:** Van Cassel demands that in order to avoid questions
                 relating to the Dreyfus verdict only the single charge brought against

GÉNÉRAL GONSE   COMMANDANT RAVARY   BERTILLON

COMMANDANT LAUTH   TRARIEUX   MAITRE LEBLOIS

L'ARCHIVISTE GRIBELIN   L'EXPERT TEYSSONNIÈRES   GÉNÉRAL DE PELLIEUX

L'AFFAIRE ZOLA

Witnesses at the Zola trial

Zola by Billot (*v.* 18 Jan 1898) should be considered. Labori and Clemenceau protest but the court accepts Van Cassel's request. Directing proceedings is therefore an impossible task for Delegorgue, who has to permit questions about Esterhazy's guilt while disallowing those concerning the innocence of Dreyfus.

As the first session ends, fights break out in the galleries. Zola is jeered at and can hardly force his way through the angry crowd. He has to be protected by friends and the police. Outside the Palais de Justice, Guérin's men insult and assault dreyfusards, shouting 'Death to the Jews!', 'Death to the traitors!' During the evening, windows of Jewish-owned shops are smashed. The demonstrations continue throughout Zola's trial.[67]

Feb 8   **The Trial, Day 2**: Labori calls the first witness, Lucie Dreyfus. He asks her to tell the Court to comment on the good faith of Zola. Delegorgue interrupts, asking what connection this has with the case. Zola intervenes, exclaiming: 'I demand to have here the freedom accorded to killers and thieves. They can defend themselves, have witnesses summoned and ask them questions.'[68] Despite his fervent protest, which precipitates the first of many noisy incidents in the courtroom, Delegorgue concludes: '*La question ne sera pas posée*' ('The question will not be raised'), a phrase that is to resonate around the courtroom throughout the trial. This means that Lucie is not to be heard on the grounds that she has 'no connection' with the case. Next to be called is Leblois who recounts the matter of the false telegrams sent to Picquart. He is followed by Scheurer-Kestner, who wishes to read out one of Gonse's letters to Picquart but is not allowed to do so by the Court.[69] Casimir-Périer, former President of the Republic, states that he comes to testify out of respect for the Court, as a simple citizen. He is applauded by revisionists. But he further declares that he can not say 'the whole truth' invoking 'the constitutional principle of non-responsibility' and the silence imposed on him about events that took place while he was president. (*v.* Appendix 21)

Feb 9   **The Trial, Day 3:** Boisdeffre maintains that Picquart's conduct in accusing Esterhazy without revealing serious evidence against him is reprehensible. Boisdeffre confirms that he does not know the identity of '*la dame voilée*', but refuses to speak about the *document libérateur* as it refers to the Dreyfus case. He is allowed to say that facts emerging after the court martial of Dreyfus confirm his guilt. Gonse repeats the statement of his superior officer. Labori questions Mercier. He erroneously describes *Ce canaille de D.* as containing that phrase as a postscript, whereas it appeared in the middle of the text. (*v.* 16 Apr 1894) Mercier seizes the opportunity to confirm that he has no knowledge of such a document. Mercier refuses to answer any of Labori's questions concerning Dreyfus' court martial. He concludes by reaffirming that Dreyfus was 'a traitor who was legally and justly convicted'.

Feb 10   **The Trial, Day 4:** The four members of the Court and d'Ormescheville, reporting judge at the court martial of Dreyfus, are called to testify.

Delegorgue rejects their evidence. Du Paty refuses to answer most of the questions. Henry staggers to the witness box, with a medical certificate to confirm his heavy cold. Questioned about the Secret Dossier, he says that he received it from Sandherr but was absent when it was removed by Picquart. He refuses to disclose its contents. Confronted with Leblois regarding his [Henry's] accusation that Picquart had consulted him [Leblois], Henry becomes confused and contradicts himself. Gonse comes to Henry's rescue and requests that he be allowed to stand down because he is seriously ill. Pellieux insists that Esterhazy is innocent and that those who judged him did so honestly and honourably. The defence calls Maître Emile Salles, who informed Demange in 1896 that he had heard about the secret transmission of documents at the court martial of Dreyfus. (*v.* 29 Oct 1896) Delegorgue refuses to hear the witness on the grounds that he has nothing to contribute to the Esterhazy case.

Feb 11   **The Trial, Day 5:** Picquart recounts his discovery of the *petit bleu* and his surprise at not finding any reliable evidence against Dreyfus in the Secret Dossier of 1894. Questioned by Labori, he confirms that no one ever claimed that Esterhazy could not be the *bordereau*'s author. Nor was he instructed to stop the investigation of him. Picquart claims that Esterhazy was being protected by the Ministry of War and adds that Ravary refused to find out who they were. Finally, Picquart declares that Pellieux showed him the *document libérateur*, which he [Picquart] describes as merely a copy of *Ce canaille de D.*, the document he was accused of showing to Leblois. These revelations anger Lauth, Gribelin, Pellieux and Ravary, who all confront him with a torrent of accusations.[70] Pellieux insinuates that Zola is disloyal to France. Furious, Zola intervenes: 'France… can be served by both the sword and the pen. General de Pellieux has doubtless won some great victories! I have won my own. Through my works, the French language has been taken to the entire world. I have my victories! I bequeath to posterity the names of General de Pellieux and Emile Zola: it will choose!' When Ravary remarks that 'Military justice does not resemble civil justice', Albert Clémenceau retorts: 'There is but one justice, the true one.'[71]

Feb 12   **The Trial, Day 6:** Picquart is confronted by Henry on the subject of the Secret Dossier. Henry repeats that he had seen the file on the desk in Picquart's office when Leblois and Picquart were in consultation there some time in November 1896. Picquart replies that Leblois was not in Paris at the time. Under cross-examination Henry says that he could even recognize the document *Ce canaille de D.* sticking out of the dossier. Picquart protests that this was impossible at a distance, but Henry insists. Picquart formally challenges Henry's statement. Henry continues to insist, adding emphatically, 'Colonel Picquart has lied.' At this insult Picquart raises his hand to strike Henry.[72] Picquart exclaims in an outburst of anger that he has been disgraced by his colleagues. They are the ones responsible for the whole business and now seek to conceal their mistakes:

> *Tomorrow, perhaps, I will be dismissed from the army that I love, to which I have devoted 25 years of my life! But that did not stop*

*me when I thought that I should seek truth and justice. I did so,
and in so doing believed I rendered a greater service to my country
and to the army. I believed that is how I should do my duty as an
honest man.*[73]

Gonse denies that Picquart has been disgraced. On the contrary, he
was sent on important missions. Labori proceeds to question Henry
further about the Secret Dossier. He succeeds in blurring the issue
with endless details, including the fact that Sandherr had another ultra
secret dossier that contained a letter damaging to Dreyfus (an allusion
to the *bordereau annoté*).[74] Jaurès gives his testimony.[75] Without
advancing new evidence for Zola's defence he emphasizes the
'mysteries' and 'scandals' and especially the irregularities at the courts
martial of Dreyfus and Esterhazy. Jaurès states that at least 40 Deputies
believe the court martial of Dreyfus was illegal and that there would
have been further protests if the elections had not been imminent.
Demange states he is certain that proceedings at that court martial
were illegal. Albert Clemenceau asks pointedly whether the illegality
was the result of a secret document being shown to the Court. Before
Delegorgue can stop him, Demange exclaims: 'Why yes, of course!'

Feb 12–17   **The Trial, Days 6–10:** Numerous experts, archivists and scholars (Paul
Meyer, Auguste and Emile Molinier, Louis Havet, Pierre-Séraphine
Célerier, Fernand Bournont, Louis Franck, Edouard Grimaux,[76]
Paul Moriaud and Arthur Giry) confirm that the handwriting of the
bordereau and that of Esterhazy's letters is identical. Bertillon repeats
his quasi-scientific, unintelligible demonstration of why the *bordereau*
must have been the work of Dreyfus. This provokes laughter in
the courtroom. Furious at this outburst and unable to answer the
questions Labori directs at him, Bertillon retreats behind the verdict
of 1894 which 'forbids discussion of the case'. As Bertillon leaves the
witness stand, Labori exclaims sarcastically: 'Here is the accusation
of 1894. There is a single charge: the *bordereau*, and there is the
principal expert!'[77] Pellieux dismisses the graphologists' conclusions,
claiming that they were amateurs whose analyses were based merely
on a photograph of the original *bordereau*. He shifts the discussion
to its contents. Pellieux declares that Esterhazy could not have written
it because he was not party to the secret information it contained.
Dreyfus, on the other hand, knew it all. In response, Picquart affirms
that Esterhazy could have procured all the information referred to
in the document. The ensuing discussion brings to light a significant
conflict over the date of the *bordereau*. To Picquart's astonishment,
Gonse and Pellieux mention that it was not written in April but in
August 1894.[78] Gonse explains that the 'note on Madagascar' referred
to could not have been written before August. Labori seizes on this
important new information to question Gonse on how the report of
d'Ormescheville could have accused Dreyfus of procuring the 'note on
Madagascar' in February 1894, as the information on the expedition to
Madagascar was not available until August of that year. Gonse falters
but maintains his statement.[79] Fearing that the defence is gaining
ground, Pellieux asks to be heard again. In a dramatic speech he

declares that the Ministry of War possesses 'absolute proof of Dreyfus' guilt', which it obtained at the time of Castelin's interpellation in 1896. (*v.* 18 Nov 1896) Pellieux then quotes the *faux Henry* from memory: 'A Deputy is going to ask questions about Dreyfus. Never disclose we had any relations with the Jew…'[80] The defence immediately demands that the document be produced before the Court. Gonse confirms Pellieux's statement but refuses to produce the document. Pellieux demands that Boisdeffre be called as a witness. Delegorgue closes the session. (*v.* Appendix 21).

That evening demonstrations outside the courtroom are fierce. An attempt is made to seize Leblois, and one of Guérin's gangs threatens to throw him into the Seine.

Feb 18   **The Trial, Day 11**: Boisdeffre makes a brief but firm statement confirming that Pellieux's deposition is 'true and authentic' in all

General de Boisdeffre

respects. He concludes his testimony with a clear message to the jurors, which forces them to choose between the army and Dreyfus: 'You are the jury, you are the nation. If the nation does not have confidence in the leaders of its army... they are ready to leave this onerous task to others; you have only to speak. I will not say one more word.'[81] Boisdeffre's statement is applauded. Labori's request to cross-examine Boisdeffre is denied.

Picquart throws serious doubt on the authenticity of the document Pellieux referred to: '...because of the terms in which it was written, absolutely improbable terms... there are grounds to consider it a forgery'. He then continues: 'It is a forgery.'[82] Esterhazy is called to testify. Instructed by Pellieux, he is on the witness stand for 40 minutes, listening to the 60 questions prepared by Albert Clemenceau, concerning his life, career, his letters to Mme Boulancy , and the *bordereau*. He answers none of them. (*v.* Appendix 21) Esterhazy receives a standing ovation from the officers.[83] That evening, outside the courtroom, Guérin's supporters carry him jubilantly on their shoulders.

Feb 19　　**The Trial, Day 12:** Stock recounts the episode concerning Esterhazy's letters to Autant regarding the lease to his appartment. (*v.* 30 Nov 1897, n. 113) Questioned by Labori, Stock asserts that he is absolutely certain about Zola's 'good faith'. When he mentions that he can simply enumerate the secret documents passed to the judges during the court martial of Dreyfus, he is interrupted by Delegorgue: 'No, this is unnecessary; we do not have the right to talk about the Dreyfus Affair.'[84]

Feb 21　　**The Trial, Day 13:** After Van Cassel's closing speech Zola reads aloud the script he has prepared. There are continuous insults and interruptions from the courtroom:[85]

> '...You are the heart and mind of Paris, of my great Paris, where I was born, that I love with infinite tenderness, that I have been studying and extolling for almost 40 years... Do me the honour of believing that I am not defending my own liberty here. In striking me, you would only enhance my stature. Whosoever suffers for truth and justice becomes noble and sacred. (Murmurs)... Dreyfus is innocent, I swear it. I pledge my life on it, I pledge my honour. In this solemn hour, before this tribunal which represents human justice, before you, gentlemen of the jury, who are the very incarnation of the country, before all of France, before the entire world, I swear that Dreyfus is innocent! And by my 40 years of work, by the authority which this labour may have given me, I swear that Dreyfus is innocent! And by all that I have achieved, by the reputation I have earned, by my works which have helped the expansion of French literature, I swear that Dreyfus is innocent. May all of that collapse, may my works perish if Dreyfus is not innocent! He is innocent!...* [86] (*v.* Appendix 21)

Feb 22–23　　**The Trial, Days 14 & 15:** Labori makes his closing speech.[87] He recounts the Affair at length, destroys the myth of the alleged confession, describes the document quoted by Pellieux as a forgery and reads from Dreyfus' letters to his wife. He ends by addressing the jurors: 'May your verdict signify several things: first, 'Long live the Army!'... but also 'Long live the Republic!' and 'Long live France!', that is, 'Long live justice! Long live the eternal ideal!'[88] (*v.* Appendix 21) There is applause and shouts of indignation as the officers in the courtroom bang their scabbards on the floor.[89]

Georges Clemenceau presents his closing speech. Frequently interrupted by Delegorgue and by increasing protests from the courtroom, he defends at length the principles of civil as opposed to military society. In conclusion, he confronts the jurors directly with their civil duty: 'It is up to you, gentlemen, to give your verdict, less upon us than upon yourselves. We appear before you. You appear before yourselves. You appear before history.'[90] (*v.* Appendix 21)

Van Cassel takes advantage of his right to reply. He reminds the jury that it should consider only one question in coming to its verdict: had Esterhazy been acquitted 'on order'. (*v.* 18 Jan 1898, n.156) Van Cassel concludes: 'France is sure of you, gentlemen of the jury! Be guided by the soul of the nation.'[91] His speech is acclaimed with shouts of 'Bravo!!', '*Vive l'Armée!* and much applause. Labori in his final statement reminds the jury that it is about to give a historic verdict: 'If you have the courage, pronounce that this man [Zola] is guilty of having fought against all passions, against all hatred, against all anger, for the cause of justice, right and liberty!'[92] Violent altercations break out in the courtroom. One of the officers, Captain Niessel, threatens anyone who applauds Labori.

Conviction of Zola

Feb 23   The jurors withdraw to deliberate. After 40 minutes the verdict is read: Zola is found guilty by a majority vote of 8 to 4. The Court sentences him to one year's imprisonment and a fine of 3000 francs, the maximum sentence for libel. Perrenx is sentenced to the same fine and four months in prison. The verdict is greeted with shouts of elation, spreading from the courtroom to the galleries and the streets around: 'Long live the Army!', 'Down with Zola!', 'Death to the Jews!' During the night and on the following day there are demonstrations in several cities (Dieppe, Béziers, Veynes) in support of Esterhazy and the army and against Zola, Dreyfus and the 'Syndicate'.[93] (*v.* Appendix 23)

Feb 8   The Government takes measures against dreyfusard activists. Professor Andrade is suspended from Rennes University (*v.* 14 Jan 1898); the correspondent of the pro-Dreyfus Swiss journal *Basler Nachrichten* is expelled from France by order of Barthou, Minister of the Interior.

Feb 9   The Chambre correctionnelle du tribunal de la Seine (the Criminal Division of the tribunal of the Seine) sentences Rochefort to five days' imprisonment and a 2000-franc fine for libel against Reinach whom he accused of fabricating the *faux Otto*.[94] (*v.* 25 Nov & 25 Dec 1897)

Feb 14 Colonel Guérin sends Saussier a long report on the degradation ceremony of Dreyfus. In it he relates the alleged confession of Dreyfus to Lebrun-Renault. [95] (*v.* 5 Jan 1898, n. 10)

Feb 15 At a public meeting in Suresnes organized by Nationalist Deputies, Lucien Millevoye refers to and pretends to quote from an alleged 'secret document' that he claims is in the possession of the General Staff. He is referring to the fictitious *bordereau annoté*.[96] (*v.* 12 Dec 1897)

Picquart is authorized to give evidence before Bertulus, who is investigating the Speranza and Blanche telegrams.[97] (*v.* 28 Jan 1898)

Protest against Pellieux's statement regarding the *faux Henry*

Feb 18 Tornielli writes to Rome expressing his indignation about Pellieux's statement at Zola's trial: 'The fact is serious. After the Government's declaration to the Italian Chamber, any new declarations on my part would be an insult, both to the dignity of the royal representative and to my own personal dignity.'[98]

Hanotaux reiterates in a Cabinet meeting that Tornielli had notified him that the document Pellieux read at Zola's trial is a forgery. (*v.* 15 & 28 Jan 1898) Billot protests and affirms its authenticity. Hanotaux insists and puts his statement in writing.

Ligue des droits de l'homme et du citoyen

Feb 20 Trarieux describes to a group of intellectuals, mainly professors at prestigious academic institutions his proposed foundation of the Ligue des droits de l'homme et du citoyen (League of the Rights of Man and the Citizen).[99] (*v.* 1 Apr 1898)

At a mass meeting of antisemites in the Salle Chayenes, Paris, Régis calls for the Crémieux Decree (*v.* 24 Oct 1870) to be repealed and for the 'mass expulsion of all the yids'. The crowd shouts 'Down with the Jews!', 'Put them on Devil's Island with Dreyfus!' Régis repeats his provocative words, 'We will water the tree of liberty with Jewish blood.'[100] (*v.* 21 Mar 1898)

Drumont demands that General Davoust, Duc d'Auerstaedt, Grand Chancellor of the Legion of Honour, expel Zola from the Legion. (*v.* 26 July 1898, Second conviction of Zola)

Feb 20 & 22 Monod writes to Hanotaux from Rome protesting against Pellieux's statement at Zola's trial:

How can the Government allow Pellieux to make such statements, ten times more dangerous than any of Zola's violence?... Among those who hold our fate in their hands, you are by far the most capable. You can save us from the abyss towards which we are heading.

Monod also conveys the indignation felt abroad against France:

The enormous error which is of concern to us in France is to believe that the passion evoked by foreigners to this affair is inspired by hostility towards France... The general question of justice and humanity dominates everything.[101]

Feb 22   In a letter to Schwartzkoppen, Panizzardi deplores Boisdeffre's statement at Zola's trial confirming the authenticity of the document mentioned by Pellieux. Panizzardi remarks that although no names were mentioned 'everybody knows that it is you and me who are concerned.' Panizzardi reiterates that 'something must be done', as 'at present, it is no longer a question of saving a man and getting the real culprit convicted but a question of protecting our honour and at the same time giving Boisdeffre a lesson... and letting the world know, especially the French, the extent to which this man is lying.' He also mentions that 'there is not a single man who believes Esterhazy is innocent' and states that it might have been better to 'admit everything from the beginning of the Affair'.[102]

Feb 24   The Chamber of Deputies debates measures to repress dreyfusard activities. Méline accuses the press, the Jews and the intellectuals for the disorder throughout the country in previous months. He declares that 'There is, at present, no Zola trial, no Esterhazy trial, no Dreyfus trial; there are no more trials...'[103] Méline announces he will apply the full weight of the law to those who 'continue the struggle'. The Chamber votes in favour of displaying Méline's speech publicly and approves the Government's statements by an overwhelming majority of 416 to 4. (*v.* Appendix 24)

Lucie appeals once more to Lebon for permission to join her husband on Devil's Island. Her request is again refused. (*v.* 24 March 1898)

Feb 25   Leblois is relieved of his functions as deputy mayor of the 7th arrondissement.[104] (*v.* 21 Mar 1898) Professor Grimaux is relieved of his post at the Ecole polytechnique as a result of his testimony at Zola's trial. (*v.* 12–17 Feb 1898, Zola's trial, n. 76)

The dismissal of Picquart from the army

Feb 26   Picquart is dismissed from the army for serious disciplinary offences and his pension is reduced. (*v.* 1 Feb 1898)

Zola and Perrenx lodge appeals before the Supreme Court of Appeal against their verdict. Zola engages lawyer Henry Mornard for the appeal. (*v.* 31 March–2 Apr 1898, Annulment of Zola's verdict; 8, 10 April, 23 May and 6 July–10 Aug 1898, Further proceedings against Zola)

Georges Clemenceau challenges Drumont to a duel over an article published in *La Libre Parole* which accuses him of cowardice during the Franco-Prussian War. Each fires three times, but neither is hurt.[105]

Feb 28   Devil's Island: Dreyfus writes to the Chamber of Deputies:

From the day after my conviction, that is already more than three years ago... I have declared not only that I was innocent, but that I demanded that light, full and shining light, be shed on the matter... I have waited for three years, in the most appalling situation that one can imagine, suffering constant blows without cause, and this research has come to nothing... Some months ago now, I appealed to the high sense of justice of the members of the Government, describing all the tragic and undeserved horror of this situation. I now also appeal to the equity of the deputies, seeking justice for my loved ones, the life of my children, and an end to this appalling martydom of so many human beings...[106]

Méline and Lebon intercept the appeal, which does not reach the Chamber.[107]

c. Feb   Through Rowland Strong, Paris correspondent of the *New York Times* and the London *Observer*, Esterhazy meets the writer Oscar Wilde, recently released from prison in England, where he was convicted for homosexuality.[108] Wilde tells Esterhazy that two of his and Panizzardi's friends, Fred C. Conybeare[109] and Carlos Blacker,[110] gave him details of Esterhazy's treason, his last visit to Schwartzkoppen (*v.* 23 Oct 1897) and papers relating to him held by the German General Staff.[111] Wilde reports his conversations to Strong, who remains in contact with Esterhazy. (*v.* 24 Aug & 1 Sept, 1898)

Mar 1   Billot tells former Foreign Secretary Jules Develle that he possesses a large file proving the treason of Dreyfus (the extended Secret Dossier). He states that he believes Esterhazy to be guilty.

Tornielli assures Trarieux that Dreyfus had no dealings with any German or Italian representatives and that it was Esterhazy who passed the documents listed in the *bordereau* to Germany.

Mar 2   Devil's Island: Dreyfus writes a letter to the Minister of War similar to the one he sent to the Chamber of Deputies. (*v.* 28 Feb 1898)

Mar 3   Lemercier-Picard is found hanging from a window of the Hôtel de la Manche in the rue de Sèvres, Paris. The circumstances of his death are unclear. Police doctors certify the cause of death as suicide.[112]

Mar 5   Picquart and Henry fight a duel with swords over the incident that arose during Zola's trial – Henry's accusation that Picquart had lied. (*v.* 12 Feb 1898) Henry is wounded in the right hand.[113]

Mar 10   Pellieux authorizes Esterhazy to initiate proceedings against Mathieu for his public denunciation. Esterhazy declares to the *Agence Nationale* that he renounces the issue 'for the moment'. But he will pursue the matter only if Matthieu makes further charges against him.

Mar 12   Devil's Island: Dreyfus appeals again to President Faure demanding a revision of his verdict. He recalls the previous appeals he has addressed (20 December 1897) to the President and to Boisdeffre. Although without a reply, he claims he has been informed that his appeal has been transferred to the Government. This leads him to believe that Boisdeffre is in favour of the revision.[114] (*v.* 4 July 1899, n. 133)

Mar 15   Bertulus dismisses the case against Mathieu and Léon Dreyfus for their alleged bribery of Sandherr in 1894. (*v.* 13 Dec 1894 & 29 Dec 1897)

Mar 16   In Algeria, Régis and Jewish Captain Lévy Oger fight a duel over insults published by Régis' newspaper *l'Antijuif.*

Mar 18 *Le Siècle* publishes Lucie's letter to Lebon (dated 24 Feb 1898), requesting authorization to join her husband.

Mar 21 Régis is arrested on a charge of incitement to murder. (*v.* 20 Feb 1898)

The Ordre des avocats in Paris (the Bar) suspends Leblois for six months for his alleged misconduct in disclosing documents to Scheurer-Kestner entrusted to him confidentially by his client Picquart.

Mar 24 *Le Petit Temps* publishes a legal analysis of the Government's rejection of Lucie's request to join her husband. Senator Léopold Thézard and Professor Leveillé, Professors of Law at Poitiers and Paris universities respectively, declare the Government's decision illegal.

The wives of certain eminent intellectuals address an appeal to French women, calling on them to support Lucie Dreyfus.[115]

Mar 27 In Algiers, a 200-strong crowd attacks and murders a Jewish worker, Shébat, when he takes a seat in a tram.

Mar Régis publishes in *L'Antijuif d'Alger* lists of women who frequent Jewish shops. The paper again appeals to readers to boycott Jewish shops and businesses. Some shops display signs with the words 'Anti-Jewish establishment' or 'Catholic establishment'. Several firms dismiss Jewish employees.[116]

The annulment of Zola's verdict

Mar 31 The Criminal Chamber of the Supreme Court of Appeal examines Zola's and Perrenx's appeal against their verdict.[117] In his closing speech, Jean-Pierre Manau, procureur général près de la cour de cassation (Principal State Prosecutor attached to the Supreme Court of Appeal) takes a clear stand in favour of a revision not only of Zola's case, but of Dreyfus' as well. He condemns the insults levelled at supporters of the revision, whom he describes as respectable people fighting indefatigably for the honour of France. Manau deplores the primarily antisemitic furore the Affair has created throughout the country and recognizes that it will not be silenced by a legal decision alone:

> We would be pleased if [the exclusively legal aspect] could dispel the irritating misunderstandings that have given this trial [the Zola trial], in itself very simple, proportions it should not have assumed. It has created deplorable divisions, even within families, forming two camps in the country and unleashing a torrent of abuse and violence which discredit our times.[118]

Apr 1 Trarieux and Paul Viollet, Catholic scholar at the Institut, draft the statutes of the League of the Rights of Man and the Citizen, which establishes it in law.[119] (*v.* 4 June 1898)

Apr 2 The Criminal Chamber of the Supreme Court of Appeal quashes the verdict of Zola and Perrenx on the technical grounds identified by

Zola's lawyer, Henri Mornard. The accusation against them should have been brought by the judges of Esterhazy's court martial, not by the Minister of War.[120] (*v.* 8 Apr 1898)

Apr 3   Von Münster sends a telegram to the Kaiser:

> *The Supreme Court of Appeal has declared the proceedings of the Zola trial illegal, they have dismissed the judgment as nul and void and decreed that Zola should not be subjected to another trial by jury. The verdict of the Supreme Court of Appeal was based on the fact that the Minister of War was not entitled to make an indictment in the name of the court martial. Consequently Zola is free unless a new indictment is made against him. That seems very unlikely. The Government's position is becoming difficult, and a Ministerial crisis is not impossible.*

Marginal note by the Kaiser: '*Bravo!*'[121]

Revelations in the press

Apr 4 & 8   *Le Siècle* publishes 'The Truth about Esterhazy', an article signed 'A diplomat from Berne'. It reveals in detail the dealings between Esterhazy and Schwartzkoppen.[122]

Apr 4   In a telegram to the German Foreign Office von Münster confirms that he was unaware of the relationships between Esterhazy and Schwartzkoppen.

Apr 7   *Le Siècle* publishes the statement Casella had intended to make at Zola's trial.[123] Based on his conversations with Panizzardi and Schwartzkoppen, Casella's statement includes the description of Esterhazy's last visit to Schwartzkoppen and Panizzardi's exclamation 'Zola speaks the truth.'[124] (*v.* 24 May 1898)

Apr 8   The judges of Esterhazy's court martial decide to file a further suit against Zola and Perrenx. They insist that Zola's name be struck off the Legion of Honour. (*v.* 26 July 1898, Second conviction of Zola)

Esterhazy's wife, the comtesse de Nettencourt, begins divorce proceedings.

Apr 9   Paul Déroulède, a Nationalist candidate in the forthcoming parliamentary elections, issues a manifesto which is distributed throughout French municipalities. It demands that no 'defender of the traitor' should be elected to the Chamber of Deputies and that all candidates sign a declaration undertaking to oppose any revision of Zola's trial.

Apr 10   The retrial of Zola and Perrenx is transferred to the Assize Court of Versailles. Zola is attacked near Médan by several individuals, including nine soldiers. (*v.* 23 May 1898)

Apr 12   Millevoye's paper *La Patrie* publishes an article based on an account in the *Berliner Tageblatt* claiming that Esterhazy had been in contact with Schwartzkoppen 'with the knowledge and authorisation of the French General Staff'.

In *L'Intransigeant* Rochefort says that 'the evidence of the guilt of Dreyfus can be weighed in kilos'.

Apr 13 Following recent press revelations, (*v.* 4 & 7 Apr 1898) Esterhazy is assaulted by journalists. He declares in *L'Agence Nationale* that he wishes to give no more interviews on the Dreyfus Affair. This wins the approval of the anti-revision press.

Von Münster telegraphs Hohenlohe:

> *The resumption of the Zola trial illustrates the French Government's weakness... Nevertheless the unpleasant issue of Esterhazy and Schwartzkoppen will again emerge. It was not right for Schwartzkoppen to get involved with that creature behind my back. He had always promised me not to meddle in any espionage. The whole diplomatic corps is greatly harmed by the wretched institution of the military attachés. It will be difficult to make this clear to the Kaiser, who still supports it. Schwartzkoppen, who I had always warned about espionage and to whom I had always made clear that I would not tolerate it, just did not care. As he was fully aware of this, he kept his relationship totally secret with Esterhazy, that Jesuit, that most dangerous breed of all schemers.*[125]

Apr 19 Picquart writes to Bertulus identifying Esterhazy as the writer of the Dixi articles published in *La Libre Parole* between 15 and 17 November 1897. (*v.* 4 May 1898)

Apr 24 *Le Jour*, *L'Echo de Paris* and *Le Gaulois* announce that Picquart was seen meeting a foreign military attaché in Karlsruhe at the beginning of April and that they have a photograph to prove this. Providing further details of this alleged meeting, *Le Jour* (28 & 30 April, 1 and 3 May) specifies that the attaché was Schwartzkoppen.[126]

Apr 25 In order to strengthen the Ministry of War's files against the dreyfusards, Gonse secretly prepares a report. It suggests that Picquart shares Panizzardi's sexual inclinations and that 'in a certain social circle Picquart is known as Georgette'.[127]

April In the month leading up to the parliamentary elections of 8 and 22 May, the dreyfusard and anti-dreyfusard press try to rekindle the Affair although it is not a main issue in the electoral campaign.

The Catholic daily *La Croix* issues a short pamphlet 'Le Complot Juif' ('The Jewish Conspiracy') outlining an alleged Jewish plan to dominate France and the world.[128]

Professor Henri Vaugeois and the writer Maurice Pujo establish a committee with the title L'Action française, aiming to influence the May elections. It publishes an appeal to French citizens to oppose the dreyfusard campaign.[129] (*v.* 20 June 1899)

April–May Christian Esterhazy, who has still not received any income from the money he entrusted to Esterhazy in October 1896 asks Esterhazy to reimburse him. Esterhazy refuses. Realising that the money has not been invested at the Rothschild's, Christian looks for a lawyer. Labori is informed by his colleague Gabriel Herbin that Christian has been swindled by Esterhazy. He agrees to meet him and Christian reveals all he knows about the collusion between the General Staff and Esterhazy. He states that '*la dame voilée*' was none other than Du Paty; the *document libérateur* a sealed envelope given by Du Paty to Esterhazy and returned unopened to the Ministry of War; and that one of the false Blanche and Speranza telegrams sent by Esterhazy at Du Paty's instigation, was written by Mlle Pays. Christian repeats this information to Trarieux, who passes it on to Zola, Picquart, Leblois and Reinach. They decide that Picquart will inform Bertulus, who since February has been in charge of investigating the false telegrams. Meanwhile, Mathieu procures a sample of Mlle Pays' handwriting for comparison.[130] (*v.* 9 & 11 July 1898, The revelations of Christian Esterhazy)

Consolidation of the Secret Dossier[131]

End April – Billot entrusts Gonse with the task of classifying all documents that
end May may relate to the Dreyfus case. He appoints Adolphe Wattine his son-in-law, a lawyer, to assist Gonse in preparing a complete inventory of this extended Secret Dossier.[132] It is to be arranged in chronological order. Undated documents are given 'new' dates; original dates are changed. Several items are forged, others are fabricated. By the time the work is finished, towards the end of May the new dossier contains 373 documents. These include over 30 memos from Guénée on moral conduct of Dreyfus; fragments of documents predating the court martial and over 70 letters intercepted at foreign embassies after the arrest of Dreyfus, none of which have any connection to the case; the so-called confession file of Dreyfus containing false reports and notes faked by Gonse; the *faux Henry* as well as other letters from Panizzardi to Schwartzkoppen.[133] (*v.* 1 June 1898)

May 4 Bertulus receives a police report confirming that the Dixi articles were dictated by Esterhazy. (*v.* 14 May 1898)

May 6 Picquart institutes libel proceedings against *Le Jour* for the publication of his alleged encounter with Schwartzkoppen. (*v.* 24 Apr 1898)

May 7 Guyot publishes the pamphlet *L'Innocent et le Traître: Dreyfus et Esterhazy – le devoir du Garde des Sceaux, ministre de la justice* ('The Innocent Man and the Traitor: Dreyfus and Esterhazy – the Duty of the Minister of Justice'). He includes details of the Affair which confirm the innocence of Dreyfus and guilt of Esterhazy. In the summary, entitled 'Duties of the Minister of Justice', he sets out the procedures for a revision of the Dreyfus verdict according to civil and military law.[134]

Pressure on Schwartzkoppen

May 7   Malwida von Meysenburg (1816–1903), a well-known novelist and personal friend of von Bülow's wife, writes to Schwartzkoppen:

> *There are moments in life when the eternal interests of humanity, when truth and justice are in danger, and when the formalities of social life must retreat to the background. It is in such a moment... that I approach you... you will guess at once with regards to what – the things that are going on in France... Sir, the decision lies in your hands. It is said that you have promised that despicable man Esterhazy not to betray him... This is no longer a matter of particular individuals, nor even of the poor victim on Devil's Island, nor of questions of nationality or political considerations, but only this – whether wickedness and baseness are to win, or truth and justice. Give a great example, even if it should cost you dearly, even your post... Name to all the world the wretch who served as tool... but do not first put your proofs in the hands of the French Government, there, they would disappear...*[135]

May 8   First round of the national legislative elections. (*v.* 22 May 1898)

May 14   Bertulus interrogates Esterhazy, who denies having written the Dixi articles but admits having given *La Libre Parole* the information on which the articles are based. He continues to maintain that he was given the information by '*la dame voilée*'.[136]

May 20   Mathieu Dreyfus approaches Schwartzkoppen via Albert Sandoz, one of his friends from Mulhouse. Sandoz writes to Schwartzkoppen hoping to persuade him to put an end to his silence.[137] (*v.* 25 Aug 1898)

May 22   The second round of the elections reflects the unpopularity of the dreyfusards. Reinach and Jaurès are defeated. The anti-dreyfusards Déroulède, Millevoye and Cassagnac are elected. Drumont is elected Deputy in Algiers.[138] However, the new Chamber shows no significant change in terms of party political representation and Méline's majority remains.

General Von Schliefen, Chief of the German General Staff, writes to Hohenlohe that in his view there was not enough material in their archives to provide convincing evidence of Esterhazy's guilt.[139]

Adjournment of Zola's retrial

May 23   Zola's second trial opens before the Assize Court in Versailles. Labori challenges the competence of the Court to try the case in Versailles, arguing that Zola lived in Paris and the charge against him was filed in Paris. The Court justly rejects his appeal. Zola immediately appeals against the rejection. (*v.* 16 June 1898) Outside the courtroom, demonstrations break out against Zola. The crowd, which includes Esterhazy, tries to attack Zola and Picquart.

May 24   Bertulus issues a ruling establishing the authenticity of Esterhazy's letters to Mme Boulancy , including the Uhlan letter.

Le Siècle publishes a second statement by Casella on his conversations with Panizzardi. (*v.* 7 Apr 1898) In it Casella asserts that Panizzardi has again recently confirmed that *Ce canaille de D.* is a forgery; Schwartzkoppen admitted to him his dealings with Esterhazy; only Schwartzkoppen could 'lift the veil' and 'open the doors of confession'.[140]

May 28 Von Süßkind who has replaced Schwartzkoppen as military attaché, remarks that he is in favour of a revision of the verdict on Dreyfus: 'This would be the best. There would be a great scandal, but then there would be an end to it.'[141]

May 30 Drumont arrives in Paris. His arrival sparks off antisemitic demonstrations.

June 1 The report by Gonse and Wattine on the documents contained in the Secret Dossier (*v.* end Apr–end May 1898) is signed by Gonse and Boisdeffre. The report concludes:

Henri Brisson

Identified by Panizzardi's letters, convicted by the bordereau, crushed by the chain of proof and the later correspondence in which he is named in full, Dreyfus certainly betrayed his country and one can affirm in soul and conscience together with the judges of the 1894 court martial: 'Yes, Dreyfus is guilty. [142]

June 2 By 282 votes to 278, the new Chamber of Deputies elects the moderate Paul Deschanel as President instead of the Radical Henri Brisson. The Republican centre group, now called the progressive centre group, begins to split. The Right sees the emergence of the Nationalists (Drumont, Rochefort, Déroulède and Barrès strongly supported by the Assumptionist 'La Bonne Presse', a powerful vehicle of antisemitic propaganda).[143] Reacting to this radicalism, several Deputies from the progressive centre group are gradually driven towards the Radicals (the Left). This disintegration of the political centre is to lead to a government crisis. (*v.* 15 June 1898, Resignation of Méline)

June 4 Reinach publishes in *Le Siècle* an article 'Les enseignements de l'histoire' ('The Lessons of History'), which quotes and analyses a passage by Conybeare that previously appeared in London's *National Review*. Conybeare refers to proof of Esterhazy's treason held by Germany:

The Emperor William II has in his hands a weapon with which, when the occasion arises, he can smite the entire General Staff... The series of secret documents sold by Esterhazy does not stop in October 1894, the date of Dreyfus' arrest, but extends on into the year 1896. It includes many important documents all in the handwriting of the bordereau. Dreyfus cannot have written these, for he was already in prison. [144] (*v.* 25 June 1898)

First meeting of the General Assembly of the Ligue des droits de l'homme et du citoyen.[145]

June 7 Devil's Island: Dreyfus sends another appeal to the President:

For many long months, I have been addressing appeals to the Head of the State, to seek a revision of my trial... From day to day, from hour to hour, I await a response which does not come. My physical and moral strength are diminishing every day... I ask now only one thing of life: to be able to descend into the tomb at peace, knowing that the name of my children has been cleansed of this horrible defilement. If it is necessary to die a victim of innocence, I will be able to do so, Mr. President, bequeathing my poor unfortunate children to my dear country, to which I have always given faithful and loyal service... But at the very least, Mr. President, may I respectfully request a reply to my requests for a revision, a reply which I will await anxiously from day to day... [146]

June 14 The Chamber of Deputies passes a motion that the Government can only approve policies which a Republican majority supports.[147] Despite Méline's protests, the motion is carried by 295 votes to 246.

Resignation of Méline

June 15   Méline tenders his resignation to President Faure. This marks the beginning of a political crisis which lasts two weeks. (*v.* 28 June 1898)

June 16   The Supreme Court of Appeal rejects Zola's appeal. (*v.* 23 May 1898) The trial is rescheduled for 18 July 1898.

June 25   By order of the Minister of War (12 June), a military board of inquiry is called to judge Deputy Joseph Reinach, also a Captain in the Reserves. The board recommends that Reinach be deprived of his rank on the grounds of a serious disciplinary offence, that being his article of 4 June affirming the innocence of Dreyfus and guilt of Esterhazy.

The Brisson Government

June 28   Brisson is elected Prime Minister. A new Cabinet is formed: Cavaignac is Minister of War, Delcassé is Foreign Secretary and Sarrien Minister of Justice.

Cavaignac is an antirevisionist and determined to prove the guilt of Dreyfus. He calls for the Secret Dossier and orders it to be examined by Captain Louis Cuignet and Colonel Guadérique Roget, head of the Quatrième Bureau. Alarmed, Boisdeffre and Gonse advise Cavaignac to remain very discreet about the content of the dossier.[148] Cavaignac asks Boisdeffre whether he has verified the authenticity of all the items. Boisdeffre merely invokes his 'unlimited trust in Henry' as a 'sufficient guarantee'.

June 30   At a public meeting in Montpellier, Jaurès declares that Dupuy, Prime Minister in 1894, had told him that Dreyfus did not make any confession to Lebrun-Renault.

Beginning July   Henry reveals to Roget that Esterhazy was in contact with the General Staff, pointing to Du Paty as the principal person responsible for the collusion.[149]

July 3   Alarmed by Cavaignac's order, Esterhazy hurries to Pellieux. He tells him that his life has 'become unbearable' and threatens that if the General Staff abandons him he will go to the press with supporting evidence about their collusion.[150] He claims that the Jews have offered him 600,000 francs to admit being the author of the *bordereau*. Concerned, Pellieux simply tries to calm Esterhazy down and suggests he should stop his press campaign against the General Staff.

In the evening Esterhazy happens to meet Picquart in the Place Victor Hugo. Probably drunk, he attacks him with his cane. Picquart retaliates with his own cane.

July 4   Picquart asks Bertulus to call Christian Esterhazy as a witness in his investigation of the Speranza and Blanche telegrams. (*v.* 9 & 11 July 1898, The revelations of Christian Esterhazy)

To reassure Cavaignac about the authenticity of the documents in the Secret Dossier, Gonse tells him that the letter mentioning the name of

Dreyfus (the *faux Henry*) has been kept in his (Gonse's) office since 2 November 1896. The same day Lebrun-Renault shows Cavaignac a page from his 1895 notebook, in which, he claims, he recorded on 5 January the exact words Dreyfus said to him on that day, amounting to a confession. (*v.* 6 Jan 1895) Cavaignac copies the entry and returns it to Lebrun-Renault.[151]

Lucie's appeal to the Minister of Justice

July 5   Lucie sends Sarrien an appeal for annulment of the 1894 verdict. The appeal is based on the grounds of legal irregularity in Dreyfus' court martial, that is, the transmission of secret documents to Court members.[152] It is published in the press on the following day. (*v.* Appendix 26)

Cavaignac, informed about Lucie's appeal, becomes increasingly determined to put an end to the campaign in favour of a revision. He meets Brisson and Sarrien to obtain their approval to reveal some of the documents in the Secret Dossier to the Government, thereby making them public for the first time. Cavaignac shows Brisson and Sarrien some 60 documents from the dossier together with Cuignet's commentary; they find the *faux Henry* of particular interest. Brisson reluctantly approves Cavaignac's plan.[153]

Cavaignac's speech in the Chamber

July 7   In the Chamber of Deputies Castelin calls for special legislation to reprimand 'the traitor's champions'. He accuses Mathieu, Reinach, Demange and Picquart of conspiracy with foreign powers, proposes to fine *Le Siècle* for publishing Dreyfus' indictment (*v.* 7 Jan 1898) and to strike Zola from the Legion of Honour. (*v.* 26 July 1898) Cavaignac first announces that 'an attempt has been made to substitute for Dreyfus an officer [Esterhazy] who tomorrow will receive the disciplinary punishment he deserves'. (*v.* 11 July 1898) He explains that the officer was acquitted in error because the Court was under the impression that no proof of his alleged crime existed. This comment is greeted with applause from Radicals and Socialists. Cavaignac goes on to state that Dreyfus was justly condemned.[154] Declaring his 'absolute certainty of Dreyfus' guilt', he promises to reveal the evidence. He reads three letters 'selected from a thousand' held at the Ministry of War exchanged between military attachés in Paris. These are the letter in which Panizzardi informed Schwartzkoppen that an individual named 'D' had brought him interesting material (the letter that Henry falsified by substituting the initial 'D' for the original 'P'); *Ce canaille de D;* and the forged letter the *faux Henry*.[155] Cavaignac confirms the 'material and moral authenticity' of these documents. He ends by giving details of what he sees as evidence of the confession of Dreyfus.[156] The entire Chamber acclaims Cavaignac's speech and unanimously votes for an *affichage*, that is for the statement and the *faux Henry* to be printed and placarded outside the town halls of each of the 36,000 *communes* of France.[157] (*v.* Appendix 27)

Reactions to Cavaignac's speech

July 8   The Nationalist press acclaims Cavaignac's speech. Drumont hails it as 'the supreme verdict'; Rochefort sees Cavaignac as a 'new Boulanger'; for the Socialist Millerand the speech eased the public conscience' (*La Lanterne*).

Dreyfusards gather in dismay at the offices of *La Revue Blanche*.[158] *Le Siècle,* on the other hand, publishes an article entitled 'La Révision s'impose' ('The revision is imperative'), and in *L'Aurore* Georges Clemenceau declares 'the revision is inevitable… today, thanks to Cavaignac himself, the whole truth emerges'. (*v.* 9 July 1898)

In an attempt to mitigate the punishment he is about to receive, Esterhazy writes to Pellieux to express his 'profound apologies' for

Godefroy Cavaignac

having put the General Staff at risk. (*v.* 3 July 1898) He promises to do nothing that might compromise the army.[159]

July 9   *La Petite République* publishes an open letter from Jaurès to Cavaignac, dated 8 July, stating that Cavaignac has unintentionally opened the way for a revision:

> *Yesterday in the Chamber, you accomplished something useful and something criminal. You did something useful for the country in exposing part of the dossier. Henceforth it will no longer be permissible to speak of the need for a closed hearing; you have made the nation itself aware of the problem.*

Jaurès then details the 'criminal' aspect of the documents quoted by Cavaignac, forged and inapplicable to Dreyfus, they confirm the illegality of the 1894 trial.[160]

Demange sends an open letter Minister of Justice Sarrien in support of Lucie's appeal for the annulment of the 1894 verdict.[161] (*v.* 5 July 1898) He states that at the 1894 court martial neither he nor Dreyfus knew of any of the documents read by Cavaignac on 7 July, and that the only legal document known to the court martial, the *bordereau*, was not even mentioned by Cavaignac. Demange appends to his letter Dreyfus' statement to Mercier of 31 December 1894, written immediately after Du Paty's visit to his cell and his unsuccessful attempt to obtain a confession.

Picquart issues an open letter to Prime Minister Brisson, writing that it is his duty to declare that two of the documents dated 1894 read by Cavaignac do not refer to Dreyfus, and that the third one, dated 1896 [the *faux Henry*], 'has all the hallmarks of a forgery'. He adds that he is prepared to defend his statement before any competent court.[162] (*v.* 12 July 1898)

The revelations of Christian Esterhazy

Christian Esterhazy testifies before Bertulus. (*v.* 4 July 1898) He reveals that he has been swindled by his cousin and, like Du Paty, used as an intermediary between the General Staff and Esterhazy. He also states that Esterhazy and Mlle Pays had told him in November 1897 that they needed to compromise Picquart and that the Blanche and Speranza telegrams were false. He states that the first was written by Du Paty, the second by Mlle Pays.[163]

July 11   Christian entrusts Bertulus with documents proving that he has been swindled by his cousin.[164] He repeats all the statements he gave to Labori regarding the collusion. (*v.* Apr–May 1898) He indicates that he was the writer of two of '*la dame voilée*' letters dictated to him by Esterhazy; that the *document libérateur* was a sealed envelope handed to Esterhazy by Du Paty; and that it was returned to the Ministry of War as such. He states that Esterhazy had only been vaguely briefed about the contents of the *document libérateur*.[165]

Bertulus informs Public Prosecutor Germain Feuilloley that he intends to arrest Esterhazy and Mlle Pays on a double charge of fraud and forgery.

Cavaignac signs an order for Esterhazy to appear before a military board of inquiry to decide the grounds on which he could be cashiered: 'habitual misconduct', 'violation of discipline', or 'violation of honour'. (*v.* 24–27 Aug 1898)

The arrests of Esterhazy and Picquart

July 12   Determined to punish Picquart, Cavaignac files a complaint with Sarrien against both Picquart and Leblois on charges of divulging and examining confidential documents at the time Piquart was head of the Section de Statistique. The complaint is based on the previous accusations brought by Gribelin, Lauth and Henry against Picquart during Zola's trial. Leblois is charged with being an accomplice.[166]

Albert Fabre is appointed examining magistrate. (*v.* 13 July–25 Aug 1898, Fabre's investigation)

Fabre orders an immediate search of Picquart's apartment, in his absence. Piquart's codicil to his will of 2 April 1897 is found there but contains nothing incriminating.

In a letter to Sarrien, Trarieux protests against the search of Picquart's apartment. He describes it as a 'violation of the law', because it was conducted in his absence. Knowing that the next step would be Picquart's arrest, Trarieux declares: 'If his arrest is to take place, I insist, in order to spare him needless humiliation that he should be taken from my home. That tells you how strongly I feel.'[167]

Bertulus orders an immediate search of Mlle Pays' apartment in the rue Douai. Starting at 6 p.m, many of Esterhazy's papers are seized and placed under seal. Esterhazy arrives at 8 p.m. to take his mistress out to dinner. On the orders of Bertulus, Esterhazy and Mlle Pays are both immediately arrested on a charge of forging the Speranza and Blanche telegrams. Esterhazy is also charged with fraud in connection with the affairs of his cousin Christian. At midnight, when the search has been completed, Mlle Pays is taken to St-Lazare prison, Esterhazy to La Santé.[168]

The imprisonment of Picquart in La Santé

July 13   Picquart is summoned by Fabre to the Palais de Justice. He is informed of Cavaignac's suit against him. He is immediately arrested. Like Esterhazy, he is taken to La Santé.[169]

La Ligue des droits de l'homme et du citoyen demonstrates against Picquart's arrest.

July 14   Picquart institutes legal proceedings against several press publications including in *Le Jour* and *L'Echo de Paris* for publishing unsubstantiated accounts of his alleged attempt to commit suicide in prison.

Cavaignac's personal inquiry

c. **July 15**   Alarmed by the arrest of Esterhazy ordered by Bertulus, Cavaignac interrogates Du Paty, a distant cousin of his. Du Paty speaks of the parc Monsouris meeting (November 1897) between himself, Gribelin and Esterhazy and confirms his dealings with Esterhazy. He states that his superior officers were aware. He denies any knowledge of the Blanche and Speranza telegrams and the *document libérateur*. Cavaignac then interrogates Gribelin, who blames Du Paty for the collusion with Esterhazy. Cavaignac, now aware of the collusion, wishes to protect Du Paty, at least until the results of Bertulus' investigation are made known. He does not inform Prime Minister Brisson.[170]

Bertulus' investigation of Esterhazy and Mlle Pays (15 July–12 August)

July 15–16   At La Santé the sealed papers seized at the apartment of Esterhazy and Mlle Pays are opened.[171] On her way to La Santé on the first day of the interrogation Mlle Pays tells Bertulus that if he had not arrested her she would have told him the whole truth. She admits that she wrote the Speranza telegram but says that Du Paty was responsible for the Blanche telegram. After being briefed by Tézenas at La Santé she retracts her statement.[172]

The opened papers shed no new light on the false telegrams and do not lead to any significant discoveries. They clearly demonstrate the collusion between Esterhazy and the General Staff.[173] Esterhazy tries to deny as much as possible. Although he admits that one of the documents was a draft of a letter he wrote to Boisdeffre, he only agrees to sign the official verbatim account of the interrogation if Boisdeffre's name is omitted.[174]

July 18–19   At Bertulus' chambers Mlle Pays and Esterhazy are confronted with Christian Esterhazy, who repeats details of their fraud and collusion. Esterhazy denies most of Christian's accusations. Mlle Pays again retracts her previous confession and claims that her knowledge of the false telegrams is based only on what she has read in the newspapers.[175]

July 18   Cavaignac sends Henry to Bertulus' chambers to ascertain whether Esterhazy's papers contain documents endangering the security of the nation. If they do, Henry is empowered to seize them. Bertulus explains that the seals can only be opened in the presence of the accused [Esterhazy and Mlle Pays] and their lawyers. He postpones the examination until 21 July, but shows Henry a number of documents that have already been unsealed,[176] outlining his conclusions about the collusion between Esterhazy and Du Paty and their collaboration in the false Speranza and Blanche telegrams. Henry admits that Bertulus is probably right in his assumptions, but asks him not to pursue his investigation without consulting General Roget (Cavaignac's private secretary). Bertulus agrees but insists that the identities of the officers involved will have to be disclosed. He adds that this includes another collaborator, Henry, saying: 'Let Du Paty blow his brains out and let justice takes its course with Esterhazy... but there is still you to think about.' He then tells Henry that he had seen Esterhazy's letter to Roche complaining about Henry as his 'debtor since 1877'. (*v.* 27 Jan 1897) Bertulus mentions how dangerous this letter could be for Henry if it fell into the hands of 'his enemies', as in view of his long collaboration with Esterhazy, it could imply that it was Henry who kept Esterhazy informed. According to Bertulus, Henry at this point breaks down in tears, crying: 'Save us, save save us, you must save the honour of the army!' Bertulus asks Henry whether Esterhazy is the author of the *bordereau.* Henry replies, 'Do not insist now... above all the army's honour must be saved.' Bertulus has Henry shown out of his chambers.[177]

Henry returns to the Ministry of War and gives Gonse and Roget a completely different version of his encounter with Bertulus. He

Paul Bertulus

reports that Bertulus burst into tears, protesting his love and respect for the army; that his order to arrest Esterhazy is just a warning, and that he is waiting for the Government to take action.[178]

July 19   Tézenas informs Cavaignac that since his arrest, Esterhazy keeps threatening to disclose to Bertulus all he knows about the General Staff's involvement in his case. Cavaignac refuses to intervene.[179]

July 21   Henry returns to the chambers of Bertulus for the official opening of Esterhazy's sealed papers. Esterhazy, Mlle Pays and Tézenas are present. On examining the papers Henry states that none of them are of interest to the Deuxième Bureau and need not therefore be confiscated. However, he seizes the two documents on which the word 'Basel' and the initial 'C' appear.[180] (*v.* 18 July 1898)

At the suggestion of Bertulus, Christian lodges an official complaint against Esterhazy for fraud. (*v.* 6–9 Nov 1899)

July 25   On Picquart's behalf, Labori lodges a complaint against Du Paty for forgery, alleging he is an accomplice of Esterhazy and Mlle Pays.[181]

Bertulus interrogates Esterhazy for the last time. Esterhazy denies all knowledge of the false telegrams. He becomes confused with his own lies and contradictions.[182]

July 26   Henry is sent once more to Bertulus for a final examination of Esterhazy's papers. He is accompanied by Junck. No more documents are seized. Bertulus accompanies Henry and Junck out of his office telling Henry: 'You see, you can criticise that man [Esterhazy] for anything you like in terms of his honesty, in terms of his financial affairs; he's an adventurer; but in terms of treason, there's nothing.'[183] In order to get more information from Esterhazy, Bertulus, back at his office, remarks to his clerk in Esterhazy's presence, that he wonders at which documents the two officers were looking. Esterhazy reponds without any explanation, 'the imperial guard' (an allusion to the *bordereau annoté*).[184]

Legal complexities

July 27   The Procureur de la République (the Public Prosecutor) Feuilloley affirms that the charge brought by Picquart against Du Paty (25 July) is not within the competence of Bertulus, since the accused, being an officer on active duty, is subject to military law. Bertulus is invited to declare the case is not within his jurisdiction.

July 28   Bertulus confirms that the matter is not within his jursidiction so long as Du Paty is considered sole author of the Blanche telegram (i.e. if there is no civilian involvement). However, the charge does fall within his jurisdiction if Du Paty is considered an accomplice to the Speranza forgery by Esterhazy, who has been cashiered, and Mlle Pays, a civilian. The ruling is published in *Le Siècle* on 30 July. The anti-revisionist press attacks Bertulus, calling for his withdrawal from the case.

July 29 Both Picquart and the Public Prosecutor appeal against the Bertulus ruling, contesting the distinction between the charges.[185] Bertulus is forced to suspend proceedings against Esterhazy.

Aug 5 La chambre des mises en accusation (the Indictments Chamber) rules that Bertulus is not competent to investigate the charge for complicity in forgery brought by Picquart against Du Paty.

Aug 7 Picquart appeals to the Supreme Court of Appeal against the ruling of the Indictments Chamber of 5 August. (*v.* 2 Sept 1898)

Aug 9 Bertulus issues a ruling that Esterhazy and Mlle Pays are to be sent before the Assize Court on charges of forgery, fraud and complicity in fraud.

Aug 12 The Indictments Chamber quashes Bertulus' ruling of 9 August on the grounds of insufficient evidence. That evening, Esterhazy and Mlle Pays are released from prison.

Fabre's investigation of Picquart and Leblois (13 July–25 August)[186]

Fabre hears all the military witnesses – Gonse, Gribelin, Lauth, Henry and Pellieux. They all confirm Picquart's misconduct over the *petit bleu* and in disclosing secret documents to Leblois. They also hold Picquart responsible for the article in *L'Eclair* (*v.* 14 Sept 1896), the publication of the facsimile of the *bordereau* in *Le Matin* (*v.* 10 Nov 1896) and for passing information to Scheurer-Kestener and Lazare as from 1896. The military witnesses base their accusations on the evidence of one of Picquart's orderlies in Tunisia, Flavian-Uband Savignaud, who states that he despatched from Tunisia (in 1896–97) four letters from Picquart to Scheurer-Kestner. Both Scheurer-Kestner and Mathieu deny this and testify that they had never seen or heard from Picquart before Esterhazy's court martial in January 1898. Fabre disregards Savignaud's evidence as false. (*v.* Rennes court martial, 24 Aug 1899, n. 41) He interrogates Leblois and Picquart several times, confronting them with the other witnesses. Picquart admits having consulted Leblois over espionage matters, especially carrier-pigeons (*v.* end Mar 1896, n. 8), but denies having broken any rule or divulging the existence of the Secret Dossier to Leblois. Picquart also admits that, sensing he was threatened, he had considered it expedient to tell Leblois about the miscarriage of justice in 1894 on condition that Leblois did not mention it to anyone except a member of the Government, if and when he judged it necessary. Mathieu and Demange were not to be informed. Fabre also examines all Picquart's correspondence held at the Ministry of War.[187]

Aug 18 Fabre concludes that the charges against Picquart and Leblois are interrelated and that Leblois should not be considered an accomplice but as having equal responsibility for divulging secret documents.[188]

Aug 25 Fabre's ruling requires Picquart and Leblois to appear on criminal charges before a civil court on 21 September 1898.[189]

Further proceedings against Zola (6 July–10 August)

July 6–9   Proceedings for libel against Zola and Perrenx, instituted on 21 January 1898 by graphologists Varinard, Couard and Belhomme, open before the 9th Criminal Division of the tribunal of the Seine. Zola is sentenced to a suspended prison term of two months and a fine of 2000 francs. Perrenx receives a 500-franc fine. Both are to pay damages of 5000 francs to each of the graphologists. (*v.* 10 Aug 1898)

July 16   *L'Aurore* publishes Zola's acerbic letter to Prime Minister Brisson: 'You used to embody republican virtue; you were the lofty symbol of civic honesty… Suddenly you fall into this monstrous Affair. You are stripped of your moral sovereignty and now you are no more than a weak and compromised man.'[190] Zola predicts in the letter that the next President of the Republic will be a politician who will grant the country the revision.

Second conviction of Zola

July 18   Zola's retrial opens before the Assize Court in Versailles. The Court again condemns again Zola and Perrenx to the maximum penalty for libel – one year's imprisonment and a 3000-franc fine. The verdict is acclaimed with shouts of 'Out of France!', 'To Venice, Italian!' (Zola's father was Italian), 'Coward!', 'Traitor!', 'Go back to the Jews!'[191] Zola appeals against the verdict (*v.* 5 Aug 1898), but in order to avoid the sentence escapes by night to London.[192]

July 20   *L'Aurore* publishes an article attributed to Zola but in fact by Clemenceau, 'Pour la preuve' ('For the Evidence'), which explains the reason for his flight:

> *I want… the Supreme Court of Appeal to pronounce on the only question which is important for me: my right to prove… Accepting the restricted hearing without doing everything possible to demonstrate the evidence, was to render useless the long effort of these last ten months. Whatever happens, next October, after the recess, I will be before my judges. Once again, I will offer the evidence.*[193]

July 26   Zola's name is struck off the roll of the Legion of Honour.[194]

Aug 1   Labori institutes libel proceedings against Ernest Judet, editor of *Le Petit Journal*, and Hyppolyte Marioni, its owner, for the campaign defaming the memory of Zola's father.[195]

Aug 3   The 9th Criminal Division of the tribunal of the Seine finds Judet and Marioni guilty of libel. Judet is to pay a fine of 2000 francs, Marioni 500 francs. They are to pay a total of 5000 francs in damages to Zola.

Aug 5   The Supreme Court of Appeal rejects the appeal of Zola and Perrenx against the judgment of the Versailles Assize Court.

Aug 10   The Supreme Court of Appeal amends the verdict of the 9th Criminal Division of the tribunal of the Seine in the case brought by the graphologists against Zola and Perrenx. Zola is sentenced by default to one month in prison and Perrenx to a fine of 1000 francs. The damages due to each of the graphologists are raised to 10,000 francs (Zola is thus to pay a total of 32,000 francs). (*v.* 6–9 July 1898 & 23/29 Sept 1898)

Aug   Jules Guérin obtains a monthly payment ranging between 15,000 and 25,000 francs from the duc d'Orléans in support of the Ligue antisémitique française. In exchange, Guérin promises to mobilize the league's supporters for the Royalist cause.[196] (*v.* 21 Aug 1898)

Aug 10   The libel proceedings instituted by Picquart against *Le jour* (*v.* 6 May 1898) are postponed to 19 October 1898.

         In *La Petite République* Jaurès begins publication of 'Les preuves', a series of articles in which he demonstrates the machinations of which Dreyfus was the victim, the illegalities of the conviction of Dreyfus and his innocence.[197]

Aug 11   At a Ministerial dinner hosted by Brisson, Cavaignac seeks the Prime Minister's approval of a vast project he has prepared to arrest the principal leaders of the revisionist camp and to accuse them of attempting to 'plot against the security of the nation'. The long list of people Cavaignac wants arrested includes Picquart, Leblois, Trarieux,

Jules Guérin (left) and the duc d'Orléans (right)

Scheurer-Kestner, Jaurès, Ranc, Reinach, Zola, Mathieu, Christian Esterhazy, Lazare, Clemenceau and Guyot. Brisson strongly objects to this 'outrageous proposition' and threatens resignation.[198]

Cuignet's discovery of the *faux Henry*

Aug 13   Instructed by Cavaignac, after his 7 July speech, to continue his careful examination of the Secret Dossier, Cuignet examines the *faux Henry*.[199] Examining the letter under his lamp he notices that the squared paper behind the heading and the signature is different from that of the main body of the letter. The colour of sections of the paper varied: part was bluish grey, part mauve. Cuignet thereby concludes that the document was pieced together from two separate letters and that its text had been inserted between the heading and signature; in other words, it is a forgery.[200]

Aug 14   Cuignet discloses his findings to Roget and Cavaignac. While acknowledging the forgery, Cavaignac orders Cuignet to continue examining the Secret Dossier. He does not immediately summon Henry, who is on leave. Nor does he inform Boisdeffre, who is still on sick-leave, Gonse, or Brisson.[201] (*v.* 30 Aug 1898)

Aug 21   Guérin publishes the first weekly issue of *L'Antijuif* in Paris. It becomes the mouthpiece of the Ligue antisémitique française, and is accompanied by an illustrated supplement, *L'Antijuif français illustré*.[202]

Aug 22   After his detailed examination of the *faux Henry*, Cuignet reconfirms to the Minister of War that it is a forgery and that the Secret Dossier contains a forged document. Roget informs Gonse.[203]

***c*. Aug 22**   Trarieux writes to Cavaignac refuting his 7 July speech and referring for the first time to Tornielli's revelations to him about the innocence of Dreyfus. (*v.* 1 Mar 1898)

Aug 23   Mathieu sends his friend Sandoz another letter pleading with him to approach Schwartzkoppen again, this time on behalf of Picquart, who is accused of fraud. Sandoz writes to Schwartzkoppen (August 25) and encloses Matthieu's letter:

> *What is going on now is breaking my heart. A new villainy is added on top of all the others: Colonel Picquart is being prosecuted in the criminal court for an alleged offence and is likely to be convicted...The greatest share in these responsibilities probably lies with the French government; but so long as Herr von Schwartzkoppen has not done what he must do, what is his duty, he too will share these responsibilities... Meanwhile Herr von Schwartzkoppen knows that Colonel Picquart is going to be convicted only because he pursued the truth and because, without hesitation, he sacrificed his position and his future at the bidding of his conscience... In a few days Picquart will be a victim, but only in our eyes... for the great majority of Frenchmen he will be dishonoured... Will Colonel von Schwartzkoppen allow himself to*

*commit this new grave injustice when he can still intervene by
stating, as a loyal soldier, that the famous petit bleu came from
him, and that Esterhazy was his informant?...*[204]

Drumont publishes an article in favour of Esterhazy and viciously
attacks Cavaignac for ordering Esterhazy to appear before a military
board of inquiry, for 'sacrificing the unfortunate Esterhazy, to the
scoundrels of the 'Syndicate'... to the Jewish and German syndicate'.
Drumont predicts that 'After Esterhazy, it will be Du Paty de Clam, after
Du Paty, Henry, Lauth, and Boisdeffre, and after Boisdefre, Mercier...
In abandoning their unfortunate colleagues, the representatives of the
army will be betraying themselves.[205]

Esterhazy's appearance before the military board of inquiry[206]

Aug 24　　　Esterhazy admits that he wrote all the Boulancy letters in 1892, except
for the Uhlan letter. He confesses to shortcomings in his private life.
He asserts that he acted on instructions from his superior officers,
repeating his claim that the Jews offered him 600,000 francs to declare
himself author of the *bordereau*. Confronted with Du Paty, Esterhazy
reveals their relationship, claiming that one of the letters he wrote
to President Faure had been dictated by Du Paty and that the Dixi
articles were also drafted with his help.[207] Du Paty admits the veracity
of most of Esterhazy's statements but refuses to reveal the names of
the officers involved. Esterhazy reveals his dealings with Henry and
Gribelin. He declares that he can produce a document in Du Paty's
handwriting which proves his statements: he is referring to the 'note
in two hands'.[208] (*v. c.* 20 Nov 1897) At the end of a ten-hour session,
the board adjourns its decision until 27 August to give Esterhazy time
to produce the document.

In the evening Esterhazy meets Strong, who leaves for London that
night.[209] (*v.* 25 Sept 1898)

Aug 25　　　Zurlinden, Military Governor of Paris, writes a report to Cavaignac on
Esterhazy's appearance at the military board of inquiry. His report on
Du Paty is severe.[210]

Aug 27　　　Esterhazy appears for a second time before the military board of
inquiry. He presents Du Paty's 'note in two hands', declaring that he
possesses other documents that prove the collusion. By 3 votes to 2,
the board recommends that Esterhazy be cashiered from the army for
'habitual misconduct'.[211]

Aug 28　　　Zurlinden reports to Cavaignac on the board's recommendations. He
points out that they contain 'grave revelations about the role of certain
officers on the General Staff' and concludes that the court's decision
shows 'a certain indulgence' towards Esterhazy.[212]

Cavaignac informs Boisdeffre of Cuignet's discovery of the *faux Henry*
and announces he intends to interrogate Henry in person.[213] (*v.* 30
Aug 1898)

La Petite République publishes an article by Jaurès entitled 'La Pièce Fausse. Un faux évident' ('The False Item. An Evident Forgery') which states that the third document (the *faux Henry*) quoted by Cavaignac in his 7 July speech is a forgery: 'This forgery is not the only one. A whole system of fraudulent fabrication was in operation. For two years the Minister of War had as an annex a forgery workshop, working to prove the innocence of a traitor.'[214]

Father Chanoine Pichot, one of the few dreyfusard Catholic priests, publishes the pamphlet *La conscience chrétienne et l'affaire Dreyfus*. It is an open letter directed to *La Croix*, the anti-dreyfusard Catholic daily. Pichot writes: 'One day, it will be good [to know that] we have spoken, protested, broken ranks.' He condemns antisemitism as a violation of the gospel.[215]

Henry's confession

Aug 30   At 2.30 p.m. Cavaignac summons Henry to his office for questioning in the presence of Generals Boisdeffre, Gonse and Roget. Cavaignac warns Henry that examination of two documents in the Secret Dossier

Major (later
Lieutenant-
Colonel)
Henry

has clearly revealed that they have been falsified. Henry denies any forgery, but, confused by Cavaignac's insistent questions and his own lies and contradictions, he admits that he altered a few sentences. He states that none of his superior officers knew about it and he only acted 'in the interests of his country'. In the end he admits his forgery. Cavaignac summarizes: 'In 1896 you received an envelope with a letter inside, an insignificant letter. You got rid of the letter and fabricated another one in its place.' Henry admits that this is true.[216] (*v.* Appendix 29)

Cavaignac instructs Henry to wait in another room under Roget's surveillance. Henry repeats to Roget that he had no accomplices.

In Cavaignac's office, Boisdeffre writes a letter of resignation:

> *Minister,*
>
> *I have just acquired proof that my trust in Colonel Henry, head of Intelligence Service, was not justified. That trust, which was total, led me to be deceived and to declare authentic, a document that was not, and to present it to you as such.*[217]

Cavaignac tries to dissuade Boisdeffre from resigning, claiming: 'Anyone can be deceived' and that it is up to him to pursue the investigation and 'preside over the suppression of the acts that led to the error which you made in all loyalty'. Boisdeffre insists: 'Anyone could indeed be led into error, but unlike me, not everyone had the misfortune to swear before a jury [a reference to his statement at Zola's trial] that a document was authentic when it was false.'[218]

Cavaignac orders Zurlinden to arrest Henry and detain him in Mont Valérien prison. Colonel Féry is to escort Henry to the prison, allowing him first to visit his home.[219]

Cavaignac informs Brisson of Henry's confession.[220]

Havas publishes the Government's official communiqué:

> *Today in the office of the Minister of War, Lieutenant-Colonel Henry was identified and indeed identified himself as the author of the letter dated October 1896 in which Dreyfus is named. The Minister of War ordered the immediate arrest of Lieutenant-Colonel Henry, who was taken for detention to Mont-Valérien.*[221]

The Government's dilemma

Aug 31   Shortly after reading the Government's communiqué, Pellieux writes a letter of resignation:

> *Duped by people without honour, unable to expect trust from my subordinates, without which no command is possible, having myself lost confidence in the orders of my superior officers who have made me work on forgeries, I have the honour to request you to settle my retirement pension according to my length of service.*[222]

Instead of passing this letter directly to Cavaignac, Zurlinden tries to dissuade Pellieux from resigning. He tells him that he will hold on to the letter so that he has a few days in which to reflect on his resignation. Brisson is not informed about Pellieux's letter to Cavaignac. (*v.* 2 Sept 1898, 6–7 Apr 1903)

The Cabinet holds four separate meetings. Ministers discuss recent events in the Affair, especially Boisdeffre's resignation. (*v.* Henry's death, n. 227, below) Brisson demands that the top echelon of the Ministry of War be replaced. Cavaignac objects and offers his resignation. It is not accepted. Ministers postpone all decisions until the return of Minister Léon Bourgeois on 3 September. At one of the meetings, President Faure signs the order handed to him by Cavaignac for Esterhazy's discharge from active service.

Henry's death

In the morning Henry sends a short letter to Gonse asking that he visit him urgently in prison.[223]

In the afternoon Henry writes to his wife:

My adored Berthe,

I see that apart from you everyone is going to abandon me, although you know in whose interest I acted. My letter is a copy and contains nothing, absolutely nothing, that is false. It only confirms the verbal information I was given a few days earlier. I am absolutely innocent; they know it, and everyone will know it later; but at the moment, I am not able to speak.[224]

Henry later begins another letter to his wife:

My beloved Berthe, I am like a madman, an appalling pain is gripping my brain. I am going to swim in the Seine...[225]

At 6 p.m. Henry is found dead, his throat slit by two razor slashes. He is stretched out on the bed covered in blood and with a cut-throat razor in his left hand.[226] (*v.* Appendix 30)

At midnight *Havas* issues a communiqué to the press: 'It has just been announced that Lieutenant-Colonel Henry committed suicide in Mont Valérien this evening. He cut his throat with a razor that he had taken into his cell.'[227]

Esterhazy in England

Sept 1   Esterhazy flees to London via Brussels.[228]

General Edmond Renouard replaces Boisdeffre as Chief of the General Staff.

Major Gallet, a judge at Dreyfus' court martial, admits to Senator Alphonse Chovet that Henry's testimony at the 1894 trial was the decisive factor in the conviction of Dreyfus.

Most of the press, anti-dreyfusard and dreyfusard (except *La Libre Parole* and *L'Intransigeant*), acknowledges that Henry's suicide makes a revision of the conviction of Dreyfus inevitable.

Sept 2　　Pellieux withdraws his resignation.[229] (*v.* 31 Aug 1898)

The Supreme Court of Appeal accepts Picquart's appeal (*v.* 29 July 1898) and annuls the verdict of the Court of Criminal Appeal of 5 August. Bertulus is declared competent to investigate the forgery charge brought by Picquart against Du Paty.

Henry's body is taken to his native village, Pogny, in the Marne, for burial.[230]

Lucie's appeal for revision

Sept 3　　Lucie despatches to Sarrien another appeal for revision based on 'new' facts: the discrepancies between the graphologists and their conclusions on the handwriting of the *bordereau*, at the court martial of Esterhazy and Dreyfus; and Henry's confession of forgery, Henry being 'one of the principal instigators and witnesses at the court martial of Dreyfus.[231]

Esterhazy before
fleeing to England

That evening Cavaignac hands Brisson his letter of resignation:

> *'I remain convinced of the guilt of Dreyfus and as resolute as ever to fight against a revision of the trial.*[232]

Cavaignac sends his letter to the press: its publication gives new impetus to the opponents of a revision.

Maurras' tribute to Henry

Sept 3–6   In the Royalist daily *La Gazette de France*, Charles Maurras publishes an article 'Le premier sang de l'Affair Dreyfus' ('The first blood of the Dreyfus Affair'), in which he introduces the idea of a 'patriotic forgery', portraying Henry as a martyr devoted to the nation's interests:

> *The energetic plebeian… had fabricated it [the forgery] for the public good, confiding in no one, not even the superiors whom he loved, agreeing to take a risk, but alone… National sentiment will awaken; it will prevail and avenge you. In life and in death you have led from the front. Your unfortunate 'forgery' will be counted amongst your finest military acts…*[233]

Sept 4–8   *La Croix, L'Eclair, La Libre Parole* and *Le Petit Journal* develop Maurras' theory of 'patriotic forgery' and threaten that 'revision means war'.

Sept 4   Trarieux demands that Colonial Secretary Georges Trouillot moderate Dreyfus' harsh and illegal treatment on Devil's Island.

Sept 5   Zurlinden replaces Cavaignac as Minister of War.[234]

Sept 6   In view of the anticipated revision of Dreyfus' verdict, Zurlinden demands that Edouard Lockroy, Minister of the Navy, prepare a ship to bring Dreyfus back to France. Lockroy orders the *Cécile*, then anchored in Toulon, to make ready.

Sept 7   Zurlinden instructs Renouard to open an investigation of Du Paty on the grounds of his dealings with Esterhazy. (*v.* 9–11 Sept 1898)

Sept 8   Labori submits Picquart's demand for temporary parole to the Public Prosecutor.[235] (*v.* 12 Sept 1898)

Sep 9   Paul von Below-Schlatau, acting German Ambassador in von Münster's absence, comments on the situation in Paris:

> *The revision of the Dreyfus case seems to be a decided fact, even though it may take some time because of the laborious legal procedures. As before, Germany can calmly await the future development of this unpleasant affair. To gloat is surely one of the ugliest expressions of human sentiment, but there are moments where it might be nearly forgivable. Such a moment has now come for us Germans. For four years now, since the first simple but clear declaration was made, that Captain Dreyfus had not been in any treacherous relationship with Germany, it has been repeatedly and more or less clearly stated here [in Paris] that one couldn't believe such a declaration by a government which has its own*

> *interests and stake … And now it has gradually come to light, in a deeply humiliating manner for any righteous Frenchman that the German declaration stated the truth … The key to this as to most other incomprehensible characteristics of this highly gifted and at times seriously thinking nation is their excessive vanity, the incredible arrogance, which would never admit a mistake or bring itself to admitting unjustness.* [236]

Renouard's investigation of Du Paty[237]

Sept 9–11   Du Paty admits entering into dealings with Esterhazy of his own accord, albeit under 'Henry's influence'. He insists that his superior officers were aware of this: he recalls that at one point he was instructed to cease direct contact with Esterhazy. (*v.* 16 Nov 1897) Gonse lies blatantly, saying he knew nothing about Du Paty's contact with Esterhazy until July 1898.

           Renouard's report of 11 September recommends that Du Paty be severely reprimanded; his devotion to the army and his seniority be taken into consideration; he should take early retirement. (*v.* 12 Sept 1898)

Zurlinden's and Picquart's letters to Sarrien

Sept 10   Zurlinden sends Sarrien a letter containing a full report on the Dreyfus case, advising him to oppose the revision. While admitting that 'grave errors, even crimes' were committed in 1896–97 (referring to Henry's forgery and Du Paty's contact with Esterhazy), Zurlinden does not consider they clear Dreyfus: 'to me the revision does not seem justified;… it could be dangerous and disturb the country'.[238]

Sept 11   Zurlinden replies to Sarrien's request for the Secret Dossier: 'there is no trace of the dossier at the Ministry of War'.[239]

Sept 12   Zulinden orders that Du Paty be reduced to half-pay.

           When Zurlinden reads out before the Cabinet Renouard's concluding report with its accusations against Du Paty the Ministers learn of the collusion between Esterhazy and the General Staff. Zurlinden argues vigorously against, Brisson strongly supports a revision. Both threaten to resign if their views are not accepted. After ten hours' deliberation, over two consecutive sessions, and to avoid a government crisis, President Faure postpones the matter until the next Cabinet meeting on 17 September.

           The 9th Criminal Division of the tribunal of the Seine rejects Labori's request to allow Picquart parole. (*v.* 8 Sept 1898)

Sept 14   On Delcassé's confidential advice, Picquart, still in prison, writes to Sarrien in an attempt to hasten the revision procedure. He details the events related to Dreyfus' arrest and court martial, revealing the content of each of the documents in the Secret Dossier and confirming its transmission to the judges. Picquart emphasizes that despite the irrelevancy of the dossier it must have had a decisive impact on the Court's verdict.[240]

Zurlinden counters this letter by sending a report to Sarrien on 'Picquart's manoeuvres while on service'. The report suggests that Picquart's motive was to incriminate someone else instead of Dreyfus. Zurlinden also mentions, for the first time officially the erasure on the *petit bleu* concluding that it appears to be a forgery. Zurlinden demands an investigation into the origin of the *petit bleu*.[241]

From London, Esterhazy writes to Sarrien of his disapproval of the Government's decision to discharge him from the army. (*v.* 31 Aug 1898) Esterhazy states that during his detention he declared himself innocent or guilty, as the Government's interest dictated. Esterhazy declares that he intends to 'break his silence'.[242]

Sept 15 Zurlinden informs Sarrien that he intends to order the acting Military Governor of Paris, General Borius, to initiate a preliminary judicial investigation of Picquart. Sarrien in turn informs Brisson, who forbids Zurlinden to act until the Cabinet has discussed the matter. (*v.* 17 Sept 1898)

A 3000-strong public meeting led by de Pressensé calls for Picquart's release and an immediate revision.

The daily *Le Rappel* publishes the results of a survey showing the recent drastic change in Parisian public opinion about the desirability of a revision of Dreyfus' verdict. In March 1898 only ten Parisian newspapers were in favour, 30 against; by September 1898, 36 papers are in favour and only 14 against. (*v.* Appendix 31)

Sept 16 Sarrien writes to Zurlinden stating that he cannot authorize a preliminary judicial investigation of Picquart. He argues that as Picquart was on active duty at the time of the alleged misdemeanours the matter as charged falls under military jurisdiction.

Zurlinden writes a second letter to Sarrien reinforcing his accusations against Picquart for forgery of the *petit bleu*. He announces that in spite of Brisson's disapproval he has instructed the Military Governor of Paris to start a judicial investigation to decide whether Picquart should be court-martialled. As for the 'Dreyfus Affair', Zurlinden declares:

'I am personally convinced that Dreyfus is guilty.'

The letter also discusses the 'Picquart–Esterhazy affair':

…when Henry discovered the manoeuvres of his superior [Picquart], he wished to react to the petit bleu by fabricating his faux Henry. Later on, Du Paty intervened to save Esterhazy … Henry has atoned for his crime through suicide, Lieutenant-Colonel Paty has been suspended from duty; Picquart has been discharged and is currently being prosecuted for the transmission of secret documents to persons not qualified to know about them. But Picquart's attempts to attribute the crime of treason to Esterhazy, [and] his fabrication and manipulation of the petit bleu … have not yet received the penalty they deserve.[243]

The resignation of Zurlinden

Sept 17   In the Chamber Zurlinden introduces the *petit bleu* as a forgery by Picquart and requests the Government's authorization to initiate legal proceedings against him. Brisson refuses to deliberate the question since it is not on the day's agenda. He diverts discussion to the still pending question of Lucie's appeal for a revision. (*v.* 12 Sept 1898) By a large majority, the Ministers authorize Sarrien to transfer Lucie's appeal to a Revision Commission. (*v.* 21–23 Sept 1898, The Revision Commission)

    Zurlinden tenders his resignation. He is replaced as Minister of War by General Charles Chanoine.[244]

Sept 19   Chanoine appoints Zurlinden Military Governor of Paris.

    De Pressensé is summoned before the Council of the Legion of Honour for publishing his letter to the Grand Chancellor (*v.* 26 July

General Zurlinden

1898, Second conviction of Zola, n. 194) and involvement in public meetings that voted offensive motions against army officers.[245]

Prince Alexandre von Hohenlohe, son of the German Chancellor, transmits to Schwartzkoppen a request he has received from Sandoz (*v.* 20 May 1898) in which the Dreyfus family asks Schwartzkoppen to supply further information: (1) Is the name of the man referred to in *Ce canaille de D.* in fact Dubois? (2) Did Schwartzkoppen write 'Picquart's *petit bleu*? (3) What was the registration number of the firing manual mentioned in the *bordereau*? The family promises to use the information as Schwartzkoppen may permit. The letter was not answered.[246] (*v.* 21 Nov 1898)

Proceedings against Picquart

Sept 20   With Chanoine's authorization, Zurlinden signs the order to initiate proceedings against Picquart on charges of forgery. [247]

A manifesto signed by the duc d'Orléans opposing a revision of Dreyfus' trial is distributed across Paris. It declares: 'on the pretext of clearing the man convicted by the military courts, it is the army they want to destroy and France they want to bring down'. It concludes that only the monarchy can protect the army's honour. [248]

Sept 21   Opening of the proceedings against Picquart and Leblois (accused by Cavaignac of transmitting secret documents: *v.* 12 July 1898) before the 8th Criminal Division of the tribunal of the Seine. Léon Siben, deputy Public Prosecutor, requests postponement on the grounds of the military proceedings initiated against Picquart for forgery (20 September), and because a revision of the Dreyfus' verdict is now imminent. Labori protests against postponement.[249] Picquart asks to speak:

> *This evening I may go to Cherche-Midi. It is probably the last time, before this secret investigation, that I can speak in public. I want it to be known that if Lemercier-Picard's shoelace*[250] *or Henry's razor are to be found in my cell, it will be murder, for never would a man such as I, even for one instant, contemplate suicide.*[251] *I will face this accusation, my head held high, and with the same serenity that I have always shown before my accusers.*[252]

After deliberation, the Court adjourns. Picquart refuses to ask for temporary parole. Applauded in Court, he returns to La Santé prison.

Sept 22   Zurlinden orders Picquart's transfer from La Santé to Cherche-Midi military prison, where he is put in solitary confinement.[253] Captain Adolphe-Arsène-Marie Tavernier is charged with the investigation of Picquart. (*v.* 23 Sept–16 Nov 1898, Tavernier's investigation of Picquart)

The Revision Commission[254]

Sept 21–23   Three sessions of the Revision Commission take place. The judges are split equally for and against a revision. Their report states that the points mentioned in Lucie's appeal (the graphological discrepancies and the *faux Henry*) can be considered as new evidence, and therefore concludes that a revision is inappropriate.[255] (*v.* 24 Sept 1898)

Sept 23   Opening of Tavernier's investigation of Picquart. (*v.* 23 Sept–16 Nov 1898)

Sept 23 &29   At the request of the graphologists, Zola's property, including his valuable library, is sequestrated for auction. (*v.* 11 Oct 1898)

Sept 22–24   The dreyfusard press vigorously condemns the Government's attitude towards the Picquart case. In *L'Aurore* Clemenceau openly denounces Brisson:

> *What can one say of Brisson, who is leading us, while lamenting his fate, towards the latest catastrophes? More stupid than cowardly or more cowardly than stupid? Both. Cowardice or stupidity? The two qualities are not contradictory... Brisson, Sarrien and Bourgeois, the entire pack of radicals, more Jesuit than all the Jesuit mafia put together...* [256]

Sept 24   Brisson, Bourgeois and Delcassé declare their support for a revision in a Cabinet meeting. Sarrien states that the division in the Revision Commission amounts to rejection. Brisson reminds the Ministers that the Revision Commission's decision is merely advisory and that the initiative for a revision lies with Government. The decision is postponed until 26 September.

Devil's Island: Desperate at not receiving a response to his appeals, Dreyfus writes to the Governor of Guyana saying that he wishes to send two last appeals to the President of the Republic and to Boisdeffre in order to leave them the bitterest of memories and to clear the names of his wife and children.[257] (*v.* 10 Nov & 26 Dec 1898)

Sept 25   In the *Observer*, Strong publishes what he claims are statements given to him by Esterhazy on 24 August 1898. These confirmed that Esterhazy wrote the *bordereau* on Sandherr's instruction in order to provide the General Staff with material evidence implicating Dreyfus, whom Sandherr suspected of espionage. *Le Temps* and *Le Figaro* repeat this information (27 September & 4 October). *La Libre Parole* immediately publishes Esterhazy's denials.[258] (*v.* Appendix 32)

Déroulède, now a Nationalist Deputy, revives the Ligue des patriotes. (*v.* May 1882) A first public meeting is held in the Salle Guyenet in Paris.[259]

Sept 26   Fayard announces that he has signed a contract with Esterhazy for 10,000 francs and a share of the profits for the right to publish *Les dessous de l'affaire Dreyfus* ('The Undercurrents of the Dreyfus Affair') in instalments. On seeing the first instalment Fayard refuses to publish because of Esterhazy's violent attacks on high-ranking military figures. (*v.* 15 Nov 1898)

Lucie's appeal reaches the Criminal Chamber

Brisson wins the case for a revision. By six to four Ministers decide to allow Sarrien to transfer Lucie's appeal to the Criminal Chamber of the Supreme Court of Appeal.[260]

Sept 27
Sarrien orders Manau, principal State prosecutor attached to the Supreme Court of Appeal, to entrust the Criminal Chamber with Lucie's appeal for a revision.[261] The Chamber is presided over by Louis Loew.[262] Loew appoints Alphonse Bard, one of the youngest judges of the Chamber, as reporting judge. (*v.* 27-29 Oct 1898)

Oct 13–19
Manau makes a demand to Sarrien that the Ministry of War's Secret Dossier on Dreyfus be handed over to the Chamber. Chanoine refuses on the grounds of state security.[263]

Oct 18
The anti-revisionist press (*L'Intransigeant, La Libre Parole, La Croix*) launches a defamatory campaign against the judges of the Criminal Chamber, who are said to be in the pay of the 'Syndicate' or the Germans. Rochefort's virulence knows no limits. After describing the judges as 'criminal', 'bar girls' available to the highest bidder, he elaborates the terrible punishment he suggests inflicting on them.[264]

Oct 26
Esterhazy writes to Manau protesting against the submission of documents to the Criminal Chamber relating to his court martial, Bertulus' investigation of him (July 1898) and Picquart's two letters to the Minister of Justice.[265] (14–15 Sept 1898)

Acceptance of Lucie's appeal for a revision

Oct 27–29
Over three sessions the Criminal Chamber examines Lucie's request for a revision.[266] Bard's report concludes that the request is justified and that the Chamber will proceed with a supplementary judicial inquiry. Lucie's lawyer, Henri Mornard, reads out his own conclusions, then pleads on Lucie's behalf, demonstrating that a revision is inevitable. Manau clarifies the two facts that have recently come to light justifying a revision – the *faux Henry* and the graphologists' contradictory reports in 1894 and 1897 of the handwriting of the *bordereau*. He recommends quashing the 1894 verdict and opening a new inquiry. In conclusion, he recalls Dreyfus' many protestations of innocence and reads a number of his letters from Devil's Island. By a majority of ten to four the Chamber approves Bard's summing up in favour of a revision of the court martial of Dreyfus and a supplementary inquiry, but refuses Manau's recommendation to quash the 1894 verdict. (*v.* Appendix 33)

Sept 29
Conybeare (*v.* Feb 1898) states in the *Daily Chronicle*, London, that Esterhazy sold Schwartzkoppen the documents listed in the *bordereau* in 1894 and received a 2000-franc monthly retainer from him up to September 1896.[267]

L'ILLUSTRATION

Prix du numéro : 75 centimes. SAMEDI 29 OCTOBRE 1898 *56ᵉ Année. — Nᵒ 2905.*

M. LŒW, président de la Chambre criminelle.

M. SALLANTIN.

M. PAUL DUPRÉ. — Phot. Pirou, Bd St-Germain.

M. ACCARIAS. — Phot. Pierre Petit.

M. BARD, rapporteur de l'affaire Dreyfus.

M. DUMAS. — Phot. Mathieu-Deroche.

M. ROULIER. — Phot. Pirou, Bd St-Germain.

M. ANDRÉ BOULLOCHE.

M. ATTHALIN. — Phot. Pirou, Bd St-Germain.

LA CHAMBRE CRIMINELLE DE LA COUR DE CASSATION. — Voir l'article, page 279.

Judges of the Criminal Chamber of the Court of Appeal

Von Bülow sends a coded telegram to Berlin stating that Germany is not dissatisfied with the troubles in France:

> *Our chief interest in the Dreyfus Affair is to stay clear of it as much as possible. A victory of the anti-revisionists is undesirable as it might lead to dictatorship and then to war with us. It should not sadden us that the French Generals and the General Staff have been discredited – and especially the chauvinistic and clerical officers who are militarily the most efficient among them... It is not to be desired that France should immediately recover liberal and Jewish sympathies by a quick and striking reparation to Dreyfus. It would be best if the Affair would continue to fester, to demoralize the army and scandalize Europe. We must not admit Mr von Schwartzkoppen's alleged relationships with Esterhazy, even if they did exist, because such an indiscretion would make it quite difficult in the future to obtain such information and agents.*[268]

Oct   Gonse, who has not resigned, is put on half-pay.[269]

Oct 2   The administrator of the Salle Wagram in Paris refuses to allow revision supporters to enter and hold a meeting there, even though they have paid for the facility. The police use violence against them. Supporters of the Ligue des patriotes summoned by Déroulède start a street fight with the dreyfusards. The police intervene. Some 40 people are arrested, including the dreyfusards de Pressensé, Vaughan and Morhardt, General Secretary of the Ligue des droits de l'homme et du citoyen. Royalists demonstrate in the Champs-Elysées. In the evening revisionists demonstrate outside the offices of *La Libre Parole*, *L'Intransigeant* and *L'Eclair*.

Oct 5   Morhardt deposits the intimidating letters he has received at the State prosecutor's office.

Oct 11   Zola's chattels are sold by public auction. Fasquelle buys a table for 32,000 francs.

Oct 19   Picquart's case against *Le Jour* (*v.* 6 May & 10 Aug 1898) is again postponed, by three weeks.[270]

Oct 20   First issue of *Le Précurseur* ('The Precursor') appears. It is the propaganda tool of Dubuc's association Jeunesse antisémitique et Nationaliste (JAN) (Antisemitic and National Youth of France). [271] (*v.* 21 Nov 1897)

Oct 21   Chanoine confides to Cuignet his intention of resigning when the Chamber reassembles. (*v.* 25 Oct 1898)

Oct 22   Déroulède calls on Parisians to demonstrate outside the Palais-Bourbon (seat of the Chamber of Deputies) in support of the army and against the 'traitors'. Members of Guérin's Ligue antisémitique incite the crowd: 'Down with the Jews!', 'Long live the Army!', 'Down with the traitors!'

Oct 24   The Ligue des droits de l'homme et du citoyen calls on Republicans to counter-demonstrate against the Ligue des patriotes and the Ligue antisémitique française. [272]

The collapse of Brisson's Government

Political events unconnected with the Affair present challenges to Brisson's Government and agitate the country throughout September and October.

Foreign Secretary Delcassé conducts tense negotiations with England. War is imminent over the critical situation in Fashoda, Egypt.[273]

From mid-September there is social unrest in France. Labourers on the site of the forthcoming Exposition Universelle (the Universal Exhibition or World Fair) in Paris organize strikes, which spread to other building trade workers. A general strike of railway employees is threatened. By early October 20,000 people are on strike. Brisson drafts 60,000 police and army personnel into the capital to occupy railway stations and guard the tracks.[274] Public opinion is explosive and on 16 October rumours spread of a military and Royalist plot against the Republic.[275] Several dreyfusard leaders (Clemenceau, Labori, Ranc, Jaurès, Millérand, Lazare and Mathieu) alert Brisson, who has already been forewarned. No incident occurs, but a state of alarm prevails across the country.

Oct 25

The Chamber reopens. In the morning a crowd gathers outside the Palais-Bourbon and in the place de la Concorde. Mounted police are stationed in the jardins des Tuileries.

The session opens with five speeches against Brisson concerning the pending revision.[276]

Brisson replies that the matter has been transferred from the political to the legal arena. Déroulède attacks Brisson, asking for the Government, and specifically Chanoine, to stand down. Chanoine makes a dramatic speech restating his belief that Dreyfus is guilty. He then resigns and there is turmoil in the Chamber. The Right and the Nationalists applaud. Brisson criticizes Chanoine's unexpected resignation mentioning that Chanoine was present when the Cabinet voted for the transmission of Lucie's appeal for a revision (26 September).[277] He asks the Chamber to support his decision to maintain the supremacy of civil authority. The session is suspended until the afternoon. Brisson and Sarrien ask President Faure about nominating a civilian as Minister of War. After the recess the Chamber unanimously passes a motion, brought by the united Republican groups, of support for the supremacy of civil authority and its confidence in the 'loyal obedience of the army to the laws of the Republic'. The Republicans request a two-day adjournment. Discussion follows and the Government is defeated by 286 to 254. The Ministers hand in their resignations to the President. The Chamber is adjourned until 4 November.

Outside the Palais-Bourbon, Guérin and his Ligue antisémitique française supporters mount a violent demonstration. The police intervene. Guérin and nearly 500 demonstrators are arrested.

Le Siècle publishes Reinach's article 'Les Complices d'Esterhazy' ('Esterhazy's Accomplices'), the first in a series developing his theory

on the complicity between Henry and Esterhazy during the Affair. [278]
(*v.* 7 Nov, 6 Dec 1898)

Oct 27   Devil's Island: Still unaware of the recent developments, Dreyfus is informed by his warders that he will soon receive a definite answer from the President to his appeals for a revision. Dreyfus writes to Lucie to tell her this news: 'I await it calmly and with confidence, not doubting that this reply will finally bring my rehabilitation.'[279]
(*v.* 5 & 16 Nov 1898)

Oct 28   To intimidate the Chamber's judges *La Libre Parole* publishes their addresses.

Oct 29   Esterhazy's name is struck off the roll of the Legion of Honour.

Oct 30   Cavaignac demands to be heard by the Criminal Chamber and protests against what he claims are errors in Bard's report and Mornard's closing speech.

NOTES

1   *Cass.*, II, 131. This was not true: Lebrun-Renault did not mention an alleged confession of Dreyfus either to Mercier or to the President. (*v.* 6 Jan 1895)

2   *Pro. Zola*, II, pp. 516–20. (*v.* 7 Apr 1898)

3   For the text of the order, see *AD*, p. 602. It originally contained the words 'for acts committed in 1894', but 'in 1894' was erased. This meant that an acquittal (*v.* 11 Jan 1898) would have absolved Esterhazy from any acts of treason he may have committed up to the day of his judgment. General Charles de Luxer, who was court president at Esterhazy's court martial, later claimed that he did not notice that the words had been removed. *3ème Cass.*, III, 353, Luxer.

4   For extracts of the letter see *AD*, pp. 605–7. On 7 January 1898 Reinach sent another letter to Billot demanding that Esterhazy's court martial should be held in open session. *HAD*, 3, p. 196.

5   *Répertoire*, p. 135.

6   Mathieu claimed that Casella showed him Schwartzkoppen's letter before his meeting with Panizzardi and invited him to take it, on the grounds that it contained proof of Esterhazy's guilt. Mathieu refused. Casella was furious with Mathieu: 'It is idiotic. When one has to struggle against adversaries as dishonest as those who want your brother to be the traitor, one should have no scruples of that sort; one defends oneself – and you are not doing so.' *ATQV*, p. 121.

7   Published in *La vérité en marche* [1901], 1969, pp. 99–109. See English text in Zola, *The Dreyfus Affair: 'J'Accuse' and Other Writings,* pp. 35–43.

8   Although Méline refused to meet Guyot, editor of *Le Siècle* (*v.* 20 Dec 1897), Guyot nevertheless decided to publish d'Ormescheville's report, previously unpublished. Guyot had received the copy from Reinach. Mathieu Dreyfus had received it from Forzinetti in January 1895. The indictment demonstrated the lack of evidence against Dreyfus. The only basis for the accusation was the *bordereau*, despite Billot's recent statements that there were many others. *Le Siècle* ran the risk of prosecution in publishing the indictment but Billot did not proceed against the paper. The following day Guyot published an analysis of the indictment, which he later included in his 1898 book *La Révision du procès Dreyfus* (Paris: *Le Siècle* et P.-V. Stock, 1898), pp. 41–56. D'Ormescheville's report is also included in the second volume of Zola's trial published by Stock the same year: *Pro. Zola*, II, 521–31.

9   The pamphlet was certainly written before Esterhazy's court martial. Lazare's preface refers to the trial as 'imminent'. However, it was not circulated until March 1898.

10   B. Lazare, *Comment on condamne un innocent* (Paris: Stock, 1898), pp. III, V. In his November 1896 pamphlet Lazare had already used the formula ('I accuse'), which was to become notorious a few days later with the publication of Zola's 'J'Accuse'. (*v.* 13 Jan 1898) Zola may have been inspired by Lazare. P. Oriol, *Bernard Lazare* (Paris: Stock, 2003), pp. 182–3.

11   That only two sessions had been scheduled for Esterhazy's court martial, indicates the summary nature of military justice. Bredin, *The Affair*, p. 237. The proceedings were not published *in extenso*. The open session of 10 January and the verdict were published in Guyot's *Révision*, pp. 100–67.

12 Esterhazy's court martial took place in the same room as that of Dreyfus.

13 Although it created ambiguity from a legal point of view, previous rulings permitted civil suits to be filed in courts martial. B. Weil, *Der Prozeß des Hauptmanns Dreyfus* (Berlin: Grunewald: Dr Walther Rothschild, 1930), p. 88.

14 Labori had been recommended by Leblois. Before taking on the case, he first asked to examine the 1894 file and learn from Demange all the case details up to Esterhazy's court martial. He then agreed to represent Lucie on condition that he received no fee. Demange objected, claiming it would harm his reputation because he had received a fee for defending Dreyfus in 1894. He threatened to withdraw from the case. Labori agreed to accept payment. M. Dreyfus, *Dreyfusards!*, pp. 123–4.

15 This meant that Picquart, the most important military witness, would not be heard in public.

16 During Pellieux's second investigation (23 Nov–3 Dec 1897) Esterhazy acknowledged having written the Uhlan letter.

17 Stock was merely asked how Esterhazy's letters to Autant (of 20 and 26 October 1897) reached Reinach. (*v.* 30 Nov 1897) Autant confirmed that Mlle Pays pleaded with him in October 1897 to transfer the lease in her name, because of Esterhazy's despair and his threat of suicide. Mlle Pays denied mentioning that Esterhazy had threatened suicide. *Révision*, pp. 155–61.

18 Picquart was not present in court when Ravary's report was read and was therefore not aware of its charges against him. *Cass.*, II, 205, Picquart.

19 Years later Esterhazy admitted that the whole procedure had been a 'predetermined comedy', in which everyone, including his lawyer, played the clown. Weil, *Der Prozeß des Hauptmanns Dreyfus*, p. 90.

20 *Déb. Cass., 1899*, 326–7; A. Dreyfus, *Cinq années de ma vie* (1901), pp. 348–9. Faure passed on to Billot two appeals from Dreyfus. (20 December 1897 and 12 January 1898) At the same time Boisdeffre and Gonse were adding material to the dossier on the alleged confession of Dreyfus.

21 Pellieux submitted the letter to the graphologists on 1 December 1897. He only received their report on 9 January 1898.

22 At the end of Esterhazy's court martial Pellieux pleaded with Esterhazy's wife, the comtesse de Nettencourt, to return to conjugal life 'for the honour of the army'. When she refused Pellieux threatened her in vain with a scandal. That same evening Esterhazy presented himself at his wife's home, but she refused to let him in. *Répertoire*, p. 139.

23 The fortress of Mont-Valérien, built in 1841, is situated between Suresnes and Rueil Malmaison, to the west of Paris. During the German Occupation (1940–44) over 1000 members of the French Resistance were executed. Today the fortress houses the 8th Signals Regiment. It is also the site of the American War Cemetery and the Memorial for Fighting France.

24 *L'Aurore* increased its circulation tenfold and organized exceptional publicity for this special issue. Several hundred *camelots* (newspaper criers) were employed and Zola's letter was also posted across Paris. More than 200,000 copies were sold by evening.

25 Certain that Esterhazy would be acquitted, Zola began writing his letter during the court martial without waiting for the verdict. Like most of Zola's previous writings on the Affair, this article was intended to be published in pamphlet form: Zola only decided to publish in the press at the last minute. On the evening of 12 January he took the letter to the offices of *L'Aurore* because *Le Figaro* had recently declared it had abandoned the dreyfusard campaign (*v.* 19 Dec 1897). It was *L'Aurore's* editor, Georges Clemenceau, who decided to add the heading 'J'Accuse' to Zola's original title 'Letter to the President of France' and to put it on the front page.

26 'J'Accuse' has been translated many times and in many languages. For the full text in English, see e.g. Zola, *The Dreyfus Affair: 'J'Accuse' and Other Writings*, pp. 43–53.

27 Throughout 1898 and 1899 articles, pamphlets, caricatures and popular songs appeared which were scornful and dismissive of Zola. For reactions to Zola's involvement in the Affair, especially after the publication of 'J'Accuse', see Emile Zola, *L'Affaire Dreyfus: Lettres et entretiens inédits*, ed. A. Pagès (Paris: CNRS Editions, 1994); A. Pagès, *Emile Zola. Un Intellectuel dans L'Affaire Dreyfus. Histoire de 'J'Accuse'* (Paris: Librairie Séguier, 1991); R. Frédéric, *Zola en chansons, en poésies et en musique* (Sprimont: Mardaga, 2001).

28 Cavaignac was referring to evidence of the alleged confession of Dreyfus, especially two documents: Gonse's recent forgery, dated 6 January 1895 (*v.* Jan 1898) which Gonse had shown to Cavaignac earlier in January, and the statement Lebrun-Renault signed in front of Gonse and Henry. (*v.* 20 Oct 1897)

29 Dupuy, who was Prime Minister in 1894–95, was present at this session and knew that no such evidence existed. He remained silent. So too did Barthou, Poincaré and Hanotaux, all of whom were Ministers in 1895 and knew that Dreyfus had made no confession to Lebrun-Renault.

30 *Pro. Zola*, II, p. 520. No letter from Panizzardi to Schwartzkoppen dated 13 January was found in Schwartzkoppen's papers. Schwartzkoppen, *The Truth About Dreyfus*, p. 116.

31 Lucy quotes this letter which states that Dreyfus made no confession to Du Paty as evidence that there were no grounds for a confession and therefore there could not have been any confession to

Lebrun-Renault. She wrote this letter on Reinach's advice. It was possibly at this time that Gonse asked Du Paty to write a note from memory on the detailed report he had sent to Mercier on 31 December 1894. (*v.* Sept 1897, n. 139)

32   The two petitions contained some 2000 signatures, including scholars (Edouard Grimaux, Louis Havet, Paul Viollet, Arthur Guy, Léon Blum, Jean Psichari, Lucien Herr, Anatole France, and from the French Academy, Elie and David Halévy); writers (Pierre Quillard, Jacques Bizet, Marcel Proust, Octave Mirbeau, Charles Péguy); artists and poets (Claude Monet, Eugène Carrière, Ratisbonne, Barbier). Many other intellectuals supported a revision of the verdict of Dreyfus, including the sociologists Emile Durkheim and Lucien Lévy-Brühl and the writers André Gide (previously an antisemite), Stéphane Mallarmé, Jules Renard, Julien Benda and Maurice Maeterlinck.

33   In using this title Clemenceau launched the term 'intellectuals' in its contemporary sense, giving it political and social connotations. It was Maurice Barrès, however, who popularized the term, protesting that 'nothing is worse than these semi-intellectuals, than these aristocrats of the mind who affirm that they do not think like the crowd' (*Le Journal*, 1 February 1898). The word thus initially had a pejorative connotation (like the word dreyfusard), and described those who upheld opinions not favoured by the majority of the nation. On this aspect see C. Charle, *Naissance des 'intellectuels' (1890–1900)* (Paris: Ed. de Minuit, 1992), mainly pp. 139–82; Pagès, *Zola, un intellectuel*, p. 303, n. 60, and annex 2 (pp. 325–10) where the first lists of signatories are reproduced. See also M. Barrès, *Scène et doctrines nationales* (Paris: Trident, [1902] 1987), pp. 38–45. The lists were published in *L'Aurore* between 14 January and 6 February and totalled 1482 signatories.

34   Cavaignac did not doubt that this evidence (Gonse's letter dated 6 January 1895) was forged.

35   *Déb. Cass., 1899*, 327; A. Dreyfus, *Cinq années de ma vie* (1901), pp. 349–50.

36   Mathieu and Lucie knew that no such testimony existed in the Ministry of War. If some document did exist, it must be dated after 1897, almost three years after the events took place. Picquart had never mentioned the existence of any such document. Had it existed, Billot would have shown or mentioned it to Scheurer-Kestner to stop his campaign for Dreyfus' revision. Méline in turn would hardly have objected to the publication of a document that supposedly proved that Dreyfus had confessed. M. Dreyfus, *Dreyfusards!*, p. 127.

37   On these riots that inflamed the country during January and February, see Wilson, *Ideology and Experience,* pp. 106–24 and Wilson's article 'The Anti-Semitic Riots of 1898 in France', *The Historical Journal* 16, 4 (1973), 789–806. See also P. Birnbaum, *Le moment antisémite, un tour de la France en 1898* (Paris: Fayard, 1998). Birnbaum refers to police reports and numerous municipal and provincial archives, including those of Bar-le-Duc, Bordeaux, Clermont-Ferrand, Grenoble, Limoges, Lyon, Marseille, Montpellier, Nantes, Orléans, Privas, Rennes, Rouen, Paris, Saint-Malo and Toulouse.

38   In 1898 directories called *Indicateurs des juifs* listing Jewish people and their business addresses were in circulation in three regions, the Loire, Saône-et-Loire and Seine-Inférieure. This was a precursor to the list of Jews to be published in Vichy France (*v.* 1940–44) and in Germany during the Third Reich. One of the main features of this campaign was an appeal to women to boycott Jewish shops. In Nantes an association of antisemitic women was formed; in Toulouse, a demonstration was organized in March outside a Jewish shop called 'Le Paradis des Dames', which was probably a reference to Zola's novel *Au bonheur des dames*. See Wilson, *Ideology and Experience*, pp. 279–90.

39   Sporadic riots involving the ransacking of Jewish shops and synagogues had already occurred in Algeria in May 1897. One of *La Libre Parole*'s principal journalists, Adrien de Boisandré, explained that in Algeria, to avoid confusion with the Arabs who are also semites, it was preferable to use the term 'anti-Judaism' or 'anti-Jewish', rather than the 'more generally accepted scientific expression, antisemitism'. This explanation is found in a short pamphlet entitled *Petit catéchisme antijuif* (pp. 7–8), published in 1899 by l'Oeuvre Nationale de propagande antijuive. It could be bought at the Librairie Antisémite at 45 rue Vivienne, Paris.

40   Despite inciting this violence, neither Régis nor the other leaders were arrested. The anti-Jewish demonstrations in Algeria continued throughout 1898. Through his street gangs, Régis popularized antisemitic songs, including 'The Marseillaise Antijuive' and the 'Marche Antisémite'. (*v.* Appendix 25) See also Whyte, *The Accused*, pp. 98, 104; Wilson, *Ideology and Experience*, pp. 208, 119–20, 230–4; and Hebey, *Alger 1898, La grande vague antijuive* (Paris: Nil, 1996).

41   By narrowing the charges to this one accusation out of the many formulated in Zola's letter, Billot intended to avoid any discussion of Dreyfus' court martial and therefore the question of a revision. He also intended to restrict Zola's trial to matters on which the defence could produce no evidence. Zola wrote to Billot protesting against what he considered an 'attempt to suppress the truth. Is it really possible that you do not accept discussion of such clearly formulated accusations, which are no less serious for the accuser than for the accused?' Zola confirmed that despite this limitation he would fight to throw light on the Dreyfus case. With faith in the public's judgement, he added: 'You have forgotten that my judges will be 12 independent French citizens' (quoted in Weil, *Der Prozess des Hauptmanns Dreyfus*, p. 94). This was precisely what Esterhazy feared, and were the reasons for his disapproval of the trial. He wrote to his cousin Christian on 28 January that the trial was a serious error. *HAD*, 3, p. 296.

42 *HAD*, 3, p. 253. The manifesto was published in the leading newspapers on 19 January.

43 The letters were published by Stock in 1898 in a book of the same title.

44 Cavaignac mentioned this time that these consisted of (1) a report by Lebrun-Renault and (2) a letter from Gonse dated 6 January 1895 attesting Lebrun-Renault's statements.

45 A prestigious academic institution founded in 1530, which still functions today as a centre of research and teaching.

46 Hanotaux told Paléologue, 'These intellectuals, who were once my friends, I now find unbearable. Their campaign is abominable.' Baumont, *Aux sources de l'affaire*, pp. 189–90.

47 This shows the ambivalent position of the Socialists, who still considered Jews as largely representative of the capitalist class.

48 Quoted in *HAD*, 3, pp. 311–12.

49 This was very unlikely. Von Bülow mentioned in his memoirs that as soon as he was appointed he wanted to be informed about the Dreyfus Affair. B. von Bülow, *Mémoires du chancelier prince de Bülow* (trans. H. Bloch and P. Roques (Paris: Plon, 1930–31) vol.I, *Le Secrétariat d'État des Affaires étrangères et les premières années de chancellerie, 1897–1902*), pp. 198–200.

50 *Die Große Politik, der Europäischen Kabinette 1871–1914*. Sammlung der Diplomatischen Akten des Auswärtgen Amtes. Im Auftrag des Auswärtigen Amtes herausgegeben von Johannes Lepsius, Albrecht Mendelssohn Bartholdy und Friedrich Thimme, 13. Band: Die Europäischen Mächte untereinander 1897–1899, (Berlin, 1924), No. 3598, p. 300. This statement was considered by Germany to be an official denial, which is why further statements were refused despite attempts by the French Government to procure them during the Rennes trial. (*v.* Sept 1899, Negotiations with Germany) As much of the French press, both pro- and anti-dreyfusard, observed, the denial was limited. It was based on a text prepared on 13 December 1897 by Chancellor Hohenlohe in reply to interpellations in the German Chamber of Deputies. The original text was a much firmer statement. Baumont, *Aux sources de l'affaire*, pp. 194–5.

51 Bertulus was the magistrate seconded to Pellieux for his investigations of Esterhazy. Bertulus' investigation lasted until July 1898; a record is published in *Cass.*, I, 207–79.

52 The army also tried to keep Panizzardi silent. At the end of January Gonse invited Tornielli to the Ministry of War to convince him of Panizzardi's dubious moral and professional behaviour. He showed him some of his letters to Schwartzkoppen. Gonse probably also showed him the forged document known as the *billet des quatorze armées*, integrated into the Secret Dossier as proof of the homosexual relationship between Panizzardi and Schwartzkoppen. Lewis, *Prisoners of Honor*, pp. 222–3.

53 Schwartzkoppen, *The Truth About Dreyfus*, pp. 118–23.

54 Baumont, *Aux sources de l'affaire*, pp. 197–8.

55 Picquart, having been transferred to the 4th Rifle Brigade and thus detached from the army's General Staff, should have been brought before a board convened by his superior in Tunis. Instead, he was designated as a staff officer and brought before a board presided over by General de Saint-Germain, a close friend of Mercier. Another board member was Colonel Boucher, a close friend of Boisdeffre. *Cass.*, II, 206, Picquart.

56 In 1887 Galliffet had been instrumental in obtaining Picquart's appointment to the General Staff; Picquart then served for five years as head of the Deuxième Bureau. Galliffet became Minister or War on 22 June 1898.

57 *Cass.*, II, 153–68, records of the board of inquiry.

58 The board could not pass judgement only make recommendations to the Minister of War. Knowing that Picquart was to be a principal witness at Zola's trial, Billot was hoping that Picquart would cooperate by showing discretion. Billot sent two officers to Mont Valérien to remind Picquart that his future depended on his favourable testimony at Zola's trial. Gonse also asked Bertulus to tell Picquart that if he remained silent his career would not suffer. Picquart replied that he would do his best to reconcile his duty as a soldier with his duty as a witness. *Cass.*, I, 221, Bertulus.

59 *Déb. Cass.*, *1899*, 327–8. Dreyfus addressed two more long letters of appeal to the President in February (dated 3 & 7 February). All these letters are reproduced in A. Dreyfus, *Cinq années de ma vie* (1901), pp. 350–2.

60 After some initial hesitation Forain became a confirmed antisemite. On Forain, see R. Byrnes 'Jean-Louis Forain, Antisemitism in French art', *Jewish Social Studies*, 12 (1950), 247–56 and J. Magne, 'Forain et l'Affaire Dreyfus', *Nouvelles de l'estampe*, 8 (1973), 9–13.

61 Emmanuel Poiré, known as 'Caran d'Ache', was born in Russia in 1858. *Karandash* is the Russian word for 'pencil'. He travelled to France in 1878 and enrolled in the army. Five years later he entered the Ecole des Beaux-Arts, then became a caricaturist for *La Vie Parisienne, Rire, Caricature, Chat Noir* and *Le Figaro*.

62 On the role of caricature in the Affair, see C. Delporte, 'La guerre des caricatures', *Histoire 173, L'Affaire Dreyfus, vérités et mensonges* (January 1994), pp. 86–9. On the imagery relating to the Affair in France and abroad, see J. Grand-Carteret, *L'Affaire Dreyfus et l'image. 266 caricatures françaises et*

étrangères (Paris: Flammarion, n.d. [1898]); S. Nathan-Davis (ed.). *J'Accuse*. Catalogue of the Exhibition of 48 Images and Caricatures from France, Germany, Austria and the United States (Basel: Basel Theatre, 1994); Whyte, *The Accused*.

63   Only the main events of the trial are given here.

64   The names and addresses of the jurors were published in the Nationalist press (*La Libre Parole* and *L'Intrangiseant*, on 8 and 9 February respectively). This enabled some readers to intimidate the jurors during the trial. On 11 February they received letters threatening their wives if they acquitted Zola. On the morning of the verdict (23 February) they each received an anonymous letter offering them 10,000 francs to acquit him.

65   Mathieu kept his distance. He even decided not to attend the trial to avoid potential complications as it took place in a particularly tense and emotional atmosphere.

66   Dr Gibert, President Faure's close friend and doctor was also called by the defence to testify. A few weeks before the trial Gibert showed Mathieu a letter he had received from Senator Jules Siegfried, a close friend of the President, saying that if Gibert mentioned his conversation with Faure of 21 February 1895 the President would treat him as a liar or a madman. Despite this threat Gibert was determined to testify but fell seriously ill on arrival in Paris and was forbidden by his doctor to appear in court. Gibert then wrote down his statement so that it could be read in court. Mathieu burnt it in order to protect Gibert. (*v.* 23 March 1899) M. Dreyfus, *'Dreyfusards!'*, pp. 60–3.

67   Guérin recruited a uniformed troop of about 50 men, mainly butchers from the abattoirs of La Villette, as shock troops for demonstrations and street fights. On 9 February Guyot was attacked on the steps of the courthouse by one of Guérin's gangs.

68   *Pro. Zola*, 94, Mlle Dreyfus.

69   Reinach published some of these letters the following day in what became known as the dreyfusard press, e.g. *Le Siècle, L'Autorité, La Petite République, Le Radical.*

70   Lauth and Gribelin repeated that Picquart had shown Leblois the Secret Dossier of 1894. They stated that Picquart had forced them to lie about how the *petit bleu* reached the Section de Statistique and made them falsify it by using photography. Lauth said that he believed it was Picquart himself who had planted the *petit bleu* among the papers delivered by Bastian via the 'normal route'.

71   *Pro. Zola*, 288–9, Pellieux; 372, confrontation Picquart, Gribelin, Ravary, Lauth, Pellieux.

72   *Pro. Zola*, 391. Confrontation Picquart, Leblois, Henry, Gonse. Picquart challenged Henry to a duel over this incident; the duel took place on 5 March 1898.

73   *Pro. Zola*, 392, Confrontation Picquart, Leblois, Henry, Gonse.

74   Neither Labori or Clemenceau understood Henry's explanations, but they let him go. *DT*, 140. Henry's allusion to this mythical document fed rumours about it, which had been circulating since November 1897. (*v.* 15 Feb 1898, p. 167)

75   Jaurès was the only well-known politician to testify in favour of Zola.

76   Grimaux, one of the signatories of the petition for the revision, made an unequivocal statement. He dismissed all the documents and charges against Dreyfus as offering no proof whatsoever of his guilt and therefore of no value. He called firmly and provocatively for a revision: 'For we belong to those who want the light, all the light, even more light! Our consciences crave justice.' *Pro. Zola*, 581, Grimaux. (*v.* 25 Feb 1898)

77   *Pro. Zola*, 469, Bertillon.

78   Until then the General Staff had officially dated the *bordereau* to April 1894.

79   Labori did not insist on this significant fact, which could have destroyed the whole prosecution case of 1894. D. Johnson, *France and the Dreyfus Affair* (London: Blandford Press, 1966), p. 125.

80   Statements by the German and Italian Ambassadors and Governments (*v.* 15 & 24 Jan; 1 Feb 1898) always denied that their representatives in Paris had had any dealings with Dreyfus. Pellieux nevertheless believed the *faux Henry* was authentic. He did not understand why his superiors never chose to make use of it as proof and preferred to use the *res judicata* as their principal weapon. *DT*, p. 140. The diplomatic consequences of his statement in Court were highly significant. It put the French Government in a difficult position vis-à-vis Germany and Italy. Although Pellieux did not name the military attachés in his speech, the reference to them was implicit. (*v.* 18 Feb 1898, p, 168, Protests against Pellieux's statement regarding the *faux Henry*)

81   *Pro. Zola*, 724, Boisdeffre. Boisdeffre's statement was probably one of the most dramatic moments of Zola's trial. It even featured in the literature of the period. Marcel Proust describes the scene in his novel *Jean Santeuil*.

82   *Pro. Zola*, 739, Picquart. Talking to Paléologue that evening Henry described as 'absurd' Pellieux's decision to disclose 'such a secret document in public' and confirmed that Pellieux had acted without consulting his superior officers. Paléologue asked Henry whether he had any doubt about the document's authenticity. Henry answered, 'None whatsoever.' When Paléologue reported his discussion with Henry to Armand Nisard, then head of the Foreign Ministry, Nisard replied, 'The document is a forgery.' Paléologue, *Journal de l'Affaire Dreyfus*, pp. 113–16.

83 Present at the trial from the first day, Esterhazy at first found the officers' attitude towards him cold and distant. He probably complained about it to Pellieux. On the third day, following Boisdeffre's example, the officers went up to shake Esterhazy's hand. *DT*, 133.

84 *Pro. Zola*, 777, Stock.

85 In his long speech Zola spoke more of himself and his work than of Dreyfus. Even Reinach mentioned that the repetition of 'I' in the speech was excessive. *HAD*, 3, p. 470.

86 *Pro. Zola*, 824–7, Zola.

87 Labori's speech extended over three sessions, from 21 to 23 February.

88 *Pro. Zola*, 980–1, Labori.

89 On the final day of the trial the courtroom was filled with soldiers in mufti. Du Paty and Gonse had written to Jules Auffray, Royalist lawyer (and later a Nationalist Deputy), asking him to fill the courtroom with officers selected by the prosecution in order to influence the jury and support the Counsel for the Prosecution. But this was discovered and became public knowledge, as one of Du Paty's letters was sent in error to the wrong lawyer, the Republican François Auffray, who passed it to the Minister of Justice. (*v.* July 1899, Intrigues in Rennes prior to the second court martial)

90 *Pro. Zola*, 1002, Clemenceau.

91 *Pro. Zola*, 1003, Van Cassel.

92 *Pro. Zola*, 1004, Labori.

93 Wilson, *Ideology and Experience*, p. 111.

94 The court also ruled that the verdict should be published in Rochefort's paper *L'Intransigeant* and in five other papers of Reinach's choice.

95 *Cass.*, II, 138–40. This report contradicts his former report written on the day of the degradation, which made no mention of this.

96 Millevoye was probably the very first to have alluded to this document. On 8 December 1896, in his newspaper *La Patrie*, he mentioned the existence of a document that could be compromising for the Kaiser. Following Millevoye's public statement at this meeting, rumours of the *bordereau annoté* continued to circulate in top Parisian social circles.

97 Picquart recounted at length details of his involvement in the Dreyfus-Esterhazy affair since his arrival at the Section de Statistique in July 1895. He was questioned by Bertulus three further times. (16, 19 and 28 February) *Cass.*, I, 207–23, Picquart.

98 Beaumont, *Aux sources de l'affaire*, pp. 198–9.

99 The league was established in direct response to the antisemitic riots that took place in January. Its objectives included the fight against antisemitism. J. and M. Charlot, 'Un rassemblement d'intellectuels: la ligue des droits de l'homme', *Revue Française de science politique*, vol. 9, No. 3, (September 1959), pp. 995–1028.

100 Régis's speech is reproduced in Hebey, *Alger 1898*, Annex: pp. 98–9. This was also the date when Régis invited Drumont to stand as Algiers' second constituency's candidate in the legislative elections (May 1898).

101 Beaumont, *Aux sources de l'affaire*, pp. 190–1. Like Scheurer-Kestner much earlier, Monod broke off relations with Hanotaux because of his attitude towards the Affair, which they both judged weak and unjust. (*v.* 23 Jan 1898)

102 Schwartzkoppen, *Die Wahrheit über Dreyfus*, p. 130.

103 *Répertoire*, p. 159.

104 Charles Risler, mayor of the arrondissement, protested against this measure and tendered his resignation, which he later withdrew at the request of the Minister of the Interior.

105 Although not directly related to the Affair, the fact that this duel was fought three days after Zola's conviction reflects the atmosphere of violence the trial inspired. Between 1898 and 1904, over 40 duels were fought between dreyfusards and anti-dreyfusards. J. Garrigues, 'Mourir pour Dreyfus', *Histoire 173, L'Affaire Dreyfus, vérités et mensonges* (January 1994), pp. 52–3.

106 A. Dreyfus, *Cinq années de ma vie* (1982), pp. 201–2.

107 This act was illegal but only revealed in 1899.

108 Wilde was then living in exile in Paris under the pseudonym Sebastian Melmoth. Neither Esterhazy nor Strong mentions the exact date when their relationship began. *Cass.*, I, 599, Esterhazy; I, 740–2, Strong. It was most probably February. (*v.* following note).

109 Frederick Cornwallis Conybeare (1856–1924) was a well-known Oxford professor, a specialist in ancient Armenian language and literature. He began to take an interest in the Dreyfus–Esterhazy affair in early 1898. In February Conybeare was about to publish some military documents 'bought' by Schwartzkoppen from Esterhazy and written in Esterhazy's hand. Although at the last minute they were not published, Conybeare's revelations in the English press about the relationship between

Schwartzkoppen and Esterhazy, as well as his book on the Affair published at the end of 1898 caused much controversy in France. Conybeare, *The Dreyfus Case* (London: G. Allen). (*v.* 4 June 1898)

110 Wilde also revealed to Strong that Panizzardi gave Blacker copies of some documents related to the Affair which Blacker intended to publish. In spring 1898 Strong published articles suggesting Blacker's documents were forgeries. The anti-dreyfusard press in Paris repeated this information and thus aborted Blacker's campaign. J.R. Maguire, 'Carlos Blacker' in M. Drouin, *L'Affaire Dreyfus de A à Z* (Paris: Flammarion, 1994), pp. 136–42.

111 Wilde later reported to his translator, Henry Davray, that Esterhazy confessed to him having written the *bordereau*, adding derisively: 'Esterhazy is much more interesting than Dreyfus, who is innocent... one is always wrong to be innocent... to be guilty one needs imagination and courage... However, it is a pity that Esterhazy has never gone to prison.' H.M. Hyde, *Oscar Wilde: A Biography* (London: Eyre Methuen, 1976), p. 447; see also R. Ellman, *Oscar Wilde* (New York: Alfred A. Knopf, 1988), pp. 563–4. The journalist Chris Healy reported another story not corroborated by any other source, regarding the involvement of Wilde, always 'a hovering presence' in the Affair. Wilde was reputedly informed by a close friend of Schwartzkoppen that the German military attaché was sorry about Zola's conviction and was ready to help him. Wilde transmitted this information to Zola, who apparently wrote to Cavaignac threatening to publish certain compromising documents and pressing him to open an inquiry. C. Healy, *Confession of a Journalist* (London: Chatto & Windus, 1904), pp. 125–6.

112 Lemercier-Picard was involved in fabricating the *faux Otto*. (*v.* 25 Nov and 25 Dec 1897) Reinach suggested he was also involved in the *faux Henry*. Mathieu Dreyfus thought that Lemercier-Picard's death was linked to the exposure of the *faux Henry* during Zola's trial, suggesting that he had been eliminated by the General Staff to prevent interrogation of him by Bertulus. Bertulus was investigating Reinach's suit against Lemercier-Picard regarding the *faux Otto*. Several newspapers suggested that Lemercier-Picard had been murdered (e.g. *La Fronde*, 7 March). For further details, see *HAD*, 3, pp. 331–5, 493–512, and *ATQV*, pp. 172–6.

113 Henry at first tried to avoid this duel by suggesting Esterhazy fight Picquart. Esterhazy sent his seconds to Picquart on 3 March but Picquart refused the challenge on the grounds that Esterhazy was a disreputable person. On the same day Picquart sent his seconds to Henry, who used the same justification to refuse to fight Picquart. After discussion with Esterhazy at Mlle Pays' apartment Henry accepted the challenge and gave notice of his seconds. On 8 March Esterhazy's seconds proposed that a jury of honour (a jury of six people, chosen by the two sides), attest the honour of the challenger to enable the duel to take place. Although the jury of honour (one of whom was Déroulède) agreed to vouch for Esterhazy, Picquart still refused to accept claiming that criminals like Esterhazy should be judged by the law alone. *HAD*, 3, p. 516; Thomas, *Esterhazy*, pp.315–16.

114 Dreyfus sent further appeals to the President on 20 March, 22 April and 26 May 1898. See letters in *Déb. Cass., 1899*, 330–2. A. Dreyfus, *Cinq années de ma vie* (1901), pp. 353–5.

115 The appeal's list of signatories included the wives of journalist de Pressené, Trarieux, scholars Louis Havet, Paul Meyer, Jean Psichari, Goerges de Hervé and Mathias Morhardt, future General Secretary of the Ligue des droits de l'homme et du citoyen.

116 Discrimination against Jewish shops was one of the main features of the anti-Jewish press campaign led by Régis, as it also was for Guérin's Ligue antisémitique. (*v.* mid Jan–mid Feb 1898, Antisemitic riots, n. 38) Several of the lists of women published in *L'Antijuif* during 1898 are reproduced in Hebery, *Alger 1898*, pp. 107–33. The campaign against Jewish businesses also intended to be financially profitable for the instigators. This was also to be used later by the Third Reich. Guérin, Régis and the Mayor of Algiers planned to create a company to buy up Jewish firms ruined by the January riots and their campaign. Wilson, *Ideology and Experience*, pp. 186, 232, 456.

117 The Criminal Chamber was one of the three divisions of the Supreme Court of Appeal. The two others were the Civil and Appeals divisions. The records of this session are published in *Pro. Zola* II [1898], 437–508.

118 *Pro. Zola* II [1898], 478.

119 Viollet openly declared himself a dreyfusard in the newspaper *La Vérité* of 18 May 1898 (*v.* 14 Feb 1899).

120 *Pro. Zola* II [1898], p. 509. Throughout April the anti-revisionist press, mainly *La Libre Parole* and *L'Intransigeant*, continuously insulted the members of the Supreme Court of Appeal calling them 'criminals, forgers, imbeciles, Prussians...' Manau in particular was attacked, and described as 'the old agent of the Syndicate' and 'collaborator of the traitors'. This campaign was renewed with more vigour towards the end of 1898. (*v.* Nov 1898–Feb 1899, First revision investigation: Criminal Chamber, p. 223)

121 *Die Große Politik*, vol. 13, No. 2599, p. 301.

122 These articles were based on information Trarieux, Scheurer-Kestner, Zola and Reinach received from Tornielli. (*v.* 1 March 1898) They were actually written by Guyot and de Pressené. *HAD*, 3, p. 559.

123 Casella's statement was in fact rejected by Zola's defence. *HAD*, 3, p. 200. It is reproduced in *Pro. Zola* II [1898], 513–20.

124 Publication of Casella's articles began in March in the *Réforme de Bruxelles*. Panizzardi wrote to Schwartzkoppen giving his word of honour that he had never talked with Casella about Esterhazy's

last visit to him. Panizzardi was instructed by his superior officers to stay away from Paris for fear of adverse press coverage and went to Bern. The German Ambassador in Rome exchanged correspondence with Italy reminding the Italian Government that it had promised to cooperate with Germany. For further details, see Baumont, *Aux sources de l'affaire*, pp. 201–6. In 1900 Esterhazy claimed that Pellieux had told him to pay no attention to Casella's statement. *3ème Cass.*, III, 766. Also see *AD*, p. 572.

125 Herzog, *Der Kampf einer Republik*, p. 703.

126 This defamatory campaign against Picquart was inspired by Henry and Esterhazy and devised by Guénée, who had noticed that Picquart was away from home during March and April. Picquart was ill at the time and staying with one of his mother's friends. *Cass.*, I, 210, Picquart.

127 Beaumont, *Aux sources de l'affaire*, pp. 15–16.

128 Wilson, *Ideology and Experience*, pp. 254–5, 409, 603–4. The pamphlet was widely circulated in provincial cities such as Perpignan, Avignon, Amiens and Laval. It contained the antisemitic text known as 'the Rabbi's speech' included in the novel of Hermann Goedsches *Biarritz*. Following publication in Berlin in 1868 (under the pseudonym of Sir John Readclif), 'the Rabbi's speech' had an immense success among the antisemitic propaganda of Europe and Russia. On this aspect see N. Cohn, *Warrant for Genocide, the myth of the Jewish world-conspiracy and the Protocols of the Elders of Zion* (London: Eyre & Spottiswoode, 1967).

129 This appeal was the sole action by the committee in 1898. The committee stagnated until the foundation of the first anti-dreyfusard league, La Ligue de la patrie française, on 31 December 1898, when Pujo called for the first time for an 'action française'.

130 In order to procure this handwriting sample Mathieu invited a friend of his to send Mlle Pays a note with some flowers, asking her to a meeting. The ploy succeeded: Mlle Pays sent a short note thanking him for the flowers and asking to know more about the mysterious sender. Mathieu took the note to Cavard, head of the Sûreté, who happened to be one of his friends. They compared the handwriting with that of the original Speranza telegram. They were identical. *ATQV*, pp. 158–61.

131 This is the dossier which included the documents transmitted to the judges at Dreyfus' court martial in 1894 – sometimes known as *le petit dossier* – to which, from September 1897, documents were continuously added. (*v.* Sept–Oct 1897, Compilation of a second Secret Dossier)

132 Wattine was soon assisted by Captain Louis Cuignet, another Deuxième Bureau officer. (*v.* 28 June and 13 Aug 1898)

133 When collating this dossier there was one major item that could not be found, Panizzardi's telegram of 2 November 1894, of which there were various decoded versions. (*v.* 2 and 11 Nov 1894) Gonse asked Henry for this document. Henry, knowing that the telegram completely contradicted his fabrication (the *faux Henry*), claimed he could not find it. Gonse then sent him to obtain a copy from the Foreign Office. There (on 20 April, according to Paléologue) instead of handing Henry a copy, Paléologue dictated to him what was considered to be the final version. On his return to Gonse, Henry nevertheless said that he had not been able to obtain a copy from the Foreign Office. Billot tried unsuccessfully to get a copy from Hanotaux. Billot then instructed Gonse to obtain the original telegram from the postal authorities. Gonse was careful not to ask the postal authorities for a copy but for the original as he knew that it could not be found. Finally, following Henry's suggestion, Gonse asked Du Paty to reproduce the version from memory. Du Paty obeyed but left out the troublesome phrase 'Our emissary has been alerted'. Gonse augmented it using the text of the falsely decoded version and added a note that it was made by Du Paty from memory. *Cass.*, I, 557, Boisdeffre; I, 561, Gonse. Paléologue, *My Secret Diary of the Dreyfus Case*, trans from French by E. Mosbacher (London: Secker & Warburg, 1957), pp. 132–3. (*v.* Nov 1898–Feb 1899, First Revision investigation: Criminal Chamber, Paléologue's depositions, n. 36)

134 The pamphlet was published jointly by *Le Siècle* and Stock.

135 Schwartzkoppen, *Die Wahrheit über Dreyfus*, pp. 159–61.

136 Bertulus was already aware of the collusion between the General Staff and Esterhazy. One incident in particular made him realize that Gonse and Pellieux were trying to mislead him. Pellieux had already implied that Madame Monnier was the *'dame voilée'*; Monnier addressed her complaints directly to Bertulus, vowing that she was the subject of machinations. She suggested that the only way her involvement with Picquart might have reached the General Staff was through her confessor, the Jesuit Father Stanislas Du Lac, who had a large spiritual following in senior army circles, and was also Boisdeffre's confessor. In December 1898 Bertulus brought this accusation before the Supreme Court of Appeal. (*Cass.*, I, 235, Bertulus) Although Du Lac firmly denied having broken the confessional confidentiality, these anti-Jesuit rumours had a deep effect on public opinion. The 1904 investigation showed that Du Lac was probably not responsible for this rumour. *3ème Cass.*, II, 531, Picquart; III, 361–6.

137 Schwartzkoppen, *The Truth About Dreyfus*, pp. 194–7. During June and July Mathieu continued to encourage Casella to put pressure on Schwartzkoppen, but to no avail. According to Mathieu, Massip, manager of *Le Siècle*, was at the same time trying to obtain an official statement from von Bülow in Berlin. Von Bülow agreed to receive Massip's assistant, to whom he dictated a statement affirming

that if the French Government were to issue an official request, the German Government would allow Schwartzkoppen to give evidence before the French Ambassador in Berlin or any other French or German authority. Mathieu communicated this to Deputies Alexandre Ribot and Léon Bourgeois in yet another attempt to make them exert their influence with the Government. *ATQV*, pp. 167–8.

138 Three other antisemitic candidates from Algeria were elected Deputies, Firmin Faure, Marchal and Morinaud.

139 Bruno Weil believed that Schlieffen's statement was misleading. General Schwertfeger who edited Schwartzkoppen's papers, considered Weil's observation unjust. Weil, *Der prozess des Hauptmanns Dreyfus*, 211, 225, 242–3; Schwartzkoppen, *The Truth About Dreyfus*, pp. 169–70, 184.

140 Schwartzkoppen, *The Truth About Dreyfus*, pp. 129–30.

141 Herzog, *Der Kampf einer Republik*, p. 712.

142 *ASD*, p. 512.

143 La Bonne Presse was at its height at this time. Its principal newspaper, *La Croix*, had a daily circulation of over 180,000 and over 100 local weekly editions. Its illustrated weekly, *Le Pèlerin*, had an average circulation of 110,000. From 1896 *La Croix* also founded comités Justice-Egalité, which functioned as an electoral committee aiming to exclude 'Jews, Masons, and Socialists' from elections at all levels. Assumptionists and Jesuits were the cause of much concern to the Republican government. (*v.* 11 & 14 Nov 1899 & 24 Jan 1900). Sorlin; *La Croix et les Juifs*, pp. 196–213; M. Larkin, *Church and State after the Dreyfus Affair: The Separation Issue in France* (London: Macmillan, 1974), pp. 67–70.

144 Conybeare, *The Dreyfus Case*, pp. 267–70.

145 The first supporters of the league included Reinach, Scheurer-Kestner and a number of eminent scholars such as Victor Basch, Emile Duclaux, Edouard Grimaux, Gabriel Monod, Arthur Giry, Lucien Herr, Louis Hevet, Paul Meyer, Jean Psichari and Paul Viollet. Branches of the league were founded in various cities. On 22 January 1899 the Rennes branch was founded, led by Jules Andrade and Victor Basch (who was to become president of the league in 1926).

146 *Deb. Cass., 1899*, 332–3. A. Dreyfus, *Cinq années de ma vie* (1901), p. 356.

147 Until then Méline had agreed to pass Government decisions backed by a right-wing majority. By proposing this motion, Brisson sought to break the Government's alliance with the Nationalists.

148 Examination of the dossier could have revealed to Cavaignac their many fabricated documents and their collusion. (*v.* 13 Aug 1898) In ordering the examination of the content of the Secret Dossier, Cavaignac was challenging the authority of the *res judicata*. But, he was overwhelmed by the apparent evidence the dossier contained against Dreyfus and planned to use it in a dramatic move against the anti-revisionists. (*v.* 7 July 1898)

149 Henry talked about Du Paty's meeting with Esterhazy at the parc Monsouris. He denied that he had any dealings with Esterhazy and stated that they had first met at his duel with Picquart. (*v.* 5 March 1898) After the Zola trial (February 1898), at which time Du Paty had conveyed to Henry his doubts about the authenticity of the document quoted by Pellieux (the *faux Henry*), Henry began to blacken the name of Du Paty to his colleagues Gonse, Lauth and Junck. Henry thereby gave Gonse the impression that Du Paty was responsible for the Blanche and Speranza telegrams. Henry related to Gonse a conversation he had overheard between Esterhazy and Mlle Pays in their apartment. She admitted that their only mistake had been the Speranza and Blanche telegrams. Du Paty denied any knowledge of this matter to Gonse. *DT*, p. 150.

150 *ASD*, pp. 513–14. Esterhazy was probably informed about Cavaignac's investigation of the Secret Dossier. Cavaignac was determined to break the 'Syndicate' and put an end to the schemes of the anti-revisionists. (*v.* 11 Aug 1898) He also planned to break Esterhazy for whom he had no sympathy. (Bredin, *The Affair*, p. 307). Pellieux later admitted that Esterhazy was in a terrible physical state that day. *Cass.*, II, 176.

151 Two or three days later Lebrun-Renault destroys the entry, considering it 'no longer relevant'. Lebrun-Renault claimed he considered the entry was no longer relevant because Cavaignac had already copied it and read it in the Chamber. (*v.* 7 July 1898) *Cass.*, I, 276, Lebrun-Renault. For the text of the note see *Cass.*, II, 141.

152 The advice to appeal to the Minister of Justice was given to the Dreyfus family by Professor Ernest Buisson, who was close to several politicians, especially Léon Bourgeois. Reinach also strongly supported this action. Demange was to write the text. Labori suggested the assistance of Maître Mornard, who had successfully defended Zola before the Supreme Court of Appeal. (*v.* 2 Apr 1898) Mornard immediately accepted. *ATQV*, pp. 168–72.

153 Brisson preferred to rely only on the *res judicata* argument as he feared that the use of documents discovered after the trial might weaken the authority of the judgment. H. Brisson, *Souvenirs: affaire Dreyfus* (Paris: E. Cornély, 1908), p. 161.

154 Cavaignac did not mention Esterhazy's name, believing in fact that Esterhazy and Dreyfus had collaborated. His examination of the Secret Dossier confirmed his view that Esterhazy had written the *bordereau* on information he received from Dreyfus. Consequently, Cavaignac could punish Esterhazy and at the same time state that Dreyfus was justly convicted.

155 This was not the first time the existence of the *faux Henry* had been made public. Pellieux had referred to it during the Zola's trial, at which time it was contested (by Picquart, Scheurer-Kestner, Tornielli, Hanotaux and the press) as being false.

156 This evidence consisted of Gonse's forged letter to Boisdeffre confirming Lebrun-Renault's statement about the confession to Casimir-Périer (*v.* Jan 1898); Lebrun-Renault's words supposedly written in his notebook on 6 January 1895 (*v.* 4 July 1898); Lebrun-Renault's previous statement (*v.* 20 Oct 1897) and the statements of a number of Lebrun-Renault's colleagues (Captain Attel and Major Mitry). See full text of Cavaignac's speech in *AD,* pp. 376–9, 730–6.

157 A total of 15 Socialists abstained from the vote in addition to former Prime Minister Méline. On hearing the content of *Ce canaille de D.* Méline knew that it was the document revealed by Tornielli to Hanotaux as a forgery. (*v.* 15 & 28 Jan 1898) He also knew that Dreyfus had never confessed to Lebrun-Renault.

158 *La Revue Blanche* was one of the most important literary and artistic magazines of the 1890s. It was founded in 1891 by Alexander Natanson. Blum recalled the moment when Jaurès entered the offices of *La Revue Blanche*: Blum was sitting with Mathieu and Lucien Herr, 'our heads in our hands… silent… immobile'. Jaurès burst out, explaining that Cavaignac's speech was a critical moment for the dreyfusard cause: 'while Méline was invulnerable because he kept silent, Cavaignac made action possible because he spoke out'. L. Blum, *Souvenirs sur l'affaire* (Paris: Gallimard, [1935] 1981), pp. 132–3.

159 Thomas, *Esterhazy*, p. 322.

160 This letter was to be the first of a series of articles by Jaurès, *Les preuves* ('The Proofs'), published in *La Petite République* (*v.* 10 August 1898). It is reproduced in *ATQV*, pp. 152–5. The complete text of the letter in English is published in Bredin, *The Affair*, pp. 313–15.

161 Published in the press on 11 July.

162 Trarieux, Demange, Picquart, Labori and Reinach decided together that Demange was to write to Sarrien and Picquart, the only one who could confront Cavaignac. Picquart knew that Cavaignac's reaction would be severe and that he was likely to be arrested. (For his letter in English, see Bredin, *The Affair*, p. 316.) Brisson regretted publication of this letter. He could not ignore it, and had to pass it to Cavaignac. H. Brisson, *Souvenirs: affaire Dreyfus*, p. 158.

163 Informed by a relative that Christian was about to testify before Bertulus, Esterhazy sent him three letters pleading with Christian not to 'give him up'. Christian did not respond and took the letters to Bertulus. In his ruling (*v.* 28 July 1898, Legal complexities), Bertulus considered these letters as proof of Esterhazy's admission of guilt. *Cass.*, II, 270–1; 277–8, Bertulus' conclusions.

164 Bertulus requested Christian to hand over the documents that Christian had already entrusted to Labori in May. Bertulus and Labori together manoeuvred this transfer: Bertulus arrived at Labori's home, accompanied by a clerk, to claim the documents. Labori protested against this seizure (arguing his rights as a lawyer) and declared that he would only give them to his client, Christian. Christian asked Labori to return the documents, and delivered them to Bertulus. *ATQV*, pp. 161–2.

165 *Cass.*, II, 229–33, Christian Esterhazy.

166 Cavaignac's initial intention was to make Du Paty bring a defamation charge against Picquart but he was dissuaded from it by the Public Prosecutor's office. Instead of filing the suit against Picquart for his open letter to Brisson (9 July), Cavaignac succeeded in obtaining the Government's approval to prosecute him under the Law relating to espionage (of 18 April 1886). Consequently, he was allowed to summon Picquart and Leblois before a tribunal de police (a criminal court of summary justice, i.e. without a jury)

167 *HAD*, 4, p. 45. The letter was not answered. Fabre gave Trarieux his word that Picquart would not be arrested immediately. *AD*, p. 738.

168 As a consequence of his imprisonment, the military board of inquiry called to judge Esterhazy on Cavaignac's instruction (11 July) cannot operate. (*v.* 24–7 Aug 1898)

169 Trarieux had probably reassured Picquart that he would not be arrested. Cavaignac later inadvertently divulged that he alone was responsible for Picquart's arrest. He stated in the Chamber on 12 January 1899 that 'when I ordered Picquart's arrest', which he immediately corrected to 'when Brisson ordered Picquart's arrest'. Brisson, *Souvenirs: affaire Dreyfus*, pp. 156–7.

170 After interrogating Du Paty, Cavaignac told Roget (his new principal private secretary) he believed Du Paty was telling the truth; Roget insisted that Du Paty was lying. (*Cass.*, I, 629, Roget) At Rennes, Gonse stated that it was only in July 1898 that he learnt about the parc Monsouris meeting with Esterhazy. He also stated that the meeting was organized without his or Boisdeffre's knowledge, and must have been Du Paty's initiative. Boisdeffre also testified that he only learnt about Du Paty's manoeuvres in October and November 1897 following his long sick-leave (June–August 1898). *Rennes*, II, 157, Gonse; *Cass.*, I, 566, Gonse; I, 559, Boisdeffre.

171 This took place in prison rather than in the magistrate's office because Esterhazy claimed he was ill and refused to be transferred from prison. Tézenas, Esterhazy's and Mlle Pays' lawyer, and his secretary Jeammaire were also present. *Cass.*, I, 223, Bertulus.

172 Mlle Pays agreed to sign the interrogation report which mentioned her admission of 'having committed but one mistake, the Speranza telegram'. *Cass.,* I, 223–4, Bertulus; *Cass.,* II, 233, Pays.

173 The papers discovered at Mlle Pays' apartment contained items from Gonse, Pellieux (the draft of Esterhazy's letter to him requesting a court martial, which was corrected by Pellieux (*v.* 2 Dec 1897, Pellieux's second investigation of Esterhazy), and letters from Du Paty, Henry and Pauffin de Saint-Morel, Boisdeffre's private secretary. The most significant document was a note written by Esterhazy containing the word 'Basel' and the initial 'C.' (Cuers). This suggested that Esterhazy may have been warned about the meeting with Cuers. (*v.* 6 Aug 1896) *Cass.,* I, 224–9, Bertulus.

174 *Cass.,* I, 224–5, Bertulus.

175 *Cass.,* II, 241–53, Esterhazy, Pays.

176 Henry was particularly alarmed by the document containing the words 'Basel' and the initial 'C.' (*v.* n. 173 above) Bertulus suggested that if Esterhazy had been informed at the time (summer 1896) about Picquart's investigations of him, as this document proved, it must have been by someone from the Deuxième Bureau. *Cass.,* I, 226, Bertulus.

177 *Cass.,* I, 227–8, Rennes, I, 345, Bertulus.

178 Gonse and Roget later confirmed Henry's composure on returning from Bertulus on 18 July. *Cass.,* I, 573–4, Gonse; I, 624, Roget. Although Bertulus' version of their encounter is likely to be authentic, the two versions are the only ones available since there were no other witnesses to the conversation. Bertulus' error was probably in letting Henry go instead of having him arrested. By the time Bertulus revealed the details of this encounter to the Criminal Chamber (December 1898) and again at the Rennes court martial (*v.* Aug 17 1899), Henry was no longer alive. (*v.* 31 Aug 1898, Henry's death)

179 Roget was present at this meeting. *Cass.,* I, 100, Roget. Cavaignac preferred Esterhazy to be prosecuted by Bertulus. Esterhazy explained to Tézenas that the enmity between Cavaignac and him was a 'family affair', going back a generation. Esterhazy, *Les dessous de l'affaire Dreyfus,* p. 26.

180 It was Esterhazy who, in the words of Bertulus, 'had the malicious pleasure' of bringing these documents to Henry's attention, suggesting that they might be of interest to the General Staff. *Cass.,* I, 228–29, Bertulus; II, 253–5, Bertulus' investigation. Henry later submitted these documents to the Criminal Chamber, but when they were later shown to Bertulus by the Chamber (December 1898), they no longer contained the word 'Basel' or the initial 'C.' Additionally they exhibited traces of erasure. Without denouncing Henry for falsifying the documents, Bertulus produced the originals. *Cass.,* II, 18–25, Roget, Gonse, Bertulus; *Rennes,* I, 349–50, Bertulus.

181 This suit, although proposed by Bertulus, was more harmful than helpful; it led to a series of legal complications involving investigations, rulings and appeals, which ended with the annulment of Bertulus' ruling on Esterhazy and Mlle Pays and their release from prison. (*v.* 27 July; 12 Aug 1898, legal complexities)

182 *Cass.,* II, 261–79, Bertulus.

183 *Rennes,* I, 650, Junck. Junck censured Bertulus for these words. (*v.* 21 Aug 1899, Rennes court martial)

184 Probably expecting a house search, Esterhazy had hidden the most important documents relating to the collusion in the lining of his kepi. Bertulus searched the kepi but did not open the lining. *Cass.,* I, 228–9, Bertulus; *Rennes,* I, 656–8, Junck.

185 Picquart's appeal maintained that Bertulus was competent to act as a civil lawyer in both cases since Mlle Pays, a civilian, was involved. The appeal of the Public Prosecutor maintains that Bertulus was not competent to proceed, since Du Paty was a soldier.

186 The records of Fabre's investigation are published in two volumes *Fabre* (see Abbreviations and Conventions) and *L'Instruction Fabre et les décisions judiciaires ultérieures. Suppléments* (Paris: Stock, 1909). See also extracts in *AD,* pp. 738–58.

187 Although impressed by the precision of Picquart's responses, Fabre was unwilling to believe that the military officers could bear false witness against their colleague. He perceived the eagerness of the General Staff to separate the charges in order to withdraw Picquart from civil jurisdiction. For more on Fabre's investigation, see DC, pp. 180–2; *DT,* pp. 163–4.

188 *Fabre,* 217–19. Cavaignac hoped that the charges would be separated so that Picquart could be court-martialled. Fabre suggested to Picquart that he should apply for temporary release from prison. Picquart refused. *HAD,* 4, p. 116 (*v.* 8 & 12 Sept 1898).

189 *Fabre,* 219–20. See also *AD,* pp. 756–8.

190 Included in *La vérité en marche* (1969), pp. 136–44. See full English text in Zola, *the Dreyfus Affair: 'J'Accuse' and Other Writings,* pp. 66–73.

191 Following an exchange of insults in Court, Nationalist Deputy Déroulède and Radical Deputy Hubard fought a duel the same evening.

192 Zola left under pressure from his friends and lawyer, who had hoped that Bertulus' investigation would bring to light new facts and allow Labori to start fresh proceedings. Other revision supporters, like Reinach, disapproved of his departure. Zola's self-imposed exile was to last 11 months. (*v.* 5 June 1899)

193 Pagès, *Emile Zola, un intellectuel*, p. 258. Clemenceau published this article without consulting Zola. He sent Lazare to London to show Zola the article on the morning of its publication. Just before leaving, Zola wrote a long article he wished to be published in *L'Aurore*. Lazare had to inform Zola that the paper judged it more judicious to publish Clemenceau's shorter text. According to Lazare, Zola accepted this, realizing Clemenceau had acted in the common interest. This article was not included in Zola's *La vérité en marche* or in Clemenceau's books on the Affair. Pagès, *Emile Zola, un intellectuel*, pp. 271–3.

194 Several intellectuals, including the poet Jules Barbier and the journalist de Pressensé, protested against this. Barbier submitted his resignation as an officer of the Legion of Honour: it was not accepted. De Pressensé wrote to the Grand Chancellor: 'I would find it repugnant to continue adorning my button-hole with a small piece of red ribbon which has become the symbol of contempt of legality and the violation of the principles of 1789, since the Council of the Order has withdrawn the right to wear it from a writer who only demanded respect for the elementary guarantees of law.' De Pressensé, a member of the Ligue des droits de l'homme et du citoyen, was one of the main organizers and orators at public meetings in favour of the revision and against Picquart's arrest. (*v.* 19 Sept & 15 Nov 1898) After the Amnesty Law (*v.* Dec 1900), Zola, although reinstated as an officer of the Legion of Honour, refused to wear the decoration. H. Troyat, *Zola* (Paris: Flammarion, 1992), p. 389.

195 Judet synchronized his press campaign with Zola's trials. The first article appeared on 23 May, the first day of the reopening of Zola's trial at Versailles; the second on 25 May; the third on 18 July, the second reopening of Zola's trial in Versailles.

196 From then until 1903 Guérin continued to receive a monthly subsidy from the Duc d'Orléans. Along with other substantial donations from Royalist Deputies this allowed Guérin to launch his newspaper *L'Antijuif* (*v.* 21 Aug 1898) and later to establish headquarters at 51 rue Chabrol, Paris. (*v.* April 1899) During 1898–99 the League reached the height of its popularity. In July 1898 the police estimated it had a total of 11,000 members. S. Wilson, 'The Ligue Antisémitique Française', *Wiener Library Bulletin,* 25 (London, 1972), pp. 33–9 ; Z. Sternhel, *La droite révolutionnaire*, pp. 221–30.

197 The series continued until 20 September 1898. The articles were assembled into a book, published in October 1898. A new annotated edition was published in 1998: J. Jaurès, *Les preuves* (Paris: La Découverte, 1998), preface by J.D. Bredin, introduced by M. Rebérioux.

198 Desachy erroneously dates this to 11 July. Cavaignac's project included summoning before the Senate constituted as an Haute Cour de justice (special court trying members of the Government) all the people he listed as responsible for the revisionist campaign. The draft of this project was published in *Le Siècle* (12 May 1903). See also Brisson, *Souvenirs: affaire Dreyfus*, p. 79 and ff, 165; *AD*, 769–72.

199 It is possible that despite his belief in the guilt of Dreyfus, Cavaignac asked Cuignet to continue the verification of the items in the dossier in view of the warnings he had received. The historian Monod (an ardent dreyfusard), who knew Cavaignac, wrote to him before and after 7 July mentioning the forgery or forgeries included in the dossier. After Zola's conviction, Du Paty also conveyed his doubts to Cavaignac about the document mentioned by Pellieux at the trial (the *faux Henry*). Johnson, *France and the Dreyfus Affair*, p. 141; *ATQV*, p. 178.

200 For Cuignet's examination of the *faux Henry*, see Roget's full report (dated 30 August 1898) in Appendix 28.

201 There may be several reasons for the delay in interrogating Henry. Cavaignac had a full programme of political engagements. He wanted to wait for the completion of Fabre's investigation of Picquart (*v.* 13 July–25 Aug) and to deal with Esterhazy. He had already ordered Esterhazy to appear before a military board of inquiry (11 July), but the order was not carried out immediately because of Esterhazy's arrest. (12 July) It was reissued after Esterhazy's release from prison. (*v.* 24–27 Aug 1898)

202 The antisémitique française was at first supported and promoted by Drumont's *La Libre Parole*. After the May election campaign, during which Guérin acted as Drumont's electoral agent, disagreements between the two antisemitic leaders escalated. Jealous of Guérin's growing success, Drumont refused to support the League in his newspaper. Guérin broke with Drumont by founding the league's own paper as a rival to *La Libre Parole*. Some 40,000 copies of *L'Antijuif* were regularly printed, half of which was distributed as free propaganda. The paper ran to 42 issues, the last one appearing on 5 February 1899. Wilson, 'The Ligue Antisémitique Française', pp. 33–9. Guérin described these conflicts with Drumont in *Trafiquants de l'antisémitisme*, pp. 104–21.

203 Roget's detailed report on Cuignet's discovery of the *faux Henry* is signed 30 August. *3ème Cass.*, I, 415–20. See also *AD,* pp. 803–6.

204 Schwartzkoppen, *Die Wahrheit über Dreyfus*, pp. 207–9.

205 Quoted in Bredin, *The Affair*, pp. 325–6. On his release from prison and notification of his forthcoming appearance at a military board of inquiry, Esterhazy sought the support of Drumont and Mayer, editor of *Le Gaulois*, in their respective papers. *Cass.*, I, 741, Strong.

206 The grounds of complaint against Esterhazy (specified in the preliminary report, dated 22 August, and signed by Colonel Kerdrain) were his letters to Mme Boulancy and to President Faure (Oct–Nov 1897), various articles in *La Libre Parole* (including the Dixi articles from November 1897), and his misconduct as an officer in his private life (living with a prostitute and disreputable financial dealings).

The records of the inquiry (held in closed sessions), including the Kerdrain's report are published in *Cass.*, II, 169–88, dossier disciplinaire Esterhazy. See also *AD*, pp. 542–6.

207 The records of this session contain the dialogue between Esterhazy and Du Paty. *Cass.*, I, 177–80. See also extracts in Thomas, *Esterhazy*, pp. 332–3.

208 This note contained the sentence 'General de Boisdeffre is not unaware that I had some indirect communications with Major Esterhazy.'(*v.* Appendix 17)

209 According to Strong, Esterhazy was furious with the General Staff. He threatened to reveal to the military board of inquiry all he knew about their manoeuvres, both against himself and Dreyfus. Strong led Esterhazy to confess that he had written the *bordereau* under Sandherr's instructions. According to Strong, Esterhazy explained that if the military board of inquiry decided to discharge him from the army, he would have to leave France because of Christian's suit against him. (*v.* 21 July 1898) He even mentioned suicide. Strong calmed him and suggested that he should publish the truth instead. Esterhazy then had the idea of selling all that he knew 'to a rich newspaper'. Strong promised to help him and introduced him to *Pall Mall Gazette* and the *London Observer*. *Cass.*, I, 742–4, Strong. (*v.* 1 Sept 1898) Esterhazy's version differs. According to him, Strong, whom he always found supportive, was the first to congratulate him on his release from prison (12 August). Once he had learned from Esterhazy that Cavaignac had ordered him to appear before a military board of inquiry, he had invited him to England, promising to publish articles to clear him and said he would find him a respectable way of 'earning his living'. *Cass.*, I, 599, Esterhazy.

210 The report was published in *Le Siècle* on 10 March 1899.

211 The board had to decide whether Esterhazy should be cashiered for habitual misconduct, grave disciplinary offences or for offences against honour. He was only found guilty on the first charge.

212 Since the board's decision was not unanimous, Esterhazy could only be subject to disciplinary punishment without dismissal. Despite this Cavaignac decided to cashier him. (*v.* 31 Aug 1898)

213 Cavaignac should have summoned the Military Governor of Paris to be present when interrogating Henry. Cavaignac admitted (before the Chamber of Deputies, 6 April 1903) that he had decided to 'abandon regular procedures'.

214 M. Dreyfus, *Dreyfusards!*, p. 167. Jaurès arrived at this conclusion by sheer reasoning and not by any knowledge of the forgery. It was another two days before Henry's confession became public, (*v.* 30 Aug 1898)

215 As a result of his pamphlet Pichot was forced to leave the Catholic seminary of Felletin where he had been teaching. The pamphlet was published in 1899. L'abbé Pichot, *La conscience chrétienne et l'affaire Dreyfus*. (Paris: Société d'éditions littéraires, 1899). Albert I, Prince of Monaco, closely following the Dreyfus Affair, a pacifist who became an ardent dreyfusard (*v.* 25 Nov 1898; 13 Feb & 3 July 1899) nominated Pichot on 28 April 1900 priest of Sainte-Dévote, a parish of Monaco. D. Dayen, 'Un prêtre creusois dreyfusard: l'abbé Pichot' in M. Cassan, J. Boutier, N. Lemaître (eds) *Croyances, pouvoirs et société. Des Limousins aux Français*. (Treignac: Les Monédières, 1988), pp. 323–2.

216 Henry's interrogation lasted about an hour. Roget was responsible for taking notes *in extenso* (Roget's report is included in *Déb. Cass., 1898*, pp. 98–104). Since his minutes were dated 3 October 1898, it has been suggested that they may not have fully reflected all that transpired. Reinach considers Roget's report however as absolutely authentic. *HAD*, 4, p. 184. Whether Henry made other revelations during his interrogation by Cavaignac, which may have necessitated his death remains unknown. Barlow suggests that Henry named one of his accomplices, probably one of the officers present at the interrogation. Barlow, *A History of the Dreyfus Case*, p. 438.

217 *HAD*, 4, p. 191; *Répertoire*, p. 196. See also *AD*, p. 316.

218 *Rennes*, I, 530, Boisdeffre. Cavaignac confided to an intimate friend that he was relieved Boisdeffre had resigned since it spared him the anguish of having to ask him to do so. H. Dardenne-Cavaignac, *Lumières sur l'affaire Dreyfus* (Paris: Nouvelles Editions Latines, 1964), p. 178.

219 Having ceased to act 'in conformity with regular procedures' (*v.* n.213 above), Cavaignac could have issued a warrant to arrest Henry. Mercier had done so in the case of Dreyfus. No formal charge was made against Henry. And he was not sent to Cherche-Midi prison, as he should have been. Before leaving the Ministry and on orders from Cavaignac, Henry went with General Gonse to his office to transfer control of the Section de Statistique. Colonel Féry reported that he heard Henry telling Gonse: 'I do not know what stops me from taking a revolver to blow my brains out.' He kept mumbling broken sentences expressing his fear of what would happen to him and repeated that he had only acted in the interests of his country and the army. Colonel Féry's report was countersigned by Zurlinden and submitted to Cavaignac. *3ème Cass.*, I, 430–2. See also *AD*, pp. 812–14.

220 That evening Cavaignac informed the Cabinet Ministers dining with Delcassé. When Ernest Vallé remarked, 'this means a revision', Cavaignac replied, 'less than ever'. *HAD*, 4, p. 201. Cavaignac still believed in the complicity between Dreyfus and Esterhazy; for him, the discovery of Henry's forgery (committed in 1896) did not clear Dreyfus (condemned for alleged treason committed in 1894). Cavaignac's certainty about the guilt of Dreyfus was based largely on Dreyfus' alleged confession (no one – neither Dupuy, Méline, Boisdeffre, nor Mercier – ever contested Cavaignac's statement

concerning the existence of 'proofs' for this. *v.* 13 Jan 1898). Like others, Cavaignac might also have believed that Henry had committed his forgery in order to conceal another top secret document, which could not be shown because of the security risk (the alleged *bordereau annoté*, signed by the Kaiser). Finally, Cavaignac was convinced of the 'Syndicate's conspiracies to save Dreyfus. *DT*, p. 169; Johnson, *France and the Dreyfus Affair*, p. 148.

221 *Répertoire*, p. 196; *AD*, p. 815. Bertulus read the communiqué of Henry's arrest on the morning of 31 August in the presence of Dr Peyrot, the doctor responsible for all Paris' hospitals and member of the Académie Française. Bertulus told Peyrot: 'I will be a terrible witness for Henry', explaining the scene in his chambers in July when Henry burst into tears. (*v.* 18 July 1898) The following day, when news of Henry's death was published, Peyrot returned to Bertulus, who related the scene in detail. Peyrot asked to take notes and told Bertulus he wished to pass the information to a member of the Government. Bertulus reported this story at the Rennes trial adding that he did not know whether Peyrot had actually done so. *Rennes*, I, 355–6, Bertulus.

222 Text of the letter as was read in the Chamber of Deputies on 7 April 1903, reproduced in *Répertoire*, p. 196. See also *AD*, p. 817.

223 The visit did not take place. Henry was already dead a few hours after sending the letter.

224 *Cass.*, I, 123, Roget. see also *AD*, p. 814. Henry's words 'you know in whose interest I acted' and 'everyone is going to abandon me' continue to provoke controversy and debate among historians as to whom the interest referred: the General Staff, especially Henry's superiors Generals Gonse and Boisdeffre, Esterhazy, or even some other associates involved in espionage. P. Miquel, *L'Affaire Dreyfus* (Paris: PUF, [1959] 2003, 10th edition), p. 74.

225 *Déb. Cass., 1898,* 84, Report of Ballot-Beaupré. See also *AD*, p. 814. Henry seemed to be in a state of confusion. The weather was exceptionally hot that day, and a half-empty bottle of rum was found in Henry's cell.

226 Because of the circumstances of Henry's death and certain irregularities connected with it, there is a possibility that it was induced suicide or even murder: the cut-throat razor identified as the fatal weapon would not have been allowed in the cell; Henry was right-handed, but the razor was found in his left hand; an autopsy was not conducted on the grounds that the death was immediately classed as suicide. All this fuelled rumours and allegations that Henry was murdered. Several reports appeared in the press about an officier d'ordonnance who visited Henry in his cell and stayed with him for one hour before he was found dead. Charpentier remarks that the denial of the government of this visit was given to the *Agence Nationale* and not to *Havas*, to whom the ministers used to give their official statements. He also refers to irregularities with the procedure to place Henry's body in the coffin. He cites independent witnesses' statements that the body was found in cell 13 on a completely dry bed, whereas a pool of blood had to be mopped up in the connecting cell, concluding that the body had been moved. Charpentier even cites witnesses who claimed having seen Henry in Buenos Aires and Paris, after his announced death. Charpentier initiated a long correspondence with Mlle Henry in 1935–36, trying in vain to obtain from her more details about Henry's death. A. Charpentier, *Les côtés mystérieux de l'Affaire Dreyfus*, pp. 125–42, 251–78. See also A. Israël, *Les vérités cachées de L'Affaire Dreyfus* (Paris: Albin Michel, 1999), 'sur la piste de l'assassinat d'Henry' pp. 241–55. The murder theory, though never substantiated, has also been suggested by several other historians. See Miquel, *L'Affaire Dreyfus*, p. 75; J. Kayser, *The Dreyfus Affair*, trans. Nora Bickley (London: Heinemann, 1951) p. 248. In her book on her father's involvement in the Affair, Cavaignac's daughter, Henriette Dardenne-Cavaignac, argues that Henry's death was certainly suicide and cites, for example, the fact that the razor used was not very sharp and there were numerous scars (seven or eight) on Henry's body. H. Dardenne-Cavaignac, *Lumières sur l'Affaire Dreyfus*, pp. 191–2. Barlow asserts that it is impossible for any person to sever with his own hands the carotid artery on both sides as Henry's wounds were originally described. He also suggests that during Henry's interrogation by Cavaignac, Henry may have named one of his accomplices, probably one of the officers present at the interrogation. George Barlow, *A History of the Dreyfus Case* (London: Simkin, Marshall, Hamilton, Kent, 1899) p. 439. Brisson later stated: 'According to constitutional law I am responsible for the death of Henry, who was sent to Mont Valérien where he was poorly guarded.' *Le Siècle*, 13 July, 1903.

227 *Répertoire*, p. 197; *AD*, p. 815. It was only at the end of the fourth Cabinet meeting that Brisson discovered one of the latest telegrams arriving that day from Mont Valérien, announcing Henry's suicide. Brisson went to see Cavaignac, who had meanwhile agreed to Boisdeffre's resignation, and insisting on discussing at length his resignation. Henriette Dardenne-Cavaignac claims that Cavaignac was not immediately informed of Henry's death because of the poor communications between Mont Valérien and the Ministry of War. She further says that Brisson asked Cavaignac whether he had absolute trust in the General Staff officers and whether they were not responsible for Henry's death as 'a guarantee of his silence'. Cavaignac protested. Dardenne-Cavaignac also reported that when her father was asked whether he had taken enough precautions to prevent the suicide, he maintained 'it is impossible to prevent a man who wants to kill himself from doing so… if it had not been a razor Henry would have hanged himself with his sheet…' Cavaignac also argued that even if he had been able to stop Henry he would not have had the right to do so. Dardenne-Cavaignac, *Lumières sur l'affaire Dreyfus*, pp. 191–2.

228 Esterhazy's escape from the rue Douai was hazardous: on his way to Brussels he first had to hide behind a furniture van, then jump onto an omnibus, then a tram, then a train, changed train several times, shaving off his moustache. He stayed in Brussels under the name of de Bécourt, before he reached London. Thomas, *Esterhazy*, pp. 345–7. Although Esterhazy's version differs from that of Strong (*v.* 24 Aug 1898, n. 209), Esterhazy had already thought of escaping from France at the end of August. He said that on hearing about Henry's death, two of his friends told him: 'with such rascals, you have only two choices: gun or flight'. *Cass.*, I, 600, Esterhazy.

229 According to Zurlinden, Pellieux withdrew his resignation after discussion with Cavaignac. Cavaignac denied his part in concealing the existence of Pellieux' resignation letter from Brisson. The investigation of 1904 revealed that Pellieux did see Cavaignac and that Cavaignac dissuaded him from handing in his resignation. Pellieux's aide-de-camp, Henri-Denis Galon, said that Cavaignac told Pellieux he should not exaggerate his responsibility regarding the *faux Henry*. Cavaignac reassured Pellieux that he trusted him. Galon also testified that Pellieux said on the morning he wrote the letter: 'from today, a revision is imperative'. *3ème Cass.*, II, 610–13, Galon. Brisson repeated several times in his memoirs the seriousness of this episode, which could have triggered an immediate revision. See *AD*, pp. 817–21.

230 The burial took place on 4 September. Monsignor Latty, Bishop of Châlons, forbade a religious service. Instead, the mayor made a patriotic speech. None of the General Staff generals attended the ceremony but many officers and villagers accompanied the coffin draped with Henry's uniform.

231 Sarrien as Minister of Justice could have precipitated the revision procedure by initiating it with a Revision Commission. He insisted on first obtaining Cavaignac's approval. As Cavaignac refused, Brisson sent Léon Bourgeois, an influential and close friend, to persuade him but this was unsuccessful. Brisson said he was willing to resign on condition that Cavaignac agreed. In a last attempt to resolve the situation, Brisson advised the Dreyfus family, through a mutual friend, Gachet, that the appeal should come from them. Lucie's appeal was finally written during a meeting between Reinach, Demange, Trarieux, Labori, Mornard, Ranc and Mathieu. *ATQV*, p. 182.

232 *Répertoire*, p. 200; AD, p. 816.

233 Maurras' 'Apologia for Colonel Henry' is considered as the starting point of the future Action Française. (*v.* 20 June 1899) E. Weber, *Action Française: Royalism and Reaction in Twentieth-Century France* (Stanford: Stanford University Press, 1962), pp. 17, 27–8.

234 Brisson believed that Cavaignac's replacement should be an army officer who approves the revision. He first offered the post to Saussier, who refused. It was President Faure who recommended Zurlinden.

235 Picquart was still under arrest. Labori's request was based on the series of 'new facts': the discovery of the *faux Henry*, Henry's death, the confirmed collusion between Du Paty and Esterhazy, the investigation of Du Paty. These could be considered to annul Fabre's investigation and ruling concerning Picquart and Leblois. (*v.* 13 July–25 Aug 1898)

236 *Die Große Politik*, vol. 13, No. 3606, p. 305.

237 The records of Renouard's investigation are published in *Cass.*, II, 189–206.

238 *Fabre*, 281–4. See also AD, pp. 822–3. Before taking any further steps towards the revision Zurlinden wanted to study the Dreyfus' case carefully. He consulted and was influenced by Roget and Cuignet, both of whom were familiar with the Secret Dossier and believed Dreyfus to be guilty.

239 *Déb. Cass., 1898*, 120, Ballot-Beaupré's report. Zurlinden's response can perhaps be explained by the fact that two copies of Du Paty's commentary had been burnt. (*v.* 17 Jan 1895–end Dec 1897) *HAD*, 4, p. 257; DC, p. 194. Zurlinden later stated that despite his searches at the Ministry he could not find any proof of the secret communication of documents to the judges at Dreyfus' court martial, which he continued, therefore might have been mere rumour. *Cass.*, I, 48, Zurlinden.

240 Picquart sent a second letter to Sarrien on 15 September, with complementary information. Picquart's letters are included in *Déb. Cass., 1898*, 108–22, Ballot-Beaupré's report. See English version in Snyder, *The Dreyfus Case. A Documentary History* (New Jersey: Rutgers University Press, 1973), pp. 147–60.

241 *Fabre*, 284–90. Zurlinden was convinced by Roget and Cuignet that Picquart had forged the *petit bleu* and that the erasure was Picquart's work. Earlier events suggest that the erasure had been made in 1896, probably by Henry (*v.* 10 Nov 1897, n. 53 the Speranza and Blanche telegrams; 20 Nov–3 Dec 1897, Pelliux's second investigation, n. 94). However, the fact that this accusation is mentioned now officially for the first time could indicate that the erasure was effected much later, after Henry's suicide. In that case, it could have been the work of Cuignet or Roget who, from early September 1898, were in charge of the examination of the Secret Dossier.

242 *Déb. Cass., 1898*, 83–5. Before Esterhazy left France he had signed a contract with the publisher Fayard for a book about the Affair, to be published in instalments. (*v.* 26 Sept & 15 Nov 1898) Upon his arrival in London Strong put Esterhazy in touch with the editor of the London *Observer*, Rachel Beer. After negotiations, Beer agreed to pay Esterhazy £500 for a series of five articles to be accompanied by documentary evidence provided by Esterhazy. (*v.* 25 Sept 1898)

243 *Cass.*, II, 124–7; *Fabre*, 290–4. See also *AD*, 823–6. In this letter there is no explicit mention of the erasure on the *petit bleu*. (*v.* 23 Sept–16 Nov, Tavernier's investigation)

244 Anticipating Zurlinden's resignation, Brisson had already been looking for a new Minister of War. He sent his personal friend Gachet to ask Mathieu to recommend a general whom he thought capable of undertaking a revision. Mathieu suggested General Darras, who in 1895 was in charge of Dreyfus' degradation ceremony. Mathieu knew from Dr Gibert that Darras was deeply troubled by the experience and believed in the innocence of Dreyfus. After reflection Darras refused the offer. Chanoine, considered to support a revision, was suggested by Bourgeois and Vallé. *ATQV*, pp. 182–3.

245 The following month (19 October), de Pressensé refused to appear before the Council again. In a letter addressed to the Grand Chancellor he claimed his right to condemn officers suspected of plotting to keep an innocent man in prison (in reference to Picquart).

246 Schwartzkoppen, *The Truth About Dreyfus*, pp. 204–6.

247 *Fabre*, 295–6. Picquart was to appear on the following day before the civil court on the charge of divulging documents. After the discovery of the *faux Henry*, Henry's death and Cavaignac's resignation, it was likely that he would be acquitted. By ordering proceedings before a military court, Zurlinden intended to keep Picquart in prison, whatever outcome of the civil court ruling. Bredin, *The Affair*, p. 340.

248 *Répertoire*, p. 207.

249 *Fabre*, 263–78.

250 Lemercier-Picard's body had been found on 3 March 1898. Although his death was deemed to be suicide, this was doubted by many.

251 Picquart had already initiated libel proceedings against several newspapers that had announced he had attempted to commit suicide in prison. (*v.* 14 July 1898)

252 *Fabre*, 279–80.

253 A military official had already presented himself at La Santé the previous day, demanding to transfer Picquart to Cherche-Midi. The prison governor had refused to do so without written orders.

254 The commission was composed of three judges from the Supreme Court of Appeal (Théophile Crépon, Emile Leppelletier and Charles Petit) and three civil representatives from the Ministry of Justice (Louis La Borde, Adrien Coutourier and Gabriel Geoffroy).

255 *Cass.*, II, 128–30. The three judges from the Supreme Court of Appeal voted in favour of a revision, the representatives of the Ministry of Justice against.

256 The escalation of the Dreyfus Affair in 1898 brought to light the marked influence of the Jesuit order, especially in the army: leading private Jesuit schools had a very high entry rate into the military college of Saint-Cyr and the Ecole polytechnique. In 1896, almost a quarter of those accepted to Saint-Cyr came from Jesuit colleges. Larkin, *Church and State after the Dreyfus Affair: The Separation Issue in France*, pp. 83–4.

257 A. Dreyfus, *Cinq années de ma vie* (1982), p. 207.

258 Strong published this article as a result of a 'journalistic war' provoked by a clash between the *Observer* and Esterhazy over the series of articles he had agreed to publish. (*v.* 14 Sept 1898, n. 242) Esterhazy claimed an advance but refused to produce an invoice. He threatened to sell his revelations to a Belgian paper. Strong and Beer, who already had some of Esterhazy's documents, delayed returning them to him. They threatened to publish the articles without waiting for his complete text. Meanwhile, Strong has already announced that the *Observer* was to publish Esterhazy's story. Esterhazy responded by giving interviews to other newspapers, announcing he had further documents that compromised the General Staff. He then threatened, via the libellous solicitor Arthur Newton, to take legal action against the *Observer*. Finally, an out-of-court settlement was reached: the paper paid Esterhazy £500 and his legal expenses. *Cass.*, I, 747–9, Strong.

259 At its numerous public meetings the league threatened leading dreyfusards, claiming that Dreyfus would be lynched if he returned to France for a revision. In February 1899 police reports estimated the league's membership at between 30,000 (15,000 in Paris alone) and 60,000. Sternhell, *La droite révolutionnaire*, p. 106.

260 Sarrien, who opposed a revision, merely transmitted the request to the Criminal Chamber instead of issuing, as would have been usual, a request for a revision on the grounds of new evidence and in his capacity as Minister of Justice.

261 The Chamber faced several problems in examining Lucie's appeal. The main difficulty was over the *bordereau*, Strong's declarations that Esterhazy claimed he had written the *bordereau* on Sandherr's orders, and Esterhazy's denials. A further difficulty was Picquart, because he was the subject of other proceedings. Finally, there was the pressure of public opinion, which was strongly divided. Johnson, *France and the Dreyfus Affair*, pp. 154–5.

262 In 1882 Loew was involved as a judge in the proceedings relating to the *Union Générale*. (*v.* end 1881) Rumours at that time suggested he was close to the Rothschilds, who were falsely accused of causing the bankruptcy of the Catholic bank. Loew was considered by many to be in league with the Jews.

He was to be harshly criticized by opponents of the revision investigation. (*v.* 18 Oct & Nov 1898–Feb 1899, First Revision investigation: Criminal Chamber, n. 5)

263 Chanoine's refusal was an insult but Brisson yielded to it. *DT*, p. 180. The eventual handover of the Secret Dossier was to arouse a major public controversy. (*v.* 14 Nov 1898, n. 8)

264 'All the members of the Supreme Court of Appeal would be lined up... A torturer, trained beforehand, would first cut off their eyelids with a pair of scissors... When it was absolutely impossible for them to close their eyes, fat spiders of the most poisonous species would be introduced... and fixed carefully behind their heads...' Rochefort continues the atrocious description of how the spiders would eat away the judges' eyes, then, blinded, how they should be dragged to the stocks erected in front of the law courts: 'and they would hang this sign around their necks: that is how France punishes traitors who try to sell their country to the enemy.' *L'Intransigeant*, October 18, 1898.

265 *Répertoire*, p. 217; *Déb. Cass.*, 1898, 85–9.

266 The records of these sessions were published shortly afterwards by Stock: *Déb. Cass., 1898*.

267 Conybeare believed that Schwartzkoppen never had the *bordereau* in his hands, but that it was taken by the German Embassy's concierge and delivered to an agent in the Deuxième Bureau. (*v.* 27 Sept 1894, n.17) Conybeare, *The Dreyfus Affair*, p. 30.

268 *Die Große Politik*, vol. 13, pp. 307–8.

269 Gonse remained in this situation, without work, until his retirement on 19 September 1903.

270 The case was not heard until 20 November 1902, after Picquart had submitted it to the civil court. *Le Jour* had to pay him a fine of 20,000 francs. *HAD*, 6, p. 177, note 2.

271 The journal's appearance varied. The group was also known as Jeunesse antisémitique de France (Antisemitic Youth of France). In 1901 it finally became the Parti national antijuif (The National anti-Jewish Party). (*v.* 4–5 May 1901)

272 A few days earlier a number of Socialists including Jules Guesde, Jean Jaurès, Aristide Briand, Alexandre Millerand and Réné Viviani decided to form a 'committee of vigilance', reminiscent of the French Revolution. For several days manifestos from both camps called on people to take part in the demonstrations. The leagues' entry into the political arena was a new phenomenon. R. Rémond, *Les Droites en France* (Paris: Aubier-Montaigne, 1982), p. 165.

273 The Fashoda crisis marked the culmination of Franco-British rivalry in the Nile basin. On 10 July the French expedition led by Captain Marchand, sent by Hanotaux in 1896, reached the village of Fashoda. On 18 September the British Sir Herbert Kitchener, who was instructed to occupy territory in the Sudan, arrived outside Fashoda at the head of 30,000 men of the Anglo-Egyptian Army. Both commanders waited for orders from their governments. After two months of negotiations Delcassé gave Marchand orders to withdraw. The incident ended with diplomatic defeat for France and failure to obtain access to the Nile. An agreement between the two countries was signed on 21 March 1899 with France renouncing all claims to Fashoda.

274 Followers of the duc d'Orléans, who were closely watched by the police, became particularly active. Guérin dispersed his men among the strikers to agitate.

275 It was rumoured that a *coup d'état* was planned by Déroulède with the anticipated participation of Pellieux and Zurlinden. The daily *Le Petit bleu* announced (15 October) that one of the meetings between Déroulède and the Generals was hosted by the well-known right-wing antisemitic writer and illustrator 'Gyp'. Gabrielle Marie Antoinette de Riqueti de Mirbeau, Comtesse Martel de Janville, was also known as 'Bob'. She became an active anti-dreyfusard and among the first members of the Ligue de la patrie française founded at the end of 1898. (*v.* 31 Dec 1898)

276 This session took place two days before the Criminal Chamber held its final meetings about the case. (*v.* 27–29 Oct 1898)

277 Chanoine abstained from voting at the meeting.

278 Reinach's series of articles was published by Stock in 1900 as *Tout le crime* ('The Whole Crime').

279 Dreyfus sent four appeals in 1897 and two more in January 1898. In October 1898 he received Lucie's letters dated August. Despite his decision not to write again (*v.* 24 Sept 1898), he regained hope with this news and sent another letter of appeal to Boisdeffre, in whom he continued to have absolute faith. A. Dreyfus, *Cinq années de ma vie* (1982), p. 207.

Part 7

INVESTIGATION and REVISION

October 1898–August 1899

L'ILLUSTRATION

Prix du Numéro : 75 centimes.　　　　SAMEDI　8　JUILLET　1899　　　　57ᵉ Année. — Nᵒ 2941.

LE RETOUR DU CAPITAINE DREYFUS

Arrivée de Dreyfus à bord du « Sfax », devant les Iles du Salut. (D'après une photographie.) — Voir l'article, page 32.

Dreyfus, aboard the *Sfax*, returning to France for his second court martial

The Government of Dupuy

Oct 31   A new Cabinet is formed. Charles Dupuy is Prime Minister,[1] Charles de Freycinet Minister of War,[2] Théophile Delcassé Foreign Secretary, Georges Lebret Minister of Justice and Florent Guillain Colonial Secretary.

Nov 4   In the Chamber, Deputies reaffirm their backing for the motion concerning the supremacy of civil authority. Dupuy's intention is to use Republican support and to ensure the country remains calm. (*v.* 25 Oct 1898) The Chamber passes a vote of confidence in the Government by 429 votes to 64. Deputy Gerville-Réache proposes a bill to transfer Lucie's appeal for a revision of Dreyfus' verdict from the Criminal Chamber to the Combined Chambers of the Supreme Court of Appeal. Dupuy refuses, but the bill is referred to a parliamentary commission. (*v.* 16 Jan, p. 234; 10 Feb & 1 March 1899)

First revision investigation: Criminal Chamber (Nov 1898–Feb 1899)[3]

Following the Criminal Chamber's ruling of 29 October, it is to conduct the investigation in plenary session rather than through a special commission. Twelve judges, including the president, are appointed.[4] At first all depositions are given only in the presence of the judges, without Dreyfus' defence lawyer. From the second half of December the Chamber allows Lucie's lawyer, Henri Mornard, to hear the depositions. The records are also given to Freycinet, who shows them to Cuignet and Roget.

Throughout November and December the anti-dreyfusard press leads a campaign against the judges of the Criminal Chamber accusing them of being bought by the Syndicate and of 'dancing to Reinach's tune'.[5] Rumours casting doubt on the impartiality of the judges adds to the tenor of the campaign. (*v.* 25, 28 Dec 1898, pp.232–3) The judges receive anonymous and threatening letters. Passages from the depositions unfavourable to Dreyfus appear in the press. They probably emanate from Roget and Cuignet. (*v.* 31 March 1899)

Nov   The Chamber discovers significant new evidence against Esterhazy. This is two letters (dated 17 April 1892 and 17 August 1894), written by Esterhazy on India-squared paper similar to paper on which the *bordereau* was written. To verify that the dates of the letters are authentic, manufacturers of similar paper are questioned. The letters are also submitted to graphological and chemical analyses. The handwriting report (dated 26 November) concludes that they were written on paper identical to that of the *bordereau*.

Nov 8–14 Five former Ministers of War, Mercier, Billot, Cavaignac, Zurlinden and Chanoine, all affirm the guilt of Dreyfus. Mercier admits that Du Paty did not obtain a confession from Dreyfus on 31 December 1894 but reaffirms his belief in Lebrun-Renault's statement of a confession. Mercier refuses to respond to any questions about any secret transmission of documents at the court martial of Dreyfus. He stresses that the grounds of Lucie's appeal for revision were only the contradictions between the graphologists' reports on the *bordereau* and Henry's forgery.[6] Most of the Ministers claim that Esterhazy could not have obtained the information mentioned in the *bordereau*. Cavaignac expounds his theory of the complicity between Dreyfus and Esterhazy, suggesting that Dreyfus wrote the *bordereau* and Esterhazy copied it.[7]

Nov 14   The Chamber demands that Freycinet hand over the secret documents related to the Dreyfus case held in the Ministry of War, considering them indispensable to the investigation.[8] (*v.* 19 Dec 1898, p. 231)

The Chamber orders Guillain, the Colonial Secretary, to inform Dreyfus as swiftly as possible of their decision of 29 October to examine Lucie's appeal for a revision.[9] (*v.* 16 Nov 1898, p. 228)

Nov 21–24   General Roget confirms Cavaignac's theory of the complicity between Dreyfus and Esterhazy. He affirms that Esterhazy could not have provided the information indicated in the *bordereau*. He repeats his accusation that Picquart had forged the *petit bleu*.[10]

Nov 23–   Picquart testifies several times before the Chamber.[11] He explains
Dec 5   precisely all he knows and relates in great detail his involvement in the Affair from the very beginning, confirming the various intrigues of his colleagues including Henry, Gonse, Lauth, Gribelin against him. He comments on the Secret Dossier, explaining that *Ce canaille de D.* reached the Section de Statistique in 1893–94 and has no relevance whatsoever to Dreyfus. He insists on the principal role of Du Paty in the collusion between Esterhazy and the General Staff.[12]

Dec 6/10   Bertulus gives details of his interrogations of Esterhazy and Mlle Pays in July 1898 as well as the incident with Henry.[13] (*v.* 18 July 1898, Bertulus' investigation of Esterhazy and Mlle Pays)

Dec 10   Esterhazy, notified by his lawyer Tézenas that he has been called to testify (on 17 January), writes to Charles Mazeau, President of the Supreme Court of Appeal, that he is willing to appear before the Criminal Chamber on two conditions. These are that he be given a safe conduct and that he or his lawyer should in advance be informed of the issues on which he is to be interrogated.[14] (*v.* 13 Jan 1899, p. 226)

Dec 12–13   Gonse is interrogated at length on the content of the *bordereau* and whether Dreyfus, as an artillery officer, could in 1894 have known about the items mentioned in it. Imprecise and contradicting himself, Gonse insists that he heard Lebrun-Renault state that Dreyfus had made a confession to him. He explains how the Secret Dossier expanded as from 1894, accruing items proving the guilt of Dreyfus but claims he cannot comment on them. He recommends that the Chamber examine the dossier. Gonse denies Picquart's description of their conversation of 15 September 1896.[15]

Dec 13 &   Boisdeffre, tired and ill, makes a short deposition.[16] He reprimands
Jan 21   Picquart for having concealed his investigation of Esterhazy from his superiors and for the methods he used. Boisdeffre also confirms that he only heard about the *bordereau annoté* from the newspapers.

When called for the second time he mentions that he learnt about Du Paty's dealings with Esterhazy only in July–August 1898.[17]

Dec 24   Forzinetti recounts in detail the imprisonment of Dreyfus at Cherche-Midi, the irregularities and unusually harsh measures imposed; his telling Boisdeffre that he believed Dreyfus to be innocent; the terrible physical and mental state of Dreyfus during the first days of his arrest. Forzinetti also confirms that Lebrun-Renault told him in 1897 that Dreyfus did not make any confession to him.[18]

Dec 26   Dupuy admits having said in Cabinet, 'I wonder if we were not victims in 1894 of a mystification.'[19]

Dec 28   Casimir-Périer declares that as President of the Republic in 1894 he knew of only two documents providing evidence against Dreyfus. Both of these were produced at the court martial, namely the *bordereau* and *Ce canaille de D.* Casimir-Périer confirms that he had no knowledge of any secret documents nor of the existence of a letter from the Kaiser naming Dreyfus (i.e. the *bordereau annoté*).[20]

Dec 30   Cuignet brings the Secret Dossier to the Chamber for the first time and begins his testimony. (*v.* 5–6 Jan 1899, below)

Dec   The graphologist Gobert declares that there can no longer be any doubt that Esterhazy's writing is identical to that of the *bordereau*.[21] Lebrun-Renault is faced with the contradictions of his own statements on the alleged confession of Dreyfus.[22] Like Casimir-Périer and Dupuy, other Ministers of 1894–95 (Poincaré, Barthou) declare that in 1894 they had never heard of the confession of Dreyfus.[23] (*v.* 28 Nov 1898, p. 230) General Gaston de Galliffet (future Minister of War) claims that he was told by the former British military attaché, General James Talbot, that several of his colleagues in foreign embassies in Paris were easily obtaining military information from Esterhazy for the sum of one or two thousand francs.[24]

1899
Jan 5   Dreyfus on Devil's Island is interrogated by means of a *commission rogatoire* (a rogatory letter). He firmly denies any confession to Lebrun-Renault or anyone else.[25]

Jan 5–6   Cuignet continues his deposition. He blames Du Paty for many of the errors, disclosures of information and forgeries during the Affair – for the arrest of Dreyfus to *La Libre Parole* in 1894; for the *faux Henry*, when Du Paty used Henry to conceal his own forgeries; for writing the articles published by *L'Eclair* in September 1896; for sending the *faux Weyler* to Dreyfus (September 1896); for sending Picquart the Blanche and Speranza telegrams (November 1897); and, with Esterhazy, for organizing the collusion.[26] Of the hundreds of items in the Secret Dossier Cuignet chooses to present only a number of unimportant documents and disregards the three documents quoted in Cavaignac's speech of 7 July 1898. Cuignet's presentation of the decoding of Panizzardi's telegram of 2 November 1894 indicates his bias: he asserts that Gonse's and Du Paty's falsified version of the telegram (*v.* end March–end April 1898, Consolidation of the Secret Dossier n. 133) is correct and thus casts doubt on the probity of the Foreign Office, although it was the decoding by the Foreign Office that was correct.[27] (*v.* April–May 1899, First revision investigation: Combined Chambers)

Jan 12–13 Du Paty maintains that he was exploited by his superior officers in his investigation of Dreyfus (1894) and in his dealings with Esterhazy (1897). He admits that Sandherr asked him in 1894 to write a commentary on the documents in the Secret Dossier but that he had no knowledge of what Sandherr had done with it subsequently. He mentions that Gonse asked him, for a reason he cannot remember, to rewrite from memory a statement relating to the report he sent Mercier on 31 December 1894 after his visit to Dreyfus' cell.[28] (*v.* c. Sept 1897, n. 139)

Jan 13 Esterhazy, in a second letter to Mazeau (his letter of 10 December 1898 remained without reply) repeats the conditions under which he agrees to appear before the Court: since he will give evidence as a witness he is not to be interrogated or to discuss the two courts martial (his own and that of Dreyfus), whose verdicts remain valid. He admits he was in contact with a foreign agent for some 18 months during 1894–95 on Sandherr's instruction; that, a month before Mathieu Dreyfus publicly accused him (November 1897), he was supported and instructed by General Staff officers; and that in July 1898 Cavaignac suddenly changed his attitude towards him.[29] (*v.* 23–24 & 30 Jan 1899, below)

Jan 16 & 19 Four artillery officers state that the inaccuracy of the technical terms used in the *bordereau* prove it could not have been written by an artilleryman. Moreover, there was nothing confidential in the information it contained: such information could have been obtained from the military press at the time, where these issues were already being discussed.[30]

Jan 14–18/
Feb 2–6 The graphologists Belhomme, Bertillon, Charavay, Couard, Teyssonnières and Varinard testify. They uphold their previous conclusions that the *bordereau* is by Dreyfus.[31] Bertillon demonstrates in his convoluted fashion his theory of the *bordereau* as the 'self forgery' of Dreyfus. When questioned about the court martial of 1894 he claims that Dreyfus' reaction seemed to him an indirect admission that the self-forgery theory was true. Two further graphologists, Gobert and Pelletier, conclude that the *bordereau* is not by Dreyfus. Charavay, who was originally equivocal (*v.* 29 Oct 1894), remains cautious and limits himself to the comment that there are now two handwritings that are very similar to the *bordereau*. (*v.* April–May 1899, First revision investigation: Combined Chambers; 28 Aug 1899; The Rennes court martial) Also called, Monod and Trarieux state that the *bordereau* had not been written by Dreyfus.[32]

Jan 23–24
& 30 The Chamber finally hears Esterhazy.[33] He states that since he is giving his deposition as a witness, not as the accused, he is free to reject questions of which he does not approve. He describes the collusion at the General Staff in detail, repeating statements the Chamber already knows from his letter. (*v.* 13 Jan 1899) He threatens his accusers with further public revelations. Confronted with the *bordereau* and his own letters, he admits the similarity of handwriting but states that he

cannot comment further since the matter has already been the subject of two judgments (at Dreyfus' and his own court martial).[34]

Jan 9, 20 25, 31 & Feb 3 With the Government's authorization, Paléologue presents to the Chamber the Dreyfus 'diplomatic dossier' (i.e. the documents relevant to the case assembled at the Foreign Office).[35] He states that Gonse's version of Panizzardi's telegram of 2 November is falsified; that on several occasions Henry concealed the correct version; and that only one official version exists, that made by the Foreign Office (and which cleared Dreyfus).[36] (*v.* 2 & 11 Nov 1894; 17 Nov 1897; end April–end May 1898, n. 133) He shows the Chamber statements by the German and Italian Ambassadors affirming that Esterhazy was receiving payment for information delivered. Paléologue also quotes a 'very well-informed' foreign source, whose identity he cannot reveal, confirming that the Ministry of War in Berlin has 225 documents delivered by Esterhazy. Paléologue confirms that the Foreign Office does not have a letter from the Kaiser concerning Dreyfus (a reference to the *bordereau annoté*) and that he has only heard about it once, from Henry.[37] (*v.* 3 Nov 1897)

Jan 31 Hanotaux gives evidence. He does not disclose his disagreements with Mercier over the decision to court-martial Dreyfus, on the grounds of the potential diplomatic difficulties involved.[38]

1898
Nov 5 Devil's Island: Dreyfus receives letters written in September, including Lucie's letter of 26 September which gives him the news that she has presented an appeal for a revision and that it has been granted by the Government.[39] (*v.* 10 & 16 Nov 1898, below and p. 228)

De Pressensé publishes *Un héros: le Lieutenant Colonel Picquart* ('A Hero: Lieutenant Colonel Picquart'). (*v.* 15 Nov 1898, p. 228)

Nov 7 A second article by Reinach on the complicity of Henry and Esterhazy entitled 'Henry espion et traître, complice d'Esterhazy' ('Henry, Spy and Traitor, Esterhazy's Accomplice') appears in *Le Siècle*. (*v.* 6 Dec 1898, p. 231)

Nov 10 Lucie is called to the Colonial Office regarding Dreyfus' letter dated 24 September. She is not shown the letter but a summary is read to her, which leads her to think her husband declared he would not write to her again.[40] Fearing that this is a sign that her husband may be dying, Lucie asks whether he was formally informed that her appeal for a revision has been transferred to the Supreme Court of Appeal. She learns that he has not, but is not authorized to telegraph him this news.

Nov 11 Reinach protests without result to Prime Minister Dupuy against the Government's refusal to allow Lucie to inform Dreyfus of the revision. (*v.* 14 Nov 1898, First revision investigation: Criminal Chamber)

Nov 12 In *Le Siècle* Reinach publishes 'Un simple récit' ('A Simple Story'), an article reporting the Government's refusal to allow Lucie to tell her husband about recent events in the case.

Nov 15	The name of de Pressensé is struck off the roll of the Legion of Honour.
	Fayard publishes the first instalment of Esterhazy's book *Les dessous de l'affaire Dreyfus*.[41]
Nov 16	Devil's Island: Dreyfus receives a telegram sent to him by the Colonial Secretary informing him that the Criminal Chamber of Supreme Court of Appeal has declared admissible his appeal for revision of his 1894 verdict and that he is invited to produce his defence.[42] (*v.* Appendix 37)
	Le Siècle devotes an illustrated supplement to caricatures of the Affair published in the international press.[43]

Tavernier's Investigation of Picquart[44] (23 Sept–16 Nov)

	Tavernier orders that Picquart be held in solitary confinement at Cherche-Midi. Picquart is allowed to receive visits only from family and a few close friends.[45] He is questioned several times by Tavernier but is not informed of the specific and new charges formulated against him concerning the falsification of the *petit bleu* and including the erasure of the name. Picquart is told only that he is accused of 'forgery of private documents … by fabricating the *petit bleu*' and is asked only whether he recognizes the document. He is not allowed to confront any of his accusers nor to consult his lawyer, Labori.[46] On 23 October Picquart writes to Tavernier asking to be informed of the names of his accusers; but he is not questioned further and is not given any more information about the progress of the investigation. On 5 November he writes to Freycinet to contest this procedure. (*v.* Dec 1898, pp. 230–1)
	Tavernier hears Lauth, Roget and Gonse, who continue to accuse Picquart of falsifying the *petit bleu* by various means.
	Tavernier appoints further graphologists to examine the *petit bleu*. They unanimously confirm that the name of Esterhazy, the original addressee, had been erased from the *petit bleu* and written in again.[47]
16 Nov	Tavernier's investigation ends.
19 Nov	Tavernier's report to Zurlinden states that notwithstanding the graphologists' conclusions, Picquart fabricated the *petit bleu*, also changing the name of the addressee. The report also accuses Picquart of concealing the document from his superiors for a long time. Tavernier recommends that Picquart be court-martialled.[48] (*v.* 24 Nov 1899, p. 229)
Nov 21	Prince Alexandre von Hohenlohe again appeals to Schwartzkoppen. (*v.* 19 Sept 1898) He declares that the question is no longer whether Dreyfus had dealings with Schwartzkoppen but whether Picquart

has falsified the *petit bleu*, for which charge he is about to be court-martialled. Hohenlohe argues that this is an opportune moment for Germany to act, for two reasons. Firstly, there has been a reversal of public opinion in France: the majority of French people now 'desire to see the truth' and support a revision of Dreyfus' conviction. Secondly, the diplomatic failure of France in the Fashoda crisis and the collapse of Brisson's Government have generated the desire for *rapprochement* with Germany. (*v.* Oct 1898) Hohenlohe suggests that Schwatzkoppen write to the president of Picquart's court martial admitting that it was he who wrote Esterhazy's name and address on the *petit bleu*. Hohenlohe concludes: 'you would be the most popular man and the German Government the most popular in France ... This would put an end [to] the Picquart affair once and for all ... but if Picquart is convicted, the anarchy, and the division in France will take on greater dimensions, the Army will be even more discredited, and who knows what the end of this will be.'[49]

Nov 24   Zurlinden signs the order to bring Picquart before the court martial scheduled for 12 December 1898. Picquart is officially accused of forging the *petit bleu* in order to incriminate Esterhazy. He is also accused of transmission of secret documents to an outsider, 'unqualified to know about this information', naming Leblois.[50]

Support for Picquart

Nov 24–28   Left-wing Deputies and Senators strongly object to Zurlinden's order. Republican groups give notice to Dupuy of imminent interpellations in the Chamber of Deputies demanding the adjournment of the court martial until the end of the Criminal Chamber's investigation. Dupuy decides to bring the matter before the Government. (*v.* 28 Nov 1898, p. 230)

The revisionists mount widespread protests. Public meetings are organized by the Ligue des droits de l'homme et du citoyen and by the Grand Orient.[51] Jaurès, de Pressensé and other leading intellectuals address devoted followers. The Ligue des droits de l'homme et du citoyen distributes lists of petitions against the persecution of Picquart, who is described as 'the heroic artisan of the revision'. These lists are also published in *Le Siècle's* supplements and are signed by thousands throughout France, including famous intellectuals, writers, artists and diplomats. Students demonstrate outside Cherche-Midi prison shouting, 'Vive Picquart!' On 28 November Clemenceau claims in *L'Aurore*: 'We will not tolerate the iniquity against Dreyfus being redeemed at the price of an even greater iniquity against Picquart.' (*v.* 15 Feb 1899, p. 236)

Nov 25   Albert I, Prince of Monaco, writes to von Münster asking him to approach Schwartzkoppen and request a specimen of his handwriting in order to compare it with the *petit bleu*. (*v.* 29 Nov 1898)

In receipt of a letter from Mathieu, Sandoz writes to Schwartzkoppen with the same request: 'We merely need a discreet verbal communication on your part to the French Minister [concerning the *petit bleu*] to avoid the impending second miscarriage of justice [Picquart's court martial].' Sandoz adds that 'the Kaiser, whose magnanimous nature is recognized by all nations, will not refuse you the authority to say the redeeming word'.[52] (*v.* 24 April 1898)

Nov 28   In the Chamber of Deputies Millerand proposes that Picquart's court martial be adjourned until the Criminal Chamber has pronounced on Lucie's appeal. When the opposition tries to focus the debate on the treachery of the Syndicate, Deputy Raymond Poincaré, Finance Minister at the time of Dreyfus' court martial, comments that 'the silence of some of us, at the present time, would be an act of true cowardice'. He names himself and his former colleagues. Dupuy, Barthou, Leygues and Delcassé. Poincaré warns Dupuy that if a judicial error was committed in 1894, the Ministers who in power at that time must now do everything possible to bring it to light. He declares that the only charge against Dreyfus of which they were aware related to the *bordereau*. They were ignorant of any secret dossier or the alleged confession of Dreyfus. Cavaignac claims it was Mercier who confirmed Lebrun-Renault's statements of a confession. Poincaré insists that Mercier never mentioned Lebrun-Renault's statement to any of the Ministers. At the end of his speech, recognizing that he was exposing himself to attack and insult, he says: 'I do not care. I am pleased, on this platform, to have seized the opportunity, for which I have waited too long, to unburden my conscience.'[53] (*v.* Appendix 34) The speech makes a deep impression and is applauded. With Dupuy's support, Freycinet explains that Picquart's court martial cannot be postponed by the Government but only by the Criminal Chamber's investigation, which would thus absolve the Government from responsibility in the matter.[54] (*v.* 8 Dec 1898) In the end, Dupuy secures a large majority: by 338 votes to 83 the Chamber rejects Millerand's motion to adjourn Picquart's court martial.

Devil's Island: Dreyfus is now allowed to walk four hours in the morning and three in the afternoon, still within strict limits. For the first time in two years he has a view of the sea.[55]

Nov 29   At the request of Prince Albert I, von Münster writes to Schwartzkoppen requesting he send the Prince a specimen of his handwriting so that the Prince can furnish it to Labori (Picquart's lawyer) in order to compare it with the *petit bleu*.[56] Von Münster also writes of the increasing enmity between France and England and France's desire to improve relations with Germany. (*v.* 7 Dec 1898)

Hohenlohe writes to Schwartzkoppen in support of Sandoz's request.[57] (*v.* 25 Nov 1898)

Nov 30   *Le Siècle* and the Ligue des droits de l'homme et du citoyen placard Poincaré's statement (of 28 November) throughout Paris.

Dec 1   The Senate adopts a motion to extend the Law of 8 Dec 1897 relating to the procedure for criminal investigations (i.e. the right of the prisoner to consult his lawyer) concerning military justice. In the same session Waldeck-Rousseau proposes a motion permitting the Supreme Court of Appeal to order the adjournment of all proceedings on matters relating to a revision. It is technically defeated by a vote of 113 to 113.[58]

Dec 2   To avoid a court martial, Labori asks the Supreme Court of Appeal to rule that all the charges against Picquart be transferred to civil criminal jurisdiction.[59] (*v.* 8 Dec 1898)

Dec 5   Nationalist Deputy Firmin Faure stirs up members of the Ligue des patriotes to attack the dreyfusards.

Dec 6   *Le Siècle* publishes another article by Reinach, 'Les deux traîtres' ('The Two Traitors'), explicitly accusing Henry of being Esterhazy's accomplice.[60] (*v.* 25 Oct, 7 Nov 1898)

Dec 7   *Le Radical* publishes a letter from Henry's widow to Reinach protesting against the 'infamous calumnies' published about her husband.

In another letter to Schwartzkoppen, von Münster writes that Labori is about to compare Schwartzkoppen's handwriting with that of the *petit bleu*. This may help prevent Picquart from being convicted and sentenced to five years' imprisonment. He then asks Schwartzkoppen to advise him whether it was he who wrote the *petit bleu,* or whether he had had it written by someone else. (*v.* early Mar 1896, The *petit bleu* n. 4) He informs him that he will pass this information to Labori in confidence.[61] (*v.* 19 Dec 1898)

Postponement of Picquart's court martial

Dec 8   The Criminal Chamber orders an examination of Picquart's case and the appropriation of his court martial files. This ruling is tantamount to an adjournment of the court martial. Picquart remains in prison.[62]

Dec 9   *Le Siècle* publishes Reinach's response to Henry's widow. The law allows her to take him to court. He is ready to appear there.[63]

Le Monument Henry

Dec 14   *La Libre Parole* launches a public subscription to help Henry's widow and orphan to file suit against Reinach. It is called 'Le monument Henry' (Henry's memorial fund). The 18 subscription lists are published in the newspaper, ending on 15 January 1899. The paper's aim is to defend 'the honour of the French officer killed, murdered by the Jews'. Throughout this month, the paper encourages people from all walks of life to contribute, however modestly: 'it is a slap in the vile face of that ignoble Reinach'.[64] (*v.* Appendix 35)

Dec 19   The Chamber of Deputies debates the conditions under which the Secret Dossier is to be made available to the Criminal Chamber. Freycinet states that specific precautions must be taken. Nothing from the dossier is to be published without his approval; the lawyers of

Dreyfus are not to inform their client of any of the documents without Freycinet's or the Chamber's authorization; Cuignet is to bring the dossier to court every morning, explain and comment on the content and return it to the Ministry every evening. Brisson claims that only the three documents read by Cavaignac on 7 July 1898 present a risk to national security. Nationalist Deputies try to prevent these procedures. By a vote of 370 to 80 the Chamber approves the procedures for the dossier, on the above conditions.

Von Münster, angry and disappointed at Schwartzkoppen's concealment of his dealings with Esterhazy and authorship of the *petit bleu*, demands an explanation:

> *If you refuse, I should regard that as dishonourable …for my part I have been placed by you in the most uncomfortable situation in the whole Affair … at present I am made to look either a fool who does not know what has been going on under my nose, or a liar! … I expect that you'll see that it is your duty as a man of honour to write to me.*[65]

Dec 22   Schwartzkoppen replies to von Münster:

> *… From the above Your Excellency can see, that I had the feeling in the Picquart matter that I should do something, so that I cannot be made responsible, if that officer is sentenced. As a fellow colleague I feel as much sympathy for the unfortunate Captain Dreyfus as for Colonel Picquart, and we on our side have never done anything for the former to help him out of his tragic situation. Here again it was the higher interest of the state which forbade any intervention. Concerning the 'petit bleu', I sent several of these to Esterhazy and it is therefore very possible, and even likely that the one which exists in the court files was written by me. Of course I cannot be certain of this, as I have not seen it and as we all know there were many forgeries in the whole Affair. But, as I said, it is very likely … I never knowingly betrayed Your Excellency. At that time I kept many things secret, but I never even thought of speaking untruthfully or of acting dishonourably! I told Your Excellency the whole truth at that time …*[66]

Dec 25   *L'Eclair* and *La Patrie* announce that Jules Quesnay de Beaurepaire, President of the Civil Chamber of the Supreme Court of Appeal, had become aware of the favouritism of the judges of the Criminal Chamber towards Picquart. Apparently, Beaurepaire heard Bard say: 'My dear Picquart, give me your opinion on this deposition.' Over the next few days other papers (*Le Gaulois, L'Echo, La Libre Parole*) repeat the story, fuelling the attack on the judges.[67]

Dec 26   Devil's Island: Dreyfus writes to Lucie that he has just received the first letter from her in two months, dated 22 November. It describes the incomplete summary she was given of his letter. (*v.* 24 Sept & 10 Nov 1898) Dreyfus reassures Lucie, 'If my voice had ceased to make itself heard, it would be because it had been extinguished for ever.' Furious at his wife being misled, he also protests in writing to the Governor of Guyana: 'There is therefore a duty of conscience for the person who committed this act – I do not know who he is and do not wish to know – but it falls to him to make reparation.'[68]

Dec 28   Beaurepaire sends Mazeau a memorandum accusing Loew and Bard of seven acts of 'favouritism' towards Picquart and the lawyers of Dreyfus.[69] It calls on the judges to respond to each of the accusations. (*v.* 3, 7, & 27 Jan 1899)

La Ligue de la patrie française

Dec 31   A group of writers and academics led by François Coppée and Jules Lemaître, both of the Académie Française, found the Ligue de la patrie française (League of the French Fatherland). The foundation of the league is a response to the dreyfusard Ligue des droits de l'homme et du citoyen: it rallies right-wing intellectuals to its cause to counter intellectuals of the Left. It initially declares itself Republican and opposed to antisemitism. The aim is to channel anti-dreyfusard intellectuals into promoting respect for the nation and loyalty to the army. The Ligue publishes an appeal in the Royalist daily *Le Soleil* signed by 22 members of the Académie Française, several dozen members of the Institut, hundreds of university professors, writers, magistrates, doctors and other members of the liberal professions.[70] In contrast to the Ligue des patriotes, with its history of agitation, this literary, academic and aristocratic league promotes its propaganda through posters, pamphlets, newspapers and public meetings. It leaves street demonstrations to the gangs of Guérin and Déroulède.

1899

Jan 3   Mazeau interrogates Bard and Loew on the accusations brought against them by Beaurepaire. (*v.* 28 Dec 1898)

Jan 5   Tornielli submits to Delcassé the extract from Panizzardi's report of 1 November 1894, where Pannizardi declares he has never had any dealings with Dreyfus.

Jan 6   Mazeau sends a report to Lebret, Minister of Justice. He concludes that all Beaurepaire's accusations against the judges of the Criminal Chamber are without foundation.

In a letter to Lebret, Beaurepaire threatens to make public further accusations against the Criminal Chamber judges.

Investigation of the judges

Jan 7   Lebret instructs Mazeau to inquire into the accusations against the judges of the Criminal Chamber. (*v.* 27 Jan 1899)

Jan 8   Beaurepaire submits his resignation.[71]

Jan 10   Ballot-Beaupré replaces Beaurepaire as President of the Civil Chamber of the Supreme Court of Appeal.

Henry's widow arraigns Reinach and the manager of *Le Siècle* before the Seine Assize Court for libel, following Reinach's articles accusing her late husband of being Esterhazy's accomplice. (*v.* 25 Oct; 6, 9 Dec 1898, p. 231; 27 Jan 1899)

Jan 11–12   In *L'Echo de Paris* Beaurepaire makes detailed accusations against the judges of the Criminal Chamber (*v.* 28 Dec 1898) and calls for the Dreyfus case to be removed from the Chamber's jurisdiction.[72]

Jan 12   An interpellation is made in the Chamber of Deputies on recent events relating to the Supreme Court of Appeal (Beaurepaire's accusations and resignation). Several Deputies insult Bard, Manau and Loew as a 'trio of scoundrels'; Lebret is asked to read the statements made by Lowe and Bard to Mazeau.[73] The Chamber decides that Lebret is to order Mazeau to form a committee and to open an investigation into Beaurepaire's accusations.

Jan 15   The subscription launched by *La Libre Parole* for the Monument Henry (*v.* 14 Dec 1898) is closed. The last subscription list brings the total to 131,100 francs.

Fayard publishes the second instalment of Esterhazy's *Les dessous de l'affaire Dreyfus.*

Jan 16   The Chamber of Deputies tables the report of the parliamentary commission on the bill proposed by Deputy Gerville-Réache to remove the Dreyfus case from the jurisdiction of the Criminal Chamber. (*v.* 4 Nov 1898) Deputy Renault-Morlière, a former Supreme Court of Appeal lawyer and the commission's reporting judge, recommends the bill's rejection. (*v.* 10 Feb 1899, p. 236)

Mazeau opens the investigation into the accusations made by Beaurepaire against the judges of the Criminal Chamber. Two senior magistrates, Rodolphe Dareste and Félix Voisin, are appointed to assist him. (*v.* 27 Jan 1899)

Judge
Ballot-Beaupré

Jan 17   Senator Eugène-Aimé Bisseuil tables a bill in the Senate aiming to remove all judicial revision cases from the jurisdiction of the Criminal Chamber.

Jan 19   The official constitution of the Ligue de la patrie française is ratified at its first general meeting, attended by some 1200 people.

Jan 27   Mazeau's investigation ends. Mazeau, Dareste and Voisin clear the judges of the Criminal Chamber from all Beaurepaire's accusations and conclude that their integrity and good faith are beyond doubt. The investigation report comments: 'We fear that, once the examination has been completed, they [the judges], deeply disturbed by the insults and outrages …, will no longer have the peace of mind and moral freedom essential to carry out the office of judge.'[74] The report recommends that the judges of the Criminal Chamber be protected from any consequences which may stem from the judgment they pronounce.

The trial of Reinach accused by Henry's widow opens at the Seine Assize Court. (*v.* 10 Jan 1899) Outside the court Guérin's troops are ready to act. Nationalist Deputy Marcel Habert and the Socialist Ernest Vaughan are also present. Labori, representing Reinach, pleads to adjourn the trial until the judgment of the Criminal Chamber on the case of Dreyfus. The Court rejects the plea. Labori then appeals to the Supreme Court of Appeal. The trial is adjourned for legal reasons.[75] The event passes without major incident, although shouts of 'Death to the Jews!' and 'Long live Henry!' are heard.

Judge
Charles Mazeau

La loi de dessaisissement (Law of Dispossession)

Jan 28   In Cabinet, Dupuy, supported by Lebret, proposes a bill ordering the submission of all current cases of appeals for revision to the Combined Chambers of the Supreme Court of Appeal (Criminal, Civil and Appeals). This is to replace such appeals being submitted to the Criminal Chamber alone. If passed, the law is to take immediate effect and would apply to the Dreyfus case. Despite strong opposition from Ministers Leygues, Delombre, and Delcassé, the Cabinet supports Dupuy and submits the bill to the Chamber.

Jan 30   The bill for the Loi de dessaisissement is referred to a parliamentary commission, chaired by Deputy Renault-Molière.

Feb 6   The commission rejects the bill by 9 votes to 2.

Feb 9   Republican Party Deputies argue against the bill.

                    Loew informs Lebret that the Criminal Chamber's investigation of the Dreyfus case is complete.[76]

Feb 10   The bill of dispossession is debated in the Chamber of Deputies. Renault-Morlière firmly opposes it: 'You are killing the very idea of justice in this country.' He is supported by Millerand and Camille Pelletan, who strongly argue against this 'extraordinary' law. Dupuy speaks in its defence, referring to the 'extraordinary circumstances' of the situation, by which he means the defamatory campaign against the Criminal Chamber and the investigation of its judges. Lebret, in favour, calls on his colleagues to think of their constituencies. The Chamber passes the bill by 324 votes to 207. (*v.* 1 March 1899)

Feb 11   The Ligue des droits de l'homme et du citoyen demonstrates against the Law of Dispossession.

Feb 13   Albert I, Prince of Monaco, writes to Joseph Reinach about his encounter with his close friend Kaiser Wilhelm II, in which he endeavoured to make the Kaiser declare that Germany had had no dealings with Dreyfus. Prince Albert recounts the Kaiser's criticism of the conduct of the French authorities in the Dreyfus case, and their antisemitism.[77]

Feb 14   Establishment of the Comité catholique pour la défense du droit (Catholic Committee for the Defence of the Law), under the presidency of Paul Viollet. It supports the cause for a revision.[78]

Feb 15   Publication of *Hommage des Artistes à Picquart*, an album of 12 lithographs by prominent artists in tribute to Picquart. Octave Mirbeau writes the preface. The album includes the signatures of the many people who protest against Picquart's detention.[79] (*v.* Appendix 36)

Death of President Faure/Election of Loubet

Feb 16   Death of President Félix Faure.[80]

Feb 19   The Chamber of Deputies and the Senate, assembled at Versailles, elect Emile Loubet by a majority of 483 (of a total of 812 votes) as President of the Republic. They also vote for a state funeral for the former president. It is proposed that after a religious service at Notre Dame, the funeral cortège will proceed to Père-Lachaise cemetery. (*v.* 23 Feb 1899)

Loubet is denigrated in the Nationalist press as a 'Panamist' and 'dreyfusard'.[81]

On arrival at the Gare St-Lazare from Versailles Loubet is jeered and booed by supporters of the leagues of Déroulède and Guérin and followers of the duc d'Orleans. Déroulède's gangs, stationed in the streets, are urged to march on the Elysée palace. Déroulède organizes a major demonstration in the place des Pyramides, next to the statue of Joan of Arc, where he repeats the call 'to the Elysée'.[82]

Feb 23   State funeral of President Faure.

Attempted *coup d'état* by Déroulède

Déroulède is counting on the army's support for a projected *coup d'état*. Pellieux, who is to command the main escort at Faure's funeral, is to deviate from the prescribed route of the cortège and march on the Elysée. Pellieux reneges at the last moment and persuades Zurlinden to put him in command of a side escort. Roget replaces him to lead the main escort. Waiting with his troops near the place de la Nation, Déroulède is surprised to see Roget leading the main escort. He keeps to his plan, however, and calls upon Roget to 'Follow us onward to the Elysée, have pity on the country, save France and the Republic'. Members of the Ligue des Patriotes are lined up all the way to the Elysée. Confusion ensues. Struggling with his frightened horse, Roget leads the regiment back into the Reuilly barracks. Déroulède follows him. He continues to shout at Roget's side and is supported by Guérin and the Nationalist Deputies Maurice Barrès and Marcel Habert. Déroulède and Habert find themselves trapped in the barracks. The rest of the supporters remain outside. Roget invites them to withdraw but Déroulède refuses, and declares himself a 'prisoner of the army', shouting that he has been 'betrayed'. Roget then issues orders to detain Déroulède until he receives further orders. Habert asks to be arrested as well. Perplexed, Roget reports the incident to Zurlinden, who informs Dupuy. Finally, shortly after midnight, Déroulède and Habert are taken by the Sûreté. They are arrested on the minor charge of 'trespassing, at the head of a crowd, and refusing to leave despite military orders'. Déroulède demands to be prosecuted for treason, for plotting 'a rebellious movement to overthrow the Republic', and asks to be judged before the Senate constituted as an *haute court de justice* (special court for trying members of the Government). But Déroulède and Habert are to be judged by an Assize Court,[83] after spending three months in the Conciergerie.[84] (*v.* 29–31 May 1899) The duc d'Orléans flees to Belgium.

Mar 1   After three days of debate the Senate passes the Law of Dispossession by 158 votes to 131. The law is to be applied to all proceedings in progress. The Dreyfus case, *ab initio*, is to be transferred to the Combined Chambers of the Supreme Court of Appeal. (*v.* 27 March–3 June 1899)

Mar 2–3   Following the appeal of Picquart's lawyer (*v.* 2 & 8 Dec 1898), the Criminal Chamber rules that all charges against Picquart are to be resubmitted to civil jurisdiction. Picquart will not therefore be court-martialled.[85] (*v.* 13 Mar 1899)

Mar 4   London's *Daily Chronicle* begins publication of a detailed report by Esterhazy on his collusion with the General Staff.[86]

Mar 6   Mazeau appoints Ballot-Beaupré, President of the Civil Chamber, as the new reporting judge for the additional investigation of the Dreyfus case by the Combined Chambers. The records of the Criminal Chamber investigation (Nov 1898–Feb 1899) are printed in a limited edition and given to the 46 judges of the Combined Chambers and to the defence counsel, Mornard. Cuignet also receives a copy, which he submits to Roget.

Mar 7   Fayard publishes the third instalment of Esterhazy's *Les dessous de l'affaire Dreyfus*. This includes an account of Esterhazy's depositions before the Criminal Chamber and a number of significant documents including Du Paty's 'note in two hands' (*v. c.* 20 Nov 1897), which prove his collusion with the General Staff.[87]

Mar 13   Picquart is transferred from Cherche-Midi military prison to La Santé.

Exposures in the press

Mar 21–30   Several papers (*Le Siècle, La Liberté, La petite République, Le Temps*) publish recent statements of captain Freystaetter, one of the judges at the court martial of Dreyfus (1894), to Deputy Antoine de Lanessan. Freystaetter states that the conviction of Dreyfus resulted from the transmission of secret documents to the judges during their deliberation.[88] (*v.* April–May 1899, First revision investigation: Combined Chambers)

Mar 23   Monod publishes in *Le Siècle* Dr Gibert's letter to him, dated 23 November 1897. The letter tells of Gibert's conversation with President Faure on 21 February 1895 and Faure's admission that Dreyfus was convicted on the basis of documents passed secretly to the Court.[89]

Mar 31   From this date and throughout April *Le Figaro* publishes the Criminal Chamber's investigation records (Nov 1898–Feb 1899).[90] The Cabinet orders an investigation into the origin of the disclosure that lay behind this publication.[91] *Le Figaro* is prosecuted and fined 500 francs.

April   Guérin transforms the Ligue antisémitique into an association he calls the Grand Occident de France, as distinct from the Grand Orient Masonic lodge. (*v.* 24–28 Nov 1898, n. 51) Its headquarters are established at 51 rue Chabrol (Paris) a large building which Guérin transforms into a fortress.[92] (*v.* 12 Aug 1899, Jules Guérin and Fort Chabrol)

Apr 7	London's *Daily Chronicle* publishes Esterhazy's letters to the President of the Republic of 29 and 31 October, and 5 November 1897.
May 1	Freycinet suspends Georges Duruy, Professor at the Ecole polytechnique, for publishing a series of articles in *Le Figaro* (February–April 1899) in which he pleaded with the army not to back Esterhazy's cause.[93]
May 2	At Dupuy's insistence, the Chamber of Deputies postpones all interpellations on the Dreyfus Affair until the ruling of the Supreme Court of Appeal.
May 5	Freycinet submits his resignation following much criticism, mainly from Radical Deputies, for his suspension of Professor Duruy. (*v.* 1 May 1899) He is replaced by Camille Krantz, then Minister of Public Works.
May 12	*Le Petit Journal* publishes the correspondence exchanged in March between Freycinet and Delcassé relating to Cuignet's statement before the Criminal Chamber regarding Panizzardi's telegram. (*v.* April–May 1899, First revision investigation: Combined Chambers)
	Cuignet admits to providing *Le Petit Journal* with the correspondence between the Ministers. Krantz dismisses Cuignet, reducing him to half-pay.

First revision investigation: Combined Chambers[94]

Mar 27	The Combined Chambers examine the Secret Dossier. The documents are presented to the judges by Cuignet and General Auguste Chamoin, private principal secretary of Freycinet. The judges of the Combined Chambers, as those of the Criminal Chamber, find that the dossier has no documentation incriminating Dreyfus.[95]
Mar 29	The Combined Chambers examine the 'diplomatic dossier' in the presence of Paléologue.
April–May	Captain Freystaetter appears in Court as a significant new witness. His deposition makes the judges aware that *Ce canaille de D.* was secretly passed to the judges at the court martial of Dreyfus. Freystaetter also admits that it was Henry's dramatic testimony that had inclined him to vote for the conviction of Dreyfus.[96] Lépine, former Prefect of Police, reveals that the police report dated 1894 confirming that Dreyfus was neither a gambler nor a womanizer was sent to the Ministry of War but was not produced at the court martial.[97] Du Paty refutes the accusations made against him by several witnesses, mainly Cuignet.[98] Monod submits a letter from Charavay who admits his error in 1894 in concluding that the *bordereau* was in the handwriting of Dreyfus. He now firmly attributes it to Esterhazy.[99] The main incident during the investigation concerns Panizzardi's telegram of 2 November 1894. Cuignet's acceptance of the false version of Gonse and Du Paty had cast doubt on the Foreign Office's reputation. Delcassé asks the postal authorities to produce the original telegram and Paléologue to present it to the Court. Paléologue concludes once again that the version held

by the Ministry of War 'was not only erroneous, but false'.[100] Mazeau also calls Cuignet, Chamoin, and Paléologue (27 April 1899) asking them as a group to decode Panizzardi's telegram. Their version, which they all sign, is identical to the correct version (i.e. that of the Foreign Office, clearing the Italian Government of any dealings with Dreyfus).[101]

Concluding sessions: Combined Chambers[102]

May 29–31   At the final session of the Combined Chambers of the Supreme Court of Appeal (46 judges) President Ballot-Beaupré reads his long closing report. The report concludes that the *bordereau* was not written by Dreyfus but by Esterhazy. Ballot-Beaupré does not ask the Court to find Dreyfus innocent but says that there is a 'new fact' which enables his innocence to be established.[103] The Court bursts into applause.

Manau reaches the same conclusion as Ballot-Beaupré, basing it not on one but 'several new facts'; he lists ten of them, (*v.* Appendix 38) then reads his closing report:

> *He [Dreyfus] waits, full of hope, for the new judgment by his peers. Will you refuse him this supreme appeal? … Gentlemen, let us make no mistake. It is a solemn moment. You will hand down your ruling … The country will hear it, the whole world will know of it, history will record it … As for us, gentlemen, having undertaken responsibility before you for our conclusions, we also undertake it as magistrates and as citizens, and with the confidence given by a feeling of duty. And here are our conclusions: We affirm that there are in this case several new facts which are likely to establish the innocence of Dreyfus … We entreat you to let justice prevail by ordering a revision. Consequently, we request that the Court should order the annulment of the verdict of 22 December 1894 and refer Dreyfus before any court martial that it may please the Court to designate.[104]*

June 1   Lucie's lawyer, Mornard, demands on behalf of Dreyfus, that her husband be judged by his peers:[105]

> *Well, gentlemen, I am sure of it – it is with joy in their hearts that the military judges, declaring that an error has been innocently committed, will state that their unfortunate brother in arms … has never been false to the law of honour … The hour of justice has sounded, and it is with full confidence that I await your ruling. I await your ruling as a new and shining testimony of your high, impartial justice … I await your ruling as the word of peace for all citizens, who, emerging at long last from the distressing enmities of yesterday, will share tomorrow, united in the love of our noble France. In short, gentlemen, I await your ruling as the blessed dawn of the day that will bathe our beloved nation in the great light of concord and truth.[106]*

The speech is warmly applauded; the judges adjourn for deliberation until 3 June.

244 — N° 2930   L'ILLUSTRATION   22 AVRIL 1899

LA COUR DE CASSATION

M. MAZEAU, *premier président.* Phot. Petit.

Né à Dijon en 1825. Ancien député et actuellement sénateur de la Côte-d'Or, ancien ministre de la justice. Entré à la Cour de cassation en 1882, premier président depuis 1890.

M. TANON, *président de la Chambre des requêtes.*

Né à Mens (Isère) en 1831. Ancien directeur des affaires criminelles au Ministère de la justice. Entré à la Cour en 1881; président de la Chambre des requêtes depuis 1893.

M. BALLOT-BEAUPRÉ, *président de la Ch. civile.*

Né à Saint-Denis (Réunion) en 1836. A été procureur général et premier président à Nancy. Conseiller depuis 1882, a remplacé comme président de la Chambre civile, M. Q. de Beaurepaire.

M. LŒW, *président de la Ch. criminelle.* Phot. Appert.

Né à Strasbourg en 1828. A été conseiller à la Cour d'appel, procureur de la République et procureur général à Paris. Président de la Chambre criminelle depuis 1886.

M. MANAU, *procureur général.*

Né à Moissac (Haute-Garonne) en 1825. A été président de Chambre à la Cour d'appel de Paris et à la Cour de cassation. Procureur général depuis 1893.

M. ACCARIAS *(Ch. cr.).* Phot. Petit.

Né à Mens (Isère) en 1830. A été professeur agrégé aux Facultés de Douai et de Paris, puis inspecteur général des Facultés de Droit. Conseiller depuis 1891.

M. ALPHANDÉRY *(Ch. des R.).* Phot. Pataqu.

Né à Salon (Bouches-du-Rhône) en 1837. A été avocat général à Aix, procureur général à Bourges et à Bordeaux. Conseiller depuis 1894.

M. ATTHALIN *(Ch. cr.).* Phot. Pirou, R. 515.

Né à Colmar en 1848. A été juge d'instruction, conseiller à la Cour d'appel, procureur de la République à Paris. Conseiller depuis 1898.

M. BARD *(Ch. cr.).*

Né à Paris en 1850. Ancien directeur des Affaires civiles au Ministère de la justice. A été procureur général à Marseille. Conseiller depuis 1892.

M. BERNARD *(Ch. des R.).*

Né à Montmorillon (Vienne) en 1844. Ancien agréé à Bordeaux. A été procureur général à Nimes, substitut du procureur général et avocat général à Paris. Conseiller depuis 1888.

M. BOULLOCHE *(Ch. cr.).*

Né à Paris en 1854. Ancien directeur des Affaires criminelles au Ministère de la justice. A été substitut du procureur général à Paris. Conseiller depuis 1896.

M. CALARY *(Ch. civ.).*

Né à Neuvic d'Ussel en 1841. A été substitut du procureur général, avocat général et président de Chambre à la Cour d'appel de Paris. Conseiller depuis 1897.

M. CHEVRIER *(Ch. civ.).*

Né à Paris en 1832. A été avocat général à la Cour de Paris et à la Cour de cassation. Conseiller depuis 1893.

M. COTELLE *(Ch. des R.).* Phot. Jullot.

Né à Paris en 1828. A été président du tribunal à Beauvais, avocat général et président de Chambre à Paris. Conseiller depuis 1885.

M. CRÉPON *(Ch. civ.).*

Né à Beaupréau (Maine-et-Loire) en 1825. A été procureur général à Lyon et premier président à Dijon. Conseiller depuis 1878.

M. DARESTE *(Ch. civ.).* Phot. Petit.

Né à Paris en 1824. Ancien auditeur au Conseil d'Etat et à la Cour de cassation; arch.-paléog. Membre de l'Institut. Conseiller depuis 1877.

Judges of the Combined Chambers of the Court of Appeal

The appeal granted

June 3   The Supreme Court of Appeal pronounces its judgment. It annuls the verdict of the 1894 court martial and sends Dreyfus before a new court martial in Rennes.[107] Dreyfus is to be judged on one question only:

> *Is Dreyfus guilty of having in 1894, contrived plots or maintained dealings with a foreign power or one of its agents, in order to urge it to commit hostilities or undertake war against France, or to procure the means for this, by passing to it the notes and documents mentioned in the aforesaid bordereau?*[108] (*v.* Appendix 38)

Despite Manau's mention of ten new facts, the court retains only two new elements: (1) the secret communication of *Ce Canaille de D.* to the 1894 court martial with the knowledge of Mercier and Boisdeffre (the Court ruled that it has been proven to be a document unrelated to Dreyfus); (2) the new graphological study of the *bordereau* (the Court ruled that it had revealed elements in its content, handwriting and paper that were not known to the 1894 court martial and which nullified the document as effective proof against Dreyfus). The Court's ruling also mentions that Lebrun-Renault's different statements (all given after the 1894 verdict) cannot be considered as a confession by Dreyfus. Nevertheless, the ruling leaves a wide discretion for the second court martial in view of its ambiguous wording: '… whereas these facts, unknown to the court martial which pronounced the conviction, tend to show that the *bordereau* could not have been written by Dreyfus'.

The Nationalist press protests vehemently against the Court's decisions, accusing it of being in the pay of the Jews. The insults are particularly targeted at Loubet, who is called upon to resign. (*v.* 4 June 1899) The dreyfusard press calls for justice and for Mercier to be convicted, as the ruling of the Supreme Court of Appeal suggested. (*v.* 5 June 1899, nn. 116, 118)

Trial of Déroulède and Habert

May 29–31   Déroulède and Habert are brought before the Seine Assize Court following their abortive *coup d'état* of 23 February 1899. The charge against them is restricted to that of incitement to riot. They are acquitted and the outcome is acclaimed by the Nationalist press.[109]

June 1   Zurlinden orders the arrest of Du Paty following Cuignet's deposition before the Criminal Chamber and in accordance with Krantz's instruction. (*v.* 5–6 Jan 1899 First revision investigation: Criminal Chamber) Du Paty is escorted to Cherche-Midi prison, accused of fraud by both Cuignet and Picquart.[110]

June 3   Zurlinden instructs Tavernier to open an investigation of Du Paty, who is charged with forging the Blanche and Speranza telegrams, the *faux Weyler* and the *faux Henry*,[111] passing *Ce canaille de D.* to *L'Eclair* in 1896, delivering the *document libérateur* to Esterhazy, and 'any further facts that might possibly be discovered'. (*v.* 31 July 1899)

Dupuy orders the cruiser *Sfax* at Fort-de-France to leave for Devil's Island to escort Dreyfus back to France. (*v.* 9 June 1899)

Esterhazy's admission of authorship of the *bordereau*

In an interview published in *Le Matin*, Esterhazy admits writing the *bordereau* at the request of Sandherr, his 'superior and friend', and with the full knowledge of Billot, Boisdeffre and Gonse.[112] The aim was to prove that a General Staff officer named Dreyfus was a traitor.

Assault on President Loubet

June 4   Outraged by the Supreme Court of Appeal's decision to retry Dreyfus, protestors greet Loubet as he arrives at Auteuil racecourse with shouts of 'Down with Loubet!', 'Down with Panama!', 'Resign!' One demonstrator, baron Fernand Chevreau de Christiani, mounts the President's podium and strikes Loubet with his cane, knocking off the President's hat. Cheered by Royalists, Christiani is arrested. Confrontations between the police, Royalist and antisemitic demonstrators continue. Fifty demonstrators are arrested, many of whom are members of the aristocracy. (*v.* 13 June 1899)

June 5   Zola returns to Paris from England. *L'Aurore* publishes an article by him entitled 'Justice' which explains the reasons for his departure and long exile from France and the joy of return:

> *I am coming back because the truth has come to light, because justice is done ... So my soul is at peace, without anger or*

Emile Loubet

resentment … I leave it to Nemesis to accomplish her work of vengeance, I will not help her.'

Aware that the sentence imposed on him by the Versailles Assize Court could still be executed, Zola writes: 'My trial is no longer useful and no longer interests me.' However, on 9 June he files an appeal against the verdict.[113]

Devil's Island: the head warder of Dreyfus gives him a telegram containing news of the Supreme Court of Appeal's ruling:

…Captain Dreyfus ceases to be subject to the regime of deportation. He becomes simply a defendant, is reinstated to his rank and can wear his uniform again …[114]

The telegram also states that Dreyfus is shortly to be taken back to France in the *Sfax*.

Dreyfus writes to Lucie:

Heart and soul with you, children, and all. I leave Friday. Await with immense joy the happy moment when I shall hold you in my arms. Love to all.[115]

The Cabinet orders Lebret, Minister of Justice, to submit to the Chamber the passage cited in the ruling of the Supreme Court of Appeal acknowledging Mercier's responsibility for passing a secret document to the judges at the court martial of Dreyfus. (*v.* 3 June 1899) The Chamber is to decide whether to initiate proceedings against Mercier.[116]

Dupuy is questioned in the Chamber of Deputies by Republicans on the incident at Auteuil and he is immediately faced with Casaignac's interpellation about Mercier's case.[117] The Chamber votes by 277 to 228 to postpone any action on the charges against Mercier until after the ruling of the second court martial of Dreyfus.[118] The Chamber also votes by 307 to 212 to advertise the ruling of the Supreme Court of Appeal of 3 June in all the *communes* of France.

June 7   The committee of the Ligue des droits de l'homme et du citoyen protests in *L'Aurore* against the 'indefinite prolongation of the detention of Colonel Picquart'.

June 8   The divorce between Madame Esterhazy and her husband is made absolute.

June 9   Devil's Island: Aboard the *Sfax*, Dreyfus leaves Devil's Island for France.[119]

The Indictments Chamber orders Picquart's release from La Santé.[120]

June 10   Trarieux hosts a dinner in Picquart's honour, celebrating his release. His release brings numerous congratulatory telegrams.

June 11   One week after the incident at Auteuil some 100,000 Republicans demonstrate at the racecourse in Longchamp in support of the Republic and in honour of Loubet. Many of the demonstrators are armed with canes and sticks. Dupuy orders the mobilization of large contingents of soldiers, police and Republican Guards. The demonstration takes place without significant incident, apart from minor scuffles with the police at the end of day.

Fall of Dupuy's Government

June 12   Socialist Edouard Vaillant complains in the Chamber of Deputies on the violence used by the police against the Republicans. Dupuy assumes full responsibility for the police and army presence. By 296 votes to 159, the Chamber carries a motion of no confidence in the Government. The Chamber declares it is resolved to 'support only governments determined to defend the institutions of the Republic vigorously and to maintain public order'. Dupuy submits his Cabinet's resignation to the President.

June 13   The Indictments Chamber dismisses all charges against Picquart and Leblois.

                 Baron Christiani is sentenced to four years' imprisonment for his attack on Loubet of 4 June. Seven other demonstrators are sentenced to brief periods in prison and minor fines.

June 18–20   The *Sfax* docks at Cape Verde. Dreyfus receives a copy of *The Times* (London),[121] where he reads about Du Paty's arrest and detention at Cherche-Midi prison.[122]

Charles Dupuy

L'Action française

June 20   Dissatisfied with the slow pace and moderate nationalism of the Ligue de la patrie française Henri Vaugeois, and Charles Maurras create an independent action group L'Action française. The initial aim of the group is to promote a patriotic spirit in France.[123] (*v.* 3–4 June 1908)

June 21   In Brest, Brittany, Socialists distribute a manifesto calling on revisionists to protect Dreyfus against hostile demonstrations on his disembarkation.[124]

The Government of Waldeck-Rousseau

June 22   A new Cabinet is formed. Waldeck-Rousseau is Prime Minister, General Gaston de Galliffet Minister of War, Théophile Delcassé Foreign Secretary, Ernest Monis Minister of Justice and Alexandre Millerand Minister of Commerce.[125] The new Cabinet adopts extreme Republican policies, subordinating the Church and the army to civilian authority and removing principal army officers and transferring them outside Paris.[126]

               The Nationalist press vigorously attacks Waldeck-Rousseau's new Government as 'the Dreyfus Ministry, sold out to Reinach' or 'the Government of treason', accusing it of 'wanting to terrorize an adored army'.

June 24   Effigies of Dreyfus and Zola are burnt in a public square in Privas, in the Ardèche region.

               Le Matin announces that Mercier intends to produce a crucial new document at the Rennes court martial received from the German Foreign Ministry (reference to the alleged *bordereau annoté, v.* 12 Dec 1897). *Le Matin* also publishes an interview with Esterhazy in which he declares he will not appear in court.

June 26   Waldeck-Rousseau's Cabinet, announced to the Chamber of Deputies in a tense atmosphere, is approved by 263 votes to 237, with more than 60 Deputies abstaining, and by 187 to 25 in the Senate.

June 28   *La Libre Parole* is fined a total of 400 francs in damages for public libel of Mathias Morhardt, General Secretary of the Ligue des droits de l'homme et du citoyen.

June 29   Lucie arrives in Rennes. (*v.* July 1899, n. 149, Rennes before the second court martial)

Arrival of Dreyfus in Rennes

June 30–   The *Sfax* is sighted by fishermen as it approaches the French coast
July 1   in the early evening. As news of its arrival spreads, a small crowd collects near the pier. At midnight, in heavy rain, Dreyfus is transferred by launch from the *Sfax* to Port Haliguen on the Quiberon peninsula. Accompanied by Léopold Viguier, head of the Sûreté, Dreyfus is escorted and is taken in secrecy by carriage and special train to Rennes. He arrives at the military prison there at 6 a.m.[127]

July 1   At 9 a.m. Dreyfus is told he is about to see Lucie. Their meeting in a prison cell and lasts only a few minutes. Dreyfus records:

> *The emotion which my wife and I felt on seeing each other again was too intense to be expressed by any human words. It included everything, joy and sorrow … We wanted to tell each other everything we had in our hearts, all the feelings we had suppressed and stifled for so many long years, but the words died on our lips. We contented ourselves with looking at each other, divining from our exchanged glances, all the power of our affection, as well as our willpower. The attendance of an infantry lieutenant, ordered to be present at our conversation, prevented all intimacy … Besides, I knew nothing of the events which had occurred in the last five years, I had come back with confidence; this confidence had been deeply shaken by the incidents of the night full of emotion I had just experienced. But I did not dare to question my dear wife for fear of causing her pain.*[128]

July 3   In Rennes 4000 copies of a virulent antisemitic pamphlet *Le péril juif* are distributed.[129]

Dreyfus is visited by Demange and Labori, who inform him in detail of the Affair.[130] Learning what has happened over the last four years, Dreyfus admits: 'My illusions concerning some of my former superiors vanished one by one, my soul was greatly troubled and pained. I was overwhelmed by immense pity and great sorrow for this army which I loved.'[131]

That afternoon Dreyfus meets his brother Mathieu for the first time since his imprisonment.

Le Figaro publishes a letter from Prince Albert of Monaco to Lucie Dreyfus inviting her husband to the château de Marchais once 'the sacred work of justice has been done'. He adds that 'the presence of a martyr, towards whom the conscience of humanity [has] turned in its anguish, will honour my home'. In the Chamber of Deputies members of the right-wing group La Défense nationale demand to debate this letter, which they consider inappropriate interference in the internal affairs of France and an absolute affront to the independence of justice.[132]

July 4   Demange and Labori show Dreyfus the records of the trials of Esterhazy and Zola, the investigation by the Criminal Chamber and the final hearings of the Combined Chambers of the Supreme Court of Appeal. Despite his frail condition, Dreyfus spends the whole night reading Zola's trial:

> *I saw how Zola was condemned for having wanted to speak out and tell the truth, I read Boisdeffre's oath attesting the authenticity of the faux Henry.*[133] *But whilst my sadness increased on reflecting with sorrow to what extent passions lead men astray, on reading all the crimes committed against innocence, a deep feeling of gratitude and admiration arose in my heart for all the courageous men, scholars and workers, great or humble, who had thrown*

> *themselves valiantly into the struggle for the triumph of justice and truth, to uphold principles which are the legacy of humanity. And history will assign to France's honour this rising of men of all classes for the supremacy of the noble ideas of justice, freedom and truth.*[134]

July 6   During a courtesy visit on board the French training ship *L'Iphigénie*, Prince Albert of Monaco asks the Kaiser to 'adopt a stance in favour of Dreyfus'.[135]

July 7   Waldeck-Rousseau instructs Lépine to find out whether recent demonstrations (23 Feb & 4 June 1899) had been planned in concert by the various leagues.[136] (*v.* 12 Aug 1899, Jules Guérin and Fort Chabrol)

July 9   Deniel, Governor of the îles du Salut, is dismissed. Albert Decrois, the new Colonial Secretary, orders an investigation into his administration.

July 12   Lebon responds to articles published in early July about the severity of the conditions suffered by Dreyfus on Devil's Island. He issues a long statement to the press describing these in detail.[137]

July 21   To avoid confrontations, Galliffet issues an order forbidding the presence of officers in Rennes after the conclusion of the depositions.

July 31   Tavernier closes his investigation of Du Paty. (*v.* 3 June 1899) Due to lack of evidence he clears Du Paty of all charges. Released from prison after 61 days, Du Paty, who is unwell, decides to retire from the army.[138]

Du Paty writes a personal letter to Mercier insisting that the version of Panizzardi's telegram he had given to Gonse a year earlier from memory was correct. (*v.* end April–end May 1898, Consolidation of the Secret Dossier; 8–11 Aug 1899, The Rennes court martial)

Le Figaro publishes Sandherr's letter of 5 January 1895 to journalist Ulric Civry, stating that Dreyfus had not made a confession. (*v.* 5 Jan 1895, Rumours of an alleged confession n. 10) According to *Le Figaro*, the letter was passed to the Minister of War and, if authentic, would be produced as evidence at the Rennes court martial.[139]

Aug 3   *L'Intransigeant* publishes a statement by Mercier: 'Dreyfus will surely be convicted again. For in this affair, there is surely a guilty party. And that guilty party is either him or me. Since it is not me, it is Dreyfus. In closed session or in public, I will speak and tell everything. Dreyfus is a traitor: I will prove it.'

Aug 4   Déroulède sends a spokesman to Mercier advising him of his readiness to march on the Elysée if Mercier speaks out at the trial.[140]

Aug 7–8   *Le Matin* publishes a letter from Esterhazy to Louis-Norbert Carrière (Government Commissioner at the Rennes court martial), dated 6 August, in which Esterhazy announces he will not testify at Rennes, despite being called to do so and having received a safe conduct. He considers the court martial biased, illegal and subject to Government pressure.[141]

L'Affaire Bastian (The Bastian Affair)

July–Aug   Mme Bastian, still employed by both the German Embassy and the Section de Statistique, returns her keys to von Münster at the German Embassy, announcing that she has been arrested and is likely to be called to testify at Rennes. Panicking under pressure from the Deuxième Bureau and private detectives, she disappears from Paris. Rumours of this appear in the press.[142] (*v.* 29 Aug–Sept 1899, Negotiations with Germany)

Rennes before the second court martial[143]

July–Aug   The anti-Dreyfus and Nationalist campaign intensifies. The press exploits the rumour of the *bordereau annoté*, revived largely by Mercier. In *L'Echo de Paris* Beaurepaire launches a vicious campaign to have Dreyfus judged under his presidency. He claims that an investigation he has been leading on the case has brought to light witnesses with devastating proof against him. In *Le Journal*, Barrès skilfully exploits the challenge facing the judges at the Rennes court martial: the inevitable choice between the honour of Dreyfus and those of the Government and army. (*v.* 3 Aug 1899) Other Nationalist papers state that if Dreyfus is acquitted, his innocence will be a 'crime against France' and 'it is the duty of every patriot to kill him.' Virulent anti-dreyfusard and antisemitic propaganda is disseminated through popular songs, caricatures, pamphlets and posters. Anti-dreyfusard leagues subsidize train journeys to Rennes for their supporters and newspapers vendors. An anti-dreyfusard enclave of army officers, Nationalist journalists and politicians is organized around the house rented by Mercier for the period of the trial. Every day the newspapers comment on the daily proceedings of the trial, offering their interpretations and predictions. Many of the trial depositions are contradicted by the newspapers.

In the weeks leading up to the trial, as the dreyfusards congregate around the house of Victor Basch, in the Hôtel de France and the Auberge des Trois Marches, their divisions and lack of a clear strategy become apparent.[144] Despite Mathieu's incessant efforts to reconcile Demange and Labori, the increasing differences between the two lawyers undermine the defence.[145]

Galliffet and Waldeck-Rousseau decide not to exercise governmental pressure and not to give written instruction to the Government Commissioner, Louis-Norbert Carrière. Unofficially they instruct him to avoid discussion of all points on which the Supreme Court of Appeal has already ruled (3 June 1899), and not to call any witnesses on those points, so as not to exercise 'excessive power' and thereby annul the charges.[146] Galliffet does not consider it necessary to appoint a civil adviser to assist the Military Prosecutor. Carrière chooses the Nationalist lawyer Jules Auffray for the task.[147] Conversely, Labori and Clemenceau call for a trial in which 'all questions should be raised' (in contrast to Zola's trial, during which the phrase 'the question will not be raised' was constantly repeated by Delegorgue, president of the Court).[148]

The police and municipality of Rennes prepare for the court martial. The mayor orders posters to be displayed throughout the city, calling on people to remain calm. Detectives are employed to protect Lucie and Mathieu, who have been in Rennes since the end of June.[149] The recently formed dreyfusard and anti-dreyfusard enclaves in the city are closely patrolled by the police. In view of warnings of violent outbreaks when the trial opens and rumours that Dreyfus will be assassinated, hundreds of policemen are mobilized around the Lycée de Rennes, where the court martial is to take place.[150] A few days before the opening of the court martial Rennes looks like a city under siege:

> *The streets are full of soldiers. Mounted patrols circulate the city. The site of the Lycée … is guarded by the military like a fortress. No one can enter. There are fears that a bomb may be placed inside, the basement and all areas are meticulously searched.*[151]

NOTES

1   Dupuy also took over the Ministry of the Interior and of Religious Affairs. He had been prime minister in 1894 when Dreyfus was convicted.

2   Freycinet had been Minister of War during the Panama scandal in 1891–92 and Prime Minister four times between 1880 and 1890. The Nationalist press criticized his appointment: *L'Intransigeant* announced (7 November): 'He is as Protestant as Dreyfus is Jewish; both faiths merging together under the pretext that one and the other are a minority in the country.' Soon after becoming Minister of War, Freycinet confided to Cuignet that he had no firm opinion about the Dreyfus Affair. He was inclined to believe in the innocence of Dreyfus. He wanted to learn about the case and be updated about events daily by Cuignet. In November, Freycinet replaced Renouard, Chief of the General Staff, with General Paul-Marie Brault.

3   The records of this investigation are included in the first volume of *Cass.* (*v.* Abbreviations and Conventions) published by Stock in 1899.

4   Louis Loew was president of the Chamber; the other judges were Sallantin, Sevestre, Chambareaud, Dupré, Accarias, Bard, Dumas, Boulloche, Laurent-Atthalin, Lasserre and Dupont.

5   On 10 November Drumont and Rochefort announced in their respective newspapers that Loew was Jewish. They describe him as 'the Jew Levy' and brother of a Prussian clerk. In *Le Matin* Paul Loew, the judge's son, asserted that his father is not Jewish.

6   Mercier went on to deny that any of the documents read by Cavaignac on 7 July 1898 were presented at the 1894 court martial. This was a lie as *Ce canaille de D.* was one of the documents in the Secret Dossier.

7   *Cass.*, I, 3–51, Cavaignac.

8   The handing over of secret documents to the Court and the conditions to be applied in such were to be debated by the Government for some six weeks. The Court thus began hearing testimonies while this issue was still in discussion. It only began to examine the dossier on 30 December 1898.

9   The decision came after the rejection of Lucie's appeal to inform Dreyfus. (*v.* 10–12 Nov 1898, p. 227) The Court also ordered the Minister to send Dreyfus both a copy of Lucie's appeal and the Court's ruling declaring it admissible.

10   *Cass.*, I, 53–124, Roget.

11   Still a military prisoner, Picquart was escorted every day from Cherche-Midi prison to the courtroom by Captain Jean-Théodore Herqué. (*v.* 25 Dec 1898, n. 67; 12 Jan 1899, n. 73)

12   *Cass.*, I, 125–214, Picquart.

13   *Cass.*, I, 219–37, Bertulus.

14   Esterhazy was informed that Bertulus was in charge of the investigation following the official case brought against him by his cousin Christian for fraud. (*v.* 21 July 1898, Bertulus' investigation of Esterhazy and Mlle Pays) In coming to France Esterhazy could have been arrested. He no longer felt safe in England, fearing extradition, he took refuge in Holland where he frequently changed addresses, registering himself under different names ('Maravelli', 'Jean Dampierre' and others). Thomas, *Esterhazy*, pp. 349–50.

15   *Cass.*, I, 237–59, Gonse.

16   Boisdeffre had by this time retired to a family mansion in Normandy. Bredin, *The Affair*, p. 367.

17   *Cass.*, I, 259–66; I, 556–60, Boisdeffre.

18   *Cass.*, I, 316–25, Forzinetti.

19   Dupuy's deposition was taken by a *commission rogatoire. Cass.*, I, 657–9, Dupuy.

20   *Cass.*, I, 327–32, Casimir-Périer.

21   *Cass.*, I, 502, Gobert.

22   Lebrun-Renault admitted that his report after the degradation ceremony stated 'nothing to report'. (*v.* 5 Jan 1895, n.104) He also stated that he had recorded his conversation with Dreyfus in his notebook and that after showing his note to Cavaignac he decided to throw it away. (*v.* 4 July 1898) *Cass.*, I, 274–8, Lebrun-Renault.

23   *Cass.*, I, 292–5, Poincaré; I, 335–7, Barthou.

24   *Cass.*, I, 215–19, Galliffet.

25   *Cass.*, I, 813–16.

26   *Cass.*, I, 338–76, Cuignet. Most of these accusations were false. They were the subject of a long report prepared by Cuignet for Freycinet and formed the basis on which the Cabinet decided, at the end of December 1898, that proceedings should be opened against Du Paty. (*v.* 1 June 1899)

27   Despite all efforts to the contrary, Cuignet's presentation of the Secret Dossier demonstrated that its contents were not relevant to the Dreyfus case. *DT*, pp. 192–3.

28   *Cass.*, I, 439–56, Du Paty. See also *AD*, pp. 297–8.

29   *Cass.*, I, 608–11. Esterhazy also reproduced this letter in his book *Les dessous de l'affaire Dreyfus*, pp. 168–70.

30   Hyppolyte Sébert and Gaston Moch (retired officers); Joseph-Jules Ducros and Gaston-Louis Hartmann (on active duty). *Cass.*, I, 473–6, Sébert; *Cass.*, I, 508–44, Moch, Ducros, Hartmann.

31   *Cass.*, I, 482–508. They had all received copies of the *bordereau*, and, for comparison, a number of Esterhazy's letters, including those dated 17 April 1892 and 17 August 1894 written on paper similar to that of the *bordereau*.

32   *Cass.*, I, 456–72, Monod, Trarieux.

33   On 15 January Esterhazy was notified by his lawyer that the Government had granted him immunity. He arrived in Paris on 18 January, a day later than the date originally scheduled for his hearing, which therefore had to be postponed. Preferring not to stay with friends or with Mlle Pays, he lodged at the clinic of the Frères de Saint-Jean-de-Dieu. On 31 January, notified that his safe conduct had expired, he immediately returned to Rotterdam. Before leaving he lodged a formal protest against Bertulus, contesting his impartiality and hostile attitude towards him. *DC*, p. 212.

34   *Cass.*, I, 575–607, Esterhazy.

35   Paléologue stated that when Delcassé and Dupuy authorized him to present the file to the Court, Dupuy said: 'This dossier … is the salvation of Dreyfus. Do not doubt it! But when we have saved Dreyfus, how will we save the army? … The generals themselves would have to admit their error, for the army will rally around them.' Paléologue, *Journal de l'affaire Dreyfus*, p. 152.

36   On 24 December Gonse visited Paléologue questioning him about the decoding of Panizzardi's telegram of 2 November 1894. Paléologue explained that he had told Henry on 20 April 1898 that he could only give him a copy of the telegram if an official written request for such had been issued, but that meanwhile he could dictate the contents of the telegram to him, which he did. Gonse stated that Henry merely told him that Paléologue refused to give him the telegram. Paléologue then realized that Henry had concealed the correct version from his superior officers. Despite this, when Gonse was recalled by the Court (21 & 27 January 1899) to clear up this contradiction, he backed Henry by maintaining that as far as he remembered two versions were submitted to Sandherr in 1894. Paléologue, *My Secret Diary*, pp. 132–3; *Cass.*, I, 560–75, Gonse.

37   *Cass*, I, 388–401, Paléologue. See also Paléologue's own description in Paléologue, *My Secret Diary*, pp. 139–50. Before his last deposition, and in order to press home that the *bordereau annoté* was mere invention, Paléologue questioned his colleague Horace Delaroche-Vernet, then embassy secretary in Berlin. Delaroche-Vernet categorically stated that no such document existed, adding: 'Tell me, are they mad in Paris? … How could any newspaper print that the German emperor writes to a spy in his own hand? … And what is even more extraordinary, how can anyone believe such absurdities.' Paléologue, *Journal de l'affaire Dreyfus*, p. 152.

38   *Cass.*, I, 641–6, Hanotaux.

39   Even after receipt of this letter, Dreyfus remained unaware that the Government has already passed Lucie's appeal to the Supreme Court of Appeal. A. Dreyfus, *Cinq années de ma vie* (1982), p. 208.

40   In the original letter Dreyfus said that he was about to stop writing until he received an answer to his appeals for revision. The summary omitted this last phrase. (*v.* 26 Dec 1898, p. 232)

41   Fayard only approved the publication of Esterhazy's book, which was due to be published in September (*v.* 26 Sept 1898), once Esterhazy had agreed that one of his relatives (M. de Faultrier)

rewrite it. Thomas remarks that the publication was a disappointment since Esterhazy reserved the most sensational revelations including his relations with Schwartzkoppen, to the last instalment. The timing of the publication was no longer propitious; by the beginning of November, the Court had already started the investigation into the appeal for a revision. Thomas, *Esterhazy*, pp. 348–9.

42 Dreyfus was still unaware of the Supreme Court of Appeal's ruling of 29 October, and that the Criminal Chamber was already hearing evidence.

43 From September 1898, after Henry's suicide and the decision of the Court to examine Lucie's appeal for a revision, the international press became increasingly interested in developments in the Dreyfus Affair. It generally adopted a dreyfusard stance, and was critical of France. On the impact of the Affair in the international press, see J. Brennan, *The Reflection of the Dreyfus Affair in the European Press, 1897–1899* (New York: Peter Lang Publishing, 1998) and M. Denis, M. Lagrée and J.-Y. Veillard (eds) *L'Affaire Dreyfus et l'opinion publique en France et à l'étranger* (Rennes: Presses Universitaires de Rennes, 1995).

44 The records of this investigation were not published separately. Details on Tavernier's investigation can be found in 'Mémoire de Picquart' included in *Supplément de l'instruction Fabre*, 51–8 and in *L'Affaire Picquart devant le Cour de Cassation* (8 décembre 1898, 2 et 3 mars 1899) (Paris: Stock, 1899).

45 During October, the *révisionnistes*, including the committee of the Ligue des droits de l'homme et du citoyen, held numerous public meetings protesting against Picquart's arrest, and the severe restrictions imposed on visits to him. (*v.* 24–28 Nov 1898, Support for Picquart)

46 In October, Labori contested to Bertrand, Principal State Prosecutor, and to Lebret, Minister of Justice, about the military authorities refusing him communication with his client. Labori requested the application of the Law of 8 December 1879, stipulating the right for a prisoner to communicate with his lawyer. Labori also sought the permission of Freycinet, Minister of War, who finally received Labori on 13 November. Freycinet refused to give Labori the required permission on the grounds that the law was applicable under civil law but did not extend to military law. Freycinet was solicited from all sides: by General Staff officers, for Picquart's court martial, by the dreyfusards, for his release. He was also continuously criticized both by the Nationalist and dreyfusard press. In the Chamber and in Senate bills were proposed for urgent consideration of the Law of 1879, but they were too late. Tavernier hurried his investigation. It was only after Zurlinden, Military Governor of Paris, had signed the order for Picquart's court martial (*v.* 24 Nov 1898, p. 229) that Labori was authorized to see Picquart. *DT*, p. 185.

47 The dating of the erasure remained a subject of debate. The photographs taken by Lauth and Gribelin in March–April 1896 proved that at that time there were no signs of erasure. This indicated that it could not have been the work of Picquart, as they claimed. During the investigation Roget stated that he had already noticed the erasure in May 1898 and had mentioned it to Gonse, who did not pay any attention to it. Gonse, lying, told Tavernier that he had never noticed any erasure and that no one had ever mentioned it to him. 'Mémoire de Picquart' (18 Mai 1899), in *Supplément de l'instruction Fabre*, 51–8. Also see: *AD*, 783–6.

48 *Fabre*, 295–314, Taverner's report. See also *AD*, 772–8.

49 Schwartzkoppen, *Die Wahrheit über Dreyfus*, pp. 207–9.

50 *Fabre*, 315–16. Zurlinden's order. See also *AD*, pp. 778–9.

51 Founded in 1733, the Grand Orient of France was in existence until the end of the 19th century, when it was the only Masonic Order in France. Both the Grand Orient and the Ligue des droits de l'homme et du citoyen supported a revision of the Dreyfus case. A. Bauer, *Le Grand Orient* (Paris: Denoël, 2001), pp. 104–5.

52 Schwartzkoppen, *Die Wahrheit über Dreyfus*, p. 223.

53 *HAD*, 4, pp. 401–5. Poincaré, a lawyer renowned for his intelligence and honesty, had represented the department of the Meuse in the Chamber of Deputies since 1887. He had previously had a reputation for abstaining from voting and playing only a small part in politics. He gradually came to the conclusion that an error had been committed at the 1894 court martial and decided to speak out. On Poincaré's involvement in the Affair, see F. Roth, *Raymond Poincaré* (Paris: Fayard, 2000), pp. 106–11.

54 The Criminal Chamber could have claimed the right to see the original documents included in the file of Picquart's court martial, thus forcing a postponement.

55 The double stockade around his cabin had been taken down a few days earlier. Trarieux requested that Dreyfus be allowed to walk wherever he liked on Devil's Island, but Deniel, officer in command of the îles du Salut, insisted on imposing limits.

56 Von Münster wrote that Labori's approach was strictly confidential and that he already had a signature and a note in Schwartzkoppen's handwriting. Schwartzkoppen, *The Truth About Dreyfus*, pp. 134–6.

57 Hohenlohe asked Schwartzkoppen to discuss the matter openly with his father, the Chancellor. He also asked Schwartzkoppen not to mention his involvement to anyone except his father, since he did not wish to be accused of interferring in events outside his competence. Schwartzkoppen, *The Truth About Dreyfus*, pp. 213–14.

58 In proposing this motion Waldeck-Rousseau demonstrated his clear allegiance to the dreyfusard camp. As Bredin remarks, three famous French lawyers, Waldeck-Rousseau, Poincaré and Millerand, found themselves on the same side, consulted each other and gained the support of different Republican groups. Bredin, *The Affair*, p. 365.

59 The charges against Picquart brought by Zurlinden (24 November 1898) included forgery and illegalities relating to espionage (transmission of secret documents). Picquart and Leblois were still to be tried before a civil court on the same charge, brought against them by Cavaignac. (*v.* 12 July & 21 Sept 1898) Their lawyers submitted request on the grounds of conflict of legal procedures.

60 Reinach had no sound evidence for his theory. He based his articles on pieces of information he had received, mainly from Tornielli, concerning sums of money Esterhazy received from Schwartzkoppen in 1895; the loss of documents in the Ministry of War since 1893; the long-standing relationship between Henry and Esterhazy (since 1877); and Henry's 'secret funds' in the Section de Statistique. *DC*, pp. 208–9; *DT*, p. 190. Reinach's articles reflect the most significant aspects of these confused months at the end of 1898 and the almost desperate need to find the true culprit. For Reinach, this was Henry; for Picquart and other General Staff officers, Du Paty; for other officers, Picquart; for the anti-dreyfusards, Reinach and the Syndicate. See Johnson, *France and the Dreyfus Affair*, pp. 160–1.

61 Mentioning that popular opinion is largely in favour of Picquart, von Münster invited Schwartzkoppen to send him a coded telegram. If Schwartzkoppen wrote the word 'good', it would mean that it was he who had written the *petit bleu*; 'fairly good' would signify that he had had it written; 'know nothing' that neither was the case. Probably instructed by von Schlieffen and von Bülow not to make any statement regarding the Dreyfus case, Schwartzkoppen replied to von Münster using the third option. Schwartzkoppen, *The Truth About Dreyfus*, pp. 137–9.

62 *L'Affaire Picquart devant le Cour de Cassation*, 1–37. This decision provoked the anti-dreyfusards to further protests against the judges of the Criminal Chamber.

63 Drumont encouraged Henry's widow to prosecute Reinach. (*v.* 14 Dec 1898) On 10 December she informed Maître Edmond Ployer that she intended to bring both Reinach and the manager of *Le Siècle* before an Assize Court.

64 The subscriptions for Henry's memorial fund were a successful campaign, illustrating the passion and militancy the Affair aroused. Within a month it had brought in 25,000 contributions; ranging from 0.15 francs to thousands of francs. Contributions came mainly from labourers and tradesmen, but also from army officers, including Mercier and 28 retired generals. The signatories also included priests, students, journalists and literary men, members of the aristocracy and politicians. The comments accompanying the contributions revealed the strength of antisemitic and Nationalist feeling. The dreyfusards called the 18 lists published by the *Libre Parole* '*listes rouges*' ('Red lists'). In 1899 the writer Pierre Quillard, an ardent dreyfusard, published his analysis of these lists, which he classified according to the professions and geographical locations of the contributors: *Le Monument Henry, listes des souscripteurs classés méthodiquement et selon l'ordre alphabétique* (Paris: Stock, 1899). Quillard considered the Henry memorial to be 'a memorial of shame, and a repertoire of ignominies'. See S. Wilson, 'Le monument Henry; le structure de l'antisémitisme en France, 1898–1899' *Annales ESC* (March–April, 1977), pp. 265–91; Pierrard, *Juifs et catholiques français*, pp. 102–7.

65 Schwartzkoppen, *Die Wahrheit über Dreyfus*, pp. 147.

66 Herzog, *Der Kampf einer Republik*, pp. 812–14.

67 Since early December both Beaurepaire and Herqué, who escorted Picquart from prison to court, spread rumours to journalists as well as to Roget and Zurlinden about what they claimed were instances of favouritism towards Picquart by several judges, such as serving him a hot drink while he was waiting to be heard.

68 A. Dreyfus, *Cinq années de ma vie* (1982), p. 210.

69 These accusations included serving refreshment to Picquart while he was waiting to testify; a conversation between Bard and Labori; the phrase 'all the Court regrets' addressed to Picquart when he had to wait a long time before being heard.

70 Among its earliest supporters were Ferdinand Brunetière (editor of the *Revue des Deux Mondes*), Maurice Barrès, Charles Maurras, Léon Daudet, Jules Verne, Gyp (Countess Martel de Janville), the poet Frédéric Mistral, scholars Henri Vaugeois, Louis Dausset and Gabriel Syveton, historians Albert Vandal, Petit de Julleville, cartoonists Forain and Caran d'Ache and the painters Jean Renoir and Paul Degas. The League's only important political figure was Cavaignac. A total of 14 lists of supporters were published in *L'Eclair* between 6 January and 1 February 1899. By February 1899 the league claimed some 40,000 supporters; by February 1900, some 500,000. Sternhell, *La droite révolutionnaire*, p. 138; M. Winock (ed.), *Histoire de l'extrême droite en France* (Paris: Seuil, 1993), pp. 104–5.

71 Following his resignation, Beaurepaire immediately joined *L'Echo de Paris* as a journalist and continued in the press his campaign against the judges of the Criminal Chamber. In the statement he submitted to Havas, he explained that his resignation was the result of a disagreement over the investigation led by the Criminal Chamber.

72 Throughout January Beaurepaire continued to publish 'revelations' on certain Criminal Chamber judges whom he accused of participating in the campaign for a judicial revision. The recently founded Ligue de la patrie française joined Beaurepaire's campaign against the Criminal Chamber and for the removal of the Dreyfus case from its jurisdiction. This forced the Government to intervene.

73   Lebret was also asked to read the report of Captain Herqué, who escorted Picquart from prison to Court. (*v.* 23 Nov–5 Dec 1898, First revision investigation: Criminal Chamber, n. 11) This report gave more details of the alleged favouritism of some judges towards Picquart and led Deputies to an undignified discussion on items such as whether a hot beverage was served in the Court waiting room only to Picquart or also to other witnesses.

74   *Répertoire*, pp. 253–4. This conclusion opened the way for Dupuy to remove the Dreyfus case from the Criminal Chamber. (*v.* 28 Jan 1899, p. 236) Loew, President of the Criminal Chamber, later published his own account of the daily campaign of defamation against the Court: *La Loi de dessaisissement par un dessaisi* (Paris: Fischbacher, 1910).

75   Reinach withdrew his appeal in May 1899. Because of complicated legal reasons, the trial finally took place in 1902. (*v.* 2 June 1902)

76   Mazeau informed Dupuy that the majority of the judges in the Criminal Chamber were in favour of a revision, but that the majorities of the two other divisions of the Supreme Court of Appeal (civil and Appeals) were against. The removal of the case from the Criminal Chamber a few days before the Chamber was expected to pass judgment was without precedent and contrary to the law. Bredin, *The Affair*, p. 371.

77   Encouraged by this meeting, Albert I obtained a hearing with President Faure and conveyed the Kaiser's word of honour that Dreyfus had never had any dealings with Germany. The meeting took place on 16 February; according to Reinach it was heated and negative. About an hour later, President Faure suddenly passed away. (*v.* 16 February 1899, p. 236) An ardent pacifist, Albert I approached the Kaiser again in the years before World War I, in an attempt to dissuade him from war. P. Miquel, *Albert de Monaco, Prince des mers* (Paris: Glénat, 1995), pp. 202–10.

78   The committee published a dreyfusard manifesto on 19 March. At its height the committee numbered only 100–200 members. P Pierrard, *Juifs et catholiques*, pp. 186–212; R. Remond, 'Les catholiques choisissent leur camp' *Histoire 173 L'Affaire Dreyfus, vérités et mensonges* (January 1994), pp. 70–3.

79   The album was published by the société libre d'édition des gens de lettres, under the direction of Paul Brenet et Felix Thureau. The 12 lithographs were by Anquetin, Hermann-Paul, Cornillier, Gumery, Luce, Manzana, Perroudon, Petitjean, Rault, van Rysselberghe, Sunyer, and Vallotton.

80   Hearing screams from the President's private office, Faure's secretary, Le Gall, found him in a critical state due to cerebral haemorrhage. The screams were in fact from his mistress, Madame Steinheil, who was usually received in his private office. Faure died within a few hours. This news gave rise to many theories concerning his death. *La Patrie* insinuated that Faure had been murdered by the Jews (18 February); *La Libre Parole*, by the dreyfusards (23 February). Drumont suggested that Faure's mistress – Delilah – was in the pay of the Jews. The news came as a relief for the dreyfusards, since, unlike Faure, the next president could – and should – be in favour of a revision. Clemenceau immediately proposed the election of Emile Loubet, then President of the Senate.

81   Loubet was an ardent Republican and had been Prime Minister during the Panama scandal. (*v.* 1892)

82   Both Déroulède's League of Patriots and the followers of the duc d'Orléans had been waiting for some time for the right moment to overthrow the parliamentary system with the help of Guérin's Antisemitic League, which was mobilized for the purpose.

83   Less than two years later Déroulède and Habert were brought to final judgment, by the Senate constituted as a special court. (*v.* 9 Nov 1899–4 Jan 1900, p. 289)

84   After Deroulède's *coup d'état* attempt his league became the rallying point for all right-wing leagues. On the day after the attempted coup, a proposal by Senator Fabre to suppress the leagues was rejected. But Dupuy's Government ordered their prosecution under Article 291 of the Law of 1834 as 'unauthorized associations of more than 20 persons'. In order to appear impartial, the Government also prosecuted the Ligue des droits de l'homme et du citoyen. However, the Court (18 April) merely imposed a fine of 16 francs on each league. B. Joly, *Déroulède, l'inventeur du nationalisme français* (Paris: Perrin, 1998) pp. 279–300.

85   *L'Affaire Picquart devant le Cour de Cassation*, 38–193.

86   This report, for which Esterhazy was paid, was also published in *L'Aurore*. Most of the information was to appear in the third instalment of Esterhazy's *Les dessous de l'affaire Dreyfus*. (*v.* 7 March 1899)

87   To reduce the impact of Esterhazy's recent disclosures in his book, Drumont announced that Esterhazy had been 'bought by the Syndicate'. Esterhazy replied that he was 'not for sale'. During March and April Esterhazy gave interviews to the British and French press in which he continued to denigrate many of those involved – Gonse, Pellieux, Billot, Cavaignac and Déroulède – with the exception of Henry, the only one in his view who deserved respect.

88   For a long time Freystaetter was convinced that Dreyfus was guilty. He began to question this conviction in 1898, after Cavaignac's speech of 7 July and Henry's suicide (31 August). *Rennes*, II, 401–2, Freystaetter.

89   Monod published this letter shortly after the recent deaths of President Faure and Gibert.

90   The decision to publish the investigation records was taken by Mathieu, Clemenceau, Lazare, Trarieux

and Reinach in order to counter the selective publications that appeared since 1898 in the Nationalist press, and to arouse public interest in some of its important findings. Mathieu, who was shown the records by Mornard had to find a way to publish them without disclosing the source. With Reinach's help the copies were given to Victorien Sardou (playwright and member of the Académie Française), who passed them to *Le Figaro*. The success of the first publications brought a significant increase in circulation to *Le Figaro* which continued to publish the records. Mornard agreed to transmit all the records to Mathieu on condition they were copied and returned to him. With the help of Labori's secretaries and five copyists (Russian Jews enrolled by Lazare), the copious records were copied each night during the month of publication. *ATQV*, pp. 200–3.

91 The offices of *Le Figaro* were searched, but the investigation yielded no result because the dreyfusards had been very careful. Sardou took with him each night the instalment planned for the next day's publication. The secrecy surrounding this publication gave birth to curious rumours in Paris: Freycinet's wife and daughter suggested that it was Sardou himself who informed *Le Figaro*; some said the documents were stolen from one of the Court's judges; others that they were delivered to *Le Figaro* by a masked man. *ATQV*, pp. 200–3.

92 The windows and doors were reinforced and a high fence built in front of the building. It housed the offices of *L'Antijuif*, its press, a 500–capacity conference hall, an armoury, a gymnasium and a first aid post.

93 These articles were later published: G. Durury, *Pour la justice et pour l'Armée* (Paris: P. Ollendorff, 1901).

94 The records of this investigation are included in the second volume of *Cass.* (*v.* Abbreviations and Conventions) published by Stock in 1899. This volume also contains the records of the Combined Chambers and documents related to previous investigations (those of d'Ormescheville, Pellieux, Ravary and Bertulus), and various appendices (including the alleged confession dossier and the disciplinary dossiers of Esterhazy, Picquart and Du Paty).

95 Surprised at the emptiness of the dossier, one of the judges asked Chamoin whether it was complete. He was inquiring specifically about a letter from the Kaiser. Chamoin confirmed that the dossier was complete. *HAD*, 5, pp. 54–5.

96 *Cass.*, II, 5–8, Freystaetter.

97 *Cass.*, II, 9–12, Lépine.

98 *Cass.*, II, 31–8, Du Paty.

99 *Cass.*, II, 341–3, Charavay's letter.

100 Paléologue, *Journal de l'affaire Dreyfus*, p. 181. This matter was the subject of a clash between Delcassé and Freycinet who at the time was still Minister of War. Since Freycinet accepted Cuignet's statement, the two Ministers exchanged strong views which became known to the public. (*v.* 12 May 1899)

101 Although this should have put an end to the matter, this issue was to be raised again at the Rennes trial leading to a significant incident. (*v.* 8–10 & 24 Aug 1899, The Rennes court martial)

102 The records of this investigation are included in the second volume of *Cass.* (*v.* Abbreviations and Conventions) published by Stock in 1899. This publication also contains the Report of Ballot-Beaupré; the conclusion of Manau; the memoir and closing speech of Mornard and the ruling of the court.

103 *Déb. Cass., 1899*, 1–198. The discovery of new facts would enable the Supreme Court of Appeal to annul the verdict and order a revision. But, if the new facts completely destroyed the basis of the accusation, the Court could annul the verdict without the need for retrial. Ballot-Beaupré explained the inherent difficulty of the Dreyfus case. If the transmission of a secret document were mentioned, the verdict would simply be annulled. If Henry's testimony were considered false, Henry would have to be tried, but he was no longer alive. Ballot-Beaupré was finally able to cite two 'new facts' not known at the court martial of Dreyfus: that the transmission of secret information continued after the arrest of Dreyfus (the *petit bleu* was discovered in 1895), and that Esterhazy lied during Ravary's investigation when declaring that he had never written anything on India squared paper, since two such letters of his, dated the same month as the *bordereau,* had been discovered. (*v.* Nov 1898, p. 225)

104 *Déb. Cass., 1899*, 321.

105 Mornard originally intended to plead only for an annulment, on the basis of a new fact that left no grounds for a retrial. He finally bowed to Lucie's and Mathieu's demand to plead for a revision.

106 *Déb. Cass., 1899*, 703.

107 The town of Orléans had also been considered as place of judgment. There were several reasons the Court of Appeal finally decided to hold the second court martial of Dreyfus at Rennes: There was a military presence in Rennes: it was the home of the 10th Army Corps. It was not far from the coast, which would reduce security problems by allowing Dreyfus to be taken to prison rapidly from his port of arrival. Rennes was also Catholic and Conservative, and mainly anti-dreyfusard. Its location far from Paris, its wide streets and well-known calm atmosphere (with its population of about 70,000) made massive anti-dreyfusard demonstrations unlikely.

108 *Déb. Cass., 1899*, 712.

109 The acquittal coincided with the return of Captain Marchand to France (*v.* Sept–Oct 1898), welcomed by supporters of the Ligue des patriotes and the Nationalist press. *L'Antijuif* of 28 May wrote: 'the friends of Dreyfus are the enemies of Marchand'.

110 A few months earlier, when Picquart was retransferred from Cherche-Midi to La Santé (*v.* 3 March 1899), he said: 'I am being taken away from here to make room; it will not be long before Du Paty takes my place.' *Le Figaro*, 10 June 1899 (article by Huret) quoted in *HAD*, 5, p. 98.

111 The charge relating to the *faux Henry* was only made by Cuignet. *HAD*, 5, p. 239.

112 The interview was given in London to *Le Matin* journalist Serge Basset, whose *nom de plume* was Paul Ribon. The *Daily Chronicle* published this statement in French, after receiving Esterhazy's signed confirmation that he had made them. *Le Temps* published the statement on 5 June and *Le Siècle* reproduced a facsimile on 8 June. (*v.* 5 Sept 1899, The Rennes court martial)

113 Zola, *La Vérité en marche* (1969), pp. 147–55. See full English text in Pagès, *Emile Zola, The Dreyfus Affair, J'Accuse and Other Writings*, pp. 126–32. On 31 August Zola's trial was scheduled for 21 November 1899, but a few days before the proposed date it was postponed indefinitely because the amnesty bill had already been tabled. (*v.* 16 Nov 1899)

114 A. Dreyfus, *Cinq années de ma vie* (1982), p. 215.

115 A. Dreyfus, *Cinq années de ma vie* (1982), p. 217.

116 The charges against Mercier came under the Criminal Code. It was therefore the Chamber of Deputies' responsibility to decide whether to issue proceedings and bring Mercier before the Senate constituted as Haute Cour de justice (Special court trying members of the government).

117 For the Republicans the incident at Auteuil proved the fragility and weakness of Dupuy's Government. Both dreyfusards and Republicans considered it a significant warning of the threat to Republican democracy from the Nationalists, the army, the Church and aristocracy. (*v.* 11 June 1899)

118 Although the Government did not discuss the issue, the ruling of the Supreme Court of Appeal was of major consequence for the second court martial of Dreyfus, in that it recognized Mercier's responsibility for the illegalities committed at Dreyfus' first court martial. It was therefore to confront the judges with the delicate dilemma of choosing between Dreyfus and Mercier, between an issue *ad personam* and the political and general cause of the honour of the army, since a decision to acquit Dreyfus would have meant committing Mercier to trial. *DT*, 211.

119 Dreyfus had spent a total of 48 months on the îles du Salut in solitary confinement and four months imprisoned in France (15 October 1894–21 February 1895). The cruiser was specially equipped for the journey: a non-commissioned officer's cabin with a barred window was prepared for Dreyfus. An armed guard was posted at the cabin door. Dreyfus was treated as an officer but under strict arrest: he was allowed to walk on deck for only one hour in the morning and one hour in the evening, and had to remain in the cabin for the rest of the time. See Dreyfus' own description in A. Dreyfus, *Cinq années de ma vie* (1982), pp. 218–19.

120 Picquart had spent a total of 384 days in detention.

121 Here and after, refer to as *The Times*.

122 Dreyfus knew very little about events in his own case. He picked up rumours from his warders about the engagement of certain intellectuals in his cause and the campaign for a revision, but he did not know about Zola, Picquart or Scheurer-Kestner. He only heard about Esterhazy and Henry's forgery and suicide just before he disembarked in France. Dreyfus realized on reading *The Times* article that his innocence was acknowledged – at least by some.

123 The development of Action Française was directly related to the Dreyfus Affair. Of the founders of the group, only Charles Maurras was a Royalist. The others, Maurice Pujo, Henri Vaugeois, François Mahy, were Bonapartists, Catholics, freethinkers, and democrats. Under the leadership of Maurras L'Action Française was to constitute the main Royalist and Nationalist group of 20th-century France, rejecting democracy and the parliamentary system. On 10 July 1899 the first issue of the bimensual *Revue de L'Action Française* was published. This paper reflected the discussions and transformations of the movement. In the early years of the 20th century Action Française sought to strengthen its influence through fortnightly dinner-lectures in which literary, philosophical, and political matters were discussed. E. Weber, *Action Française: Royalism and Reaction in Twentieth-Century France* (Stanford: Stanford University Press, 1962) pp. 5–43. Sternhell, *La droite révolutionnaire*, pp. 348–400.

124 The Government originally instructed the *Sfax* to dock in Brest, but, fearing demonstrations, it ordered the cruiser to dock at Quiberon instead.

125 All the new Cabinet members were known to be loyal to Waldeck-Rousseau and supporters of Dreyfus.

126 Zurlinden was replaced by General Brugège as Military Governor of Paris (7 July). Following an inquiry into the conduct of Pellieux in the 1897 Esterhazy investigation, he was transferred to command a brigade in Quimper, Britanny (25 July). Roget was transferred to Belfort. Lépine returned as Prefect of Police, replacing Charles Blanc who had failed to protect Loubet. When taking up his post as Minister of War, Galliffet informed Boisdeffre and Gonse that they would remain on half pay, but he would not initiate any action against them. Boisdeffre was grateful for this. Not long before, he

had asked his confessor, Father Du Lac: 'Give me your blessing as to a man awaiting the firing squad.' Although the influence of Father Du Lac on the General Staff officers has been debated by historians, both Reinach (who met Du Lac on 10 June 1899) and Caperan confirm this episode. *HAD*, 5, p 148; L. Caperan, *L'anticléricalisme et l'Affaire Dreyfus* (Toulouse: Imprimerie régionale 1948), pp. 274–5.

127 The knowledge that Dreyfus was to arrive in Rennes had already drawn many journalists to the city and created a commotion on the night of 30 June. Antisemitic students were heard singing the 'Marseillaise antijuive' within earshot of Lucie. (*v.* Appendix 25) C. Cosnier, *Rennes pendant le procès Dreyfus* (Rennes: Ouest France, 1894), pp. 36–7.

128 A. Dreyfus, *Cinq année de ma vie* (1982), p. 221. After this first meeting Lucie was allowed to see Dreyfus each day for one hour. Detention for 52 months in solitary confinement had had a devastating effect on his mental and physical health. The almost total silence, poor nutrition and malaria had seriously diminished his faculty of speech and when he enunciated words by making a hissing sound; his vocal cords and larynx were damaged, his gums inflamed, his teeth rotting. His capacity for recalling words and his concentration were impaired. His hair had turned completely white; his clothes hung from his emaciated body; he had become an old man at only 39. He was still suffering from sudden bouts of fever and nightmares. *DFA*, pp. 247–8.

129 The pamphlet was published by the antisemtic organization L'Oeuvre Nationale de propaganda antijuive in Paris, in collaboration with *La Libre Parole*. The same pamphlet was reissued during the legislative election campaign in 1902. Pierrard, *Juifs et catholiques*, p. 150.

130 On Mathieu's suggestion, the prudent Demange was assisted by the more aggressive Labori. Instead of complementing each other, the two lawyers were temperamentally different and disagreed on strategy. Demange adopted a moderate strategy, to avert hostility from both witnesses and judges. He suggested discussion be limited to the doubts and questions left open by the ruling of the Supreme Court of Appeal. Labori preferred an uncompromising and dramatic approach, with a desire to involve as many people as possible, sparing neither Government nor army. (*v.* July 1899, Rennes before the second court martial) P. Vidal-Naquet, 'Dreyfus dans l'affaire et dans l'histoire' preface to A. Dreyfus, *Cinq années de ma vie* (Paris: Maspero, 1984), p. 19. See also Bredin, *The Affair*, pp. 398–9.

131 A. Dreyfus, *Cinq années de ma vie* (1982), p. 222.

132 *Répertoire*, p. 320.

133 Throughout his detention Dreyfus continued to believe in Boisdeffre's integrity and honesty. He was certain that Boisdeffre was one of those who fought in favour of the revision. On his journey back to France from Devil's Island Dreyfus asked to send a telegram to Boisdeffre to thank him. M. Dreyfus, *Dreyfusards!*, p. 211.

134 A. Dreyfus, *Cinq années de ma vie* (1982), pp. 222–3. Throughout July Dreyfus continued to prepare his defence. He received thousands of letters of support from friends as well as people he did not know from across the world. He particularly appreciated those of Anatole France, Scheurer-Kestner and Reinach. (For English translations of these letters, see Snyder, *The Dreyfus Case*, pp. 266–7.) Towards the end of July Dreyfus suffered from a high fever and became bedridden. Only with careful medical treatment was he able to continue to prepare his defence, and during the court martial itself he adhered to a diet of milk and eggs, with a supplement of cola nut to help him cope with the strain and withstand the long sessions.

135 Baumont, *Aux sources de l'affaire*, p. 245.

136 The police had been informed of the attempt in mid-June to unite the leagues of Guérin, Déroulède and the Royalists into a federation. Although the project failed, collaboration between these leagues for future alliance was not ruled out. From early July Déroulède began to call on the supporters of his own league to revolt against the Republic and he renewed his promises for a second *coup d'état*. He still wavered about the right timing – either at Mercier's deposition at the court martial of Dreyfus or at the time of the verdict. (*v.* 4 Aug 1899) Joly, *Déroulède*, pp. 307–13.

137 The articles were written by Louis Havet and published in *Le Temps* (6 July) and *Le Figaro* (10 & 12 July).

138 Angry with his superior officers for casting blame upon him, Du Paty wrote to his brother Auguste (2 August) that: 'those scoundrels whose incredible cowardice sent me to Cherche-Midi really hoped that I would leave my bones there.' Auguste sent the letter to a journalist of *La Lanterne* along with a note insisting that his brother was too ill to go to Rennes and that if his evidence were required, it could only be given in Paris. (*v.* 26 Aug & 6 Sept 1899, The Rennes court martial). *HAD*, 5, p. 240.

139 The letter was not exhibited at Rennes, only at the 1904 investigation. *3ème Cass., 1904*, I, 425. It was published (in English) in W. Harding, *Dreyfus: the Prisoner of Devil's Island* (New York: Associated Publishing Company, 1899), pp. 97–8.

140 With little of substance to reveal, Mercier gave an evasive answer, following which Déroulède decided to postpone his *coup d'état* from 12 August, which was the day planned for Mercier's deposition, to the day of the verdict. The police continued to believe 12 August a likely date for the coup.

141 In this letter Esterhazy reiterates his version of the history of the *bordereau*: i.e. that it was dictated to him by Sandherr, 'taken' by an Intelligence agent from a pigeon-hole at the German Embassy and torn

up by Intelligence to make it look as if it had come via the 'normal route'. The letter was published in *Le Figaro* (8 August). It is reproduced in *Répertoire*, pp. 342–4.

142 Various witnesses at the 1904 investigation confirmed that the disappearance of Mme Bastian abounded with contradictory detail. On 26 July she received an unexpected visit by someone claiming to have been sent by Waldeck-Rousseau, who wished to question her about her work at the German Embassy. Frightened, Mme Bastian held a knife to the visitor and forced him to the local police station. The following day, police headquarters and the Sûreté were informed; the visitor was identified as a former Sûreté agent who had been engaged by Reinach through the journalist Marguerite Durant. Mme Bastian informed both the Deuxième Bureau and the Sûreté of this, while Reinach and Galliffet informed Waldeck-Rousseau. Von Münster and Galliffet instructed the Sûreté to make inquiries; neither obtained reliable information as to Mme Bastian's whereabouts. The only certain fact was that on 22 August Mme Bastian registered in the village of Marly under the name of Zimmermann. According to Reinach the Deuxième Bureau had taken her there much earlier. Shortly before the opening of the Rennes trial Mercier warned Mme Bastian that he might have to denounce her in the forthcoming trial, but told her that she would continue to receive an army pension. This was not true: the army abandoned her, and did not continue to pay her pension as Mercier had promised; she was only 'saved' by a Mme Jourdain, who, via the intervention of journalist Ernest Judet, supported her for several years. For the testimonies of François, Mercier, Bastian, Jourdain, Reinach, Galliffet, see *3ème Cass.*, II, 225–9; I, 459–64; 452–6; III, 340–3; I, 108–10; II, 639–40.

143 For the tense atmosphere in Rennes before and during the second court martial of Dreyfus, see C. Cosnier, *Rennes pendant le procès Dreyfus* (Rennes: Ouest France, 1894); C. Cosnier & A. Hélard, *Rennes et Dreyfus en 1899. Une ville, un procès* (Paris: Pierre Horay, 1999); J. Guiffan, *Les Bretons et l'affaire Dreyfus* (Rennes: Terre de Brume, 1999).

144 For dreyfusard activities before and during the Rennes trial, see Stock, *Memorandum d'un éditeur*, pp. 111–28. See also the recently published letters of Victor Basch, a principal dreyfusard and future president of the Ligue des droits de l'homme et du citoyen. L. Crips and P. Gruson, *Victor Basch, un intellectuel cosmopolite* (Paris: Berg international, 2000) and F. Basch and A. Hélard (eds) and *Le deuxième procès Dreyfus, Rennes dans la tourmente – Correspondances de Victor Basch* (Paris: Berg international, 2003). (*v.* Appendices 39 and 51)

145 Labori left many notes on these differences, which became increasingly apparent and sharp. He also described the split in the dreyfusard camp that occurred after the Rennes trial. These notes were collected and published by Labori's wife: see M.F. Labori, *Labori. Ses notes manuscrites. Sa vie* (Paris: Victor Attinger, 1947).

146 After examining the Secret Dossier and realizing its irrelevance to Dreyfus, Galliffet believed that the trial would be a mere formality before Dreyfus was finally acquitted. Waldeck-Rousseau was less convinced of an obvious acquittal. On 16 July he wrote that Dreyfus had only a small chance of success, and that even this would be reduced if the dreyfusard press continued to attack the army and the defence lawyers did not restrict themselves to matters left open by the Supreme Court of Appeal. After the court martial, Labori and Picquart accused Waldeck-Rousseau of betraying the dreyfusards by misleading them with his optimism and thus disarming the defence. (*v.* 7 Apr 1899, n. 6, The Rennes court martial)

147 *3ème Cass.*, II, 645, Galliffet. Auffray had previously collaborated with the General Staff: he had been asked to fill the courtroom with soldiers during Zola's trial. (*v.* 23 Feb 1898, n. 89)

148 Paradoxically Clemenceau became the perfect spokesman for the anti-dreyfusards, who were pleased to reopen all issues including those which the ruling of the Supreme Court of Appeal had already dismissed, such as Dreyfus' alleged confession and the document *Ce canaille de D.* (*v.* 3 June 1899, The appeal granted).

149 Lucie and Mathieu were both of interest to the many journalists and reporters who poured into the city. Lucie's daily visits to see Dreyfus in prison were a great opportunity for photographers and journalists. Lucie tried to avoid this publicity, assuring journalists that the Dreyfus family did not want to create a fuss. Her calm avoided a potential cause for public animosity. Forced to move out of her hotel room she eventually found accommodation, via the help of Paul Collet, a local Protestant pastor, with a Madame Godard, who was herself criticized in the anti-dreyfusard papers for her hospitality. Unlike Lucie, Mathieu was still presented in the papers as one of the main instigators of the Jewish 'Syndicate'. He was more unpopular than Lucie both with the public and the police. The Dreyfus family hired its own private security, in addition to the police detectives assigned to watch Mathieu. Cosnier, *Rennes pendant le procès Dreyfus*, pp. 34–6. DFA, pp. 220, 241–2.

150 The court martial was initially to have been held on the order of General Lucas, Commander of the 10th Army Corps, in a room of the artillery stores, in order to reduce the number of spectators. Following strong protests by Labori and the journalists, the location was changed to the *salle des fêtes* of the Rennes Lycée, which could hold several hundred people. DT, p. 228.

151 *ATQV*, p. 207.

Part 8

SECOND CONVICTION, PARDON and AMNESTY

August 1899–December 1900

Ce numéro est accompagné d'un supplément de deux pages en couleurs hors texte.

L'ILLUSTRATION

Prix du Numéro : 75 centimes.　　　SAMEDI　16　SEPTEMBRE　1899　　　57ᵉ Année. — N

Colonel Jouaust, President of the Rennes court martial

The Rennes court martial (7 August–9 September 1899)[1]

At 7 a.m. the court martial of Dreyfus opens at the Lycée de Rennes.[2] The Court consists of President Colonel Albert Jouaust, Major Lancrau de Bréon, Lieutenant-Colonel Brogniart, Major Maurice Merle, Major Profillet, Captain Parfait and Captain Beauvais. Also present are Major Carrière (Government Commissioner or Military Prosecutor), General Chamoin, representing the Ministry of War, Delcassé and Paléologue, representing the Foreign Office. The *salle de fêtes* (public room), transformed into a courtroom, is full to capacity with over 100 witnesses,[3] some 300 French and international journalists, soldiers, politicians and writers including Jean Jaurès, René Viviani, Maurice Barrès, Bernard Lazare, Anatole France, (*v.* Appendix 40) Marcel Prévost (correspondent of the *New York Herald*), Theodor Herzl, Victor Basch and many other foreign correspondents.[4] The trial also attracts professionals of the new media, photographers and the first documentary film-makers including the cinema pioneer Georges Méliès.[5] For security reasons gendarmes are stationed amongst the public and soldiers are armed.

Aug 7

At a roll of drums the Court falls silent. Jouaust orders the prisoner to be brought in. All eyes are turned to the right. (*v.* Appendix 39) Almost everyone is standing. A frail Dreyfus enters the courtroom followed by a gendarme. After reading d'Ormescheville's indictment of 1894, the Supreme Court of Appeal's ruling (3 June 1899) and the witness list, Jouaust questions Dreyfus and shows him the *bordereau*.[6] Dreyfus denies having written it, denies knowledge of the information it contains and denies making any confession to Lebrun-Renault. He repeats his declaration of innocence: 'I have endured everything for five years, Colonel, but one more time, for the honour of my name and that of my children, I am innocent …'[7]

Aug 8–11

The Court sits in closed session to examine the diplomatic dossier and the Secret Dossier presented by Chamoin and Paléologue respectively. Dreyfus remains silent during the proceedings, unable to see a link between the documents under examination and his own case. A significant incident occurs during this examination. On 8 August Labori notices that one of the documents in the Secret Dossier is unnumbered; he wishes to examine it more carefully but Chamoin asks him not to. On 10 August Chamoin regretfully acknowledges that on the opening day of the court martial Mercier had handed it to him and asked him to insert it into the dossier.[8] Chamoin asks Labori how he should proceed. Labori advises reporting the incident in the next open session, after Mercier's deposition (14 August).[9] The Court asks Paléologue to produce the *bordereau annoté* (the alleged letter from the Kaiser) from the diplomatic dossier: Paléologue affirms that no such document exists.[10]

Aug 12

Second public session (opening 6.30 a.m.): Casimir-Périer declares he will speak 'without reserve' and tell 'the whole truth, in its entirety', out of respect for his conscience, for the judges and 'the judgement of men of good faith'. (*v.* 8 Feb 1898, Casimir-Périer's deposition in

Zola's trial) He states that at the first court martial of Dreyfus, Mercier informed him about *Ce canaille de D.* and its transmission to the court but not that it was to be passed in secret to the judges. He refers to the press rumour in 1895 of the 'diplomatic incident' regarding Germany's involvement in the Affair, stating that there had never been any risk of war between Germany and France. He confirms that Lebrun-Renault, brought before him by the Minister of War (6 January 1895), did not report any confession by Dreyfus. Mercier's eagerly awaited deposition lasts four and a half hours. To support his claim that an espionage network under Schwartzkoppen's direction existed in 1894 he cites several documents.[11] He admits that a Secret Dossier was passed to the judges at the court martial of Dreyfus, claiming that this was justified by the fear of war. He then reproaches Casimir-Périer for omitting from his deposition a 'major event'. This was the 'fatal night' when he, Casimir-Périer and Dupuy waited in the Elysée palace until after midnight to hear if war was to be declared as a result of exchanges between the Kaiser and the German Ambassador over rumours of German involvement in the Dreyfus Affair. Mercier dates this 'historic night' to before the conviction of Dreyfus, but he cannot remember the date exactly.[12] (*v.* 14 Aug) Instead of producing the *bordereau annoté* he merely alludes to the Kaiser's personal involvement in espionage activities. Mercier also states that the similarity between the paper of the *bordereau* and that used by Esterhazy in the same period is unimportant, since India-squared paper is widely used. He further states that the *bordereau* is without doubt the work of Dreyfus and that *Ce canaille de D.* can be applied to Dreyfus despite the ruling by the Supreme Court of Appeal of 3 June 1899. Mercier finally concludes: 'if the slightest doubt had crossed my mind, gentlemen, I would be the first to tell you so, for I am an honest man … I would come before you to say to Captain Dreyfus, 'I was mistaken in good faith.'' Dreyfus gets up and shouts: 'That is what you should do! It is your duty.' Applause breaks out in the courtroom, but Mercier coldly repeats this statement: 'No, the belief I have maintained since 1894 has not changed in the slightest, [on the contrary], it has been strengthened … despite the huge and repeated efforts, despite the millions foolishly spent.[13] (*v.* Appendix 41) Casimir-Périer demands to be heard again, in confrontation with Mercier. (*v.* 14 Aug 1899) As Mercier leaves, protected by gendarmes, the public jeers and hisses.

Jules Guérin and Fort Chabrol (12 August–20 September)

On Waldeck-Rousseau's instruction, several dozen Nationalist, Royalist and antisemitic leaders are arrested in Paris suspected of planning a *coup d'état.*[14] Those arrested are to be prosecuted by the Senate.[15] Only a few avoid immediate arrest, including Habert, who flees to Belgium, and Guérin, who barricades himself with some 15 colleagues at 51 rue Chabrol, headquarters of the Ligue antisémitique. Waldeck-Rousseau advises against an immediate attack on this

THE GRAPHIC

Only once during the public sitting of the court-martial at Rennes on the opening day was there anything like a dramatic scene, and that was at the beginning of the hearing. The *bordereau* having been handed to Captain Dreyfus, he examined it, and then, in a voice husky with emotion, and with his left hand upraised, while in his right he held the document, he said : " I am innocent. I swear it, Colonel, as I affirmed it in 1894. I can bear everything, Colonel, but once more, for the honour of my name and my children, I am innocent"

THE SECOND COURT-MARTIAL ON CAPTAIN DREYFUS: THE ACCUSED AVERRING HIS INNOCENCE

FROM A SKETCH IN COURT BY OUR SPECIAL ARTIST

Dreyfus averring his innocence

'fortress'. He orders the police to cut the telephone wires and cordon off the street. Guérin and the others are besieged by the forces of the police for 38 days. Guérin's neighbours supply him with provisions. On 20 September the water supply is cut off and Waldeck-Rousseau orders the police to break the siege.[16]

Assassination attempt on Labori

Aug 14   Just after 6 a.m. Labori is shot in the back in Rennes from a distance of three or four metres while walking to the courtroom along the canal de la Vilaine with Picquart and Gast (Picquart's cousin). His assailant, a 30–year-old man, runs off shouting: 'I have just murdered the Dreyfus! I have just murdered a Dreyfus!' Picquart and Gast chase him, but he disappears into the forest surrounding the city.[17] At first the wound seems fatal but within 48 hours doctors announce that the bullet, which was lodged between his fifth and sixth ribs, stopped a few millimetres from Labori's spine and that he will soon recover. The assassination attempt creates turmoil in Rennes. The Prefect of Police, Mayor and Deputies of Rennes condemn the attack and call on residents to resist provocation and remain calm.[18] On 25 August *La Libre Parole* publishes the song 'La chanson de l'assassiné bien portant' (to the music of the popular air, 'Le Patriote Breton'). The refrain is 'As-tu vu / Le trou d'balle, le trou d'balle / As-tu vu / Le trou d'balle à Labori?'[19] ('Have you seen/ The bullet hole of Labori?').

Third public session: Despite Labori's absence, at 6.35 a.m. Jouaust opens the session with a warning that if further interruptions occur (as at the close of the previous session), he will be forced to empty the room and continue the trial in closed session. The hearing is about to commence when news of the assassination attempt reaches the Court. At Demange's request the session is adjourned. However, it recommences at 7.15 a.m. Mercier confronts Casimir-Périer. This time he dates the 'historic night' to 6 January 1895, the day after the degradation ceremony of Dreyfus. Casimir-Périer demolishes Mercier's deposition by stating that Boisdeffre was not in Paris that night. Mercier then admits that the 'historic night' may have occurred on another date. Demange asks Mercier how, if the date of 6 January 1895 is correct, it justifies the transmission to the court martial of the Secret Dossier in December 1894. Mercier replies that the events of January were simply the closing episode of a long crisis.[20] Demange asks Mercier why he destroyed Du Paty's commentary. Mercier replies that he considered the commentary was intended for his 'personal use' and that he therefore had the right to do so. Former Ministers of War Billot, Chanoine and Zurlinden testify. They repeat their previous statements to the Supreme Court of Appeal, that Dreyfus was Schwartzkoppen's agent and author of the *bordereau*. Cavaignac repeats the General Staff's arguments. He recalls the alleged confession of Dreyfus. Hanotaux hands the Court a copy of an official memorandum he wrote on 7 December 1894 which detailed his objections to proceeding against Dreyfus. But Hanotaux does not mention the numerous messages he received from Tornielli, von Münster and Monod since 1897 regarding the innocence of Dreyfus. (e.g. *v.* 30 Nov 1894; 28 Nov 1897; 15 Jan & 18 Feb 1898)

Aug 15[21]   Dreyfus requests in writing that the Court adjourn the trial until Labori has recovered.

Aug 16   **Fourth public session:** Demange presents the request of Dreyfus for adjournment. The request is rejected.[22] André Lebon, former Colonial Secretary, is questioned on the severe and inhumane measures he had ordered to be imposed on Dreyfus on Devil's Island. Lebon states that these measures, and especially the double shackles, were only introduced in September 1896. He justifies them as a response to rumours of attempts to arrange the prisoner's escape. Asked to comment on this deposition, Dreyfus exclaims: 'I do not come here, Colonel, to speak of the tortures or atrocious suffering inflicted for five years on a Frenchman who is innocent … I am here only to defend my honour. And so I will not speak, Colonel, of anything that happened during those five years on Devil's Island.' *(Great commotion)*[23] At Demange's request Lebon's official report on the treatment of Dreyfus on Devil's Island is read out. The public gasps in indignation. (*v.* Appendix 41) Henry's widow, dressed in mourning, recounts her husband's devotion to the army, stating that he had acted purely 'in the interests of the country', and denies any dealings with Esterhazy. Roget's long deposition lists his reasons for believing that Dreyfus is guilty. He argues that Esterhazy, in spite of his dissolute life, could not be the author of the *bordereau.* Further, he suggests that he was in the pay of the Jews and refers to documents allegedly attesting to the treason of Dreyfus.[24] Dreyfus interrupts forcefully: 'I cannot bear listening for hours to depositions in which my heart and soul are torn out. Never has a man, an innocent man and loyal soldier, been put in such an appalling situation.'[25] *(Applause in the courtroom)*

Demange receives a threatening letter which he submits to the head of the Sûreté.

Aug 17   **Fifth public session:** Bertulus relates events in his office with Henry on 18 July 1898. He gives a full account of his investigation of the Blanche and Speranza telegrams and of his intervention in the Affair. With magisterial authority and eloquence he concludes that Dreyfus is innocent. He explains that the *bordereau* is not by Dreyfus and that the Supreme Court of Appeal has said it was by Esterhazy. Why, he asks, if Dreyfus is guilty, did the General Staff need to plot against Picquart and Dreyfus and protect Esterhazy? He states there was absolutely no motive for Dreyfus to betray his country: 'without a motive, there is no crime'. The deposition of Bertulus causes a reaction in the courtroom. Henry's widow asks to speak again and gives her version of Henry's encounter with Bertulus. (18 July 1898) She claims that Bertulus was extremely friendly, greeting Henry with open arms and the kiss of friendship, and that she then asked her husband: 'Are you sure of this man? I am afraid it was the kiss of

Judas!' Bertulus counters that it is to be expected Henry's widow should protect her late husband's name and honour. He also points out that there is nothing spontaneous in her statement. He hands to the Court a letter he received the previous day warning him that Mme Henry intended to 'create a scene' and describe him [Bertulus] as a 'Judas'.[26] Picquart, in civilian clothes, begins his deposition. He recounts the role he has played in the Affair since 1894, and reveals the faults of the Ministry of War. He blames Du Paty for many of these. Picquart recalls the deep impression caused by Henry's testimony at the court martial of Dreyfus (1894) and analyses the *bordereau* in situ to prove that Dreyfus could not have written it.

Aug 18   **Sixth public session:** Picquart continues his deposition, which lasts almost five hours. In a meticulous analysis of the Secret Dossier of 1894, he proves that none of its four documents can be related to Dreyfus.[27] He describes his discovery of the *petit bleu* and the subsequent manoeuvres against him. Roget and Mercier both try to trap him on minor inaccuracies in his deposition.

Aug 19   **Seventh public session:** Cuignet's deposition is a long and detailed indictment of Dreyfus. He gives three reasons for his belief in the guilt of Dreyfus: Lebrun-Renault's confession; the technical nature of the *bordereau*; and the Secret Dossier, which, according to him includes items directly implicating Dreyfus. At the end of Cuignet's deposition Dreyfus exclaims: 'I protest against the witness's singular state of mind that we have been listening to here for an hour and against a testimony in which the full relentlessness against an innocent man is unleashed.'[28] Boisdeffre in his summary repeats his belief in the guilt of Dreyfus. He asserts that the Dreyfus family accused Esterhazy in order to find a scapegoat for Dreyfus. He confirms that in 1894 Picquart did not question the guilt of Dreyfus. Finally, he confirms the account of the 'historic night' given by Mercier.[29] Gonse passes from one subject to another. Questioned by the Court and Demange, he falters and contradicts himself.[30]

Aug 21   **Eighth public session:** Fabre and d'Aboville recall the negative impression Dreyfus made on his colleagues and superior officers as a probationer. They considered him arrogant and pretentious. They recount the arrival of the *bordereau* at the Ministry of War and the reasons which led them to believe it was written by Dreyfus. Cochefert describes the dictation and the arrest of Dreyfus. He states that he, like Du Paty and other observers in the room, believed Dreyfus showed signs of unease from the beginning of the dictation. He confirms his belief in the guilt of Dreyfus. (*v.* 7 Sept, Cochefert's second deposition) He confesses, however, that had he known Esterhazy's handwriting at that time he would have tried to restrain the Minister of War from arresting Dreyfus. Gribelin is also convinced of the guilt of Dreyfus. He insists that when Dreyfus denied the charges made against him at the time of his arrest, he declared himself ignorant of matters that would have been known to any officer. Regarding his meetings with Esterhazy in November 1897, Gribelin admits having confused the intrigues of Du Paty with those of Henry. Lauth and Junck again accuse Picquart of falsifying the *petit bleu*. Junck also attacks Dreyfus and Bertulus.[31] Bertulus declares dramatically:

> *My conviction on this point [that Esterhazy is a traitor] ...*
> *gentlemen, has been fully founded since 12 July, the day I had*
> *him [Esterhazy] arrested. I arrested him, because deep in my heart*
> *I was convinced I was in the presence of a traitor, the only traitor,*
> *and that here was the key to this entire case that was destroying*
> *France ... I say because I believe it: 'Esterhazy is the traitor and I*
> *will say it in spite of everyone!'* (Sensation)[32]

Aug 22–23   **Ninth & tenth public sessions:** Labori's return to Court (August 22) is greeted with cheers and a standing ovation. Many witnesses and Court officials, including Billot and Mercier, ask after his health. Jouaust opens the session with words of welcome. Labori's short, emotional response is met with further applause.[33] More than a dozen former colleagues and superiors of Dreyfus are heard, along with other minor witnesses. Most testify against him, describing him as a pretentious, untrustworthy libertine and gambler, and denouncing his conduct in 1894 and prior to that date.[34] Dreyfus protests strongly after each deposition. Du Breuil, a civilian, accuses Dreyfus of dining in 1886 with a German attaché whose name and exact position he cannot recall, at the house of Mme Bodson, one of Dreyfus' lady friends. Dreyfus exclaims to President Jouast: ' ... it is facts and precise testimonies we must discuss here, not idle gossip. What has to be determined is the name of the person in question, the quality of the person with whom I am supposed to have dined, so that we finally know who is telling the truth.'[35] As Esterhazy and Mlle Pays are not present, their depositions before the Criminal Chamber are read out. (*v.* 23–24, 30 Jan 1899) At Labori's request, Esterhazy's letters to Faure (October–November 1897) and the Dixi article (15 November 1897) are also read. Gonse denies some of Esterhazy's statements about the collusion. He is handled harshly by Labori and finally admits to facts which confirm rather than refute the General Staff's protection of Esterhazy.[36]

Aug 24   **Eleventh public session:** Under pressure from Labori, Maurel, president of the first court martial of Dreyfus, admits that the Secret Dossier was transmitted to him by Du Paty. Refusing to reveal its contents, he describes how the dossier was presented to the judges. Maurel contradicts himself. He first explains that he only read aloud one document from the Secret Dossier. He did not however listen when the others were read by his colleagues since he had already made up his mind on the guilt of Dreyfus from the discussions in court. Later he declares that reading this one document was enough to convince him, implying he was not yet then convinced of Dreyfus' guilt and that the Secret Dossier influenced his decision. Labori asks that Mercier be recalled.[37] The cross-examination becomes so intense that it provokes interventions from Roget, Gonse, Chamoin, Gribelin and Lauth. (*v.* Appendix 41) Several contradictions are revealed: the

importance of the information referred to in the *bordereau*; whether
the rank and position of Dreyfus would have given him access to
that information; his alleged confession; Mercier's destruction of Du
Paty's commentary on the Secret Dossier (*v.* 17 Jan 1895 & end Dec
1897); and the incident that occurred in closed session concerning the
falsified translations of Panizzardi's telegram.[38] (*v.* 8–11 Aug) General
Risbourg, Commander of the Republican Guard, recounts the alleged
confession of Dreyfus to Lebrun-Renault.[39] Dreyfus relates at length
the exact content of his conversation with Lebrun-Renault and recalls
his appeal to Du Paty (31 December 1894) to open an investigation
to find the true traitor. He protests dramatically: 'When such an
appalling and dishonourable accusation hangs over a man, when he
has struggled against it for five years, I find it is a duty of conscience
that when witnesses speak of their convictions, they should bring
proof, positive proof! Otherwise I do not understand.' *(Prolonged
commotion)*[40] Demange seeks further explanation from Mercier.
Why, if he believed in the alleged confession, did he not call Lebrun-
Renault in again to follow up the matter? Mercier hesitates. Dreyfus
renews his protest, and recalls his numerous letters to the Minister of
War, the President of the Republic and Prime Minister confirming his
innocence. He demands to know why for four years he heard nothing
about this 'fiction of a confession', which he could have immediately
refuted. Police official Desvernine testifies to Esterhazy's two visits
to the German Embassy on 23 October 1897. Savignaud, Picquart's
former orderly in Tunis (in 1896), testifies that Picquart sent letters to
Scheurer-Kestner in 1897.[41]

Aug 25   **Twelfth public session:** a medical certificate is read out stating that
Du Paty is unable to appear before the Court.[42] Journalist Rowland
Strong speaks of his dealings with Esterhazy in 1898 and his intention
to publish Esterhazy's confession to authorship of the *bordereau*. As
Maurice Weil is not present, claiming to be ill, his deposition given
to the Criminal Chamber is read out. It reveals that in 1894 Esterhazy
had told Weil he believed that although Dreyfus was innocent he
would probably be convicted because of the climate of antisemitism
in France. (*v.* early Dec 1894) Gobert describes the conditions under
which his examination of the *bordereau* took place in 1894 (*v.* 11–12
Oct 1894) on instructions from Mercier, Boisdeffre and Gonse. He
also describes his conversation with Guérin (then Minister of Justice)
on the day of the arrest of Dreyfus. (*v.* 15 Oct 1894) He affirms
clearly why he was, and still is, absolutely certain that Esterhazy,
not Dreyfus, wrote the *bordereau*. Bertillon begins his deposition,
repeating his theory of the 'self forgery'. Despite laughter from the
public he strives to prove his convoluted theory by using charts,
diagrams, photographs and other documents.[43]

Aug 26   **Thirteenth public session:** Captain Valério, an artillery officer called
by the prosecution, asserts the validity of Bertillon's theory. He states
that Esterhazy could not be the author of the *bordereau* and concludes
that thanks to Bertillon the Court now has material proof of Dreyfus'
guilt. Valério adds that the only way Esterhazy could have written

the *bordereau* was by tracing the writing of Dreyfus. He implies that there were two *bordereaux*, reviving suspicions of the existence of the mythical secret document, the *bordereau annoté*. Freystaetter's short deposition provides a moment of drama. He admits that his belief in the guilt of Dreyfus at the first court martial was based largely on the Secret Dossier: he acknowledges the deep impression this made on him and the other judges. Freystaetter enumerates the documents included in the dossier, claiming that one of them was the falsified translation of Panizzardi's telegram of 2 November. Maurel and Mercier immediately refute this statement. Maurel explains that when he claimed (24 August) he had read only one document, he did not mean that the dossier contained only one document, but that he simply ignored the others. Freystaetter maintains that Maurel read and commented on all the documents. Mercier denies that Panizzardi's telegram was included in the dossier, claiming that Freystaetter's memory must be hazy.[44] Labori repeats his demand for Du Paty's medical condition to be reassessed. He considers Du Paty's presence in court essential since it was he who wrote the commentary on the dossier. Mercier claims Sandherr was responsible for the dossier's content, at which Labori exclaims: 'Always the dead! Colonel Sandherr is dead, Colonel Henry is dead, M. Du Paty de Clam refuses to appear.' *(Prolonged agitation)*[45] Jouaust agrees to interrogate Du Paty in Paris under a rogatory letter, led by Tavernier.[46] (*v.* 6 Sept) Mathias-George Paraf-Javal, a draughtsman called by the defence, refutes Bertillon's pseudo-scientific system and, with the aid of a blackboard, demonstrates its incoherence, fallacies and absurdities.

Aug 28 **Fourteenth public session:** The entire session is devoted to graphological analyses. Claude-Maurice Bernard, an engineer, proves that Bertillon's system is based on false calculations.[47] Graphologists Teyssonnières, Charavay, Pelletier, Couard and Varinard confirm their previous depositions given before the Criminal Chamber. (*v.* 18 Jan 1899, First revision investigation: Criminal Chamber) Charavay states that it was only after becoming familiar with Esterhazy's handwriting that he realized it was identical to that of the *bordereau*. He states: '**...** I have recognised my error, and it is a very great relief to my conscience to be able before you, gentlemen, and above all before the victim of that error, to declare that I was mistaken in 1894 and that today I consider the writing on the *bordereau* is not in the hand of Captain Dreyfus, but that of Major Esterhazy.' *(Commotion)*[48]

Aug 29 **Fifteenth public session:** Released from his oath of professional secrecy, Lieutenant-Colonel Cordier, former deputy of Sandherr, reveals details of the 'normal route' procedure.[49] He states that *Ce canaille de D.* reached the Deuxième Bureau in 1891 or 1892. Although connected in general with espionage matters, it could obviously not have had any connection with the Dreyfus Affair. Cordier explains that his belief in the guilt of Dreyfus has reversed since 1894 because of the campaign against Picquart, led mainly by Henry, and the 'false' date (April) given by the General Staff to the *bordereau*, which he knew had arrived in September. (*v.* 26 Sept 1894, n. 15 & 12–17 Feb 1898, Zola's trial) Cordier also discloses that from 1895 Henry, Lauth and Gribelin plotted against their superior Picquart. Cordier's evidence provokes vehement protest, especially from Lauth, Roget and Gribelin.[50]

Aug 30   **Sixteenth public session:** Paul Meyer, August Molinier and Arthur Giry, members of the Institut, demonstrate the invalidity of Bertillon's system and declare categorically that the *bordereau* was written by Esterhazy.[51] Emile Picot, mathematician and also member of the Institut, recounts his conversation with Colonel Schneider of May 1899 in which Schneider seemed convinced of the innocence of Dreyfus. Schneider also confirmed Esterhazy's dealings with Schwartzkoppen, and the latter's dissatifaction with the information he had received from Esterhazy.[52] General Deloye, Chief of Artillery, gives technical information on the 120mm short cannon mentioned in the *bordereau* and explains that in 1894 its development was highly secret.[53]

Aug 31   A three-hour discussion takes place in closed session by order of the Ministry of War regarding artillery matters referred to in the *bordereau*. Major Louis Hartman asserts that a captain of Dreyfus' rank could not have been familiar with its highly secret information regarding the mechanism and development of the cannon. General Deloye firmly contradicts him.[54]

     Seventeenth public session: Lebrun-Renault repeats his statement concerning the alleged confession of Dreyfus but, cross-examined by Labori and Demange, stumbles and contradicts himself. Forzinetti declares that in 1897 Lebrun-Renault admitted that Dreyfus had never confessed to him. Lebrun-Renault finally acknowledges Forzinetti's evidence. Gonse and Mercier admit that they treated the matter of the confession casually. Forzinetti describes Du Paty's attitude toward Dreyfus while interrogating him in prison and the alarming mental and physical state of Dreyfus. He confirms that he told Boisdeffre he believed Dreyfus was innocent. (*v.* 27 Oct 1894) Boisdeffre denies this, but Forzinetti reconfirms his statement.

Sept 1   **Eighteenth public session:** The depositions of several secondary witnesses, mainly former colleagues of Dreyfus, prove contradictory.[55] They are followed by depositions from a number of artillery officers. Lieutenant Fernand-Lucien Bernheim asserts that he provided Esterhazy with a book on firing which was never returned. Mercier denies that this book contained the information relating to the Firing Manual referred to in the *bordereau*. Lieutenant Louis-Joseph Bruyère testifies that since the Field Artillery Firing Manual was already in circulation in 1894, information about the 120mm short cannon could have been obtained quite easily, even by non-artillery officers, who were sometimes present when the cannon was in operation. (*v.* 7 Apr 1894) Captain Julien Carvalho confirms that no special precautions were taken to keep the mechanism of the 120mm cannon secret. General Hyppolyte Sébert demonstrates at length that the inaccuracies and imprecise expressions of the *bordereau* mean it could not have been written by an artillery officer or an officer who had studied at the Ecole polytechnique. (*v.* 7 Mar–19 Nov 1904, Second revision investigation: Combined Chambers' investigation) Major Ducros declares that when he worked at the arms factory at Puteaux (1891–94), where secret gun parts were manufactured, he had twice invited Dreyfus to see the manufacturing process but that Dreyfus had never visited there.

Sept 2   **Nineteenth public session:** Major Hartman insists that the *bordereau*'s inaccuracies would have been unacceptable for an artillery officer, implying that it could not have been written by Dreyfus.[56] He states that any officer present at the camp in Châlons could have obtained sufficient information to write notes on covering troops and Madagascar. General Deloye is confronted with Hartman. Questioned by Demange, Deloye declares that since he has not been involved in the Dreyfus Affair and has only been called to testify as a technical witness, he can give his opinion with an easy conscience. He states that he has no single proof of the guilt of Dreyfus: 'If I had such proof, I would most certainly give it, but I do not have it.' In response to Labori, Deloye declares that the guilt of the accused could never depend on 'pseudo-scientific or mathematical analysis of the *bordereau*'. Still dissatisfied with this answer, Labori continues to press Deloye, asking whether the documents referred to in the *bordereau* were of great importance. Deloye suddenly bursts out: 'Oh! Do not insist! Do not insist! … You see, this *bordereau* contains things which mark it as the work of a master, a gentleman … It gives proof that the person who wrote it was at the source. He had an official document.'[57] Louis Havet, member of the Institut, demonstrates that from a grammatical point of view the *bordereau* resembles the epistolary style of Esterhazy more than that of Dreyfus. At Labori's request, selected letters from the correspondence between Gonse and Picquart (September 1896) are read out. Labori insists that they do not refer to the alleged confession by Dreyfus. Gonse replies that this was because he advised Picquart not to mix the Esterhazy and the Dreyfus cases; but under Labori's questioning, and confronted with Picquart, Gonse and Roget have difficulty explaining the various stages of the conspiracy against Picquart. Artillery officer Captain François de Fonds-Lamothe[58] raises the matter of the last phrase of the *bordereau*: 'I am leaving on manoeuvres'. He asserts that in 1894 probationary officers serving on the General Staff were informed, according to Boisdeffre's order of 17 May, that they were not to go on manoeuvres. This shows, he continues, that Dreyfus could not have been the author of the *bordereau* since it has been proven to date from September. Fonds-Lamothe also advances the idea that if the *bordereau* were still to be considered to date from April, Dreyfus could not have spoken about the Firing Manual printed in May. (*v.* 19 Dec 1894, The first court martial of Dreyfus). There follows a heated confrontation with Mercier and Roget, who struggle to find minor points in Fonds-Lamothe's evidence that they can refute.

Sept 4   **Twentieth public session:** An unexpected prosecution witness is presented, former Austrian officer Eugène Lazare de Cernuski.[59] Cernuski claims his limited French does not allow him to testify orally, and his evidence is read by the Court's clerk. Cernuski declares that in August 1894 one of his friends at the Foreign Office of a central European power confided to him the names of four persons engaged in espionage in France on Germany's behalf. These included Dreyfus. He states that a month later this information was confirmed to him by a high-ranking officer on the German General Staff, who showed him several secret documents as proof. After this evidence has been read, both Cernuski and the Government Commissioner demand that the rest of the deposition be heard in closed session. (*v.* 6 Sept) Labori seizes on this development to declare that since the prosecution has called a witness of foreign nationality, he demands the Court make formal application to the appropriate authorities (Germany and Italy) to permit the appearance of Panizzardi and Schwartzkoppen as witnesses to verify whether the documents enumerated in the *bordereau* were delivered to any foreign power and, if so, by whom. (*v.* 12 Aug–8 Sept 1899, Negotiations with Germany) Mathematician Paul Painlevé demolishes Bertillon's theory, referring to the views of another distinguished mathematician, Henri Poincaré, in order to support his conclusions. A subsequent confrontation with Gonse, Roget, Cuignet and Chamoin reveals the dubious nature of the compilation of the extended Secret Dossier. The discussion is interspersed with clashes between Labori and Jouaust. Police official Tomps describes how he accompanied Lauth and Henry to Basel to interview Cuers, and how Henry declined his offers to extract information from Cuers. (*v.* 6 Aug 1896, n. 20) Tomps also recounts that in November 1896 Henry wanted him to say that the copy of the *bordereau* printed in *Le Matin* had not been provided by Teyssonnières but by Picquart. (*v.* 21 Nov 1896)

Sept 5   **Twenty-first public session:** Labori submits his demand to the judges that the Government should procure the documents listed in the *bordereau*, if they exist, from the foreign power via diplomatic channels. At the end of the session Jouaust reads out the Court's decision to reject Labori's demand. Labori also informs the Court that he has notified Government Commissioner Carrière of two additional witnesses for the defence he wishes to call, Panizzardi and Schwartzkoppen.[60]

Serge Basset, a journalist for *Le Matin* writing under the name of Paul Ribon, reports his interviews with Esterhazy of May 1899. He explains that Esterhazy gave him full consent to publish his statement that he had written the *bordereau* on Sandherr's instructions and that he was appalled that the General Staff had rejected him. (*v.* 3 June 1899, Esterhazy's admission of authorship of the *bordereau*) In response to Labori, Basset reveals that Esterhazy has been writing letters to Roget since the beginning of the Rennes court martial. Labori insists that the letters be included as evidence. Jouaust, who is also in receipt of letters from Esterhazy, asserts that they contain only personal recriminations of no interest to the Court. [61] (*v.* 7 Sept) Roget admits that he considered Esterhazy's confession of no value. He stumbles when Labori asks him if he believed Esterhazy was a scapegoat and, if so, why this was not mentioned in 1894 or at Zola's trial. Trarieux begins his long and eloquent deposition. He describes what prompted him to cast doubt on his initial belief in the guilt of Dreyfus and how he finally became totally convinced of his innocence and thus supported a revision. He cites the violent antisemitic attacks against Dreyfus; the secret transmission of documents to the judges at the first court martial; Scheurer-Kestner's campaign; the manoeuvres against Picquart; and the various forgeries emanating from the Deuxième Bureau. But above all, Trarieux asserts, he was convinced by information obtained from a foreign ambassador (Tornielli), who confirmed that Dreyfus never had any relations with a foreign military attaché; that Tornielli saw a letter from Schwartzkoppen asserting Esterhazy's guilt; and, long before Henry's confession, that the *faux Henry* was a forgery.

Sept 6   Cernuski now takes the oath in closed session. He gives the names of his alleged informers but breaks down under questioning. The session is suspended. After the recess Jouaust receives a police report on the witness prepared after Cernuski was called to testify which establishes that Cernuski has been suffering from mental problems, has numerous debts and has committed perjury several times.[62]

Maître Labori

Twenty-second public session: Trarieux declares that the *petit bleu* is authentic, not falsified by Picquart. He draws attention to the role of Lauth in the manoeuvres against Picquart. Lauth protests, but Zurlinden, trapped by Labori's questions, admits that Picquart could not have made the falsification. Labori calls Paléologue, who states that the Secret Dossier contains a document confirming the authenticity of the *petit bleu*.[63] Trarieux reads out the letter he sent Billot on 6 January 1898 before Esterhazy's court martial. The lettter denounces the travesty of justice which was being prepared in order to achieve the acquittal of Esterhazy. Billot, called to reply, describes Trarieux's deposition as a plea for the defence, for Picquart and an arraignment of former Ministers. He then returns to the theory that Esterhazy and Dreyfus were accomplices. This provokes a vehement protest from Dreyfus and an argument between Labori and Jouaust.[64]

Coupois, clerk of the Court, reads Du Paty's deposition taken by Tavernier. (*v.* 26 Aug) This is merely a repetition of Du Paty's former evidence before the Supreme Court of Appeal.

Sept 7   **Twenty-third public session:** Labori, having been informed that Schwartzkoppen and Panizzardi cannot appear personally in Court, proposes that questions be telegraphed to them so that their evidence may be received.[65] Called to give his opinion, Paléologue does not object, but expresses reservations about the use of telegrams. Carrière accepts the procedure on condition that the Military Code of Justice is respected (i.e. that proceedings are not interrupted for more than 48 hours). Jouaust refuses the proposal. Labori submits a formal application, which the Court rejects after deliberation.[66] (*v.* 5–8 Sept, Labori's appeal) Cochefert, contradicting his former deposition regarding the dictation scene (*v.* 21 Aug), admits that he did not notice that Dreyfus was troubled until Du Paty began to question him. He adds that Dreyfus' reply to Du Paty when he noticed the gun on the table ('I do not want to kill myself because I want to live to establish my innocence') was missing in the report of the arrest, despite Cochefert having mentioned it to Mercier and Boisdeffre. Mercier asks to be heard again. He explains that Freystaetter's evidence (*v.* 26 Aug) might have cast doubts on his own deposition and integrity.[67] He again denies that the translation of Panizzardi's telegram of 2 November was part of the Secret Dossier. (*v.* 26 Aug, n.44) He harshly condemns Freystaetter in his absence as mentally troubled, immoral and with close Jewish connections.[68] Finally, Mercier recapitulates the army's arguments against Dreyfus and begs the Court to consider his own evidence with all the confidence and authority they would have attributed to it had the 'Freystaetter incident never occurred'. There follows a reading of the graphologists' reports. These conclude that the *bordereau* was written on paper similar to that used by Esterhazy. Labori calls attention to one of the documents in the Secret Dossier presented by Chamoin to the Court in closed session. This is a note sent to Schwartzkoppen on 29 October 1894 concerning information on manoeuvres in Toul and Paris, which was intercepted by the Section de Statistique. Labori establishes that this is proof that disclosures continued after the arrest of Dreyfus. It also refers to the last sentence of the *bordereau* ('I am leaving on manoeuvres') and demonstrates that Dreyfus could not have been its author. At Labori's request, further documents are read, describing how Esterhazy employed officers to copy military documents. In resonse to Labori's request, sections of Esterhazy's letter to Roget are read.[69] Jouaust announces the end of the depositions. Following Galliffet's orders (*v.* 21 July & 5 Sept), all military witnesses rise and leave the courtroom. Carrière delivers his closing speech. It reiterates the arguments of the General Staff in confused and disorganized manner. He ends with an affirmation of the guilt of Dreyfus and demands the application of Article 76 of the Penal Code.[70] (*v.* 22 Dec 1894, n. 125)

Sept 8　　**Twenty-fourth public session:** Demange's closing speech for the defence.

Sept 9　　**Twenty-fifth public session:** Security measures are reinforced for this final session. Soldiers are stationed throughout the city. The infantry guard outside the courtroom is quadrupled. The public is meticulously searched: even objects such as opera glasses and women's parasols are confiscated. Numerous public figures arrive to hear the verdict, including the antisemitic agitator Max Régis from Algiers and Lord Russell of Killowen, Lord Chief Justice of England, sent by Queen Victoria.

Demange continues his closing plea, which lasts five hours. After reviewing and refuting the prosecution case and Bertillon's theory, he addresses the Court. He stresses that the judges must rely only on evidence and their consciences must be free from doubt in giving their verdict:

> *You are about to enter the chamber where you will make your deliberations, and then what are you going to ask yourselves? If Dreyfus is innocent? No … you have only to ask yourselves whether he is guilty … and having heard the defence which, whilst certainly powerless to shed complete light on the affair, came, I beg you believe, from an honest and convinced heart, you will say to yourselves: we do not know. Someone else could have been the traitor, but not him … And you will say further to yourselves: this writing is not his … At that moment, I swear it, there will be doubt in your minds. That doubt, gentlemen, is enough for me. That doubt is an acquittal. That doubt does not allow honest and loyal consciences to say that this man is guilty.*[71]

Labori waives his right to make a closing speech.[72] Carrière claims his right to reply to Demange. The session is briefly adjourned. Shouts of 'courage' are addressed to Dreyfus as he is taken from the courtroom. The Court resumes at 3 p.m. Carrière makes his final statement, arguing that in criminal matters proof has no specific legal form since 'proof is everywhere; it is in the whole'; the law does not ask how a verdict is reached, nor does it tell the judges that they are obliged to ascertain fully each and every fact mentioned. It asks only one important question, which summarizes the Court's duty: 'Do you have a deep-felt conviction?' He concludes by reiterating his demand for the application of Article 76 of the Penal Code.[73] Demange responds as follows:

Gentlemen, in reading the text of the law, the Government Commissioner reminded you of what we all know: that you must only account for your judgement to your own conscience and to God. What I also know, and this is my last word in this affair, is that men of loyalty, men of uprightness such as military judges, will never elevate such possibilities or presumptions as those brought here to the status of proof. I have confidence in you because you are soldiers.[74]

Asked for his final words in defence, Dreyfus says in a weak voice:

I will only say one very simple thing: that I am absolutely sure, that I affirm before my country and before the army that I am innocent. It was with the sole aim of saving the honour of my name, and saving the honour of my children's name, that for five years I suffered the most monstrous tortures. That aim, I am

THE MARTYRDOM OF ALFRED DREYFUS
A HISTORICAL SUMMARY OF THE WHOLE CASE

CAPTAIN ALFRED DREYFUS, THE MARTYR OF THE CENTURY

Dreyfus awaiting the verdict in Rennes

convinced I will attain today, thanks to your loyalty and your justice.[75]

Second conviction of Dreyfus

After deliberation, the Court resumes at 4.45 p.m. for the reading of the verdict. This is carried out in the absence of the accused, as prescribed by military law: 'The court martial declares … by a majority of five votes to two: "Yes, the accused is guilty"; … that there are extenuating circumstances.'[76] (*v.* Appendix 42) The Court sentences Alfred Dreyfus to ten years' detention.[77] Demange falls back in his chair, in tears, his head in his hands. He asks Labori to tell Dreyfus, stating that he cannot bring himself to do so. On seeing Labori, Dreyfus immediately understands. He embraces Labori and asks him

Maître Demange
on hearing the
verdict

to take care of his wife and children. The verdict is then read to him as he stands still and rigid. That evening, Dreyfus signs an appeal for a revision. (*v.* 8–19 Sept, The pardon)

Negotiations with Germany

Aug 12   Waldeck-Rousseau informs von Münster in confidence that the lawyers of Dreyfus will probably ask him to obtain an official declaration from Germany stating which of the documents cited in the *bordereau* are held in Berlin, and whether they were delivered by Esterhazy after 15 October 1894 (the day Dreyfus was arrested). Waldeck-Rousseau explains that he will only issue an official demand if he knows in advance what the German reaction will be.[78]

Aug 13   Von Bülow informs Count Metternich (minister plenipotentiary and the Kaiser's counsellor) of Walseck-Rousseau's discussion with von Münster. He suggests that Germany should only repeat its previous official denial of any dealing with Dreyfus. (*v.* 24 Jan 1898) He adds:

> *The pending case in Rennes is not about Esterhazy but about Dreyfus. Previously I have publicly declared with the approval of the highest authorities that Dreyfus had neither any direct or indirect relations with German government. If these categorical declarations do not carry any weight in France it may be assumed that any disclosures demanded of us now would also be doubted. I have above all the military point of view in my mind that the work of our military intelligence service would be greatly impeded, if we lifted the veil of our information system and revealed one of our agents.*[79]

Aug 14   Baron von Richthofen, German Under-secretary of State for Foreign Affairs, instructs von Münster to convey to Waldeck-Rousseau that if the French Government requires an official denial, Germany would only reiterate von Bülow's official declaration made in the Reichstag on 24 January 1898.

The Nationalist daily *Le Gaulois* publishes an 'Open letter to General Mercier', reiterating and enlarging on the myth of the *bordereau annoté*. It claims that Mercier has a copy and calls on him to produce it before the Court.[80]

Aug 21–28   Waldeck-Rousseau repeatedly approaches von Below-Schlatau, *chargé d'Affaires* in Paris, to obtain an official statement of denial from Germany. He is not successful. Von Below-Schlatau states that since France ignored Germany's previous statement, Germany cannot intervene further in what is now an 'internal French matter'. Waldeck Rouseau emphasizes that there is a fundamental difference between the present French Government and that of Méline in 1898. Von Bülow also reaffirms Germany's refusal to issue a further statement.[81] (*v.* 5 Sept 1899, Labori's appeal)

Aug 29–Sept 1 *The Times* names Mme Bastian in connection with the Deuxième Bureau and its procedure of 'normal route'. It states that for several years she has been employed as a cleaner at the German Embassy.[82]

Sept 1   Following an urgent demand of the Kaiser for a detailed account of revelations in the press, von Below-Schlatau reports to Berlin:

This woman [Madame Bastian] who never gave rise to any suspicion here and was considered absolutely safe (the Kaiser makes exclamation marks on the margin with the words: 'incomprehensible negligence') *returned the keys [of the German Embassy] in her possession on the eve of the Rennes court martial. She made it known that she had been arrested and that she had to be taken to Rennes. On the orders of the ambassador, the police had been questioned on this matter. Lépine, the prefect of police, presented himself personally at the Embassy to explain that after the investigation he had instigated Madame Bastian had not been arrested* (exclamation marks by the Kaiser on the margin) *but left for the country in the company of her husband, without saying*

Kaiser Wilhelm II

where. Since that time, one has no idea where she is. The newspapers
claim that she is to appear as a witness in Rennes. (The Kaiser notes:
'a wonderful disorder reigns at the Embassy. That must change').[83]

Sept 3   Von Below-Schlatau confirms in a report to von Münster that Mme
Bastian could have had access to official papers in the German
Embassy. However, no papers were reported missing. Von Below
also mentions that Mme Bastian was illiterate and could not make an
educated selection of the documents she found.[84]

German Secretary of State von Bülow sends secret instructions to the
German Embassy issued by the Kaiser to ensure that the embassy is
protected from espionage. These state that the embassy is to employ
only German employees 'who do not know French, and who are
preferably former soldiers'; the military attaché's office must be
exclusively within the embassy; no documents are to be held at the
attaché's private home; no documents, even drafts, are to be thrown
away into wastepaper baskets but burnt instead; embassy employees
are to be put under surveillance.[85]

Labori's appeal to the Kaiser and the King of Italy

Sept 5   Labori telegraphs Schwartzkoppen and Panizzardi asking them to
testify before the Court at Rennes.[86] Without consulting his colleague
Demange, but with Mathieu's consent, Labori telegraphs the Kaiser
and the King of Italy asking them to grant Schwartzkoppen and
Panizzardi permission to testify.[87]

Upon receiving Labori's telegram, Count Metternich informs the
German Foreign Office that the Kaiser regards Labori's request as
'an impertinence'. He further states that 'it is obviously impossible to
accede to this request'.[88]

Galliffet repeats his order of 21 July for all military witnesses,
including generals, to leave Rennes within two hours after making
their depositions.

Sept 6   *La Libre Parole* publishes an article entitled 'The two *bordereaux*'.
The article claims that the *bordereau* exhibited in the court martial
is merely a facsimile or a copy of the 'original and true one', which
includes annotations, not written in French but which mention the
name of Dreyfus. The paper claims that diplomatic considerations
have prevented the transmission of this document to the Court.

Instructed by Waldeck-Rousseau, Galliffet, not yet knowing the
Kaiser's decision, talks unofficially with Major Baron von Süßkind,
German military attaché expressing the hope that the Kaiser will
answer Labori's request positively or at least allow Schwartzkoppen
to testify at Rennes. Süßkind telegraphs von Bülow. The text of the
telegram, annotated by the Kaiser, shows both Galliffet's technique of
working on the Kaiser's vanity and the Kaiser's scornful and shrewd
remarks.

He [General Galliffet] asks His Majesty to have the grace not to blame the government for the numerous regrettable incidents in Rennes. People like Mercier should be kicked like a mouse that wants to gnaw on one's boot and moreover they should be snubbed. (The Kaiser's marginal note: 'No, that is not enough! Such vermin has to be crushed!')

… The plea to His Majesty [for Schwarztkoppen to testify in Rennes] put forward by the lawyer Labori provides three options:

1. Refusal.

2. Colonel Schwartzkoppen to appear in Rennes.

3. The provisional interrogation of Colonel Schwartzkoppen in Germany according to German legal procedures.

… If His Majesty had the grace to fulfil his earnest request in order for the third option to be taken, His Majesty would earn recognition in re-establishing order in France. (The Kaiser's marginal note: 'That's none of my business. I'm not the Emperor of the French! Besides, the Court martial does not want it!')

… If Dreyfus was sentenced again, it seems to him [Galliffet] that a revolution with incalculable consequences is to be feared. (The Kaiser's marginal note: 'Correct!') He said that the survival of France was in danger. (The Kaiser's marginal note: 'Yes!')[89]

Sept 8   The German Government publishes a statement in the official section of the *Reichsanzeiger* (Monitor of the German Empire) confirming that no German agent had any dealings with Dreyfus. The article repeats

René Waldeck-Rousseau

von Münster's earlier statements (Dec 1894 and Jan 1895) and von Bülow's statement in the Reichstag (24 Jan 1898). Paléologue passes the article to the Rennes court martial on the morning of 9 September, before the trial's last session opens.[90]

World reactions to the Rennes verdict

With the exception of the antisemitic newspapers, the French press is united in its consternation at the Rennes verdict. *L'Aurore* describes the judgment as 'abominable' and an 'iniquity'; for Yves Guyot it is 'a model of cowardice and jesuitism'. Various papers describe the judgment as 'disgraceful', 'shameful', and 'proof of flagrant 'injustice'. Jaurès calls for the abolition of military tribunals, which he considers relics of medieval prejudice.

12 Sept   In *L'Aurore*, Zola publishes the article 'Le cinquième acte' ('The Fifth Act'), severely condemning the verdict:

> *I am in terror. It is no longer anger or vengeful indignation, the need to cry out against crime and to demand its punishment in the name of truth and justice; it is terror, the sacred terror of the man who sees the impossible being realised, streams running back to their sources, the earth tumbling into the sun. And at what I cry out is the distress of our generous and noble France, it is fear of the abyss into which it rolls. We had imagined that the Rennes trial was the fifth act of the terrible tragedy we had lived through the last two years … How have we been deceived; a new turn of the wheel has taken place, the most frightful of all … The trial at Rennes was only the fourth act. Great God what will be the fifth? Of what new sorrows and suffering will it be composed? To what extreme expiation will it throw the nation? Is it not so?[91]*

The daily *L'Avenir* publishes a letter signed by 70 dreyfusards who declare that the Rennes court martial reconfirms the innocence of Dreyfus. They express their profound sorrow at the verdict, promising not to abandon Dreyfus and to continue to fight for justice and truth.

Von Below-Schlatau writes to Hohenlohe:

> *From whichever point of view one considers the verdict pronounced in Rennes – human, legal, military or political – it is and remains a monstrosity, and as such it will be condemned by the public opinion of the entire civilized world except France who thereby excludes itself from the rank of civilized nations.* (The Kaiser's marginal note: 'Yes!') *The mixture of brutality and cowardice is the seal of barbarity as is the signature on the verdict of the judges of Rennes. Brutal enough to condemn for a second time a man of whose guilt they were not or not sufficiently convinced, they did not have the courage to return him to Devil's Island and, for the crime of treason, which Dreyfus was supposed to have committed, they decided on extenuating circumstances.[92]*

The antisemitic *La Libre Parole*, following the second conviction of Dreyfus, inset with portrait of Drumont

Around the world the verdict provokes a wave of indignation against France. The German press unanimously describes the verdict as cowardly, criminal and a grave political error. The press in England is condemnatory: 'Rennes is France's moral Sedan' (*Daily Mail*); 'The infamous judgment disgraces France, dishonours her army, insults the Kaiser, and offends the best principles of humanity' (*Daily Telegraph*); 'We do not hesitate to pronounce it [the Rennes verdict] the biggest and most appalling prostitution of justice the world has witnessed in modern times' (*The Times*). There is also condemnation from British clergymen. Lord Russell of Killowen, in a harsh report to Queen Victoria tries to explain some of the reasons of the 'erroneous judgment' of Rennes: '[the judges] were unversed in the law, unused to legal proceedings, with no experience or aptitude to enable them to weigh the probative effect of testimony; they were steeped in prejudice and concerned in what they regarded as the honour of the army ... and thus they gave undue weight to the flimsy rags of evidence ...'[93] Queen Victoria telegraphs Lord Russell to express her 'profound sorrow upon hearing the news', qualifying the verdict as 'defiance of good sense', and hoping that the 'poor martyr would appeal to better judges'. Theodore Roosevelt, Governor of the State of New York, states on 13 September: 'We have watched with indignation and regret the trial of Captain Dreyfus. It was less Dreyfus on trial than those who tried him. It was due in part to the bitter religious prejudices of the French people.'[94] The *New York Times* reports: 'It is incredible that the Supreme Court of Appeal in France will do injustice with all the world looking on, with all the evidence on display and with the public judging the judges. If Dreyfus is crushed his country will be crushed with him and France will be the scorn of the civilised world.'[95] (*v.* Appendix 43)

In Brussels, Milan, Budapest, London, New York and other cities and towns across the globe there are popular anti-French demonstrations. Some 40,000 demonstrate in London's Hyde Park. In Indianapolis and Chicago the French flag is publicly burned. French Embassies and Consulates are besieged or stoned. Performances of French plays are disrupted or cancelled. Businesses are ordered to cease importing from France. Strong threats came from the United States, where appeals were made to Congress for an official withdrawal from the Paris Universal Exhibition due to open in 1900. Numerous threats to boycott the exhibition are expressed in cities worldwide. [96]

The pardon[97]

Sept 8　　　In a letter to Waldeck-Rousseau Gallifet warns against allowing an appeal to the Supreme Court for revision in the event of the conviction of Dreyfus. He explains that such an appeal would only lead to a third court martial and undoubtedly another conviction. It would put the Government in a dangerous position, which must be avoided: 'On one side there will be the entire army, the majority of the French (not to mention the deputies and senators) and all the agitators; on the other, the Ministry, dreyfusards and foreign countries.' Galliffet also mentions in this letter that 'we must not forget that the great majority of people in France are antisemitic'.[98]

Sept 10 Waldeck-Rousseau and Mornard explore the possibilities of quashing the Rennes verdict without recourse to a third trial. Both agree that an appeal is unlikely to succeed. Mornard points out that Dreyfus is not physically fit and that his morale may not be strong enough to withstand further imprisonment. Waldeck-Rousseau suggests a presidential pardon.

Visiting Dreyfus in prison, Mathieu promises that the fight will continue. He urges his brother to endure all the suffering, even a second degradation, with stoicism. Dreyfus exclaims: 'I will never endure another degradation. I will not put on my uniform, it will not be sullied for a second time. I will make them drag me, they will have to carry me by force; not that, never, never.'[99] For the first time since his return to France, Dreyfus asks for his children to be brought to Rennes. Mathieu goes to Paris to discuss with friends how his brother's honour can be preserved without his life being sacrificed.[100]

The judges of the Rennes court martial unanimously decide to send a request to the President of the Republic that Dreyfus be spared a further degradation.

General de Galliffet

Sept 11   In an article in *Le Siècle* entitled 'Il faut dégager l'honneur de la France' ('The honour of France has to be redeemed'), Reinach proposes an immediate pardon of Dreyfus as a solution.[101] He suggests a pardon as the most honourable response the Government can make to the verdict, which it cannot annul but has no obligation to accept. Reinach considers a pardon as only a 'transitional measure', a 'preface to rehabilitation'.

Mathieu discusses the presidential pardon with Reinach, Lazare and Clemenceau. He explains that his brother will not survive six months in prison: 'What an indelible blemish on the country if he dies in prison.' Lazare, sensitive to Mathieu's argument about his brother's physical condition, accepts the proposal of a pardon. Clemenceau is hesitant: 'My heart says yes, but my reason no'. He states it will be impossible to continue the fight and mobilize support once Dreyfus is at liberty. The pardon would be seen as a 'solution', putting an end to the Affair.[102]

Reinach discusses the matter with Waldeck-Rousseau, who agrees to try to convince the Cabinet and President Loubet.

Millerand, Minister of Commerce, reveals that a pardon can only be secured if Dreyfus withdraws his appeal.[103]

Mathieu meets a number of dreyfusards including Jaurès, Clemenceau and de Pressensé. On being informed of Millerand's advice he protests: 'No, I will never advise my brother to withdraw his appeal.' Clemenceau tells him: 'Ah, that's the way to talk … You are a courageous man … I expected no less from you.'[104] Mathieu is urgently called to the Ministry of Commerce, along with Reinach. Facing the legal difficulty, Millerand and Reinach invite Mathieu to convince his brother to withdraw his appeal. Unable to decide alone, Mathieu asks for Clemenceau and Jaurès to be present. After a tense discussion well into the night, they accept the solution of a pardon on condition that the fight for a revision continues.[105] Mathieu asks Jaurès to write the declaration that Dreyfus will publish once he receives a pardon and is at liberty. It reads:

> *The Government of the Republic gives me back my freedom. It is nothing to me without my honour. From today on I shall continually work towards the reparation of the frightful miscarriage of justice of which I am still the victim. I want all France to know by a definitive judgement that I am innocent. My heart will never be appeased until there is not a single Frenchman who attributes me with the abominable crime that another has committed.*[106]

Mathieu leaves immediately for Rennes. Before departing he receives Millerand's word of honour that he will approach the President and the Ministers the next day and that if the pardon is not signed immediately, he will resign.

Sept 12   After a two-hour conversation, Mathieu succeeds in convincing Dreyfus to withdraw his appeal for a revision in order to accept a presidential pardon.[107]

Dreyfus five years after the Rennes verdict

At a Cabinet meeting, President Loubet hesitates over the signing of the pardon despite the Ministers' approval. He fears that the army will resent the Government's intervention in a military affair so soon after the verdict. Millerand offers his resignation, claiming that he has given Mathieu his word of honour. Galliffet and Waldeck-Rousseau follow his example. Mathieu is recalled from Rennes and in order to prevent a ministerial crisis absolves Millerand from his pledge.

Sept 14   Dr Pierre Delbert goes to Rennes to examine Dreyfus. He reports that if Dreyfus is not freed, his health will deteriorate further 'without hope of recovery'.[108] The report is submitted to Loubet, who announces that the pardon will be signed at the next Cabinet meeting, scheduled for 19 September.

Sept 19   President Loubet signs the letter of pardon submitted to him by Galliffet. It reads:

> *... The highest function of Government is to ensure respect for the decisions of justice, without distinction and without reservation. In its resolve to fulfil this duty, it must also take into account the counsels of clemency and the public interest ... Information obtained reveals that the health of the prisoner has been seriously damaged and that he would be unable to endure a prolonged detention without the greatest danger to himself ... Apart from these considerations of a nature to arouse concern, there are others of a more general nature which point to the same conclusion. A higher political interest and the need to recover all their powers have always directed governments after difficult crises, and with regard to certain sequence of events, measures of clemency or omission. The Government would respond poorly to the wishes of a country eager for the re-establishment of peace if, by the acts in its power to accomplish, whether on its own initiative or by a proposal to Parliament, it did not strive to efface all traces of a painful conflict.*[109]

Scheurer-Kestner dies of cancer after many months fighting the disease.[110]

Sept 20   Léopold Viguié, head of the Sûreté, and a number of inspectors escort Dreyfus from Rennes to Nantes, where they meet Mathieu. Mathieu takes his brother to the family home in Carpentras, belonging to their brother-in-law Joseph Valabrègue.[111]

Sept 21   Dreyfus meets his children, Pierre (now eight) and Jeanne (six), for the first time since his arrest in 1894.

Galliffet sends an order to the army:

> *The incident is over. The military judges, surrounded by the respect of all, delivered their verdict in complete independence. Without any reservations, we bowed before their decision. And in the same way, we will also accept the act dictated to the President of the Republic by a sentiment of profound pity. There can no longer be any question of reprisals of any sort whatsoever. And so I repeat, the incident is over. I ask of you, and if it were necessary, I would*

> *order you, to forget the past in order to think only of the future.*
> *With all my comrades, I shout with all my heart, 'Vive l'armée!*
> *– that army which belongs to no party but only to France.*[112]

Sep 22

The first interview of Dreyfus after his release is published in the *New York Herald.*[113]

L'Aurore publishes 'Lettre à Madame Alfred Dreyfus', Zola's letter to the Dreyfus family. The letter expresses his compassion for Lucie, his understanding of her joy in seeing Dreyfus return to his family but also his resentment of the pardon and his strong desire to see the honour of France restored.[114]

Sep 1899–
Apr 1900

Dreyfus stays with his family in Villemarie outside Carpentras.[115] Many dreyfusards go to visit him there, including Forzinetti, Grimaux, Monod and Reinach. He receives letters of support and sympathy from all over the world, and starts working for the revision of his case.[116]

Oct 6

Reinach publishes in *Le Siècle* and *Le Figaro* a statement of the Austrian Albert Mosetig who, according to Cernuski's deposition at Rennes (*v.* 4 & 6 Sept 1899) attested that Dreyfus was a spy. Mosetig's statement in the press denies Cernuski's allegations.[117] (*v.* 22 & 28 May 1900)

Nov 6–9

Christian Esterhazy's proceedings for fraud against his uncle (Esterhazy) are heard in the Criminal Chamber in Paris. Esterhazy is sentenced in his absence to three years in prison.[118]

Trial of Nationalists and Royalists (9 November 1899–4 January 1900)

The trial of Paul Déroulède, André Buffet, Jules Guérin and 14 other Nationalists accused of conspiracy against the Republic (*v.* 12 Aug 1899, Jules Guérin and Fort Chabrol) lasts for almost two months. The courtroom is guarded by some 1000 police. After 47 sessions, during which more than 300 witnesses are called and 30 lawyers engaged, Déroulède, Buffet and Guérin are found guilty. Déroulède and Buffet are sentenced to 10 years in exile, Guérin to ten years' imprisonment.[119] Habert, who was close to Déroulède in the leadership of the Ligue des patriotes, gives himself up during the trial.[120]

Nov 10

In a letter to Waldeck-Rousseau, Esterhazy threatens publication of new accusations against General Staff officers.[121] (*v.* 21 Nov 1899)

Nov 11

Waldek-Rousseau orders a search at the headquarters of the Assumptionists, suspected of subsidizing anti-republican propaganda. Nearly 2 million francs are found in the offices of *La Croix,* the principal newspaper subsidized by la Bonne Presse. (*v.* 2 June 1898, n. 143) Waldeck-Rousseau files a suit against the congregation. (*v.* 24 Jan 1900)

Nov 14

In pursuit of his Republican and anticlerical policy, Waldeck-Rousseau proposes a bill to reduce the influence of and retain government control over religious associations.[122]

Nov 16   Waldeck-Rousseau presents his political programme to the Chamber of Deputies. Its primary aim is to separate Church and State. It is accepted by 317 votes to 211. (*v.* 3 July 1905)

The Law of Amnesty

Nov 17   Waldeck-Rousseau proposes a general amnesty bill 'for all criminal or unlawful acts connected with the Dreyfus Affair or included in any proceedings relating to one of those acts'. However, in order to allow Dreyfus to pursue a revision, the bill stipulates the Rennes verdict as an exception.[123]

Picquart publicly discloses his letter to Waldeck Rousseau protesting against the amnesty: 'I am concerned to demonstrate that the accusations made against me rest on fraud and falsehood ... I protest against the amnesty with all my strength. To grant an amnesty when a man has been unjustly accused is to deprive him of the moral reparation to which he has a right.'[124] Picquart calls for a judicial investigation of Gonse for his role in the affair of the *faux Henry,* and of Gribelin for his secret manoeuvrings at the Ministry of War.

Clemenceau and Jaurès protest against the amnesty bill and request that a legal action be brought against Mercier, whom they describe as the 'main criminal' in the Dreyfus Affair. Clemenceau considers the amnesty bill an 'error', a 'crime', a 'disgrace' and calls it the 'villainous amnesty'. He writes in *L'Aurore*: 'They [the government] become the villains' accomplices ... They adjourn the desire, they adjourn courage and they call that governing the Republic of France ...'[125]

Nov 21   Esterhazy writes to Clemenceau that he also strongly opposes the amnesty bill. He suggests that Clemenceau 'collaborates': if Clemenceau sends him 'a safe man', Esterhazy will reveal more of the crimes of the 'real culprits' (i.e. the officers on the General Staff). Clemenceau publishes the letter in *L'Aurore* (23 November) and shows it to the Senators and the Deputies who are considering the amnesty bill.[126] (*v.* 26 Jan 1900)

Dec 13   Labori's suit against *La Libre Parole* reaches the civil court. Millot, owner of the paper, is fined 2000 francs. As part of the compensation due to Labori, the verdict is to be published in 40 newspapers in Paris and 200 in the provinces.[127]

1900   Publication of *Musée des horreurs,* 52 anti-dreyfusard lithographs by Lenepveu depicting the main dreyfusard characters as bestial images. This was followed by three images entitled *Musée des Patriotes.*

Jan 24   The Assumptionist congregation is dissolved, its leaders having been accused by the Seine Assize Court of collaborating in a conspiracy against the Republic. Father Bailly, owner of *La Croix,* is removed from his post and the paper placed under secular management.

Jan 26   Esterhazy writes again to Waldeck-Rousseau stating that he is ready to return to France and be judged.

Jan 28   Mercier is elected Senator of the Loire-Inférieure region by 700 votes to 300.[128]

Feb 22–Mar 5 With authorization from Waldeck-Rousseau, André Lequeux, French Consul in London, takes Esterhazy's verbal depositions, given over four sessions. Esterhazy repeats information already given regarding his collusion with the General Staff, writing the *bordereau* under Sandherr's instructions and the means by which it reached the Deuxième Bureau. Esterhazy attaches to his depositions copies of documents he claims as proof of the collusion but refuses to submit the originals. Waldeck-Rousseau considers Esterhazy's depositions to be worthless. He does not recall him to France so as not to reopen the Affair without reason.[129]

Mar 1   The amnesty bill comes before the Senate. A select committee is appointed to examine it under the presidency of Senator Jean-Jules Clamageran. (*v.* 13 Mar; 1–2 June 1900)

Mar 8   Dreyfus protests against the bill to Clamageran:

> *This bill puts an end to public actions from which I hoped to see the emergence of revelations, perhaps even confessions, which would have allowed me to refer my case to the Supreme Court of Appeal … The right of the innocent is not clemency, it is justice … The amnesty strikes at my heart; it would be to the sole benefit of General Mercier … I implore the Senate to grant me my right to truth, to justice …*[130]

Mar 13   The Senate select committee hears Picquart and Reinach.[131]

Esterhazy writes to Clamageran protesting that the amnesty was decided 'by order', to protect Reinach and Picquart. This accusation appears in the Nationalist papers.

Mar 14   *L'Echo de Paris* publishes an article describing the amnesty as 'perfidious and shameful, … prepared by Waldeck-Rousseau, and his colleagues Dreyfus, Reinach, Picquart and Zola'. Picquart and Reinach commence proceedings against the paper.[132]

Opening of the Paris Universal Exhibition

Apr 15   The Government celebrates the opening of the Universal Exhibition in Paris as a symbol of 'reconciliation' among the French people. Waldeck-Rousseau greets the event as 'the testimony that moral peace has been restored'. At the ceremony of inauguration, President Loubet declares: 'France wishes to make a dazzling contribution to the advent of concord amongst people.'[133]

Apr 20   Dreyfus moves to Switzerland. He stays at the home of Hélène and Eugène Naville, near the village of Coligny above Lake Geneva.[134]

Against the *'reprise de l'affaire'* ('revival of the Affair')

Apr 24   In an address to the Ligue des droits de l'homme et du citoyen Reinach states that for 'the historical honour of France' the Rennes verdict must be annulled by a further ruling. Until then, dreyfusards must continue the fight against the amnesty 'which strangles justice and suffocates truth'. Reinach promises an 'armistice' of this campaign during the Universal Exhibition.[135]

The speech fuels the Nationalist campaign for the forthcoming municipal elections. In Paris the Ligue de la patrie française and the Ligue des patriotes placard the slogan 'reprise de l'affaire' accusing dreyfusards and Republicans of a 'new plot'. Waldeck-Rousseau is accused of complicity with Reinach.

May 4   In Paris' municipal elections, 45 Nationalist Deputies are elected, 35 Republicans. In the provinces, Republicans win with a large majority.

May 21   *L'Eclair* announces that it has evidence of Waldeck-Rousseau's role in a plan involving the police to quash the Rennes verdict. Sûreté officers were to obtain information from double agent Cuers (*v.* 10 July 1885; June 1896) proving that the testimony of Cernuski was false.[136]

May 22   Waldeck-Rousseau is questioned in the Chamber of Deputies about Reinach's speech. By 425 votes to 60, the Chamber passes a motion that the Government is to 'oppose vigorously the resumption of the Dreyfus Affair, from whatever source it might come'. Deputy Alphonse Hubert refers to an article published in the press mentioning the existence of letters from Tomps, proving that attempts have been made by officers of the Deuxième Bureau to obtain information on Cernuski.[137]

May 28   The Chamber debates the conduct of Deuxième Bureau officer Captain Fritsch, who disclosed the information regarding Cernuski's testimony to *L'Eclair*. (*v.* 21 May 1900) Galliffet states that he has punished Fritsch. Waldeck-Rousseau describes Fritsch's action as 'felony'. The Nationalists vigorously protest. They ask Waldeck-Rousseau to retract his words and Galliffet to protect the army. Léon Bourgeois proposes a motion to approve the Government's action. The motion is passed by 286 votes to 234. Galliffet tenders his resignation.

May 29   General Louis André, an ardent Republican and anticlerical, is appointed Minister of War.[138]

L'Aurore publishes Zola's 'Lettre au Senat', strongly critical of the amnesty bill:

> *The amnesty was made against us, the defenders of right, in order to save the true criminals, closing our mouths with an act of hypocritical and insulting clemency, lumping together decent people and scoundrels, a supreme ambiguity which will end up rotting the national conscience … You are making this law of amnesty for them [the enemies of the Republic], to save the leaders from the penal colony … You are traitors, the ministers are traitors, the President of the Republic is a traitor. And when you have voted in the law, you will have done the work of traitors in order to save traitors … In this grave danger, there was only one thing to do: to accept the struggle against all the united forces of the past, to change the administration, to change the magistrature, to change*

> *the high command, since it all appeared in its clerical rottenness.*
> *To enlighten the country by acts, to speak the whole truth, to*
> *deliver complete justice … what we want is for the Dreyfus Affair*
> *to end with the only outcome that can give back strength and calm*
> *to the country; that is, that the culprits are punished, not for us*
> *to take delight in their punishment, but so that the people finally*
> *know the truth and so that justice, the only true and solid way,*
> *may bring appeasement … Vote in the law of amnesty, Senators,*
> *complete the strangulation, say with President Delegorgue that the*
> *question will not be put … and if France is one day dishonoured*
> *before the whole world, it will be your work … The law of amnesty*
> *will be a civic treason, the relinquishment of the Republic into the*
> *hands of its worst enemies …*[139]

June 1–2   The Senate debates the amnesty bill. Trarieux, in opposition, explains
the injustices the law would entail – the transfer of the trials of Zola
and Reinach from criminal to civil jurisdiction (where neither proof
nor the interrogation of witnesses are necessary); the annulment of
Piquart's court martial, depriving him of a true judgment; but especially
leaving the principal culprits, above all Mercier, unpunished. Mercier,
now a Senator, states that all his actions in 1894 were committed out
of conviction that he was serving his country. Whilst acknowledging
that the reasons of the opponents of the amnesty are legitimate,
Waldeck-Rousseau summarizes: 'The amnesty does not judge, it does
not accuse, it does not exonerate, it does not convict: it does not
know, and is inspired only by public interest.' The Senate passes the
bill by 231 votes to 32.[140] (*v.* 6–18 Dec 1900)

Nov 25   At Mathieu's suggestion Dreyfus returns from Switzerland to Paris,
where he settles at his father-in-law's apartment in the rue de
Châteaudun.[141]

The parting of Labori and the Dreyfus family

Dec   Forcefully opposing the amnesty, Labori insists that Mathieu must
break with Demange.[142] Mathieu refuses. On 14 December, after a
heated meeting between Mathieu and Labori, Mathieu leaves: 'All is
over between us … *Au revoir Monsieur.*' Despite an exchange of
letters and the intervention of Dreyfus himself, the rift between Labori
and the Dreyfus family is final.[143]

Dec 6–18   The amnesty bill is debated in the Chamber of Deputies.[144] Drumont
supports the proposal to extend the amnesty to Déroulède and
Guérin. Waldeck-Rousseau refuses. On the night of 18 December the
Chamber passes the bill by 155 votes to 2.[145]

Dec 22   *L'Aurore* publishes Zola's open letter to President Loubet: 'I have fulfilled
my entire role as honestly as I could, and now I am withdrawing definitively
into silence.'[146]

Dec 25   In a public letter to Waldeck-Rousseau, Picquart again protests against
the amnesty and the Government's intention to promote his [Picquart's]
military career.[147]

Dec 26   Dreyfus writes to Waldeck-Rousseau requesting a judicial investigation:

> *... My innocence is absolute and to my dying day I will pursue*
> *the legal recognition of that innocence through a revision. I am*
> *no more the author of the bordereau annotated by the Kaiser,*
> *which is merely a forgery, than I was of the original, authentic*
> *bordereau, which was by Esterhazy ... I retain the right of every*
> *man to defend his honour and have the truth proclaimed. And so I*
> *retain the right, Mr President, to ask you for an investigation, and*
> *I have the honour to solicit it ...*[148]

Dec 27   The Senate passes the amended amnesty law by 194 votes to 10.

NOTES

1   Only the main events of the court martial are given here. The full proceedings were published by Stock in three volumes: *Rennes* (see Abbreviations and Conventions). There is as yet no full English translation of the court martial, but extracts exist in: (1) Harding, *Dreyfus: the Prisoner of Devil's Island*, pp. 111–333. The American journalist Harding covered the court martial for the Press Association; (2) Snyder, *The Dreyfus Case, a Documentary History*, pp. 268–336.

2   Because of the hot summer in Rennes, hearings took place only from morning to noon.

3   The main absentees were Esterhazy, Pays, Du Paty and Weil.

4   The Rennes court martial was a milestone event in the history of journalism. Specially constructed telegraph lines were laid to carry press despatches. On the opening day, about 650,000 words were transmitted in this way. The correspondent of the *New York Sun*, H.R. Chamberlain, wrote about the special problems encountered by the reporters. Snyder, *The Dreyfus Case*, pp. 329–34.

5   Attempts to film the court martial failed for technical reasons. Méliès, a dreyfusard, was the first to produce a cinematographic reconstruction of the trial. He produced the film *L'Affaire Dreyfus* in 1899 while the court martial was still in progress. Divided into 12 short episodes, this was the longest (15 minutes) and most realistic of his films to date. Soon after filming had been completed, Méliès' rival Pathé shot another, much shorter reconstruction of the trial. According to Méliès' grandmother, when the film was first shown in 1899 it aroused such strong emotions, dividing dreyfusards and anti-dreyfusards, that the police had to intervene and the film was censored. (*v.* 1915) S. Bottomore, 'Dreyfus and documentary', *Sight and Sound* 53, 4 (1984), pp. 290–3; E. Ezra, *Georges Méliès. The Birth of the Author* (Manchester: Manchester University Press, 2000), pp. 68–77; J. Barnes, *The Beginning of the Cinema in England 1894–1901*, vol. 4, 1899 (Exeter: University of Exeter Press, 1996), pp. 68–76; S. Sand, 'Dreyfus in Hollywood', in *L'Histoire* 173 (January 1994) pp. 120–3.

6   According to French law, when a new case is opened a new indictment must be presented. But since the Rennes court martial did not represent a new case, there was no new indictment, despite the ruling of the Supreme Court of Appeal that the 1894 indictment was no longer applicable. Although the Government had the right to instruct Carrière to drop all charges relating to the 1894 indictment, he was allowed to take them up again since Galliffet and Waldeck-Rousseau did not want to give the judges the impression that the Government was 'inviting' them to acquit Dreyfus. The result was that the validity of all previous accusations, put forward in particular by Mercier, made it more difficult for the judges, who had to choose between Dreyfus and Mercier.

7   *Rennes*, I, 20–1, Dreyfus.

8   The document was Du Paty's note to Mercier of 31 July 1899, containing the falsified version of Panizzardi's telegram of 2 November, which Du Paty asserted was correct.

9   Mercier's deposition began on Friday 12 August. Labori was prevented from cross-examining him fully because of the assassination attempt on his life (*v.* 14 Aug). Chamoin reported the disclosure and existence of the document to Galliffet, who considered the matter unimportant. Mathieu and his friends seized the opportunity to write to Waldeck-Rousseau requesting the arrest of Mercier: they did not receive a reply. Labori, *Labori. Ses notes manuscrites. Sa vie*, pp. 102–6; ATQV, pp. 214–16. The document was not examined in Court until 24 August. (*v.* n. 38)

10   Paléologue commented that the Court assumed he was concealing the truth or simply ignoring the existence of the document. Paléologue, *My Secret Diary*, pp. 174–5.

11   One of the new documents Mercier produced was a copy of a report supposedly written by Colonel Schneider, Austrian military attaché to his superiors saying that the German and Italian military attachés had admitted the guilt of Dreyfus. (*v.* 17 Aug) Colonel Schneider telegraphs *Le Figaro* to say that he did not write the report mentioned by Roget in his deposition and also by Cavaignac and Mercier. It

is a forgery. Over the following days the French newspapers continued to publish official and semi-official Austrian communiqués confirming this denial. On 28 August a communiqué established that the report was actually one of Schneider's many draft reports, which he decided not to send. Although misdated, the letter was not a forgery *per se*. (*v.* 30 Aug, Picot's deposition)

12   Mercier 'chose' two dates for his 'historic night', either 13 December 1894 or 8 January 1895. He mentioned that he had even ordered Boisdeffre to wait with the necessary officers that evening in the Ministry of War, in case an order for immediate mobilization was to be issued. Casimir-Périer objected twice during this dramatic account, once with gestures of denial, once requesting to speak.

13   *Rennes*, I, 143, Mercier. Mercier's last phrase was a reference to the Syndicate, accused by anti-dreyfusards of financing the revision. Mercier also claimed that Freycinet stated in May 1899 that his Government knew that 35 million francs had come from Germany and England alone in support of the pro-Dreyfus campaign. A few days later (29 August) Freycinet answered Mercier stating that he had only repeated statements he had heard from well-informed agents. Freycinet described the dreyfusard campaign in France as disinterested and prayed it would cease because it was harmful to the country. Trarieux, much less hesitant in his deposition (5–6 September) than Freycinet, completely denied Mercier's allegation. He submitted to the Court a recent letter from Waldeck-Rousseau and another from Barthou, former Minister of the Interior, confirming that no official report of foreign funds supporting a revision of the court martial of Dreyfus had been found.

14   Waldeck-Rousseau received ministerial authorization on 10 August for a major police operation against the leagues, based on police information about Déroulède's plan for a Nationalist conspiracy. Among those arrested were Déroulède and Guérin; the main gang leaders, Dubuc and Cailly (leaders of Jeunesse antisémitique); and André Buffet, Sabran-Pontevès, Guixiou-Pagès (Royalist supporters of the Ligue antisémitique et nationaliste). Joly, *Déroulède*, pp. 313–14.

15   By the decree of 4 September the Senate was constituted as a special court for trying members of Government, and started preparations for the trial, which opened on 9 November 1899. Of the 67 arrested, only 17 were finally brought before the court.

16   In the end the Fort Chabrol episode was not a serious threat to the Republic. Guérin's intention, to divert attention from the Rennes court martial, did not succeed. However, the term 'Fort Chabrol' entered the French language as a descripiton of political and criminal resistance to the police.

17   On the previous day Labori had received two letters containing death threats. He did not pay much attention to them as he had become used to threats of this nature over the previous two years. The police did not succeed in apprehending his assailant. It was only in 1905 that Labori was able to trace the identity of his assailant. In the confession, which Labori made him sign, the assailant declared having acted at the instigation of Devos, then administrator of *La Libre Parole* as well as of an officer of General Staff. Devos denied this allegation. The police established that he (the assailant) was active in Jules Guérin's Ligue antisémitique, and involved in another assassination attempt with Guérin. He was also implicated in a plot to kidnap Reinach during the Rennes court martial. Labori, *Labori. Ses notes manuscrites. Sa vie*, pp. 230–6.

18   After the incident, Labori received thousands of telegrams and letters of support from army officers, famous writers and artists including Claude Monet, Edmond Rostand, Marcel Proust and Léon Daudet, an ardent anti-dreyfusard, lawyers, magistrates, doctors and many ordinary people, some of whom he did not know. For reactions to the assassination attempt on Labori see Cosnier, *Rennes pendant le process Dreyfus*, pp. 113–22; ATQV, pp. 216–18; Labori, *Labori. Ses Notes manuscrites. Sa vie,* pp. 107–30.

19   *La Libre Parole* published the same week several articles alleging that the assassination attempt on Labori was sham, invented by Labori himself in order to draw public attention. Labori lodged a suit against the paper for libel. (*v.* 13 Dec 1899)

20   During the recess the judges of the court martial questioned Paléologue on the 'historic night'. He confirmed that there was no fear of war on the night of 6 January 1895. Paléologue, *My Secret Diary*, p. 181.

21   The Day of the Assumption. There was no hearing on this day, or on Sundays during the court martial.

22   According to the military code of justice proceedings could not be interrupted for more than 48 hours without having to be recommenced. Mathieu Dreyfus requested Mornard to replace Labori.

23   *Rennes*, I, 247. After each deposition the accused was asked whether he had any comments.

24   These were: (1) an alleged report by Panizzardi in which he admitted that Dreyfus had betrayed his country but was not working for Italy; (2) a report already mentioned by Mercier (dated 30 November 1897) that Roget attributed to Colonel Schneider supposedly mentioning his belief in the guilt of Dreyfus. (nn. 11, 52) Panizzardi telegraphs *Le Figaro* protesting against the passage in Roget's deposition (16 August) that refers to a report that Roget alleges Panizzardi sent to the Italian Ambassador on relations between Schwartzkoppen and Dreyfus.

25   *Rennes*, I, 309, Roget.

26   *Rennes*, I, 366–8, Bertulus, Mme Henry.

27   Picquart admitted that his memory had momentarily betrayed him into thinking that Mercier had asked him to deliver the Secret Dossier to Maurel. He confirmed that at the time of the court martial of Dreyfus he did not know the dossier's content. He only discovered this and its irrelevance to the Dreyfus case in 1896. (*v.* 20 Dec 1894, n. 119; 21 Dec 1894)

28   *Rennes*, I, 516, Cuignet.

29   Boisdeffre also dated that night to early January 1895 but was not able to recall the exact day.

30   Gonse confirmed that when Picquart first told him that Esterhazy's handwriting was identical to that of the *bordereau*, he ordered him not to worry about this. In answer to Demange's questions, however, Gonse admitted that when he first saw Esterhazy's writing he was struck by its resemblance to the *bordereau*.

31   Junck asserted that Dreyfus, while a probationary officer, spent a great deal of money on women and gambling, and also frequented men's clubs of dubious character. Dreyfus firmly denies all Junck's allegations. Junck further alleged that Bertulus was very friendly with Henry during the investigation of Esterhazy. (*v.* 26 July 1898)

32   *Rennes*, I, 658, Bertulus.

33   From the day Labori returned to court, he adopted an even more combative style than before, attacking witnesses rudely and mercilessly in cross-examination and arguing with the Court President. His differences with Demange and the antagonism between them became obvious and increasingly harmful to the cause of the defence.

34   The officers included Lieutenant-Colonels Bertin-Mourot, Gendron, Jeannel, Captains Besse, Duchatelet, Valdant, Le Rond, Majors Rollin (Head of the Intelligence service), Boullenger, Maistre, Roy and General Lebelin de Dionne. Their accusations included the alleged interest of Dreyfus in secret documents, taking some home, entering the Ministry of War at unusual hours and dining with foreign attachés. Closely questioned by Labori, the witnesses were taken aback at Labori's ferociousness. Gonse and Mercier intervened in an attempt to defend them.

35   *Rennes*, II, 110, Breuil.

36   After that day's session (23 August), Boisdeffre went into Paléologue's office in a state of great fatigue and said: 'This morning's hearing … what pain … what an abomination!' Placing his trust in Paléologue, Boisdeffre asked him: 'Why did Henry … and perhaps others as well commit all these aberrations, since the guilt of Dreyfus is not in doubt? Paléologue answered: 'My answer is simple. I have only to put your question the other way round. Why would Henry, and certainly others as well, have committed all these aberrations if they had not feared that you and General Gonse would consider Dreyfus innocent?' Paléologue, *Journal de l'affaire Dreyfus*, p. 227.

37   Because of the attempt on his life and his absence from court, Labori had not yet had the opportunity to cross-examine Mercier on his deposition (12 and 14 August).

38   Mercier and Chamoin covered up for each other in this incident on matters relating to the attempt to infiltrate the unnumbered document into the Secret Dossier. (*v.* 8–11 Aug) Chamoin took full responsibility for the irregularities he committed in agreeing to present the document and he apologized for his ineptness and 'ignorance of legal procedures'. Mercier explained that he was unaware of the exact content of the document. He claimed that since it was a note from Du Paty received on 31 July 1899, he had considered it private and had simply handed it to Chamoin without indicating it should be presented to the judges. This was the second document Mercier had deemed 'private'; the first was Du Paty's commentary on the Secret Dossier, which he had burnt. (*v.* 14 Aug)

39   The Combined Chambers had already ruled on this matter, declaring that no confession had been made by Dreyfus. (*v.* 3 June 1899)

40   *Rennes*, II, 236, Risbourg.

41   Savignaud's previous evidence against Picquart had already been disregarded by Fabre. (*v.* 13 July–25 Aug 1898, Fabre's investigation of Picquart) Trarieux, who testified on 5–6 September, had rejected this testimony as false, citing Savignaud's disreputable record and the fact that he [Savignaud] had been visited by two officers, on Cavaignac's orders, before the opening of the Rennes trial. Savignaud's testimony at Rennes, later proven to be false, was one of the grounds on which Dreyfus appealed for a second retrial. (*v.* 26 Nov 1903)

42   Insisting on the importance of Du Paty's testimony, Labori asked Jouaust to send two reputable doctors to examine him. Jouaust refused. (*v.* 26 Aug)

43   Many members of the public left the courtroom during Bertillon's incomprehensible explanation. See two reports on his evidence, written by *The Times*' special correspondents at Rennes, in Snyder, *The Dreyfus Case*, pp. 300–6.

44   On this issue Mercier and Maurel were right, since the Secret Dossier did not include Panizzardi's telegram. Worried by the strong impression that Freystaetter's testimony might have had on the judges, Mercier was to return to this incident later in the trial, attacking Freystaetter's sanity and honesty. (*v.* 7 Sept)

45   *Rennes*, II, 403–4, Freystaetter.

46 This was one of the dramatic confrontations of the court martial.

47 Bertillon requested permission to respond. He was quickly interrupted by Maurel, who – to loud laughter from the courtroom – did not allow him to continue. Bertillon resumed his seat.

48 *Rennes*, II, 466, Charavay. Charavay was seriously ill at this time and died a few weeks later.

49 Cordier had already been called to testify on 24 August but asserted that he could not do so until he was released from his oath of professional secrecy. At the request of Jouaust, the Minister of War agreed to release him.

50 Lauth remarked that while Cordier affirmed there were no antisemites on the General Staff – a statement that Lauth supported – there was an exception – Cordier himself, who did not hide his antipathy to the Jews and was an avid reader of *La Libre Parole*. Cordier replied: 'I was an antisemite, but my antisemitism never went – and never would go – as far as giving testimony against a Jew because he is a Jew: I am an honest man; I have a conscience.' *Rennes*, II, 528, Cordier.

51 All three were graphologists who had studied the *bordereau* in 1897, and in 1898 testified at Zola's trial.

52 Picot was called by the defence after it had been established that the report attributed to Schneider was not a forgery but one of Schneider's unsent notes. (*v.* 12 Aug, n. 11). Picot attributed the contradiction between Schneider's unsent report and his oral statement to him, to Schneider having changed his mind. This was also why he had decided not to send the report in question. Schneider also confirmed that the *petit bleu* was a letter in which Schwartzkoppen wanted to inform Esterhazy that he was reducing his pay. Schwartzkoppen finally threw the letter away and it reached the Deuxième Bureau via the 'normal route'.

53 This was a crucial issue as it concerned both the essence of the *bordereau* – the information it promised – and the question of whether it could or could not have been provided at that time by an artillery officer such as Dreyfus.

54 This information on the closed sessions of the Rennes court martial is provided by Paléologue. The discussion was highly charged, revealing technical disagreement and confrontation between two officers of unequal rank. Hartman made a decisive distinction between secret information on the 120mm short cannon, that was highly confidential and could only have been known to four or five people at the time, and general information which had already been circulated and was thus easily available. Paléologue, *My Secret Diary*, p. 204.

55 Some witnesses – all from Mulhouse – asserted that Dreyfus attended German army manoeuvres; others denied this. The depositions included those of George-Eugène Germain (a friend and 'recruit' of Beaurepaire who took it upon himself to 'assist' the General Staff in Rennes), François d'Infreville, Paul Kulmann, Captain Auguste-Victor-Jean-Baptiste Lemonnier, Claude-Emilien Voillon and Louis Fischer.

56 A crucial point raised by Hartman and other officers, a cause of discord and confusion, was the incorrect use in the *bordereau* of the term 'hydraulic brake' in relation to the 120mm short cannon. This cannon had a 'hydropneumatic brake' (common to the 120mm long cannon). Mercier retorted that the term 'hydraulic brake' could be explained as that used by the Germans for similar brakes. Hartman explained that the German brake was invented before the French version, which thus excluded the question of treachery by a French officer. Hartman later (7 September) refuted Mercier's statement on the German use of the term 'hydraulic brake'.

57 *Rennes*, III, 236–8, Hartmann. All observers mention the deep impression made on the public and judges by Deloye's successive contradictory statements. This incident was a significant example of how the differing approaches of Demange and Labori damaged the defence. Deloye's answer to Demange could have been crucial for the defence as a clear acknowledgement of 'no proof against Dreyfus', but his subsequent exclamation to Labori reversed the situation, since the Court was likely to apply the phrase 'the work of a master' to Dreyfus. Paléologue admits that he immediately applied the phrase to the existence of a 'fourth party to the treason' (a fourth man he believed to be connected to Esterhazy, Henry and Weil). According to Reinach, Labori was unsuccessfully and imprudently trying to pressure Deloye to say what he certainly did not want to say – or could not – that in espionage, even documents without value (such as those referred to in the *bordereau*) could be bought by foreign agents. During the recess the Clerk of the Court, Coupois, admitted to Paléologue, 'Deloye has just pronounced the verdict of guilty.' Paléologue, *Journal de l'affaire Dreyfus*, p. 241.

58 Fonds-Lamothe served with Dreyfus as a probationary officer on the General Staff in 1894. He later became Freycinet's principal private secretary. Until the investigation of the Combined Chambers in 1899 Fonds-Lamothe was convinced that Dreyfus was guilty.

59 Cernuski, scion of a Serbian dynasty, married since 1895 to the daughter of illegitimate son of the Count Sérurier (a Marshal of the Empire) was an adventurer and a gambler. From 1894 he took refuge in France and lived on his wife's dowry. Cernuski was in contact with a group of doubtful characters, gamblers and spies, some of whom were later found also to be 'employed' by the General Staff. These included the Polish Stanislas Przyborowski, Bavarian Mathilde Baumler, a professional spy, an ex-German lieutenant Helmuth Wessel. Before the Rennes court martial, in debt from gambling, Cernuski claimed that he had evidence against Dreyfus, and offered himself to the ardent antidreyfusard and

former magistrate Quesnay de Beaurepaire, who was looking for ways to 'help' the General Staff to prepare the Rennes court martial. Having failed to inform Cavaignac, Roget and Mercier of Cernuski's potential testimony, Beaurepaire made Cernuski write directly to Major Carrière, who finally agreed to introduce him as a witness. Carrière did not, however, check the information given by the witness or any details about him. In Court, Jouaust introduced Cernuski informally, and not under oath. The 'Cernuski Affair' which abounds with conflicting evidence, was one of the grounds for the second revision. It was examined in detail during the 1904 investigation. It also led to the discovery of more of the General Staff embezzlements with the Section de Statistique's secret funds. (*v.* 7 Mar–19 Nov 1904, Second Revision investigation: Criminal Chamber)

60 Jouaust consulted Paléologue about Labori's request. Paléologue assured the Court that the Government would refuse to send such a request. (*v.* 5–8 Sept, Labori's appeal to the Kaiser and King of Italy)

61 Roget admitted that after opening just one of Esterhazy's letters he handed the others unopened to Jouaust. Carrière also admitted having received letters from Esterhazy that he did not open, considering them of no importance. In addition to insults, Esterhazy's letters also contained threats to send Demange further documents incriminating the General Staff. In a long letter addressed directly to Jouaust, Esterhazy reiterated that the *bordereau* was not the only proof of Dreyfus' guilt, implying that Mercier still had documents he had concealed from the Court (a reference to the *bordereau annoté*). Esterhazy also threatened to publish a document that he claimed was in his possession, which would be dangerous for State security. No attention was paid to these threats. The aforementioned letters are reproduced in *3ème Cass.*, III, 676–87, 690–741.

62 The hearing of Cernuski was to be continued the following day. But Cernuski did not appear in court. Jouaust read out a letter from the witness who claimed that he was ill. Cernuski was never seen in Rennes again. Labori then showed the Court further evidence of Cernuski's involvement with dispreputable people and of his mental condition, implying that his testimony could not be admitted by the Court. Cernuski's evidence was found to be false, and was one of the factors that precipitated the revision of the eventual Rennes verdict. (*v.* 6 Oct 1899 & 23 Nov 1903)

63 This is a note dated 15 April 1899 concerning a conversation between von Münster and Delcassé, in which von Münster said that Schwartzkoppen had admitted having written various *petits bleus* to Esterhazy. (*v.* 22 Dec 1898)

64 After this confrontation Labori was convinced that the Court was utterly hostile to him and that conviction was certain. He wished to retire from the case and to announce this the following day. After a long discussion with Mathieu, Labori agreed to remain in court on condition that he received a request in writing from Mathieu. In his letter Mathieu sympathized with Labori's sentiments, but pleaded with him to 'make this enormous sacrifice' and to defend his brother to the very end. M. Dreyfus, *Dreyfusards!*, pp. 218–19.

65 On the previous evening Paléologue had informed Demange that the only possible way to procure Panizzardi and Schwartzkoppen's evidence was to send them a rogatory letter. (Paléologue had received a telegram on the matter from Delcassé). Demange agreed, but confessed that he was no longer able to discuss anything with his 'irascible colleague' Labori. Paléologue promised to speak to Labori and went to see him just before the opening of the 7 September session. He first tried to persuade Labori to abandon the appearance of Panizzardi and Schwartzkoppen, then suggested the solution of a rogatory letter. Paléologue, *My Secret Diary*, pp. 216–17.

66 The Court's decision concluded that only the president – not the Court as a body – was authorized to order a rogatory letter in this case. Labori asked Jouaust if he still held to his refusal. Jouaust answered in the affirmative and thus excluded Schwartzkoppen and Panizzardi's evidence.

67 Mercier commented that after Freystaetter's deposition the dreyfusard newspapers again bombarded him with accusations of fraud and forgery.

68 Mercier read a report to the Court that while in Madagascar Freystaetter was guilty of executing 30 natives without trial. Mercier's speech caused such disquiet in court that Jouaust asked him not to enlarge on the subject. As Freystaetter had already left Rennes he was not able to respond to these denunciations.

69 The letter contained a long list of insults, mainly directed at General Staff officers and certain members of the court martial. Esterhazy described Bertillon as 'a miserable madman', Boisdeffre as 'a miserable lunatic'. He concluded that although he remained 'like a faithful dog', he had been basely abandoned by his superiors whom he deemed 'stupid like General Billot' and 'cowardly like Boisdeffre and Gonse'.

70 Carrière's speech provoked laughter among the public and was considered by most observers extremely weak, full of unfounded hypotheses and lacking in substance. Chamoin confided in Paléologue that day: 'After a closing speech for the prosecution of such total nullity the acquittal of Dreyfus is certain. I have just telephoned General de Galliffet to tell him.' Paléologue replied: 'And I have just telephoned M. Delcassé to say that a conviction is inevitable.' Paléologue, *Journal de l'affaire Dreyfus*, pp. 256–7.

71 *Rennes*, III, 742–3, Demange.

72 At 4 a.m. on 8 September, a letter from Reinach (in Paris) was delivered to Mathieu telling him that in order to prevent the conviction of Dreyfus some of the principal dreyfusard leaders closely related to the Government suggested that Labori should either considerably soften the tone for his final plea or withdraw from making a plea. However, only one person dared to write such a letter to Labori, Joseph Cornély, political editor of *Le Figaro*. Reinach enclosed Cornély's letter, leaving it to Mathieu to judge whether to pass it on to Labori. After much hesitation, Mathieu handed both letters to Labori, who decided to waive his right to plead. During the day Mathieu and Demange tried in vain to persuade Labori otherwise. For Reinach and Cornély's letters and more details on this incident, see M. Dreyfus, *Dreyfusards!* pp. 224–8; Labori, *Labori. Ses notes manuscrites. Sa vie*, pp. 152–65. In February 1900 Labori published the notes he had prepared for his final plea in his monthly paper *La Grande Revue* (founded in 1896 as the *Revue du Palais*). These notes are also included in the third volume of the Rennes trial, published by Stock: *Rennes*, III, 755–807.

73 *Rennes*, III, 744–6. Carrière's speech was prepared with the assistance of his lawyer, the Nationalist Jules Auffray.

74 *Rennes*, III, 746. Demange pleaded with Labori to respond to the Government Commissioner, but he refused. Labori considered Demange's closing speech extremely weak and insufficient. Labori, *Labori. Ses notes manuscrites. Sa vie*, pp. 165–8.

75 *Rennes*, III, 746.

76 Jouaust and Bréon were in favour of an acquittal.

77 Espionage can have no 'extenuating circumstances'. To arrive at this verdict the Court had to refer to several articles of the Military Code. Dreyfus was thus sentenced to ten years of 'simple detention' (applicable within French territory), and was given credit for the five years he had already served. However, the verdict implied a further degradation ceremony. The Rennes verdict was a major compromise. It implied an admission that an error had been made at the first court martial in 1894; but it did not proclaim the innocence of Dreyfus. Martin, 'The Dreyfus Affair and the Corruption of the French Legal System', p. 46.

78 Baumont, *Aux sources de l'affaire* pp. 246–7.

79 *Der Kampf einer Republik. Die Affäre Dreyfus*, p. 867.

80 The letter also appeared in other newspapers. Its publication puzzled the judges, who again questioned Paléologue about it. Paléologue repeated that no such document existed and suggested Mercier be recalled for questioning. Paléologue, *My Secret Diary*, pp. 187–8.

81 Baumont, *Aux sources de l'Affaire*, pp. 248–51.

82 On 29 August Cordier revealed the 'normal route' procedure before the Rennes court.

83 Baumont, *Aux sources de l'affaire*, pp. 274–5.

84 Baumont, *Aux sources de l'affaire*, pp. 275–6. The fact that Mme Bastian was illiterate has been confirmed. *3ème Cass.*, III, 344, Jourdain.

85 Baumont, *Aux sources de l'affaire*, pp. 276–7.

86 Baumont, *Aux sources de l'affaire*, p. 259.

87 Mathieu agreed that Demange should not be consulted, predicting that he would not agree to this. ATQV, p. 223.

88 Herzog, *Der Kampf einer Republik. Die Affäre Dreyfus*, p. 882; Baumont, *Aux sources de l'affaire*, p. 259.

89 *Die Große Politik* vol. 13, 3635, pp. 327–31.

90 This statement which finally came as a reply to Labori's demand that Schwartzkoppen's and Panizzardi's evidence be included in the trial, arrived 'too late'. The Court had already concluded the hearing of depositions.

91 Quoted in *The Jewish Chronicle* of 15 September 1899. The text is included in *La Vérité en marche* (1969), pp. 157–66. See full text in English in Zola, *The Dreyfus Affair: J'Accuse and Other Writings*, pp. 136–43 for more reactions to the verdict.

92 *Die Große Politik*, vol. 13, 3640, pp. 335–6.

93 Quoted in Burns, *France and the Dreyfus Affair*, pp. 152–5.

94 Quoted in Harding, *Dreyfus, the Prisoner of Devil's Island*, p. 380; pp. 334–42, 379–86.

95 Quoted in E. Feldman, *The Dreyfus Affair and the American Conscience 1895–1906* (Detroit: Wayne State University Press, 1981), p. 27; see also pp. 30–1, 49–50, 104–5, 128–9.

96 Calls to boycott the Universal Exhibition in Paris over the Affair's violation of human rights had been voiced since 1898 in Holland, Switzerland and Germany. It was in this last phase of the Affair that the word 'boycottage' entered the French language. Although most of these threats were not official they came from exhibitors and visitors. They carried weight since they represented the popular face of the universal exhibitions. This pressure had a considerable influence on President Loubet's decision to pardon Dreyfus. (*v.* 19 Sept 1899) See R. Mandelle, 'The Affair and the Fair: Some Observations on the

Closing Stage of the Dreyfus Case', *Journal of Modern History* 37 (1967), pp. 253–65; M. Burns, 'The Policy of Pardoning: Dreyfus and the World's Fair in 1900', in M. Denis, M. Lagrée and J.Y. Veillard (eds) *L'Affaire Dreyfus et l'opinion publique en France et à l'étranger* (Rennes: Presses Universitaires de Rennes, 1995), pp. 27–36; Harding, *Dreyfus, the Prisoner of Devil's Island*, pp. 387–90.

97 The Rennes' verdict – both in its abnormality and the uproar it created – dictated the Government's reaction. A presidential pardon as a solution to this politico-legal imbroglio required not only a great deal of manoeuvring with Government members, but also within the dreyfusard camp and with Dreyfus himself. For details on the events concerning the pardon and the different positions of those involved see P.V. Naquet, preface to *Cinq ans de ma vie* (1982), pp. 19–25.

98 HAD, 5, pp. 579–81.

99 ATQV, p. 237.

100 Mathieu was extremely worried about his brother's condition. He stated that Dreyfus' request to see his children in his present condition could only be 'the last wish of a man who felt his end was near'. ATQV, p. 238.

101 A pardon had to be processed immediately, within 48 hours of the judgment, and addressed to the President by the Minister of War.

102 ATQV, pp. 238–39.

103 Millerand was an ardent defender of Dreyfus and the first Socialist Minister in the Third Republic. He discovered a formal irregularity (*vice de forme*) in the Rennes verdict in that the Court forgot to stipulate the type of surveillance Dreyfus would be subjected to during his detention. In the case of a further court martial, this legal point alone would be disadvantageous to Dreyfus.

104 HAD, 5, pp. 552–3.

105 Clemenceau and Jaurès were hostile to the concept of a pardon, which for them was the sacrifice of an ideological cause for the sake of an individual. They were finally won over by practical and humanitarian considerations. Clemenceau told Mathieu, 'If I were the brother, I would accept.' ATQV, p. 242.

106 A. Dreyfus, *Cinq années de ma vie* (1982), p. 226.

107 Dreyfus claimed he had no need of a pardon but 'thirsted for justice'. His brother convinced him that there was very little hope that he could withstand a long imprisonment in his state of health, and that liberty would allow him to continue the fight for justice. Dreyfus stated that it was also the thought of his wife and children, whom he did not want to deprive any further of his presence, that led him to agree to withdraw his appeal. A. Dreyfus, *Cinq années de ma vie* (1982), p. 226.

108 This examination was Waldeck-Rousseau's plan in order to convince Loubet of the need for a pardon. The medical report confirmed that, along with malnutrition and malarial fever, Dreyfus showed symptoms of tuberculosis of the spinal marrow. Delbert forecast that Dreyfus would die within months if he remained in prison. ATQV, p. 245.

109 HAD, 5, pp. 582–4. The pardon caused a serious split in the dreyfusard camp: Clemenceau, Jaurès, Labori, Picquart, Guyot, Zola and other dreyfusards opposed the idea, considering it a betrayal of their long fight for justice. For them Dreyfus ceased to be the noble victim for whom they were struggling. Mathieu and Reinach were accused of negotiating with Waldeck-Rousseau and opening the way for an eventual amnesty, which would absolve Mercier and the other politicians and military personnel involved in the Affair. For this split in the dreyfusard camp, see ATQV, pp. 251–78 and Labori, *Labori. Ses notes manuscrites. Sa vie*, pp. 242–67, 321–32.

110 His funeral took place on 25 September, with many of the Ministers and the President of the Senate present.

111 The police were meticulous in supervising the route for this journey. There was some public curiosity but no violent incident. ATQV, pp. 246–50.

112 Galliffet's military orders reducing the 'Affair' to an 'incident' became famous, reflecting the Government's desire to calm the mood in the country. HAD, 6, p. 3. Galliffet issued this order without consulting Waldeck-Rousseau, who reprimanded him and refused its publication in the *Journal Officiel*.

113 For the full text of the interview see Snyder, *The Dreyfus Case*, pp. 350–9.

114 *La Vérite en marche* (1969), pp. 167–77. See English version in Pagès, *Emile Zola, The Dreyfus Affair, J'Accuse and Other writings*, pp. 143–50. Zola wrote the letter on 19 September the day after Loubet signed the pardon. Dreyfus and Lucie received it on 22 September, the day after their arrival in Carpentras. Dreyfus was deeply moved; his reply to Zola (30 September) was highly charged and expressed his deep respect for Zola's actions and words. For extracts, see A. Dreyfus, *Carnets (1899–1907), ed.* P. Oriol (Paris: Calman-Lévy, 1998), pp. 289–90.

115 Carpentras was chosen largely because of the calm family environment and its mild climate. It was the perfect place to improve his health after his long imprisonment. Nevertheless, he continued to suffer from fevers and nightmares. DFA, pp. 274–5, 283–4.

116 Mathieu was now well-known and also received many letters, as did Lucie who was given encouragement and advice about how to build up her husband's health. One such letter came from the famous Australian soprano, Nellie Melba; another from an associate of Dr Gibert (one of the first dreyfusards, *v.* Feb 1895), hoping to treat Dreyfus with hypnosis; the American writer Mark Twain suggested the services of Dr Kellgreu, a physician who can 'cure diseases where no physician can do so ...' Twain asked his publisher and Zola to pass on his message to Lucie. See letters in Snyder, *The Dreyfus Affair*, pp. 362–5.

117 This could prove that Cernuski's testimony was false and thus be considered as 'new fact' which enabled a revision of a case. However, Mornard held the view that since Cernuski's testimony was given in closed session (and thus had no written record), it could be the subject of contestations and the witness could be acquitted. He feared that this acquittal would be harmful to Dreyfus as it would certainly be used against him. Charpentier, *Historique de l'Affaire Dreyfus* (Paris: Fasquelle, 1933), p. 242 (chapter not translated in the English edition of the book).

118 Reinach asked the Government to demand Esterhazy's extradition from England to stand trial (*Le Siècle*, 8 November). Waldeck-Rousseau and Monis (Minister of Justice) refused to make the application.

119 Déroulède chose Saint-Sébastien in Spain as his place of exile. Despite repeated efforts Déroulède did not succeed to revive the Ligue des patriotes. He founded a daily newspaper *Le Drapeau*, which failed within a few months (May–December 1901). The legislative elections in May 1902 brought defeat for the Nationalists. After two difficult years (1902–04), during which Déroulède suffered depression, an amnesty for him was voted (30 October 1905), ending his years of exile. Déroulède received an enthusiastic welcome on his return to Paris. Déroulède, still in exile in December 1904, was challenged by Jaurès to a duel after a vicious exchange over an article published in the Socialist *Humanité*, commenting on a patriotic demonstration of the Ligue des patriotes near the Statue of Jeanne d'Arc. The duel took place in France on 6 December 1904. Prime Minister Combes was much criticized for according Déroulède a safe conduct for 24 hours. Guérin spent one and a half years in Clairvaux prison before his punishment was commuted to exile. He also finally received an amnesty in 1905. Joly, *Déroulède*, pp. 323–49.

120 Habert, who fled to Brussels in August, presented himself to the police on 19 December 1899. He was tried by the Senate for conspiratorial activities (19–23 February 1900) and sentenced to five years in exile and joined Déroulède in Spain. Joly, *Déroulède*, pp. 321–2.

121 At the same time Esterhazy advised Boisdeffre and Gonse that he had entered into negotiations with the Government to hand over documents in his possession compromising the General Staff.

122 The bill was approved on 28 June 1900. The Law was finally approved on 28 June 1901, after passionate debates. (*v.* 15 June 1902, n. 7)

123 The tabling of the amnesty bill entailed the suspension of all trials in progress: Zola's trial before the Assize Court in Versailles, scheduled for 21 November; Henry's widow's case against Reinach, scheduled for 21 December; and Picquart's pending court martial. An exception was made for Labori's suit against *La Libre Parole.* (*v.* 13 Dec 1899)

124 HAD, 6, p. 52.

125 HAD, 6, p. 54.

126 Lazare suggested that Mathieu should buy Esterhazy's papers. Mathieu refused, anxious not to arouse accusations against the 'Syndicate'. HAD, 6, p. 76.

127 See extracts of depositions in Labori, *Labori. Ses notes manuscrites. Sa vie*, pp. 212–29. On 18 December Henry's widow complained to Waldeck-Rousseau that unlike her proceedings against Reinach, Labori's trial had not been adjourned because of the pending amnesty bill. Several adjournments meant that her case did not reach court until 1902. (*v.* 2 June 1902)

128 Mercier avoided attending the sessions at the Senate. He first appeared there for the debate on the amnesty bill. (*v.* 1–2 June 1900)

129 During March–April Esterhazy continued to send insulting and indignant letters to Waldeck-Rousseau. Esterhazy sold his depositions in two slightly different versions, to *Le Siècle* and *L'Indépendance Belge*. They were published in 1900 and 1901. Both texts were also published together as a pamphlet (Brussels: G. Fischlin). Esterhazy's depositions are included in *3ème Cass.*, III, 742–69. See also AD, pp. 550–75.

130 The letter was published in *Le Siècle* of 10 March 1900. See full text in A. Dreyfus, *Carnets (1899–1907)*, pp. 32–3. For Dreyfus' letter in English, see Snyder, *The Dreyfus Case*, pp. 367–8.

131 They protested against the implications of the amnesty bill. The cancellation of penal actions connected to the Affair meant the annulment of Picquart's court martial and the transfer of the trials of Zola and Reinach to civil courts (instead of the Supreme Court of Appeal). Henry's widow, however, would be able to pursue her suit for damages against Reinach.

132 The case was brought to court on 11 and 18 June 1900. Labori was their counsel. *L'Echo de Paris* was fined and had to pay damages.

133 When Zola appeared before the select committee of the Senate, he said: 'The amnesty is sought so as not to offer the spectacle of our discord to the foreigners who will visit the exhibition. Above all, France needs to appear before the world as having accomplished its great work of justice.' HAD, 6, p. 85.

134 Like many other Swiss and French Protestants, the Navilles became dreyfusards from 1897, following Scheurer-Kestner's campaign. Eugène, who was in contact with Mathieu, Reinach, Jaurès and others, supported the Dreyfus cause in the *Journal de Genève*. Under the pseudonym Villemar, Hélène, published a short history of Alfred Dreyfus' life in 1898, *Dreyfus Intime* and *Un essai sur le colonel Picquart*. The Navilles were the hosts to the frequent visits of close friends and Picquart.

135 The event took place in Digne, the district which Reinach represented as a deputy in the Senate until May 1898. HAD, 6, pp. 86–7.

136 The Sûreté began to obtain information from Cernuski's accomplices (Przyborowski, Mathilde and Wessel). (*v.* following note)

137 The article was instigated by one of the officers of the Section de Statistique, Captain Jules Fritsch, after a series of incidents occurred between the Intelligence and the Sûreté. Galliffet, informed about this, dismissed Fritsch. In September 1899, immediately after the verdict of Rennes, Galliffet had ordered the removal of espionage and counter-espionage from the Deuxième Bureau and transferred it to the Sûreté police. In November 1899 he replaced the head of the Section de Statistique Rollin with Captain Marcelin François. The other members of the Service were Captain Fritsch, Captain Henri Mareschel (who replaced Lauth in December 1897) and archivist Grégoire Dautrich (who replaced Gribelin in December 1898). The new espionage department now situated in the Sûreté was put under the civil direction of Cavard and Tomps. Tomps was poorly regarded by the offices of the Section de Statistique. (*v* 21 Nov 1896, n. 87)

138 As commander of an infantry division in 1899, André had forbidden the reading of antisemitic newspapers.

139 Zola, *La Vérité en marche* (1969), pp. 179–93. See full text in English in Pagès, *Emile Zola, The Dreyfus Affair, J'Accuse and Other Writings*, pp. 154–64.

140 The Senate approved the placarding of Waldeck-Rousseau's speech (by 169 votes to 41). It also rejected a counter-proposal to apply the amnesty to the Nationalists and Royalists condemned by the Senate in January 1900 (by 161 votes to 102).

141 Dreyfus' stay in Switzerland was misinterpreted by several dreyfusards who considered his absence from France as an abandonment of his fight for justice. Havet told Mathieu 'Esterhazy in London, and Dreyfus in Switzerland, that does not sound good.' ATQV, pp. 262–3.

142 After the Rennes trial, Labori's bitter disapproval of the attitude of Demange and Mathieu became ever more harsh. Labori considered Demange an ally of Waldeck-Rousseau's policy of caution. He warned Mathieu, 'It is either him, or Picquart and me … Choose. We have no confidence in him [Demange]. Everything we decide he communicates to Waldeck-Rousseau.' ATQV, pp. 251–61.

143 Labori agreed to meet Dreyfus only in the presence of Picquart. He repeated all his grievances and stated that as a lawyer he could not continue to represent Dreyfus. According to Labori, Dreyfus burst into tears. A year later Labori also broke with Reinach. Labori, *Labori. Ses notes manuscrites. Sa vie*, pp. 241–76. M. Dreyfus, *Dreyfusards!*, pp. 247–8.

144 The Chamber delayed debate of the amnesty bill (passed by the Senate in June) until after the Universal Exhibition, the summer recess and the Senate's examination of a related amnesty bill concerning misdemeanours of the press and facts related to strikes.

145 As the wording of the law was slightly modified, it had to be resubmitted to the Senate for approval. (*v.* 27 Dec 1900)

146 Zola, *La Vérité en marche* (1969), pp. 194–210. See English version in Zola, *The Dreyfus Affair: J'Accuse and Other Writings*, pp. 164–75.

147 Picquart was informed that his appeal to the Senate Council protesting against the decision to remove him from military service would probably be accepted and that he would even be given a post of command. In his letter he stated that he had no wish to receive anything from the Government. The letter remained unanswered.

148 The letter was published in *Le Siècle* of 28 December 1900. Dreyfus wrote it in response to a series of articles published by Rochefort earlier in December which revived the saga of the *bordereau annoté*. Dreyfus did not receive a reply. See A. Dreyfus, *Carnets (1899–1907)*, pp. 76–7.

Part 9

EXONERATION

1901–JULY 1906

Georges Clemenceau

1901
Feb 16   Fasquelle publishes *La vérité en marche*, Zola's collection of articles and letters on the Affair.[1]

Cinq années de ma vie

May   Fasquelle publishes Dreyfus' memoirs of the Affair, entitled *Cinq années de ma vie* ('Five Years of My Life').[2] Reinach's first volume of his *Histoire de l'Affaire Dreyfus* is published.[3]

May 4–5   An antisemitic congress is held in Paris, with some 200 delegates. Dubuc announces that the Jeunesse antisémite et nationaliste has become the Parti National Antijuif (Anti-Jewish National Party). Dubuc is elected its leader.

May 7–10   *Le Siècle* publishes the correspondence between Leblois and Scheurer-Kestner.[4] (*v.* Aug 1897)

1902
The Government of Emile Combes

April–May   Legislative elections take place. Victory goes to Waldeck-Rousseau's party of the Left which obtains 370 seats out of 588. Georges Clemenceau is elected Senator for the Var region. (*v.* 15 June 1902)

June 2   The suit of Henry's widow against Reinach comes before the Civil Court of the Seine.[5] The Court rules that Reinach is to pay only minimum indemnities to Henry's widow and child, 500 francs for each, instead of the 200,000 francs Henry's widow had claimed.[6]

June 3   Although gaining a large majority, Waldeck-Rousseau tenders his resignation.

June 15   A new Cabinet is formed with Emile Combes as Prime Minister and Minister of Interior. General André remains Minister of War. Combes pursues the anticlerical policy of the previous government. This is to lead to the Law of Separation between Church and State.[7] (*v.* 3 July 1905)

Death of Zola

Sept 29   During the night of 28/29 September Zola dies at his home in Neuilly-sur-Seine (west of Paris), asphyxiated by fumes escaping from the chimney flue in his bedroom.[8] (*v.* 1957)

Oct 5   A crowd of more than 20,000 mourners, including Dreyfus, Jaurès and Lazare, attend Zola's funeral at Montmartre cemetery.[9] Anatole France delivers a speech at the graveside, recalling Zola's struggle for truth and justice in the Dreyfus Affair and concluding his oration: '*Il était un moment dans la conscience humaine*' ('He was a moment in the conscience of mankind').[10]

Oct   In his continuous search for new facts to allow Dreyfus to apply for a revision of the Rennes verdict, Mathieu asks his friend Dr Roger Dumas to approach Major Maurice Merle, a judge at the Rennes court martial, for information. Dumas has several meetings with Merle in Avignon and Montpellier, which seems to suggest that the doubted document known as the *bordereau annoté* could have been shown to the judges during their deliberation.[11]

Nov 12   In a long letter to Mornard, Dumas reports his conversations with Merle.[12]

1903   Publication of the orchestral work *Hymn à la justice* by the French pro-dreyfusard composer Alberic Magnard.

               First appearance of the *Protocols of the Learned Elders of Zion* (extracts) in the Russian newspaper *Znamia* ('Banner').[13]

April   *Vérité*, the third volume of Zola's *Quatre Evangiles*, a novel inspired by the Affair, is published posthumously.[14]

Jaurès' interpellation in the Chamber of Deputies

Apr 6–7   In the Chamber of Deputies Jaurès takes the opportunity offered by the debate on the election of Deputy Gabriel Syveton – a matter completely irrelevant to the Dreyfus Affair – to raise the question of the *bordereau annoté*.[15] In a speech lasting the entire session of 6 April and more than two hours on 7 April, Jaurès exposes the intrigues and crimes committed during the Affair, dwelling insistently on the various forgeries fabricated by the General Staff and especially the damaging use of the 'monstrous forgery' of the *bordereau annoté* (claimed by the Nationalists and their press to exist).[16] Jaurès demonstrates the innocence of Dreyfus conclusively. He describes Henry's confession of his forgery. When Jaurès reads Pellieux's letter of resignation of 31 August 1898 addressed to Cavaignac, Brisson intervenes, declaring that his Government was never informed of the existence of Pellieux's letter.[17] Cavaignac takes full responsibility for the events that occurred under his administration. There is a violent exchange between Cavaignac and Brisson.[18] Jaurès concludes his speech on 7 April, calling for the Government to initiate a new investigation of the actions of the Deuxième Bureau in the Dreyfus case. In the name of the Government, André, Minister of War, agrees to proceed with an investigation. Encouraged by his success, Jaurès proposes a motion to put the Government's statement on record. A confused series of motions follows including: (1) that a general inquiry be held on the irregularities committed by the military authorities in the Dreyfus Affair and on the proceedings of the courts martial; (2) a motion of confidence in the Government recommending that the Dreyfus Affair should not be removed from the realm of legal jurisdiction. The Chamber passes this last motion by a vote of 304 to 196, a result that conflicts with the first motion proposed by Jaurès.[19]

Apr 21   Dreyfus sends André a request to open an investigation into his case based on new elements that have come to his attention.[20]

End Apr   Following the request of Dreyfus, Prime Minister Combes authorizes André to proceed with a personal investigation. He is to start as soon as the session adjourns for the summer recess so as to avoid any questions in the Chamber.

General André's investigation (4 June–19 October)

André delegates one of his subordinates, Captain Antoine-Louis Targe, to assist him in the investigation. Despite the dispersal of the files after the Rennes court martial Targe endeavours to reassemble them. He succeeds in locating documents not included in the Secret Dossier, i.e. documents which Henry, Gonse and Cuignet had concealed because they appeared to support Dreyfus.[21] André examines the Secret Dossier by himself, then calls for the assistance of Gribelin, who on this occasion reveals the truth. As a result, André has no difficulty in finding two major forgeries in the dossier in addition to the *faux Henry*.[22] Gribelin also discloses his own falsification, made on Henry's orders, of Deuxième Bureau secret fund accounts in order to conceal the payment of a monthly allowance to Val Carlos from 1894 to 1897. He reveals how Henry falsified the amounts expended by Picquart to suggest he was embezzling the secret funds.[23] Gribelin also admits that it was Du Paty who sent the Speranza telegram to Picquart in Tunis and Henry who gave Esterhazy the *document libérateur*. The investigation also leads Targe to find Guérin's note to Saussier after the degradation ceremony, in which he wrote that there was 'No other incident' to report. (*v.* 5 Jan 1894, n.10) Targe further discovers that '1894' has been erased from the indictment of Esterhazy given to the president of his court martial. (*v.* 2 Jan 1898, n. 3) As to the *bordereau annoté*, no copy or trace of this document is found.

Oct 19   André delivers his report, presenting to the Prime Minister the newfound elements, which demonstrate the gravity of the situation. He concludes that he deliberately limited himself to enumerating the main elements (documents that had been hidden, falsified or forged and various schemes) confirming that a further investigation will bring many others to light.[24]

Sept 1   Lazare dies of cancer at the age of 38. Only a few people attend the funeral (4 September). Mathieu is present, Dreyfus is absent.[25]

Nov 21   André obtains the Government's permission to submit his report (of 19 October) to Ernest Vallé, Minister of Justice, who has the power to initiate a Revision Commission.

Nov 22   Jaurès informs Dreyfus that André's report is with the Minister of Justice.

The appeal of Dreyfus for a revision

Nov 26   Dreyfus sends Vallé an appeal for a revision of the Rennes verdict. The appeal (dated 25 November) is based on several arguments: Jaurès' disclosure of 'an audacious fabrication' (the *bordereau annoté*) which might have affected the decision of several judges; the false testimonies of Cernuski and Savignaud at the Rennes court martial;

von Münster's letter to Reinach attesting Schwartzkoppen's confession to his former ambassador that his contact was Esterhazy; and finally, the probable outcome of André's investigation.[26] (*v.* Appendix 44)

Nov 27   The Government decides that Vallé is to put forward a request to the Revision Commission.[27]

Dec 24   The Revision Commission states unanimously that there are grounds for a revision.

Dec 25   Vallé refers to Manuel Achille Baudouin, Principal State Prosecutor attached to the Supreme Court of Appeal, the results of André's investigation as well as Dreyfus' appeal for a revision of the Rennes verdict.[28]

Aug 1903–   Esterhazy, in London, acts as the London correspondent of *La Libre*
Jan 1906   *Parole* under the pseudonym Patrick Sullivan.[29]

1904
Jan 17   After a thorough examination of the Dreyfus case, Baudouin presents his application to commence proceedings before the Criminal Chamber. He concludes that the Rennes verdict was based on forged documents and invalid testimonies, confirming the Government's request for a revision of the case. The President of the Criminal Chamber, Jean-Antoine Chambareaud, appoints Pierre-Auguste Boyer as reporting judge of the case.

Jan 30   Mornard, Dreyfus' lawyer, submits his statement demanding that the Supreme Court of Appeal accept Dreyfus' appeal for a revision and proceed with a new investigation.[30]

Second revision: Criminal Chamber's hearing [31]

Mar 3–5   Boyer's report stipulates the need for a supplementary investigation. He dismisses the theory of Dreyfus and Mathieu on the passing of secret documents and the *bordereau annoté* to the judges at the Rennes court martial. Boyer retains as a 'new element' the forgery of Panizzardi's letters (the *faux Henry*). Baudouin also concludes on the need for a supplementary investigation of the case. Affirming that Dreyfus is innocent, Baudouin argues for a revision without a new trial. Mornard is the last to plead the case.[32]

Mar 5   The Criminal Chamber declares the appeal for revision admissible and orders a fresh investigation.[33]

Mar 13   Trarieux dies in Paris.

Second revision investigation: Criminal Chamber (7 March–19 November) [34]

The Chamber examines the files relating to the Affair and hears witnesses. Targe testifies to Gribelin's falsification, ordered by Henry, of the secret funds account books to conceal the dealings with Val Carlos. He confirms that Val Carlos was selling information to the General Staff. Targe also exhibits the various false documents he had uncovered in his investigation.[35] Gribelin, although attempting to deny the falsifications, when faced with the documents is obliged to admit them.[36] Val Carlos firmly denies he ever received monthly payments. He claims that he had only received from Henry the sum of 1500 francs, in several payments, which he was to transfer to Mestre Anabile, in Cuba, who spoke several languages and could be a valuable agent for the Deuxième Bureau.[37] Val Carlos also denies that he had stated in 1894 that there was a traitorous officer on the General Staff. (*v.* March 1894) This proves Guénée's falsification of his 1894 reports and that Henry's testimony at the first court martial of Dreyfus was false. Du Paty confirms that in 1894 Mercier asked him to write a memorandum (commentary) on the four documents included in the Secret Dossier. He claims that its content was dictated to him by Sandherr, then copied and subsequently altered by his superior officers. (*v.* Nov–Dec 1894, Du Paty's commentary, n. 99) He further confirms that it was on the instructions of Gonse that he entered into dealings with Esterhazy in 1897; that he was the author of the 'note in two hands'; (*v. c.* 20 Nov 1897) and that he had read and corrected the Dixi article. (*v.* 15 Nov 1897) He further admits giving to Esterhazy a draft of the first letter Esterhazy sent to President Faure (29 October 1897), but claims he was not involved with the Blanche and Speranza telegrams; that he never saw the *document libérateur* and believed that Esterhazy never received it; and that the *bordereau annoté* never existed.[38] The three experts from the Académie française, Jean-Gaston Darboux, Paul-Emile Appel and Henri Poincaré appointed to study Bertillon's theory on the *bordereau* deliver a report proving the absurdities of Bertillon's system.[39] Mercier continues to uphold Bertillon's theory, describing it as irrefutable; but has no evidence to give against Dreyfus. The previous Ministers of War and General Staff officers persist in their claim that Dreyfus is guilty. Their testimonies are vague, their previous arguments having been demolished.[40] Cuignet, resentful, casts doubt on the good faith of the Criminal Chamber, Delcassé, André and Targe, accusing them of ludicrous indiscretions and falsifications. Contradicting his testimony at the Rennes trial, Roget pays tribute to Picquart and withdraws many of the accusations he had formerly made against him.[41] Picquart gives evidence with his usual precision. He maintains his view that Weil was Esterhazy's accomplice or informer. (*v.* Aug 1896) He also reveals his disagreements with Mathieu and Demange, both of whom had asked him during the Rennes trial not to accuse the General Staff nor use the words 'false testimony' or 'fraud'.[42] The Chamber hears Weil, whose evidence does not help to clarify Picquart's view of Weil's complicity.[43] Reinach refers to his various correspondence and conversations with Tornielli and von Münster, who had repeatedly denied having any dealings with Dreyfus. He claims that he had established that in October 1897 Schwartzkoppen admitted to von Münster his connection to Esterhazy. Reinach also relates his investigation of Mme Bastian.[44]

The Chamber decides that while Targe's investigation found no evidence of a *bordereau annoté*, in view of its importance and the credence given to it during the Rennes court martial, a thorough examination of it should take place. All witnesses able to shed light on this mysterious document are called to testify.[45] The Chamber concludes that no such document ever existed (i.e. a *bordereau* annotated by the Kaiser, mentioning the name of Dreyfus). It further concludes that a forgery was probably fabricated by Henry or Lemercier-Picard and that one or several copies of this forged *bordereau annoté* must have circulated among General Staff officers and journalists before being destroyed.

The Chamber entrusts Judge Atthalin with the investigation of the testimony of Cernuski in the Rennes court martial. Atthalin interrogates numerous witnesses (Deuxième Bureau officers and Cernuski's accomplices: Przyborowski, Mathilde Baumler and Helmuth Wessel) in court and via rogatory letters. Cernuski, who had taken refuge in London, only agreed to send a letter to the Chamber. Cernuski withdraws his testimony given in Rennes, confirming it was false. Captain Mareschal admits having had contact with one of Cernuski's accomplices, Przyborowski, to whom he paid a sum of money from the secret funds. Following this admission, Atthalin extends the investigation to Dautriche, who is responsible for Deuxième Bureau accounts. Atthalin discovers traces of erasure which prove Dautriche had falsified the accounts to conceal certain significant remittances to secret agents. On 26 May 1904 Dautriche admits to his falsification.[46] Atthlain also interrogates General Galliffet and all the officers of the General Staff and Sûreté officers involved.

Before closing the investigation the Court examines the technical aspect of the *bordereau*. The relevant military authorities deliver a report which categorically refutes the validity of charge originally brought against Dreyfus on the basis of the *bordereau*. The report concludes that the language in which the *bordereau* was drawn up could never have been that of an artilleryman. It further states that the three 'notes' mentioned in the *bordereau* on new artillery were related to technical aspects tested in 1894 during manoeuvres in Châlons, where Esterhazy was present. It also concludes that the Firing Manual was not a confidential document and that the claim of the informer about difficulties in procuring it was solely a way of extracting a greater financial reward.[47]

Nov   In accordance with the Law of Dispossession (*v.* 1 March 1899), the Criminal Chamber forwards the case to the Combined Chambers of the Supreme Court of Appeal.[48]

Oct 28 &   Two turbulent sessions take place in the Chamber of Deputies over the
Nov 4   discovery of André's method of advancing the careers of Republican officers in the army, to the detriment of Royalist or Catholic officers.[49] Despite the scandal, the government of Combes secures a fragile majority of two votes. This leads, however, to the fall of Combes' Government.

Nov 15   André tenders his resignation.

1905

Jan 23   Combes resigns. A new Cabinet is formed, with Pierre Maurice Rouvier as Prime Minister.

May 14   Judge Clément Moras is appointed reporting judge for the revision of the case of Dreyfus before the Combined Chambers.[50]

Law of Separation of Church and State

July 3   After more than three years of debate and successive proposals, the bill for the separation of Church and State is finally passed in the Chamber of Deputies by 341 votes to 233. The law represents the culmination of Republican struggle against Nationalism, clericalism and antisemitism. The key figures in promoting the law are the Socialists Aristide Briand, Jean Jaurès and Francis de Presenssé (president of the Ligue des droits de l'homme et du citoyen since 1903).[51]

Sept 25   Death of Godefroy Cavaignac.

Nov 15   Eugène Etienne is appointed Minister of War.

Dec 9   The bill for the separation of Church and State is passed in the Senate by 181 votes to 102. It appears in the *Journal Officiel* and becomes law on 11 December.

Jean Jaurès

1906

Jan 17   The seven-year term of office of President Loubet ends. Armand Fallières, a left-wing candidate, is elected President of the Republic.

Mar 7   Prime Minister Rouvier resigns.

Mar 14   A new Cabinet is formed, with Jean Ferdinand Sarrien as Prime Minister. The new administration includes several dreyfusards – Louis Barthou, Aristide Briand, Raymond Poincaré and Georges Clemenceau.

May 6 & 20 General legislative elections are held. The Left's majority is strengthened; it now holds 420 seats. The Right and Centre lose more than 50 seats.

Second revision: Combined Chambers' hearing (15 June–12 July)[52]

June 15–16 The Combined Chambers examine the Secret Dossier in closed session.

June 18–22 The public hearings of the Combined Chambers are attended only by the Dreyfus family and a number of lawyers and former militants, including Demange, Mme Zola and Picquart.[53] Judge Moras reads his long report in four sessions. It forms a precise and meticulous analysis of the case. He asserts that the writing of the *bordereau* and its delivery are a crime and that it has never been proven that it was committed by Dreyfus. Demolishing one by one all the charges against Dreyfus, Moras concludes that Dreyfus is innocent. He enumerates three 'new elements' revealed by André's investigation.[54]

June 25– July 5 Baudouin presents his closing speech in eight sessions. It is an indictment of each and every one of those involved in the Affair, including Mercier, Du Paty, Cuignet, Gribelin and Gonse.[55] Baudouin enumerates six new elements in the case. He concludes by asking the Combined Chambers to quash the Rennes verdict *sans renvoi* (without a retrial).[56]

July 5–7 Mornard presents his conclusions, demonstrating that no charge remains against Dreyfus. Like Baudouin, and unlike his previous plea (*v.* 1 June 1899), Mornard appeals for the Rennes verdict to be quashed without retrial. He reveals that Dreyfus, seeking only to regain his honour, foregoes any monetary compensation due to him in law and simply requests that the Combined Chambers' ruling be published in the *Journal Officiel* and a number of newspapers.[57]

July 9 Picquart and Gonse fight a duel with pistols provoked by their conflict in 1896. (*v.* 15 Sept 1896) Gonse misses and Picquart does not fire.

Proclamation of the innocence of Dreyfus

July 12 Before a standing and hushed courtroom, Ballot-Beaupré reads the ruling of the Supreme Court of Appeal. It quashes the Rennes verdict without a new trial, pronounces the rehabilitation of Dreyfus and proclaims his innocence.[58]

July 13 The Chamber of Deputies discusses proposals for two bills: one to invest Dreyfus with the rank of chef d'escadron (major) with immediate effect and with the cross of the Legion of Honour; the other to reinstate Picquart in the army, promoting him retrospectively to the rank of Brigadier-General, as from 10 July 1903.[59] The Chamber approves the motion on Dreyfus by 432 to 32. The motion on Picquart is adopted by 449 votes to 26.[60]

The Chamber of Deputies passes a third bill by 316 votes to 165, which relates to the removal of Zola's ashes from Montmartre cemetery to the Pantheon.[61] (*v.* 4 June 1908)

The Senate discusses the two motions concerning Dreyfus and Picquart. Mercier dares to speak against the bill for the reintegration of Dreyfus into the army, accusing the Supreme Court of Appeal of irregularity, claiming that it did not study all the evidence. Indignant protests however remind him of the crimes he had committed in 1894. Mercier tries to respond but is jeered by the Senators. The bill is approved by 182 votes to 30. Picquart's reintegration is adopted by 184 to 26.[62]

In the Senate, Ernest Monis proposes a resolution on behalf of the left-wing groups: 'The Senate, wishing to pay tribute to the civic courage of two of its lamented former members, Auguste Scheurer-Kestner and Ludovic Trarieux, resolves that busts of these two great citizens will be placed in the gallery outside the Senate chamber.' The Senate approves the motion by 181 votes to 29. Mercier abstains.[63]

July 16 Leblois is appointed honorary mayor of the 7th arrondissement of Paris.

July 20 The Council of the Legion of Honour approves the Government's proposal for the decoration of Dreyfus. President Fallières decides that Targe is also to be decorated with the rosette of the Legion of Honour.

Exoneration of Dreyfus

July 21 Dreyfus' rehabilitation ceremony takes place in the Cour des jardins, a small courtyard at the Ecole militaire.[64] On the order of Etienne the ceremony is held in the presence of only a small number of witnesses – the Dreyfus family, Picquart, Baudouin, Anatole France, a number of journalists and photographers.[65] Two batteries of artillerymen and two squadrons of cuirassiers are lined up in the courtyard. The ceremony opens to the sound of trumpets. Both Dreyfus and Targe, in ceremonial uniform, take up their positions in front of General Gillain, commandant of the First Cavalry Division. Gillain decorates Targe. He turns to Dreyfus. Lowering his sword onto the shoulder of Dreyfus he announces: 'In the name of the President of the Republic, and by virtue of the powers invested in me, I appoint you, Major Dreyfus,

Chevalier of the Legion of Honour.' To the sound of a brass band, the troops march forward. They raise their sabres and salute Dreyfus as they pass in front of him. Congratulatory shouts are heard from the witnesses: 'Long live Dreyfus!', 'Vive Picquart!' Dreyfus replies: 'Long live the Republic!', 'Long live Truth.'[66] (*v.* Appendix 45)

July 25   Reinach presents Dreyfus to President Fallières. Dreyfus tells the President that he intends to retire from the army the following year.[67]

Oct 25   A new Cabinet is formed with George Clemenceau as Prime Minister. Clemenceau appoints Brigadier-General Picquart as Minister of War.[68]

Late Nov   Dreyfus makes formal requests to Picquart for promotion to the rank of lieutenant-colonel, Believing his seniority entitles him to this rank. Picquart rejects the request.[69]

During 1906   Esterhazy and the French journalist Paul Desachy begin a voluminous correspondence.[70] (Desachy was a dreyfusard but had won Esterhazy's confidence. In Esterhazy's letter to him he divulges many details about his life.)[71]

NOTES

1   The book ran into several editions, with different prefaces and commentaries: e.g.: Paris: J.J. Pauvert, 1965 (introduced by J.-P. Legal); Paris: Garnier-Flamarion, 1969 (chronology and preface by C. Becker); Paris: Imprimerie national, 1992 (introduced with comments by J.D. Bredin).

2   When in Rennes, Dreyfus had already begun to receive tempting contracts from English and American literary agents, but he decided to publish his memoirs in France. The publisher Pierre-Victor Stock, who had been devoted to the Dreyfus cause and had already issued hundreds of publications supporting the cause from the very beginning of the Affair, (*v.* pp. 484–8, Publications of P.-V. Stock on the Dreyfus Affair) was offended that Dreyfus chose another publisher for his work. The book was an immediate success and was soon translated into many languages. It has been noted with surprise the absence of any references to his Judaism or to the antisemitism, which was one of the main elements of the Affair.

3   The other six volumes were published between 1901 and 1906. Dreyfus and Reinach corresponded throughout 1900, sharing information with each other for their respective publications. After Reinach's fourth volume was published in 1904 Labori criticized the work, describing it in parts as erroneous, and misleading. Labori's notes on Reinach's four volumes were shown to Picquart who completed his listing of Reinach's erroneous information or misinterpretation. Labori, *Labori. Ses Notes manuscrites. Sa vie*, pp. 343–61. Nevertheless, the six volumes of Reinach's history of the Affair remains the most significant and most detailed historical work on the Affair.

4   The correspondence was published in the same year in the pamphlet *Lettres de M. Scheurer-Kestner et de M. Leblois. Août-octobre 1897,* by the Ligue des droits de l'homme et du citoyen.

5   The Amnesty Law allowed Henry's widow to transfer the case from criminal to civil jurisdiction. This also applied to Picquart's suit against *Le Jour* and to that of the handwriting experts accused by Zola.

6   The Court decided on this symbolic amount having concluded that Reinach's articles were published 'in good faith', without intending to harm Henry's memory.

7   On 27 June a decree ordered the closure of 120 establishments of religious education; on 7 July 1904 a law forbade all teaching by religious congregations; such congregations were subsequently dissolved. In total about 30,000 members of religious communities left France. On 30 July diplomatic relations with the Vatican and France were broken. J. Baubérot, *Histoire de la laïcité française* (Paris: PUF 'Que sais-je', 2000), pp. 81–9.

8   Rumours that Zola was murdered by right-wing Nationalists were dispelled by the autopsy, which determined that he had died of carbon monoxide poisoning. However, whether his death was a mere accident remains unresolved, especially since one of the flues leading to his room, although recently cleaned, was found blocked.

9   Zola's death prompted a wave of criticism and slanders in the press. Worried that Dreyfus' presence at the funeral would provoke demonstrations, Mme Zola, Reinach and the Paris Prefect of Police urged him not to attend. Dreyfus insisted on paying his respects to Zola's memory. *DFA*, pp. 299–300.

10   The speech was published in *L'Aurore* of 6 October 1902. See extracts in English in Burns, *France and the Dreyfus Affair*, pp. 167–8.

11   Since the Rennes verdict Mathieu had suspected that, as in the first court martial, secret documents were shown to the Court during its deliberation. In this case he suspected also that photographs of the *bordereau annoté*, which he was convinced was an outright forgery, were shown. Mathieu found out which two members of the Court voted in favour of the acquittal (Jouaust and Bréon). When Mathieu approached Jouaust via a friend asking for a formal statement of what had happened during the deliberation, Jouaust only agreed to say that he was writing his memoirs and that the truth will be known after his death. Jouaust, however, never published his memoirs. Informed that Merle changed his mind at the last minute and voted against the acquittal, Mathieu decided to approach him. *ATQV*, pp. 279–85.

12   *3ème Cass.*, III, 293–6, Dumas. According to Dumas' letter, when Merle was questioned as to whether there was any truth in the story of a *bordereau*, on heavy paper, annotated by the Kaiser and mentioning Dreyfus' name, he was dumbfounded and replied: 'What? What are you saying? … Don't talk about such an affair. You must never talk about it. This affair could resurface.' Despite Dumas' insistence on getting more information, Merle refused. When called to testify before the Criminal Chamber in 1904, Merle deemed Dumas letter as 'pure imagination'. *3ème Cass.*, III, 298, Merle. However, Mathieu mentioned that on receiving a registered letter from Dumas containing a record of their conversations, Merle did not issue a formal denial. *ATQV*, pp. 285–6.

13   An unknown author working in Paris at the time of the Dreyfus Affair (probably 1897) began writing the antisemitic forgery to be known as the *Protocols of the Learned elders of Zion*. It claimed to record an alleged conference of the leaders of world Jewry to achieve world domination but in reality it was an adaptation of an old French pamphlet by Maurice Joly on Napoleon III and other antisemitic tracts. Published in its full version in Russia in 1905 appended to a religious tract by Serge Nilus. The Protocols have been denounced as a blatant forgery and established as such by court proceedings in Berne in 1934. It has been translated into numerous languages and still being published and has become the classic of antisemitic literature. The first translations of the protocols into English and other languages included the word '*Learned*'. *Encyclopaedia Judaica* (Jerusalem: Keter, 1978), vol. 6, cl. 581–3. See also N. Cohn, *Warrant for Genocide, the myth of the Jewish world-conspiracy and the Protocols of the Elders of Zion* (London: Eyre & Spottiswoode, 1967). H. Ben-Itto, *The Lie That Wouldn't Die: The Protocols of the Elders of Zion*, Preface by Lord Wolf; Foreword by Edward R. Korman (London: Vallentine Mitchell, 2005).

14   Only notes exist for the fourth volume, which was to be entitled *Justice*.

15   Syveton was an ardent anti-dreyfusard and treasurer of the Ligue de la patrie française. In the May 1902 elections he was elected by a large majority in the 2nd arrondissement. Because of a poster issued by Jules Lemaître during the campaign which referred to Waldeck-Rousseau's administration as 'the Ministry of Foreigners', a parliamentary commission was appointed to investigate the validity of Syveton's election. Its report, supporting his election, reached the Chamber on 6 April. Jaurès had been planning for several months to use this opportunity to raise the issue of the Dreyfus Affair and ask the Government to open a new investigation into the case. He consulted Waldeck-Rousseau, Clemenceau, Combes and Brisson, who all gave their approval and support. In February 1902 Jaurès gave an outline of his intended speech to Dreyfus, who found it appropriate.

16   The speech of Jaurès was published in full in J. Jaurès, *Le Faux impérial: discours prononcé à la Chambre des députés, séances des 6 et 7 avril 1903* (Paris: Société nouvelle de librairie et d'édition, 1903).

17   According to Dreyfus, the intervention had been planned between Brisson and Jaurès. A. Dreyfus, *Souvenirs et correspondance publiés par son fils*, p. 353.

18   Cavaignac was insulted by many left-wing Deputies. Aristide Briand, hinting at Cavaignac's complicity in Henry's death, shouted: 'You sent the razor to Henry.' Cavaignac made an impassioned speech against the revival of the revisionists and the scheming of the Republicans.

19   In this confused session the Chamber also approved (by 281 votes to 228) a second motion by Jaurès, declaring Syveton's election to the Chamber invalid. Syveton was re-elected on 21 June 1903.

20   Combes and Mornard suggested that Dreyfus should wait until the Ministers clarified the implication of the motion. However, Dreyfus decided to take the risk and lodge his appeal. The 'new elements' on which Dreyfus based his appeal were the allegations in the Rennes court martial of the *bordereau annoté* and Cernuski's false testimony. *AD*, pp. 947–9.

21   These documents included (1) A report by Colonel Paul Phillipe Alexandre de Fontenillat of his conversation with Panizzardi on 6 November 1897, when the latter had given his word of honour that neither he nor Schwartzkoppen had ever had dealings with Dreyfus; (2) A note written by Henry giving the translation of a coded telegram sent from the Italian General Staff to Panizzardi on 31 December 1894 (after Dreyfus' conviction) instructing Panizzardi to cease relations temporarily with

an unnamed dubious person (the date of this telegram proves that the agent with whom Panizzardi had been in contact could not have been Dreyfus); (3) a note written by Henry confirming that he had received a letter from a Deuxième Bureau agent (Edmond Lajoux) in April 1895, with a recognizable description of Esterhazy as the informer in Schwartzkoppen's pay; (4) three of Schwartzkoppen's notes on the master plans. These confirmed that he had already received them in 1892 (long before Dreyfus' attachment to the General Staff as an officer on probation) and that this traffic continued after the arrest of Dreyfus. All these documents are published in *3ème Cass.*, I, 8–20.

22   These were (1) Panizzardi's letter to Schwartzkoppen including the phrase 'P ... has brought me many interesting things' in which Henry had erased the letter 'P' and substituted 'D' (this was one of the items read by Cavaignac in the Chamber of Deputies on 7 July 1898); (2) Panizzardi's letter to Schwartzkoppen on the organization of railways, dated 28 March 1895, which date was changed by Henry and Gribelin to April 1894. (*v.* Sept–Oct 1897, Consolidation of the Secret Dossier) *3ème Cass.*, I, 20–1.

23   Report (dated 4 November 1903) of Louis-Charles Crétin, Contrôleur général of the army, who was appointed to assist André's investigation. *3ème Cass*, I, 21–6.

24   *3ème Cass.*, I, 5–10. See also *AD*, pp. 950–3.

25   Lazare's friends erected a modest monument to his memory in Nîmes. (*v.* 11 Feb 1908, n. 4) In 1910 Charles Péguy published a poignant portrait of Lazare in *Notre Jeunesse*. An English translation can be found in A. Aronowitz, *Jews and Christians on Time & Eternity. Charles Péguy's portrait of Bernard Lazare* (Stanford: Stanford University Press, 1998), pp. 44–71. (*v.* Appendix 49)

26   *3ème Cass*, I, 26–38. Dreyfus was aware of the results of André's investigation from Jaurès, who had been informed of them unofficially. Dreyfus wrote the appeal with Mornard after consulting his friends, including Reinach, Demange, Leblois and Mornard.

27   The Government hesitated on how to proceed, fearing questions in the Chamber on André's investigation, which was to be considered 'personal' (*v.* 21 April 1903). For legal purposes, the request therefore only retained as new elements the two forgeries found by André in the Secret Dossier.

28   *3ème Cass.*, I, 38–44. Also in *AD*, pp. 954–9.

29   Esterhazy's articles for *La Libre Parole* appeared intermittently. He wrote on various subjects, including the Zionist movement (3 September 1903) as well as Jews and antisemitism in England (17 and 22 August; 8 September; 1 November 1903). He was very modestly remunerated. In 1906, after Dreyfus was reintegrated into the army, Drumont ended his collaboration with his London correspondent Esterhazy-Sullivan. Thomas, *Esterhazy*, 372–3.

30   The text was written by Dreyfus and completed by Mornard. See *AD*, pp. 960–2.

31   The records of the hearings were published in *Déb. Cas. 1904.* (*v.* Abbreviations and Conventions) This volume also contains Baudouin's written closing speech (of 17 January).

32   A few days before the hearing Labori informed Mornard that he agreed to be involved in the Affair again. Remembering Labori's harsh attitude towards Dreyfus, Mornard refused. Demange, Labori and Picquart were present at the public hearing. According to Reinach there was an incident: when Mornard's speech emphasized the shy and sensitive personality of Dreyfus, which he declared Demange and Labori could confirm, Labori left the courtroom. This incident is mentioned in *HAD*, 6, p. 293 but not in Labori's notes (published by his wife): *Labori. Ses notes maniscrites. Sa vie.*

33   For the text of the ruling see *AD*, pp. 962–3.

34   Only the main elements of the investigation are given here. The full records were published in *3ème Cass.* (3 vols).

35   *3ème Cass.*, I, 61–182; II, 727–47; 760–78, Targe.

36   *3ème Cass.*, I, 182–212; II, 657–75, Gribelin.

37   *3ème Cass.*, I, 219–24; II, 373–87, Val Carlos.

38   *3ème Cass.*, I, 233–97, 366–76; II, 675–727, Du Paty.

39   *3ème Cass.*, III, 500–600, Graphologists' report.

40   *3ème Cass.*, I, 298–353, Gonse; I, 376–437, 459–64; II, 140–4, Mercier; I, 501–26, Zurlinden; I, 668–96, Billot; I, 723–48, Boisdeffre; II, 394–530, Cuignet.

41   *3ème Cass.*, II, 158–213, Roget.

42   *3ème Cass.*, II, 249–79, 291–309, 530–51, Picquart.

43   *3ème Cass.*, II, 309–30, Weil.

44   *3ème Cass.*, II, 88, 128, Reinach. The Chamber also interrogated the officers of the General Staff and the agents of the Sûreté involved in the disappearance of Mme Bastian during the Rennes court martial. Mme Bastian was heard as well.

45   The Chamber interrogated Casimir-Périer, Hanotaux, Dupuy, Jaurès, Dr Dumas, Major Merle, Baron Stoffel, the various journalists who spread the rumour Rochefort and Millevoye (Papillaud from *La Libre Parole* refused to testify). All the military witnesses, when asked about the *bordereau annoté,*

confirmed they had only heard about it during the Rennes trial, and believed it never existed.

46 *3ème Cass.*, III, 80–265. After Dautriche's admission, he was arrested and sent to Cherche-Midi and an investigation was opened by Captain Vidal Cassel. Cassel ordered the arrest of the other officers involved in the monetary irregularities, Mareschal, François and Rollin. In his concluding report, Cassel argued for the case to be dismissed for lack of evidence. However, General Jean-Edouard Dessirier, Military Governor of Paris, ordered Dautriche to be court-martialled on 8 October 1904. At the end of the court martial (7 November) all the officers were acquitted. The proceedings were published in *Procès Dautriche* (8 October–7 November 1904) (Paris: Société nouvelle de librairie et d'édition, 1904).

47 *3ème Cass.*, II, 733–47, Targe.

48 Ballot-Beaupré, President of the Supreme Court of Appeal, nominated three reporting judges, all of whom declined to act for reasons of health. (*v.* 14 May 1905)

49 In order to learn about the conduct of the army officers, Captain Mollin, André's aide-de-camp, a Freemason (and son-in-law of Anatole France), sought the assistance of the Masonic lodges. Over four years a 25,000-card index was assembled, which was divided into two categories: 'Corinthe' (officers who were promoted) and 'Carthage' (officers whose careers were damaged). The discovery of this '*affaire des fiches*' created scandal and confusion. Jaurès defended André, recalling that he had been appointed after the Rennes court martial in order to restore Republican spirit in the army. During the Chamber's 4 November session, André was attacked by Nationalist Deputy Syveton. This was praised by Déroulède and Barrès. On the evening following Syveton's appearance in court, he was found dead. The Nationalist press claimed the death as a 'Masonic crime'.

50 Baudouin and Mornard had by that time already written their statements. Moras completed his statement by December 1905. Yet 12 months separated the appointment of Moras and the meeting of the Combined Chambers. (*v.* 18 June 1906) Baudouin's conclusions were published in *La Révision du procès de Rennes. Réquisitoire écrit de M. le procureur général Baudouin (de 1905)* (Paris: Ligue française des droits de l'homme, 1907). Mornard's statement was published in *La Révision du procès de Rennes. Mémoire de Maître Henri Mornard pour M. Alfred Dreyfus (de 1905)* (Paris: Ligue française des droits de l'homme, 1907).

51 See J. Baubérot, *Vers un nouveau pacte laïque* (Paris: Seuil, 1990), pp. 49–80. Larkin, *Church and State after the Dreyfus Affair*, pp. 111–16; 144–69.

52 The records of these sessions were published in *Déb. Cass., 1906* (2 vols). (*v.* Abbreviations and Conventions) The Dreyfus case finally reached the courts more than two years after his appeal for a revision (*v.* 26 Nov 1903), and more than a year since the case was transferred to the Combined Chambers (19 Nov 1904). These long delays were probably due to the juridical debate whether or not Dreyfus should be sent to a third court martial. There were also political considerations: the debate over the Law of Separation (*v.* 3 July & 9 Dec 1905); the conflict with Germany over Morocco; the Government preference to delay until the General Elections (May 1906). Picquart and Clemenceau continued the campaign for justice, claiming that Dreyfus was to be judged by his peers and not by civilians. Picquart exhibited some of his antisemitism: in *La Gazette de Lausanne* (2 April 1906) he remarked that 'the best share of the booty [of the Affair] has gone to the Jews who have been promoted, particularly in the army'. This article was quoted by Drumont in *La Libre Parole*.

53 Ballot-Beaupré was President of the three courts. The Civil Chamber was chaired by Albert Sarut, one of Scheurer-Kestner's former advisors; the Criminal Chamber by Alphonse Bard (reporting judge for the Dreyfus case in 1898); the Appeals Court by Louis Tanon. Labori was not present. Mathieu attempted to shake hands with Picquart, but Picquart refused.

54 These were: the letter in which the letter 'D' was substituted for the letter 'P'; the falsification of the date on Panizzardi's letter on railway organization; and the rediscovery of the note on artillery. *Déb. Cass., 1906*, I, 5–368, Moras' report.

55 Baudouin's address revived public interest and provoked protest. Cuignet protested before the Minister of Justice; Zurlinden and Gonse published public protests; Du Paty filed a complaint before the Minister of Justice and published an open letter to Ballot-Beaupré in *La Libre Parole*; Drumont published a furious letter sent by Esterhazy from London (*v.* Appendix 46) and challenged Mercier to respond to the accusation in Ballot-Beaupré's indictment. Obliged to react, Mercier sent a letter to Ballot-Beaupré (6 July), protesting only against some minor points. All these protests are published in *Déb. Cass., 1906*, II, 666–85.

56 *Déb. Cass., 1906*, I, 369–639; II, 5–272, Baudouin's closing speech.

57 *Déb. Cass., 1906*, II, 273–480, Mornard's conclusions.

58 *Déb. Cass., 1906*, II, 481–502. See also *AD*, pp. 981–1000. The annulment of the Rennes verdict, without retrial, was voted by 31 to 18. The proclamation announcing Dreyfus innocent of all charges was voted unanimously. In order to reach the decision not to send Dreyfus before a third court martial, the Court formulated its own interpretation of Article 445 of the Criminal Code which stipulated that a verdict of no retrial was only possible when the accused was dead or no punishable crime existed after the judgement, i.e. if no treason had been perpetrated in 1894. The Court's

decision was political. It was highly criticized in the Nationalist press, which described the proceedings of the Supreme Court of Appeal as 'illegal' and 'falsified'. For L'Action française, the verdict fuelled a new campaign which was to continue until World War I. Article 445 became their rallying cry in their attacks on the Republic. (*v.* 11 Sept 1908) (Martin, 'The Dreyfus Affair and the Corruption of the French Legal System', pp. 47–8; E. Weber, *Action Française*, pp. 39–42). The judgement stipulated that the verdict was to be advertised in Paris and Rennes, and published in the *Journal Officiel* as well as five other newspapers. Dreyfus was further authorized to publish the verdict in 50 newspapers of his choice at the Government's expense.

59   These proposals treated Picquart and Dreyfus differently, favouring the former. While Picquart regained the seniority he would normally have reached, Dreyfus' career was damaged. Dreyfus considered this a further injustice. If he had not been convicted, he would already have been promoted to major in 1901 and would probably have become a lieutenant-colonel soon after. (*v.* Appendix 47) The Minister's proposals probably influenced by Clemenceau, who had lost interest in Dreyfus after the pardon. But Etienne also took into account the degree of indulgence toward Dreyfus that the army and Government would tolerate: his reintegration was primarily a political necessity. *DFA*, pp. 311–12.

60   *Déb. Cass., 1906*, II, 508–30. A tumultuous debate followed a proposal by Deputy Pressensé to sanction officers found guilty of fraud and criminal acts after the amnesty of 1900. Sarrien (both Prime Minister and Minister of Justice) denounced these criminal acts but refused the proposal, preferring to pursue a policy of 'pacification and social calm'. Pressensé's proposal was rejected by 338 votes to 194. *Déb. Cass., 1906*, II, 554–89.

61   *Déb. Cass., 1906*, II, 590–9. The Senate passed the bill on 12 December 1906, by 150 to 107. *Déb. Cass., 1906*, II, 610–65. Because of Nationalist protests and administrative delays, the transfer only took place in spring 1908.

62   *Déb. Cass., 1906*, II, 530–46.

63   *Déb. Cass., 1906*, II, 503–7. All these debates in the Chamber of Deputies and the Senate of July 1906 are also published in *Jean Jaurès Cahiers trimestriels 147 : Le parlement et l'Affaire Dreyfus. Douze années pour la vérité (1894–1906)* (Paris: Assemblée nationale ; Société d'étude Jaurésienne, 1998).

64   At first Reinach had proposed that the ceremony should take place in the grand Cour Morland, the location of Dreyfus' ceremony of degradation 11 years earlier; Dreyfus declined because he was afraid that his memories would overwhelm him.

65   Mornard, Demange, Reinach, Jaurès and André were not informed about the ceremony.

66   At the close of the ceremony, after shaking hands with and embracing all the witnesses including Picquart and his children, Dreyfus was overwhelmed by emotion. He began to suffer sharp pains in his chest and asked to be escorted home. A. Dreyfus, *Souvenirs et correspondences publiés par son fils*, pp. 434–7;

67   Dreyfus was appointed major in the artillery, first in Vincennes (east of Paris), then in Saint-Denis (north of Paris).

68   Picquart was informed of his appointment while at the Vienna State Opera listening to Wagner's *Tristan and Isolde* conducted by Gustav Mahler. Picquart was a pianist himself and a fine musician. A. Mahler, *Gustav Mahler, Memories and Letters,* trans. B. Creighton (New York: Viking Press, 1946), p. 93.

69   Having served as artillery major for some months, Dreyfus appealed for promotion – he could no longer tolerate the fact that his five years on Devil's Island were discounted from his career record. Picquart, who had already received requests for Dreyfus' promotion from other quarters, including Reinach and Zola, believed that the campaign for his promotion was organized by Dreyfus himself. *DFA*, p. 325.

70   Desachy had already published two major works on the Dreyfus Affair in 1905: *Répertoire de l'Affaire Dreyfus 1894–1899* (a detailed chronology) and *Bibliographie de l'affaire Dreyfus* (including 728 titles).

71   Just before the beginning of World War I, Esterhazy bequeathed his papers to Desachy on condition that they would be transferred to the Bibliothèque Nationale de France (BNF) after Desachy's death. The Esterhazy–Desachy papers may be consulted at the BNF's *Fonds des nouvelles acquisitions françaises.*

Part 10

LEGACIES, MEMORIES and REPERCUSSIONS

1907–2006

Theodor Herzl in Basel, by the Rhine

1907	Pathé produces *L'Affaire Dreyfus*, a new film on the Dreyfus Affair,[1] directed by Lucien Nonguet. The screenplay is by Z. Rollini, a pseudonym of the brother of Ferdinand Zecca, Pathé's main director. The film is dreyfusard and the first to show a 'happy ending' to the Affair, with a reconstruction of the solemn military ceremony reintegrating Dreyfus into the French Army.[2] (*v.* 1915)
July 26	Dreyfus submits his request to Picquart for retirement and a pension fitting with his seniority.
Oct 25	Dreyfus retires from the army with the rank of captain, and with a pension of 2350 francs for his period of service (30 years, 10 months and 24 days).[3]
1908 **Feb 11**	A statue in honour of Scheurer-Kestner is erected in the Jardins du Luxembourg. Those present include President Fallières and members of the Government, presidents of the Senate and of the Chamber of Deputies, Brisson and Clemenceau.[4]
Mar 21	Maurras transforms the *Revue de L'Action française* into a daily newspaper of the same name, described as the 'organ of Nationalism'. The first issue calls upon all good Frenchmen to oppose the Republic.[5]

Transfer of Zola's ashes to the Pantheon/Assassination attempt on Dreyfus

June 3	Hundreds of Nationalists march through the Quartier Latin in Paris shouting 'Spit on Zola'. In *L'Action française* Léon Daudet begins his attack on 'foreigners within the country'. He calls on 'patriotic students' to demonstrate the following day against the transfer of Zola's ashes to the Pantheon.[6]
June 4	Official ceremony for the transfer of Zola's ashes to the Pantheon. Dreyfus with his family and other dreyfusards including Clemenceau, Picquart and Jaurès attend the ceremony. A crowd of student supporters of L'Action française greet the arrival of President Fallières with shouts of 'Down with Zola!', 'Down with Dreyfus!' During the ceremony, Louis-Anthelme Grégori, a 66–year-old military journalist and admirer of Drumont, fires two shots at Dreyfus. Dreyfus is wounded in the upper left arm.[7] (*v.* 11 Sept 1908)
June 5	The Nationalist press acclaims Grégori's assassination attempt as 'a courageous attack', 'a very French gesture', 'a patriotic achievement'. Dreyfusard newspapers condemn it as 'the most odious and cowardly assault'.
June 6	The actress Sarah Bernhardt writes to Dreyfus:

> *You have suffered again. We have cried again. But you should no longer suffer, and we should no longer cry. The flag of truth is placed in the hand of the illustrious man resting under the [Pantheon's] glorious arches … Suffer no more, our dear martyr. Look around you, close by, then farther on and farther on still*

> *and see this crowd of people who love you and defend you against*
> *cowardice, lies, and the quest to forget. Your friend is among*
> *them.*[8]

Sept 11   Grégori is arraigned before the Seine Assize Court. In his defence he argues that he 'did not aim at Dreyfus but at dreyfusism', and that 'it was a purely symbolic act'. Grégori brandishes as his 'talisman' Article 445 of the Criminal Code, which since 1906 had symbolized for anti-dreyfusards the 'illegality' of the Republic's conduct in 1906. (*v.* 12 July 1906, n.58) The jury unanimously acquits Grégori by answering 'no' to the four questions presented to them: 'Is Grégori guilty of attempting to murder Dreyfus?'; 'Was the attempt premeditated?'; 'Is Grégori guilty of wounding and shooting the person of Dreyfus?'; 'Were the wounding and shooting premeditated?' Applause bursts out in the courtroom, with shouts of 'Vive le jury! Vive la Nation!' [9]

The Camelots du Roi

Nov 16   Maurice Pujo founds the Camelots du Roi as an auxiliary group to L'Action française. The Camelots are young Royalists, mainly recruited from the wealthy 17th arrondissement of Paris. They also include working-class supporters, such as butchers and carpenters. They assist student members of L'Action française in selling copies of the group's daily paper. The Camelots are equipped with hawker's licences from the police.[10] (*v.* 1911 & 1931 theatre riots)

End of 1908   Esterhazy, under the name of Fitzgerald, settles in the village of Harpenden in Hertfordshire, 30 kilometres north of London. He takes lodgings with Mr and Mrs Humphrey. Esterhazy shares his life there with Mme de Voilement, whom he has recently met.[11]

1909   Publication of *Précis de l'Affaire Dreyfus* by Colonels Larpent and Delebecque (under the pseudonym of Dutrait-Crozon), dedicated anti-dreyfusards and supporters of L'Action française. The rationale behind the book inspired by Major Cuignet is that the reintegration of Dreyfus into the army and Picquart's appointment as Minister of War are humiliating for the French Army and a sign of its decadence.

Feb   A gang of 60 youths from the Camelots du Roi attempt to force their way into the apartment of Dreyfus in Paris, shouting 'We must have the Jew!' The demonstrators reach the lift, which they vandalize, before they are evicted.

July   Collapse of the Clemenceau Government.

         Picquart takes up command of the 2nd Army corps in Amiens.

May 29   Congress of the Ligue des droits de l'homme in Rennes. (*v.* Appendix 51)

1910

June 30   Labori is appointed President of the Bar in Paris.

End of 1910   Esterhazy, assuming the name of Count Jean de Voilemont, moves to a cottage in Harpenden.

1911	In Paris the Comédie française performs *Après moi* by the Jewish playwright Henri Bernstein. The Camelots du Roi demonstrate both inside and outside the theatre. Their protest is largely antisemitic. After two days the play is withdrawn. The *Paris Daily Mail* declares that antisemitism is a political weapon wielded by two minorities, L'Action française and a handful of revolutionaries.[12]
1913	Roget Martin du Gard publishes the novel *Jean Barois*, which summarises the experiences of young intellectuals during the Dreyfus Affair. It is firmly based on the historical documents available at the time.
Mar	Léon Daudet, one of the main figures of *L'Action française* since 1904, publishes *L'Avant-Guerre* ('Before the War'). It accuses Germans and 'German-Jewish spies' of preparing the ground for an enemy invasion. It is a publishing success, selling 25,000 copies.
May 15	Esterhazy, alias Count Jean de Voilemont, purchases a large property, in Harpenden.[13]
1914 **Jan 19**	Picquart is killed in a riding accident. He is given a state funeral.

Outbreak of World War I

June 28	Assassination of Archduke Franz Ferdinand, Crown Prince of the Austro-Hungarian Empire, in Sarajevo by Gavrilo Princip, a member of a secret Bosnian nationalist organization.
July 28	Austria-Hungary mobilizes and declares war on Serbia.
July 31	Assassination of Jean Jaurès by Raoul Villain, a 20-year-old member of L'Action française.
	General mobilization in Germany.
Aug 1	General mobilization in France. Germany declares war on Russia.
	Emile Dreyfus, son of Mathieu, joins the 32nd Artillery in Fontainebleau. Ado Reinach, Mathieu Dreyfus' son-in-law (son of Joseph and husband of Marguerite Dreyfus, Mathieu's daughter, married in 1912) enlists in the Meuse region (between Bar-le-Duc and Verdun); Pierre Dreyfus, son of Alfred enlists with the 7th Artillery and is stationed near the German border.[14]
Aug 2	Alfred Dreyfus receives his mobilization orders. He is posted as artillery officer in the fortified zone north of Paris, near Saint-Denis.
Aug 3	Germany declares war on France.

The Dreyfus family during World War I (1915–18)

Emile Dreyfus is wounded by a shell during the battle of Champagne on 27 September 1915. He dies from war wounds on 22 October, a few days after he is named Chevalier of the Legion of Honour.

Ado Reinach is reported missing at the end of August 1914. His fate cannot be ascertained. Eugène Naville, Director of the International Agency of Prisoners of War, asserts that all search efforts have failed. Pierre Dreyfus serves throughout the war and fights in some of the fiercest battles including those of the Oise, Champagne, and Verdun. In August 1914 he participates in the French invasion of Mulhouse, which then becomes French territory after a lapse of 44 years. This lasts for only 48 hours, before it is recaptured by the Germans. In 1918 Pierre is wounded by poison gas, but returns to the front after six weeks. Pierre obtains five promotions and three citations for courage in combat.[15]

1915   In the midst of the battles of World War I, Heinrich Mann writes an essay to be published in Rene Schickele's *White Sheets*. It is a 'hymn' to Zola.

The French Government bans all motion pictures on the Dreyfus Affair as part of its policy of suppressing political conflict during the war. The two French films on the subject, those of Méliès (1899) and Nonguet (1907) are banned.[16]

1916
Dec 3   Death of Du Paty de Clam at the age 63; his death is the result of war wounds at the battle of the Marne and other battles.

1917
Jan 8   Schwartzkoppen, after active combat on the Eastern Front from the beginning of the war, and having suffered from war wounds, is taken ill. He is sent to Berlin and enters the Elisabeth Hospital, where he dies. Just before his death he cries out in delirium: 'Frenchmen, listen to me! Dreyfus is innocent! He has never committed anything. It was all intrigue and fraud. Dreyfus is innocent.'[17]

Feb   Dreyfus is posted to the Eastern Front. At the side of his son Pierre he takes part in the 'Nivelle offensive' at Verdun. He also fights in the battle of the Chemin des Dames.

Feb 6   Death of Edouard Drumont at the age of 73. Hundreds of mourners attend the funeral at the cemetery of Père-Lachaise.[18]

July   Dreyfus returns to his original post near Paris.

Nov 16   Georges Clemenceau is elected Prime Minister for the second time. He plays a significant role in the victory of France in World War I and becomes known as *Père-la-Victoire*.

Esterhazy–Waverly–Smith articles (1911–1917)

Esterhazy, alias Waverly, publishes 'The unknown England', a series of articles in *L'Eclair*, the paper owned by Ernest Judet. All the articles – on a variety of subjects such as prostitution in London, the social situation, Irish nationalism and many others – are tinged with Esterhazy's strong criticism of and hostility towards England. When World War I breaks out, Judet cannot order another series from

Esterhazy. It is only in 1915 that he engages Esterhazy again to write in his newspaper but on a less regular basis and on condition that he changes the anti-British tone of his articles, as England and France are now allies. He may however, express his pro-German sentiments. In October Judet himself is suspected of being involved with German agents. He flees to Switzerland, from where he continues to manage his paper. Esterhazy continues his involvement but as 'Mr Smith'. At the end of 1917 Judet is forced to sell the paper. The new owner, René Wertheimer, changes the paper's policy and puts an end to the collaboration of most of its former correspondents, including that of Esterhazy–Waverley–Smith.[19]

1918
Sept   Dreyfus is promoted lieutenant-colonel in the reserves.

Nov 11   The Armistice is signed. End of World War I.

1919
Jan 12   Opening of the Paris Peace Conference. The conference is to discuss the postwar world. Political leaders of 32 countries attend.

June 28   Signature of the Treaty of Versailles, a peace settlement imposed on Germany by the Allied powers. It demands heavy reparations from Germany, territorial, military, financial and general. Clemenceau plays a prominent role in formulating the treaty.

July   Dreyfus becomes Officer of the Legion of Honour.

1921
Apr 19   Death of Joseph Reinach.

1923
May 21   Death of Esterhazy, alias Count Jean de Voilemont. He is buried in Kent.[20] His last words to his daughter Everilda state: 'No one knows, no one will ever know the truth about the Dreyfus Affair' and refer to its 'terrible secret'.[21]

1924
May–June   Victory of the Cartel des Gauches, a left-wing coalition led by Edouard Herriot, who becomes Prime Minster.

1925
Feb 11   Death of Demange.

                  A statue is erected in the memory of Zola in the Avenue Emile Zola, in Paris.

1926
Dec   Pope Pius XI condemns L'Action française. The publications of Charles Maurras are placed on the Index.[22]

1927   25th anniversary of Zola's death. In a commemorative speech at the Sorbonne, Edouard Herriot (then Minister of Education) describes

Zola as an 'athlete of the novel', who had always provoked criticism and who had referred to himself 'as the steward of his time'.

1929

Nov 24   Death of Georges Clemenceau.

Nov 25   Première of 'René Kestner's' play *Die Affäre Dreyfus*, at the Berlin Volksbuehne. 'Kestner' was the pseudonym chosen by authors W. Herzog and H.G. Rehfisch as a sign of respect for Scheurer-Kestner.[23]

1930   German director Richard Oswald makes a talking film *Dreyfus*, based on *Prozess des Hauptmanns Dreyfus*, the book published in the same year by Bruno Weil: a French soundtrack is prepared but the film is banned by French censorship for 'fear of riots'.[24]

Oct 22   Death of Mathieu Dreyfus, at the age of 73. Eugene Naville records in his diary: 'A man of noble character endowed with integrity and fraternal devotion.'[25]

1931
Theatre riots

Feb–Mar   On 1 February a French adaptation by Jacques Richepin of the successful German play *Die Affäre Dreyfus* opens in Paris at the Théâtre de l'Ambigu.[26] At the instigation of Charles Maurras, members of L'Action française, the Camelots du Roi and other Nationalist groups disrupt the performances, protesting against the 'German Jewish play'.[27] (*v.* Appendix 50)

English film directors F.W. Kraemer and Milton Rosmer complete the film *The Dreyfus Case* based on the play of Herzog and Rehfisch. The film is banned in France.

1933
Jan 30   Adolf Hitler is appointed by President Paul von Hindenburg German Chancellor. Dawn of the Third Reich.[28]

1934
L'Affaire Stavisky

Jan   A financial scandal at the crédit municipal de Bayonne (Bayonne's municipal pawnshop) – the Stavisky Affair[29] – leads to accusations of corruption against Chautemps' Government and forces his resignation. Chautemps is replaced by Edouard Daladier. The Stavisky Affair fuels a virulent anti-republican campaign, led by Maurras and Daudet. Throughout January, L'Action française and right-wing leaders demonstrate across Paris.

Assault on the Palais Bourbon

Feb 6   A vast demonstration organized by L'Action française leads thousands of Parisians and war veterans in an assault on the Palais Bourbon. A dozen people are killed and thousands injured in the scuffles which follow. Daladier represses the riots but is forced to resign. He is replaced by Gaston Doumergue and a right-wing government of national unity.

Formation of the Popular Front by a group of left-wing politicians, led by Léon Blum (*v.* 4 June 1936), Edouard Daladier, Maurice Thorez and Edouard Herriot. The Popular Front includes the Communist Party, the Socialist Party and the Radical Party.

1935   In reaction to the Popular Front, a group of former Royalists and members of ultra right-wing leagues form the clandestine anti-republican and paramilitary organization CSAR (Comité secret d'action révolutionnaire: Secret Committee for Revolutionary Action), also known as the Cagoule. Its head is Eugène Delonche, a former Polythequenicien, vice-president of one of the Paris sections of L'Action française. Most CSAR members come from L'Action française and the Camelots de Roi. The main purpose of the CSAR is to antagonise Communists, strike back at them and foil a mythical 'Communist plot'.[30]

Death of Dreyfus

July 12   Death of Alfred Dreyfus, at the age of 75. Dreyfus is buried on 14 July in the Jewish section of the cemetery of Montparnasse. The Chief Rabbi Julien Weill conducts a simple religious service. The ceremony is attended only by close family members.

Sept 15   The Nuremberg Laws are enacted in Germany. Jews become second-class citizens and are forbidden marriage or sexual relations with German Aryans.

1936   *Souvenirs et correspondences publiés par Pierre Dreyfus*, the reminiscences of Alfred Dreyfus and his son on the Affair, are published in Paris by Grasset.[31]

Government of Léon Blum (1936–37)

May 3   Victory of the Popular Front in the general election.

June 4   Léon Blum, leader of the Socialist Party, is elected France's first Jewish Prime Minister.

1937
June 22   As result of the crisis over government policy towards the Spanish Civil War, Blum tenders his resignation.[32] He is succeeded by the Radical Camille Chautemps.

1938   Daladier, the new Prime Minster, prohibits the screening of the recent American motion picture *The Life of Emile Zola* (1937) by the German director William Dierterle, winner of three Oscars. (*v.* 1952) Following Daladier's claim that the film 'injured the honour of the French Army', it is withdrawn from the official selection for the Venice Film Festival of 1938. [33]

Nov 9–10	Kristallnacht (Night of the Broken Glass), the Nazi pogrom conducted throughout Germany and Austria, during which over 7500 Jewish shops are destroyed, 400 synagogues burnt, 91 Jews killed and thousands are sent to concentration camps.[34]
Nov	Promulgation of racial laws in Italy, inspired by the Nazi legislation. These prohibit sexual relations between Jews and 'Aryans', placing Jews under further restrictions including banishment of alien Jews, expulsion of Jewish students and teachers from schools and universities.

1939
Outbreak of World War II

Sept 1	Germany invades Poland, declaring war.
Sept 3	England and France declare war on Germany. Commencement of World War II.

1940

May	Lucie and her family seek refuge in the south of France.[35]
June 14	The German Army enters Paris.

Léon Blum

June 18   General Charles de Gaulle, member of the French Government in exile who had escaped to England from the German occupation of France, speaks to the French people via the BBC. De Gaulle asks French men and women to join in the fight against the Nazis. By his 'Appel du 18 juin' ('Appeal of 18 June') De Gaulle founds the Free French Forces.

June 22   France signs an armistice with Germany and Italy. As a result, France is divided into an occupied zone in the north (three-fifths of France) under German authority, and an unoccupied zone, (*zone libre*) under French control, with Vichy as its capital.

Fall of the Third Republic: Foundation of Vichy France

July 9–10   The National Assembly gives 84-year-old Marshal Philippe Pétain (Prime Minister since June) the legislative and executive powers necessary to revise the constitution of the Third Republic. The vote passes by 569 votes to 80.

July 11   Establishment of the Vichy regime with Marshal Pétain as Head of State. Pétain issues the three first Constitutional Acts, which suspend the Constitution of the Third Republic, the Chamber of Deputies and the Senate, transferring all powers to himself.

July 12   Pétain appoints Pierre Laval as his deputy.

Aug 27   Vichy abrogates the Marchandeau decree of 1939, which prohibited the expressions of racism and antisemitism in the press.[36]

Aug 29   Foundation of La Légion française des combattants, the only legal civic action group under the Vichy regime. The legion becomes a governmental instrument in promoting the politics of national revolution.[37]

Oct 3   Promulgation of the first Statut des Juifs (Jewish Decrees), antisemitic legislation stipulating the definition of a Jew – those with three grandparents of 'Jewish race', or two if the spouse was also Jewish – and the exclusion of Jews from public life, forbidding their activities in public services, the army, commerce, industry; and forbidding participation in various professions, including teaching, medicine, law, cinema, theatre and the press. The legislation applies to both the occupied zone and the *zone libre.*[38]

Oct 7   Vichy annuls the Crémieux Decree (1871), thereby withdrawing French nationality from all 'native Jews' of Algeria.[39]

1941
Mar 29   Formation of the Commissariat Général aux questions juives (Commissariat for Jewish Affairs), responsible for all legislation and measures concerning Jews in France. Xavier Vallat is nominated head of the Commissariat.

June 2   A second Statut des juifs replaces the first, increasing professional restrictions on Jews and enlarging the definition of Jews to those with two grandparents who belong to the 'Jewish religion' or not being converted to any other religion before 25 June 1940.[40]

July 22   Vichy inaugurates a programme of Aryanization, confiscating Jewish-
                owned property.

1942
Jan 20   During the Wannsee Conference on the 'Final Solution',[41] leaders
                of the Third Reich decide on a policy of deportation and eventual
                extermination of the Jews in Europe.

May   Jean-Pierre Reinach (Mathieu Dreyfus' grandson), who had joined the
                Free French Forces in England, is parachuted into France and dies in
                combat.

                Louis Darquier de Pellepoix, a convinced racist and antisemite,
                replaces Xavier Vallat as head of the Commissariat Général aux
                questions juives. Vallat is considered by the SS as too moderate.[42]

May 29   In the occupied zone all Jews over the age of six are officially obliged
                to wear on the left side of their outer garment the yellow star of
                David, upon which is written in black letters the word *Juif* or *Juive*
                ('Jew' or 'Jewess'). The law comes into force on 7 June.[43]

June   The family of Pierre Dreyfus secures an exit visa and leaves for New
                York via Casablanca.

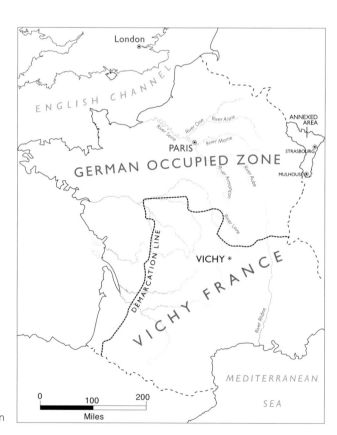

Map of divided
France in 1940
following the
German occupation

La rafle du Vélodrome d'Hiver (or du Veld'hiv)

July 16   Beginning of a vast *rafle* (round-up) organized by the French police in collaboration with the Germans, in which 13,000 Jews living in Paris are seized. They are interned for several days in the Vélodrome d'Hiver sports arena and subsequently transferred to the concentration camps of Drancy (in the north-east of Paris), Compiègne, Pithiviers and Beaune-la-Rolande.[44]

July 19   The start of French deportations to the extermination camps of Auschwitz-Birkenau.

               A total of 75,721 Jews are deported from France; 2654 returned.[45]

Nov 11   Occupation of Vichy France by the Germans.

Dec 11   By order of Pellepoix, identification papers of all Jews are to be stamped with *Juif* or *Juive*. Jews are forbidden to circulate in certain regions of France.

               Lucie adopts her sister's married name Duteuil and takes refuge in Valence, Provence. She is directly affected by the new measures against Jews and the outbreaks of popular antisemitism in the south of France.[46]

1943
Jan 30   Official formation of the French Milice as a substitute police force which is to 'take active part in the political, social, economical, intellectual and moral reorganization of the country'. The head of the Milice is the Head of State. The Milice becomes the spearhead of Vichy and enforces its racial policies.[47]

Nov 3   Madeleine Lévy, the 25-year-old granddaughter of Dreyfus and member of the Resistance, is arrested in Toulouse and interned in Drancy.

Nov 20   Madeleine Lévy is deported to Auschwitz, where she perishes.[48]

1944
Jan 10   Victor Basch, president of the Ligue des droits de l'homme et du citoyen, and his wife are murdered by the Milice in Lyon; they are both over 80 years old. (*v.* Appendix 49)

Feb   Charles Du Paty de Clam (son of Du Paty de Clam) replaces Pellepoix as head of the Commissariat Général aux questions juives.

Aug 25   Liberation of Paris by the Allies.

1945
Conviction of Maurras

Jan 27   Charles Maurras is convicted for 'intelligence with the enemy' (i.e. collaboration with the Germans). He is sentenced to life imprisonment and to 'national degradation'. Upon hearing the verdict, Maurras exclaims: 'This is the revenge of Dreyfus.'[49]

               Liberation of Auschwitz by the Soviet Army.

May 8	Capitulation of Germany.
Aug 15	Marshal Pétain is condemned to death. His sentence is commuted to life imprisonment.
Oct 9	Pierre Laval is condemned to death. He is executed on 15 October.
Dec 14	Death of Lucie Dreyfus in Paris, at the age of 76.

1946

Oct 13	Establishment of the French Fourth Republic.
Oct 27	The first article in the preamble to the constitution of the Fourth Republic declares:

> *The French people proclaim once more that every human being, regardless of race, religion or creed, possesses inalienable and sacred rights. It solemnly reaffirms the rights and freedoms of man and the citizen laid down in the 1789 Declaration of Rights and the basic principles recognized by the laws of the Republic.*

1947

Nov 29	United Nations General Assembly Resolution 181 calling for the partition of the British-ruled Palestine Mandate into a Jewish state and an Arab state is approved with 33 votes in favour, 13 against, 10 abstentions and 1 absent. The resolution is accepted by the Jews but rejected by Arabs and the Arab states.

1948

Declaration of the State of Israel

May 14	Declaration of the establishment of the State of Israel. The declaration of Independence is read in Tel-Aviv by David Ben-Gurion, who becomes the country's first Prime Minister.

1952

50th anniversary of Zola's death/Cause of Zola's death questioned (1952–53)

	The Paris cinema Studio 28 (in Montmartre) shows German director William Dieterle's film *The Life of Emile Zola*. (*v.* 1938) French censorship authorizes the showing only under certain restrictions: it is to be shown without subtitles, certain sections are to be cut and a warning projected before each screening.[50]
Sept 29	Day of the 50th anniversary of Zola's death. The French newspaper *Libération*[51] publishes a leader by the editor Jean Guignebert dedicated to Zola. The article praises Zola's heroic intervention in the Dreyfus Affair and repeats the official version of his death, asphyxiation overnight at his home.

1953

Jan	*Libération* receives a letter signed by Pierre Haquin announcing that Zola's death was not an accident but a 'political assassination'. Haquin declares that 25 years after Zola's death (1927) a person involved in this supposed plot confided in him. Guignebert entrusts journalist Jean Bedel to pursue an investigation of Zola's death.

Sept–Oct   *Libération* publishes a series of articles in which journalist Jean Bedel reveals his 'scoop' concerning Zola's death, claiming it was a criminal act. Bedel's conclusions are based on information he received from an informer, to whom one of the chimneysweeps in Zola's building had confessed in 1927 that the flue had been deliberately obstructed. Bedel preserves the anonymity of both his informer and the chimneysweep. (*v.* 2002)

1958
Oct 5   Following the Algerian crisis and a referendum in which a new constitution is supported by a large majority, de Gaulle proclaims the establishment of the Fifth Republic.

1959   French censorship authorizes for the first time the unrestricted screening of a film on the Dreyfus Affair – the American film *I Accuse* (1957), directed by and starring José Ferrer.[52]

1965   Release of a short French documentary, *L'Affaire Dreyfus*, by de Jean Vigne. The film is intended for educational use.

Oct 28   *Nostra Aetate*, the Declaration on the Relation of the Church to Non-Christian Religions at the 21st Ecumenical Council of Vatican II (1962–65), declares that Jews cannot be charged with the crime of deicide. It further states:

> *Indeed, the church reproves every form of persecution against whomsoever it may be directed. Remembering, then, its common heritage with the Jews and moved not by any political consideration, but solely by the religious motivation of Christian charity, it deplores all hatreds, persecutions, displays of antisemitism levelled at any time or from any source against the Jews.*[53]

1971
May 28   The City Council of Rennes names the lycée where Dreyfus' second court martial took place in 1899 as the Lycée Emile Zola. The City Council report states: 'Even though there is no direct connection between the famous writer and Brittany or the city of Rennes, the historical event [Dreyfus' second court martial] which emanated from his intervention ['J'Accuse'] justifies the decision of City Council, dedicating the school in his name.'[54]

1974   Release of the French documentary, *Dreyfus ou l'intolérable vérité* ('Dreyfus or the Intolerable Truth'), produced by Jean Cherasse. [55]

1978   Release of a film in four parts for French television, *Zola ou la conscience humaine* ('Zola or the Human Conscience'), produced by Antenne 2, directed by Stellio Lorenzi. It is based on the book by Armand Lanoux, *Bonjour monsieur Zola*.

1985
June 24   Founding in Paris of the Société Internationale d'Histoire de l'Affaire Dreyfus. The society aims to disseminate and develop research on the history of the Dreyfus Affair.[56]

The Dreyfus statue

1984–88 In 1984 the French Government and President François Mitterrand decide to honour the memory of Captain Alfred Dreyfus. Jack Lang, Minister of Culture, commissions a sculpture from the political cartoonist, painter and sculptor Louis Mitelberg, better known as 'Tim'. The statue is finally unveiled by Jack Lang in a corner of the Jardins des Tuilleries on 9 June 1988.[57] (*v.* Oct 1994)

1987
Sept 13 The major exhibition 'The Dreyfus Affair: Art, Truth and Justice', curated by Norman L. Kleeblatt, opens at the Jewish Museum in New York. The opening address is given by the grandson of Dreyfus, Jean-Louis Lévy. (*v.* Appendix 55)

1988
June 20 Dreyfus' grave in the Montparnasse cemetery is desecrated. It is daubed with expletives and the sign of the swastika, '*Sale Juif*' ('Dirty Jew') in green, '*Juden Raus*' ('Out with the Jews') and '*Sieg Heil*' (the Nazi salute) in black. The colours green and black probably represent French and German vandals.

Oct 9 Pope John Paul II addresses the leaders of the Jewish community in Strasbourg: 'I again repeat to you the strongest condemnation of antisemitism and racism, which are opposed to the principles of Christianity.'[58]

1990
July 13 Promulgation by the Government of Prime Minister Michel Rocard and President François Mitterrand of the Loi Gayssot, a law against acts of racism, antisemitism and xenophobia.[59]

1991 American production of a television film devoted to Picquart, *Prisoner of Honor*, director Ken Russell.

Sept 'The Dreyfus centenary' initiative is launched in London by George R. Whyte to create and monitor commemorative events for the Dreyfus Centenary 1994. (*v.* Appendix 53)

1992
May 'Gedenken an Dreyfus 1894–1994' ('Remembrance of Dreyfus') initiative is launched in Bonn by Barthold C. Witte (former Director General of Cultural Affairs at the German Foreign Office) and George R. Whyte to create and monitor commemorative events in Germany for the Dreyfus Centenary 1994. (*v.* Appendix 53)

Oct 5 Centenaire de l'Affaire Dreyfus Comité Français is established in Paris.[60]

1993
July 29 The activities of the London–Bonn Dreyfus Centenary initiatives are taken over by the newly formed Dreyfus-Stiftung für Menschenrecht und active Toleranz, the Dreyfus Society for Human Rights. The objectives of the society are to support programmes and projects for the Dreyfus Centenary; projects aimed at fighting xenophobia, racism and antisemitism; and to establish a Dreyfus Study Centre.[61]

Sept 23–25   The Emile Zola Centenary Internationaal Conference organized by the Emile Zola Society, l'Institut français de Londres, le Service Culturel de l'Ambassade de France à Londres.

1994

Jan 31   Colonel Paul Gaujac, head of SHAT (Service historique de l'armée de terre), publishes in the French Army's weekly magazine *SIRPA Actualité* a summary of the Dreyfus Affair discounting the crimes of the General Staff, describing the dreyfusard campaign as attempting to destabilize and vilify the army. The article ends with the provocative conclusion: 'Today, Dreyfus' innocence is the thesis generally accepted by historians and still, to this day, no one is prepared to state whether Dreyfus had been a conscious or unconscious victim.'[62]

Feb   François Léotard, Minister of Defence, relieves Colonel Gaujac of his functions.

Oct   Tim's sculpture of Alfred Dreyfus is unveiled in the Square Pierre Lafue in Paris' 6th arrondissement, close to the site of the former Cherche-Midi prison where Dreyfus was arrested. The unveiling takes place in the presence of Prime Minister Jacques Chirac, the Mayor of Paris and many other official and government representatives.

The Dreyfus centenary 1994

A series of international commemorative events are held throughout the year. (*v.* Appendix 53)

1995

Sept 7   Special screening of Yves Boisset's film *L'Affaire Dreyfus* at the Hôtel de Ville, Paris. It is organized by the Consistoire in the presence of 2000 people. General Jean-Louis Mourrut, head of SHAT, declares that Dreyfus was a victim of 'a military conspiracy, in part based on fraudulent documents, which led to the deportation of an innocent man'.[63]

1998

Centenary of Zola's 'J'Accuse'

A series of international commemorative events are held throughout the year. (*v.* Appendix 54)

Mar 16   The Vatican Commission for Religious Relations with the Jews issues the document *We Remember: A Reflection on the Shoah* [Holocaust], in which it categorically deplores the unspeakable iniquity of the Shoah and reflects on the influence of the long-standing anti-Jewish prejudices embedded in the Christian world and of racial and modern antisemitism. The authors represent the failure of the Christian world to protest strongly against the Nazi's persecution of Jews, as a heavy burden of conscience:

> *At the end of this millennium, the Catholic Church desires to express her deep sorrow for the failure of her sons and daughters*

> *in every age ... we pray that our sorrow for the tragedy which the Jewish people has suffered in our century will lead to a new relationship with the Jewish people. We wish to turn awareness of past sins into a firm resolve to build a new future in which there will be no more anti-Judaism among Christians or anti-Christian sentiment among Jews ...Finally, we invite all men and women of good will to reflect deeply on the significance of the Shoah ... To remember this terrible experience is to become fully conscious of the salutary warning it entails: the spoiled seeds of anti-Judaism and antisemitism must never again be allowed to take root in any human heart. The Pope, in his letter to Cardinal Cassidy dated 12 March states his fervent hope that the document will 'enable memory to play its necessary part in the process of shaping a future in which the unspeakable iniquity of the Shoah will never again be possible.*[64]

2000
July 12   On the occasion of the 65th anniversary of the death of Dreyfus, the city of Paris dedicates a square in his name situated at the junction of rue Emile Zola and rue du Théâtre (in the 15th arrondissement). Jean Tiberi, Mayor of Paris unveils the plaque 'Place Capitaine Dreyfus', in the presence of members of the Zola and the Dreyfus families.

2002   On the centennial anniversary of Zola's death and 50 years after his first success, journalist Jean Bedel publishes the full story of his investigations into Zola's death. (*v.* Sept–Oct 1952) Bedel reveals for the first time both the name of his informer – Pierre Hacquin – and that of Henri Buronfosse, one of the presumed collaborators in Zola's assassination who had confessed to Hacquin having participated in obstructing the flue in Zola's home. According to Bedel, Hacquin authorized him to reveal the name of Buronfosse only after his (Hacquin's) death. Bedel's book introduces further suspicions about Zola's death, all of which imply a criminal act.[65]

Feb 6   The statue of Dreyfus (in the 6th arrondissement) is smeared with yellow paint, images of the star of David and antisemitic slogans such as '*sale traître*' ('dirty traitor').

2003
Feb 3   Promulgation by the Government of Jean-Pierre Raffarin and President Jacques Chirac of the Loi Lellouche, reinforcing the punishment for crimes and misdemeanors of racism, antisemitism and xenophobia.[66]

A further cast of Tim's sculpture of Dreyfus is erected in the courtyard of the Musée d'art et d'histoire du judaïsme. (in the 3rd arrondissement)

A 15-minute documentary *Dreyfus aujourd'hui* is made by Michel Grosman, produced by the Musée d'art et d'histoire du Judaïsme.

2005   Desecration of Drancy memorial to the deported.[67]

2006   Centenary of the exoneration of Dreyfus.

Tombstone of Dreyfus in the cemetery of Montparnasse, Paris

NOTES

1   Pathé's earlier film was produced shortly after that of Méliès in 1899. (*v.* 7 Aug–9 Sept 1899, the Rennes court martial, n. 5)

2   S. Sand, 'Les sosies cinématographiques de Dreyfus', in L. Gervereau and C. Prochasson (eds), *L'Affaire Dreyfus et le tournant du siècle (1894–1910)*, (Nanterre: BDIC, 1994), pp. 224–7.

3   Dreyfus received no compensation for his time in prison or on Devil's Island. The report of his current superiors closing his dossier mentioned his 'excellent conduct' and concluded that 'despite his age, Dreyfus was perfectly suited to render the finest service to the artillery or to the General Staff as a major or lieutenant-colonel in the reserve'. Dreyfus was appointed major in the military command of Paris.

4   A statue in honour of Trarieux was also erected nearby at Denfert-Rochereau. Both statues, as well as that of Bernard Lazare in Nîmes, were attacked with stones and hammers by Royalists that year.

5   The paper was partly financed by the Duc d'Orléans, who also supported other Royalist publications – *Le Soleil, Le Gaulois,* and *La Gazette de France. L'Action française* continued publication until the summer of 1944. Weber, *Action française*, pp. 50–3.

6   For several weeks members of L'Action française condemned the Government's decision to transfer Zola's ashes to the Pantheon scheduled for 4 June. They called on their supporters to protest. Zola's wife received anonymous warnings of a 'bloody drama'.

7   Grégori probably acted on his own. However, in a private meeting of the leaders of L'Action française prior to the ceremony André Gaucher, a writer for the Royalist *Soleil,* volunteered for the task of assassinating Dreyfus, but Maurras objected. Weber, *Action française*, p. 42.

8   A. Dreyfus, *Souvenirs et correspondance publiés par son fils,* p. 442.

9   *Procès du panthéon (4 Juin–10 & 11 Septembre 1908). Grégori, Dreyfus et Zola devant le jury* (Paris: *La Libre Parole*, 1908), 166–7. Grégori's acquittal was a great victory for the Nationalists and L'Action française. It also confirmed that public opinion was prepared for anti-Republican ideas. *Le Gaulois* exclaimed: 'Grégori's courageous attack struck Dreyfus in the arm. The verdict struck dreyfusism in the heart.' Grégori published a letter in *La Libre Parole* thanking his friends for their moral support. Drumont opened a subscription for Grégori in remembrance of Henry's memorial fund.

10 The number of Camelots increased rapidly. In December there were several dozen. Within a year there were 600 members in Paris alone, and 65 Camelots branches throughout France. The Camelots sold the daily *L'Action française* on Sunday mornings and were called to participate in demonstrations. In 1910 an elite was created within the group: the Commissaires, who armed with loaded canes, were to maintain order during meetings and gatherings, and protect L'Action française leaders during parades. Weber, *Action française*, pp. 54–5.

11 Esterhazy remained extremely secret about this relationship. Hardly any details (dates of birth and death, nationality etc.) are known about Madame de Voilemont. Thomas, *Esterhazy*, pp. 378–79.

12 Weber, *Action française*, p. 83.

13 The purchase of the property was most probably by Madame de Voilemont, in view of Esterhazy's financial situation.

14 *DFA*, p. 360.

15 *DFA*, pp. 360–400.

16 A law on cinematographic censorship came into force in 1919. It also applied to foreign pictures and remained in force until the 1950s. (*v.* 1930; 1931, 1938; 1952)

17 Schwartzkoppen, *Die Wahrheit über Dreyfus,* p. XI.

18 After Drumont's death, his paper *La Libre Parole* gradually fell into decline, ceasing publication in 1924. In its last phase, with the collaboration of members of L'Action française, the paper supported fascism, and in its final issue denounced the revision of the Dreyfus verdict. In 1928 *La Libre Parole* was relaunched by the young right-wing Ploncard d'Assac. On the development of the paper after Drumont's death, see F. Busi, *The Pope of Antisemitism, the Career and Legacy of Edouard-Adolphe Drumont* (Lanham: University Press of America, 1986), pp. 156–69.

19 Thomas, *Esterhazy*, pp. 383–7.

20 According to the newspapers, he had grown rich as a travelling salesman, or had fallen into dissolution as a drug-addicted manager of a brothel. It has been suggested that Esterhazy received regular monthly payments through the local post office from a source which has not been identified.

21 Thomas, *Esterhazy*, p. 399.

22 The Vatican feared the popularity of Maurras and the increasing power of his movement both in the political and social spheres. It was seen as a potential threat to the pope's spiritual authority. The interdict on the L'Action française was lifted on 7 July 1939. Weber, *Action française*, pp. 219–55.

23 Herzog, *Der Kampf einer Republik*, p. 963.

24 A French translation of Weil's book was published by Gallimard in the same year.

25 *DFA*, p. 416.

26 The text was translated into French by J. Richepin, and published in 1930 by Albin Michel.

27 Weber, *Action française*, pp. 298–9; M. Knobel, 'Des incidents au théâtre de l'Ambigu', *Revue d'Histoire du théâtre*, 1989, pp. 264–70 ; Herzog, *Der Kampf einer Republik*, pp. 964–8.

28 Third Reich: period of Nazi rule in Germany between 1933 and 1945.

29 The Jewish financer Serge Alexandre Stavisky was found dead, either having committed suicide or murdered by the police on 9 January.

30 The name Cagoule was given to CSAR by Maurice Pujo, a member of L'Action française. During 1937, the Cagoule led several terrorist attacks and plotted to overthrow the Republic. Its principal leaders were arrested. M. Winock (ed.) *Histoire de l'extrême droite en France* (Paris: Seuil, 1993), pp. 177–8.

31 In 1931, with the help of his son, Dreyfus prepared a book of his recollections. The book contained a re-edition of his *Cinq années de ma vie*, slightly modified, as well as extracts from his memoirs and letters from the years after the Rennes trial. The project, however, did not materialize. The manuscript of this book is at the Musée d'art et d'histoire du judaïsme in Paris.

32 Blum was re-elected Prime Minister and served in that capacity between March and April 1938. In 1940 he was deported to Buchenwald, one of the first and largest Nazi camps, established on German soil near Weimar. He was again Prime Minister between December 1946 and January 1947.

33 More on this aspect see S. Sand, 'Dreyfus, made in Hollywood', in *L'Histoire*, 173 (January 1994), pp. 120–3; P. Erens, *The Jew in American Cinema* (Indiana: Indiana University Press, 1984), pp. 161–3.

34 Nazi Party: political party in Germany between 1933 to 1945 known as National Socialism. The party was governed by totalitarian methods and practised an anti-Jewish policy of extermination.

35 What was known as *l'exode* started in May: about 8 million French people (1 million Parisians, including tens of thousands of Jews) fled from the north of France to the south. Lucie first took refuge in Toulouse. For two years (1940–42) she travelled across the south, where she took cures for a respiratory illness. On Lucie's life during the war years, see *DFA*, pp. 462–70, 485–6.

36 This was one of the first measures against the Jews in France which had already started before the capitulation of France to Germany. They were enforced by the Vichy Government independently of German influence. Vichy also revised the laws of naturalization, which left thousands of Jews who had escaped from Germany to France during the 1930s stateless.

37 The legion developed into a 'unique party' (1942), gave birth to the SOL (Service d'Ordre Légionnaire) which served as the embryo of the Milice. (*v.* 30 Jan 1943)

38 The law was drafted by Raphaël Alibert, Minister of Justice, a dedicated follower of Charles Maurras. Within 14 months, 60 decrees and laws, directly or indirectly relating to Jews in France, were issued, establishing their exclusion. C. Singer, *Vichy l'université et les juifs. Les silences et la mémoire* (Paris: Belles lettres 'Pluriel', 1992), pp. 71–138.

39 The Crémieux Decree was reintroduced in Algeria on 21 October 1943.

40 Only a certificate of baptism was accepted as a renunciation of the Jewish faith. Further decrees completed this law. The restrictions imposed on Jews during 1940–41 effectively deprived half the Jewish population of France of its means of existence. M. Winock, *La France et les Juifs, de 1789 à nos jours* (Paris: Seuil, 2004), pp. 218–28.

41 A suburb of Berlin.

42 Pellepoix was responsible for accelerating Vichy's anti-Jewish policy in 1942–44, in conjunction with the German authorities. L. Joly, *Darquier de Pellepoix et l'antisémitisme français* (Paris: Berg International, 2002).

43 The measure provoked some manifestations and sympathy towards Jews. Vichy did not officially impose the star in the *zone libre*. The measure did not extend to the south, even after its occupation by the Germans. (11 Nov 1942) But other methods were used by Vichy to help identify the Jews. (*v.* 11 Dec 1942) M.R. Marrus and R.O. Paxton, *Vichy France and the Jews* (New York: Basic books, 1981), pp. 235–40; S. Klarsfeld, *Vichy-Auschwitz*, Vol. 1 (Paris: Fayard, [1983] 2001), p. 203.

44 Auschwitz-Birkenau, Nazi Germany's largest concentration and extermination camp, was located near the town of Oswiecim in Southern Poland; Sobibor was a Nazi German extermination camp near the village of Sobibor in the Polish province of Lubin; Theresienstadt a concentration camp and transit camp to Auschwitz and other extermination camps.

45 The first round-up of Jews began in May 1941, but from the summer of 1942 these deportations from France to Nazi Germany escalated dramatically. Drancy was the main transit camp. Between 1942 and 1944 65,000 Jews left Drancy in 64 transports. Of these transports, 61, comprising 61,000 deportees, went to Auschwitz; the rest were sent to the extermination camp of Sobibor. Of a total of 80,000 victims deported from France 10,750 were children and 9,700 were over 60 years old. See S. Klarsfeld, *Vichy-Auschwitz*, 2 vols (Paris: Fayard, 1983 and 1895).

46 Lucie remained in hiding in Valence until late summer 1944. After the liberation of Provence in 1944 she returned to Paris.

47 In 1944 the General Secretary of the Milice, Joseph Darnand, took an oath to Hitler, which reinforced the collaboration of Vichy and the SS. P. Giolitto, *Histoire de la Milice* (Paris: Perrin, 1997), pp. 127–30; M. Cointet-Labrousse, *Vichy et le fascisme* (Paris: Complexe, 1987), pp. 232 5.

48 Madeleine was deported on convoy No. 62 from Drancy to Auschwitz, where she perished in January 1943. *DFA*, pp. 481–3; Whyte, *The Accused*, p. 152. Other members of the Dreyfus family who were deported and never returned included Alfred's nephew René Dreyfus; Julien Dreyfus the son of Rachel Dreyfus-Schil; Alice May, the widow of Alfred's brother, Léon; and Joseph Reinach's niece, Fanny, who was deported in the same convoy as Madeleine.

49 Weber, *Action française*, pp. 474–5; *Charles Maurras et Maurice Pujo devant la Cour de justice du Rhône: les 24, 25, 26 et 27 janvier 1945* ([Lyon: Vérités françaises, 1945] Reprint. Paris: Trident, 1994).

50 H. Dumont, *William Dieterle. Antifascismo y compromise romantico* (Filmoteca Espanola, 1994), pp. 91–9.

51 Founded under the German occupation, *Libération* became a daily newspaper on 24 August 1944, the eve of the Liberation of Paris. It continued publication until 1956. Following social upheavals in Paris in May 1968, the philosopher Jean-Paul Sartre created a new daily under the same name, which is still in existence today.

52 The film was based on the book by Nicholas Halasz, *Captain Dreyfus. The Story of a Mass Hysteria* (New York, Simon & Schuster, 1955). This was the first film to emphasize the Jewish origins of Dreyfus.

53 Austin Fannery, OP [Order of Preachers] (ed.) *Vatican Council II, Constitutions, Decrees, Declarations. The basic sixteen documents. A Completely Revised Translation in Inclusive Language* (New York: Costello Publishing Company/Dublin: Dominican Publications, 1996), p. 573.

54 When suggestions were first put forward in 1960 for a new name for the school, the name of Dreyfus had been suggested. When the school was transferred to a new building in 1971 the name of Dreyfus was mentioned again, but was rejected a second time for fear of provocation; even the decision to name it after Zola was disputed. The decision was narrowly accepted by 15 votes to 13, with 8 abstentions.

55 In an interview given to *La Presse nouvelle hebdomadaire* (13 December 1974), Jean Chérasse related the obstacles he encountered while making the film. The next year Chérasse published the interviews included in his film in *Dreyfus ou l'Intolérable vérité* (Paris: Pygmalion, 1975).

56 Founder members: Eric Cahm (deceased), Catherine Coquio, Michel Drouin, Marc Knobel, Jean-Yves Mollier and Philippe Oriol; President: Marcel Thomas; Vice-Presidents: Madeleine Rebérioux, Maurice Agulhon, Jean-Denis Bredin and Michael R. Marrus.

57 Tim's bronze sculpture represents Dreyfus holding a broken sabre, symbolizing his unjust disgrace. Tim first proposed to install it in the courtyard of the Ecole militaire, where 90 years earlier Dreyfus was degraded. In the name of the army, Charles Hernu, Minister of Defence, refused this location under the pretext that the courtyard is closed to the public, and proposed to erect the statue in the gardens of the Ecole polytechnique, where Dreyfus had studied. Tim then suggested the statue be placed in the place Dauphine, in front of the Palais de Justice. Articles in *L'Express* on this issue (9–15 August, 1985) were entitled 'Une nouvelle affaire Dreyfus' ('A New Dreyfus Affair').

58 *Insegnamenti* 11/3, 1988, 1134.

59 Loi No. 90–615 tendant à réprimer tout acte raciste, antisémite ou xénophobe. ('Law aiming to repress all acts of racism, antisemitism and xenophobia') For the full text of the law, see <www.legifrance.gouv.fr>.

60 Founding members: Jean-Denis Bredin, Jacques Durin, Jean-Louis Lévy, George R. Whyte.

61 President: Barthold C. Witte, Chairman George R. Whyte, members include Ignatz Bubis, Prof. Ernst-Otto Czempiel, Horst Dahlhaus, Prof. Götz Friedrich, Hans-Dietrich Genscher, Prof. Dr Hermann Lubbe, Zurich, Prof. Dr Julius Schoeps.

62 For extracts of the article in English, see Burns, *France and the Dreyfus Affair*, pp. 189–90. The article was prepared by officers serving in the SIRPA (Service d'Information et de Relation Publiques des Armées) who based their information on two French dictionaries, *Petit Mourre, dictionnaire de l'Histoire* (1993 edition) and *Quid* (by Dominique and Michèle Fremy). Various personalities, including journalists and historians, responded to this article. See M. Knobel, 'En cette année 1994 … L'Affaire Dreyfus' in *Cahiers Naturalistes* 69 (1995), pp. 303–5.

63 *Libération*, 12 September 1995.

64 *We Remember: A Reflection on the Shoah*. Document under the signatures of Cardinal Edward Idris Cassidy (President of the Vatican Commission for Religious Relations); Reverend Pierre Duprey (Vice-President); Reverend Remi Hoeckman (Secretary).

65 J. Bedel, *Zola assassiné*, introd. H. Mitterand (Paris: Flammarion, 2002).

66 Loi No. 2003–88, visant à aggraver les peines punissant les infractions à caractère raciste, antisémite ou xénophobe ('with the aim of intensifying the rigour of the punishment for the offence of a racial, antisemitic or xenophobic nature'). For the full text of the law, see <www.legifrance.gouv.fr>.

67 Incendiary attack 22 Feb 2005, on the memorial exhibit of a railway wagon used for the deportation of Jews from Drancy to the Nazi death camps of Eastern Europe.

APPENDICES

Appendix 1: The Declaration of the Rights of Man and the Citizen (Déclaration des droits de l'homme et du citoyen) Approved by the National Assembly of France, 26 August 1789

The representatives of the French people, organized as a National Assembly, believing that the ignorance, neglect, or contempt of the rights of man are the sole cause of public calamities and of the corruption of governments, have determined to set forth in a solemn declaration the natural, inalienable, and sacred rights of man, in order that this declaration, being constantly before all the members of the Social body, shall remind them continually of their rights and duties; in order that the acts of the legislative power, as well as those of the executive power, may be compared at any moment with the objects and purposes of all political institutions and may thus be more respected, and, lastly, in order that the grievances of the citizens, based hereafter upon simple and incontestable principles, shall tend to the maintenance of the constitution and redound to the happiness of all. Therefore, the National Assembly recognizes and proclaims, in the presence and under the auspices of the Supreme Being, the following rights of man and of the citizen:

Articles

1. Men are born and remain free and equal in rights. Social distinctions may be founded only upon the general good.

2. The aim of all political association is the preservation of the natural and imprescriptible rights of man. These rights are liberty, property, security, and resistance to oppression.

3. The principle of all sovereignty resides essentially in the nation. No body nor individual may exercise any authority which does not proceed directly from the nation.

4. Liberty consists in the freedom to do everything which injures no one else; hence the exercise of the natural rights of each man has no limits except those which assure to the other members of the society the enjoyment of the same rights. These limits can only be determined by law.

5. Law can only prohibit such actions as are hurtful to society. Nothing may be prevented which is not forbidden by law, and no one may be forced to do anything not provided for by law.

6. Law is the expression of the general will. Every citizen has a right to participate personally, or through his representative, in its foundation. It must be the same for all, whether it protects or punishes. All citizens, being equal in the eyes of the law, are equally eligible to all dignities and to all public positions and occupations, according to their abilities, and without distinction except that of their virtues and talents.

7. No person shall be accused, arrested, or imprisoned except in the cases and according to the forms prescribed by law. Any one soliciting, transmitting, executing, or causing to be executed, any arbitrary order, shall be punished. But any citizen summoned or arrested in virtue of the law shall submit without delay, as resistance constitutes an offense.

8. The law shall provide for such punishments only as are strictly and obviously necessary, and no one shall suffer punishment except it be legally inflicted in virtue of a law passed and promulgated before the commission of the offense.

9. As all persons are held innocent until they shall have been declared guilty, if arrest shall be deemed indispensable, all harshness not essential to the securing of the prisoner's person shall be severely repressed by law.

10. No one shall be disquieted on account of his opinions, including his religious views, provided their manifestation does not disturb the public order established by law.*

11. The free communication of ideas and opinions is one of the most precious of the rights of man. Every citizen may, accordingly, speak, write, and print with freedom, but shall be responsible for such abuses of this freedom as shall be defined by law.

12. The security of the rights of man and of the citizen requires public military forces. These forces are, therefore, established for the good of all and not for the personal advantage of those to whom they shall be entrusted.

13. A common contribution is essential for the maintenance of the public forces and for the cost of administration. This should be equitably distributed among all the citizens in proportion to their means.

14. All the citizens have a right to decide, either personally or by their representatives, as to the necessity of the public contribution; to grant this freely; to know to what uses it is put; and to fix the proportion, the mode of assessment and of collection and the duration of the taxes.

15. Society has the right to require of every public agent an account of his administration.

16. A society in which the observance of the law is not assured, nor the separation of powers defined, has no constitution at all.

17. Since property is an inviolable and sacred right, no one shall be deprived thereof except where public necessity, legally determined, shall clearly demand it, and then only on condition that the owner shall have been previously and equitably indemnified.

Source: The Avalon Project at Yale Law School www.yale.edu/lawweb/ avalon/rightsof.htm.

* Author's emphasis.

Appendix 2: Statutes of the Ligue nationale antisémitique de France, 1899: founded by Edouard Drumont, the marquis de Morès and Jacques de Biez

The national league of anti-Semites in France has the purpose of defending the spiritual, economic, industrial, and commercial interests of our country with all appropriate means.

The league is an instrument of national revival, of protection of the conscience of each individual, of mutual and fraternal assistance.

Our intentions are patriotic without reserve, and social.

Members of the league are entitled to any political and religious freedom.

Propagating the truth in broad daylight and employing social means, the league will fight the pernicious influence of the financial sway of the Jews whose clandestine and merciless conspiracy jeopardizes the welfare, honour, and daily security of France.

Membership

Excluded from membership are:

1 Jews

2 Jewish renegades

3 He who has lost his rights as citizen because of a dishonourable penalty.

However, article 33 of the constitution said: Excepted are all those members of the league who were sentenced to a dishonourable penalty by courts whose presidents had been Jews or whose judges had had relations with Jews. Excepted also are the active members of the league, particularly if the sentences aimed at their punishment were for actions or offences committed in speeches or writings against the Jews and for the welfare of the league.

Source: W. Herzog, *From Dreyfus to Pétain 'The Struggle of a Republic',* trans. W. Sorell (New York: Creative Press, 1947), pp. 30–1.

Appendix 3: Extracts from *La Libre Parole's* campaign against Jewish officers in the army, May 1892

The army has been protected from Jewish influence for longer than the rest of contemporary society... Why would it have wanted yids in its ranks? ...

If the Jews cared little for enlisting, the army was even less keen to receive them. Apart from all religious considerations, amongst the huge majority of soldiers there is an instinctive feeling of repulsion towards the sons of Israel. They see in them the usurer who causes the ruin of the debt-laden officer, the supplier who speculates on a soldier's stomach, the spy who traffics shamelessly in the secrets of national defence. Everywhere and always, in peace and in war, the army saw the Jew rebel against it, against its duties, against its well-being, against its honour ...

No sooner had the Jews gained a foothold in the army than they sought by all possible means to acquire influence in it ... Already masters of finance and of administration, dictating rulings in the tribunals, they will finally become the masters of France on the day they command the army. Rothschild will have the mobilisation plans sent to him, one can well imagine with what aim ...

Appendix 4: Du Paty's and Cochefert's reports on the arrest of Dreyfus; first interrogation of Dreyfus by Du Paty, 15 October 1894

War Ministry
Articles 85 and 86 of the Military Code
Army General Staff

REPORT OF ARREST

In the year 1894, 15 October, at nine o'clock in the morning.

In the presence of us, Monsieur Du Paty de Clam, qualified head of battalion employed by the Army General Staff, acting in accordance with articles 85, 86 and 87 of the Military Code of Justice and delegated by the War Minister, as a police detective officer, assisted by M. Gribelin, principal archivist, second-class, of the Army General Staff, acting as clerk, to whom as a preliminary we have sworn an oath to carry out the duties well and faithfully, and in the presence of Mr Cochefert, police superintendent of the City of Paris, head of the Detective Force, in the office of the Chief of the Army General Staff.

We had brought before us M. Alfred Dreyfus, qualified captain of the 14th artillery, probationary officer with the Army General Staff, for the purpose of proceeding to his arrest.

Captain Dreyfus having been brought in, we invited him to complete a sheet of notes and to write at our dictation a letter beginning with these words: 'Having the most serious interest, Sir...' and ending: '... a note on Madagascar'.

These two documents are attached to the dossier.

When the writing of this letter was found to be incorrect after the fourth line, we called upon Captain Dreyfus to ask him the reasons for this. He replied, 'My hands are cold.'

We then proceeded immediately to arrest him in the name of the War Minister.

In witness whereof we signed, along with the witnesses.

Police detective officer	The Clerk
Signed: Du Paty de Clam	Signed: Gribelin
Police Superintendent	
Signed: Cochefert	

Reports of interrogation by the police detective officer [Cochefert]

REPORT

In the year 1894, 15 October,

We, Armand-Constant Cochefert, police superintendent of the City of Paris, head of the Detective Force and a police detective officer, assistant to the Public Prosecutor;

In view of the attached order in which Division General Mercier, War Minister, charges us to proceed with urgency to all useful searches and the interrogation of Mr Dreyfus (Alfred), captain of the 14th artillery regiment, probationary officer of the Army General Staff, accused of high treason and acts of espionage.

Having gone, accompanied by our secretary Mr Boussard, to the offices of the War Ministry on Boulevard Saint-Germain;

We were put in contact with M. Du Paty de Clam, head of an infantry battalion, on special assignment, attached to the Army General Staff, acting in conjunction with us, in pursuance of the above mentioned order.

There, we were taken into the office of General Le Mouton de Boisdeffre, head of the Army General Staff.

At nine o'clock precisely, Captain Dreyfus having in turn been brought into the office, M. Du Paty de Clam, assisted by Mr Gribelin, assigned to him in the capacity of clerk, proceeded with the first interrogations, general statements and the placing under arrest of Captain Dreyfus (Alfred).

The arrest thus being an accomplished fact, we continued, in the presence of the above-mentioned witnesses, with the interrogation of Captain Dreyfus as follows:

Q: What is your civil status?

A: Dreyfus (Alfred), aged 35, born 9 October 1859 in Mulhouse (Alsace-Lorraine) of the late Raphael and late Jeannette Lippmann; I opted for French nationality through the paternal line on 1 October 1872 in Mulhouse.

I married Miss Lucie Hadamard, with whom I have two children.

I am a Captain of the 14th artillery regiment, a probationary officer in the Army General Staff, and I live at no 6, Avenue du Trocadéro.

Q: You are charged with the crime of high treason and espionage on behalf of a foreign power.

During your service at the Army General Staff, you have been in a position to know certain secrets relating to national defence.

You have had documents in your hands, of which you were able to take copies, with the help of which you were able to draw up notes which were handed or communicated to foreign agents.

A long inquiry was started against you, at the hands of the military authority, as a result of serious suspicions which had first been raised against you; and this long enquiry has finally led to indisputable evidence, about which you will be informed in the course of the examination of the case currently started against you.

Q: Explain yourself on the facts of which you are accused.

A: I am totally innocent and I protest vehemently against the rigorous measures taken against me. Never have I communicated to anyone at all even the briefest note relating to my service at the General Staff.

I am not in relation with any foreign embassy and if the facts of which I am accused were established, I would be a scoundrel and a coward.

It is my honour as an officer that I am defending and however painful my situation might be, I will defend myself to the end.

I sense, however, that an appalling plan has been prepared against me, for a purpose I do not understand, but I want to live to establish my innocence.

Q: We implore you to speak the truth.

Documents written in your handwriting, as confirmed after expert analysis, are in the power of the military authority. These documents, or at least one of these documents, has reached the foreign person to whom it was addressed and it gives indications about the military defence of our territory.

Have you never confided to people outside the army, notably to a woman, notes and documents of the kind we are discussing, which could be put to harmful use against our country?

A: Never, I affirm it again, I have not committed the slightest error, nor acted even remotely in the sense which you indicate.

After due reading, M. Dreyfus persisted in his statement and signed it in our presence, along with Mr Du Paty de Clam and the appointed witnesses.

Signed: A. Dreyfus, Gribelin, Boussard, Du Paty de Clam, Cochefert.

In view of the preceding:

And reserving the right to continue subsequently with our other acts of procedure in execution of the aforementioned order.

We order that the present document be transferred urgently to the War Minister for due purposes.

Police superintendent

Signed: COCHEFERT

Ministry of War
Articles 85 and 86 of the Military Code

REPORT OF INTERROGATION

The year 1894, 15 October at nine o'clock in the morning.

In the presence of us, M. Du Paty de Clam, qualified head of battalion at the Army General Staff, acting in accordance with articles 85 and 86 of the Military Code of Justice and delegated by the War Minister as a police detective officer, assisted by M. Gribelin, principal archivist, second-class, of the Army General Staff, acting as clerk, to whom as a preliminary we have sworn an oath to carry out the duties well and faithfully, and in the office of the Chief of the Army General Staff, we had brought before us for the purposes of interrogation Captain Dreyfus of the 14th artillery regiment, probationary officer at the Army General Staff, charged with high treason.

In consequence, the above-named accused was brought before us and we questioned him as follows:

Called upon to declare his surname, first names, age, place of birth, civil status, profession and residence, he replied:

My name is Alfred Dreyfus, Captain of the 14th artillery regiment, son of the late Raphaël and late Jeannette Lippmann, aged 35, born 9 October 1859 in Mulhouse (department of Haut-Rhin); my profession is that of Captain of the 14th artillery, domiciled before my entry into service, in Paris; I am currently a probationary officer of the Army General Staff, garrisoned in Paris.

Q: You are charged with high treason, a crime provided for and punished by Article 76 of the Penal Code. What do you have to say in your defence?

A: I do not know what I am charged with and I demand some explanations.

I swear upon all that I hold most sacred in the world that I have never had any dealings with the agents of a foreign power, that I have never written, nor ever removed a document from the offices of the Army General Staff.

Q: Have you travelled with the General Staff and at what period?

A: In the second half of June.

Q: You supervised a run of documents in the geographic service?

A: Yes.

Q: What documents?

A: Instructions relating to the covering troops.

Q: When?

A: In the month of September.

Q: At the time you were employed on the Army General Staff (Deuxiène and Troisième Bureaux), did you know of a note relating to Madagascar?

A: No, I have never known of a note on Madagascar.

Q: Do you have any enemy likely to have conspired to create the documents which were seized and caused your arrest?

A: I am not aware of having any enemies.

Q: Do you have knowledge of our landings, concentrations and cover?

A: I know nothing of our landings or our concentrations. I only acknowledge having had in my hands a secret document on cover.

Q: Your reply is definite on this point?

A: Yes, I deny ever having knowledge of a secret document concerning concentration and landings.

Q: Do you have knowledge of our landings, concentrations and our cover?

A: No.

Q: Some people state, however, that you know our landing plan by heart?

A: This statement is inaccurate, I do not have knowledge of our landing plan.

Q: Do you have knowledge of a draft Artillery Firing Manual of 14 March 1894?

A: No, I have never heard of it; I did not even know it had been done.

Q: Do you have dealings with the technical section of the artillery?

A: When I was in the Deuxième Bureau, I was charged with a piece of work on German artillery which I communicated to Colonel Naquet.

I went for a second time to the technical section, when I was in the 3rd bureau, to see Colonel Naquet.

Signed Du Paty de Clam, Dreyfus, Gribelin.

Source: 3ème Cass., III, 601–7.

Appendix 5: **Interrogation of Dreyfus conducted by Du Paty (de Clam) in Cherche-Midi prison Handwriting Test, 18 October 1894**

Q: Will you write some pages at my dictation?

A: I will write anything you like; all I ask is that light is shed on this matter.

At that point, I, M. Du Paty de Clam, described above, dictated to Captain Dreyfus the text of the documents attached to the present report, which are numbered from one to ten, classified and signed by myself, the clerk and the accused, as listed below:

Document No. 1 was written seated;

Document No. 2 was written standing;

Document No. 3 was written seated;

Document No. 4 was written standing;

Document No. 5 was written seated and wearing a glove;

Document No. 6 was written standing and wearing a glove;

Document No. 7 was written seated and using a round-ended pen;

Document No. 8 was written standing and using a round-ended pen;

Document No. 9 was written seated, wearing a glove and using a round-ended pen;

Document No. 10 was written standing up, wearing a glove and using a round-ended pen.

We will take care of the aforementioned documents in the presence of our clerk, by keeping them in a safe place and under our own seal.

Source: 3ème Cass., III, 608.

Appendix 6: Forzinetti's account of the detention of Dreyfus in Cherche-Midi prison

On October 14, 1894, I received a secret message from the Minister of War informing me that on the morrow, at 7 p.m., a superior officer would arrive at the prison to make a confidential communication. Lieutenant-Colonel d'Aboville arrived in the morning and handed me a message dated the 14th, informing me that Captain Dreyfus of the Fourteenth Artillery, probationer on the General Staff, would be incarcerated in the morning, charged with the crime of high treason, and that I was to be held responsible for him. Colonel d'Aboville asked me to give him my word of honour to execute the orders, both verbal and written, of the Minister. One of the communications ordered me to place the prisoner in the most complete secrecy, and not to allow him to have by him either paper, ink, pens, penknife, or pencil. He was likewise to be fed like an ordinary criminal; but this measure was annulled later on, as I pointed out that it was irregular. The Colonel ordered me to take whatever precautions I might think necessary for keeping the fact of Captain Dreyfus' presence there secret. He asked me to visit the apartments destined for officers at the prison, and select the room to be occupied by Captain Dreyfus. He put me on my guard against the probable efforts of the 'upper Jewdom' as soon as they should hear of the imprisonment. I saw no one, and no such efforts were made, in my case, at all events. I may add that all the time the prisoner was in the Cherche-Midi Prison I never entered or remained in his cell without being accompanied by the chief military officer at the prison, who alone had the key in his possession.

Toward noon, Captain Dreyfus arrived, in civilian clothes, accompanied by Major Henry and an agent of the secret police. Major Henry gave the order of imprisonment, which was signed by the Minister himself, and the fact that it was dated the 14th proves that the arrest had been decided upon before the Captain had been called to the Ministry of War and charged with the crime of high treason.

The chief military police officer of the prison, to whom I had given my instructions, took the Captain to the cell which had been selected for him.

From that moment Dreyfus was entombed alive between its four walls, no one could see him. The door of his cell could be opened only in my presence during the entire length of his stay in the Cherche-Midi Prison.

Shortly afterward I went to see Captain Dreyfus. He was in a state of extraordinary excitement. He looked like a madman; his eyes were bloodshot, and the things in his room had been upset. I had great difficulty in calming him. I had then the intuition that this officer was innocent. He begged me to give him writing materials, or to write myself, to ask the Minister of War for an audience, either of him or of one of the Staff officers.

He told me the details of his arrest, which were neither dignified nor military.

Between the 18th and the 24th of October, Major Du Paty de Clam, who had arrested Dreyfus at the War Office, came twice with a special authorization from the Minister to examine him. Before seeing Dreyfus he asked if he could enter his cell softly, carrying a lamp powerful enough to throw a blaze of light on the face of the prisoner, whom he wished to surprise and embarrass. I said this was impossible. He had two sittings with him, and each time dictated to him passages from the incriminating document, with the object of comparing the handwriting.

Captain Dreyfus was still frightfully excited. From the corridor he was heard to groan, to talk in loud tones, and to protest his innocence. He struck against the furniture and the walls, and appeared not to know when he had injured himself. He had not a moment's rest, for when overcome by his sufferings, he flung himself, dressed, upon the bed, his sleep was haunted by horrible nightmares. In fact, he struggled so in his sleep that he often fell out of bed. During these nine days of agony he took nothing but beef-tea and sweetened wine. On the morning of the 24th his mental state, bordering on madness, appeared to me so grave that, anxious as to my own responsibility, I made a report to the Minister as well as the Governor of Paris. In the afternoon I went to see General de Boisdeffre, having been ordered to do so, and accompanied him to the Minister. In response to the General's question I replied unhesitatingly: 'You are off the track; this officer is not guilty.' This was my conviction, then, and it has only been confirmed since.

The General went in alone to see the Minister, came out shortly afterward, looking much annoyed, and said: 'The Minister is off to his niece's wedding, and leaves me *carte blanche*. Try to manage with Dreyfus until he gets back; then he will deal with the question himself.' I was inclined to think that General de Boisdeffre had nothing to do with the arrest, or that he did not approve of it. The General, nevertheless, ordered me to have the Captain secretly visited by the prison doctor, who prescribed calming potions and recommended that constant watch be kept over him.

From the 27th on, Major Du Paty de Clam came almost daily to examine him and to obtain copies of his handwriting, his one object now being to obtain from Dreyfus a confession, a procedure against which Dreyfus constantly protested. Up to the day when the poor man was handed over to the Judge Reporter of the Court Martial, he knew that he was accused of high treason, but had no idea of the specific nature of the charge. The preparation of the indictment was long and minute, and all the while Dreyfus so little believed that he would be sent up for trial, much less condemned, that more than once he said: 'What redress shall I ask for? I shall solicit a decoration, and resign. This is what I said to Major Du Paty, who put it into his report. He could not find a single proof against me, for there can be none, any more than could the Reporter, who proceeds by inductions and suppositions, without saying anything precise or definite.'

A few moments before appearing in Court he said, 'I hope that finally my martyrdom is to end, and that I shall soon be back in the bosom of my family.'

Unfortunately this was not to be. After the verdict, Dreyfus was taken back, at about midnight, to his room, where I awaited him. On seeing me he exclaimed: 'My only crime is to have been born a Jew. To this a life of work and toil has brought me. Great heavens! Why did I enter the War School? Why didn't I resign, as my people wished?' Such was his despair that, fearing a fatal ending, I had to redouble my vigilance.

On the morrow his counsel came to see him. On entering the room, Maitre Demange opened his arms and, in tears, embracing him, said, 'My poor boy, your condemnation is the greatest infamy of the century.' I was quite upset. From this day on, Dreyfus, who had heard nothing from his family, was authorized to correspond with them, but under the supervision of the Judge Advocate. I was present at the only two interviews which he had with his wife, and at that with his mother-in-law; they were moving.

After Dreyfus' appeal, Major Du Paty came back with a special authorization from the Minister allowing him free communication with Dreyfus. After having inquired as to the prisoner's *état d'âme,* he went into his room ordering the chief policeman of the prison service to remain within call, in case of necessity. In this last interview, as is shown by a letter written immediately by Dreyfus to the Minister of War, Major Du Paty sought to obtain a confession of guilt, or at least of an imprudent act, of laying a trap. Dreyfus replied that never had he made any such attempt, and that he was innocent.

On the 4th of January, 1895, I was relieved of the heavy responsibility that had been laid upon me. After having shaken hands with Captain Dreyfus, I handed him over to the gendarmes, who led him away, hand-cuffed, to the Military School, where he underwent, while proclaiming his innocence, the degradation, a torture more terrible than death or exile. I have had to fulfil a mission that was extremely painful, having lived, so to speak, for nearly three months the very existence of this poor man, for I had received formal orders to be present at all his meals, which I was to watch over most carefully, lest any writing reach him from outside hidden in his food.

During the years that I have spent as the head of various military prisons, I have acquired a great experience of prisoners, and I do not fear to say, and to say deliberately, that a terrible mistake has been made. I have never regarded Captain Dreyfus as a traitor to his country and uniform.

From the very first my immediate chiefs and others knew my opinion. I affirmed it in the presence of high officials and political personages, as well as of numerous officers of every rank, of journalists, and of men of letters. I will go even further. The Government, as well, knew my opinion, for on the eve of the ceremony of the degradation, the head of one of the departments of the Home Office came to me, sent by his Minister, M. Dupuy, to ask me for information in regard to Dreyfus. I made the same reply. This official certainly repeated it to his chiefs. Now, I assert that up to the 5th of last November, never did I receive from any of my chiefs the slightest intimation or order to keep silent, and that I have always continued to proclaim the innocence of Dreyfus, who is the victim either of an inexplicable fatality, or of a machination concocted wittingly and impossible to unravel.

I must say also that if Dreyfus did not commit suicide, it was not from cowardice, but because he was so placed as to be absolutely incapable of doing so, and because he yielded to my exhortations and the supplications of his despairing family …

All convictions are worthy of respect when they are disinterested and sincere, and it will be admitted that if there are people convinced of the guilt, there are also, as I can affirm, a very great number, in the upper civil and military circles, who, like me – and to the same extent – are convinced of the innocence of Dreyfus. But fear of consequences has prevented them from saying so publicly. I have not cared to be of that number.

An eminent politician, still a member of Parliament, whom I must not name, said to me: 'The Dreyfus trial is an anti-Semite trial, grafted upon a political trial!'

This is my opinion.

God grant that the poor man, who is wearing out his life in agony on a rocky isle, may one day be rehabilitated, for the honour of his family, of his children, and also for the honour of our army!

FORZINETTI,

Major (Retired),

Ex-Governor of the Paris Military Prisons

Source: Published in *Le Figaro* of 21 November 1897. A. Dreyfus, Captain, *Five Years of my Life. The Diary of Captain Alfred Dreyfus.* Intro. N. Halasz (New York/London: Peebles Press, 1977).

**Appendix 7: Verdict of the first court martial of Dreyfus,
Paris, 22 December 1894**

In the name of the people of France, on this day, 24 December 1894, the first permanent Court Martial of the military government of Paris, having met in camera, delivered its verdict in public session as follows:

The following single question was put to the members of the Court:

Is Captain Alfred Dreyfus, Captain of the 14th Artillery Regiment, a certified General Staff officer and probationer of the Army's General Staff, guilty of having delivered to a foreign power or to its agents, in Paris in 1894, a certain number of secret or confidential documents concerning national defence, and of thus having maintained secret relations with this power or its agents, in order to obtain for that power the means to commit hostilities or undertake war against France?

Votes were taken in compliance with the law, beginning with the lower rank, and the President having been the last to give his view, the Council declared unanimously, 'Yes, the accused is guilty.'

Acceding to the conclusions of the Government Commissioner, and having read to the Court the articles of law to which he referred, the President again took votes on the application of the penalty, beginning with the lower rank and the President voting last.

The Court unanimously sentences Alfred Dreyfus, whose titles are listed above, to the penalty of deportation to a fortified enclosure, and applying articles 76 of the Penal Code, article 5 of the Constitution of 4 November 1848, article 1 of the law of 8 June 1850, and articles 189 and 267 of the Military Code of Justice …

Pronounces the discharge of Captain Alfred Dreyfus and orders that his military degradation should take place at the first military parade of the Paris garrison.

The Court declares him stripped of his decorations and privileges and of the right ever to bear arms; and it sentences him to pay costs to the State.

It calls upon the Government Commissioner to read this verdict immediately to the convicted man, before the assembled armed guard, and to inform him that he has twenty-four hours in which to appeal for a review.

Source: AD, p. 327.

**Appendix 8: The degradation of Dreyfus. Ecole militaire,
Paris, Saturday, 5 January 1895.
Descriptions of the ceremony by
Maurice Barrès, Alfred Dreyfus, Léon Daudet and Theodor Herzl**

Maurice Barrès,

'THE PARADE OF JUDAS' (Memories of the degradation of Alfred Dreyfus at the Ecole Militaire, 5 January 1895).

… My imagination … persists in taking me back to that cold January morning when I watched the degradation of Dreyfus …

When the clock struck nine and the general drew his sword, when the orders rang out, when the foot soldiers presented arms and the cavalry drew their swords, the little squadron moved away from the corner of the immense square. Four men: in the middle the traitor, quite upright, to one side the executor, a veritable giant. The five to six thousand people present, moved by this tragic wait, were all of one mind: Judas walks too well!

… In this desert, he walked with a firm step, his chin held high, his body straight as a rod, his left hand on the hilt of his sword, his right hand swinging… This sinister group approached diagonally, stopping suddenly four paces from the General, immobile on his horse. The four artillerymen took a few steps back, the clerk spoke, the rigid silhouette did not flinch except to raise an arm and utter a cry of innocence while the officer of the Garde Républicaine, terrifying in his height and magnificent in bearing, stripped him so quickly – and yet so slowly – of his buttons, his stripes, his epaulettes, his red bands, tugged him, flayed him, plunged him into mourning. The most terrible moment was when he broke the sword over his knee.

After a few seconds, when he remained dishonoured and disarmed, the crowd's instinctive pressure demanded with yet more fury that he should be killed… But the law protected him in order to make him suffer the regulation insults.

… He marches past.

… The wall of soldiers around which he marches contains its rage, but seems ready to burst with fury. At every moment, I think a sword is going to be raised. The crowd at the gates, on the rooftops, still demands his death.

As he came towards us, his kepi pulled down over his forehead, his pince-nez on his ethnic nose, his eyes furious and dry, his whole face hard and defiant, he cried out – what am I saying? – he ordered in his unbearable voice, 'You will tell all of France that I am innocent.'

'Judas! Traitor!' There was a storm of outcry… His face of foreign race, his impassive uprightness, his whole being revolted even the most self-controlled of spectators…

… In three years, someone said, he will be an Uhlan cavalry captain. Oh no, there is certainly no group in the world that would accept this creature. He was not born to live socially. Alone in a wood, disparaged, a tree branch reaches out to him.. So that he can hang himself.

… Ten minutes past nine! The parade is over… At the end of his sinister march past, Dreyfus is pulled up over there into a black van, pushed in by the police. The military bands play the march, 'Sambre et Meuse', spreading honour and loyalty over the area to sweep away the stench of treason. The battalions march past, bristling with rifles and fine French faces. Very good! But we are not sure of each other. A handful of men here and there are bringing small patches of corruption into our admirable race…

… That is what I saw and felt in 1895.

Source: Scènes et Doctrines du Nationalisme (Paris: Félix Guven, 1902), pp. 134–7. These recollections were first published in *Le Journal,* 4 and 7 July 1899.

Alfred Dreyfus

ACCOUNT IN *FIVE YEARS OF MY LIFE*

The degradation took place on Saturday 5 January; I endured that appalling torture without weakness.

Before the sorrowful ceremony, I waited for an hour in the room of the garrison adjutant at the Ecole Militaire. During those long minutes, I summoned all the strength of my being; the memories of the atrocious months I had just lived through came back to me, and in broken sentences I recalled Major Paty de Clam's last visit to my prison. I protested against the vile accusation made against me, I recalled that I had again written to the minister to tell him that I was innocent. It was in distorting these words that Captain Lebrun-Renaud, with a rare lack of thought, created or caused the creation of the legend that I had confessed – whose existence I only discovered in January 1899. If I had been told of this before my departure from France, which only took place in February 1895, that is more than seven weeks after the degradation ceremony, I would have sought to nip that legend in the bud.

I was then led, between four men and a non-commissioned officer, to the centre of the square.

Nine o'clock struck; General Darras, commanding the parade, gave the order to raise arms.

I was suffering agonies, but steeled myself to concentrate all my strength. To sustain myself, I evoked the memory of my wife and children.

As soon as the sentence had been read out, I called out, addressing myself to the troops: 'Soldiers, you are degrading an innocent man; soldiers, you are dishonouring an innocent man. Long live France, long live the army.'

An adjutant of the Republican Guard came up to me. Rapidly, he tore off buttons, trouser stripes and the insignia of my rank from my kepi and sleeves, then he broke my sword. I saw these tatters of honour fall at my feet. Then with an appalling shudder of my whole being, but with my body erect and head held high, I shouted again and again to the soldiers, to the assembled crowd, 'I am innocent.'

The ceremony continued. I had to march around the soldiers' square formation. I heard the yells of the deluded throng, I sensed the shiver of thrill which I knew must be going through the crowd since they were being presented with a man convicted of treason, and I tried to transmit another feeling to them: that of my innocence.

The parade around the square finished; the torture was over, at least I thought so.

Source: A. Dreyfus, *Cinq années de ma vie* (1982), pp. 80–1.

Léon Daudet
LE CHÂTIMENT ('THE PUNISHMENT')

Eight o'clock. It is a sharp, rainy Paris morning … Big livid clouds hang in a dull sky. Passers-by hurry towards the Ecole Militaire. Place Fontenoy has already been invaded by a tumultuous crowd which the police is controlling… The neighbouring streets are rivers of anxious faces.

Behind the big gate, on the vast, solemn Morland square, troops begin to mass. The companies march past. I hear a single step, made up of hundreds of steps, brief commands, the rustle of rifles, leather equipment and swords. I see the surroundings: on the sides the squat buildings which will enclose the drama, ochre-coloured and chalky-white, their windows lined with faces. In the background, the Ecole de Guerre, its central clock, its columns, a deserted courtyard… and by the side pillars, military and civilian spectators… Not a murmur is to be heard …

With every minute that passes the regular-shaped compound is becoming fenced with soldiers bearing all manner of arms, who take their place methodically… Trumpets resound quite nearby, others further away, and still more seem to reply to them. Now the spectacle is ready. The courtyard is surrounded by a long geometric ribbon of cloth, bodies and steel, infantry, cavalry, artillery… in fine, strict discipline; but despite the variety of uniforms, it all merges into a mass of greyish blue…the central space remains empty, immense and gleaming with mud. It is here that destiny must be fulfilled.

All eyes are fixed on the large clock which swallows up time slowly. Over there, in the right hand corner, lies a dark and guarded door, through which he will have to come out… In a side road, between two buildings there is a gleam of armour beside a black van which will be the exit of shame. Five cavalrymen arrive, a general, two officers and two dragoons… Only a few minutes to go… Only two minutes… Nine o'clock strikes. The general draws his sword. The drums roll. Their dull rumble reflects the contained shudder of all that silent assembly. The fateful door opens and the terrible procession emerges: four artillerymen, the culprit between them; and nearby, the executioner, an officer of the Republican Guard. This sombre little group moves forward at a march, diagonally. It stops a few metres from the general. All hearts tremble. A stormy silence prevails. The clouds roll away; a brief and bloody ray of sunshine casts a little life on this death that is worse than death itself.

The clerk appears. He reads the judgement. But his voice is lost in space, like that of the general. At once the executor, a sort of helmeted giant, approaches the convicted man, a rigid, dark silhouette upon whom all attention is focused. He does not hesitate and sets to work on the kepi: he tears off the insignia, the fine strips of gold, the decorations of the jacket and sleeves. The mannequin-victim cooperates with this atrocious task: he even raises his arms. He shouts a few words; 'I am innocent!.. innocent!… Long live France!'…

Outside, on the square, at the rear, on the pedestals, the crowd gets restless and shouts angrily. People scream and boo. It is a hurricane of mingled, strident insults…

But within no one flinches among the soldiers who witness and judge I take some opera glasses… The condemned man… submits like a puppet frozen to the spot. I catch sight of his sly and wan face, raised in ultimate defiance. But his body catches my attention: this disparaged, lying body which is being stripped piece by piece of everything that gave it social value, rank and its undeserved grade.

Now the executor stoops over completely. Actively, with meticulous care, he seeks out, slashes and pulls off the reddish stripes on the trousers. Are these objects falling to the ground, or scraps of a life, shreds of honour?

The general and his retinue remain firmly on horseback. The military compound is impassive and tense… It is the end of the physical torture. The giant draws the sword of the man who was once a captain, and with a single sharp snap, a last flash of steel, breaks it over his knee. The remains lie on the ground, lamentable rags …

What else can be inflicted on this small, automaton-like man, now completely in black, stripped of everything, what can be done to this hideous beast of treachery who remains standing upright, having survived this catastrophe?… He will now be exposed to the scorn of those who were his comrades, whose defeat he was planning, all those courageous officers, all those humble soldiers who stand immobile and terrified… He will march before these honest people, before uprightness, before discipline, before duty, before potential heroism, all sentiments that are deprived of meaning for him the traitor whose mind was clouded by monstrous moral deviation and incomprehensible, covetous perversity.

The funereal procession begins to move again. It proceeds around the military enclosure… He approaches between his guards, a walking corpse, marching automatically as if on parade, frail to all appearances but magnified by his shame… Near to us, he still finds the strength to call out, 'I am innocent…' in a blank, precipitate voice. And there he is before me, at the moment when he passes dry-eyed, his gaze lost no doubt in the past, since his future is dead along with his honour. He no longer has any age. He no longer has a name. He no longer has a complexion. His is the colour of treason. His face is grey, flattened and base, showing no sign of remorse, a foreigner certainly, a wreck from the ghetto. A stubborn, determined audacity persists, banishing all feeling of compassion… This is his last walk among human beings and yet he seems to be profiting from it, so great is his self-control and defiance of ignominy. It is a terrible sign that his will has not sunk into the mud, that there has been neither collapse nor weakness In these tragic circumstances, tears would not have appeared cowardly.

The angry shouts of the crowd have ceased. The little sun has disappeared. We are nervously exhausted. It is time for the drama to end. The degradation and march past have lasted just ten minutes but our emotions have gone right around the clock. The end of that sinister march is the black van waiting over there in the little avenue where the corpse finally arrives and disappears inside, lifted in by the policemen. We are relieved of his presence.

Life resumes. The troops disband, beat drums, sound the fanfare! Cast your proud and sonorous mantle over this vile burial. Rifles bristle. The soldiers march briskly and this spectacle is forever fixed in their eyes.

For the idea of the homeland is so deep-rooted and proud that it draws strength from its antithesis and any attacks directed against it cause an excess of excitement. Above the wreckage of so many beliefs, a single faith remains true and sincere, that which safeguards our race, our language, the blood of our blood, which unites us in solidarity. These serried ranks are ours. That wretch was not a Frenchman. We have all understood this from his action, from his appearance, from his face. He has plotted his own downfall but his crime has exalted us. And as I leave that accursed spectacle, amongst the tumult, the commands, the warlike march, I see rising up before me the lofty, simple column 'In memory of army and naval officers and soldiers who were killed in action in defence of our country.'

Source: Le Figaro, 6 January, 1895.

THEODOR HERZL

On that dreary winter morning, numerous curious onlookers gathered around the Ecole Militaire, situated near the 1889 Exhibition building, in order to witness the Captain's degradation. A large number of officers were recognisable, some of them accompanied by their wives. At the courtyard entrance, however, only officers and a few journalists were admitted. The usual crowd was waiting outside, the gawping spectators who usually attend executions… The police was present in strength.

At 9 o'clock the huge courtyard was filled with detachments of soldiers who formed up in a square, five thousand men in all. In the middle of them, there was a general on horseback. A few minutes after nine o'clock, Dreyfus was led into the yard wearing his captain's uniform. Four soldiers flanked him before the general, who shouted out: 'Alfred Dreyfus, you are unworthy to bear arms. I degrade you in the name of the French people. Let the judgment be executed.' Dreyfus raised his right hand and called out: 'I swear that you are degrading an innocent man. Long live France.' At that moment, the drums began to roll, and a military court clerk began to tear the buttons and stripes of his uniform, which had been partially unstitched beforehand.

Dreyfus maintained a dignified bearing throughout this procedure which lasted scarcely more than a few minutes. Then there was the march past the assembled troops.

Dreyfus' attitude was that of a man conscious of his innocence. Passing before a group of officers who called out 'Judas! Traitor!', Dreyfus shouted in reply: 'I forbid you to insult me.' At 9:20, the parade ended.

Then, in shackles, Dreyfus was handed over to the policemen. From that moment, he would be treated as a civilian prisoner. The crowd thronged at the gate to witness the prisoner's departure. Shouts filled with hate were heard. 'If they ever let him out, he'll be torn apart.'

I would like to add that as Dreyfus passed in front of the soldiers, among whom were numerous young recruits, he often shouted, 'I am innocent.' Stopping before a group of journalists, he exclaimed, 'You will tell the whole of France that I am innocent.' Some of them heaped abuse on him. Shouts went up from the crowd following the ceremony from outside, through the railings: 'Death to the traitor'.

Note: 'Death to the Jews' shouted by the crowd at the degradation was either deliberately left out by Herzl or excised by his editors.

Source: Published in *Neue Freie Presse* (Vienna), 5 January 1895.

Appendix 9: Letter from Dreyfus, on île de Saint-Martin-de Ré, to Charles Dupuy, Prime Minister and Minister of the Interior 26 January 1895

LETTER TO MR. CHARLES DUPUY

Minister of the Interior, Prime Minister
Depot of Saint-Martin-de Ré, 26 January 1895

Minister,

I have been convicted of the most infamous crime that a soldier can commit, and I am innocent.

After my sentence, I resolved to kill myself. But my family and friends convinced me that if I were dead, everything would be over: my name, the name carried by my dear children, would be dishonoured for ever.

So I had to live!

My pen is powerless to recount for you the agony I am enduring; as a Frenchman, your heart will make you sense it better than I ever could.

You know, Minister, of the letter that constituted the accusation formulated against me.

That letter was not written by me.

Is it apocryphal? Was it really sent, along with the documents listed in it?… Was my handwriting copied in order to target me individually? Or is it simply a fatal similarity of handwriting …

So many questions which my brain alone is powerless to answer.

I ask you here, Minister, not for pardon or pity, but only justice…

In the name of my honour as a soldier which has been torn from me, in the name of my unfortunate wife, and finally in the name of my poor children, I beg you to continue the investigation to find the real culprit.

In a century like ours, in a country like France, imbued with noble ideas of justice and truth, it is impossible that with the powerful means of investigation at your disposal, you do not succeed in clarifying this tragic story, in unmasking the monster who has brought misfortune and dishonour to an honest family.

I entreat you once again, Minister, in the name of all that you yourself hold dearest in this world, for justice, justice through the pursuit of research.

As for myself, I seek only oblivion and silence about my name, until the day that my innocence is recognised.

Until I arrived here, I was able to write and work in my cell, correspond with the various members of my family and write to my wife every day. It was a consolation for me in the appalling situation in which I find myself – so appalling, Minister, that no human mind could possibly imagine a more tragic one.

Yesterday, still happy, with nothing and nobody to envy! Today, having done nothing to deserve it, an outcast of society! Ah, Minister, I believe that no man in our century has endured such martyrdom. To have one's honour as highly placed as anyone else in the world and to be deprived of it by one's peers; is there a more monstrous torture for an innocent man?

Night and day, Minister, I am alone in my cell with my brain, without any occupation. My mind, already deeply shaken by these catastrophes – as tragic as they were unexpected – is no longer very stable. So I ask you to kindly give permission for me to write and work in my cell.

I also ask that you allow me to correspond from time to time with the various members of my family (parents-in-law, brothers and sisters).

Finally, I was informed yesterday that I will only be able to write to my wife twice a week. I beg of you to allow me to write more often to this unfortunate child who has such need of consolation and support in the appalling situation which fate has brought upon us.

Justice therefore, Minister, and work – that is all that is asked of you by the most unfortunate of Frenchmen, to allow his mind to await the shining hour when his innocence will be recognised.

I beg of you, Minister, to accept the assurance of my highest respect.

Alfred Dreyfus

Source: A. Dreyfus, *Cinq années de ma vie* (Paris: La Découverte, 1982), pp. 231–3.

Appendix 10: Henry's statement concerning secret information received from an agent [Edmond Lajoux, working as a double agent] in April 1895

You have in Paris a gentleman who is admirably informed and in the pay of Lieutenant-Colonel von Schwartzkoppen.

The latter has at his disposal some quite considerable funds, obtained from the intelligence service in Berlin, by means of which he has organised a veritable espionage service in Paris.

On all these questions, Lieutenant-Colonel von Schwartzkoppen corresponds directly with the head of the General Staff, without going through the intelligence service.

The person who passes him information in Paris is decorated with the Legion of Honour and aged about 45. But it is not known whether he is a civilian or a serviceman.

The person often goes to the embassy on rue de Lille, wearing the Legion of Honour ribbon in his buttonhole.

He passes numerous reports to Lieutenant-Colonel von Schwartzkoppen. The last one he handed over concerned the production of new artillery equipment in France.

All these reports are much appreciated at [German] General Staff headquarters.

Source: 3ème Cass, I, 19.

Appendix 11: Picquart's first report on Esterhazy, 1 September 1896

Intelligence Service note on Major Esterhazy, 74th Infantry

NB: Ellipsis marks indicate the omission of passages, the inclusion of which could present problems for the Intelligence Service.

1. At the end of the month of April 1896, the service was given possession of a missive originating from Embassy X addressed to 'Major Esterhazy, 27 rue de la Bienfaisance, Paris'. The contents of this missive reveal the existence of shady negotiations between the embassy and the addressee. (See Doc No. 1 and 1A, photographs).

2. At the end of the month of June 1896, an agent… presented himself to Mr N… and made, among others, the following revelations:

'For two or three years, Mr A…. a foreign agent, has been given information by a French major who has supplied him with the most diverse indications and has notably given him the Ecole normale firing course manual from the Châlons camp, and a great deal of information about artillery. This latter fact even aroused suspicion; questions were asked as to how this Major could be informed in this way and it was thought it could very well be a case of a hoaxer or an agent provocateur.'

The French service in Paris having made contact with the employee in question, he made similar statements to the two officers charged with interrogating him. (See report of 6 August 1896, Document 2).

3. Although Major Esterhazy is considered a bad officer by his colleagues, caring little for his profession, it has been noticed that he continually sought to obtain information about certain military questions. Thus, for several years running (1893, 1894 and, it is believed, 1895) he asked to go to the artillery firing schools. There he made friends with artillery officers and had no qualms about asking them numerous questions on the progress of their weapons. In his regiment, he was on the lookout for the firing school course manuals from the Châlons camp and all other documents from that school. He had copies of documents made in his office by soldiers who can easily be found. He was not always in a position to return all the documents lent to him to their owners, and he got out of it by claiming to have lost them. Finally his insistence on obtaining documents of this type was noticed and officers instinctively only lent him their copies with great reluctance.

4. In the middle of 1894, the intelligence service was given possession of an anonymous note addressed to Mr A… (a foreign agent*), with which various confidential or secret documents were being sent to the latter.

The author of this note, speaking of the artillery firing manual, said that if it was desired, he could have it copied in extenso. He ended his note by saying, 'I am leaving on manoeuvres.'

Comparing the handwriting of this note with Major Esterhazy's usual writing, one finds between them such a similarity that it is striking even to the least expert eye, and certain words of one are an absolute copy of certain words of the other.

At that time, Esterhazy was a major and could easily have had a copy made of a document as voluminous as the firing manual.

Finally, around the middle of the year; the manoeuvres in question could only be manoeuvres involving officers. Major Esterhazy precisely took part in manoeuvres with officers from 21–26 May 1894 (see Documents No 3 and 3a (anonymous note), 3b and 3c (the Major's handwriting), No. 4 (summons to manoeuvres).

5. Although he is married and a father, Major Esterhazy leads a disorderly life. He maintains a woman at 49 rue de Douai (see Document No. 5) and spends all his evenings in night-haunts such as the Moulin Rouge etc.

His creditors complain about him and he has recently received some summonses before the justice of the peace for old and minor debts (see Documents 6 and 7).

On several occasions, messengers from various credit establishments have been seen to present themselves in vain at his home, seeking payment. (See among others Document No 8.)

He has been going into No. 6, Boulevard Poissonnière, where there is a gaming-house. There is no proof, however, that he gambled. (See Document No.. 8).

Finally, he is thought to concern himself with speculation and frequents assiduously a certain Count X… considered as suspicious by the Prefecture of Police.

It has not been possible to investigate things more deeply in a preliminary enquiry, which, in order to remain secret, has necessarily been conducted with limited means. But the facts indicated seem serious enough to merit a more detailed enquiry. Above all, it would be necessary to seek some explanations from Major Esterhazy about his relations with the embassy and the use he made of the documents which he had copied. It would also be interesting to question his secretaries. But it is indispensable to operate by surprise, with both firmness and caution, because the Major is known as a man of unequalled audacity and trickery.

* This note has already served as the basis for other enquiries, which does not prevent the existence of the facts indicated. (It is the *bordereau*.)

Source: Cass, II, 87–9.

Appendix 12: Lucie's appeal to the Chamber of Deputies for a revision of the Dreyfus verdict at the 1894 court martial, 18 September 1896

Deputies,

In its issue of Tuesday 15 September… in defiance of all contrary evidence, *L'Eclair* announced that there was irrefutable, material proof of the guilt of my husband in the hands of the War Ministry, which they had transmitted confidentially, during the deliberation, to the judges of the court martial; and it had shaped their conclusions, without either the defendant or his lawyer having any knowledge of it.

I refused to believe such a fact and awaited the usual denial with which the officious Havas Agency normally responds to all false items of news, even ones of lesser importance than this.

The denial did not come. And so it is true that after debates shrouded in the most complete mystery because of the closed hearing, a French officer has been convicted by a court martial on a charge produced by the prosecution without his knowledge, which therefore neither he nor his counsel were able to discuss.

It is the denial of all justice.

I have been subjected myself to the most cruel martyrdom for almost two years – like the man in whose innocence I have absolute faith. I remained silent despite the odious and absurd slanders propagated amongst the public and in the press.

Today it is my duty to break that silence, and without comment or recriminations, I address myself to you, Gentlemen of the Chamber of Deputies, the only power to whom I can have recourse, and I demand justice.

Lucie Dreyfus

Source: ATQV, p. 83.

Appendix 13: Lucie's supplication to Pope Leo XIII, September 1896

Most blessed Father,

Lucie Eugénie Dreyfus, wife of a captain holding a brilliant position in the French Army, of Jewish birth, begs and implores the intervention of the Most Holy Father, Leo XIII, under the following circumstances: Alfred Dreyfus, a soldier most devoted to his country, was tried, before a special court-martial, on evidence both fallacious and frivolous, and condemned by his judges to perpetual exile, accompanied by the severest form of punishment.

A doubt exists as to the crime of Dreyfus, and increases day by day. Moreover, Christian minds are filled with a grave misgiving that antisemitic prejudice has had much to do with the matter. Experts in handwriting have shown singular hesitation in forming their decisions. Proofs, documents, and signs alleged before the secret court were insufficient. After the terrible sentence, no one was allowed in the presence of the prisoner who, snatched from the bosom of his family, was conveyed to Devil's Island, where he endures a wretched existence.

Lucie Eugénie Dreyfus, prostrate at the feet of your Holiness, most humbly supplicates the mercy and compassion of the Father of the Catholic Church. She declares that her husband is innocent, and the victim of a judicial error. Snatched from all association with humankind as he is, this petition is signed by his grief-stricken wife, who, in tears, looks towards the Vicar of Christ, even as formerly the daughters of Jerusalem turned to Christ Himself.

Signed Lucie Eugénie Dreyfus

Source: Written in Latin. Published in English on 5 December 1897 in the *Sunday Special.* Published in French on 8 December 1897 in *La Libre Parole.* English translation: G. Whyte, *The Accused: The Dreyfus Trilogy* (Bonn: Inter Nationes, 1996), p. 105.

Appendix 14: Codicil to Picquart's will, 2 April 1897

The Codicil

In case of the death of the undersigned, please deliver this letter to the President of the Republic, who alone should know of its contents.

G. PICQUART

Lieutenant-Colonel with the 4th Regiment of *Tirailleurs* (Colonial Infantrymen)

Sousse, 2 April 1897

I, the undersigned Marie-Georges Picquart, Lieutenant-Colonel with the 4th *Tirailleurs* (Colonial Infantrymen), formerly Head of the Intelligence Service at the Ministry of War, certify on my honour the accuracy of the following information, which in the interests of truth and justice it is impossible to 'stifle,' as has been attempted.

In the month of May 1896 my attention had been drawn to Major Walsin-Esterhazy of the 74th Infantry, to whom a card-telegram containing highly suspect information, had been written by a person in the German Embassy (probably the military attaché Lieutenant-Colonel Schwartzkoppen). From the in-depth investigation which I undertook, the results of which are recorded in a note of 1 September 1896, which I conveyed to General Gonse, it is clear that Major Walsin-Esterhazy is an agent for Germany. There is abundant proof of this; and Esterhazy's desperate financial situation, together with his absolute lack of scruples in the ways he chooses to obtain money, only corroborate the material evidence collected.

In the months of August or September Esterhazy caused several Deputies to act on his behalf and through his friend (and possible accomplice), Lucien Weil, he even induced General Saussier to help him obtain a position in the Infantry's head office or in the Intelligence Service at the War Ministry. My report to the Minister on the subject of Esterhazy thwarted this ambition, despite his numerous and insistent approaches.

In studying the Esterhazy Affair I was struck by the following: that certain facts attributed to *Dreyfus* in fact fitted perfectly with facts relating to Esterhazy.

When Dreyfus was accused of writing a document addressed to the German military attaché in Paris, I was curious to compare Esterhazy's handwriting with the writing of that document. To my great stupefaction they were identical.

Three experts (out of 5) had declared that the incriminating document was the writing of Dreyfus, *modified* or *disguised*. But I found that this was Esterhazy's *natural* handwriting.

Not wishing to rely only on my own knowledge, I took a sample of Esterhazy's handwriting to one of the experts, Mr Bertillon, the one who was most convinced, without telling him of its provenance. Mr Bertillon declared immediately and without hesitation that this was the writing of the Dreyfus document. He even pressed me with questions to find out from where I had obtained this sample, finding, he said, 'that the disguises which Dreyfus had used were so well copied in this writing that the person who had written it must have undertaken very special studies.'

Moreover, all the samples of Esterhazy's handwriting (and I have samples from various periods) are identical.

I reported these facts first to General Boisdeffre, then with his agreement to General Gonse and finally to the Minister General Billot. General Boisdeffre and General Gonse, who in short ordered the Dreyfus trial under the direction of General Mercier, appeared quite embarrassed. The Minister accepted all my proofs, and told me that if need be, he would get his clutches into Esterhazy. For the time being I was to continue my investigations.

Meanwhile, the press campaign in favour of Dreyfus took place, as well as the questioning of Castelin. General Boisdeffre saw the Minister and after their meeting, the latter seemed to have quite turned around. He told me very openly (and I take the liberty of believing it was not true) that he had evidence of the guilt of Dreyfus from his special police, but he did not tell me what it was.

General Gonse asked me with a certain anxiety if I really believed what the Minister had told me. As I always stated that I was convinced of the evidence I had gathered, I was sent away one day (November 16) on a special mission to the 6th Corps; then I was sent to the 7th, then the 14th, then the 15th. Finally I was detailed to the 4th *Tirailleurs* (Colonial Infantrymen), all this without allowing me to draw breath for a moment and with the obvious intention of distancing from the Intelligence Service someone who had just made a troublesome discovery.

Moreover, all the proofs that I had in hand, which were taken away from me a few days before I was sent on the so-called mission, demonstrate in the clearest fashion:

1. That Walsin-Esterhazy (and perhaps also his friend Weil) is an agent for Germany;

2. That the only tangible facts blamed on Dreyfus are attributable to Esterhazy;

3. That the trial of Dreyfus was handled in an unprecedentedly superficial manner, with the preconceived idea that Dreyfus was guilty, and with a disregard for due legal forms. (A secret *dossier* transmitted in the court chamber to the judges consisted of four documents, one of which related to Esterhazy, another to an individual designated by the letter D, which could not have been Dreyfus given the documents indicated, and the two others having no importance whatsoever, based simply on gossip.) It was this dossier *not communicated* to the accused or his lawyer which led to the conviction of Dreyfus. It had an impact on judges who were undecided, had no one to enlighten them and were obliged to make a rapid decision. It cannot withstand any reasoned discussion and the lawyer would certainly have refuted it in the most complete fashion.

I repeat: all these documents were taken away from me successively by General Gonse as and when I made my discoveries. I even fear that the documents contained in the dossier transmitted to the court chamber may also have been destroyed.

G. Picquart

Source: HAD, 2, pp. 701–4.

Appendix 15: Letter from Dreyfus on Devil's Island to the President of the Republic, 8 July 1897

Îles du Salut, 8 July 1897

To the President of the Republic

Mr President,

I permit myself to appeal once more to your great equity, to throw at your feet the expression of my profound despair, the cries of my immense grief.

I will open my heart fully to you, Mr President, certain that you will understand me. I appeal simply for your indulgence as to the form, the possible disjointedness of my thoughts. I have suffered too much, I am too broken, morally and physically, my mind is too crushed to be able to continue making the effort to collect my ideas.

As you know, Mr President, accused and then convicted on the evidence of handwriting for the most abominable crime, the most heinous crime that a man, a soldier, can commit, I wanted to survive to await the explanation of this appalling drama, to see my dear children again, on the day when honour is returned to them.

What I have suffered, Mr President, since the beginning of this sorrowful drama, only my heart knows! I have often called upon death with all my strength, and then I steeled myself again, still hoping in the end to see the light of justice dawn.

I submitted completely, scrupulously, to everything, I defy anybody to reproach me for any incorrect practice. I have never forgotten, I will not forget until my dying breath that a dual interest is at stake in this frightful affair: that of the homeland, mine and that of my children; one is just as sacred as the other.

Most certainly, I have suffered in being unable to alleviate the appalling sorrow of my wife and my family; I have suffered in being unable to devote myself body and soul to the discovery of the truth; but never did the thought occur to me, nor will occur to me, to arrive at this truth by means which might be harmful to the superior interests of the country. I would remain silent about the purity of my thought if I did not have as warrant the loyalty of my actions since the beginning of this sorrowful drama.

I have permitted myself, Mr President, to appeal to your high justice, in order to seek this truth; I have also entreated the Government of my country because I thought that the Government would find it possible to reconcile at once the interests of justice and compassion necessarily inspired by such an appalling and atrocious situation, with the interests of the country.

As for me, Mr President, confronted with the most abominable abuse, when my pain became such that death would have been a kindness, when my reason was collapsing, when everything within me was tearing apart at seeing myself treated like the last miserable wretch on earth, when finally a cry of rebellion escaped from my heart at the thought of my children growing up, their name dishonoured... it was to you, Mr President, it was to my country's Government that my cry of supreme appeal was addressed, it was in that direction that I always directed my eyes, my tearful glance. I hoped at least, Mr President, that I would be judged on my actions. Since the beginning of this sorrowful drama, I have never deviated from the line of conduct I had mapped out for myself, that my conscience inflexibly dictated. I have suffered everything, endured everything, I have been struck pitilessly without ever knowing why… and strengthened by my conscience, I was able to resist.

Ah! yes indeed! I had moments of anger, reactions of impatience. I sometimes let my cankered heart gush forth all its bitterness, consumed by the insults, its most intimate sentiments torn asunder. But I have never forgotten for a single moment that the homeland comes above all human passions.

And yet, Mr President, the situation imposed on me became more atrocious every day; the blows continued to rain down on me without respite, without my understanding why, without my ever having provoked them by my words or actions.

Add to my own sorrow, so atrocious and intense, the torture of infamy, that of the climate, of quasi-solitary confinement, of seeing myself an object of scorn – often not concealed – and of constant suspicion by those who guard me night and day, is that not too much, Mr President… for a human being who has always done his duty in all directions?

And what is appalling for my mind, already suffering from hallucinations, already numb and reeling from the blows which strike it constantly, is to see that an honest man, a loyal Frenchman, whose rectitude of conduct, his invincible desire that no torture will undermine, and whose wish is to die as he lived, is to see himself treated, as I said, every day more harshly, more wretchedly.

My misery cannot be compared with any other; there is not one minute of my life that is not agony. Whatever the conscience, the strength of spirit of a man may be, I am collapsing and the tomb would be a kindness to me.

And so, Mr President, in this profound distress of my whole being, crushed by the tortures, by this situation of infamy which is breaking me, by the suffering which strangles my throat and suffocates me, my mind hallucinating from all the blows which strike me without respite, it is to you, Mr President, it is to the Government of my country that I utter this cry of appeal, certain that it will be heard.

My life, Mr President, I will not describe. Today as yesterday, it belongs to my country. What I ask it simply, as a supreme favour, is to take it quickly, not to leave me to die so slowly in atrocious agony, enduring so many ignominious tortures that I have not deserved, that I do not deserve.

But what I also ask of my country, is to shed complete and full light on this frightful drama; for my honour does not belong to the country, it is the legacy of my children, the property of two families.

And I also entreat, with all the strength of my soul, that consideration be given to the atrocious and intolerable situation, worse than death itself, of my wife and family; and also to think of my children, my dear little children who are growing up, who are pariahs; that every possible effort should be made, everything in a word that is compatible with the interests of the country, to bring an end as soon as possible to the torture of so many human beings.

Confident of your equity, I beg of you, Mr President, to accept the expression of my respectful sentiments.

Source: Cinq années de ma vie (1982), pp. 234–7.

Appendix 16: Letter from Esterhazy to the President of the Republic, 5 November 1897

Mr President,

Please excuse me for troubling you once again, but I fear that the War Minister may not have transmitted my last letters to you, and I insist that you should be well informed about the situation. It is, moreover, the last time that I shall address myself to the public authorities. The woman who warned me of the horrible plot hatched against me has given me, among others, a document that offers me protection since it proves the villainy of Dreyfus. It is also a danger for my country because if it is published along with the facsimile of handwriting, France will either be forced into humiliation or into war...

You who are above the futile party quarrels in which my honour serves as ransom; do not force me to choose between two equally horrible alternatives.

Force the Pontius Pilates of politics to make a clear and precise declaration instead of manoeuvring to preserve the voices of the friends of Barrabas. All the letters I have written will be entrusted to one of my relatives, who this summer had the honour of receiving two emperors.

What will people think throughout the entire world when people hear of the cowardly and cold cruelty with which I have been left to struggle in my agony – without support, without counsel! My blood will be on your hands. And when the letter, of which the Government is aware, is published – which is one of the proofs of Dreyfus' guilt – what will the whole world say about this miserable Parliamentary tactic, which has failed to impose silence by a few energetic words on the pack of hounds?

I appeal to you in the words of the old French cry, 'Haro, my Prince, come to my rescue!' I address my appeal to you, Mr President, since before being Head of State, you are an honest man who must be profoundly sickened, to the depths of your soul, by the cowardice you see.

Defend me, and I will return the document to the War Minister without anyone in the world having laid eyes on it. But defend me quickly for I can wait no longer, and I will stop at nothing to defend or avenge my honour, which has been unworthily sacrificed.

I am, etc

Esterhazy.

Source: Répertoire, 104–5.

Appendix 17: Du Paty's 'note in two hands' sent to Esterhazy during the Pellieux investigation, *c.* 20 November 1897

If General de Pellieux were to ask me if I have had dealings with you, I intend to say the following, which is more or less true:

'As soon as we were informed anonymously of the plot hatched against Major Esterhazy, I understood how important it would be to warn him, to prevent an act of desperation.

I thus entered into relations with him, by means which I do not wish to reveal, in order not to compromise third parties to whom I am bound by honour. I must say, however, that the *dame voilée* is completely unconnected with the events just related...

The effect of my relationship with Major Esterhazy was to prevent him from taking extreme measures, for he had been warned for his part and wanted...

As soon as I knew that he possessed a secret document, all my efforts were focused on making him return it, by appealing to his sense of patriotism; and I was successful, moreover, without difficulty.

My intervention thus served to curb a very legitimate exasperation. I abstained from communicating anything of a secret nature to him. Any information of this nature which he may have had came from another source. I am not involved in the campaign against Picquart. On the other hand, General Boisdeffre is not unaware that I have had indirect relations with Major Esterhazy.

From the moment when Major Esterhazy had supporters and a lawyer, and wrote articles in the newspapers, I ceased my relations, which were no longer useful.

Since he made an honourable commitment to me, I will release him from his word by a message, if you wish; for without that, he will feel obliged to deny these relations, but his word of honour, like mine, will remain with respect to third parties:

Consequently

1. Until you have received an official letter from me, you are not supposed to know me;

2. Remain silent on the nature of the relationship that we have had, by hiding behind your commitments towards third parties;

3. Insist that this relationship consisted purely of acts of encouragement, advice of moderation and appeals to your finer sentiments to return the document, and is completely unconnected to the business of the veiled woman;

4. Never have I revealed anything confidential to you, and I was not the one who denounced Picquart to you.

That is the line I will take: take good heed of all the parts I have ticked in red and destroy this. You understand how important it is to be completely in agreement, for you and for me.

All is well: the person who went to fetch Picquart's famous letters, as agreed, is precisely the author of the telegram signed Blanche, which is in the person's handwriting, but slightly disguised.

The police has laid hands on her. She is a friend of…

We will be able to prove that the Rumanian gave you nothing.

Source: Esterhazy, *Les dessous de l'Affaire Dreyfus* (Paris: Fayard, 1899), vol. 3, pp. 190–2.

Appendix 18: Investigation reports on Esterhazy by Pellieux and Ravary; extracts from the conclusions of the three reports, Nov-Dec 1897

Pellieux's Report of 20 November 1897

… An officer, head of the intelligence service at the War Ministry [Picquart], becomes the agent – unconsciously one hopes – of the defenders of Dreyfus, defenders of good faith or not, it matters little. He delivers to a third party Section letters, directly from his superior, probably secret documents which do not belong to him. He commits a serious lapse of professional duty and must be punished. With what aim did he compile the Esterhazy dossier? It is not up to me to find out, but I can say that he compiled the Leblois dossier, against his leaders, against the Minister.

This related question, which makes the whole affair a Dreyfus/Esterhazy/ Piquart question, seems to me to call for a prompt and radical solution, and in my soul and conscience, I say:

Esterhazy seems to me to be in the clear. However unworthy he may be because of serious lapses in his private life, he cannot, *in my opinion*, be accused in this case of treason.

Picquart seems to be guilty. Unfortunately, I think that the documents which exist at the General Staff allow no doubt of this (intercepted letters and telegrams).

Should the enquiry be continued and extended? If Picquart is questioned in Tunis, it will be said that we are afraid to bring him here. If we question him here as a witness, it will be very difficult to keep him away him from his advisers.

It seems to me that Lieutenant-Colonel Picquart should be brought before a commission of inquiry, and that he should be questioned in conditions of the utmost secrecy. Governor, that is my conclusion and I submit it for your approval, declaring my enquiry finished.

Signed: DE PELLIEUX

Source: 3ème Cass., III, 392–7.

Pellieux's Report of 3 December 1897

My conclusions, based on the various depositions, are as follows:

As far as Esterhazy is concerned in the present case, subject to the expert analysis of the bordereau, there is no evidence to support the Dreyfus accusation; no evidence of the accusations of Lieutenant-Colonel Picquart; but nevertheless there is a need for complete and full light to be shed on the matter, in a public hearing; this senior officer is to be brought before a court martial and the procedure continued to its conclusion, conviction or acquittal.

However, because of the inanity of some of the accusations, I ask that Major Esterhazy should be left temporarily at liberty during the examination, at least until the time when the results of the new expert analysis are known; besides, the reporting judge is free to have him imprisoned before, if this was felt to be necessary.

As far as Lieutenant-Colonel Picquart is concerned, it is easy to recognise that his depositions are a tissue of deliberate and calculated inaccuracies, perfidious insinuations against his superiors and his subordinates. The basis of his creation against Esterhazy is a document which has no authenticity or verisimilitude, that I would like to think was not fabricated for the needs of some cause or other. As I said in my first report, this senior officer seems to me to be the agent – unconsciously, I hope – of a person who, knowing his belief in the innocence of Dreyfus, has pushed him down a path which, I fear, has made him come close to dishonour.

Whatever the facts may be, his depositions themselves contain the confession of a military error of exceptional gravity: this superior officer, head of the intelligence service at the War Ministry, if he did not actually transmit secret or other documents relating to the Section, has certainly passed on knowledge of them to a third person outside the Ministry, whom he often received in his office [Me Leblois]. He handed over to this person correspondence between himself and his superior, General Gonse, deputy head of the Army General Staff, a correspondence which cannot be considered personal since it deals with his Section and a confidential mission; and he did that with the avowed aim of using it, he says, as a defence against his superiors and his subordinates.

That represented a strange concept of military honour and his professional duties, and I conclude that this officer should be sent immediately before a commission of inquiry, called to rule on whether there is a case for discharging him from the army for infringements of honour, or at least for serious misconduct in the service.

Signed: DE PELLIEUX

Source: 3ème Cass., I, 101–3.

Ravary's Report of 31 December 1897

Certainly the private life of Major Esterhazy could not be held up as a model to our young officers. But from these lapses, even of the most reprehensible kind, one should not necessarily conclude that he is guilty of the greatest crime that a soldier and a Frenchman can commit.

Besides, the duty of impartiality requires mention of the fact that the personal notes about the accused are full of praise up to 1896, the year in which he was suspended from duty on the grounds of temporary infirmities, and a number of letters written by his former superiors bear witness to their feelings of esteem for him. In short, what remains of this sorry affair, which was so skilfully plotted? A painful impression that will elicit a distressing response in all truly French hearts. Of the protagonists brought on stage, some acted in the open, others remained in the wings; but all the means employed had the same objective: the review of a judgement that was legally and justly delivered.

In conclusion, we would say that whilst the accusations against Major Esterhazy were made with a precision and stage-direction that was liable to move and trouble public opinion, in reality, no convincing, legal proof of his guilt has been established, and the laborious examination which we have made has been unable to gather sufficient charges to support the indictment for high treason directed against the accused.

In consequence we are of the opinion that a ruling of discharge for lack of evidence should be made in this case.

Reporting judge: Major Ravary

Source: Révision, pp. 115–22.

Appendix 19: Debate in the Chamber of Deputies, 4 December 1897

Latest Intelligence
The case of Captain Dreyfus
DEBATE IN THE CHAMBER

… The sitting was then suspended till the arrival of General Billot, the Minister of War. On the resumption of the sitting General Billot, said:-

'The Prime Minister has told you that, in the circumstances, there is no Dreyfus affair. A year ago, in reply to M. Castelin, the Minister of War had occasion to say to you that Dreyfus had been judged, well judged, and condemned unanimously by seven of his peers on the testimony of 27 officers called as witnesses. Questioned once again the other day, the Government, by the mouth of the Minister of War, declared to you that it considered that the Dreyfus affair had been regularly and justly judged. As for me, in my soul and conscience as a soldier, as head of the army, I consider the judgement as having been well deserved, and Dreyfus as guilty. (*Loud cheers from the Centre, Right, and a portion of the Left.*)

I pass to the Esterhazy affair. An officer has been the object of a denunciation. The head of the army prescribed immediately the regulation extra-judicial inquiry. That inquiry was conducted loyally and speedily by General de Pellieux under the high direction of the Military Governor of Paris. As a result of this inquiry an order to institute a formal inquiry was issued this morning by the Military Governor of Paris. I hope that the Chamber will understand that the Minister of War, that the Government, that the Chamber itself would exceed their rights and duties if they were in any way to influence the action of justice, especially, when it is proceeding under the supreme direction of a man like General Saussier, General-in-Chief of your armies, covered with years and glory, whose character has never been misunderstood nor disputed by any one, and whose authority extends, not merely over the entire army, but beyond our frontiers. (*Loud cheers.*)

I come now to the odious accusations which too long have been directed against the heads of the army, and, in particular, against its eminent head of the staff. (*Loud cheers.*) I have regretted from the bottom of my heart that I am disarmed by the law and cannot punish as they deserve certain insinuations which are as perfidious as they are culpable. You will permit the *doyen* of the French Army, who has the honour of being today its head, to say to you that for 19 months he has been at work with his eminent associate, General de Boisdeffre, in putting France into readiness for all emergencies. It is painful to read such outrages, to have to look on while a campaign, which I do not know how to characterize, is carried on against the national honour and the honour of the army. In the name of the army I beg the Chamber, which has given me its confidence for 19 months, to end this campaign as soon as possible.'

Source: The Times, 6 December 1897.

Appendix 20: Article by Theodor Herzl on the situation in France in 1897

The Situation in France

Some faithful and courageous men have tried to raise the heavy stone which covers his grave. But a frenzied pack threw themselves on the liberators and pushed them aside. The tombstone thus returned to its former position and the human being continues to remain buried. Such is the current aspect of the Dreyfus Affair, of sad renown. The people of France, so generous, so eager for justice, the people of Human Rights who review all trials and never allow an irrevocable verdict, these people decline to cast doubt on the guilt of the Jewish captain.

The noisy demonstrations in the streets, the patriotic declamations in the Chamber, the insults of the newspapers, all of these together pursue only one objective: to keep this Jew on Devil's Island. They are killing him again, though he is already buried. One should think of this proverb: 'When one is dead, it is for a long time.' All the more so if it is the fate of a living being, for he is certainly cut off from the living for a long time...

But the facts are as follows. They are refusing to hold another trial because Captain Dreyfus must not be found to be innocent... The Dreyfus Affair is not at all finished because the poor man is dying slowly on that island where fever is rife. The bitter suffering of that man has raised another question of no less considerable importance: For whom is he paying? For whom?…

All the unleashed fury has been reserved for Dreyfus. If it had been possible, the rabble would have rolled him in tar, quartered him, committed I know not what torture! And why? They were no longer cries of vengeance for a military treason which normally would barely excite the mob in times of peace. This explosion of anger was of a quite different nature and was like the excesses of a gang of rioters and people in revolt. They took scant account of the accusation. They were not screaming 'Down with Dreyfus!' but 'Down with the Jews!' It was like that from the beginning and so it continued…

Since they could not seize hold of the people they hated, they hated the one who could be seized. Thus, the Dreyfus Affair revealed in France such an accumulation of hatred against the Jews that one could not divine a priori who bore responsibility for it. Certainly not this courageous artillery captain, a native of Alsace, who was ready to lay down his life for France on the battlefields…

Do people really believe that the devourers of Jews, who have tested their strength on the unfortunate Dreyfus, will be content with a single victim? They have acquired a taste for blood and will ask for more, with all the more assurance and avidity since they have become aware of their own irresistible power…

Source: Die Welt (Basel), 24 December 1897

Appendix 21: Summons of Emile Zola, 20 January 1898 and extracts from Zola's trial 7–23 February 1898

Summons of Emile Zola, 20 January 1898

On 20 January 1898, at the request of the Public Prosecutor at the Court of Appeal of Paris, who elects domicile at the public prosecutor's office located in this city, at the Palais de Justice, acting in his capacity on the complaint filed on 18 January 1898, by the Minister of War, under article 47 of the law of 29 July 1881, in the name of the first Court Martial of the military government of Paris, having judged Major Esterhazy on 10 and 11 January 1898, in the court under his jurisdiction.

I, Charles-Marie-George Dupuis, court usher at the Court of Appeal of Paris, residing in the same town, at the Palais de Justice, undersigned,

Summon: 1. Mr A. Perrenx, manager of the newspaper *L'Aurore*, residing in Paris at 142, rue Montmartre, having been there and spoken first to an employee of the newspaper, then to him in person; 2.° Mr Emile Zola, man of letters, residing in Paris at 21bis, rue de Bruxelles, having been there and spoken to a person in his service, to appear before the Seine Assize Court, located at the Palais de Justice, Paris, on Monday, 7 February 1898, at eleven thirty in the morning,

As charged:

I - J.-A. Perrenx, Of having, in his capacity as manager of the newspaper *L'Aurore*, published in Paris less than three months ago, in number 87 of the second year of the paper, dated Thursday 13 January 1898, which issue was sold and distributed, put on sale and displayed in public places or meetings, the following passages contained in an article signed Emile Zola and entitled: 'Letter to Mr. Felix Faure, President of the Republic.'

First column of the first page:

'A Court Martial has just, by order, dared to acquit Esterhazy, a supreme affront to all truth, to all justice. And it is the end, France bears this defilement on its cheek. History will record that it was during your presidency that a social crime of such nature could be committed.'

Sixth column of the first page:

'They delivered this iniquitous sentence which will forever hang over our Courts Martial, which henceforth will sully all their rulings with suspicion. The first Court Martial may have been unintelligent, the second is necessarily criminal.'

Second column of the second page:

'… I accuse the second Court Martial of having concealed this illegality under order, committing in turn the legal crime of knowingly acquitting a guilty party.'

The aforesaid passages containing the imputation of facts liable to undermine the honour of the military government of Paris, which sat on 10 and 11 January 1898, and relating to its functions, and thus to have publicly libelled it, with regard to its functions;

II-Emile Zola

Of having, at the same time and same place, been an accessory to the offence specified above, by giving either to Mr. Perrenx, manager of the newspaper *L'Aurore*, or to any other editor or employee of the said paper, for transmission to the said manager, and in order to be published, the writings containing the passages referred to above, and of having thus procured the means which served to commit the offence, knowing that they had served that purpose.

Offences dealt with and punished by articles 23, 29, 30, 31, 35, 42, 43, 45, 47 clause 52 of the law of 29 July 1881, and articles 59 and 60 of the Penal Code

In order that the above-named should be fully informed, while speaking as above, I have also left them copy of the present summons.

M. President – M. Perrenx and M. Zola, you are warned that in an article of the newspaper *L'Aurore* entitled 'J'accuse', you have libelled the members of the first Court Martial who acquitted Major Esterhazy. We will proceed to call witnesses.

Source: Pro. Zola, pp. 20–1.

Extracts from Zola's trial, 7-23 February 1898

CASIMIR-PÉRIER CAUSES A STIR

There was much stir in court when it was announced that M. Casimir-Périer, the former President of the French Republic, would be the next witness. When he was called the presiding Judge said: 'You swear to speak without animus and fear, and to speak the truth and nothing but the truth.'

M. Casimir-Périer at this point interrupted the Judge, saying: 'Pardon me. I cannot swear to tell the truth, because I cannot do so. It is my duty not to tell it.' This statement caused a commotion among the audience. The presiding Judge resumed, remarking: 'The law compels you, before even speaking or refusing to testify, to take the oath.' M. Casimir-Périer then submitted, raised his hand and took the oath.

Source: New York Daily Tribune, Wednesday 9 February 1898.

Latest Intelligence

THE DREYFUS TRIAL

What took place during this interval no one has been able to discover. Of one thing there is absolute certainty; there was a council of war in the lobbies, for when the sitting was resumed General de Pellieux advanced to the railing and asked to be heard. The scene which ensued was extraordinary.

Thus far, he said, we have remained within the legal forms. But the defence, as has already happened during the trial, has publicly read a passage of the report of the Dreyfus affair. I, therefore, ask leave to speak, and I will repeat the very typical phrase of Colonel Henry. 'You have forced me to it. Well, so be it.' At the time of the Castelin interpellation a very serious incident occurred. Positive proof of Dreyfus's guilt came to light, and that proof I myself have seen. I can, therefore, give you some information on that document. It was a paper, the source of which cannot be doubted. [Pellieux quotes the faux Henry]. The letter is signed with a name little known, but this important document is supported by a visiting card with an insignificant appointment at the back, bearing the name of the person given at the foot of the letter. This is the truth. I make this statement on my honour as a soldier and General de Boisdeffre can confirm me.'

M. Labori seemed in no wise disconcerted.

> 'This document,' he cried, 'so long as it is not publicly known does not count. Let it be brought in here. The obscurities and doubts in this whole affair are being daily increased. Whether Dreyfus be guilty or innocent, whether Esterhazy be innocent or guilty, we shall continue to have divergent opinions and we cannot but persist in them if light be not thrown on this business. Already revision of the trial has become certain. (Loud protests from the public at the back of the hall.) The protests of the crowd show well enough that it has no conception of the meaning of this debate from the everlasting point of view of justice and humanity. We must have light – justice and humanity require it – and then we will return to our long labour of peace – or of war. But war, whatever the Generals may say, is remote, and we will not allow the country to be frightened by allusions to it. This document must be brought to us and discussed here.'

General Gonse. - 'I absolutely confirm what General de Pellieux has just said. He did well to say it, but we must be prudent. There are other documents. I doubt whether documents so delicate can be brought here.' (Murmurs.)

General de Pellieux. - 'I have precipitated this incident only because I was obliged to do so. You talk of revision, and of a secret document rendering the first trial illegal. Where is your proof? Not enough attention has been paid to Colonel Henry's statement that Colonel Sandherr made before the trial a *dossier* of secret documents for the Dreyfus affair. This *dossier* was put under seal before the court martial. Now let General de Boisdeffre be sent for.' Turning to the little knot of officers on the witnesses' bench, he gave an order that he should be fetched. Continuing, the witness said: – 'The report of M. d'Ormescheville as published in the papers is mutilated. I ask that he be called.'

M. Labori. - 'The word of General de Boisdeffre, any more than that of General de Pellieux, will not suffice for us. As long as you do not bring in this document your statements are worthless. Moreover, why did not General Billot make this statement in the Chamber; why did he not show his proofs to M. Scheurer-Kestner?'

The witness. - 'I do not know what General Billot should or should not say, but I know that he affirmed that Dreyfus was justly and legally condemned.'

M. Labori. - '"Legally" is false; judge as to the other affirmation!'

General de Pellieux.- 'Prove it.'

The President - 'Call another witness.'

M. Labori. - 'Oh, no; you can understand that the incident is too grave for us to remain there. We must have General de Boisdeffre here, we must discuss the terms of his statement, and we must insist on the communication of this document thus so suddenly flung into the debate.'

The President. - 'Call another witness, and Major Esterhazy entered, perfectly calm and self-contained.'

'I tell you,' said M. Labori, 'that we refuse to question the witness until we have had before us General de Boisdeffre. We shall put in our applications.'

The President. - 'Do as you like; meanwhile, we suspend the sitting.'

It is unnecessary to attempt to describe the extraordinary excitement which prevailed in Court at this moment. What did it all mean? Conjecture jostled conjecture in vain inquiry. Then the bell rang and the Judges entered. To the astonishment of every one, although it was said that General de Boisdeffre had arrived, the President said, 'In the absence of General de Boisdeffre, the sitting is adjourned until to to-morrow.'

Source: The Times, Friday 18 February 1898.

The Dreyfus case

ESTERHAZY ON THE STAND PROTECTED IN A REFUSAL TO ANSWER QUESTIONS - LITTLE HOPE OF GETTING AT THE TRUTH -

ZOLA'S COUNSEL REPEATEDLY SILENCED AND HIS REQUESTS DENIED - PUBLIC INTEREST INCREASING

When General Boisdeffre, in full uniform, took the stand, the Presiding Judge addressed him as follows: 'General, an incident which we did not anticipate occurred yesterday. A desire was manifested that you should be examined and the Court has acceded to it.'

The Presiding Judge then read the shorthand report of General Pellieux's statement and asked the witness what he had to say on the subject. General Boisdeffre replied:

'I confirm fully the authenticity of General Pellieux's statement. I do not wish to add a word to it, but, gentlemen of the jury, you are the nation here, for you represent it. If the nation has not confidence in the chiefs of the army, let it say so, and we are ready to leave to others the burden of our responsibility.'

This statement caused a prolonged sensation.

'Yes,' exclaimed the General, 'Vive l'Armée!' (Cheers.)

As General Boisdeffre was leaving the stand, M. Labori, counsel for M. Zola, rose and said:

'I should like to question General Boisdeffre.'

'You cannot,' replied the Presiding Judge.

'What!' exclaimed M. Labori.

'No,' vehemently retorted the Presiding Judge, 'you cannot. Call the next witness.'

Labori protests in vain

M. Labori vainly protested against this ruling, but an usher called Major Esterhazy, who immediately appeared, and, amid profound silence, took the stand.

'What questions have you to put?' asked the Judge, addressing M. Labori.

'I am drawing up a formal application to cross-examine General Boisdeffre,' replied counsel for the defendant.

'Very well,' said the Judge; 'then I will put my own questions.'

Turning to Major Esterhazy, the Judge thereupon said:

'It is said that you are the author of the *bordereau*. What have you to answer?'

'First,' replied Major Esterhazy, 'I have a statement to make. Gentlemen of the jury, on a shadow of proof this miserable Mathieu Dreyfus has accused me of being guilty of his brother's crime. I have been judged by my peers, who have acquitted me; but to-day I am summoned as a witness so that he may reaccuse me when I have neither advisor nor counsel to defend me. I will answer any questions you put to me, gentlemen of the jury, but as for those people,' turning to M. Zola and his counsel, 'I won't reply to them.' (Sensation.)

The Judge then turned to M. Labori and asked:

'Have you any questions to ask Major Esterhazy?'

'I am still drawing up my application,' answered M. Labori, 'and I shall not ask any questions until the Court has given a decision upon it.'

'Put your questions immediately,' exclaimed the Judge, 'or you will not put any.' (Murmurs.)

'I can say nothing for the moment,' replied M. Labori, 'but I protest against this attitude'

Zola's counsel scores a point

Counsel for M. Zola retorted: 'The Generals came into court in full uniform, and wearing their decorations, in order to make speeches for the prosecution.' (Uproar.) M. Labori also said: 'The defence is reproached with attempting to secure a revision of the Dreyfus case, but the Generals have harangued against a revision of the trial of Major Esterhazy, who was acquitted. Let his judges bear the responsibility.' (Uproar.) M. Labori alluded to the 'man suffering on Devil's Island,' adding 'though his sufferings, doubtless, do not interest the men who are howling at the back of the courtroom.' The counsel concluded by imploring the Court to rise 'superior to demonstrations upon the part of the people who do not know what they are talking about.' (Increased uproar.)

'Gentlemen of the jury,' M. Labori added, 'I entreat you most earnestly to rise above the emotions of the misled public, and to consider that we are perhaps at a turning point in our history, and that your decision will have consequences which no one to-day can measure.' (Prolonged sensation).

Source: New York Daily Tribune, Saturday 19 February 1898.

Refusal of Eterhazy to answer any questions (18 February)

Mᵉ Labori. - Major Esterhazy has declared that he will not answer my questions. Thus, in accordance with the law, I address no questions to him. For this reason, I ask the President of the Court to put to him the question I have just indicated, and to point out to Major Esterhazy that it is the President of the Assize Court who is asking him the question.

Court President. - I am quite willing to repeat the question to Major Esterhazy. (*Turning towards the witness*) You are asked what you think of the handwriting of the *bordereau.*

Major Esterhazy. - Although you do me the honour of communicating this question, Mr President, it is still Mᵉ Labori's question; and consequently, I shall not reply.

Court President. - Do you wish to answer?

Major Esterhazy. - My answer, Mr President, is that I shall not answer any questions put to me. It is clear!...

Court President - Did you hear the question?

Major Esterhazy. - I shall not answer.

Mᵉ Labori. - Well, gentlemen, I believe it is useless to prolong the experience; as far as I am concerned, I have finished. I think that Mᵉ Clemenceau will also have some questions to put to the witness; they will, moreover, be of a very different nature.

Mᵉ [Albert] Clemenceau. - I shall carry on with the experience; and as the witness has the right to change his mind, I ask your permission, Mr President, to put all the questions that I have to articulate through you. The witness will answer or remain silent: we will see...

Mᵉ Clemenceau. - At what time was the witness part of the Intelligence Service in France? Didn't he say that he was part of the Intelligence Service twenty years ago? Didn't he make that statement to the court martial?

Court President - Mr Esterhazy has just told you that he will not answer. Consequently, it is pointless to wait for his response.

Mᵉ Clemenceau. - Nevertheless, I am going to continue with my questions, if you allow it. Did the witness know a person answering to the name of Mme de Boulancy?

Court President. - Do you wish to answer this question?

Major Esterhazy. - No, Mr President, nor any question. (*Signs of approval in the courtroom.*) ...

Mᵉ Clemenceau. - Another question: does the witness admit having written a letter to Mme. de Boulancy containing the following passage? 'The Germans will put all those people (referring to the French) in their rightful place before too long.'

Court President. - Major Esterhazy has declared that he will not answer.

Mᵉ Clemenceau. - Then I point out that the witness has admitted the accuracy and authenticity of this letter... (*Murmurs in court.*) I affirm an indisputable fact. I continue...

Mᵉ Clemenceau. - Is it not a fact that another reason for his surprise was his habit of playing the Stock Exchange described by the witness Mr de Castro?

(*Major Esterhazy, turning his back on Mᵉ Clemenceau, continues to remain silent.*) May I carry on, Mr President?

Court President. - Yes, carry on!...

Me Clemenceau. - May I request now that you ask the witness how he found out that he was suspected of having written the famous *bordereau*?

Court President - Carry on!

Me Clemenceau. - On what date did he find out?

Court President. - You can continue, the witness has told you that he will not answer.

Me Clemenceau. - Did the witness not state that he discovered this from a letter signed *Speranza* [Hope], received at his country home on 20 October 1897, which reported that Colonel Picquart had bribed soldiers to obtain samples of his handwriting? ...

Court President - Carry on!

Me Clemenceau. - Mr President, would you put the following question to the witness: is it correct, as stated in *La Patrie*, [Millevoye's newspaper] that Major Esterhazy has admitted that he had infrequent, but not secret, relations, with Colonel Schwartzkoppen, whom he said he had met in Carlsbad?

Court President. - No, I will not ask the question.

Me Clemenceau. - How is it that in a legal hearing one cannot speak of an act committed by a French officer?

Court President. - Because there is something that comes above that: it is the honour and security of the country! (*Long acclamations and prolonged applause throughout the courtroom.*)

Me Clemenceau. - Mr President, I understand then that the honour of the country allows an officer to accomplish such acts but does not allow them to be spoken of! (*Shrill cries dominate the general noise.*)

Court President, to the court usher. - Remove the person who is shouting like that.

Me Clemenceau. - Those...

Court President, *to the court usher.* - Call another witness.

Source: Pro. Zola, pp. 742–54.

Zola attacks the premier

When the session was resumed, M. Zola read an address to the court in which he said that the Premier, M. Méline, 'had the air of giving the jury, who are charged to avenge the national honour, the order to find me guilty.' (*Loud protests*)

The Presiding Judge said: 'You cannot say that the Premier has given an order to condemn you.'

Continuing, M. Zola said: 'Such proceedings are an abominable piece of political manners. I have never insulted the army, as has been said, but I have raised a cry of alarm, and I leave history to judge me and to appreciate my acts.'

'Those who dishonour France,' M. Zola remarked, 'are those who mingle cries of 'vive l'Armée!' with 'A bas les Juifs!' ('Down with the Jews!') and 'Vive Esterhazy!' after the letters he has written. (*Murmurs.*) If I am here, it is because I wished it. It is I who asked to appear before you, who are the voice of justice. It is for you, gentlemen, that I raise the cry of alarm, and that

I wish to bring out the truth, perhaps unsuccessfully, but here I stand before you and await your justice.'

M. Zola then complained of the prevailing state of lassitude, and exclaimed:

'Your thoughts, which I think I can read on your faces, are: 'We have had enough of it. The matter must be brought to an end!'

'I am not defending my liberty, gentlemen,' M. Zola explained to the jury, 'in presenting myself before you. I am defending the truth. Look me in the face, gentlemen. Have I been bought, or am I a traitor? I am a free writer, who intends to resume his vocation and again take up his interrupted labours.'

Source: New York Tribune, Tuesday 22 February 1898.

Zola's closing speech (22 February)

You are the heart and mind of Paris, of my great Paris, where I was born, that I love with infinite tenderness, that I have been studying and extolling for almost 40 years... Do me the honour of believing that I am not defending my own liberty here. In striking me, you would only enhance my stature. Whosoever suffers for truth and justice becomes noble and sacred. (Murmurs)... And so, I am not defending myself. But what an error you would commit if you were convinced that by striking me you would re-establish order in our unfortunate country!

...A judicial error has been committed and since then, in order to conceal it, it was necessary every day to commit a new attack against common sense and justice. It is the conviction of an innocent man that has led to the acquittal of the culprit. And now today, you are asked to condemn me, because I have shouted out in anguish, seeing my country take this appalling path. Condemn me then! But it will be another error, in addition to the others, an error for which later you will bear the burden of history

...Alas, gentlemen, you, like many others, are perhaps awaiting a bolt from the blue, the proof of the innocence of Dreyfus, descending from heaven like thunder! Truth does not normally proceed in this way, it requires some research and intelligence... This truth... will be known by all in future. And if at this moment it is impossible for us to go and seek it out where it exists, protected by insurmountable formalities, the government which knows everything, the government which is convinced as we are of the innocence of Dreyfus (loud protests) will be able, without risks when it so desires, to find the witnesses who will finally cast light on the matter.

Dreyfus is innocent, I swear it. I pledge my life on it, I pledge my honour. In this solemn hour, before this tribunal which represents human justice, before you, gentlemen of the jury, who are the very incarnation of the country, before all of France, before the entire world, I swear that Dreyfus is innocent! And by my 40 years of work, by the authority which this labour may have given me, I swear that Dreyfus is innocent! And by all that I have achieved, by the reputation I have earned, by my works which have helped the expansion of French literature, I swear that Dreyfus is innocent. May all of that collapse, may my works perish if Dreyfus is not innocent! He is innocent!

Source: Pro. Zola, 824–7.

George Clemenceau's closing speech (23 February)

Well, what are the facts which emerge from the depositions at this bar? What was the origin of the movement in favour of Dreyfus? I do not speak of his family who believe him innocent and would naturally move heaven and earth to exonerate the head of the family. But apart from the Dreyfus family, who were the first to give substance to the hypothesis of his innocence? You know, gentlemen, that doubt was first raised in the army itself. It was Colonel Picquart, whom I did not know before seeing him here, who, I declare openly, seems worthy of all respect; it was Colonel Picquart who first pointed to Major Esterhazy, whose name was found inscribed on the *petit bleu* which came from the famous basket Me Labori described to you. It was Colonel Picquart who conceived the first doubts.

Mr. Zola. - And he is an antisemite!

Me Clemenceau. - Mr. Zola tells me that he is an anti-semite, I knew nothing of that, but that only makes it the more significant. It was Colonel Picquart who expressed his doubts to his superior, General Gonse, and it was from the scruples of those two men, revealed in the letters which you are aware of, that the whole affair emerged which brings us here today...

One speaks of the equality of the law. It is simply a word. We await its reality. It is to obtain this equality of law, it is to obtain a legal judgement, it is to obtain the common rule of justice that we are here before you today. You cannot refuse our request without doing harm to yourselves. We are accused of having contravened the law. On the contrary, we present ourselves at this bar in the interests of the law, and if some other means of obtaining justice had been available to us, we would not be here...

We stand before you, gentlemen; you will give your verdict shortly. All we ask is that you should demand and uncover the truth. The truth belongs to no party; it is the right of all men. Without the truth, Mr Zola can do nothing. With a grain of truth, he is invincible. Give us, give to the people of France who await it, the truth, the whole truth. France's good reputation in the world demands this...

And above all beware of this line of reasoning, which at the moment exists in too many minds: 'It is possible that Dreyfus was convicted illegally, but it was justly done; that is enough, let us speak no more of it.'

It is a serious error. An illegality is a form of iniquity, since the law is a guarantee of justice.

Gentlemen, all the generals and all the magistrates together cannot claim that illegality arising from a defective form of justice is not imperfect justice with insufficient guarantees, because the law is merely a guarantee of justice. No one has the right or power to do justice outside the law.

If in the present circumstances you wish to render a supreme service to your country, see to it that the supremacy of the law is undisputed; and through the law and supremacy of justice rid our hearts of this respect for reasons of State that is absurd in a democracy

In a democracy, reasons of State are merely a contradiction, a vestige of the past... At the present moment, I accept that you are faced with an acute and distressing problem. It is painful for us and for you to find ourselves in conflict with good people who are soldiers, people who believed they were doing the right thing, want to do the right thing, but believing they were doing the right thing, did the wrong one. That can happen to civilians without uniform, it can happen to civilians in military uniform, for soldiers are only fallible men like others...

Without giving your verdict on the faults of anyone, or on the inherent errors of human judgement, it is for you to determine whether you wish to seek the truth for its own sake, to do justice for the sake of justice, as the law gives you the right to do, as the interests of our country impose the duty on you. Put aside, then, all considerations of people.

Here today, you do not have to judge General de Boisdeffre or General de Pellieux who will explain themselves to their superiors, that is not your business. It is not up to you to approve or blame them. Whatever you decide, the only danger which could be the result is if you yourselves abandon the cause of the law of justice which you represent. That you will not do. You will put civil law above all prerogatives. You will keep intact the store of our conquests of freedom and equality, beyond all considerations of race or belief. Thus you will render the invaluable service of repressing these first movements of religious war which would bring dishonour upon this country... (*Murmurs*).

You protest, so much the better! I sincerely want to believe that you have no intention of restarting the wars of religion! Yet when I see in France, in our French Algeria... when I see that Jews guilty of fetching bread for their families have been massacred, I have the right to say that religious wars presented scenes like that in history. That is why I ask the members of the jury today, when giving their verdict in the spirit of freedom and justice for all, even for the Jews, to put an end to these excesses, to say to the instigators of these brutalities: 'In the name of the people of France, you will go no further!'

Gentlemen, we are the law, we are tolerance, the tradition of the French spirit, we are the defenders of the army... (*Laughter and murmurs.*) Yes, the army, in the interests of which preventions of the spirit of solidarity deceive you, for we do not separate justice from patriotism since the army will only be strong if it is controlled and respected, and on condition that it draws its strength from respect for the law. Yes, gentlemen, we are the defenders of the army when we ask you to drive Esterhazy from it. (*Noises, shouts.*) And those who propose to drive Picquart out of the army in order to retain Esterhazy are its enemies, whether conscious or unconscious... Gentlemen, I have spoken. In this century we have undergone terrible ordeals, we have known all manner of glories and disasters, at this tragic moment of our history we are faced with the unknown, caught between all our fears and all our hopes. Seize the moment, as we have seized it ourselves, be masters of your own destinies. For this is a majestic moment: the people judging itself; and it is also an awesome moment: the people deciding its future. It is up to you, gentlemen, to give your verdict: not so much on us, but more on yourselves. We appear before you. You appear before yourselves. You appear before history. (*Applause and clamours.*)

Source: Pro. Zola, pp. 981–1002.

The trial of M. Zola

'Need I speak', said M^e. Labori in conclusion, 'of the partial secrecy – more hypocritical than entire secrecy, for it allowed the attack but stifled the defence – and of the officers' enthusiastic reception of Esterhazy? When, next day, Colonel Picquart is put under arrest, the cup is brimful, and uneasiness gives place to indignation. M. Zola then launches his famous letter. It was violent, and had to be so. In some parts it was exaggerated, but it was true in substance. It was courageous and sublime. (*Murmurs.*) Confining myself to the narrow ground of General Billot's plaint, I maintain that in 1894, in the absence of proofs, an ephemeral Minister took upon himself to condemn one of his officers. Everything that has been done since has been done to screen and conceal the mistake. M. Zola's letter was a cry for justice and truth. (*Murmurs.*) In spite of certain agitators, it has won the support of all the chivalry and greatness of France. Do not allow yourselves to be intimidated. The honour of the army is not in question. Dangers of war have been spoken of. Do not credit them. All these brave officers, though they may have been mistaken, would fight with the firmest courage and lead us to victory. Do not punish Emile Zola. You know that he is an honour to France. (*Murmurs.*) Victories are won by the heart, by moral forces. I too cry "Vive l'armée!" in asking you to acquit Zola. I cry at the same time "Vive la République!" "Vive le droit!" "Vive l'idéal éternel de justice et de vérité!" and it is with tranquil confidence that I await your verdict.'

Loud applause followed, but vociferous protests were soon mingled with it, and there were for some minutes conflicting cries of 'Vive Labori!' 'Vivent les généraux!' 'Vive l'armée!' 'A bas Reinach!' 'Vive la France!' 'Vie la République !'

Source: The Times, Thursday 24 February 1898.

Appendix 22: The Dreyfus agitation, 22 January 1898

The Dreyfus agitation

VIOLENT SCENES IN THE FRENCH CHAMBER

…M. Cavaignac thereupon withdrew the interpellation, his purpose, he said, having been attained, but M. Jaurès took it up, and he twitted M. Méline with having effected a diversion which had rallied all his friends of the Right. He taunted General Billot with following the traditions of the generals of the Empire, and he criticized the emasculation of the Zola prosecution.

Here M. de Bernis exclaimed:- 'You belong to the Dreyfus syndicate.'

'What is that you say?' asked M. Jaurès.

'I say,' rejoined M. de Bernis, 'that you must be in the syndicate, that you are probably counsel for the syndicate.'

Upon this M. Jaurès retorted: - '*Vous êtes un misérable et un lâche.*'

Uproar followed, and M. Gérault-Richard, rushing from his place among the Socialists to the front bench on the Right and going up to M. de Bernis, exclaimed:- '*Vous êtes un gredin.*'

M. de Bernis smiled and made no reply. Exasperated at his silence, M. Gérault-Richard struck M. de Bernis in the face with his fist. Several Deputies standing near tried to get between the disputants, but M. Coutant and other Socialists threw themselves on M. de Bernis and attempted to drag him outside the hall. M. Jaurès remained meanwhile at the tribune. President Brisson, quite taken by surprise, sent for his hat and twisted it nervously round on his hands till, mastering his excitement, he clapped it on his head and without uttering a word quitted the hall.

M. Jaurès, having collected his notes, was now descending the tribune on the left when M. de Bernis, having shaken off his assailants, rushed up the steps on the other side, struck him violently on the back of the head and kicked him in the legs. M. Jaurès stumbled down the three remaining steps, and then, picking himself up and turning round, saw M. de Bernis hastening off amid the crowd of Deputies. Unable to overtake him, M. Jaurès threw a knotted handkerchief at him, reascended the tribune, and received the congratulations of his friends. Some people in the galleries also applauded him. Several Socialists advanced threateningly to the Ministerial bench, but they were dissuaded from further hostilities, and the galleries being cleared, the Deputies retired into the lobby.

There the ushers, who were themselves being pushed and squeezed, had great difficulty in preventing fighting. M. de Bernis was in a committee room, blood from his cheek falling on his shirt-front, when a Socialist Deputy, exclaiming '*Misérable*', threw an inkstand at him, but fortunately missed his aim. Loud altercation went on elsewhere and experiences were related. M. Chaulin Servinière states that in trying to part M. de Bernis and M. Gérault-Richard, he received an unintentional blow on the shoulder and was near having his leg broken. The office-bearers of the Chamber eventually met and resolved on reporting M. de Bernis and M. Gérault-Richard to the Public Prosecutor.

Source: The Times, 24 January 1898.

Appendix 23: **World reaction to the verdict at Zola's trial**

The *Figaro* believes that the result of the trial will surprise no one. The jury could give no other verdict, especially in view of the pressure exercised upon it by public opinion. The journal adds that though M. Zola has been justly condemned, no one doubts his disinterestedness and his courage.

The *Gaulois* says that the jury's reply was that of good sense and patriotism given to professional rhetoricians, and if the polemic still continues it will be between those who do not want a revision of the Dreyfus trial and those who do – that is 'between good Frenchmen and the others.'

The *Soleil* says that the author of the 'Débâcle' has shown a malevolent spirit from the social point of view, and declares that the verdict was dictated by good sense and honourable feeling.

The *Aurore* says that it is proud 'to have been struck in company with the glorious defender of liberty.'

The *Siècle* says that M. Zola will pay in prison the penalty for an act of courage and revolt nobly accomplished, and that his work will survive...

The *Post* says that the judgement of the world will be anything but favourable when it reviews the incidents of the last few weeks and the convulsions which have shaken popular feeling in France. It goes on to say: 'Details of the life and the ways of officers of the general staff have been revealed and the intellectual capacity of the leaders of the French army has been exhibited in the worst light. The Sandherrs, the Du Paty de Clams, and the Esterhazys will remain standing types of French officers of the present epoch and will afford a standard for measuring their worth ... A Republic in which the army is Sovereign is a monstrosity ... Although at present we have no reason to view the development of the situation in France with anxiety, yet we cannot but reflect that that country might enter upon another path, and where it would lead is beyond our knowledge. Watchfulness continues to be a dictate of duty for Germany.'

The *National Zeitung* is convinced that 'the military reign of terror has carried the day in France.'

The *Voissiche Zeitung* says of M. Zola: 'He is not fallen. Crowned with the halo of the noblest heroism and the most genuine humanity his figure towers into that immortality which his writings may, perhaps, have failed to achieve. What he has done with such courage for the sake of truth, justice, and humanity is as surely immortal as the action of Voltaire in the case of Jean Calas, performed as it was under far less difficult conditions.'

The *Berlin Liberal* organ thinks that the French nation will yet acknowledge with shame the services of the man 'who is about to forfeit a precious year of a life dedicated to the national glory for his bravery as the champion of truth.'

The *Berline Neueste Nachrichten* asserts that the elementary principles of civilization have been trodden under foot by the people who claim to lead the vanguard of progress. 'Anti-Semitism celebrates its worst orgies, and wherever there is the faintest allusion to hated Germany every spark of reason and of honour is extinguished.'

The *Berliner Tageblatt* goes even further. Beginning with the taunt that 'the French army yesterday won its first victory since its defeat in 1870–71', it proceeds: 'For us Germans the trial has a special lesson. Zola receives the blows, but they are meant for Germany. Yesterday we had finally to bury the hope of ever achieving an honourable peace with France. The revision of the Dreyfus verdict has been refused. Will the revision of the peace of Frankfurt be obtained?'

The *North-German Gazette's* only comment is that Zola appears to have misjudged his countrymen, since in every sensational case in France a verdict and sentence are expected which embody the spirit and temper of the nation, whether it is a question of acquitting a murderess or of withholding clemency from a man who happens to be unpopular. 'The Court accommodated itself to the temper of the jury and passed the heaviest sentence that the law allowed.'

In the severity of the German comments there is manifestly something more than an ordinary sense of outraged justice. The Anti-Semitic character of the agitation against M. Zola and his friends and the Anti-German attitude of the French military and Chauvinist parties have given a peculiar intensity to the bitterness with which German journals of various shades of opinion have commented upon this unhappy episode in French public life.

The *Neue Freie Presse* says: 'France will some day bitterly repent of this sentence, the responsibility for which falls upon the whole French people … The French have lost all sense of genuine freedom … Zola, Picquart, and Dreyfus have been sacrificed to reasons of State … That is a return to barbarism, for nowhere is the principle acknowledged that the individual must surrender his life, honour, and freedom because the public welfare prohibits the rectification of a judicial error … A nation whose sense of justice is shaken is always in danger of decay.'

The *Neues Wiener Tagblatt* says: 'Although he has been condemned, our sympathies remain with him of whom Victor Hugo would have said that, as he stood head and shoulders above the crowd, they cut his head off. We take our place beside the man with whom all those must elect to stand who remember the past, who have not forgotten what mankind was before the feeling of humanity got the upper hand, beside the man who seeks to make France once more the land of justice where the fraternization of nations is promoted. If it be a dishonour to follow in his footsteps, then every man of courage will claim a share in this dishonour, and will pray to Providence that he may long participate in that disgrace of which the standard-bearer was yesterday condemned in Paris.'

The *Pester Lloyd* remarks: 'To what low depths must the nation have sunk which raises Rochefort on to a pinnacle and casts Zola into prison! What has become even of French good taste, now that a Court of justice does not hesitate, according to all appearances, for purposes of revenge to condemn to severe punishment a man whom the world respects as the most prominent and important representative of contemporary French literature, and whose fault, if it can be called one, consists exclusively in believing, as do millions of people outside France, in the innocence of Dreyfus? What has become of the commonsense of the rulers of France, if they imagine that the condemnation of Zola will dispose of the Dreyfus affair?'

The Times: 'M. Zola has been tried as he desired, he has been condemned, as he must have known for a long time that he would be, and he has failed to make the trial, as he hoped, an opportunity for a practical revision of the

Dreyfus judgement by a French Court of Law. But in a far larger sense he has succeeded, and that with a completeness that may well console him for what he will have to suffer in person, in pocket and in popularity. He has procured revision of the Dreyfus case, not indeed in the sense of repairing the wrong done to an individual, but in the far more important sense of exposing the perils that assail the foundations of society in France. He has been served by M. Labori with extraordinary ability, ingenuity, perseverance, and eloquence. It has been a rare intellectual treat for educated men everywhere to watch the splendid fight made by M. Zola's counsel against the heaviest odds... The question of the innocence or guilt of Dreyfus stands very much where it did. If the great combination against which M. Zola has been struggling are content with the gratification of vindictive feelings against the prisoner of the Île du Diable, that satisfaction is theirs. But M. Labori's conduct of the trial has made it clear beyond the reach of controversy that Dreyfus, innocent or guilty, was illegally tried and illegally condemned.'

The *Standard*: 'The very form of the indictment never gave M. Zola free play, since it covered a corner only of his letter to the *Aurore*. Witnesses summoned by him were allowed to absent themselves on the most trivial excuses, or no excuse at all. The President made little semblance of keeping order, and permitted the most unseemly interruptions of M. Zola and his Counsel, Maitre Labori, to pass without so much as a word of rebuke. Worse than that, he shut the mouths of the Defendant's Witnesses whenever they came near the Dreyfus case, whereas the Witnesses against him were allowed to drag in Dreyfus, *bordereau* and all, at pleasure. Colonel Picquart was brow-beaten, almost placed on his trial, for breathing suspicion of Major Esterhazy. When General de Pellieux or General de Boisdeffre condescended to give evidence, they immediately assumed complete direction of the whole affair. The Court of Justice became a Court-martial, and a very French Court-martial too. The speech of the Advocate-General evidently carried far less weight with the Jury than that abrupt appeal of General de Pellieux to the sacrosanctity of the Esterhazy tribunal, and the effect of a slur upon the good fame of the Army in the hour of danger, which might be more imminent than blameless citizens imagined...'

The *Daily News*: 'The sentence is brutal, cruel and barbarous. It may be received with enthusiasm by excited crowds of the most turbulent classes in Paris. It will not be upheld by the sober sense of the French nation... But M. Zola has not been altogether unsuccessful. He has made it extremely difficult for the French Government to persist in refusing Dreyfus a new and public trial. The question, be it observed, is not whether Dreyfus was guilty or innocent, but whether he was fairly tried. Upon the first question, no one who is unacquainted with the evidence laid before the Court Martial can form an opinion of any value. Upon the second, there is little room for doubt. If a man can be condemned to a living death on testimony not produced to him he might as well, and perhaps better, be hanged without trial, or shot on site. Sooner or later that idea will penetrate to the French mind in spite of all the furious prejudice against Jews, which the worst part of the French press has fostered and encouraged.'

The *Daily Chronicle*: 'The jury have undoubtedly been influenced by the prevalent opinion in Paris that the army is above the law. When it is safe to cry "Vive l'Armée!", but distinctly unsafe to cry "Vive la République!" nothing but a miracle could have induced twelve French jurymen to acquit M. Zola. The popular attachment to the army is sincere enough... An unhappy complication has been made by the anti-Semitic frenzy. Dreyfus is a Jew, and most Frenchmen believe that he is befriended by an iniquitous "syndicate", which somehow comprised the flower of intellectual France, including staunch Protestant Scheurer-Kestner. Against such bigotry it is useless to argue. M. Méline and his colleagues are on the eve of the elections, and they have 'obvious reason' not to run counter to popular feeling. But we trust that long before M. Zola has served his term of twelve months' imprisonment the better mind of France will assert itself above fanatical passion and the necessity of satisfying reason and conscience as to the truth about Captain Dreyfus will be acknowledged. If not, France must suffer, as she is suffering to-day, from the suspicion that she has lost control of her destiny, that she is in the hands of men unworthy to represent any considerable country in the world, and that in the process, she has abandoned the ideas which had made her the greatest intellectual force of the century.'

Source: The Times and the *Jewish Chronicle*, 24 and 25 February 1898.

Appendix 24: **Debate in the Chamber of Deputies:**

The Trial of M. Zola, 24 February 1898

...'It is with sadness,' he said [Socialist Deputy Viviani], 'that I once more ascend the tribune to return to this painful business which has so long troubled the country, and which would become, were it to continue, a real public danger. Civil justice in its most democratic and most popular form has just pronounced and proclaimed that the military judges are honest men who obeyed their conscience. This verdict is the more striking as everything had been done to make the jury lose sight of the true question. But it was impossible to get the better of their penetration and sense of justice. This far-resounding trial has turned to the confusion of those who braved the laws of the land. In order to weaken the effect of the verdict, an effort is being made to maintain that it was secured by an abusive military intervention.

'The Government is asked whether it authorized the Generals who gave evidence to assume the attitude they did and to utter the language which they uttered. M. Hubbard has made a serious blunder from the judicial point of view. He has spoken of subordinates of the Minister of War. Before the Assize Court there are no subordinates. There are witnesses, to whom the Minister has no orders to give. I recognize that the Generals may have been carried further than they would have wished to be, but the defence drew them upon this ground. This shows once more the necessity of the *huis clos* when it is a question of the defence of the country.

I come to the deposition of a general accused of having exercised pressure on the jury. Certainly, in other circumstances, I might have said that in this deposition there was a superfluous phrase, but I perfectly well understand what must have passed in the soul of a soldier who for a week was on the rack and treated as a suspect, almost as a culprit. This soldier returns home humiliated, exasperated. Then a day comes when a party leader, all whose words are acts, launches against him before France and the foreigner this monstrous charge that he is preparing defeat by his incapacity.'

M. Jaurès.- 'Not at all. I said, and I maintain, that it is the irresponsibility of the high military authorities which is preparing the disasters of the fatherland.'

'You said it, and you are surprised that this General, finding himself once more before the Judges who heard the accusation, uttered this indignant exclamation:- "If we are as incapable as you pretend we have only to disappear, for we should no longer have the necessary authority." It is a retort which you yourselves provoked, and you have only reaped what you have sown.

The army, whatever may be said, is the respectful servant of the nation and the law. Since 1870 it has held aloof from parties, and the lamentable fall of the only general who has not accepted this principle is a lesson of history. No, never will our army be made an army of Pretorians. It is the army of the Fatherland. There is now no longer a Zola affair, an Esterhazy affair, or a Dreyfus affair. Those who should keep up the present agitation would foment a party war, a racial war, and would expose the internal and external security of France to the greatest perils. The extent of the mischief which has for four months suspended the life of the nation can be measured. The uneasiness has become general, business has slackened, the ill-humour of the nation might have found vent in violence. Nor is this all. The affair has had a sad echo abroad. A portion of the foreign Press has seized on it and turned it against us. It will ever be the punishment of those who speak ill of France to receive such plaudits. This campaign has been as violent as it was unjust. It was an affair which concerned ourselves only, and which those who were acquainted with the *dossier* or who heard the witnesses could alone judge. There are constantly such affairs abroad; there was even one in which some of our countrymen were involved. You remember the officer who was condemned in a neighbouring country to 14 months' imprisonment, but was afterwards proved to be innocent and pardoned. The French journals then protested, but with moderation. There was then no such campaign here as that which has been conducted in the foreign Press on the Dreyfus affair. Our Press held no such language when Captain Romani was tried abroad.' (M. Jourdan.- 'He had no money.')

'The conclusion to be drawn from all this is that there must be a stop to it. It must stop in the interest of all, in the interest of the army, and in that of the public peace and national industry, as well as of our dignity and our external security. Let us no longer compromise the admirable situation which for two years we have enjoyed. It must stop, in the interest even of those who have so senselessly, so imprudently, carried on this campaign. They ... course of reviving in our country animosity which had ceased to exist. This escapes the ... actual *elite* which from the recesses of a private study fails to see whither it is marching or what passions it lets loose when it seems to delight in preventing such a wound from healing. The mission of the Government will be to enforce pacification on all.' (M. Méry.- 'It is an amnesty for the syndicate.') 'The Government will enforce the laws and the disciplinary measures dictated by the circumstances. From tomorrow none of those who should continue this conflict can allege good faith. It would be wilfully troubling the internal peace of the country and risking the creation of embarrassments abroad. We shall apply to them all the severities of the laws, and if these are not sufficient we shall ask for others. There are laws which protect communities as well as individuals, and when it is a question of that community called the Fatherland everybody should defer to it. We ask for the co-operation of the Chamber, which will be testified by its vote. It will thus be seen abroad that France can command herself in formidable crises, and that when patriotism is at stake there is no longer any division of parties, but everybody marches under the flag.'

Source: The Times, 25 February 1898.

Appendix 25: Antisemitic songs

'The Anti-Jewish Marseillaise'	*'La Marseillaise Antijuive'*
Start trembling Yids and traitors	*Tremblez, youpins, et vous, perfides,*
Despised by one and all	*L'opprobre de tous les parties,*
If the Jews rise up against us	*Contre nous de la juiverie*
The avenging hordes will roar (*repeat*)	*Le troupeau hurlant s'est levé* (bis*)*
...	...
Frenchmen it's an outrage	*Français, pour nous, ah! quel outrage*
Our weakness has allowed	*D'être insultés par ces bandits,*
Let's rid ourselves of outlaws	*Balayons donc tous ces youdis*
May Jews be disavowed.	*Que notre faiblesse encourage.*
...	...
To arms anti-Semites! Form your battalions!	*Aux armes, antijuifs, formez vos bataillons.*
March on, march on	*Marchons, marchons,*
May our fields be drenched with their tainted blood.	*Qu'un sang impur abreuve nos sillons.*
...	...
And how this rotten race	*Eh! Quoi cette race pourrie*
Of Dreyfus and the likes	*De Dreyfusards, de va-nu-pieds*
Insult our homeland	*Insulterait notre Patrie,*
Dictating all our lives! (*repeat*)	*Ferait la loi dans nos foyers!* (bis*)*
Bite the dust, you Jews, you thieves	*Aux juifs fais mordre la poussière,*
We'll drive you from our shores	*Fais rendre gorge à ces voleurs*
You will not profit from your vice	*De notre or de notre honneur*
Just stay with you and yours.	*Puits chasse-les hors la frontière.*
To arms anti-Semites! Form your battalions	*Aux armes, antijuifs, formez vos bataillons*
March on, march on	*Marchons, marchons,*
May our fields be drenched with their tainted blood.	*Qu'un sang impur abreuve nos sillons.*

Zola shut your trap	*Zola Ferm'ta boîte*
When, when, shall we see the end	*Quand donc finiras-tu, dis?*
Of Zola defending his Yid friends?	*Zola d'défendr' les Youdis:*
If you don't want a kick up the arse	*Si tu n'veux plus qu'on t'emboîte,*
Shut your trap!	*Ferm'ta boîte!*
You'll be out of the Academy	*Tu n' s'ras pas d' l'Académie*
It is now very clear,	*Maint'nant, c'est bien entendu,*
Finish your comedy	*Finis donc ta comédie:*
You've betrayed us quite enough!	*T'as assez vendu!*
You've betrayed us quite enough!	*T'as assez vendu!*
Shut your trap!	*Ferm'ta boîte!*
Shut your trap!	*Ferm'ta boîte!*
You've betrayed us quite enough!	*T'as assez vendu!*
Now that you are as rich as Croesus	*Maint'nant qu't'es rich' comm' Crésus*
Do not put blame on Jesus	*N'viens pas la faire au Jésus:*
Don't preach in Holy tones	*Ne prêch' pas d'ta voix benoîte;*
Shut your trap!	*Ferm'ta boîte!*
Of the innocence of your traitor	*De l'innocence de ton traître*
You're the only one convinced	*Tu restes le seul convaincu;*
They're probably laughing at you	*Au fond d'en rigol's peut-être;*
You've betrayed us quite enough!	*T'as assez vendu!*
Shut your trap! Shut your trap!	*Ferm'ta boîte! Ferm'ta boîte!*
You've betrayed us quite enough!	*T'as assez vendu! Assez vendu!*

Whyte, *The Accused*, pp. 36; 104.

Appendix 26: Lucie's appeal to the Minister of Justice for the revision of the Dreyfus verdict at the 1894 court martial, 5 July 1898

Minister,

You alone have the power to refer to the Supreme Court of Appeal verdicts which were delivered in violation of the law.

The only right which I possess is that of begging you to make use of this power; I beg you to refer to the Supreme Court the verdict which sentenced my unfortunate husband on 22 December 1894.

He had been brought before the first Court Martial of the Government of Paris as the author of the *bordereau*, the only document which was communicated to him, the only document referred to in the indictment, the only document upheld by the Government Commissioner after a long examination and long proceedings. However, this document was not written by him, and this was demonstrated after the contradictory expert reports of 1894 made by the highest authorities of science.

In the almost four years of my husband's appalling martyrdom, he has not ceased for a single day or a single hour to protest his innocence.

The recent proceedings at the Assize Court have proved clearly that the Court Martial had ruled on secret documents.

It emerges from revelations made during this trial that the verdict pronounced against my husband rested on accusations provided to the judges of the Court, in violation of article 101 of the military code, without having been brought to the attention of the accused or his defence.

It is up to you, Minister, to refer this breach of defence rights, in the formal text of the law, to the Supreme Court of Appeal. in accordance with article 441 of the Code of Criminal Procedure. You alone can do this

The good faith and loyalty of the officers who convicted my husband are beyond suspicion; they would not have convicted him had the accused been able to discuss the documents which were secretly invoked against him, which were not related to him at all, and of which several may be apocryphal.

I express but one wish: that the man whose name I bear should be judged again, with reference to all the documents which can be charged against him, in the light of proceedings with due hearing of the parties, convinced that his innocence will burst forth to broad daylight.

Confident of your spirit of justice, I beseech you, Minister, to take all necessary measures to order the annulment of a verdict which was illegally delivered.

Be assured, Minister, of my highest regard.

Lucie Dreyfus.

Source: ATQV, pp. 171–2.

Appendix 27: Cavaignac's speech in the Chamber of Deputies, 7 July 1898

The Dreyfus case

In anticipation of M. Castelin on the Dreyfus affair the Palais Bourbon was crowded today, the diplomatic boxes and the front rows of the galleries being filled with spectators, whose efforts to procure cards of admission during the past week have been nothing short of desperate.

...

M. Cavaignac then immediately ascended the tribune and said:–

'It has been the first anxiety of the Government to consider by what means it could put an end to the agitation on this subject. It might, perhaps, have simply affirmed its respect for the *chose jugée* and its resolution not to shrink from any duty for ensuring that respect. I believe the public conscience to be so convinced of the necessity of obtaining the guarantees necessary for its tranquillity that such a declaration would have sufficed. That will, perhaps, be the work of tomorrow; but today we have to do more. We are bound to offer the Chamber and the country all the truth that we can. What is the situation? The honest men composing the Court-martial judged according to their conscience and without passion. There has been an attempt to impeach their decision by substituting for Dreyfus an officer who will be visited tomorrow by the disciplinary punishment which he has merited. (Cheers.) The members of the second Court-martial held in their conscience that it was not for them to consider the proofs of crime imputed to that officer, which, moreover, would not have made Dreyfus innocent. Nothing that has been attempted can impeach the decisions of the Courts-martial. We shall know how to enforce respect for their decisions and for themselves.

At the same time, we hold that the most ample recognition of the authority of the *chose jugée* cannot prevent us from bringing before you the facts which have come to confirm it.

...

Having said this I bring to the tribune the facts which I am at liberty to bring. They are of two classes. First the Intelligence Department of the War Office has collected during six years more than 1,000 documents and letters, emanating from persons whose business is espionage. These documents, in the light of their origin, their number, their aspect, and the tests which may be applied to them, can leave no doubt as to their authenticity or as to the identity of those who write them or receive them. Among these there are some which are insignificant, there are some which are important. I will not dwell on the former. I will call the attention of the Chamber to only three documents. The first two were exchanged between certain persons who have been mentioned and refer to a person designated by his initial D. Here is the first letter. It received the date of March 1894 when it reached the Intelligence Department of the War Office:

"Last evening I finally decided to send for a doctor, who forbade me to go out. Being unable to go and see you tomorrow, I beg you to come to me in the morning, for D. has brought me a number of very interesting things, and we must divide up the work as we have only 10 days' time."

The second, dated April 16, 1894, is in the following terms:–

"I exceedingly regret not having seen you before my departure. However, I shall be back in a week. I enclose 12 plans of ..." here he gives the name of one of our fortresses which I omit – "which *Ce canaille de D.* gave me for you. I told him you had no intention of resuming relations. He alleges that there has been a misunderstanding and that he will do all in his power to satisfy you. He says he was obstinate and that you will not bear a grudge against him. I replied that he was mad and that I did not believe you cared to resume relations. Do as you like."

Although it is certain in my view that this refers to Dreyfus, owing to the confirmation afforded by a comparison of the less important documents which I have mentioned, I will read a third document, which contains the full name Dreyfus. When, in October or November, 1896, M. Castelin put in his first request to interpellate the Government, the two correspondents of whom I am going to speak became anxious as to what was going to take place, and one of them wrote to the other:–

"I have read that a Deputy is going to make an interpellation on Dreyfus. If' – here is a portion of a phrase which I am unable to read – "I shall say that never have I had any relations with this Jew. That is understood. If you are asked, say the same, for nobody must ever know what has occurred with him." (M. Humbert.– "That is clear enough.")

The material authenticity of this document is evident, not merely from the circumstances which I have related, but from the striking similarity between it and a document written on the same paper and with the same blue pencil, dated 1894, which has not since been out of the War Office archives. The moral authenticity is established by the correspondence exchanged between the same persons in 1896. The first writes to the other, who replies in terms which leave no obscurity on the cause of their common uneasiness. Thus the guilt of Dreyfus is clearly proved by a document of 1896, which perfectly fits in with a previous correspondence, and which proves that guilt in an irrefutable fashion. (Cheers.)

…

I have done. Fortified not only by a resolution which nothing can shake, but by what is better, with a sense of the truth and justice of the cause we defend, we shall not permit any injury to be done to the national interests of which we have the keeping. (Loud cheers and cries of "Vive la France!") I have now but one wish to express – it is, perhaps, only an illusion; it is in any case an ardent hope – namely, that tomorrow all Frenchmen may join in proclaiming that this army, which is their pride and which is their hope (loud cheers), is powerful, not merely because of its own strength and because of the confidence of the country, but also because of the justice of the acts which it has had to fulfil.'

Loud and prolonged cheers burst from the entire House. Never was a Minister more generally acclaimed. Then, amid the tumult of applause, the voice of M. Mirman was heard proposing the placarding of this speech throughout France, and someone asked for a public vote.

Source: The Times, Friday 8 July 1898.

Appendix 28: General Roget's report on Captain Cuignet's examination of the *faux Henry*, 30 August 1898

Paris, 30 August 1898

As soon as he arrived at the Ministry, the Minister ordered an overall enquiry and report, as complete and detailed as possible, on the Dreyfus affair. This report was in particular to present, for each document included in the dossier, all the arguments which could prove its authenticity.

This work had been entrusted to Captain Cuignet, the Minister's aide-de-camp, under the direction of General Roget, principal private secretary.

On Saturday 13 August, Captain Cuignet was proceeding with his work, around 10 o'clock in the evening, in the aide-de-camp's office. He was proposing to group together the existing arguments about the authenticity of one of the documents in the dossier, seized in October 1896.

It was a letter written in blue pencil, on squared paper, beginning with the words: 'My dear friend, I have read that a deputy intends to raise the Dreyfus case in the Chamber', and signed with a pseudonym. It had arrived at the Bureau of Information torn into tiny pieces; it had been reconstituted and the fragments were held together using bands of gummed paper.

Looking at this document in the light of the lamp, Captain Cuignet thought at a certain moment that he noticed a strange characteristic which it presented.

The squaring of the top fragments, on which were written the words 'My dear friend' and that of the fragments containing the signature seemed to him to have a bluish grey tint; whilst on the contrary, the squares on all the other fragments which formed the body of the document seemed to him to be purple or wine-red.

Very disturbed by the discovery he had just made, Captain Cuignet referred immediately to another document which had been seized as far back as June 1894, which, by its strong resemblance to the first, could serve as a point of comparison.

This document was also written in blue pencil, on identical squared paper. It began with the same words 'My dear friend' and was signed with the same pseudonym. Finally, it had arrived at the Bureau of Information in the same way and in the same state as the 1896 document, torn into tiny pieces: it had been reconstituted and the fragments had been held together following the process already described, i.e. with the help of bands of gummed paper.

On this second document, Captain Cuignet made the opposite discovery to the one made on the first. The fragments with the words 'My dear friend' and the fragments of the signature seemed to him to be squared in purple, while the fragments of the body of the letter appeared to be on bluish grey squares.

He then examined the two documents at length and attentively, both separately and by bringing them closer together and comparing them. It seemed to him increasingly evident that the fragments of heading and signature had been exchanged between the two. Nevertheless, still not daring to believe in the reality of what seemed, however, certain to him, the captain thought that he could be under the influence of a hallucination brought about by fatigue. He had, indeed, been working all day on the comparison of the documents and the drafting of his report; he had prolonged this work late into the evening. He decided to put the two documents back in place in the dossier and resolved to re-examine them the next morning in daylight.

The following day, Sunday 14 August, at 7 o'clock in the morning, Captain Cuignet took out the two documents once again and noted on each one the same characteristics which had struck him the day before.

He informed his superior, General Roget, principal private secretary of the minister, as soon as the latter arrived in his office. He gave him both documents and described the observations which he had made about them. The General, who had never had to examine the documents and saw them in daylight, did not initially have a very clear perception of the colour characteristics which were pointed out to him. He wanted to experience the same conditions of light as Captain Cuignet the day before. He went into Cuignet's office which had previously been darkened by closing the shutters and drawing the curtains, and was lit by two lamps. The result of the General's subsequent examination convinced him of the accuracy of the observations made by the captain and he resolved to inform the minister immediately.

The General revealed to the minister the result of Captain Cuignet's remarks and the minister himself examined the two suspect documents thoroughly, both in the light of day and in lamplight, but he was less struck than the General by the characteristics noted.

He instructed him to continue the verifications and to check in particular whether or not some other suspect indication, apart from the colour of the squaring, could be discerned. This work was entrusted to Captain Cuignet.

This officer used the following days above all to complete the overall report, for which the minister had made him responsible. In the meantime, he also examined the two documents again and thus noticed on the 1896 document some new characteristics liable to render its authenticity suspect.

1. The upper right fragment, squared in purple like the body of the document and consequently belonging to this body section, showed a margin above the first horizontal line of the squaring. The upper left fragment which, after being pieced together, should of necessity be at the same height as the right fragment and should have shown the continuation of this margin, bore no trace of it. The horizontal lines existed at the normal interval throughout the whole fragment; the upper edge had been visibly cut following one of those lines, and some elements of this could still be seen with the naked eye. This certainly proved that the horizontal margin did not continue on this fragment which, consequently, could not have been in the place indicated by the reconstitution before the document was torn.

2. On the heading, the horizontal lines of the fragments squared in bluish grey were well lined up with the horizontal lines placed at the same height on the fragments squared in purple. But the vertical lines of the first fragments did not line up with those of the fragments of the body of the document placed below;

3. An anomaly of the same kind was noted on the bluish grey fragments of the signature.

Captain Cuignet reported his observations to General Roget as and when he noted them. On Thursday 18 August, the minister asked to see the suspect documents around 10 o'clock in the evening, and examined them in one of the salons of the building in electric light. He focused his attention on the characteristics of the colour of the squaring which had been indicated to him, and asked Captain Cuignet to inform him of his new observations which are reported herein.

Concerned to arrive at a certainty without any material operation damaging the suspect documents, the minister then ordered General Roget to have all the fragments traced, reproducing the squaring and the words written in blue pencil; and to check whether in reproducing the documents using these tracings, it was possible to transfer to the 1896 document the heading and signature of the 1894 document, and vice versa to transfer to the 1894 document the heading and the signature of the 1896 document.

This lengthy and meticulous operation required several days. As the minister had to go to Le Mans in the meantime to chair the Sarthe area general council session, Captain Cuignet's work could only be submitted to him on his return, on Wednesday 24 August. The reproduction of the two documents using fragments of tracing paper, made in accordance with the minister's instructions, i.e. by transferring to each document the fragments which seemed to belong to it on the basis of the colour of the squares, showed that the heading and the signature of one document matched the other perfectly, both with regard to the squares and the joins of the torn paper.

The minister then ordered them to undertake a counter-proof, i.e. to reproduce the two documents on fragments of tracing paper such as they existed in the original, leaving the same heading and the same signatures.

This new work was submitted to the minister on Saturday 27 August; from the point of view of the mismatching of the squares, it highlighted the same anomalies already noted on the original documents. The minister was then convinced.

By telegram, he summoned Generals Boisdeffre and Gonse who were in the country. They arrived in Paris, and on Monday 27 August, at five o'clock in the evening, they were received by the minister, who informed them of the observations made with regard to the two documents.

It was decided that Lieutenant-Colonel Henry would be invited to provide explanations. It was indeed Henry who had received the documents torn into tiny pieces from an agent of the Bureau of Information, reconstituted them and then presented them to his superiors.

Lieutenant-Colonel Henry was on leave, but it was known that he was to be in Paris the following day, on Tuesday. The minister informed him via General Gonse that he should attend on Tuesday around 2 o'clock at his office in the ministry. Lieutenant-Colonel Henry obeyed this instruction to attend, but was unaware of the reason for it. On arriving at his office, at around 2.30 on Tuesday 30 August, he found General Gonse there, who took him to the minister's office, where Generals Boisdeffre and Roget were already waiting with the minister.

Following an interrogation conducted personally by the minister, which lasted approximately ¾ of an hour, Lieutenant-Colonel Henry was led to declare that the 1896 document had been fabricated by him.

The General,

principal private secretary of the Minister of War.

Signed: ROGET.

Source: *3ème Cass*, III, 415–20.

Appendix 29: Henry's interrogation by Minister of War Cavaignac on the *faux Henry*, 30 August 1898

The Dreyfus case

M. BARD'S REPORT

... At this point M. Bard read the report of the examination of Colonel Henry when that officer was informed that the examination of the two documents in blue pencil which reached the Intelligence Department in June, 1894, and on October 31, 1896, had revealed the fact that one of them contained words belonging to the other and *vice versa*, and that they had consequently been seriously tampered with.

Cavaignac – When and how did you reconstitute the document of June, 1894? When and how did you reconstitute that of 1896?

Henry – I received the first piece in June, 1894; I myself put it together, like the majority of the pieces having the same origin when written in French. I dated it at the moment of receiving it. As for the piece of 1896, I received it on the eve of All Saints' Day, and put it together myself. I myself put on the date.

Cavaignac – Did you never ungum them and put together again the piece of 1894?

Henry – I never ungummed and regummed this piece. Why should I have done so? It had no importance. It had been classified in the *dossier* of 1894. I am sure I never ungummed it. Moreover, that is a thing I never do.

Cavaignac – Do you now and again keep pieces of paper for some time without putting them together, and sometimes for a certain time, long enough to find out what there is in the papers?

Henry –But I do not remember having kept bits of paper in disorder for more than eight or ten days.

Cavaignac – Did you have the piece of 1896 in your possession after you had handed it to General Gonse?

Henry – No.

Cavaignac – How do you explain, then, that the piece of 1894 contains portions belonging to that of 1896 and *vice versa*?

Henry – I cannot explain it; it appears to me materially impossible. The piece of 1896 never passed out of General Gonse's possession. As for that of 1894, the existence of which you know at the archives, I had it looked up a few days after having handed it to General Gonse. It was not then known where it was, and I had to have a search made for it.

Cavaignac – Was its date inscribed on the piece itself, or on a memorandum?

Henry – There was no memorandum, but a *dossier* containing the unimportant documents.

Cavaignac – What you say is impossible. There is material proof that certain bits were interchanged. How do you explain it?

Henry – How? Why if it exists I must have myself made the intercalation. I cannot, however, say I fabricated a document. I did not fabricate. It would also have been necessary to fabricate the envelope. How could that be?

Cavaignac – The fact of the intercalation is certain.

Henry – I put the pieces together as I received them.

Cavaignac – I remind you that nothing is graver for you than the absence of all explanation. Tell me what you did.

Henry – What do you want me to say?

Cavaignac – To give me an explanation.

Henry – I cannot.

Cavaignac – The fact is certain, reflect on the consequences of my question.

Henry – What do you wish me to say?

Cavaignac – What you have done.

Henry – I have not forged papers.

Cavaignac – Come, come! You have put fragments of one into the other.

Henry – (After a moment of hesitation). Well, yes, because the two things fitted admirably. I was led to this. I received the first document in June, 1894, and I then reconstituted it. When the document of 1894 arrived there were some words which I did not quite understand. I took some cuttings from the first document and put them in the second.

Cavaignac – You forged the document of 1894.

Henry – No, I did not forge it.

Cavaignac – What did you do?

Henry – I added a few words to the document of 1896 which were in the other. I arranged phrases, 'Il ne faut pas qu'on sache jamais,' but the first phrase was correct, the name of Dreyfus was really there.

Cavaignac – You are not telling the truth.

Henry – I tell you I only arranged these phrases at the end.

Cavaignac – Who suggested it?

Henry – Nobody ever spoke to me of it. I did it to give more weight to the document.

Cavaignac – You are not telling everything. You concocted the whole document.

Henry – I forged nothing. Dreyfus's name was in the document of 1896. I could not have taken it in the document of 1894 for it was not there. I had not three documents at my disposal, but only two. I swear that is how it was.

Cavaignac – Your explanation is contrary to the facts; tell me all.

Henry – I am telling you all; I added only that phrase.

Cavaignac – Then your explanation is that you forged the final phrase, 'Il faut pas qu'on sache jamais.'

Henry – I cannot say that I made the phrase. When I found the paper of 1896 I was startled. There was, 'J'ai vu qu'un député va interpeller sur Dreyfus.' Then after a certain phrase I could not find the continuation, and I took from the document of 1894 a few words which completed the sense.

Cavaignac – It is not true. You concocted the document.

Henry – I swear not. I added the phrase, but did not concoct the document.

Cavaignac – What you have said is not possible. Confess the whole truth.

Henry – I took part from the document of 1894 and put the words at the end, 'Il faut qu'on sache jamais.'

Cavaignac – Why did you forge those words?

Henry – To give more weight to the document.

Cavaignac – What words did you forge?

Henry – I do not remember. I ungummed part of the document of 1894, and then the whole document. It is possible I put the words of one document into the other. I fabricated part of the last phrase.

Cavaignac – You forged the whole document.

Henry – I swear not. The other documents which we had at that time proved the authenticity of the letter which followed, 'C'est fâcheux que nous n'ayons pas eu la fin de la lettre de ____' (here the name of a foreign officer). I swear that the beginning of the letter in blue pencil is authentic.

Cavaignac – The beginning has also been invented, but tell the whole truth.

Henry – No, I only put the last phrase. I wrote it without tracing.

Cavaignac – Come, come, confess, for the documents speak for themselves.

Henry – There are words in the body of the letter which come from the other, but the beginning is in the very writing of ____ (here the name of a foreign officer).

Cavaignac – What gave you the idea?

Henry – My chiefs were very uneasy, and I wished to pacify them. I wished to restore tranquillity to men's minds. I said to myself, 'Let us add a phrase. Suppose we had war in our present situation.'

Cavaignac – Did that idea induce you to forge the letter?

Henry – I did not forge it. How should I have imitated a signature like that? It was the beginning which gave me the idea of making the end.

Cavaignac – Is that your language, 'Il faut pas qu'on sache'?

Henry – Yes, because I knew how he wrote.

Cavaignac – You did not date in 1894 the document which bore that date?

Henry – Yes, I dated it in 1894; I do not think I dated it afterwards, but I do not recollect.

Cavaignac – You were the only one to do this?

Henry – Yes, Gribelin knew nothing about it.

Cavaignac – No one knew it, no one in the world?

Henry – I did it in the interest of my country. I was wrong.

Cavaignac – Come, tell the truth, the whole truth. Tell me what took place.

Henry – I swear that I had the beginning; I added the end to give more weight.

Cavaignac – Was the piece of 1896 signed?

Henry – I do not think I made the signature.

Cavaignac – And the envelopes?

Henry – I swear I did not make the envelopes. How could I have done so?

Cavaignac – It is very improbable you added only the final phrase.

Henry – I swear it was the beginning that gave me the idea.

Cavaignac – Come, come, one of the documents is water-marked in pale violet, the other in blue grey, which shows there were bits that were regummed, but your explanation is impossible, the intercalations do not correspond to what you say.

Henry – What are the bits which you suppose intercalated?

Cavaignac – I do not ask you to question me, but to reply. You concocted the whole letter.

Henry – I swear I did not. It would have been necessary to have the names that are in that of 1896. Why take a portion of the piece of 1894 to put it in the other?

Cavaignac – You will not tell the truth.

Henry – I cannot say anything else. I cannot say I wrote the whole of it. The first one I found, the second I intercalated, adding only the end.

Cavaignac – All you were able to get hold of was the superscription and signature.

Henry – I received the first part.

Cavaignac – Or you received nothing whatever.

Henry – I had the first part, the superscription and signature.

Cavaignac – That is impossible; you aggravate your position with these reticences.

Henry – I acted for my country's good.

Cavaignac – That is not my question. What you did was taken out of the documents themselves. Tell all.

Henry – But I cannot say a thing I did not do. When I had the first part –

Cavaignac – That is not possible. It is clear on the face of it that it would be better to tell the whole truth.

Henry – So you are convinced it was I.

Cavaignac – Tell the truth. You received the envelope and superscription?

Henry – Yes.

Cavaignac – What was there? Only 'Mon cher ami'?

Henry – I have told you – the first portion.

Cavaignac – There was only 'Mon cher ami.' You are putting yourself, I repeat, in the worst position.

Henry – Well, this is what happened. I received the beginning and a few words.

Cavaignac – What words?

Henry – Other things having nothing to do with the affair.

Cavaignac – So this is what happened? You received in 1896 an envelope with a letter inside, an insignificant letter. You suppressed the letter and fabricated the other.

Henry – Yes.

Thereupon Colonel Henry was asked to withdraw to the next room, where he was watched by General Roget.'

M. Bard added:– 'This series of facts indicates the motive of Colonel Henry in doing all in his power to prevent the condemnation of Esterhazy. Henry had given the *bordereau*. If Esterhazy were condemned, the head of the Intelligence Department was thereby compromised. Hence the reassuring forgery and the obstinate denials. It should also be noted that Colonel Henry had been entrusted with Dreyfus's incarceration. The *bordereau* is the essential document of the case against Dreyfus, and Colonel Henry's word was the only guarantee as to its origin.' M. Bard then discussed the letter addressed to M. Sarrien by Colonel Picquart, who, while attributing indiscreet interference in other people's business to Dreyfus, acquitted him of the authorship of the *bordereau*, and attributed all the mischief to M. Du Paty. M. Bard described M. Du Paty as an author and poet, and as too imaginative. He urged that if there was a secret document it might have been shown to Dreyfus without danger to the national defence, and he insisted that the proper forms ought to have been observed. The Minister of War, however, on September 11 assured the Minister of Justice that there was no trace at the War Office of a secret *dossier* having been communicated to the Court-martial.

At this point the Court adjourned.

Source: The Times, 28 October 1898.

Appendix 30: The death of Henry: report of the commander of arms of Mont Valérien

31 August 1898, 7.30 in the evening, Mont-Valérien

General,

Lieutenant-Colonel Henry committed suicide this afternoon.

He cut his throat between three and six o'clock in the afternoon.

He had locked his door, and at half past six, the duty lieutenant was notified that the orderly who took the lieutenant-colonel's meal could not open the door; he went up, forced the lock, opened the door and saw Lieutenant-Colonel Henry stretched out on his bed, covered in blood, his throat slit.

The lieutenant came to inform me, and I confirmed the facts.

I am informing the government by telegram as follows:

31 August 1898, 7.20 in the evening, Mont-Valérien.

Grave event which I am reporting by letter to the general, commander of *La Place [de Paris]*. The letter leaves at 7.30 this evening, by bicycle. It would be fitting if an officer from *la place* came to Mont-Valérien immediately.

Walter

Official Report

31 August 1898, Mont-Valérien

The undersigned, Walter, artillery squadron leader, commander of arms of Mont-Valérien; Variot, lieutenant of the Republican Guard, duty officer in *la place de Paris*; Fête, lieutenant of the 16th foot artillery battalion, went today at 8.30 in the evening into the room occupied by Lieutenant-Colonel Henry, head of the Bureau of Information at the Ministry of War, currently detained in the military prison of Mont-Valérien.

They saw for themselves that Lieutenant-colonel Henry was stretched out on his bed, after having slit his throat with a razor which he was still holding in his left hand.

The doctor called in to confirm the death had not yet arrived.

The body was cold, as had already been noted at seven o'clock by the commander of arms.

Lieutenant-Colonel Henry must have committed suicide around three o'clock in the afternoon.

Two letters were found on the table, one closed, addressed to Mme Henry, and the other open, consisting of incoherent words

In addition, a letter addressed to Mr J Henry, 13 avenue Duquesne and a visiting card were found in the pockets of his clothes.

All these objects were entrusted this evening to Lieutenant Variot, who will deliver them to the general in command of *la place de Paris*.

Finally, a card case containing a 100-franc note, an identity card and some visiting cards were also given to Mr. Variot, together with the wallet and watch of Lieutenant-Colonel Henry.

The wallet contains 265 francs.

Except for these items, no other paper was found in the room or in the clothes of Lieutenant-Colonel Henry.

Mont-Valérien, 31 August 1898

Source: HAD, 4, pp. 619–20.

Appendix 31: The evolution of French press opinion

Le revirement de l'opinion

Six months ago [March 1898]:		Today [September 1898]:	
For the Revision	Against Revision	For the Revision	Against Revision
Le Rappel	*L'Autorité*	*Le Rappel*	*La Croix*
Le XIXe *siècle*	*La Cloche*	*Le XIX*^e *Siècle*	*L'Eclair*
L'Aurore	*La Croix*	*L'Aurore*	*L'Evénement*
Les Droits de l'Homme	*Le Courier du Soir*	*L'Autorité*	*Le Gaulois*
La Fronde	*L'Echo de Paris*	*La Cloche*	*Le Gil Blas*
La Lanterne	*L'Eclair*	*Le Courier du Jour*	*Intransigeant*
La Paix	*L'Evénement*	*L'Echo de Paris*	*Le Jour*
La Petite République	*L'Estafette*	*L'Estafette*	*La Libre Parole*
Le Radical	*La France*	*La France*	*La Patrie*
Le Siècle	*La France Militaire*	*La France Militaire*	*Le Petit Caporal*
	Le Figaro	*La Fronde*	*Le Petit Journal*
	Le Gaulois	*Le Figaro*	*La Presse*
	Le Gil Blas	*Le Journal*	*République Française*
	L'Intransigeant	*Le Journal des Débats*	*Le Soir*
	Le Jour	*La Lanterne*	
	Le Journal des Débats	*La Liberté*	
	La Liberté	*Le Matin*	
	La Libre Parole	*La Paix*	
	Le Matin	*La Petite République*	
	La Patrie	*Le Petit Parisien*	
	Le Petit Caporal	*Le Paris*	
	Le Petit Journal	*Le Petit Bleu (nouveau)*	
	Le Petit Parisien	*Le Siècle*	
	Le Paris	*Le Soleil*	
	La Presse	*Le Temps*	
	République Française	*Le Voltaire*	
	Le Soleil		
	Le Soir		
	Le Temps		
	Le Voltaire		
10 newspapers	**30 newspapers**	**26 newspapers**	**14 newspapers**

Source: Le Rappel, 16 September 1898.

Appendix 32: Extracts from the *Observer* article on Esterhazy's authorship of the *bordereau*

Extracts from article by special correspondent [Rowland Strong]
LIGHT UPON THE DREYFUS CASE.
THE AUTHORSHIP OF THE BORDEREAU

Count Ferdinand Esterhazy came from Paris to London with the object of making certain disclosures. The principal disclosure which he made (and this to more persons than one) was that he was the author of the *bordereau*…

'I wrote the bordereau' he said 'at the request of Colonel Sandherr who is now dead.'

It is unfortunate that both Colonel Sandherr and Colonel Henry should be dead, for they both knew the facts; but it is quite possible to prove that I did write the bordereau in spite of the disappearance of those two witnesses.

The *bordereau* was intended to constitute the material proof of Dreyfus's guilt. All that the Intelligence Department had managed to find out against Dreyfus was in the nature of moral proof. It was known through the French spy services in Berlin that certain documents had reached the German General Staff which Dreyfus alone could have obtained. And it was the list of these documents, whose arrival in Berlin had been signalised to our Intelligence Department, which constituted the *bordereau*. Dreyfus had been tested in several ways. For instance a plan of the concentration of troops on the south-eastern frontier had been dictated to him which was quite fantastic. A short time afterwards our spies in Italy informed us that the Italian Staff was making certain modifications in the fortifications around Nice which corresponded to the changes announced in the imaginary scheme dictated to Dreyfus. Then Dreyfus managed to spend long holidays in Alsace without being apparently found out by the German authorities – a very suspicious sign in itself for it is almost impossible for a French officer to remain any length of time in the conquered provinces without being discovered. In fact there was considerable moral proof against Dreyfus before his trial took place; but there was not material proof. Colonel Sandherr, who was an Alsatian, like Dreyfus, but intensely anti-Semitic, determined to forge this proof. He was personally convinced of the accused man's guilt, and he would not allow him to escape. Since circumstantial evidence was not enough, it was necessary for the purposes of the Court-martial that documents should exist. I was at that time attached to the Intelligence Department, my duty being to watch the movements of the military attachés accredited by the Powers of the Triple Alliance, and also to make voyages to foreign countries, where I was never supposed to be a French officer, partly owing to the fact that I speak Italian and German very well – and then my name, Esterhazy, made everybody believe I was an Austrian.

When Colonel Sandherr told me to write out the *bordereau* I did so without the slightest compunction or hesitation. I am one of those men who are soldiers by profession, and who cling to the old medieval traditions of military discipline. When I received an order I obeyed it implicitly, and without any sort of question. I wrote the *bordereau* because Colonel Sandherr told me to do so. I knew, of course, the purposes it was intended to serve. I knew that I was committing a forgery, but I also knew that all intelligence departments in all countries in the world are run on precisely the same lines as our own, and that it is impossible to achieve practical results in any other way… It is nearly always necessary to manufacture the material evidence against spies, because otherwise they would never be punished. They never, or very rarely, leave written evidence of their nefarious work.

'The *bordereau* then, having been written by me, it became necessary to give it the indispensable air of an authentic document. As you know, it was supposed to have been stolen from the German Embassy. Colonel Schwartzkoppen, however, denied having ever seen it. I believe he gave his word of honour to that effect. What he said was perfectly true. He never did see the bordereau. It was handed by an agent of our Intelligence Department to the porter of the German Embassy, who is a spy in our service, and the porter gave it to another agent whose name is Genest, and by him it was brought back to the Intelligence department, and there duly docketed and numbered as a document which had been obtained from the German Embassy in the usual course. It thus received the official baptism. Now, it was exclusively upon the evidence of the *bordereau* that Dreyfus was condemned. The document privately shown to the officers of the Court-martial was fetched from the War Office during the *huis clos,* with the object of convincing the judges, should they show any signs of wavering. It was the famous letter containing the phrase, *Ce canaille de D.* Now this letter, which is genuine, and was really written by Schwartzkoppen, did not refer to Dreyfus at all, and the General Staff was absolutely aware of the fact. The 'D' in question was a certain Dollfus, a building contractor, who years before the Dreyfus affair had supplied the German military attaché with plans of the fortifications near Nice.'

The ex-Major concluded his conversation by bitterly inveighing against the General Staff which had, he said, abandoned him. He told the whole story of the Speranza and Blanche forgeries, and said that the judges of the Court of Indictment had quashed the case against him in defiance of all law and justice. He also described his relations with Colonel Du Paty de Clam and said that the veiled lady was none other than the Colonel's wife, the Marquise Du Paty de Clam.

We think that it may now be said, with M. Zola, that nothing will prevent the truth in this lamentable affair from ultimately being told.

Source: The Observer, 25 September 1898.

Appendix 33: The ruling of admissibility of Lucie's appeal for revision (5 July 1898), 29 October 1898

In view of the letter of the Minister of Justice, dated 27 September 1898;

In view of the closing speech of the Public Prosecutor at the Supreme Court of Appeal denouncing to the Court the condemnation pronounced by the first court-martial of the Military Court of Paris, on December 22, 1894, on Alfred Dreyfus, then captain of artillery, attached to the General Staff of the Army;

In view of all documents of the case, and of Article 443 to 446 of the Code of Criminal Procedure, amended by the law of June 10, 1895, on the formal admissibility of the demand for a review;

Whereas the Court is vested by its public prosecutor, in virtue of an express order from the Minister of Justice, acting after having taken the advice of the commission instituted by article 444 of the Code of Criminal Procedure;

Whereas the application falls within the cases provided for by the last paragraph of article 443; whereas it was introduced within the time limit fixed by article 444; whereas finally the verdict which is the subject of an appeal for review has the force of a *res judicata;*

On the status of the procedure:

Whereas the documents produced do not place the Court in a position to give a ruling on the merits of the case, and that there are grounds to proceed to a supplementary investigation;

On these grounds

The Court declares the application in proper form and admissible;

It states that it will institute a supplementary investigation;

and declares that there are no grounds at present for a ruling on the Public Prosecutor's application concerning the suspension of the penalty.

Source: Déb. Cass. 1898, 266–8.

Appendix 34: The Speech of Deputy Poincaré in the Chamber of Deputies, 28 November 1898

M. Raymond Poincaré and the Dreyfus Case
THE PICQUART PROSECUTION

'The time has come' he said in substance, 'when silence for some of us would be utter cowardice. For the last two years, with almost everyone else and with the majority of my colleagues, I have wished for the truth, but I have held that the authority of a judicial decision could not be shaken by illegal and almost revolutionary means. I have however, always asked the Government to put and end to certain intolerable abuses committed in certain bureaux at the War Office.' (Cheers.)

'Today an effort is being made without the responsibility of the Government – a final and supreme effort – to prevent all these abuses from becoming known. It is strange that now for the third time Colonel Picquart should be prosecuted, and I cannot help affirming that these prosecutions have always taken place in conditions giving them, I will not say the character, but the aspect of reprisals. He has been kept in secret imprisonment quite beyond all reasonable bounds, and while this ex-officer is being prosecuted, other more serious acts are unaccountably allowed to go unpunished. The authors of a number of forged documents are not in prison; only M. Picquart is there. These methods are such as finally to make even the calmest minds revolt. (Cheers.) It is the duty of the men who held office in 1894 at all events not in any way to prevent the discovery of the truth. In 1894 I, like many of my colleagues, knew of Dreyfus's arrest only a few days after it had taken place through a newspaper article'

There were loud cheers and general expressions of astonishment, while M. Barthou, one of the colleagues in question, jumping up in his place, exclaimed: – 'It is the language of truth. I applaud it and support you in your attitude.' (Cheers.)

'If,' continued M. Poincaré, 'if I have hesitated to make a public declaration, it is because no competent jurisdiction has had the case in hand. At present everyone who possesses a single particle of the truth is bound to make it known'. (Cheers.) 'The Ministers of 1894 never heard mention of any other definite charges than that of the *bordereau*, and never did the then Prime Minister (it was M. Dupuy) nor any of his colleagues hear of any such thing as confessions made by Dreyfus to Captain Lebrun-Renault.' (loud cheers.)

M. Cavaignac, rising in his place: 'General Mercier received these confessions.'

– 'I willingly accept this correction, but he made no mention of it to his colleagues, and Capitan Lebrun-Renault, when summoned by the Prime Minister, never mentioned any such confessions. It was not for any one of us in 1894 to substitute our opinion for that of a Court-martial, but today fresh facts have been revealed. The Court of Cassation is examining them, and what we ask is that it should be left to examine them in complete independence, all procedure connected with it being adjourned until later on. In acting as I have acted I consider that I am following our national traditions of justice and liberty (loud cheers); and I am happy to have seized the opportunity, too long awaited, thus to ease my conscience.'

Source: The Times, 29 November 1898.

Appendix 35: Le monument Henry:
Extracts from remarks accompanying contributions to Henry's
subscriptions, December 1898–January 1899

The contributions are accompanied by signatures or commentaries such as:

'Concierge for Jews, disgusted by the Yids'

'A French Catholic full of hatred for the Jews and Freemasons'

'Feutrier, photographic dealer and antisemite, victim of Jews'

'A Priest praying for a bedside carpet made of Yid skin'

'A military physician who would vivisect Jews rather than harmless rabbits'

'An Artillery lieutenant ashamed to see so many Jews in his army'

'Resident of Baccarat, keen to put all the Yids, young and old, into glass furnaces'

'A cook, wants to roast the Jews'

'An Alsatian robbed several times by the Jews'

'Ex-civil servant, financial and administrative victims of the Jews and Freemasons'

'A miserable commercial traveller, enemy of all Jews and foreigners'

'A subscriber asking why the Jews want to be French? Negroes aren't white'

'Lydia M., aged twenty, rich only in hatred of the Yids'

'A French Catholic, out of hatred for the Jews and Protestants, enemies of France'

'L.M. the authentic antisemitic café-owner'

'A group of candidates for the Ecole Polytechnique' protest against 'the Jewish invasion'

'An anti-Jew who never buys from the Jews at any price'

'A French Captain, victim of the English and the Jews'

'A subscriber, who thinks it should be forbidden for any Jew to travel in France without a yellow robe'

'Henri Loubeau, a small winegrower, enraged by the thought that the Yids can drink the excellent Montreuil-Bellay wine'

'A little Gentile, out of hatred of the deicide Jew, the cause of all our misfortunes'

'An inmate of La Salpêtrière [Parisian hospital] who wants to see all the Jews crucified'

'A subscriber, convinced the Jew is a stinking and dangerous beast and destruction is necessary'

'A medical student who would like to dissect all the Yids in France'

'A patriot who would like to see all Jews nailed to the wall'

'A subscriber who would like to eat some Jew to shit him out'

In several commentaries Jews are described as: 'the cosmopolitan gang' 'bought by foreigners', 'the race of traitors', 'the horrible spider which is sucking all the blood of our country', or referred to as animals: 'chimpanzees', 'pigs', 'these bugs', 'the Jewish microbes', 'Synagogue lice', 'Jewish plague', 'the cancer', 'vile spiders'. 'I hold a Jew in less esteem than the lowest of the animals that I have on my farm'

Source: S. Wilson, *Ideology and Experience*, pp. 136–53.

Appendix 36: *Derrière un grillage* ('Behind Bars'): extracts from Octave Mirbeau's preface to *Hommage des Artistes à Picquart*, February 1899

More than six long months have passed since Colonel Picquart was put in prison.

He is in prison because he refused to be associated with a crime; he is in prison because he proclaimed the innocence of a man condemned to the worst possible torture. He is in prison because he demanded the very thing that nowadays is banished from all form of life – justice! When in the future, the indifferent, the neutral, that mass of human larvae called wise men, realise what they have allowed to happen and be said, perhaps they will be appalled!

More than six long months have passed since Colonel Picquart was put in prison, and as for the traitors, they are quite at ease. They come and go freely, boldly! Sure of their own impunity, they dictate the conditions for justice and deal with the law as between powers… It is not enough!… In an astounding perversion of patriotic duty, they are protected, defended, acclaimed. They receive the accolade of princes. Writers, artists, philosophers, high-ranking civil servants, presidents of the Bar fraternise with them… And that is not all… Statues are erected to these glorified forgers; swords of honour are bestowed upon them, incomes from the state, the thanks of the nation… The army honours them with a triple column of rifles, cannons and flags. The Church exalts and in a way beatifies them. The forger is a saint, the traitor a martyr. The officer's jacket and the monk's habit, the sword of one and the cross of the other cover them to impose on the world the new dogma of the Immaculate Treason of Esterhazy. And on all sides, a cry goes up from the ignorant and deceived crowd, a cry of shame – the shame of which will remain forever on the face of France.

Long live the forgers and glory be to the traitors!

If a man today simply shows some humanity, some pity, if he is enamoured of justice, if in one way or another, he should seek the truth in the Dreyfus affair, that is sufficient for him to be discredited, covered in abuse, pursued by boos, threatened with death! And if a man suddenly cries out in the crowd, 'I'm a traitor as well, I too have sold my country', that is sufficient for him to be immediately surrounded by frenzied cheers and carried aloft in triumph by the patriots!

Long live the forgers and glory be to the traitors!

And by virtue of this odious cry, more than six long months have passed since Colonel Picquart was put in prison…

More than six long months have passed since Colonel Picquart was put in a prison cell. He has not deceived himself, nor did he deceive his persecutors on the firmness of his spirit. Nothing could sap his gentle, resigned energy: nothing could throw a shadow of sadness over his strong, peaceful, serene cheerfulness. His character as a free man has not changed in captivity... He never complains and he waits... He awaits deliverance, calmly; he awaits the worst without anguish...

I saw him again yesterday.

The visiting room is dark. Daylight scarcely penetrates this room; and through the only window which lights it, one's glance is confronted with the very high, very black, infinitely sad wall of the prison. The prisoner is at the far end of the visiting room, between bars, in a sort of cage like an animal, separated from the visitor by quite a wide corridor screened with metal grills. The impression is really painful. The mesh of the double grill is so fine that at first one sees nothing. Then little by little one perceives a vague figure coming and going behind the grill, a distant figure almost without contours, a figure that fades like a shape disappearing into the mist... In fact, at certain times of day, or when the clouds hang low, on filthy days like yesterday, one can only distinguish two eyes, two clear, limpid, happy eyes which offer you a friendly greeting...

Francis de Pressensé said that Colonel Picquart was a hero. He inscribed this word at the front of his well-known book devoted to Picquart. I offer my apologies to my dear and noble fellow campaigner, but I myself dislike heroes and know what blind, bloody brutes those people that we call heroes – those nefarious, generally military men – have been throughout history. And so I would rather say that Colonel Picquart is a man! In these times of decline and degradation, to be a man seems to me more moving and more rare than to be a hero... Humanity dies from having heroes; it is re-invigorated when it has men....

Source: Hommage des artistes à Picquart. Album of 12 lithographs. Preface: Octave Mirbeau. (Paris: Société libre d'édition des gens de lettres, 1899).

Appendix 37: Extracts from the correspondence between Dreyfus and his wife Lucie and from his Devil's Island diary: 7 December 1894–6 June 1899

Letters 7 December 1894 – 12 March 1895

Alfred to Lucie. Cherche-Midi prison, 7 December 1894:

My beloved Lucie....Dear France, you whom I love with my whole soul, with all my heart, to whom I have dedicated all my strength, all my intelligence, how could I be accused of such an appalling crime?

...At last the day of my appearance before justice draws near...I have come to the end of this moral torture...I shall be tried by soldiers who will listen to me....tomorrow I shall appear before my judges, my head held high, my soul at peace...I am ready to appear as a soldier who has done nothing wrong....they will see it in my face...I have nothing to fear.

Alfred to Lucie. Cherche-Midi prison, 23 December 1894:

To be innocent...to see oneself convicted of the most monstrous crime... .Whatever happens to me...to seek out the truth...to move heaven and earth to discover it...to rehabilitate my name...this undeserved stigma must be removed.

Lucie to Alfred. Paris, 23 December 1894:

My Darling…What misfortune…what torture…what ignominy…wherever you may be sent I will follow you…I cannot do without you…accept the undeserved punishment…do it for me …for your children…I weep, I weep… live for my sake, I beseech you…I should die of grief if you were no longer alive….Rest assured, I will never bow my head…I do not sleep, and it is to you that I return.

Alfred to Lucie. Cherche-Midi prison, 27 December 1894:

…and so I shall fight to my last breath…to my last drop of blood…

Lucie to Alfred. Paris, 31 December 1894:

My Dearest…I see that you have regained your courage and have given some back to me…Endure this dreadful ceremony valiantly…head high and declaiming your innocence…

Alfred to Lucie. Cherche-Midi prison, 3 January 1895:

…the supreme humiliation is set…I was prepared…yet the blow was violent…

Alfred to Lucie. La Santé prison, 5 January 1895:

…In promising that I will live…to hold out until my name is rehabilitated…I will tell you, when we are happy again, what I suffered today…how my heart bled…I seemed to be the victim of an hallucination, but alas my torn and defiled uniform reminded me of the brutal reality…

Alfred to Lucie. La Santé prison, 5 January 1895, 7 o'clock in the evening:

I do not have the right to give up as long as breath remains in my body…I will fight…

Lucie to Alfred. Paris, 5 January 1895, evening:

…What a horrifying morning…what appalling times…I cannot think…it hurts too much

Alfred to Lucie. La Santé prison, 9 January 1895:

….when I think of it again…how could I have promised to go on living after my conviction…that Saturday is engraved on my mind in letters of fire…I have the courage of a soldier…but alas, have I the soul of a martyr?…

Alfred to Lucie. Ile de Ré, 23 January 1895:

…I am …the victim of the most appalling error…But whatever happens …in our fine country of France…there will arise a man honest and courageous enough to discover the truth…Yes, my darling, I have to live…I have to suffer to the end for the sake of the name borne by the dear children…I weep when I think of our past happiness…

Lucie to Alfred. Paris, 28 February 1895:

…My Dearest Love, I cannot describe the grief I feel as the distance that divides us grows greater and greater I pass my days with dreadful thoughts, my nights with frightful dreams…

Alfred to Lucie. Ile de Ré, 12 March 1895:

...Beloved Lucie...I am incapable of writing to you all...my mind is too weary...my despair too great...it is time that this horrible drama came to an end...but for God's sake hurry and work hard ...When you have some good news send a telegram; I await it every day like the Messiah.

From the time of Dreyfus' arrival on Devil's Island letters took 2–3 months to reach him. All letters were first directed to the central department of penal administration, where they were read and inspected before being forwarded to Dreyfus. All his own letters were also censored. This procedure, due to be put in place on 23 March 1895, was definitively enforced on 12 May 1895.

Extracts from the Diary 14 April 1895 – 10 September 1896

14 April 1895, Devil's Island:

Today I begin the diary of my sad and appalling life....I worshipped reason...I believed in logic...I believed in human justice...the physical and mental tortures ...have been worse than I even expected...today I am broken in body and spirit... ...my horror of life is such that I considered not seeking medical help thus putting an end to this martyrdom...

Oh how I wish to live till the day of my rehabilitation...Shall I survive till then? I often have my doubts...

Night of 14 – 15 April 1895:

Impossible to sleep...the guard walks up and down...the itching from insects which run over my skin...the anger stirring in my heart at being reduced to this...an atrocious thought to be convicted of such an abominable crime without knowing the reason why!...

19 April 1895:

...still no news from my loved ones...what I find inhuman....is that they are intercepting my correspondence...to bury me alive...to prevent all communication is contrary to all justice...

20 April 1895, 2 o'clock in the afternoon

To think that in our century, in a country like France imbued with ideas of justice and truth, things of this sort, so utterly undeserved, can happen, I have written to the President of the Republic, I have written to ministers, always asking them to uncover the truth... it is justice that I clamour for...

Lucie to Alfred. Paris, 21 April 1895:

... I cry to God with unceasing supplications that this year may bring our happiness back to us...

28 April 1895:

A storm is brewing...gusts are buffeting everything...causing violent clashes...just like the state of my soul, sometimes in its violent fits of anger...

2 May 1895:

> *The boat...is in sight...my heart is beating to the point of bursting... bringing letters from my wife?...*

9 May 1895:

> *Appalling day. Fits of weeping...hysterics...but it has to be mind over matter...*

Friday 10 May 1895:

> *Acute fever during the night*

16 May 1895:

> *Continual fever...*

29 May 1895:

> *Continuous rain...heavy weather...stifling...nerve-wracking*

1 June 1895:

> *The mail boat from Cayenne has passed...Shall I at last have news of my wife and children? Since I left France on the 20 February I have had no news of my loved ones...*

2 June 1895:

> *Nothing. Nothing....the silence of the grave...*

3 June 1895:

> *...A traitor! At the very word all my blood rushes to my head, my whole being shivers with anger and indignation, a traitor, the lowest of the low...*

(Letter from Alfred to Lucie, 3 June 1895:

> *Do you remember those lines of Shakespeare from Othello...:*
>
> *Who steals my purse steals trash; 'tis something, nothing;*
> *'Twas mine, 'tis his, and has been slave to thousands:*
> *But he that filches from me my good name*
> *Robs me of that which not enriches him*
> *And makes me poor indeed.*
> *Ah, yes, the wretch who has stolen my honour has certainly made me 'poor'.*

5 June 1895:

> *No news from my loved ones...for three and half months....*

9 June 1895:

> *My heart bleeds so much that death would be a deliverance...Still no letters from my loved ones.*

12 June 1895:

> ....*finally some letters from my wife and family....so it takes more than three months...*

19 June 1895:

> ....*when will they find the culprit...when shall I finally know the truth... will I live to see that day...my poor dear Lucie and my children....*

10 July 1895:

> *Irritations of every kind....I may no longer walk around my but...no longer sit facing the sea where it is cool ...*

14 July 1885:

> *I saw the tricolour flying...this flag which I have served with loyalty and honour. My pain is such that my pen falls from my hand; some feelings cannot be expressed in words.*

16 July 1895:

> *...heat intolerable...nothing to read...always this silence*

29 July 1895:

> *A heavy, stifling day, harrowing...my nerves are stretched like violin strings.*

31 July 1895:

> *Last night I dreamed of you, my dear Lucie, and of our children....I await the mail from Cayenne with feverish impatience...*

1 August 1895 midday:

> *Mail has arrived from Cayenne...Has it brought me my letters? and what news...?*

1 August 1895 4.30pm:

> *Still nothing....terrible waiting...*

1 August 1895 9 o'clock in the evening:

> *Nothing...what bitter disappointment.*

2 September 1895:

> *It has been long since I added to my diary. What is the point?...*

22 September 1895:

> *Convicted on the evidence of handwriting...I have been seeking justice for almost a year...what I demand is ...the discovery of the wretch who wrote that infamous letter...*

27 September 1895:

> *Such torment…goes beyond human endurance…the daily renewal of agonising anguish….is sending an innocent to his grave…a Government has all means to clarify…*
>
> *It has an absolute duty to do so…*

29 September 1895:

> *Violent palpitations…I was suffocating…the machine is struggling on… but for how much longer?*

5 October 1895:

> *….letters from my family…agonising cries of such distress arise from these letters that my whole being is shaken… I have just sent the following letter to the President…*

4 November 1895:

> *Terrible heat…nothing consumes the heart and mind as much as these long agonising silences…never a human voice…never a friendly face…*

15 November 1895:

> *…I will carry on to the limits of my declining strength…a relentless struggle against isolation…a climate that saps all energy…nothing to read…nothing to do…*

13 December 1895:

> *They will kill me by this endless torment or force me to kill myself as an escape from insanity…*

30 December 1895:

> *My blood burns and fever is eating me up…when will this torture end?*

12 January 1896:

Reply from the President to my petition of 5 October 1895:

Rejected, with no comment.

7 September 1896:

> *Yesterday I was put in shackles…why? Since my arrival I have fully observed all orders…how did I not go mad during that long, atrocious night…?*

Later the same day:

> *…my suffering is dreadful…but I no longer feel anger towards those who cause an innocent man to suffer…I pity them…*

8 September 1896:

> *These nights in shackles!…without knowing why! What horrible and atrocious nightmare have I been living in for nearly two years?*

Same day, afternoon:

My mind is so stricken, so overwhelmed ...that I can go on no longer...I am failing.

...why am I not in the grave?...when light has been shed on this affair, oh! I bequeath my children to France, to my dear homeland. My dear little Pierre, my dear little Jeanne, my dear Lucie, all of you whom I love from the depth of my heart, with all the ardour of my soul, believe me, if these lines reach you, that I will have done all that is humanly possible to hold out.

9 September 1896:

The commander of the islands came yesterday...he explained that the action taken was not a punishment but a 'security measure'...putting in shackles a security measure...when I am guarded day and night by a guard armed with revolver and a rifle! The truth must be told...it is a measure of hatred, of torture, ordered from Paris...I am so depressed, so overwrought, so crushed that I cannot think...and always the appalling enigma...

10 September 1896:

I am so weary, so broken in body and spirit that I am stopping this diary today, unable to judge how long my strength will last, or on which day my mind will collapse...

I end it by addressing this supreme appeal to the president of the republic in case I should die before seeing the end of this frightful drama.

'Mr President...' (v. Chronology, Part 4, pp. 80–1)

End of diary.

From the end of 1896 the surveillance of Dreyfus' correspondence became more stringent: all letters addressed to him were copied. He no longer received any of the originals.

Letters 5 February 1897 – 6 June 1899

Alfred to Lucie. Devil's Island, 5 February 1897:

My Dearest...Facing the greatest suffering, the vilest insults, when the ferociousness stirred by bestial inhumanity caused my reason to waver– when blood flooded my temples and my eyes–I have thought of death with longing...but my mouth is sealed because I want to die not only an innocent man, but also as the good and loyal Frenchman who has never for one moment forgotten his duty towards his country...

Alfred to Lucie. Devil's Island, 10 August 1897:

My beloved Lucie...once again I tell you of my deep affection, infinite tenderness, my admiration for your noble character; I open my soul to you and I will acquaint you with your rights and obligations, the rights which can only be abandoned when confronted by death. And this inalienable right, both for my country and for all of you, is to demand that full light is shed upon this frightful drama...And on the day when the whole truth is uncovered–as it must be, for neither time, patience or will

> *must be spared...if I am no longer alive, it will be up to you to (cleanse my memory) clear my name ...and I repeat, however outrageous the suffering and torture inflicted upon me...I have never forgotten that far above men and the passions (and errors) which may lead them astray is our country. It rests upon her to be my final judge...*
>
> *My deepest affection to you and our beloved children...*

Lucie to Alfred. Paris, 6 October 1897:

....I did not succeed in expressing....the great confidence...that I felt that our happiness will return....

Lucie to Alfred. Paris 7 January 1898:

My Darling,...Have courage! Have courage! I see the moment when we will finally be reunited, cleansed of this frightful stain....all that will remain will be a painful memory, which alas will never disappear...

> Alfred to Lucie. Devil's Island, 26 January 1898:
>
> *....I understand...I believe that General Boisdeffre has never been against doing us justice...we request him to shed light on this affair. It was no more in his power to act than it was ours....*

> Alfred to Lucie. Devil's Island, 26 May 1898:
>
> *....As I told you, I have written to the President (of the Republic) asking for a review of my trial...I am still totally in the dark...I do not know the definitive results of the request....I have been expecting a reply daily for several months...*

Lucie to Alfred. Paris, 10 August 1898

...how difficult it is to have an error acknowledged. The human mind welcomes evil with enthusiasm and prejudice is more difficult to root out because it has been accepted easily...and has become legend, an acquired fact....

Telegram Governor, Cayenne, 16 November 1898:

Governor to the deported convict Dreyfus, via the officer in command of Devil's Island

Informs you that Criminal Division of Supreme Court of Appeal has declared admissible in present form the appeal for review of your judgement and instructed that you be informed of this ruling and invited to produce your pleas of defence.

> Telegram Alfred to Lucie. Cayenne, 6 June 1899:
>
> *Madame Dreyfus. Devil's Island 5 June. Heart, soul with you, children, all. I am leaving on Friday. Await with immense joy the moment of happiness of holding you in my arms. Love to all. Alfred.*

Appendix 38: Ruling of the Supreme Court of Appeal annulling the verdict of the 1894 court martial of Dreyfus and the ordering of a second court martial to be held in Rennes, 3 June 1899

In the name of the People of France

The Supreme Court of Appeal has delivered the following decision following the speech of the Public Prosecutor, the content of which is as follows:

The Public Prosecutor at the Court of Appeal states that the following facts result from the documents of the dossier and in particular the inquiry made by the Criminal Division and by the Combined Division, which summarize the principal elements of the appeal for review of the verdict of the Court Martial of 22 December 1894, condemning DREYFUS to deportation and degradation for the crime of treason.

1. The faux Henry renders suspect the sensational testimony given by Henry before the Court Martial;

2. The date of the month of April assigned to the *bordereau* and to the despatch of the documents, used both in the trial of Dreyfus and that of Esterhazy, served as a basis for the conviction of one [Dreyfus] and the acquittal of the other [Esterhazy], whilst today that date is deferred to the month of August, removing all legal basis from the verdict of 1894;

3. The obvious contradiction existing between the expert report of 1894 in the trial of Dreyfus, and that of 1897 in the trial of Esterhazy, and, moreover, the new opinion of one of the experts of 1894, resulting in the overturning of most of the expert report of 1894;

4. The absolute identity of the India paper on which the *bordereau* is written with the India paper which was used by Esterhazy to write two letters in 1892 and 1894, which he recognized as his own;

5. The absolute proof, resulting from several letters by Esterhazy, of the fact that he was present at the August manoeuvres in Châlons in 1894, and of other documents proving that he alone could have written that sentence in the *bordereau*: 'I am leaving on manoeuvres', whilst it emerges from an official circular of 17 May 1894, not produced at the trial in 1894, that not only did Dreyfus not go on these manoeuvres, nor to later ones, but that he was well aware that he was not to go there, and that consequently he was not able to write that sentence;

6. The official report from Police headquarters, not produced in the proceedings of 1894, establishing that contrary to the information provided by Guénée and used as moral arguments by the prosecution, it was not Dreyfus who frequented gambling circles and that there had been a confusion of names;

7. The highly dramatic scene which took place in the office of Mr. Bertulus and justifies the most serious assumptions on the guilty conduct of Henry and Esterhazy;

8. The telegram of 2 November 1894, the meaning of which is agreed by all today, not produced at the trial, and from which it emerges, in conjuncture with another telegram that was invoked against Dreyfus, that Dreyfus had had no dealings with the foreign power indicated in this telegram;

9. The official documents which establish that Dreyfus had no dealings, direct or indirect, with any foreign power;

10. Lastly, the serious protests and presumptions of innocence resulting from the documents of the dossier and from Dreyfus' correspondence, showing that Dreyfus never confessed, nor could confess his guilt;

And whereas in terms of article 443 of the Code of Criminal Procedure, § 4, a review can be requested:

'When, after a conviction, a fact comes to light or is revealed, or when documents unknown at the time of the proceedings are produced which are liable to establish the innocence of the accused.'

Whereas all these facts specified above constitute new facts or new documents, in the meaning of the law, it is therefore right to admit them and consequently to quash the verdict of 22 December 1894:

On these grounds

The Public Prosecutor

In view of the documents of the dossier and the inquiry

In view of articles 443, § 4, 444, 445 of the Code of Criminal Procedure

Asks that it may please the Court,

To admit the new facts and new documents referred to above as being liable to establish the innocence of Dreyfus,

And in doing this, to declare admissible in substance and legally justified the appeal for a review of the verdict of the Court Martial dated 22 December 1894:

To SET ASIDE and ANNUL the aforesaid verdict, and to return the case of the accused Dreyfus before any such Court Martial as it would be pleased to designate.

Delivered by the Public Prosecutor's Department, 27 May 1899.

Public Prosecutor

Signed: J. MANAU

The Court

Having heard President Ballot-Beaupré in his report, the Public Prosecutor Manau in his submissions, and Maitre Mornard, lawyer of Madame Dreyfus in his capacity, delivers its conclusions;

In view of article 443, § 4, of the Code of Criminal Procedure, namely: 'Review can be requested when, after a conviction, a fact comes to light or is revealed, or when documents unknown at the time of the proceedings are produced which are liable to establish the innocence of accused;

In view of article 445, modified by the law of 1 March 1899;

In view of the ruling of 29 October 1897, according to which the Criminal Division, ordering an enquiry, declared admissible and in due form the request for a review of the trial of Alfred Dreyfus, convicted on 22 December 1894 to the penalty of deportation to a fortified enclosure and to military degradation for the crime of high treason;

In view of the official reports of the aforesaid enquiry and the enclosures;

ON THE PLEA THAT THE SECRET TRAP, THE DOCUMENT CALLED 'CE CANAILLE DE D.' WAS ALLEGEDLY COMMUNICATED TO THE COURT MARTIAL

Whereas this communication is proven, both by the deposition of President Casimir-Périer and by that of Generals Mercier and Boisdeffre themselves;

Whereas, on the one hand, President Casimir-Périer declared that he had learned from General Mercier that the document containing the words '*Ce canaille de D.*', considered then to indicate Dreyfus, was disclosed to the Court Martial;

And whereas, on the other hand, Generals Mercier and Boisdeffre, invited to reveal whether they knew that this communication had taken place, refused to answer; and thus recognized it implicitly;

Whereas the revelation, after the verdict, of the communication to the judges of a document which could have made a decisive impression on them and which is today considered inapplicable to the convicted man, constitutes a new fact liable to establish his innocence;

ON THE PLEA CONCERNING THE BORDEREAU

Whereas the crime Dreyfus was charged with consisted in the fact of having delivered to a foreign power or its agents some documents, confidential or secret, relating to national defence, the despatch of which was accompanied by a letter missive or *bordereau*, which was undated, unsigned and written on India paper 'watermarked in outline after manufacture with lines in each direction making up four-millimetre squares';

Whereas this letter, the basis of the accusation made against him, had been successively submitted to five experts charged with comparing the handwriting with that of Dreyfus, and that three experts, Charavay, Teyssonnières and Bertillon, had attributed it to him;

Whereas, moreover, nothing had been discovered in his possession, nor proved that he had used any paper of this type, and that research undertaken to find similar paper at a number of retailers had been fruitless; whereas, however, a similar sample, but of different format, had been supplied by the house called Marion, a wholesaler, in the Bergère district, where they had declared that 'the sample was no longer current in the trade.'

Whereas in November 1898 the enquiry revealed the existence and led to the seizure of two letters on squared India paper, whose authenticity is in no doubt, dated 17 April 1892 and 17 August 1894, the latter contemporary with the despatch of the *bordereau*, both emanating from another officer who in December 1897 had expressly denied ever having used tracing paper;

Whereas on the one hand, three experts commissioned by the Criminal Division, Professors Meyer, Giry and Molinier of L'École des Chartes were in agreement to affirm that the *bordereau* was written in same hand as the two letters referred to above, and that Charavay endorsed their conclusions after examining this writing, which was unknown to him in 1894;

Whereas on the other hand, three experts also commissioned: Putois, president, and Choquet, honorary president of the Trade Union for paper and its manufacturing industries, and Marion, wholesale dealer, affirmed that in terms of its external measurements and the measurements of the squares, in terms of shade, thickness, transparency, weight and sizing, in terms of raw materials used in its manufacture, 'the paper of the *bordereau* presented characteristics of the greatest similarity' to that of the letter of 17 August 1894;

Whereas these facts, unknown to the Court Martial which pronounced the conviction, tend to show that the *bordereau* could not have been written by Dreyfus;

That they are also, consequently, liable to establish the innocence of the convicted man;

That consequently they fall within the category provided for by paragraph 4 of article 443;

And that one cannot dismiss them by invoking other facts subsequent to the verdict, such as the remarks made by Dreyfus on 5 January before Captain Lebrun-Renaud;

That one cannot, indeed, consider these remarks as a confession of guilt, since they not only begin with a protestation of innocence, but it is also impossible to establish the exact and complete text because of the differences existing between the successive declarations of Captain Lebrun-Renaud and those of other witnesses;

Whereas there are no grounds to consider further the deposition of Depert, which is contradicted by that of the Depot director who was with him on 5 January 1895;

And whereas by application of article 445, new oral proceedings must be heard;

On these grounds, and without need to rule on the other pleas;

The Court QUASHES and ANNULS the verdict of conviction delivered on 22 December 1894 against Alfred Dreyfus by the 1st Court Martial of the military Government of Paris;

And returns the accused before the Court Martial of Rennes, designated after special deliberation taken by the Court to consider the following question: Is Dreyfus guilty of having in 1894, contrived plots or maintained dealings with a foreign power or one of its agents, in order to urge it to commit hostilities or undertake war against France, or to procure the means for this, by passing to it the notes and documents mentioned in the aforesaid *bordereau*?

And states that this present ruling will be printed and transcribed on the registers of the first Court Martial of the military Government of Paris, alongside the quashed verdict;

In the presence of: MM. MAZEAU, First President; BALLOT-BEAUPRÉ, reporting judge; LŒW, TANON Presidents; PETIT, SALLANTIN, DARESTE, LEPELLETIER, VOISIN, CRÉPON, SEVESTRE, GEORGE-LEMAIRE, CHAMBA-REAUD, LARDENOIS, COTELLE, .DENIS, FAURE-BIGUET, BERNARD, PAUL DUPRÉ, DURAND, RUBEN DE COUDER, PAYE, ACCARIAS, LOUBERS, MARIGNAN, BARD, LETELLIER, DUMAS, SERRE, CHÉVRIER, REYNAUD, ALPHANDERY, ROULLIER, FALGIMAIGNE, FAUCONNEAU-DU-FRÉSNE, RAU, FOCHER, FABRE-GUETTES, BOULLOCHE, ZEYS, GALARY, MAILLET, ATTHALIN, DUVAL, LASSÈRRE, DUPONT, LE GRIX, Advisers; MANAU, Public Prosecutor; MÉRILLON, Counsel for the Prosecution; MÉNARD, Chief clerk; SAIGE and TOURNIER, clerks.

In consequence, the President of the French Republic instructs and orders all court ushers and bailiffs, as requested by this order, to carry out the said ruling; Public prosecutors of the Republic in courts of first instance to give assistance; All commanders and officers of the public forces to come to their aid when legally requested to do so.

In faith of which, the present ruling was signed by the First President, the Reporting Judge and the Chief Clerk.

Signed: MM. MAZEAU, First President;
              BALLOT-BEAUPRÉ, reporting judge,
              and L. MÉNARD, Chief clerk.

For certified copying:

              L. MÉNARD, Chief clerk of the Supreme Court of Appeal.

Source: Déb. Cass., 1899, 705–11.

Appendix 39: Victor Basch: opening of the Rennes court martial, August 1899

From the first days of July, the normally sleepy town of Rennes had taken on an unaccustomed aspect. Swarms of reporters from all over the world, men and women onlookers, pretentious men and women, and above all, the most passionate protagonists of the two causes at issue, not to mention a veritable army of policemen, had descended on the capital of Brittany. There was a heavy atmosphere of storm and feverishness. Everywhere, secret discussions were being held, camps were being formed, battle plans being sketched out....

It was in this feverish, anguished atmosphere that the court martial's first session opened on 7 August... On the stage, in the front row, the court martial officials; in the second row their deputies and behind them a few privileged guests... At the sides, the journalists. At the back of the room, controlled by policemen, the general public...

Obstinately, passionately, their eyes were riveted on a little door on the right-hand side. That was where the man at the centre of the Agony was going to appear. None of us had ever seen him. But for more than a year and a half, we had lived with him, we had suffered with him. At the moment when we were going to see him, all his lamentable and prodigious agony was revived in our memories: the catastrophe befalling him in the midst of his happiness, the interrogation of Du Paty de Clam, the agony of the Cherche-Midi prison, the martyrdom of the degradation, the separation from his wife without being allowed to kiss her or shake her hand, and then the superhuman torture of five years on Devil's Island, the physical, degrading pain added to the moral suffering, Lebon's double shackles, the cowardly harassment of his subordinates, the heart-rending cry of innocence repeated tirelessly for five years. (*Applause*) Ah, we had despaired of ever catching sight of his face...

And after an agonising hour of waiting, he appeared to us. And it was Lazarus, indeed, Lazarus as Giotto depicts him in the sublime fresco of the Arena. Instead of the ghostly bandages, it was a uniform which floated around him, a uniform he did not seem to fill, which did not appear to be part of him, from which he was separated in fact by layers of cotton wool designed to mask his emaciation. He moved forward with a straight step, automatically, like a ghost. It seemed as if his limbs did not make up an organic whole and that each one was operating separately. His face was yellow and only streaked with red on his cheeks. He let himself sink slowly, heavily onto his chair. One had the feeling that this was no living being before us, but a man who had come back from the land from which one does not normally return. And this sensation intensified to the point of pain when he began to speak. No, it was not a human voice which emerged from that throat. It was a strangely husky, toneless voice, like that of a deaf mute, the voice of someone who had not spoken for five years and no longer knew how to speak...

Source: 'Discourse of Victor Basch on the Dreyfus Affair pronounced during the Congress of the Ligue des Droits de l'Homme in Rennes (29 Mai 1909)', quoted in F. Basch, *Victor Basch de l'Affaire Dreyfus au crime de la milice* (Paris: Plon, 1994), pp. 354–5.

Appendix 40: Anatole France: 'La séance d'aujourd'hui à Rennes', extracts from 'Le Bureau', article in *Le Figaro*, 16 August 1899

... And yet it is quite true that at the far end of a Ministry corridor, along thirty square metres of waxed parquet floor, military bureaucrats – some lazy and deceitful, others bustling and turbulent – have, with their treacherous and fraudulent piles of paperwork, failed justice and misled an entire great people. But if this affair, above all the affair of Mercier and the Bureaux, has revealed nasty habits, it has also inspired some fine qualities of character.

And in this very Bureau there was a man who in no way resembled those bureaucrats. He had a lucid mind with sharpness and depth, a fine character, a patient, largely humane soul of unfailing gentleness. He was rightly considered one of the most intelligent officers in the army. And although these exceptional qualities found in too rare a breed of men could have proved harmful to him, he was the first officer of his contemporaries to be promoted to lieutenant-colonel and all boded well for the most brilliant future in the army. His friends were aware of his slightly mocking leniency and his solid goodness. They knew he was gifted with a superior sense of beauty, capable of deep sensitivity to music and literature and of living in the higher world of ideas. Like all men whose inner life is profound and reflective, he developed his intellectual and moral faculties in solitude. This tendency to withdraw into himself, his natural simplicity, his spirit of renunciation and sacrifice and his fine candour – which sometimes remains like a gift of grace in the minds of those most aware of universal evil – all these qualities made of him one of those soldiers seen or imagined by Alfred de Vigny, those calm, everyday heroes whose inner nobility is transmitted to the most humble tasks they perform, for whom the fulfilment of regular duties is the familiar poetry of life.

Having been called to the Deuxième Bureau, this officer discovered one day that Dreyfus had been convicted for the crime committed by Esterhazy. He informed his superiors. They tried – first gently, then with threats – to stop him from pursuing research which in discovering the innocence of Dreyfus, would also reveal their errors and their crimes. He sensed that by persevering he was causing his own downfall. He persevered. With calm, slow and sure reflection, with tranquil courage, he pursued his work for justice. He was sent away. He was sent to Gabès and even as far as the Tripoli frontier on a poor pretext and solely in order to have him murdered by Arab bandits.

Having been unable to kill him, they tried to dishonour him, they attempted to ruin him with a profusion of slander. With treacherous promises, they thought they could stop him from testifying at Zola's trial. He testified. He testified with the tranquillity of a righteous man, with the peace of mind of a soul without fear or desires. There was neither weakness nor excess in his words. The tone of a man who is doing his duty that day as on other days, without for a moment considering that this time, it takes unusual courage to do it. Neither threats nor persecutions made him hesitate for a moment.

Several people commented that in order to accomplish his task, to establish the innocence of a Jew and the crime of a Christian, he had had to overcome clerical prejudices and conquer antisemitic passions rooted in his heart from his youngest years, growing up in that region of Alsace and France which then gave him to the army and homeland. Those who know him are aware that this is far from the truth; that he possesses no fanaticism of any sort, that he never has a single sectarian thought, that his superior intelligence raises him above hatred and partiality; and that finally he is a free spirit.

Source: Le Figaro, 16 August 1899.

Appendix 41 Extracts from the Rennes court martial, 7 August–9 September 1899

The Dreyfus trial
THE SCENE IN COURT

Only once after the entrance of Dreyfus was there an essentially dramatic incident, and that was in what I venture to call the really heart-rendering cry, *un cri de Coeur,* with which Dreyfus at the opening of the long list of formally prepared questions with which he was plied by the President exclaimed in a voice husky with pent-up emotion, now at last allowed to burst its barriers before the world, that he had no knowledge of the *bordereau*, that he was innocent. The tones in which he made this declaration, adding:- 'For five years I have suffered everything that a man can suffer, but for the honour of my name and that of my children I am innocent, my colonel,' were agonizing in their high-pitched sobbing pathos. He held the *bordereau* in his hand. The little messenger in uniform had carried it to him with visible emotion at being the bearer of so portentous a document; but Dreyfus took it from him without a tremor, and it was thus that, holding it in the right hand with less agitation than is manifested by a Deputy unrolling his notes at the tribune of the Chamber, he raised the other with half-clenched fist in the irrepressible gesture of protest of a man who swears by all the gods that what he says is true. This moment was, indeed, dramatic, and it was attended by a general thrill throughout the Court.

Source: The Times, Tuesday 8 August 1899.

The Rennes trial: important evidence

M. CASIMIR-PERIER AND GENERAL MERCIER

In conclusion, General Mercier said:-

'To my mind the treason clearly results – first, from the prisoner's contradictions and perpetual falsehoods; next, with moral certainty, from the technical examination of the *bordereau*. It results with material certainty from the cryptographic examination of the *bordereau*. It results from the confessions. Let me add one word. I have not reached my age without having had the sad experience that all that is human is liable to error. If, moreover, I am weak-minded, as M. Zola has said, I am at least an honest man and the son of an honest man. When, therefore, the revision campaign began I watched with poignant anxiety all the controversies and discussions. If the slightest doubt had crossed my mind I should be the first to declare it to you, and to say before you to Captain Dreyfus:- "I have been honestly mistaken."'

Captain Dreyfus. – 'It is what you ought to say.'

Witness. – 'I should come and say to Captain Dreyfus:- "I have been honestly mistaken. With the same good faith I come and acknowledge it, and I will do all that is humanly possible to retrieve a terrible mistake."'

Captain Dreyfus. – 'It is your duty.'

Witness. – 'Well, it is not so. My conviction since 1894 has not undergone the slightest change. It has been strengthened by the most thorough study of the *dossier*. It has been strengthened also by the inanity of the results obtained for proving the innocence of the condemned man, in spite of the immensity of the accumulated efforts, in spite of the enormous millions senselessly expended.'

Source: The Times, Tuesday 14 August 1899.

Extract from the Official Report on Dreyfus' detention on Devil's Island, signed by Jean Decrais, private secretary to the Colonial Secretary,

READ IN SESSION OF 16 AUGUST 1899

…I come now to the attitude of Dreyfus during his four years in detention. It can be clearly characterised: he did not cease to affirm his innocence, to call for "full light to be shed on the appalling miscarriage of justice of which he was victim". His tenderness towards his loved ones did not fail for an instant; he retained a submissive attitude, without the slightest inclination towards revolt or any attempt at escape.

On 7 March 1895, before his transfer from his cell on the Ile Royale to the hut on the Ile du Diable, he was informed that any attempt to effect an escape from the implementation of his penalty would be repressed with the utmost severity. He replied 'that he submitted unreservedly'....

On 2 July 1895, questioned about the state of his health, Dreyfus replies:

'I am well at the moment... It's my heart that is sick... Nothing...' His words become unintelligible and are interrupted with sobs. He weeps profusely for about a quarter of an hour. (*July monthly report)...*

On 7 September: he receives ten letters and weeps profusely as he reads them.

On 2nd, about six o'clock, the convicted prisoner had a spasm; he began to sob, saying that this could not go on any longer, that his heart would eventually burst. (*Report of September 1895)*

On 2 October, he receives 14 letters, begins to read them immediately and, after a few moments' reflection, says: 'I would have shot myself in the head long ago if I didn't have my wife and children'. (*Report of October 1895)...*

On 31 December, he asks to send a telegram to his wife, saying: 'Received letters, health good, love'. But the senior administrative director considers that 'that there is no reason at all to act upon the prisoner's request.' (*Report of December 1895)...*

In August 1896, at the beginning of the month, he receives his correspondence. 'He wept profusely as he read it.' (*Report of August 1896)*

His general attitude remains the same: submissive and deferential. (*September 1896)....*

He never voiced any complaints or requests. (*April 1996)...*

In fact, Mr Deniel sometimes completed, and always paraphrased the reports of the head guards and tried to interpret the actions of the deported convict with a view to deducing his motives, not only for himself, but – more seriously – in the reports he addressed to his superiors.

An enforcer of the law, he set himself up – without anyone having asked or encouraged him – as a criminologist.

Is Dreyfus weeping? It is because he is putting on an act.

Does he write to his wife and children? It is out of self-interest and vile calculation, to ask them to help him escape.

Does he speak of killing himself to be released from the appalling martyrdom to which he is subjected? M Deniel only considers that a pretence to conceal his true plans.

If Dreyfus retains a gentle and submissive attitude, it is as a result of the moral cowardice of a guilty party who knows his crime is proven...

One can see that the interpretation of Dreyfus' actions and movements is never in his favour.

Whatever he does, 'his actions are considered as signs of his guilt, emanating from a fundamentally base and hateful nature'; that is what emerges from the long commentaries of M. Deniel, insofar as it is possible to understand the thought behind them...

M. Deniel overestimated the importance of his own duties.

He believed he was invested with a higher mission, and in order to fulfil it, in every monthly report he repeated his assurance that he was ready 'to sacrifice his life and health'.

By nature as unstable as he was conceited, he did not hesitate to attach considerable significance to the slightest incident.

The merest glimpse of a sail on the horizon, the lightest wisp of smoke breaking the monotony of the sky in the distance were taken as definite signs of a potential attack, provoking rigorous measures and new precautions...

* * *

The monthly reports of the head guards give us the following indications:

On 15 May 1895, a few days after his arrival on the Ile du Diable, Dreyfus says that he is ill. On 29th, 'during the day, he says he has had two violent attacks, like at the beginning of the month.'

In October 1895, 'questioned about his state of health, he replies that in spite of the heart problem from which he suffers, he is keeping reasonably well'.

In December 1895, 'he complains of headaches, of fever.'

On 12 February 1896, he complains of fainting fits, breathlessness. He talks of heart palpitations, blood rushing to the brain and adds: 'You can't do anything about it: it is the result of my mental condition.'

He asked for a doctor to be brought to see him; but as he did not seem ill, the request was refused.

In April 1896 'Dreyfus suffers several nervous attacks.'

In June 1896 'he had violent bouts of fever, accompanied by cerebral congestion. One night, about half past eleven, when he tried to stand up, he fell over hitting his face on a little bucket placed at the back of the hut. His face and forehead were grazed in this fall. The guard on duty had to lift him up... On his request, the prisoner, who can no longer eat preserved food, received some eggs. He refuses to take a tonic medicine prescribed for him by the doctor, on the pretext that he feels too weak to be able to take it. Dreyfus is deeply affected; and he is declining every day.'

In July 1896, 'Dreyfus, very tired after a bout of fever, declares that he cannot prepare his food and asks to receive them every day from the hospital, on a refundable basis.'

In October 1896, the 'prisoner had several attacks of nerves'.

Several months pass; 'the health of the deportee is very much undermined; he complains of heart palpitations, pains in his head, nervous tension.' (*Report of 26 May 1897*)...

On 1 October, at eight o'clock in the morning, the prisoner Dreyfus collapsed in his hut in a fainting fit which lasted about three minutes. After examining him, the doctor stated that the prisoner Dreyfus had probably suffered from a cerebro-cardiac neuropathy, of mental origin, caused by the refusal to make medicines available to him. On 29th in the morning, contrary to his usual attitude, the prisoner Dreyfus had made a strong protest on this subject. Attack of short duration...

In March 1898: 'Dreyfus is still in a great state of agitation and with his mental state affecting the physical, his health is less satisfactory.' (*Report of 23 March 1898*)

The heart disorders (palpitations, breathlessness etc) are still the same and, according to the prisoner, have even increased. (*Report of 15 April 1898*)

On 11 November 1898, 'he had a very clear bout of swamp-fever.'

On the night of 23 January, among others, he is haunted by nightmares, he shouts out, 'he sits up straight, gasping for breath, then lies down again on his bed, without saying a word, but not without first looking around the room with anxiety.' (*Rapport Officiel, January 1899*)

Source: Rennes, I, 248–58.

The court-martial: General Mercier questioned.

M. Labori requested the President to ask General Mercier to go to the bar as he had questions to put to him respecting the communication of the secret *dossier*, and the General accordingly did so.

M. Labori. – 'Do you acknowledge having given orders to communicate the secret *dossier* to the members of the Court-martial?'

Mercier. – 'Yes; I gave the moral order to make that communication.'

Major Carrière. – 'This looks like discussion, and if we enter on that path, we shall never get out of it.'

M. Labori. – 'But I am confining myself to putting questions and hearing the answers.'

Major Carrière. – 'My remark will surprise nobody.'

M. Labori. – 'What is your meaning?'

Major Carrière. – 'You are entitled to put questions but not to make reflections.'

M. Labori. – 'I do not accept that remark; and I have not to be taught my duty by Major Carrière.'

The President. – 'I recommend M. Labori to confine himself to questions, and not to discuss.'

M. Labori. – 'Quite so. If I begin discussing you will be good enough to stop me, and I shall bow respectfully. I ask General Mercier whether at the beginning of the affair, at the time of his conversation with M. Hanotaux, there were any charges against the accused besides that of having written the *bordereau*?'

'There were others, those of the secret *dossier*.'

M. Labori. – 'Why did you not tell M. Hanotaux that there were others?'

Mercier. – 'It is a political question; I shall not answer.'

M. Labori. – 'I have already stated that I had many questions to put to General Mercier and that he would refuse to answer some of these. I do not insist. The Court will judge. I now ask him why, if there were other charges against Dreyfus, he proceeded to the dictation test, and whether he acknowledges having said that if that test succeeded he would immediately have Dreyfus arrested.'

Mercier. – 'It was an additional charge.'

M. Labori. – 'Then the charges were insufficient?'

Mercier. – 'I repeat that it was an additional charge, that is all.'

M. Labori. – 'Did you say that he would not be arrested if the dictation ordeal did not succeed?'

Mercier. – 'It is possible.'

M. Labori. – 'Then you were not yet convinced of his guilt?'

Mercier. – 'No, there were only presumptions.'

M. Labori. – 'Why did you, according to your own expression, precipitate Dreyfus's arrest?'

Mercier. – 'As there was treason it was important to arrest the delinquent.'

M. Labori. – 'Why not keep a strict watch?'

Mercier. – 'That was impossible in the circumstances.'

M. Labori.– 'Were you aware of the tone of the Press towards you before the Dreyfus affair?'

Mercier. – 'There is at the War Office a Press bureau where newspaper cuttings are sent to the Minister, who reads them when he has time.'

M. Labori. – 'Do you know of violent articles about you in the *Libre Parole?*'

Mercier. – 'I am used to Press attacks, and paid no attention to those of the *Libre Parole.*'

M. Labori. – 'Do you remember an article of October 6, 1894, which styled you a *vrai coquin?*'

Mercier. – 'I do not recollect, and I care nothing about it.'

M. Labori. – 'The day after Dreyfus's arrest was the *Libre Parole* full of deference to you?'

Mercier. – 'I paid no attention to it.'

M. Labori. – 'Are you aware of the indiscretion committed at the General Staff by which Dreyfus's arrest was revealed to the Press?'

Mercier. – 'I know of an indiscretion committed by the Press, but not by the General Staff.'

M. Labori. – 'Who committed it?'

Mercier. – 'It might have emanated from the Dreyfus family, or from the experts.'

M. Labori then read a letter addressed, on October 28, 1894, when Dreyfus's arrest was not yet known, to M. Papillaud, of the *Libre Parole.* It said:-

Mercier. – 'My dear friend, - I told you so yesterday. It is Captain Dreyfus, living at 6, Avenue du Trocadéro, who has been arrested October 15 for espionage, and who is in prison at Cherche-Midi. He is said to be on a journey, but it is a falsehood, because there is a desire to hush up the affair. All Israel is astir. Yours, Henry. Complete my little investigation as soon as possible.'

Mercier. – 'How is it signed?' asked the President.

M. Labori. – 'It is signed "Colonel Henry." Does General Mercier believe that this letter emanated from the Dreyfus family?'

Mercier. – 'I do not know whether it emanated from the Dreyfus family, but I have heard say that it was not Colonel Henry.'

M. Labori. – 'Then I ask the President kindly to have a judicial commission sent to Paris, so that M. Papillaud may produce this letter, and that an expert's report, a report on the handwriting, be made.'

Mercier. – 'Is that necessary?' asked the President. 'Will it not prolong the trial?'

M. Labori. – 'I wish to enlighten the Court-martial on the part played by Colonel Henry and Colonel Du Paty de Clam in this affair, and I ask General Mercier what he thinks of this indiscretion.'

Mercier. – 'I gave no order to have this letter written, and I do not believe that there could have been found among the officers who were with me, one capable of writing it.'

M. Labori. – 'Will you say what you think of Esterhazy?'

Mercier. – 'I think nothing and I know nothing of him and his trial.'

(Exclamations of surprise.)

M. Labori. – 'What? You know nothing of the trial of 1898?'

Mercier. – 'I am not bound to explain or give an account of my ideas to anybody.'

M. Labori. – 'I do not ask what you think of it, but whether you are cognisant of it.'

Mercier. – 'I am responsible to nobody for my thoughts.'

M. Labori. – 'But you are cognisant of it.'

Mercier. – 'The Esterhazy trial? Not at all.'

M. Labori. – 'You did not watch its vicissitudes?'

The President. – 'General Mercier was not then Minister.'

M. Labori. – 'I am not asking him as a Minister, but as a witness.'

Mercier. – 'As a witness I abide by the decision of the Court-martial, which acquitted Esterhazy.'

The President. – 'General Mercier is not bound to have an opinion on it.'

M. Labori. – 'What is your authority for saying that the treason syndicate has expended 35 millions for saving Dreyfus?'

Mercier. – 'I have already given it.'

M. Labori. – 'It does not emanate from M. de Freycinet or General Jamont?'

Mercier. – 'I have said that it was a verbal testimony.'

M. Labori. – 'And what is it?'

The President. – 'You are recommending the deposition.'

M. Labori. – 'No; and the proof is that General Mercier refuses to reply.'

Mercier. – 'I do not refuse to answer for my acts, but only for my thoughts.'

M. Labori. – 'Are you cognisant of Esterhazy's *role* and the manoeuvre employed for screening him?'

Mercier. – 'No. Question those who are acquainted with them.'

M. Labori. – 'The Court will judge. It is a way of cutting short my *interrogatoire*.'

Mercier. – 'I protest against the word *interrogatoire*. I am not an accused man.'

(Murmurs.)

M. Labori. – 'I am not treating him as an accused man. I mean questioning, and I think that in good French you have a right to say *interrogatoire*.'

The President. – 'Yes, but it is open to a certain interpretation'.

M. Labori. – 'What has been done with the 35 millions spoken of?'

Mercier. – 'I might perhaps ask you that.'

M. Labori. – 'What do you mean by that?'

The President. – 'Be good enough to have no altercation with the counsel.'

Mercier. – 'I beg pardon.'

The President. – 'The question is too important to be omitted. Kindly say how the 35 millions have been expended.'

Mercier. – 'I cannot give the details, but what is certain is that for a year there has been an enormous outlay in all directions.'

The President. – 'Has it been employed in printing or in bribery?'

Mercier. – 'I will not say anything.'

Source: The Times, Friday 25 August 1899.

Appendix 42: Verdict of the Rennes court martial, 9 September 1899

Upon resumption, the President reads out the following verdict:

In the name of the people of France

On this day, 9 September 1899, the Court Martial of the 10th region of the army corps, deliberating in camera.

The president asked the following question;

Is Alfred Dreyfus, certificated captain of the 14th artillery regiment, probationer with the General Staff of the Army, guilty of having, in 1894, contrived plots or maintained dealings with a foreign power or one of its agents, in order to urge it to commit hostilities or undertake war against France, or to procure the means for this, by passing on to it the notes and documents mentioned in the above-mentioned bordereau?

Votes were taken separately, beginning with the lower rank and the least senior in each grade, the president having given his opinion last,

The Court decides on the question by a majority of five votes to two: 'Yes, the accused is guilty'. By majority vote, they agree there are extenuating circumstances;

After which, on the closing submission of the Government Commissioner, the President asked the question and again took votes in the manner indicated above.

In consequence, the Court convicts Dreyfus (Alfred), by a majority of five votes to two, to the penalty of ten years' detention by application of article 76 of the Penal Code, article 7 of the law of 8 October 1830, article 5 of the Constitution of 4 November 1848, article 1 of the law of 8 June 1850, articles 463 and 20 of the Penal Code, and articles 189, 267 and 132 of the Military Code of Justice, whose terms are as follows;

Article 76 of the Penal Code. – Whosoever contrives plots or maintains relations with foreign powers or their agents, in order to urge them to commit hostilities or undertake war against France, or to procure them the means to do so, will be punished by death. This provision will remain in effect even in cases where the aforesaid plots or relations have not resulted in hostilities;

Article 1 of the law of 8 June 1850 – In all the cases where the death penalty has been abolished by article 5 of the Constitution, this penalty is replaced by that of deportation to a fortified enclosure designated by law, outside the continental territory of the Republic. — Deportees will be given there all freedom compatible with the need to ensure their supervision. — They will be subjected to a regime of police and supervision determined by a ruling of public administration

Article 463 of the Penal Code. – In the event of extenuating circumstances… if the penalty is that of deportation to a fortified enclosure, the court will apply that of simple deportation or detention.

Article 20 of the Penal Code. – Whosoever is sentenced to detention will be confined in one of the fortresses located on the continental territory of the kingdom which are determined by royal order, delivered in the due form of public administration rulings.

Detention cannot be pronounced for less than five or more than twenty years;

Article 189 of the Military Code of Justice. – The penalties of forced labour, deportation, detention, solitary confinement and exile are applied according to the provisions of the ordinary Penal Code. They have the effects determined by the Code and comprise, in addition, military degradation;

Article 267 of the Military Code of Justice – The military tribunals apply the penalties incurred by ordinary criminal laws for all crimes or offences not covered by this Code, and, in that case, if there are extenuating circumstances, article 463 of the Penal Code is applied to soldiers.

Article 139 of the Military Code of Justice – The verdict which pronounces a penalty against the accused condemns him to the payment of costs to the State. In addition, it orders in cases provided for by the law, the confiscation and restitution of goods seized, either for the benefit of the State or for that of the owners, of all objects or products seized at the trial as exhibits;

It fixes at a minimum the duration of detention in accordance with article 9 of 22 July 1867, modified by that of 19 December 1871;

It calls upon the government commissioner to have the present verdict read immediately in the presence of the convicted man, before the assembled armed guard, and to point out that the law grants him a delay of twenty-four hours to make an appeal.

The President, – The Court remains in session until the room is completely empty; I ask the public to leave in orderly fashion and in silence, in order not to give rise to any repressive measures.

The Court rose at five o'clock.

Source: Rennes, III, 747–8.

Appendix 43: Reactions to the Rennes verdict, September 1899

Notice published in Hatzvi

DREYFUS WILL BE FREE

Translated by our special correspondent A. Ludvipol*

By virtue of the Law reducing the years of punishment of an individual whose verdict resulted in a reduced sentence and who had previously been detained in circumstances more severe than those which his judgement required, *freedom will be given to Dreyfus.*

In these circumstances, his liberty is approaching.

A. Ben Yehouda.

* Avraham Ludvipol was not the special correspondent of *Hatzvi* (weekly representing the nationalist and progressive branches of the Zionists in

Palestine), but of *Hamelitz* (representing the 'Hovevei Zion' ('Lovers of Zion' Zionist movement) a paper edited by Leon Rabinovitz. Ludvipol nevertheless came to be regarded in the emerging Hebrew press as a 'specialist' of the Dreyfus Affair. G. Koutz, 'La Presse hébraique au début de l'affaire Dreyfuss', *Reeh* 1 (Paris, 1996), pp. 51–4.

Source: Notice published in the Zionist weekly *Hatzvi*, ed. Eliezer Ben Yehouda, Palestine, 12 September 1899.

Theodor Herzl, 'Five Against Two'

September 9 1899 was that memorable Saturday when the whole world heard the astounding news. It has been established that justice could be refused to a Jew for the sole reason that he was a Jew; that he could be tortured as if he did not belong to the human race; that despite his innocence he could be sentenced to a dishonouring penalty...

Five against two! What a memorable lesson of contemporary civilization can be learnt from this number! It was a painful discovery to note that such an adventure could happen in our century...

And so there is no valid grounds for further concern. One had to read the newspapers published abroad. In publishing long, daily reports on the Rennes trial, they proclaimed the innocence of the accused everywhere...

Thus, so-called French patriots are not bound by the humanitarian duties observed by the hereditary enemy when they are judging a Jew...

Such were the criticisms that one could read in all the newspapers insofar as they were not infested with the antisemitic virus. The conclusions commenting on the verdict were clearly identical: Berlin and Rome, London and New York uttered a unanimous cry of horror. In these papers we read first of their astonishment at the discriminatory treatment of a Jew, then of their certainty of an acquittal; and finally that the whole of Europe, Asia and even Polynesia were outraged by this Affair...

... the importance of the Dreyfus Affair, which has become an abstract symbol representing the Jew in the modern world, who had tried to assimilate into his environment, who speaks its language, approve its ideas, conforms to its spirit and finds himself suddenly exposed by violence. Dreyfus 'signifies a strategic position which has been fought over, is still fought over, but is already lost... let us admit it frankly.'

Source: Die Welt (Basel) 37, 15 September 1899.

Sermon preached by the Chief Rabbi at the Great Synagogue in London on the Day of Atonement (Yom Kippur) 5660 (September 1899)

My dear Brethren,
    ...

Righteousness exalteth a nation, but wickedness leads to its ruin. What is morally wrong cannot be politically right. There is one immutable Divine law which underlies all history, that a nation can only endure so long as it preserves truth and venerates justice, that falsehood and injustice may prosper for a time, but that their doom is certain. There is a retribution which sooner or later overtakes every nation that forgets and rejects the eternal distinctions of right and wrong. Neither from the east, nor from the west, nor from the south does greatness come. But God is the Judge, and abaseth the one and exalteth the other. ...

One of our ministers is reported as having said, that Saturday last was the bitterest day in modern Judaism. From this view I entirely dissent. It was certainly gloomed by keenest disappointment. Our hearts went out in deepest pity for the prolonged agony with which our brother in faith was being tortured, the renewed anguish which his devoted wife and kinsfolk were made to suffer. But unto us Jews it was not a day of unalloyed bitterness. It was the bitterest day in modern France, more disastrous than Waterloo, more humiliating than Sedan. For France, once so chivalrous, sometime fired with more generous impulses; France, the first country to abolish disabilities of race and faith, and to give to the Jews the rights and privileges of free citizenship; France had broken the Divine law of righteousness. Her judges in one and the same breath branded an innocent man as an odious traitor to his country and at the same time pronounced the pestilential doctrine that for treason there could be extenuating circumstances. Verily, judgment is turned away backward, and justice standeth afar off, for truth is fallen in the street, so that equity cannot enter. To us Jews it was not a day of bitterness. There is, I hope and believe, not one member of the House of Israel worthy of the name who would not rather share the fate of the heroic Dreyfus than allow his conscience to be burdened with such guilt as defiles the soul of his judges. Centuries of persecution have taught us that it is better to suffer injustice than to commit injustice; that the martyr is precious in the sight of the Lord, but that the inquisitor is hateful in His eye. And whilst this stirring world-drama is fraught with many a circumstance that causes the Angels of Justice and Mercy to weep bitterly, it presents also incidents to cheer and to console. Its central figure, with his dauntless courage and dignified patience, serves as a truer representation of the modern Jew than the caricature presented by prejudiced writers. We have seen the German Emperor proving himself worthy of his noble and never-to-be-forgotten father, and his august kinswoman, our dearly beloved and venerated Queen, in that he has braved obloquy and scorned insult in the cause of justice and of truth. And is not the great heart of civilised mankind throbbing with noble indignation at the crime perpetrated in Rennes, huge and dark as the mountain? And does not the newspaper Press outside France voice this horror with an emphasis and unanimity almost without precedent? Aye, and in France there are still good men and true who have not yet been hypnotised by the sickly and unholy blend of militarism and clericalism, who will not rest until they have vindicated the majesty of the law, not by obtaining a pardon – such an offer would be rejected with scorn – but a reversal of that most iniquitous verdict. And we feel assured that the God of Justice will bless these efforts. It is not for the first time in history that we have seen:

Truth on the scaffold wrong upon the throne.
But the scaffold sways the future,
And behind the dim unknown,
Standeth God within the shadow,
Keeping watch above His own.

The God of Judgment will not leave the righteous in the hand of the wicked, nor condemn him when he is judged. And it is ardently to be hoped that the mock trial at Rennes, and the terrible miscarriage of Justice will convince the world of the folly and the savagery of anti-Jewish hatred, that a vile unreasonable sentiment as this cannot but lead to cruelty and wrong, that anti-Semitism is but another name for the defiance of law and order, and that the violation of truth and honour. It is, therefore, my most fervent desire, as it must be of all ministers of religion, and true friends of humanity, that the righteous anger which animates mankind may not engender evils similar to those which we now so deeply deplore and anxiously deprecate. Condemn falsehood, fraud, and forgery with the strongest emphasis. But do not visit the sins of the guilty upon the innocent: do not let us stain the fair name of England by breaches of hospitality and lack of international courtesy. Above all, let us take to heart the cardinal lesson of the Dreyfus Case, the lesson of the guilt and the peril of unreasoning prejudice, of racial hatred, and of religious ill-will...

Source: Jewish Chronicle, 22 September 1899.

Appendix 44: Dreyfus' appeal to the Minister of Justice, 26 November 1903

Paris, 25 November 1903

To the Minister of Justice

Minister,

I have the honour to beg of your Justice a review of the judgement of the Rennes court martial, which, on 9 September 1899, by a majority of 5 votes to 2, declared me guilty, 'with extenuating circumstances', of having contrived plots or maintained secret dealings with a foreign power.

This verdict, which is inexplicable after the judgement of 3 June 1899 by the Combined Chambers of the Court of Appeal, was pronounced on the basis of false documents and perjuries, and new facts demonstrate that, although clearly innocent, I have been convicted for a second time.

During the hearings which took place in the Chamber of Deputies on 6 and 7 April 1903, Deputy Jaurès established that an audacious forgery had weighed on the conscience of certain judges. This forgery is a document attributed to the German Kaiser, which was allegedly used without the knowledge of the defence, who were unaware of its existence.

On 21 April 1903, I had the honour of sending to the War Minister, the administrative head of the services responsible for military jurisdiction, a request for an inquiry into the serious errors committed to my detriment by the services under his control.

The results of this inquiry – which could not be refused me – have not yet been conveyed to me, but I have reason to believe that they fully justify the review I am seeking.

The War Minister, to whom my request for review will certainly be communicated, will not fail moreover to inform you of the results of the enquiry which he undertook following my request of 21 April 1903.

In addition to the decisive results of this enquiry, a review is also justified by the following considerations.

I. – Perjuries and false documents

Perjury by Czernuski: Mr *Czernuski*, a new witness called to Rennes by the prosecution, had stated that he had been told by Dr. Mosetig, an Austrian Aulic Councillor, that I was a spy in the pay of Germany. This deposition was false. Its falseness is evident from an authentic statement by Dr. Mosetig, which I attached to my request for an enquiry of 21 April 1903.

In that request, I indicated to the War Minister the serious revelations of a certain Mr Wessel concerning the machinations of Intelligence service agents with the perjured witness. These revelations are confirmed by a memorandum Wessel wrote to his lawyer, Raimondo, conveyed to Maître Mornard, which I attach to this request.

They are also confirmed by a letter from Mme Wessel to Mr. Gabriel Monod, sent by the latter to the War Minister.

Perjuries of Savignaud and Gribelin: Savignaud was a witness recruited by the prosecution to destroy the authority of Lieutenant Colonel Picquart, who had discovered the error made by the judges in 1894 and the manoeuvrings directed against me.

The archivist Gribelin had been called to make depositions in a similar vein.

The perjury of Savignaud is established by letters of M. Scheurer-Kestner to Maître Leblois. Gribelin himself has admitted his own perjury.

False documents: The secret dossier used against me contained documents that had been altered. Moreover, those who used the documents must have known that they were false.

The document attributed to the German Kaiser, the existence of which was formally recognized by a letter of M. Ferlet de Bourbonne, is a forgery. The letters sent by Dr. Dumas to Maître Mornard, which my lawyer conveyed to the War Ministry show the use which was made of this document at the Rennes trial.

II. – New facts

Colonel von Schwartzkoppen and Colonel Panizzardi, who according to the prosecution, were the agents of the foreign power to whom I allegedly delivered secret documents, have both given assurances that they had no dealings with me.

A letter from Colonel Chauvet of the Swiss army to Professor Andrade, sent by M. Andrade to Monis, Minister of Justice, after the Rennes trial, records the solemn affirmations of Colonel von Schwartzkoppen.

Colonel von Schwartzkoppen's word of honour that he never had any dealings with me, either direct or indirect, was also known to the prosecution, who concealed it from the judges. The War Minister has proof of this in his records.

A letter from Count von Münster to Mr. Joseph Reinach contains the same statements and, for the first time, reveals that Colonel von Schwartzkoppen confessed to his Ambassador that his spy and informant was Esterhazy, and that their dealings went back to 1893. I am attaching this letter to my request, which the recipient was good enough to let me have; it was published in *Le Temps* on 25 April 1903.

As for Colonel Panizzardi, the telegram so often referred to in the hearings would have had a decisive effect on the minds of the Rennes judges, had the prosecution not tried by illicit means to falsify it during decoding. And yet the War Ministry at the time possessed documents concealed by my accusers which established that Colonel Panizzardi's agent and informant continued his relations with him after my arrest.

My conviction, so painfully extracted from judges whose doubts were expressed in the form of 'extenuating circumstances,' is therefore the product of forgeries and falsehoods.

I request a review of my trial because I must have back my full honour, for the sake of my children and myself, and because I have never failed in any of my duties as a soldier and a Frenchman.

Please accept, Minister, this assurance of my deep respect.

Signed: Alfred Dreyfus

Source: 3ème Cass, I, 26–9.

Appendix 45: Rehabilitation of Dreyfus:
Journal Officiel and Dreyfus' diary description of the ceremony of 12 July 1906

Decoration of Major Targe and Major Dreyfus

On 14 July 1906, the *Journal Officiel* published the following decision:

"By ministerial decision dated 13 July 1906 and in pursuance of the specifications of article 16 (paragraph 4) of the decree of 28 December 1900, the following are officially inscribed on the appointments board:

Officer of the Legion of Honour: M. Targe, major with the 13th artillery.

Knight (Chevalier) of the Legion of Honour: M. Dreyfus, certificated artillery major, on special duties."

The *Journal Officiel* of 21 July 1906 published the following decrees:

LEGION OF HONOUR: By decree of the President of the Republic, dated 20 July 1906, issued on the recommendation of the Minister of War, in view of the declaration of the Council of the Order of the Legion of Honour of the same date, whereas the promotion of the present decree is carried out in conformity with the laws, decrees and rulings currently in force, the following has been promoted to the rank of Officer of the Legion of Honour:

ARTILLERY

13th regiment: M. Targe, major commanding the artillery of the 1st cavalry division; 23 years' service, 1 campaign. Knight, 13 July 1895.

By decree of the President of the Republic, dated 20 July 1906, issued on the recommendation of the Minister of War, in view of the declaration of the Council of the Order of the Legion of Honour of the same date, whereas the promotion of the present decree is carried out in conformity with the laws, decrees and rulings currently in force, the following has been promoted to the rank of Knight of the Legion of Honour:

ARTILLERY

Special General Staff. M. Dreyfus: certificated major, at the artillery command at Vincennes; 30 years' service.

Dreyfus' diary description of the ceremony of 12 July 1906

On the morning of 20 July, *Le Journal Officiel* published news of my appointment as a chevalier of the Legion of Honour... The Council's decision was unanimous.

On that same day, in the afternoon, the ceremony for the award of my decoration took place in the artillery courtyard at the Ecole Militaire.

The appearance of the grey, dilapidated walls of the square of the Cour Desjardins had remained the same since the days when I was a lieutenant with the horse batteries at the Ecole Militaire.

For this act of reparation, they did not choose the square beside this one: the Ecole Militaire's great courtyard where twelve years earlier the atrocious first parade had taken place. This was at my request, for I feared that the emotion of my memories would impose a burden upon me which was beyond my strength and overcame my courage.

At half past one, the troops ordered to render the honours, the two horse batteries and two squadrons of the First Cuirassiers [Armoured Division] formed up parallel to the three sides of the courtyard. They were placed under the orders of Lieutenant-Colonel Gaillard-Bournazel of the First Cuirassiers.

At five minutes to two, the fanfare of trumpets sounded. General Gillain, commander of the first cavalry division, a white moustache, marched into the courtyard on foot. He strode before the troops. Silence lay heavy, impressive, and in the silence my thoughts wandered headlong, recalling the dormant memories of twelve years before: the screams of the crowd, the atrocious ceremony, my stripes unjustly torn from me, my sword broken and lying in pieces at my feet... My heart was beating as if it would burst, blood rushed to my head, sweat covered my brow... I had to make a huge effort of willpower to manage to recover my self-control and not proclaim my past agonies.

The order to 'Sound the drum' forced me from my painful daydream and brought me back to the reality of the act of reparation. With a fine gesture, General Gillain drew his sword and first handed the cross of an officer of the Legion of Honour to Major Targe. Then the drum roll stopped, then started again straightaway for me. This time General Gillain pronounced the ceremonial words with emotion and pinning on the insignia of the honour, said to me softly, 'Major Dreyfus, I am happy to have been entrusted with decorating you; I know what excellent memories remain of you in the 1st Cavalry Division.' Then he embraced me wholeheartedly and his eyes filled with tears. The troops then went to mass at the rear. The order 'Parade, forward, march' echoed in the yard. And with the Lieutenant-Colonel at their head, preceded by the brass band, the troops marched before General Gillain, before Major Targe and before me, the officers saluting with their swords as they passed by. The brass sang high and clear on that joyful day.

The troops disappeared. People surrounded me immediately, shouting 'Long Live Dreyfus'. 'No', I cried, 'Long live the Republic, Long live the truth.' Hands were eagerly stretched out towards me. I shook them in a nervous clasp, I embraced friends... And it was all so moving that words are inadequate to describe the feeling...

Anatole France approached me in turn and said, 'I am very happy and very moved. I do not know how to pay tribute to the steadfastness you have shown through so much suffering, allowing us to accomplish the work of justice and reparation which is crowned by today's solemn ceremony. And so I shake your hand without saying another word.'

Then my son threw himself into my arms. Then it was the turn of my wife and my loved ones. Delightful embraces from all those I loved, for whom I had had the courage to go on living.

I went to find General Picquart who had been present at the ceremony and shook me warmly by the hand. I expressed all my gratitude to him, as well as to M. Baudouin who was present. But all these emotions were too strong. I suffered a temporary problem with my heart... When I was feeling better, I left by car with Georges Bourdon from *Le Figaro* and my son...

It was a fine day of reparation for France and the Republic.

My affair was over. Lieutenant-Colonel Picquart had been reinstated in the army with the rank of brigadier as compensation for the persecutions he had suffered as a result of defending me from the moment he became convinced of my innocence. If all those who had fought for justice and were still alive were not able likewise to receive their reward for the sufferings they endured for truth, it is certain that they would find it in the quiet satisfaction of their consciences, and in the esteem their sacrifices had earned them from their contemporaries. And even if they appeared to be forgotten, they were not poorly rewarded for they did not fight only for a particular cause but contributed largely to one of the most extraordinary struggles for rehabilitation that the world has witnessed, one of those struggles which resound into the far distant future because they have marked a turning point in the history of humanity, an imposing step towards an era of immense progress for the ideas of freedom, justice and social solidarity.

At the beginning, in fact, for most of those who took part in it, the Affair was only a question of justice and humanity. But as the struggle proceeded against all the combined forces of oppression, it assumed an unsuspected scope which continued to increase until full light was shed on it, bringing with it a significant change in ideas. Discoveries were made in succession, bringing new substance each day, forcing minds to reflect and gradually to change their ideas on a whole host of questions which otherwise would not have concerned them. Education took place progressively, traditions died away. All the important reforms which were implemented successively in the governments of Waldeck-Rousseau and Combes would never have been accepted without the Affair, which slowly but surely prepared the minds of the public for them.

Source: A. Dreyfus, *Carnets (1899–1907)*, *Après le procès de Rennes*, pp. 263-65.

Appendix 46: Letter from Esterhazy in London to *La Libre Parole*, 3 July 1906

Letter of Mr. Esterhazy

London, 29 June 1906

Sir,

Alone, abandoned by all, in the most atrocious situation, I had promised myself that I would not say a word during all the proceedings of the Dreyfus Review. But my attention has been brought to the abominable outrages, the nameless insults with which in their true panic even those who should have defended me condemn me or have me condemned, and I cannot remain silent. I ask you for access to the pages of *La Libre Parole*, to try and make my protest heard, in despair in the face of such cowardice and stupidity. From the very start in 1897, I wanted to tell the truth, believing that it was the best thing to do. I was ordered to remain silent, to obey, with a formal assurance that 'my superiors would protect me'. I obeyed, as I had throughout my life and I think that at that point any man in my place would have done the same. But I considered the course of action taken to be absurd and shared my feelings on this matter with those I trusted or believed I could trust and told them the truth;

However, as long as my superiors did not abandon me and kept their commitments towards me, which they repeated to my friends and at my trial, all went well. With M. Cavaignac, everything changed; he immediately lost his head, and badly advised, believed he played a master stroke by throwing Henry and myself overboard. Everyone knows what followed;

A campaign of vile abuse even more abominable than that peddled by the defenders of Dreyfus – who at least were fighting for their man and their cause – began against me; and from one day to the next, those who carried or had me carried in triumph, threw themselves upon me like howling dogs. Never has one seen a faster or more cynical about-turn. 'They abandoned him, they are lost', said *L'Aurore*, and one had to be foolish not to see that each blow they aimed at me, struck them as well;

I endured all these appalling cowardly acts without saying anything. During the enquiry of the Supreme Court of Appeal, in 1899, my lawyer M. Cabanes – whose letters testify to this – received on my behalf all manner of assurances from high-ranking figures, saying that they regretted what Cavaignac had done, and, through him, I was pressed with fine promises to remain silent. Trusting my lawyer, I foolishly believed them; thus it was with great indignation that I read the depositions before the Court which they had thought should remain secret.

Outraged, I broke my silence.

Since then, in Rennes, I overwhelmed the President of the Court Martial, the Government Commissioner and the Generals with letters reminding them of the truth, entreating them to speak it, since they knew it as well as I did. There was nothing doing. They wanted to destroy themselves. Later, at my urgent request – because in the face of so many lies, I wanted a trace of the truth to remain – I appeared before the General Consul of France. I told him everything – not in the presence of a solicitor, as someone said who does not even know what a solicitor and an affidavit are – but before the General Consul, whose chancellor recorded my deposition without deletions or corrections, and copied the documents I presented. Those who had received my confidences in 1897 could see that this deposition was the faithful reproduction of what I had always said. It is the truth – the truth which explains everything, whereas the other versions leave a thousand points obscure.

M. Cavaignac had invented a system that did little honour to his intelligence, not to mention his courage and heart. To Me Cabanes, who was telling him that he was going to force me to speak in spite of myself, he [Cavaignac] had answered that measures had been taken and that I would be discredited to the extent that nobody would believe me any more. A stupid policy which all have followed blindly since then and is the cause of their ruin today.

That I was the author of the *bordereau*, everyone knows; and even more so those who impudently deny it, whether they are from the [Ecole] Normale, Polytechnique or Charenton. The director of the paper which today attacks me with the filthiest of assaults knew about it through a friend who told him at the time when Cavaignac was beginning his fine manoeuvres against Henry and me, which have worked so successfully!

Everyone knew about it from the beginning. Yes, I obeyed the orders of Colonel Sandherr, with whom I had dealings, to whom I took documents, who passed me replies to lists of questions. Yes, I was a counter-espionage agent, and it is a strange error to say that no officer ever performed this service. There were (Agents), and always will be in all the armies of the world, because it is an effective means of counterattacking the intentions of the enemy. I performed important services; I believe it and have been told so.

One only needs to reread my deposition at the General Consulate and refer to the records of the General Staff that I indicate, to see the manoeuvres of the highest authorities in 1897, in order to conceal this act which I had carried out on a precise order. Many of those who scurrilously attack me today with astounding cowardice, pampered me at the time, sought the communications which I took, on order, to newspapers, and were the first to tell me then that they knew the role I had played.

Today when the stupidity and cowardice of the protagonists have made them lose the game, I am the one they still pursue, and they return to this 'substitution' – as they call it – one of the most improbably stupid inventions of this affair, in which there is a heap of stupidities. I do not speak of the material fact; discussing it would be grotesque, if it were not so lamentable. But the reasons invoked to support it are even more unbelievable.

If I was an actor in this saga, I would have asked for payment, I suppose. I had no money at the time when the supporters of Dreyfus represented me as selling my country for the weight of gold. For eight years now, I have been in the greatest penury, since the time when the inventors of this substitution represented me as having forged the means to have him rehabilitated.

All that of course, for nothing.

Even more stupid than scoundrels are the people with their so called superior knowledge from the Ecole Normale, Polytechnique and Charenton. All those who know me here know of my poverty, the painful life which I lead, very often deprived of the most essential items; they can tell how often I have been without bread or a fire.

In abandoning me as they did, those who should have defended me, those who had linked their cause to mine, who had lavished their assurances and promises to my defenders, are abominable cowards: they have committed an infamy with respect to the memory of my family, valiant soldiers who were their leaders, whose son they had promised to protect. They have destroyed themselves because cowardice never leads to victory. And if I were the 100,000th part of the man they themselves represent, they would be poor nameless wretches, for they would have used me like a shield to save their skin and cast me off afterwards.

But if the masters are wretched people without courage, they believed they were saving their own skin. What should one say of the lackeys? They can heap on me their most disgusting infamy, they will never reach the names they deserve.

Cowards who do not even remember their own baseness towards me; cowards who, in high-sounding words, sought for me a commission as Lieutenant-Colonel and who now have me affronted by stupid imbeciles; cowards even down to their puerile quibbling, of which they do not believe a single word!

For eight years, I have suffered all that a human being can suffer; I have not seen my dear children, whom I left as little girls and are now women.

On various occasions, offers of money were made to me; I refused them and, yet I was in the deepest penury. *La Libre Parole* once published proof of this, and the German who came from Berlin to make me accuse Henry, unmasked by his name, breathed not a word of it.

I have never betrayed my country; it is not true; I have served it as a soldier on the battlefield, and I have also served it elsewhere, as I had agreed to conceal this fact from the superior, the friend whose orders I was carrying out; and there too, I have given service.

I have never deserved the horrible destiny which befell me. If there is inherent justice, it will cruelly strike those who treated me in such cowardly and unworthy fashion; it is their cowardice towards me which has destroyed them, which has destroyed France; and their sorry lackeys will invent in vain all the most cowardly stupidities against me; for the more they strike me, the more they lose the cause which would surely have triumphed with a little more heart and intelligence.

Major Esterhazy

Source: Déb Cass, 1906, II, 675–8.

Appendix 47: **Extract from the diary of Dreyfus, 1907**

I left on July 25 with my family for Villers-sur-Mer.

I received there a letter from the 19th brigade's chief officers and the head artillery office of Vincennes which informed me that when I left the army, they would be very pleased to offer me a farewell dinner. I replied that I was very touched by their kind thought, but that I was to stay in Villers until the end of September.

I was struck off as an artillery officer on 25 August, and on 25 September 1907, the *Journal Officiel* announced the appointment of my replacement to command the artillery of the district of Saint-Denis. The reasons which motivated the decision that I had to take can be summarized as follows:

The draft bill concerning my promotion to the rank of artillery major was proposed by the government to the members of the Chambers on 13 July 1906, detailing their reasons as follows:

The Combined Chambers of the Supreme Court of Appeal have by decree of 12 July 1906, quashed without referral the verdict given against Captain Alfred Dreyfus on 9 September 1899 by the Court Martial of Rennes.

The innocence of the man convicted is legally and definitively established by this decision, which ipso facto leads to the reinstatement of this officer within the ranks of the army and erases all the effects of the conviction pronounced against him.

The government is powerless to repair the immense harm, both material and moral, which the victim has suffered from such a deplorable miscarriage of justice. It wishes at least to replace Captain Dreyfus in the position he would have reached if he had pursued the normal course of his career.

Yet, on 13 July 1906, more than one hundred artillery officers, less senior than me as captains, were already majors. In appointing me a major, the law recognized that with my ranking when I left the École supérieure de guerre, my personal dossier, the same would also have applied to me. Consequently it would have been equitable to give me my legitimate position in seniority among the officers of my weapon-section.

On the date of 13 July 1906, M. de Laguiche, an artillery officer of notably less seniority than me as a captain, was already a lieutenant-colonel. But I had not sought an exceptional promotion.

Among the hundred or more majors of lesser seniority than me as captains, the first promoted to commander was on 12 October 1901. It would thus simply have been fair to give me, at the time the law was voted, the same seniority as major.

An injustice was thus clearly committed in the bill relating to me when, instead of being replaced, as outlined in the reasons, in the situation where I would have found myself on 13 July 1906 if I had pursued the normal course of my career, I only took the rank of major on the very day the law was voted, that is with a delay of almost five years on my rights.

When informed by members of the Parliament of the injustice committed, the Government, whilst recognizing the material circumstances, declared that it had no possibility to repair it.

I considered then that I could not accept a moral diminishment, and that I could only remain in the army in possession of my full rights. I thus found myself forced to take early retirement.

I had hoped, on 12 July 1906, that the formal proclamation of my innocence would put an end to my trials. It was not to be, I was to remain the victim right to the end. But I comfort myself by thinking that the iniquity from which I suffered so prodigiously will have served the cause of humanity and developed sentiments of solidarity in society.

Alfred Dreyfus

4 October 1907

Source: A. Dreyfus, *Carnets (1899–1907), Après le procès de Rennes,* pp. 283–5.

Appendix 48: Edmond Fleg: extracts from his works and correspondence

Edmond Fleg to his mother
Leipzig, Sunday 9 January 1898

...This Dreyfus Affair has moved me deeply; the article which you sent me this morning gave me a great deal of food for thought. If there is manoeuvring by powerful people, whose interest and desire is to persecute us, the future of Judaism in France and Europe is frightening.

Edmond Fleg to his mother
Leipzig, 16 January 1898

... It is horrible to feel powerless when such things are happening. I would never have believed that human stupidity and the injustice of men could go so far and I fear for the Jews that there will be even more hideous moments to endure... It is certain that in France the majority of the population is already against them: the students in Paris are beginning an almost revolutionary movement; twenty years from now, it could end in a general massacre.

Edmond Fleg to his mother
Berlin, 25 February 1898

... The outcome of the Zola trial has devastated me. This affair took hold of my imagination to the point of preventing me from sleeping; and all this has caused me much pain as if it were a personal misfortune. And it is indeed, for each one of us, a personal misfortune, a great misfortune that antisemitism has made such progress, and that on the first occasion we have the prospect of massacres which will equal those of Armenia...

Edmond Fleg to his mother
Paris, 9 December 1898

...Everyone at the *Ecole [Normale]* is fanatically pro-Dreyfus and I have never anywhere else seen a hatred of antisemitism comparable to the one prevailing in this milieu. If instead of bowing their heads and remaining silent, the Jews had protested right from the beginning of the antisemitic campaigns five or six years ago, showing a little dignity, matters would not have gone so far. But we all show prudence verging on cowardice; we try to slip unnoticed amongst the crowd; yet we are seen nevertheless and our hypocritical humility is what does us the greatest harm...

Edmond Fleg to Lucien Moreau [1]
19 December 1898

... I am more and more absorbed in Zionism and it is a total renewal, a total rejuvenation. I find in it the calm and strength which I have long lacked; and later on, I will find in it, I think, a precise purpose to which I can apply my intellectual efforts, an aim such as I have needed to guide my life and give it a social meaning... Since I read the phrase of Bernard Lazare: 'Judaism is a nation', I have a better understanding of my past... The Jewish question is of supreme importance, not only for the Jews, but for all the countries that provide shelter for Jews. And the Jews alone will be able to offer a reasonable solution to the question: the creation of a new homeland.

Source: Correspondance d'Edmond Fleg pendant l'Affaire Dreyfus. Présentée, datée et annotée par A. E. Elbaz; préf by J. Madaule (Paris: A.-G. Nizet, 1976), pp. 63, 64, 72, 125, 128.

…In 1928 Edmond Fleg published *Pourquoi je suis juif* ('Why I am a Jew'), in which he recounted his spiritual evolution as a result of the Dreyfus Affair with a simplicity that often betrays deep emotion. He ended this autobiography with a universalist credo in which he affirms his faith in the permanence of Judaism and the unity of man:

I am a Jew because having been born a child of Israel and having rediscovered my Judaism, I felt it rekindled within me, more alive than myself.

I am a Jew because having been born a child of Israel and having rediscovered my Judaism, I want it to live beside me, more alive than myself.

I am a Jew because the faith of Israel demands of my heart all sacrifices.

I am a Jew because wherever suffering weeps, the Jew weeps.

I am a Jew because at all times whenever hopelessness cries out, the Jew hopes.

I am a Jew because the promise made to Israel is the universal promise.

I am a Jew because for Israel, the world is not completed: humanity is completing it.

I am a Jew because for Israel, man is not created: humanity is creating him.

I am a Jew because above all nations and Israel, Israel places Man and his Unity.

I am a Jew because above Man, image of the divine Unity, Israel places the divine Unity and its divinity.

'And I hoped, and still hope… for this Jewish dream that is both earthly and divine, of justice and peace, in a land made divine. And more than ever, despite all the sarcasm, I put my hope in Man.'

'Le dernier quart d'heure', interview by Pierre Lhoste.

Source: E. Fleg, *Pourquoi je suis juif* (Paris: Les belles lettres, [1928] 1995), pp. 100–1.

Notes to Appendix 48.

1   Longstanding friend of Edmond Fleg. Moreau, one of the first admirers of Charles Maurras and Maurice Barrès, became an ardent nationalist, anti-dreyfusard and antisemite. It was Moreau who introduced Fleg to nationalism. Fleg became an ardent supporter of Jewish nationalism. Despite their growing ideological divergences, Fleg and Moreau continued to correspond until Moreau's death in 1932.

Appendix 49: Charles Péguy: extracts from *Notre Jeunesse* ('Our Youth'), 1910

… Should one note once more that within this Dreyfus affair, there was, there is and will be for a long time, perhaps forever, a singular virtue. I mean a singular force. We can easily see it today. Now that the affair is over. It was not an illusion of our youth. The more this affair is over, the clearer it is that it will never be over. The more it is over, the more it proves. And first one should note that it proves that it had a singular *virtue*. In the two senses. A singular virtue of virtue as long as it remained in the realm of mysticism. A singular virtue of malice as soon as it entered into the world of politics...

The Dreyfus affair, Dreyfusism, mysticism, dreyfusard mysticism were a culmination, a culminating confluence of at least three mysticisms: Jewish, Christian and French. And as I will show, these three mysticisms did not tear themselves apart over it, they did not destroy each other, but on the contrary, through an encounter, through an intersection, they converged in an encounter and intersection that was perhaps unique in the history of the world...

The anti-Dreyfusards and we the Dreyfusards spoke the same language. We spoke on the same wavelength. We spoke exactly the same patriotic language. We spoke on the same patriotic wavelength. We had the same premises, the same patriotic assumption. Whether in fact we or they were the better patriots, that was the precise subject of the debate; but the fact that it *was* the subject of the debate, proves precisely that we were patriots on both sides...

We were heroes. We have to say it very plainly for I believe it would not be said on our behalf. And this is precisely how and in what way we were heroes. In all the world which we frequented, in all the world where we were then completing our years of apprenticeship, in the whole milieu we frequented, where we operated, where we were still growing up and completing our development, the question being asked in those two or three years of that rising curve, was not at all to know if *in fact* Dreyfus was innocent (or guilty). It was to know if one would have the courage to recognise it, to declare him innocent. To demonstrate his innocence. It was to know if one would have double courage. First, the initial courage, the external courage, the raw courage which was already difficult, the social and public courage to demonstrate his innocence to the world, in the eyes of the public, to admit it to the public, (to glorify him), to admit it publicly, to declare it publicly, to bear witness for him publicly. To venture on it, to wager on him everything one possessed, all one's miserably earned money, all the money of the poor and wretched, all the money of the little people, of misery and poverty; all the time; all one's life, all one's career; all one's health, all one's body and soul; the ruin of the body; all manner of ruin; heartbreak; the dislocation of families, the denial of one's close family and friends, eyes (and glances) turning away, silent or frenzied disapproval, silent *and* frenzied disapproval, isolation, all manner of quarantine; the break-up of friendships of 20 years' standing, in other words the friendships of our entire lives. All one's social life. All one's emotional life, in fact everything. And secondly, the second and more difficult courage, the internal courage, the secret courage to admit to oneself, within oneself, that he was innocent. To renounce for that man all peace of mind...

... About Dreyfus himself, to go to the heart of the debate, to the object, to the person himself, about Dreyfus it is clear that I wanted to say nothing, that I said nothing and could say nothing, that touched the private man. I am well aware of all that is tragic and fatal in the life of this man. But what is most tragic and most fatal is precisely that he does not have the right to be a private individual. It is that we have an incessant right to call him to account, the right and the *duty* to call him to account in the most rigorous manner...

What was he doing becoming a captain? What was he doing in the offices of the General Staff? That is the fateful calamity. What was he doing acquiring a reputation, celebrity and worldwide glory? A victim despite himself, a hero despite himself, a martyr despite himself...

Extracts from Péguy's 'portrait of Bernard Lazare' in Notre Jeunesse:

Operating and working the same subject matter, developing within the same subject matter, there were at least two Dreyfus affairs, elaborating the matter of the same story. That of Bernard-Lazare, our story, was innocent and has no need of defence. And in another sense, there were very definitely two Dreyfus affairs, the one emanating from Bernard-Lazare and the one emanating from Colonel Picquart. The one emanating from Colonel Picquart was very good. The one from Bernard-Lazare was infinite…

I can still see him [Bernard-Lazare] in his bed. That atheist, that professional atheist, that official atheist in whom resounded with incredible strength and gentleness the eternal Word; with eternal strength; with eternal gentleness; whose like I have found nowhere else. I still have imprinted upon me, in my eyes, the eternal goodness of that infinitely gentle gaze, that goodness which was not thrust forward, but poised, informed. Infinitely disillusioned; infinitely informed; infinitely indomitable itself. I can still see him in his bed, that atheist streaming with the Word of God. In death itself all the weight of his people rested on his shoulders. One was not allowed to tell him that the responsibility was not his. I have never seen a man so weighed down, so weighed down with a burden, with an eternal responsibility. Just as we are and feel burdened with our children, with our own children in our own family, he felt as much, exactly as much, exactly burdened with his people.

Source: C. Péguy, *Notre Jeunesse* (Paris: Gallimard, [1910] 1933), pp. 51–2, 63, 150–1, 163–4, 191, 194, 94, 105.

Appendix 50: Antisemitic riots in Paris, Théâtre de l'Ambigu, January–February 1931

1931

January: Great excitement in Paris due to the planned production of the German play *The Dreyfus Affair* on a Parisian stage.

Alfred Dreyfus asks Henry Torrès who wants to translate the piece for the French stage not to do so without knowing the play apparently suspecting that he is depicted on stage. Yet in *Paris-Midi* (of January 29th 1931), he declares he will not object to the planned production, instead he says it gives him great satisfaction that the translator of the play will not be Torrès, but the son of Jean Richepin, one of the sternest 'Anti-dreyfusards' during the 'Affair'.

February: Première of the French version of *The Dreyfus Affair* in the Paris Théâtre de l'Ambigu. The adaptation, totally distorting the German original, is by Jacques Richepin.

During almost all performances, there were violent clashes inside the theatre and outside on the street. Supporters of the Action française, members of the chauvinist organisation Croix de feu[1] and Camelots du roi tried to storm the theatre, attacked the actors and threw teargas bombs in the auditorium to forcibly bring the performance to an end. Despite repeated demonstrations reminiscent of 30 years ago, the run continued until the end of March. Finally, the director of the theatre had to bow to the threats made against his theatre – threats against which the theatre was not being protected. He publicly declared that this was the sole reason that forced him to bring the run to an end.

Dormant emotions re-awoke or erupted again for several weeks. Again, two opposing camps faced each other. Again, a newspaper war broke out. Debates in the chamber. Turbulent assemblies. Clashes between nationalists and pacifists. Like 30 years ago.

Again attempts to confuse the public. Sensation chases sensation. Every day, French and German newspapers print stirring news items: 'Stink bombs against *The Dreyfus Affair...*' 'over one hundred people arrested and taken into police custody, several dozens jailed for resistance to state authority'... 'Esterhazy's daughter tries to hit Richepin with a riding whip!'... 'Dreyfus' as a radio drama on the Eiffel Tower high above any stink bombs. After numerous battles around the performances of the play *The Dreyfus Affair*, the Théâtre de l'Ambigu had to close down for 24 hours. The theatre administration explained the auditorium had to be repaired and disinfected. In the meantime, to replace the cancelled stage performance, *The Dreyfus Affair* was broadcast on radio from the Eiffel tower... The Paris correspondent of a German national paper in Berlin reports: 'The reaction of the audience was extraordinary. It is astonishing how alive people's memory of this affair is which unleashed such passions. The stalls were clearly divided into parties for and against Dreyfus, for and against the leaning of the play.'

The demonstrations of the royalists recur every night. Their spiritual fathers, the leaders of the Action française, pride themselves on equalling the activities of the German nationalists who have stopped the showing of the remarkable film *All quiet on the Western front* with violence and stink bombs. The Action française celebrates the clashes in the theatre as their victory and encourages its readers to hold demonstrations more regularly and in greater numbers. Their slogans are successful. Their victory cannot be denied. The Laval government gives in. The performances are stopped. The monarchist papers declare their triumph in giant letters: 'A victory for the Camelots du roi. The performances of the Boche-play at the 'Ambigu', which have been forcefully prevented by the Camelots du roi over the last few days will be discontinued on order of the police prefect.'

Censorship does not exist in France, neither does the law permit the police prefect to give such an order. Yet it was sufficient for him to declare that he could not guarantee peace and order and provide troops of several hundred men every night. It was sufficient for the director of the theatre to receive numerous letters daily – threatening, as the *Petit Parisien* reported, to bomb his theatre or set it on fire if he continued to play the piece. He subsequently went to see the police prefect and asked for the protection he was entitled to. After this meeting, in which the police prefect in no way prohibited the performances, the director withdrew the play from his repertory.

A survey approaching numerous personalities of public life - senators, MPs, writers and artists - asked whether they were for or against the performances. The outcome was that, like 30 years ago, there were two parties diametrically opposed to each other. Nationalist writers like Claude Farrère or Rosny the Elder spoke out against it. General Oberfils stated: 'it is wiser to let such embarrassing affairs be forgotten in the silence of history'. Meanwhile , the dramatist Lenormand, Zola's friend and biographer Paul Brulat, Clemenceau's colleague at the *Aurore* Urbain Gohier, and the president of the Deputies' Chamber Ferdinand Buisson asked in surprise with what right such a play was being suppressed or its performances sabotaged by a small, politically irrelevant group. None of them objected to it. The young Jean Painlevé, son of the former prime minister, answered: '*The Dreyfus Affair* is a symbol which stays alive and must do so.'

19th March: In the chamber, MP Guernut questions the Laval government about the 'ban' of the Dreyfus Affair. He asks if the government intends to leave the streets to organised gangs or if Laval intends to do anything about securing the freedom of speech and assembly as well as the independence of theatres – which are all inextricably linked to the republican order. MP Planche then states that they are obviously witnessing a renaissance of 'French chauvinism'. He exclaims that the former frontline fighters who are now pacifists demand the immediate revival of the play. Laval interrupts him: 'The theatre can resume the performances whenever they want.'

MP Planche: 'I will hold you to your word. It is nonetheless true that the police prefect has forbidden the performances.'

Laval: 'There has been no such order!'

M. Herriot, leader of the radical socialists, intervenes. He accuses the government of playing the case down, but that it remains abominable and grotesque. Laval's statements, he says, are mere excuses. It is true that the play has not been formally banned, but it has been declared that if the theatre carries on performing, it is at its own risk. 'This equals a ban!' exclaims Herriot, then turning against a 'policy of needle pricks', which, he says, has distorted the true face of France and has something unbearably ridiculous about it.

Laval stresses again that there has never been a formal ban. On the contrary. During the 32 performances that have taken place, he has provided the theatre with several hundred-strong police units. The theatre is free to revive the play at any time. Even though he has to point out that Dreyfus' son himself had demanded for the performances to be stopped. Furthermore, he has to state that the film *All quiet on the Western front* is strictly banned in Germany, whereas it is shown in the entire French territory. Under such circumstances, how can there be talk of an infringement on the freedom of theatre? He finishes by saying he wishes that *The Dreyfus Affair* may continue to be performed under peaceful circumstances. 'However, if the performances should trigger more violence, if public order should suffer, who could blame the police prefect if indeed he did order the play to be stopped? The freedom of the theatre is granted; but only if public order is respected.'

26th March: The Théâtre l'Ambigu resumes the performances. There are new demonstrations by the Camelots du roi, encouraged by Léon Daudet of the Action française. Proper fights ensue. The papers report: 'Violent scuffle at the theatre. Another theatre battle in Paris'… 'Pacifists put Dreyfus-troublemakers to flight'. A Berlin paper writes: 'One of the young men who shouted and threw stink bombs, a certain Count de Harcourt, was grabbed by the pacifist frontline fighters and dragged onto the stage. They bared his bottom in front of the whole audience and gave him a good spanking.' For oddity's sake, it shall be mentioned that the count initiated legal proceedings and chose the socialist Paul-Boncour as his lawyer.

31st March: The paper *Frankfurter Zeitung* reports from Paris: 'The director of the theatre has today written to the play's translator, saying that they had the satisfaction of performing *The Dreyfus Affair* without major interruptions last night, but that it was enough now, that he, the director, could no longer bear to witness how the Parisians were fighting each other like bitter enemies in his theatre. Thus he was ending the run.'

We see: what was once played out as a tragedy is repeated as a farce. Also in 1931, the republicans, tired of fighting, backed down against a few hundred active enemies of the republic. Led by Léon Daudet, the violent nationalists who still consider Dreyfus guilty, Zola damaging, and Colonel Henri a patriotic hero are the factual winners – even though they are a tiny minority. The republic settles for a compromise. It does not deem it worthwhile to carry on fighting. So it bows to the demands of nationalist 'phraseurs'. In 1931 as in 1901, when Waldeck-Rousseau passed the – as Zola called it – despicable amnesty law to calm down the population.

Times change. Yet people do not change with them.

Notes on Appendix 50.

1   Veteran association created in 1927 by the writer Maurice Hanot to represent holders of the Croix de feu. Declaring itself apolitical, the organization maintained nationalist and anti-parliamentary ideals. M. Winock (ed.) *Histoire de l'extrême droite en France* (Paris: Seuil, 1993) p. 165.

Source: W. Herzog, *Der Kampf einer Republik: Die Affäre Dreyfus* (Zürich/Vienna/Prague: Büchergilde Gutenberg, 1933), pp. 964–8.

Appendix 51: Victor Basch and the Dreyfus Affair

The Dreyfus Affair, a fundamental and paradigmatic event in the lifetime of Victor Basch, preoccupied him all his life. A starting point for his intervention in city affairs, the Affair determined his system of values, the terms of his political action and was the catalyst for his passion for justice. A synthesis of the principles of the French Revolution and republican values, the Affair was an essential point of reference in his great speeches as a member of the League, the echo of an unforgettable drama and a vital message. [A, 30]

For him, as for the founders of the League of Human Rights, the Affair also dictated the principles of the organisation of which he was a member till the end of his life. For Victor Basch, a League member from its inception, the Affair incarnated the defence of the rights of the individual, from the most humble to the most well known, whether from an ethnic group or from an oppressed state. '... As long as there remained a single victim of social iniquity... the Dreyfus Affair was not over,' Basch stated in 1909, highlighting the symbolic significance of the event... [A, 30]

On 11 January 1944, at the side of *Route Nationale* 84, some passers-by discovered the bodies of two people, a man and a woman, aged 81, shot dead with several revolver bullets... Amongst other documents found on the victims' bodies were Victor Basch's identity card issued by the Croix-Rousse police station, containing the word JEW in big red capital letters, and a will in his own hand, bequeathing all his property to his wife... [A, 14]

The murderers had surprised the couple 'as they were having dinner in the dining room'... They were forced to get into a vehicle... When they arrived at the Chemin de Barrye near the village of Neyron, the two old people were told to get out of the car; they had scarcely walked ten metres or so along a little path when Joseph Lécussan fired at Victor Basch and Henri Gonnet at Ilona Basch. Killed by two bullets to the head, according to the autopsy report, they had also received two violent blows from a blunt instrument... [A, 331]

The killers of Victor Basch and their accomplices shared a far-right past and ideology... before joining the *Milice* they had been pre-war members of *L'Action française*, *La Cagoule* and the *La Croix de feu*. These far right movements had always considered Basch as the enemy to be killed, being a Jew, pro-Dreyfus a supporter of Franco-German rapprochement till 1930, a leader of the Popular Front and an antifascist militant... [B, 258]

Victor and Ilona (Hélène) Basch... lie in the military cemetery in Lyon. At the scene of the murder, in Neyron, in the Ain region, there is a stone slab among the shrubs and loose stones: the inscription has survived: 'To honour the martyrs of 10 January 1944: Victor Basch, professor at the Sorbonne and President of the League of Human Rights (1863–1944) and his companion Hélène Furth (1863–1944), who were savagely murdered by the *Milice*'. [A, 14]

Sources: (A) F. Basch, *Victor Basch ou la passion de la justice de l'Affaire Dreyfus au crime de la milice* (Paris: Plon, 1994); (B) F. Basch, *'Le Juif paye toujours'*, in F Basch, L. Crips and P. Grusan (eds) *Victor Basch 1863–1944: un intellectuel cosmopolite* (Paris: Berg International, 2000).

Appendix 52: Speech by Prime Minister Menachem Begin at the Knesset on the occasion of the visit of President François Mitterrand to Israel, 4 March 1982

Already in my youth, my father, my teacher, taught me to love and respect France. He used to recite whole paragraphs of '*J'accuse*' into his children's ears. The tragic and terrible episode of the Dreyfus case has engraved itself upon the memories of many inside and outside France as being the landmark of the outburst of antisemitism, which, although already in existence, was lying dormant.

This is the infectious illness which is passed on from generation to generation especially amongst nations where young children were taught the sickening prayer which begins thus: 'Let us pray for the hypocrite Jew…'.

This same prayer had poisoned the wells until the great Pope Johannes 23rd abolished it once and for all.

Thus, another man, the kind who is only born once in hundreds of years, Theodor Herzl, stood and watched the Dreyfus case and came to the conclusion that a Jewish State had to be established in the National Historical homeland of our people. As Herzl listened to the cry of the enraged masses calling upon 'Death to the Jews', a cry coming from the heart of world culture, Paris, the City of Cities, his soul became stricken with grief, and he sat down in his small hotel to compose the revolutionary book *The Jewish State* 'JudenStadt'. And thus he heard the wings of history beat as he was seized by a burning fever emanating from this great creation.

As tens of years passed, perhaps because of the healing process of each wound, perhaps because of the generous nature of a Jews' heart to forget the bad and remember the good, the Dreyfus case took a completely different turn. And so we saw the tremendous effort of the French people to see Justice done. A tremendous battle between truth and its opponent, between light and darkness, between love and hate, between justice and injustice began. And I have not the slightest doubt, my dear friend, François Mitterrand, that the hearts of our friends were alive then and beating next to those of Zola, Clemenceau, Jaurès, Labori and Colonel Picquart. I shall make clear today, in front of the Knesset, the main facts which show how the victory of righteousness shines [shone] amongst the French People.

On the 23rd December 1894 Alfred Dreyfus was condemned to life imprisonment on Devil's Island. In March of 1896 Colonel Picquart discovered the letter to Esterhazy named the *petit bleu*. In 1898 Zola published '*J'accuse*' against his government and his army, in the name of his People, out of respect for his country, and in the name of justice.

On the 9th of September 1899, the second trial of Alfred Dreyfus took place and he was condemned to ten years in prison. Ten days later he received a Pardon from the French President.

But the forces of justice did not rest, for the truth has no respite.

Truth triumphs. In 1903, there was yet another call to trial. In 1906 the truth triumphed, and the trials were abolished once and for all.

Twelve years of silence since Dreyfus had been tried on a sickening and disgraceful basis. And the French people did not rest until justice was brought to the miserable man, the miserable Jew. For despite everything, truth is a definite category and works outside, above and beyond time.

Appendix 53: Commemorative events of the Dreyfus centenary 1994[1]

The Dreyfus centenary 1994

Jan 1   The Dreyfus Centenary Bulletin is published in London listing the events planned for the Centenary year in France, Germany, Great Britain, Israel and Switzerland. Editor George. R. Whyte.

Jan 10   Paris Cinémathèque: Tribute to Victor Basch. Projection of the film *L'Affaire Dreyfus* by Meliès.

Jan 16   Toulouse:

Inauguration of an exhibition in the *Bibliothèque municipale de Toulouse* devoted to the various manifestations of antisemitism in the Toulouse region at the time of the Dreyfus Affair.

Exhibition at the Cultural Center Saint Jérome *Pour en finir avec l'antisémitisme* ('For an end to antisemitism'), retracing the pogroms and persecutions of Jews over two millennia.

The *Centre Maimonide* organizes a cycle of conferences about the Dreyfus Affair, on the subject of 'Catholics and the Dreyfus Affair' and 'Jewish-Christian relations'.

Jan 28–30   Mulhouse (Dreyfus' birth place): *VIe symposium humaniste international* (International Symposium): *L'Affaire Dreyfus – Juifs en France*. Colloquium organized with the support of the city of Mulhouse, the Conseil Général du Haut-Rhin, the Conseil Régional of Alsace, under the patronage of the Conseil Représentatif des Institutions Juives de France (CRIF).[2]

Jan 30   London: Seminar *The Dreyfus Affair: Jews, anti-Semitism and politics in modern France*, organized by the Institute of Contemporary History and the Wiener Library

Mar 21–22   Tel-Aviv University: International symposium *The Dreyfus Affair – 100 years, Nationalism, Raisons d'Etat and Human Rights*, organized by the Faculty of Humanities. The symposium emphasizes the importance of the Dreyfus Affair in the ideology of political Zionism and the formation of the State of Israel.

Apr 7–June 30 Paris: Musée d'Histoire contemporaine (Hôtel National des Invalides): Inauguration of the exhibition *L'Affaire Dreyfus et le tournant du siècle 1894–1910* organized with the collaboration of the city of Rennes and the Musée de Bretagne. Various films on the Dreyfus Affair are also projected.[3]

The vidéothèque de Paris screens films on the Dreyfus Affair.

Apr 28   Duisburg: University of Duisburg: Conference conducted by Jean-Louis Levy, grandson of Alfred Dreyfus, 'Le pouvoir et la morale dans l'affaire Dreyfus' (Power and Ethics in the Dreyfus Affair), organized by the Deutsch-Französische Gesellschaften (Franco-German Association) and Beate Gödde-Baumanns.

May 8   Berlin: World première of the Opera in two acts *Dreyfus – Die Affäre* by George Whyte; music by Jost Meier under the direction of Prof. Götz Friedrich.[4]

Berlin: inauguration of touring exhibition *'J'Accuse'*, compiled by George Whyte, curated by Sarah Nathan-Davis in collaboration with Diane Buckingham. Inaugural address and exhibition catalogue foreword by Norman Kleeblatt, director of the Jewish Museum, New York on 'Racism and Degradation: Distorted Realities during the Dreyfus Affair'.[5]

May 9–12   Potsdam: University of Potsdam: International symposium *Dreyfus und die Folgen* (Dreyfus and the consequences), organized by the Moses Mendelssohn Zentrum Europäisch-jüdische Studien.

May 12–July10 Geneva: Museum Petit Palais: Inauguration of the exhibition *Switzerland and The Dreyfus Affair*. The exhibition illustrates the role of the Naville Family (*v.* 20 Apr 1900) and the fight for the Dreyfus cause in the Swiss press.

Sept 4 Bonn: World première of *J'Accuse* in the Oper der Stadt Bonn, a dance drama; televised by WDR Cologne and Swedish television.[6]

Sep 21 Rennes: The Universities 1 and 2. Amphitheatre is named after Victor Basch.

Sept 22–23 Rennes: Musée de Bretagne: International conference *L'opinion publique et l'Affaire Dreyfus en France et à l'étranger.*[7]

Paris: Palais de Luxembourg: Conference *Une Affaire Dreyfus est-elle encore possible aujourd'hui?* ('Is a Dreyfus Affair still possible today?'), organized by the Mouvement contre le Racisme et pour l'Amitié entre les Peuples (MRAP).

Rage and Outrage, a French-German-British television production of a musical satire in one act by George Whyte, based on original texts by Edouard Drumont, Emile Zola, Alfred Dreyfus, and 'chansons' of the day on the Dreyfus Affair. (La Sept-ARTE/Channel 4)[8]

Paris. 'Memoire 2000' Screening and open forum on *Rage and Outrage*.

Oct 1–23 Mulhouse: Cultural Center *filature de Mulhouse*: Inauguration of the exhibition *Antisemitism at the time of the Dreyfus Affair.*[9]

Oct 2 Médan: Zola museum: Opening of the exhibition *Emile Zola dans L'Affaire*, in the presence of Mme France Beck (grand-daughter of Mathieu Dreyfus and Joseph Reinach).

Oct 15–Nov 30 Paris, Hôtel de ville: 11th arrondissement: Inauguration of the Exhibition *Les Juifs de France et l'Affaire Dreyfus: Une tragédie de la belle époque.* Exhibition under the patronage of the Grand Rabbin René Samuel Sirat, organized by Professor Béatrice Philippe, and a committee of historians.[10]

Oct 16 Paris: Nouvelle Ecole du Louvre (art school): Conference organized by the CRIF and the Institut National des Langues et Civilisations Orientales (INALCO) on the dangers of a miscarriage of justice, with the participation of Robert Badinter, Président du Conseil Constitutionnel; Jacques Toubon, Minister of Culture and of the Francophonie; Pierre Drai, First President of the Supreme Court of Appeal.

Oct 18 London: French Institute: Round table *The Dreyfus case and the Dreyfus Affair: the early years.* Organized by the Emile Zola Society, with the participation of George Whyte, (Chairman of the Dreyfus Society), Dr Nelly Wilson, (Bristol University) Professor Robert Wistrich (Hebrew University, Jerusalem).

Nov 6–10 Jerusalem: Hebrew University: International conference *Le Centenaire de l'Affaire Dreyfus*, organised by the Department of Political Science.[11]

Nov 17–19 Saint-Cyr-sur-Loire: International symposium at the City Hall *Les représentations de l'Affaire Dreyfus dans la presse en France et à l'étranger*, organized by the research group Histoire de l'intelligence européenne des Lumières à nos jours, the Société d'études de la fin du xixe siècle, and the University of Tours.[12]

Nîmes: Conference in the Chambre de agriculture *La France de l'Affaire Dreyfus*, organized by the Férération du Gard, the Ligue des droits de l'Homme and the Comité départemental de la Culture du Gard, under the patronage of the Conseil Général du Gard.

Nov 18 Tel Aviv: Museum of Jewish Diaspora *Beth Hatfutsoth*: Inauguration of the exhibition *The Dreyfus Affair-The battle for public opinion*, covering the prevailing antisemitism in France before and during the Dreyfus Affair.

Dec 13–15   Tel Aviv: Bar-Ilan University: International interdisciplinary congress *The intellectuals and the Dreyfus Affair, then and now*, organized by the Faculties of literature, social studies and Jewish studies.[13]

Grenoble: University Mendès-France: Symposium *Comment devient-on dreyfusard?* ('How does one become a dreyfusard?'), dealing with the subject of collective and individual support of the Dreyfus cause.

Dec 16–19   Berlin: Moses Mendelssohn Zentrum and the Old Synagogue: Conference *Die Dreyfus-Affäre und ihre Aktualität am Ende des 20 Jahrhunderts* ('The Dreyfus Affair and its relevance at the end of the twentieth Century'), organized by the Evangelische Akademie Arnoldshaim (Protestant Academy of Arnoldshaim); the Bundesverband Jüdischer Studenten in Deutschland (Federal Association of Jewish Students in Germany) open to Jewish and non Jewish students.

• A television documentary *Dreyfus. The Odyssey of George Whyte* (WDR Cologne).[14]

• The French government officially supports a television film *L'Affaire Dreyfus* (in two parts) directed by Yves Boisset. The screenplay, by the Spanish writer Jorge Semprun, is based on the book of Jean-Denis Bredin *L'Affaire Dreyfus*.[15]

• Release of a documentary film *La raison d'état: chronique de l'affaire Dreyfus (1894–1899)* written and produced by Pierre Sorlin and Lily Scherr. The documentary reconstructs the chronology of the Dreyfus Affair and is interspersed with interviews of Léon Blum from the 1930's in which he states the importance of the Affair in his political career.[16]

• In Bielefeld, Germany, production of Chamber opera 'Dreyfus' by Moshe Cotel and Mordecai Newman. The work focuses on the role of Herzl.

Notes to Appendix 53.

1   For more details on the commemorations held in 1994 see *The Dreyfus Centenary Bulletin,* London (1994) (*v.* 1 Jan 1994); *Jean Jaurès. Cahiers trimestriels* No. 136, Le centenaire de l'Affaire (1994–95) (April–June 1995), pp. 4–60 ; M. Knobel, 'Chronique dreyfusienne: En cette année 1994… L'Affaire Dreyfus', *Cahiers naturalistes* No. 69 (1995), pp. 302–10. On the various books and publications published in 1993–94 on the Dreyfus Affair see J.-Y. Mollier, 'Chronique Dreyfusienne, L'Affaire Dreyfus un siècle après', *Cahiers naturalistes* No. 69 (1995), pp. 280–91

2   Proceedings: *L'affaire Dreyfus: juifs en France: actes du 6e symposium humaniste international de Mulhouse, 28, 29 et 30 janvier 1994* (Mulhouse: Cêtre, 1994).

3   Catalogue: *L'affaire Dreyfus et le tournant du siècle, 1894–1910*. Catalogue edited by L. Gervereau and C. Prochasson (Nanterre: BDIC, 1994).

4   Conductor: Christopher Keene; stage director: Torsten Fischer, set and costumes: Andreas Reinhardt. Paul Frey (Dreyfus), Aimée Willis (Lucie), Artur Korn (Zola). Illustrated programme with reflections on the Affair. The opera was performed 12 times in Basel. English version 'The Dreyfus Affair' was premiered in New York on 2 April 1996, preceded by two presentations under the Guggenheim's museum series 'Works and Process' (March 17–18).

5   The exhibition tour: Berlin, May 8, 1994; Bonn, September 4, 1994; Basel, October 17, 1994; New York, April 2, 1996.

6   Scenario: George Whyte; music: Alfred Schnittke; choreography: Valery Panov; set design: Josef Svoboda; costumes: Yolanda Sonnabend.

7   Proceedings published: M. Denis, M. Lagrée, and J.-Y. Veillard (eds) *L'Affaire Dreyfus et l'opinion publique en France et à l'étranger* (Rennes: Presses Universitaires de Rennes, 1995).

8   Orchestration: Luciano Berio. Conductor Diego Masson. Piano: Jeff Cohen. Director: Raoul Sangla. Cast: Ute Lemper (artiste); Lambert Wilson (Drumont); Jean-Marc Bory (Zola). Male chorus (members of Opera Comique) and orchestra. Televised throughout Europe.

9   *Dreyfus avant Dreyfus. Une Famille juive de Mulhouse.* Catalogue de l'exposition tenue du 1er au 23 Octobre 199 à la Filature, 20 allée Nothan Katz, Moulouse. O. Jurbert and M.-C. Waill (eds) (Mulhouse, 1994).

10 The exhibition includes rare items e.g. the religious certificate (Ketubah) of Dreyfus and Lucie's marriage; the order for the ceremony of Dreyfus' degradation; the faux Henry, Dreyfus' notebook from Devil's Island. Catalogue: *Une tragédie de la belle époque. L'Affaire Dreyfus* (Paris: Comité du centenaire de l'Affaire Dreyfus, 1994).

11 The object of the conference is a consideration of the Affair as a universal phenomenon and a warning of the crises of the twentieth century, an investigation of the nature of the Affair, its intellectual, cultural and political dimensions, and its implications and long term influences in France and elsewhere in Europe.

12 The symposium includes conferences on the Dreyfus Affair in the feminist, anarchist, Hebrew, medical, and international press. Proceedings published: E. Cahm and P. Citte (eds) *Les représentations de l'affaire Dreyfus dans la presse en France et à l'étranger* (Tours: Imp. L'université de Tours, François-Rabelais, 1997).

13 Koren R., and Michman D. (eds) *Les intellectuels face à l'Affaire Dreyfus alors et aujourd'hui: perception et impact de l'Affaire en France et à l'étrange*. Actes du colloque de l'Université Bar-Ilan, Israel, 13–15 décembre 1994 (Paris/Montréal: L'Harmattan, 1998).

14 Production: Brook Associates, Inter Nationes, Artial. Director: Udi Eichler. Transmitted in Germany, Sweden, Finland, Hungary.

15 Yves Boisset received the permission of the French government to film in the Palais de Justice (where Zola's trial took place) and in the Cour Morland (Ecole Militaire), with present day soldiers of the Republican guard. A co-production with France 2 and the German-French channel Arte.

16 Film produced by the Centre National de Documentation Pédagogique (CNDP) and the Institut National des Langues et Civilisations Orientales (INALCO).

Appendix 54: Commemorative events 1998

Centenary of Zola's 'J'Accuse'[1]

Jan 11–13   A series of ceremonies in honour of Emile Zola under the high patronage of President Jacques Chirac.

11 Jan   Inauguration in the Bibliothèque nationale of an exhibition devoted to the manuscript of '*J'Accuse*' and notebooks of Alfred Dreyfus entitled: 'Hommage au Capitaine'.

12 Jan   Commemorative plaque is affixed to the building where Emile Zola lived in Paris from 1899 until his death (in this house) in 1902 (21 bis rue Bruxelle in the 9th arrondissement).

13 Jan   Colloquium in the Bibliothèque nationale de France: 'Zola in the Dreyfus Affair'.

Ceremony in the Panthéon, under the presidency of Prime Minister Lionel Jospin and in the presence of members of the government.

Laurent Fabius, President of the Chamber of Deputy opens the debates with a speech in honour of Emile Zola's intervention in the Dreyfus Affair.

A reproduction (150 square meters) of Zola's '*J'Accuse*' is draped on the front of the National Assembly in Paris for ten days accompanied by a soundtrack of the text of '*J'Accuse*', read by Philippe Torreton from the Comédie Française.

In a ceremony under the presidency of Alain Richard, Minister of Defence, and in the presence of members of the Dreyfus and Zola's families, a commemorative plaque is affixed in the courtyard of the Ecole Militaire. The text of the plaque mentions both the ceremonies of Dreyfus' degradation and reintegration in the French Army, as well as Zola's '*la vérité est en marche, et rien ne l'arrêtera*'. ('The truth is on the march and nothing will stop it').

President Jacques Chirac addresses a public letter to the descendants of the Zola and the Dreyfus families, expressing France's gratitude for their courage in their fight against hatred, injustice and intolerance.

The Catholic daily *La Croix* apologizes for its antisemitic editorials during the Dreyfus Affair.

Feb13–15   New York: Columbia University, Departments of French and Center for French and Francophone studies hold an International conference: *The*

Dreyfus Affair: Memory and History in France and the USA. Organized by Professor Henri Mitterand, President of the Société littéraire des Amis d'Emile Zola and Professor Jean-Yves Mollier from Université de Versailles-St-Quentin en Yvelines.[2] Exhibition curated by Lorraine Butler.

Feb 17   Washington: Georgetown university. Conference: *The Dreyfus case. Human rights vs. prejudice, intolerance and demonization,* organized by Jean-Max Guieu.[3]

Feb 21   Paris: Public event in the grande salle des Assises du Palais de Justice, where Zola's trial took place (7-23 Feb 1898), organized by the Ligue des Droits de l'Homme and the Ordre des avocats à la Cour d'appel de Paris.

Mar 7   London: International Colloquium: *'J'Accuse...!': A Centenary* is organized in the French Institute in London, by the British Emile Zola Society, and the Cultural Service of the French Embassy in London, under the presidency of David Baguley.

Mar 27   Valenciennes: University of Valenciennes: a study day devoted to *'J'Accuse'* Organized by Karl Zieger and the Faculty of literature.[4]

May 30   Médan: a study day devoted to Zola's *'J'Accuse'* and *Les preuves* by Jean Jaurès (*v.* 11 Oct 1898) in the Zola museum. Organized by the Société d'études jaurasiennes, the Société littéraire des Amis de Zola, L'Association du Musée Emile-Zola and the Centre d'Etudes sur Zola et le naturalisme.

Notes to Appendix 54.

1   On these events see *Cahiers naturalistes* No. 72, (1998), pp. 4–36, 427–42; *Cahiers naturalistes* No. 69, (1995), pp. 255–6.

2   A number of papers are available in: <www.columbia.edu/cu/french/maison/conferences/jaccuse/COLL.html>. See also programme in *Cahiers naturalistes* No. 72 (1998), pp. 430–1.

3   Proceeding published in *Intolérance and Indignation. L'Affaire Dreyfus* (Paris: Editions Fischbacher, 2000).

4   Publication: K. Zieger (ed.) *Emile Zola, 'J'accuse'...! Réactions nationales et internationales* (Valenciennes: Presses Universitaires de Valenciennes, 1999).

Epilogue

Appendix 55: Opening of the Dreyfus Exhibition at the Jewish Museum in New York (12–13 September 1987): inaugural address by Dr Jean-Louis Lévy, grandson of Dreyfus

This Exhibition draws our attention to a strange phenomenon, the ongoing relevance, in today's world, of the Dreyfus Affair.

Neither the genocide of 6 million Jews, nor two world wars have succeeded in obliterating the Dreyfus Affair with the ashes of forgetfulness.

The Dreyfus Affair, just like great ancient myths, offers an inexhaustible reserve of examples and symbols to our imagination. An extraordinary confrontation unfolds in front of our eyes. The confrontation between an unconquerable will and the forces of inhumanity. The inhumanity of those who persecuted Dreyfus and were eager to bring dishonour upon him; the will of one who pledged to prove his innocence. A confrontation which lasted 12 years.

During 1237 days, Dreyfus, isolated on Devil's Island, was ignorant of the Affair's vicissitudes. How did he survive? How did he fight against illness, against mental disease, against the temptation to let himself die,

He had sworn an oath to his wife and children to regain the honour of his name. Under a distress of unbearable proportions, he was torn between two images of himself: the honest soldier he was and 'the vile rascal' he represented. 'My life belongs to my country, but not my honour.'

On September 14 1896, after 18 months of deportation, he reaches the extreme limits of his strength. Completely exhausted, he stops keeping his diary.

Then, one night, he sees 'the guiding star':

Today, more than ever, you must not desert your post. More than ever, you do not have the right to shorten your sad and miserable life, even by one single day. Whatever tortures are inflicted upon you, you must walk upright until they throw you into your grave. You must stand tall in front of your torturers so long as you have a shadow of strength left continuing to live however desolate, leaving engraved in their mind's eye the intangible supremacy of the soul.

He inherited from Judaism, of which he knew little, the strength of being a man 'with a stiff neck' unable to break, unable to submit.

May I conclude with a frail hope? The Dreyfus Affair remains an example of a power that is deeply rooted in each one of us; the resilience of the human mind, that mysterious fortitude which resists and says No; NO to force, NO to injustice, NO to tyranny. Each one of us has this potential power.

During the Dreyfus Affair, an explorer was caught in the Polar ice. When he was rescued his first question was:

Is Dreyfus free?

We must never stop asking ourselves that very question:

Is Dreyfus free?

BIOGRAPHICAL PROFILES

ALBERT OF MONACO, Prince, born Albert Honoré Charles Grimaldi (1848–1922)

Prince and Ruler of Monaco.

1870 joins French navy in Franco-Prussian War; awarded the Legion of Honour; founds Oceanographic Institute in Monaco; 1889 marries Marie Alice Heine, duchesse de Richelieu, an American of German-Jewish descent who develops Monaco into a cultural centre with an opera, theatre and ballet under the direction of Russian impresario Sergei Diaghilev; 1899 visits the Kaiser in Berlin who assures him that Dreyfus had no contact with Germany; calls on President Faure to plead the case of Dreyfus. Offers Dreyfus the hospitality of Château Machais; welcomes Forzinetti and takes him into his service; 1909 becomes member of the British Academy of Sciences; 1911 grants Monaco a constitution; 1920 awarded the Gold Medal of the American Academy of Sciences. A staunch, loyal and devoted dreyfusard.

ANDRE, Louis-Joseph Nicholas (1838–1913)

Career soldier. General at the time of the Affair.

1900 appointed Minister of War; 1903 conducts a preliminary investigation after second appeal by Dreyfus for a revision; 1904 resigns; Republican and anti-clerical.

BALLOT-BEAUPRE, Jules Marie Claire Clément Alexis (1836–1917)

Judge.

1894 reporting judge at the Supreme Court of Appeal; 1899 President of the Criminal Chamber of the Supreme Court of Appeal; announces the annulment of the Rennes verdict; in favour of a revision.

BARRES, Maurice (1862–1923)

Author, journalist and politician.

1889 Boulangist Deputy for Nancy; 1894 founder, editor and contributor of anti-dreyfusard articles to the Boulangist paper *La Cocarde;* labels Dreyfus as Judas; 1898 founder member of the Ligue de la patrie française; rejects Léon Blum's approach to support Dreyfus; 1906 member of the Académie française; 1914 succeeds Déroulède as President of the Ligue des patriotes; as Deputy of Paris closely associated with Charles Maurras; member of L'Action française; fervent Nationalist, anti-dreyfusard and antisemite.

BASCH, Victor (1863–1944)

Professor, philosopher, humanitarian.

Born into a Hungarian Jewish family; 1866 moves with his family to France; 1881 studies German and philosophy at the Sorbonne; 1885 marries Ilona Furth in Budapest; 1887 naturalized French citizen; 1894–1899 staunch dreyfusard; 1887–1906 Professor of Aesthetics and Philosophy at Rennes University; 1912 engages in Zionist movement; 1926 elected President of the Ligue des droits de l'homme et du citoyen; 1937 denounces Nazism; 1940 moves with his wife to Lyon; 1944 murdered with his wife by the French Milice.

BASTIAN (Mme), née Marie-Caudron (1854–?)

Cleaning woman and agent for the Section de Statistique

Recruited by the Section de Statistique as an agent working under the pseudonym Auguste; 1889 becomes cleaner at the German Embassy in Paris and eventually *concierge* there; passes papers and fragments of documents found in wastepaper baskets at the embassy to the Deuxième Bureau (a procedure known as *la 'voie ordinaire'* or 'the normal route', generally considered to have led to the discovery of the *bordereau*); 1899 abruptly leaves her employment at the German Embassy.

BEAUREPAIRE, Jules Quesnay de (1837–1923)

Judge and journalist.

Prosecutor in the Boulanger case; involved in the Panama trials; 1896 appointed President of the Supreme Court of Appeal; attempts to involve the civil court in the Dreyfus Affair; active in the press campaign against the judges of the Criminal Chamber; anti-Socialist; committed anti-dreyfusard and anti-revisionist.

BERTILLON, Alphonse (1853–1914)

Criminologist.

Chief of the Identification Department at the Préfecture de Police in Paris; inventor of anthropometry, a method of identifying criminals; 1894 appointed by Mercier as expert graphologist to appraise authorship of the *bordereau*; elaborates a convoluted theory of self-forgery by Dreyfus to demonstrate his guilt; 1904 his system examined by experts including the mathematician Henri Poincaré and is considered absurd.

BILLOT, Jean-Baptiste (1828–1907*)*

Career soldier. General at the time of the Affair.

Graduate of the military academy of St-Cyr; 1871 elected to the Chamber as radical Republican; 1882 Minister of War; 1896 Minister of War in the Méline Cabinet; 1898 files suit against Zola after publication of 'J'Accuse'; opponent of the revision.

BLUM, Léon (1872–1950)

Statesman, politician and lawyer.

Under the influence of Jaurès becomes dreyfusard and Socialist; in conflict with Barrès over the Dreyfus Affair; collaborates with his brother René, co-founder of the pro-Dreyfus publication *La Revue Blanche*; 1936 becomes France's first Jewish and Socialist Prime Minister, forming the Front Populaire Government; 1938 Prime Minister between March and April; 1940 deported to Buchenwald; his brother René perishes in Auschwitz; 1946 Foreign Secretary in the first government of the Fourth Republic; Prime Minister for a third time between December 1946 and January 1947.

BOISDEFFRE, Raoul François Charles Le Mouton Néraud de (1839–1919)

Career soldier. General at the time of the Affair.

1879–80 French Ambassador to Russia; 1887 Brigadier-General; 1892 Major-General; 1893 Chief of the General Staff; ignores Picquart's insistence on the innocence of Dreyfus and protects his own subordinates; 1898 testifies for the army at Zola's trial; 1898 resigns on Henry's confession of forgery but remains confirmed anti-dreyfusard; 1899 testifies against Dreyfus at his second court martial at Rennes; devout Catholic; his confessor was the influential Jesuit Père du Lac.

BRISSON, Eugène Henri (1835–1912)

Politician.

1881 elected President of the Chamber of Deputies; 1885 Prime Minister; 1894 President of the Chamber; 1898 Minister of the Interior and then Prime Minister; approves and promotes the revision of the Dreyfus verdict following the discovery of the *faux Henry*; 1899 intervenes with Loubet to pardon Dreyfus; 1904 and 1906 President of the Chamber; Freemason; anti-clerical; Radical; promotes the Law of Amnesty.

BULOW, Bernhard Heinrich Martin Karl, Prince von (1849–1929)

German diplomat and statesman.

1894 German Ambassador to Rome; 1897 Secretary of State; supports strengthening of German navy; 1894 dissuades the Kaiser from involvement in the Dreyfus Affair; 1900–09 Chancellor and Prussian Prime Minister under Kaiser Wilhelm II; pursues policy of German aggrandisement; 1914 ambassador to Rome.

CASIMIR-PERIER, Jean Pierre Paul (1847–1907)

Statesman.

Graduate in Literature and Law; Infantry Captain; awarded the Croix de Guerre; 1893 Prime Minister; 1894 President of the Republic at the time of the arrest of Dreyfus; 1895 resigns; testifies at Zola's trial but does not disclose events which occurred during his presidency; 1899 testifies in Dreyfus' second court martial in Rennes, rejects the statements made by General Mercier.

CAVAIGNAC, Jacques Marie Eugène, known as Godefroy (1853–1905)

Politician.

1882 Deputy; 1885 Under-secretary for War; 1895 Colonial Secretary and Minister of the Navy; 1895 Minister of War; 1898 Minister of War; presents the *faux Henry* before the Chamber of Deputies as incontrovertible proof of the guilt of Dreyfus; Captain Cuignet, his secretary, discovers it is a forgery; orders Henry's arrest; resigns after Henry's sudden death but continues to oppose the revision; 1899 joins the Ligue de la patrie française; strongly anti-dreyfusard; cousin of du Paty du Clam; fervent Catholic; Père du Lac is his confessor and spiritual guide.

CLEMENCEAU, Georges Benjamin (1841–1929)

Statesman.

1865 medical studies in Paris; 1855 begins sojourns in England and the United States; 1870 Mayor of the 18th arrondissement; 1871 Radical Deputy for Paris; 1876 re-elected to the Chamber and becomes leader of the Radicals; 1880 founds the newspaper *La Justice*; opposes French colonial policy; anti-Boulangist; 1893 loses his seat following the Panama scandal and reverts to journalism to become an influential political writer; from 1894 onwards writes over 600 controversial pro-Dreyfus articles; 1897 editor of *L'Aurore* and campaigns for the revision of Dreyfus' verdict; 1898 *L'Aurore* publishes Zola's letter to the President, which Clemenceau entitles 'J'Accuse'; 1899 opposes acceptance of presidential pardon for Dreyfus; opposes the amnesty bill; 1902 elected Senator for the Var; 1904 Minister of the Interior; 1906 Prime Minister; appoints Picquart Minister of War; promotes separation of Church and State; 1917 called on by Raymond Poincaré to become Prime Minister; forms a Cabinet which leads France to victory over Germany in World War I; prominent figure at the Versailles Peace Conference; 1918 elected to the Académie française; 1920 loses presidential election and returns to writing career.

COMBES, Justin Louis Emile (1835–1921)

Politician.

1894 President of the Senate; 1902 Prime Minister; plays significant role in initiating final appeal for the revision of Dreyfus' verdict; 1903 promotes bill for the separation of Church and State, which passes a few months after his administration (1905). Anti-clerical, dreyfusard.

CUIGNET, Louis Benjamin Cornil (1857–1936)

Career soldier. Captain at the time of the Affair.

1893 appointed to the Quatrième Bureau of the General Staff; 1898 secretary to Cavaignac; instructed to examine the Secret Dossier; discovers the *faux Henry.* Anti-dreyfusard.

DAUDET Marie Alphonse Vincent Léon (1867–1942)

Journalist and novelist.

Son of the novelist Alphonse Daudet. Marries and later divorces the granddaughter of Victor Hugo; 1908 co-founder (with Charles Maurras) and editor of the right-wing daily L'*Action française.* Forceful critic of the Third Republic and democracy; 1919 elected Deputy; 1927 fails to win election. Fierce royalist, anti-dreyfusard and antisemite.

DEMANGE, Charles Gabriel Edgar (1841–1925)

Criminal lawyer.

1862 member of the Paris Bar; 1870 obtains acquittal of Prince Pierre Bonaparte, who killed the Republican Victor Noar; 1882 elected member of the Conseil de l'Ordre; 1892 defends the marquis de Morès in his trial for having killed Captain Mayer in a duel; 1894 Defends the anarchist writer Félix Fenéon; recommended by Waldeck-Rousseau as defence counsel for Dreyfus at his first court martial; tries in vain to lift the court ruling on a closed session; declares publicly after the verdict that he is convinced of the innocence of Dreyfus; convinces Scheurer-Kestner to reveal in the Senate information proving the innocence of Dreyfus; 1898 represents Mathieu Dreyfus at Esterhazy's court martial; 1899 Counsel for the Defence with Labori at the second court martial of Dreyfus in Rennes; 1919 re-elected member of the Conseil de l'Ordre, 1920 defends Joseph Caillaux, accused of espionage.

DEROULEDE, Paul (1846–1914)

> *Politician and Poet.*

> 1870 fights in the Franco-Prussian War; 1882 co-founder and head of the Ligue des patriotes; supporter of General Boulanger; 1889 elected Deputy; 1890 member of the Paris Bar; 1898 re-elected deputy; 1899 attempts *coup d'état* during the funeral of President Faure which fails; plans major demonstration at Rennes court martial but is arrested the previous night; 1900 sentenced to ten years' exile; from his exile in Spain continues to animate the Ligue des patriotes, founds its daily *Le Drapeau*; 1905 returns to France after he is granted an amnesty. Ultra-Nationalist and prominent anti-dreyfusard.

DREYFUS, Alfred (1859–1935)

> *Career soldier. Captain at the time of the Affair.*

> Born in Mulhouse, Alsace, into an assimilationist Jewish family; 1878 enters the Ecole polytechnique; 1882 promoted lieutenant; 1889 captain; 1890 enters Ecole de guerre; 1890 marries Lucie Hadamard; 1891 birth of son Pierre; 1893 birth of daughter Jeanne; 1893 becomes probationary officer on the General Staff at the Ministry of War – the only Jewish officer there; 1894 arrested and charged with delivering secret military documents to Germany; declared guilty by court martial; 1895 publicly degraded and deported to Devil's Island for term of life imprisonment; 1899 returned to France for second court martial in Rennes and again found guilty; pardoned; 1906 guilty verdict quashed; rehabilitated and re-integrated into the army; awarded the Legion of Honour; 1914 appointed second in command of the Artillery of the Northern Zone of the Paris Defences; requests to be sent to the front; commands the Artillery depot of the 168th Division attached to the 20th Corps; participates in the Battle of the Chemin de Dames; 1917 the 20th Corps relieves the 7th including the battery of '75's' commanded by his son Pierre; serves in World War I and fights in the battle of Verdun with his son Pierre; serves at headquarters; promoted to lieutenant-colonel and to Officer of the Legion of Honour. Leads secluded life. 1935 buried in the Jewish section of the cemetery of Montparnasse; 1988 his grave is desecrated.

DREYFUS, Lucie (1869–1945)

> *Wife of Alfred*

> Born Lucie Hadamard into a traditional Jewish family; an observant Jewess devoted to biblical study and prayer; accomplished pianist; 1890 marries Alfred Dreyfus; bears two children, Pierre and Jeanne; displays unshakeable loyalty to her husband and exhibits formidable strength of character throughout the Affair; serves as volunteer nurse in the Saint Louis hospital, Paris during World War I; in hiding during World War II; works for Jewish charitable causes.

DREYFUS, Mathieu (1857–1930)

> *Industrialist. Alfred's older brother*

> 1894 relinquishes responsibility in the family firm in Mulhouse to his brothers Jacques and Léon in order to devote himself to the rehabilitation of his brother; 1895 meets Bernard Lazare; 1896 denounces Esterhazy as the author of the *bordereau*; 1899 persuades Dreyfus, as a result of his physical and mental state, to accept a pardon after the second Rennes verdict.

DREYFUS, Pierre (1891–1946) **and Jeanne** (1893–1981)

> *Children of Alfred and Lucie Dreyfus.*

Pierre serves as captain in World War I and is decorated with the Croix de Guerre; marries Marie Baur, with whom he has four children; Jeanne marries Pierre Paul Lévy with whom she has four children; her daughter Madeleine is arrested in World War II as both a Jewess and member of the Resistance; she is interned in Drancy concentration camp and deported from there to Auschwitz, where she perishes in 1944. She shares a headstone with Alfred Dreyfus in the cemetery of Montparnasse in Paris.

DRUMONT, Edouard Adolphe (1844–1917)

> *Antisemitic activist and writer.*

Popularly known as the Pope of Antisemitism; employed by the Prefecture of Police; works for the Jewish bank Pereire but is dismissed for embezzlement; from 1870 becomes active in satirical journalism; criticizes the admission of Jewish officers into the army; 1886 writes *La France Juive*, a violent anti-Jewish diatribe which ignites French political antisemitism; further similar publications follow; 1890 founds la Ligue nationale antisémitique française; 1892 launches the newspaper *La Libre Parole* subtitled *La France aux Français* purchased from his confessor Père du Lac; launches a campaign against Jews in the army; 1894 publishes first news item on the arrest of Dreyfus justifying his stand against Jews in the French Army; continues violent antisemitic and anti-dreyfusard campaign throughout the Affair in *La Libre Parole*; 1898 elected Deputy for Algiers following the city's antisemitic riots; declares himself leader of the Anti-Jewish Party, supported but later challenged by similar movements, overtaken by the daily *L'Action française*, first published in 1908; 1902 appointed honorary president of the Partie nationale antijuif and then of the Fédération nationale antijuive. His fame revives during World War II and Vichy officials pay homage to him at his graveside.

DU PATY *see* PATY de CLAM

DUPUY, Charles Alexandre (1851–1923)

> *Politician.*

1893 Prime Minister; 1894 Prime Minister at the moment the *bordereau* is discovered. Does not follow Hanotaux's warning and agrees to the arrest of Dreyfus; 1895 collapse of his government; 1898 elected Prime Minister again; 1899 supports the Law of Dispossession which is passed during his administration, delaying the revision of the Dreyfus case; protects the army's reputation. Maintains a moderate position; 1899 collapse of his government, replaced by Waldeck-Rousseau.

ESTERHAZY, Marie Charles Ferdinand Walsin (assumes title of Count) (1847–1923)

> *Career soldier. Major at the time of the Affair.*

Son of General Walsin Esterhazy, an illegitimate descendant of the illustrious Esterhazy family; 1865 studies law in Paris; 1866 fails entry examination for St-Cyr military academy; 1868 joins the Papal Zouaves; 1869 2nd Lieutenant; 1870 joins the Foreign Legion; participates in the Franco-Prussian War; 1874 aide-de-camp to General Grenier; speculates on the stock market; 1877 joins the Deuxième Bureau as German translator; meets Henry; 1880 participates in the Tunisian campaign; 1881 becomes lover of his cousin Mme de Boulancy; 1882 meets Sandherr in Tunisia and is frequently in the company of Prince von Bülow there; 1886 marries Anne, daughter of the marquis de Nettancourt; Major in 74th Infantry Regiment; continuing financial difficulties;

1894 beginning of contact with German Embassy and Schwartzkoppen; 1895 meets Marguerite Pays; 1897 denounced by Mathieu Dreyfus as author of the *bordereau*; 1898 acquitted by court martial of treason; discharged after discovery of the *faux Henry* and flees to England; accused by his cousin Christian of fraud and arrested; 1899 condemned, *in absentia*, to three years in prison; declares having written the *bordereau* under Sandherr's orders; 1903–06 London correspondent of *La Libre Parole*; lived in Harpenden, Hertfordshire, until his death under the alias Count Jean de Voilemont.

FAURE, Félix François (1841–1899)

Statesman.

Wealthy businessman in Le Havre; 1881 elected Radical Deputy for the Seine-Inférieur; 1894 Minister of the Navy; 1895 President of the Republic; consolidates the Franco-Russian alliance; reveals existence of the Secret Dossier to Dr Gibert and then Mathieu; 1898 becomes less hostile to a revision; 1899 Nationalist demonstrations at his state funeral. Anti-dreyfusard and at first hostile to revision.

FLEG, Edmond (pseudonym of E. Flegenheimer) (1874–1963)

Poet, author and playwright.

Born in Geneva into a Jewish family; educated at the Ecole normale supérieure in Paris; his assimilationist tendencies reverse during the Dreyfus Affair; becomes aware of his Jewish heritage and espouses the cause of Dreyfus and then Zionism; author of moving works on the subject of Jewish identity; 1943/44 Fleg and his wife sought by the Gestapo and live in hiding.

FORZINETTI, Ferdinand Dominique (1839–1909)

Prison administrator.

1894 Governor of Cherche-Midi military prison where Alfred Dreyfus is imprisoned; convinced of the innocence of Dreyfus and informs the General Staff accordingly; active in bringing about a revision; 1896 supports Bernard Lazare in publication of his pamphlet; 1897 relieved of his duties; Prince Albert of Monaco takes him into his service; publishes an account of Dreyfus' captivity in *Le Figaro*, accusing du Paty du Clam of maltreating Dreyfus. Committed dreyfusard.

FRANCE, Anatole François Thibault (1844–1924)

Poet and novelist.

1896 elected member of the Académie française; vigorous defender of both Dreyfus and Zola; 1898 signs the petition of the intellectuals and refuses to wear the decoration of the Legion of Honour after Zola was struck off; famous oration at Zola's funeral describing him as a 'moment in the conscience of mankind'; several of his works relate closely to the Affair; 1904 appointed to the central committee of the Ligue des droits de l'homme et du citoyen; 1921 awarded Nobel Prize for Literature.

GALLIFFET, Gaston Alexandre Auguste de (1830–1909)

Career soldier. General at the time of the Affair.

1871 earns reputation for brutality in the repression of the Paris Commune; 1899 Minister of War; proposes a presidential pardon for Dreyfus; promotes the amnesty bill; 1900 resigns; ardent Republican.

GONSE, Charles Arthur (1838–1917)

> *Career soldier. General at time of the Affair.*

1893 Deputy head of the General Staff directly in charge of the Denxième Bureau; 1894 charges du Paty with examining the *bordereau*; 1896 instructs Picquart to separate the Esterhazy and Dreyfus affairs; attempts to dissuade Picquart from investigating Esterhazy; removes Picquart from his post as head of intelligence; covers up Henry's machinations; involved in all the intrigues of the Dreyfus Affair; 1898 after Henry's death transferred to reserve duty; tries to clear the name of Esterhazy; 1903 retires from army; 1906 fights duel with Picquart. One of the army's typical anti-dreyfusards.

GRIBELIN, Félix

> *Archivist.*

Archivist in the Section de Statistique, at the Ministry of War; 1894 present at the handwriting test of Dreyfus; involved in the General Staff's various manoeuvres against Dreyfus; participates in the parc Montsouris meetings with Esterhazy; on Henry's instruction falsifies the account books held at the Section de Statistique; testifies against Picquart; loyal to his superiors.

GUERIN, Jules Napoléon (1860–1910)

> *Antisemitic agitator. Political activist.*

1897 Revives the Ligue antisémitique de France founded by Drumont in 1890 and becomes its flamboyant leader; 1898 founds the weekly *L'Antijuif* ('the Anti-Jew'); masterminds street violence with his gangs known as 'the people's army'; receives financial support from the duc d'Orléans; 1899 participates in Déroulède's *coup d'état* at the time of Félix Faure's funeral; establishes headquarters at Fort Chabrol, Paris; to avoid arrest, barricades himself in the Fort Chabrol but surrenders after a 38-day siege by the police; 1900 sentenced to 10 years' imprisonment; released after five years. Committed antisemite and Royalist.

GUYOT, Yves (1843–1928)

> *Journalist and politician.*

Appointed to the Rennes Bar; establishes Radical paper *Le Droit de l'Homme*; 1885 Municipal Counsellor for Paris; opposes Boulangism; 1885 Deputy for the Seine; 1890 Minister of Public Works; 1892 political editor of *Le Siècle*; 1898 serializes in his paper *Lettres d'un Innocent*, the letters of Dreyfus from Devil's Island to Lucie; 1898 attempts to obtain adjournment of the case against Picquart; demands proceedings against Mercier; prominent and active dreyfusard.

HANOTAUX, Gabriel (1853–1944)

> *Statesman and historian.*

1886 Deputy; 1894/1896/1898 Foreign Secretary; 1897 member of the Académie française; 1894 opposes arrest of Dreyfus; 1898 informs the Government of the German and Italian denials of any dealing with Dreyfus.

HENRY, Hubert Joseph (1846–1898)

> *Career soldier. Major (later Lieutenant-Colonel) at the time of the Affair.*

Son of a farmer; 1865 volunteers for the army; passes through the ranks and is commissioned 2nd Lieutenant; 1870 wounded in the Franco-Prussian war; 1874 Lieutenant; 1876 aide-de-camp to General Miribele, Chief of the General Staff;

1877 appointed to the Section de Statistique, where he becomes acquainted with Esterhazy; 1879 Captain; 1884 posted to Oran; awarded the Croix de Guerre; 1887 posted to Tonkin and cited for bravery; 1890 Major; 1893 engaged at the Section de Statistique under Sandherr; 1894 intercepts the *bordereau* and participates in manoeuvres against Dreyfus; gives false testimony at the first court martial of Dreyfus; 1895 officer of the Legion of Honour; hostile to Picquart's appointment to Sandherr's former post; becomes central figure in the intrigues of the army against Dreyfus and helps to compile the Secret Dossier against him; 1896 fabricates the *faux Henry*; 1897 Lieutenant-Colonel; 1898 confesses his forgeries to Cavaignac during intensive interrogation; found dead with his throat cut in his cell at Mont Valérien prison the following day.

HERR, Lucien (1864–1926)

Literary figure.

Born in Alsace; 1888 Chief Librarian at the Ecole normale supérieure; profound knowledge of German philosophy; influenced a whole generation of young Socialists at the time of the Affair, including Charles Péguy and Léon Blum, and his home in the rue de Val de Gras, Paris became a forum of intellectual and liberal discussion; an early contributor to the paper *L'Humanité*; signed many petitions in favour of the revision and was one of the first Socialists to engage openly in support of Dreyfus.

HERZL, Theodor Benjamin Ze'ev (1860–1904)

Journalist, playwright, Zionist political leader.

Born in Budapest; educated in Vienna; degree in law; holds Jewish assimilationist views; correspondent of the Austrian newspaper *Neue Freie Presse* in Paris; 1895 witnesses degradation ceremony of Dreyfus in Paris and becomes convinced of the need for a Jewish homeland; 1896 publishes *Judenstadt*, elaborating the concept of a Jewish State; 1897 organizes First Zionist Congress in Basel; 1898 Second Zionist Congress with focus on the Dreyfus Affair; 1899 attends the Rennes court martial; 1901 continues negotiations for the establishment of a Jewish State; 1904 dies in Vienna; 1943 his daughter Trude and her husband Richard Neumann perish in Theresienstadt; 1949 Herzl's remains are transferred to the State of Israel, in accordance with his wishes; his tomb is situated on Mount Herzl, near Jerusalem.

HOHENLOHE, Clovis Charles Victor, Prince de Schillingfürst (1819–1901)

German statesman and Imperial Chancellor.

Enters Prussian diplomatic service; 1843 Referendar; 1845 Prince of Hohenlohe-Schillingfürst; 1846 member of Bavarian Reichstag: 1866 head of Foreign Office.

JAURES, Jean Léon (1859–1914)

Statesman, journalist, historian. Leading French Socialist.

Born in Castres; son of a farmer; brilliant student at the Ecole normale supérieur; Professor of Philosophy; 1885 Socialist Deputy for the Tarn; 1893 defends miners in the Carmaux strike; elected Deputy for Carmaux; 1894 hostile to Socialist involvement in the Affair; convinced by Bernard Lazare of the innocence of Dreyfus, becomes a prominent dreyfusard critical of the Government's attitude; 1898 demands indictment of Mercier; loses his seat in the elections due to his support for Dreyfus; becomes political editor of *La Petite République*; publishes *Les Preuves*, a series of articles demolishing the charges against Dreyfus; 1903 spearheads campaign in the Chamber of Deputies for a second revision of the Dreyfus case; 1904 founds the daily *L'Humanité;* fights for the separation of the Church and State; 1914 assassinated by the fanatic Raoul Villain, a member of L'Action française who considered Jaurès a traitor.

LABORI, Fernand (1860–1917)

> *Criminal lawyer.*

1880 enters Paris Law school; 1884 admitted to the Bar; editor in chief of *La Gazette de Paris*; 1894 defends the anarchist Auguste Vaillant; 1897 founds literary review *La Revue du Palais*; 1898 represents Lucie Dreyfus at the Esterhazy court martial; defends Zola; defends Picquart; 1899 represents Reinach in the suit brought against him by Mme Henry; with Demange represents Dreyfus at his second court martial in Rennes; shot and wounded there in an assassination attempt; in continuous conflict with the President of the Court; in disagreement with Demange; opposes Dreyfus' acceptance of a presidential pardon; breaks off relations with the Dreyfus family; opposes the Law of Amnesty; 1906 elected independent Deputy; supports first Clemenceau Government; strongly favours devolution of ecclesiastical property and elimination of courts martial; 1911 President of the Bar; 1914 obtains acquittal of Mme Caillaux, the assassin of Joseph Calmette; director of *Le Figaro.* Warmly received in England and North America.

LAC de FUGERE, Stanislas du, known as Père du Lac (1835–1909)

> *Jesuit priest.*

Of noble descent; 1853 enters the novitiate at the Society of Jesus in Alsace; 1869 studies theology at Laval; ordained priest; 1870 Rector of the Collège Sainte-Croix, Mans; 1871 Rector of the Ecole St-Geneviève in the rue des Postes in the Quartier Latin (Paris), an institution preparing candidates (known as Postards) for the great military academies of France; teaches students to be fearless Catholics; 1880 founds St Mary's College, Canterbury, England; 1889 continues as preacher and spiritual guide in Paris and in France; a powerful and mysterious figure in the higher echelons of the army; father-confessor to Boisdeffre, Cavaignac and other senior army officers, as well as Drumont. Considered by many to play a covert but influential role in the Dreyfus Affair.

LAUTH, Jules Maximilien

> *Career officer. Captain at the time of the Affair.*

1893 serves in the Section de Statistique; close friend of Henry; collaborates with Henry, Gribelin and du Paty in intrigues against Dreyfus and Picquart following Guenée's false reports. Untruthful and fanatical antisemite.

LAZARE, (BERNARD-LAZARE), Lazare Marcus Manassé Bernard, known as Bernard-Lazare (1865–1903)

> *Writer and journalist.*

Born in Nîmes of Jewish parentage; 1890 involved in anarchist and symbolist circles; 1890 begins to publish on antisemitism; 1895 meets Mathieu Dreyfus and becomes one of the first dreyfusards; 1896 in dispute with Drumont; publishes in the paper *Le Voltaire*; fights a duel with Drumont; writes the influential *Une erreur judiciaire* claiming to prove the innocence of Dreyfus; Castelain seeks to indict him but Méline refuses; 1897 publishes second edition of *Une erreur judiciaire*; in later years involved in Zionism; Charles Péguy described his participation in the Affair as 'pure'; 1908 monument erected in his honour in Nîmes which was demolished by the Germans during World War II.

LEBLOIS, Henry Louis (1854–1928)

Lawyer.

Son of a pastor; schoolfriend of Picquart at the Lycée of Strasbourg; 1871 studies law in Paris; 1878 member of the Bar; 1880 deputy public prosecutor in Dijon and then Nancy; 1890 leaves judiciary to act as a lawyer; 1897 Picquart confides to him his discoveries concerning Esterhazy and entrusts him with documents relating to the intrigues of the General Staff against him; passes information to Scheurer-Kestner with whom he is friendly; becomes committed dreyfusard and battles for revision of Dreyfus' verdict; discharged from his post as Deputy Mayor of the 7th arrondissement in Paris; suspended by the Association of Barristers for six months; Cavaignac launches a suit against him; becomes advisor to Jaurès and Clemenceau; 1903 supports Jaurès for a second revision; makes financial contribution to *L'Aurore* to foster Clemenceau's political career; 1929 his monumental work on the Dreyfus Affair, *L'Affaire Dreyfus, l'iniquité, la réparation*, is published posthumously.

LOUBET, Emile (1838–1929)

Lawyer, politician.

Doctor of Law; Mayor of Montélimar 1876 Deputy of the Drôme; joins Republican movement; 1892 Prime Minister; 1896 President of the Senate; 1899 President of the Third Republic; demonstration against his presidency by the Ligue des patriotes; 1899 attacked and insulted at the Auteuil races; signs decree pardoning Dreyfus and calls for an amnesty on all proceedings relating to the Affair; 1900 champions Universal Exhibition in Paris; pursues rapprochement with Italy and the Entente Cordiale with England; 1906 retires.

MAURRAS, Charles Marie Photius (1868–1952)

Journalist, writer. Political activist.

Born in Martignes into a Catholic, monarchist milieu; 1885 arrives in Paris; 1888 journalist; 1892 contributes articles to the Royalist *Gazette de France*; 1894 collaborates with Maurice Barrès; takes firm anti-dreyfusard position; 1898 after the death of Henry, describes the *faux Henry* as a 'patriotic forgery' in his famous article 'Le Premier Sang'; 1908 becomes leading voice of Action française; 1926 condemnation of Maurras and l'Action française by the Pope; 1941 key supporter of the Vichy regime and its antisemitic policies; 1945 arrested and sentenced to death; commuted to life imprisonment and deprivation of civil liberties. Prominent figure of the French Right.

MELINE, Félix Jules (1838–1925)

Politician.

1896 Minister of Agriculture, Prime Minister; 1897 claims that there is no Dreyfus Affair and that Dreyfus was properly and justly condemned; anxious not to antagonise the army but after the death of Henry supports the revision; moderate Republican.

MERCIER, Auguste (1833–1921)

> *Career soldier. General at the time of the Affair.*

Trains at the Ecole polytechnique; takes part in the Mexican campaign and later in the Franco-Prussian War; 1883 Colonel; 1885 General; 1889 director of administrative services in the army; 1893 Minister of War; 1894 personally responsible for the arrest, court martial and conviction of Dreyfus as well as the illegal transmission of documents to the judges at his court martial; vigorous anti-dreyfusard and opposed to any revision; 1898 retires from the army; 1900 Senator; 1906 opposes the bill to rehabilitate Dreyfus; 1907 awarded the Médaille d'Or by L'Action française for his stand in the Affair; staunch Republican.

MIRBEAU, Octave (1848–1917)

> *Journalist, novelist and dramatist.*

Attends Jesuit school of Vannes, pupil of Père du Lac; 1866 studies law in Paris; begins to write for *L'illustration* (supports the Impressionists); 1877 secretary to the Prefect of Police in Ariège; publishes articles in *Le Figaro, Le Matin* and later *L'Aurore*; 1894 acquires strong dreyfusard commitments, writes numerous pro-Dreyfus articles; 1899 undertakes vigorous campaign in favour of revision; 1899 is author of moving preface to *L'Hommage des Artistes à Picquart*; considers the Affair to have been the result of a Jesuit plot. Vigorous and active dreyfusard.

MORNARD, Henry (1859–?)

> *Criminal lawyer at the Supreme Court of Appeal.*

1898 supports Zola's appeal against his verdict; supports the appeal of Lucie Dreyfus to the Ministry of Justice for the annulment of the 1894 verdict; 1898 asked by Mathieu Dreyfus to assist Demange; represents Dreyfus in the hearings of his first and second appeals before the Supreme Court of Appeal.

MUNSTER, Georges de (1821–1902)

> *German Diplomat.*

Born and educated in England; 1867 Conservative Liberal in the Reichstag of North Germany; 1871 Deputy at German Reichstag; 1873 ambassador to London; 1885 ambassador to Paris; 1894 initially unaware of Schwartzkoppen's dealings with Esterhazy; 1900 dismissed from his post as ambassador in Paris and takes early retirement; improves Franco-German relations; Anglophile.

ORLEANS, Louis Philippe Robert duc d' (1869–1926)

> *Pretender to the French throne during the Third Republic.*

Born in England, the eldest son of Louis Philippe Albert, Count of Paris and great-grandson of Louis Philippe; 1886 banished from France as a threat to the Republican regime; 1890 returns to France, arrested, imprisoned and later exiled; 1894 after the death of his father, he is recognized by French royalists as the rightful king; 1898 supporter and financier of Jules Guérin and his 'people's army'; 1914 refused permission to serve in French or allied armies.

ORMESCHEVILLE, Bexon d'

> *Career soldier. Major at the time of the Affair.*

1894 conducts first judicial investigation into allegations against Dreyfus; recommends a court martial; his report serves as the indictment of Dreyfus; reporting judge at the court martial of Dreyfus.

PALEOLOGUE, Georges Maurice (1859–1944)

> *Diplomat and author.*

1880 enters the Foreign Office; posted to the political department; diplomatic missions to Italy, Morocco, China and Korea; 1894–1899 follows Dreyfus Affair at close quarters; 1906 appointed French Minister in Sofia; 1914 French Ambassador to St Petersburg; 1920 Foreign Secretary; 1928 member of the Académie française; his insights into the Affair are published in *Journal de l'Affaire Dreyfus 1894–1899. L'affaire Dreyfus et le Quai d'Orsay.*

PATY de CLAM, Armand Auguste Charles Ferdinand Marie Mercier, marquis du (1853–1916)

> *Career soldier. Lieutenant-Colonel at the time of the Affair.*

Graduate of St-Cyr and the Ecole d'état major; cousin of Cavaignac; enters the army during the Franco-Prussian War, at the age of 17; 1894 officer on the General Staff and deputy head of the Troisième Bureau at the Ministry of War; in the capacity of criminal police officer he is charged with the preliminary investigation of Dreyfus; conceives theatrical scenarios to entrap Dreyfus (the handwriting test, disguises and meetings at the parc Montsouris, etc.); writes commentary on the Secret Dossier; involved in intrigues between Esterhazy and the General Staff; 1899 arrested and imprisoned in Cherche-Midi but discharged for lack of evidence; 1905 takes compulsory retirement; 1914 resumes active service during World War I and fights courageously in a regiment commanded by one of his sons; awarded Legion of Honour; 1916 dies of war wounds; his son becomes head of the Secretariat of Jewish Affairs in Vichy in 1943.

PEGUY, Charles (1873–1914)

> *Poet and humanitarian writer.*

Born into poverty and educated by his mother; 1894 wins scholarship and enters the Ecole normale supérieure in Paris; 1895 espouses Socialism as the means to overcome poverty; abandons Roman Catholicism but remains deeply religious; 1896 alerted by Herr and Monod of the irregularities of the court martial of Dreyfus, and enters the Dreyfus camp in the name of Socialism, idealism and anti-militarism; his library in the rue Cousin becomes the centre for the young dreyfusards of the Latin Quarter, Paris; 1900 begins publication of *Cahiers de la Quinzaine*; publishes *Notre Jeunesse,* a recollection of the Dreyfus Affair; writes for *La Revue Socialiste* and *La Revue Blanche*; dies in World War I in the first battle of the Marne.

PELLIEUX, Georges Gabriel de (1842–1900)

> *Career soldier. General at the time of the Affair.*

Military Commander of the Département de la Seine; 1897 conducts judicial investigation of Esterhazy and concludes there are no grounds on which to charge him; at Zola's trial refers to the *faux Henry* and thereby weakens the arguments of the General Staff; resigns after Henry's confession but withdraws his resignation; 1899 dismissed by the Minister of War and posted to Quimper in Brittany.

PERRENX, Alexander (1842–1900)

> *Journalist, editor.*

> Manager of the dreyfusard daily *L'Aurore*; 1898 publishes Zola's 'J'Accuse'; prosecuted with Zola and defended by Albert Clemenceau; sentenced to four months in prison and a fine of 3000 francs.

PICQUART, Marie Georges (1854–1914)

> *Career soldier. Major (later Lieutenant-Colonel) at the time of the Affair.*

> Born in Strasbourg into a distinguished family of magistrates and soldiers; school friend of Leblois; 1872 enters St-Cyr military academy; 1874 enters the Ecole de guerre; 1878 sees active duty in Africa; 1885 fights in the Tonkin War and promoted to major; 1890 appointed to the Ecole supérieure de guerre teaching topography where Alfred Dreyfus was one of his students; attached to the General Staff of General de Galliffet; 1894 participates in the investigation of the *bordereau*; attends the court martial and degradation of Dreyfus; 1895 succeeds Sandherr as head of the Section de Statistique; eventually convinced of Esterhazy's guilt; 1896 in conflict with his superior officers and sent away first to Eastern France and then Tunisia; 1897 increasingly involved in the Dreyfus investigations; 1898 relieved of his duties and arrested; incarcerated at La Santé prison and then at Cherche-Midi; 1899 the case against him is dismissed; Reinach labels him '*une conscience*'; 1906 fights duel with Gonse; reintegrated into the army with the rank of Brigadier-General; promoted to Major-General; Minister of War in the Clemenceau Government; 1910 transferred to reserve duty in charge of 2nd Army Corps; 1914 killed in a riding accident; is given a state funeral. An outstanding officer who, although exhibiting antisemitic traits, fought fiercely for justice; intellectually gifted; a polyglot, accomplished musician and pianist; friend of Gustav Mahler.

PRESSENSE, Francis Charles Dehault de (1853–1914)

> *Journalist. Politician.*

> Son of the eminent Protestant pastor Edmond de Pressensé; 1879 secretary at the French Embassy in Constantinople, then Washington; 1897 contributes to *L'Aurore*; 1898 after Zola's trial becomes an ardent dreyfusard, rejects his Legion of Honour decoration on hearing that Zola is stricken from the list; dedicates book to Picquart entitled *Un Héros*; 1902 Socialist Deputy for Lyon; 1903 succeeds Trarieux as President of the Ligue des droits de l'homme et du citoyen; close to Jaurès, one of the artisans of the Law of separation of Church and State; devoted pacifist in the years before World War I.

RAVARY, Alexander-Alfred (?–1913)

> *Career soldier. Major at time of Affair.*

> 1894 reporting judge at the first court martial of Dreyfus; 1897 appointed by General Saussier to conduct investigation of Esterhazy; his report absolves Esterhazy and accuses Picquart.

REGIS, Max (Massimiliano Milano) (1873–1950)

> *Political activist. Antisemitic agitator.*

> Son of Italian immigrant; studies Law in Algiers; expelled for agitation against Professor Levy; 1897 founds the journal *L'Antijuif* in Algiers; 1898 becomes president of the Ligue antisémite d'Alger; invites Drumont to represent Algiers

in forthcoming elections; arrested for incitement to murder; acquitted; elected Mayor of Algiers; suspended and arrested for undemocratic conduct; 1899 attends the Rennes court martial; organises an Algerian Fort Chabrol; flees to Spain; 1900 re-elected Counsellor for Algiers.

REINACH, Joseph (1856–1921)

Writer, lawyer, historian, politician.

Born into a Jewish family, son of a banker; studies Law; writes for Gambetta's *La République*; 1881 principal private secretary in Gambetta's Ministry; secretary of the Ligue des patriotes but breaks with the organization to fight Boulangism; 1889 Deputy for Digne in the Basses-Alpes; 1894 prominent supporter of Dreyfus and convinced of his innocence; writes in *Le Siècle*; intervenes with President Casimir-Perrier against a closed session at the court martial of Dreyfus; 1897 collaborates with Scheurer-Kestner for a revision; arouses violent criticism in the Nationalist press; 1898 loses his seat in the Chamber of Deputies and is stripped of his rank in the Territorial Army; sued by Mme Henry following his accusation that Henry was in league with Esterhazy; accused and vilified by the antisemitic press; 1902 defeated in elections; 1906 re-elected Deputy for Digne; 1901–1911 his monumental *Histoire de l'Affaire Dreyfus* is published; 1912 his son Adolphe marries Margaret Dreyfus, daughter of Mathieu; 1914 he chronicles World War 1 for *Le Figaro*; 1914 his son Adolphe is killed in battle. Supported by his brothers Théodore and Salomon in his loyalty to Dreyfus.

SANDHERR, Jean Robert Conrad Auguste (1846–1897)

Career soldier. Colonel at the time of the Affair.

Born in Mulhouse into a Protestant family but converts to Catholicism. Receives strongly antisemitic education; 1866 graduates at St-Cyr; 1868 enters the Ecole de guerre; 1894 appointed head of the Section de Statistique; fervent antisemite.

SAUSSIER, Félix Gustave (1828–1905)

Career officer. General at the time of the Affair.

Bachelor and *bon vivant*; 1884 Military Governor of Paris; 1894 advises Mercier not to pursue Dreyfus but eventually signs the order to prosecute him; refuses permission for Rabbi Zadok Kahn to visit Dreyfus in prison; 1897 instructs Ravary to prosecute Esterhazy; the wife of Maurice Weil is assumed to be his mistress.

SCHEURER-KESTNER, Auguste (1839–1899)

Politician.

Born in Mulhouse into a Protestant family of industrialists; studies in Strasbourg under the mathematician pastor Leblois, father of Louis; pursues scientific studies in Paris; 1862 sentenced to a four-month prison term for Republican propaganda; 1867 participates in the Geneva International Congress for Peace under the presidency of Victor Hugo; 1870 in charge of pyrotechnic installation in Sètes; on the outbreak of the Franco-Prussian War takes over from his father-in-law as head of the Kestner factory; 1871 elected Republican Deputy for the Haut-Rhin; elected Deputy for the Seine in tribute to Alsace-Lorraine, annexed by Germany; 1875 Senator for life; 1879 through his friendship with Gambetta becomes political editor of *La République Française* and with Clemenceau establishes L'Union Républicaine; 1895 Vice-President of the

Senate; approached by Mathieu Dreyfus; begins to gather information on the Affair; espouses the Dreyfus cause after Leblois relates Picquart's information; campaigns vigorously for a revision; slandered by the Nationalists; persuades Zola to join the Dreyfus camp; 1897 publishes a letter in *Le Temps* indicating that new facts have come to light confirming the innocence of Dreyfus; 1898 fails to be re-elected as Vice-President of the Senate; assists in the presidential pardon of Dreyfus; dies on the day of the pardon; 1908 a monument is erected in his honour in the Jardins du Luxembourg. Recognized as a moral authority in the field of politics.

SCHWARTZKOPPEN, Maximilien von (1850–1917)

Career soldier. Colonel at the time of the Affair.

Born in Potsdam; 1868 joins Sixth Infantry Regiment of Westphalia; 1870 participates in the Franco-Prussian War; 1882 Captain on the General Staff; 1888 Major; 1891 military attaché at the German Embassy in Paris; 1893 Lieutenant-Colonel; 1894 first contact with Esterhazy; 1897 full Colonel; 1897 leaves Paris; 1907 General; 1908 retires from the army; 1916 returns to the army and commands 20th Infantry Division in World War I; suffers war wounds; 1917 dies at l'Hôpital Elizabeth in Berlin; in his diary (published posthumously) he declares the innocence of Dreyfus.

STOCK, Pierre-Victor (1861–1943)

Publisher.

1877 chairman of Stock, the French publishing house; gains reputation as the leading publisher of the Dreyfus Affair; publishes numerous pamphlets, brochures and books on the Affair; staunch dreyfusard.

TORNIELLI-BRUSSATI, Giuseppe di Vergano (1836–1908)

Italian Ambassador to France during the Affair.

Born in Novara. Studies Law in Turin. 1859 embarks on diplomatic career. 1860 attaché in Constantinople; 1863 attaché in St Petersburg; 1864 attaché in Athens; 1869 in charge of Political Affairs in the Foreign Ministry; 1876 General Secretary of the Foreign Ministry; 1879 Senator; 1887 ambassador to Madrid; 1889 ambassador to London; 1894 ambassador to Paris during the Affair. Repeatedly states publicly, to Hanotaux and Trarieux, that Dreyfus has no relations with Italy. Believes in Dreyfus' innocence.

TRARIEUX, Ludovic (1840–1904)

Lawyer and politician

1877 President of the Bar of Bordeaux; 1897 Republican Senator; 1895 Minister of Justice before the Affair; fights ardently for revision; 1898 founder of the Ligue des droits de l'homme et du citoyen and its first president until 1903. Continues to fight until his death for Dreyfus' rehabilitation, which he does not live to see. Early and loyal dreyfusard.

VAL CARLOS, Raimundo Guell y Borbon, marquis de (1849–?)

1894 attaché at the Spanish Embassy in Paris;

Born in France to a Catalan family; 1863 enters military college in Valladolid. 1867 Second-lieutenant; 1876 Captain, second military attaché at the Spanish

Embassy in Paris; 1885 Captain; 1890 Chevalier of the Legion of Honour; 1894 an undercover agent of the Section de Statistique reporting to former police officer Guénée, Henry's 'right-hand man'. His statements are falsified by Guénée, included in the Secret Dossier to incriminate Dreyfus and used by Henry as a basis of his false testimony at Dreyfus' first court martial. The exact terms of his 'employment' by the Section de Statistique remain a subject of controversy. Val Carlos consistently denied being on the payroll of the Section de Statistique.

WALDECK-ROUSSEAU, Pierre René (1846–1904)

Lawyer and statesman.

Born in Nantes. Elected to the Bar of Rennes; 1879 elected Deputy for Rennes; 1881 appointed by Clemenceau Minister of the Interior; 1883 establishes the Grand Cercle Républicain; 1894 Senator for La Loire; 1894 advises Mathieu to engage Demange for the defence of Dreyfus at his first court martial; 1899 elected Prime Minister, tables law in favour of Picquart's case; helps negotiate pardon for Dreyfus after the Rennes court martial; imposes authority of the Republic on the leagues and religious associations.

WILHELM II, (Frederick Wilhelm Viktor Albert of Hohenzollern) (1859–1941)

Kaiser Wilhelm II. German Emperor and King of Prussia.

Nephew of Queen Victoria; 1890 dismisses Bismarck and embarks on personal rule, adopting warlike attitude to international affairs; exponent of *Weltpolitik*, 1894 watches development of the Dreyfus Affair but without official involvement; 1908 the *Daily Telegraph* Affair; 1914 pledges support to Austro-Hungarian Empire in the international crisis leading to World War I; 1918 exiled to the Netherlands and abdicates the same year; admired by Hitler for his antisemitism and militarism; buried with full military honours during the Third Reich.

ZOLA, Emile (1840–1902)

Major French novelist and literary figure.

Son of Venetian father and French mother; leader of the Naturalist School; 1894 elected President of the Société des gens de lettres; 1897 espouses the Dreyfus cause, which he defends in a series of articles, pamphlets and letters to the nation; denounces antisemitism in *Le Figaro*, 1898, following the acquittal of Esterhazy, his famous 'J'Accuse' is published in *L'Aurore*, an open letter to the President of the Republic; tried for libel and condemned with the maximum sentence of 12 months in prison and a fine of 3000 francs; stripped of the Legion of Honour. His appeal against his verdict is upheld but he is again condemned and flees to England, returning to France in 1899; writes *Vérité*, closely related to the events of the Affair (published 1903); 1902 found dead by asphyxiation (later evidence suggests foul play); 1908 ashes transferred to the Pantheon; during the ceremony an attempt is made to assassinate Dreyfus.

ZURLINDEN, Emile (1837–1929)

Army officer. General at the time of the Affair.

1898 Minister of War for short period; appointed Military Governor of Paris; orders prosecution of Picquart; continues to believe in the guilt of Dreyfus after the discovery of the *faux Henry*; opposes the revision; resigns 1898.

LIST OF GOVERNMENTS DURING THE DREYFUS AFFAIR

Presidency of Casimir-Périer
(27 June 1894 - 17 January 1895)
Cabinet of Charles Dupuy
(30 May 1894 - 26 January 1895)

Charles Dupuy	Prime Minister & Minister of Interior
Eugène Guérin	Minister of Justice
Gabriel Hanotaux	Foreign Secretary
General Mercier	Minister of War
Théophile Delcassé	Colonial Secretary

Presidency of Félix Faure
(17 January 1895 - 16 February 1899
Cabinet of Alexandre Ribot
(26 January - 1 November 1895)

Alexandre Ribot	Prime Minister
Ludovic Trarieux	Minister of Justice
Gabriel Hanotaux	Foreign Secretary
General Zurlinden	Minister of War
Georges Leygues	Minister of Interior
Emile Chautemps	Colonial Secretary

Cabinet of Léon Bourgeois
(1 November 1895 - 29 April 1896)

Léon Bourgeois	Prime Minister & Minister of Interior
Jean Sarrien (from 28 March 1896)	Minister of Interior
Louis Ricard	Minister of Justice
Marcelin Berthelot (1st Nov l895-28 March 1896)	Foreign Secretary
Léon Bourgeois (from 28 March 1896)	Foreign Secretary
Godfroy Cavaignac	Minister of War
Paul Guieysse	Colonial Secretary

Cabinet of Jules Méline
(29 April 1896 - 28 June 1898)

Jules Méline	Prime Minister
Darlan (29 April 1896-2 Dec 1897)	Minister of Justice
Milliard (from 2 Dec 1897)	Minister of Justice
Gabriel Hanotaux	Foreign Secretary
Louis Barthou	Minister of Interior
General Billot	Minister of War
André Lebon	Colonial Secretary

Cabinet of Brisson
(28 June - 1 November 1898)

Henri Brisson	Prime Minister & Minister of Interior
Jean Sarrien	Minister of Justice
Théophile Delcassé	Foreign Secretary
Godfroy Cavaignac (28 June-5 Sept 1898)	Minister of War
General Zurlinden (5 Sept- 17 Sept 1898)	Minister of War
General Chanoine (from 17 Sept 1898)	Minister of War
Georges Trouillot	Colonial Secretary

Cabinet of Charles Dupuy
(1 November 1898 - 22 June 1899)

Charles Dupuy	Prime Minister & Minister of Interior
Georges Lebret	Minister of Justice
Théophile Delcassé	Foreign Secretary
Charles de Freycinet (1 Nov 1898- 6 May 1899)	Minister of War
Camille Krantz (from 6 May 1899)	Minister of War
Guillain	Colonial Secretary

Presidency of Emile Loubet
(18 February 1899 - 18 February 1906)
Cabinet of Pierre Waldeck-Rousseau
(22 June 1899 - 3 June 1902)

René Waldeck-Rousseau	Prime Minister & Minister of Interior
Ernest Monis	Minister of Justice
Théophile Delcassé	Foreign Secretary
General de Galliffet (22 June 1899-29 May 1900)	Minister of War
General Louis André (from 29 May 1900)	Minister of War
Albert Decrais	Colonial secretary

Cabinet of Emile Combes
(7 June 1902 - 1 Jan 1905)

Emile Combes	Prime Minister & Minister of Interior
Ernest Vallé	Minister of Justice
Théophile Delcassé	Foreign Secretary
General Louis André (7 June 1902-15 Nov 1904)	Minister of War
Maurice Berteaux (From 15 Nov 1904)	Minister of War
Albert Decrais	Colonial Secretary

Presidency of Armand Fallières
(18 February 1906 -18 February 1913)
Cabinet of Maurice Rouvier
(24 Jan 1905 - 7 March 1906)

Maurice Rouvier	Prime Minister & Minister of Interior
Jacques Chaumié	Minister of Justice
Théophile Delcassé	Foreign Secretary
Maurice Berteaux (24 Jan–15 Nov 1905)	Minister of War
Eugène Etienne (from 15 Nov 1905)	Minister of War

Cabinet of Jean-Marie Ferdinand Sarrien
(13 March 1906 - 20 October 1906)

Jean-Marie Ferdinand Sarrien	Prime Minister & Minister of Justice
Léon Bourgeois	Foreign Secretary
Georges Clemenceau	Minister of Interior
Eugène Etienne	Minister of War

Cabinet of Georges Clemenceau
(25 October 1906 - 20 July 1909)

Georges Clemenceau	Prime Minister & Minister of Interior
Jean François Edouard Guyot-Dessaigne	Minister of Justice
Stephen Pichon	Foreign Secretary
General Georges Picquart	Minister of War

GLOSSARY

Acte d'accusation	(bill of) indictment, charge
Avocat général	Counsel for the Prosecution
Bâtonnier	Chairman of the Bar
baccalauréat	final school examinations in France
bar mitzvah	Jewish coming of age ceremony
Blanche telegram	anonymous telegram signed 'Blanche' sent by Esterhazy to Picquart in Tunis on 10 November 1897, with the intention of incriminating him
bordereau	an official note or memorandum; the basis of Dreyfus' conviction
bordereau annoté	apocryphal note from the Kaiser mentioning the name of Dreyfus
bulletin de renseignements	memorandum used by the Section de Statistique when reporting to the Minister of War
cahiers de doléances	petitions of complaint issued prior to the French Revolution
Camelots du roi	right-wing support group of L'Action française created in 1908.
Ce canaille de D.	'That scoundrel D.'; the document in the Secret Dossier wherein the letter 'D' was falsely attributed to Dreyfus
Chambre des Députés	Chamber of Deputies
Chambre des mises en accusation	Court of Indictment
9ème Chambre correctionnelle du tribunal de la Seine	9th criminal division of the Tribunal of the Seine
Chef de Cabinet	Minister's Principal Private Secretary
Chef du service des renseignements	Head of the Section de Statistique
la chose jugée	*res judicata*
Commandant supérieur des îles du Salut	officer in charge of the îles du Salut
Commissaire du Gouvernement	Government Commissioner; reporting official. In military courts, known as the military prosecutor
Commission de l'armée	Army Committee
Commission rogatoire	rogatory letter; delegation of judicial powers by a judge

Commission de la révision	Revision Committee
Conseil d'enquêtes	board of military inquiry
Cour d'Assise	Court of Assizes
Cour de cassation	Supreme Court of Appeal
Chambre criminelle de la court de cassation	Criminal Chamber of the Supreme Court of Appeal
Chambre civile de la cour de cassation	Civil Chamber of the Supreme Court of Appeal
Chambre de Pétitions ou de Requêtes de la cour de cassation	Appeals division of the Supreme Court of Appeal
Chambres réunies de la cour de cassation	Combined Chambers of the Court of Appeal
Croix de feu	association of veterans with nationalist and antiparliamentary ideals, created in 1927
CSAR (Cagoule) (Comité secret d'action révolutionnaire)	Secret Committee for Revolutionary Action; ultra right-wing clandestine and paramilitary body, founded in 1935 by former Royalists
la 'dame voilée'	the 'veiled lady'; name given to a fictitious character whom Esterhazy claimed had warned of a plot against him
Deuxième Bureau	one of the four bureaux (departments) of the Ministry of War, dealing with Intelligence
Directeur de l'administration pénitentiaire	Head of Penal Administration
document libérateur	name of misleading document devised by Esterhazy
Dossier Secret	*see* Secret Dossier
Espérance letter	anonymous letter signed 'Espérance' ('hope') sent to Esterhazy by the General Staff on 18 October 1887 warning him that he will be publicly denounced
état signalétique	official report of a prisoner's conduct
faux et usage de faux	forgery and intent to defraud
faux Henry	a forgery incriminating Dreyfus fabricated by Henry on 1 November 1896
Gouverneur militaire de Paris	Military Governor of Paris
heder	Jewish primary school
Inspecteur en tournée	visiting Inspector
journal de mobilisation	regimental papers

Juge d'instruction	examining magistrate; a judge who conducts investigations
ketubbah	Jewish certificate of marriage
Knesset	Parliament of the State of Israel
Magistrat	court judge
Milice	paramilitary police created by the Vichy Government in 1943; active in enforcing anti-Jewish policies
Ministre des Colonies	Colonial Secretary
Ministre des Affaires étrangères	Foreign Secretary
Ministre de la Guerre	Minister of War
Ministre de la Justice (Garde des Sceanx)	Minister of Justice
Ministre de l'Intérieur	Minister of the Interior
Officier de police judicaire	judicial police officer with special powers
Officier d'ordonnance	aide-de-camp
Ordre des avocats	the Bar
papier pelure	India squared paper
le petit bleu	the telegram (on blue paper) from Schwartzkoppen to Esterhazy, which led Picquart to the discovery of Esterhazy's treason in March 1896
plaidoirie	counsel's plea
Préfecture de police	Prefecture of Police; police headquarters
Préfet de police	Prefect of Police
Président du conseil	Prime Minister
prisonnier d'état	prisoner of State
Procureur général près de la cour de cassation	Principal State Prosecutor attached to the Supreme Court of Appeal
Procureur de la République	Public Prosecutor attached to a lower civil court
rapporteur	reporting judge
réquisitoire	(public) prosecutor's opening address, indictment
révision	revision, a judicial review*
révisionnistes	revisionists; those in support of the revision of Dreyfus' verdict

Rorschach test	a personality test in which subjects describe their reactions to ink blots
sans renvoi	without further appeal
Secret Dossier	dossier made up of documents allegedly incriminating Dreyfus; the dossier was transmitted secretly and illegally to the judges at Dreyfus' first court martial (1894); from 1897, hundreds of documents were added to the dossier by Dèuxieme Bureau officers
Section de Statistique	secret branch of the Deuxième Bureau dedicated to espionage and counter-espionage, created after the Franco-Prussian War
Speranza letter	forgery by Henry to incriminate Picquart
Speranza telegram	anonymous telegram sent by Esterhazy to Picquart to incriminate him
stagiaire	probationary officer on the General Staff
St-Cyr	leading french military academy
Sûreté	judicial police
Le Syndicat or Syndicat juif	the Syndicate, or Jewish Syndicate; terms used by anti-dreyfusards to refer to the dreyfusards; no such organization existed.
la 'voie ordinaire'	The 'normal route'; the procedure whereby the Deuxième Bureau received documents collected by its agents from the German Embassy
troupes de couverture	covering troops
vice de forme	procedural irregularity

*The French term is '*révision*', and those in supporting it were called '*révisionnistes*'. Throughout this Chronology the word 'revision', rather than the legal term 'review', has been chosen in order to reflect contemporary usage and to avoid confusion when using related terms such as 'revisionists' and 'anti-revisionists'. A revision is therefore taken here to mean a judicial review of an original case, trial or verdict, which may lead to a retrial, a confirmation of the original verdict, an annulment or a declaration of not guilty.

Sources (legal terms): *The Council of Europe French-English Legal Dictionary* (CELD); *An English Reader's Guide to the French Legal System* (ERGFLS); *The French Judicial System* (FEU 31); The French Embassy, London.

BIBLIOGRAPHY

PRIMARY SOURCES
Archives and libraries with special collections on the Dreyfus Affair

ENGLAND   The British Library, London
                Leo Baeck Library, London
                The Jewish Chronicle Library, London
                Wiener Library Institute of Contemporary History, London

FRANCE   Archives Départementales de la Haute-Garonne, Toulouse
                Archives Départementales du Haut-Rhin, Colmar
                Archives Diplomatiques: le Ministère des Affaires étrangères, Paris
                Archives d'Outre-Mer, Aix-en-Provence
                Archives Municipales de Mulhouse
                Archives Municipales de Rixheim
                Archives Nationales, Paris
                Archives de l'Alliance Israélite Universelle, Paris
                Archives de la Préfecture de Police, Paris
                Archives du Service Historique des Armées, Vincennes
                Archives du Secrétariat d'Etat des Anciens Combattants, Fontenay-sous-Bois
                Bibliothèque de Documentation Internationale Contemporaine, Nanterre
                Bibliothèque de la Société Industrielle de Mulhouse
                Bibliothèque de l'Institut
                Bibliothèque Historique de la Ville de Paris
                Bibliothèque Méjanes, Aix-en-Provence
                Bibliothèque Nationale de France, Paris
                Bibliothèque Victor Cousin, Paris
                Centre de Documentation Juive Contemporaine, Paris
                Institut d'Histoire du Temps Présent, Paris
                Musée de Bretagne, Rennes
                Musée Clemenceau, Paris
                Musée d'art et d'histoire du Judaïsme, Paris

GERMANY   German Diplomatic Archives (ex-Wilhelmstrasse), Bonn
                German Diplomatic Archives, Koblenz
                Kunstbibliothek und Staatsbibliothek der Stiftung Preußischer Kulturbesitz, Berlin.
                Zentrum für Antisemitismusforschung, Technische Universität, Berlin

ISRAEL   The Hebrew University, Jerusalem
                The Sourasky Central Library, Wiener Library Institute of Contemporary History, Tel-Aviv
                University, Tel Aviv

ITALY   Archivio Segreto Vaticano, Rome

SWITZERLAND   Bibliothèque Cantonale et Universitaire, Lausanne
                Fondation Bellanger-Martiny
                The Whyte Archives, Crans-sur-Sierre

USA   American Jewish Archives, Cincinnati, Ohio. *Gotard Deutsch Papers*
                Archidocese of Baltimore, Baltimore, Maryland. *James Cardinal Gibbons Papers*
                Houghton Library, Harvard University, Cambridge, Massachusetts. *Lee Max Friedman
                Papers*

Jewish Museum, New York

Leo Baeck Institute, New York

Library of Congress, Washington DC. *John Hay Papers, William McKinley Papers*

Massachusetts Diocesan Library, Boston. *William Lawrence Papers*

New York Public Library, New York. *John Durand Papers. Heber Newton Papers*

Ohio Historical Society, Columbus. *Washington Gladden Papers*

State Historical Society of Wisconsin, Madison. *Henry Demarest Lloyd Papers*

Yale University Library, New Haven, Connecticut. *Chauncey M. Depew Papers*

Proceedings and Investigations

Proceedings of Dreyfus

La Révision du Procès Dreyfus à la Cour de Cassation (27-29 octobre 1898) compte rendu sténographique *in extenso* (Paris: Stock, 1898).

La Révision du Procès Dreyfus. Débats de la Cour de Cassation (Paris: Stock, 1899).

La Révision du Procès Dreyfus. Enquête de la cour de cassation (Paris: Stock, 1899), 2 vols.

Le procès Dreyfus devant le Conseil de Guerre de Rennes (7 août-9 septembre 1899) (Paris: Stock, 1900), 3 vols.

La Révision du Procès Rennes. Débats de la Cour de Cassation (3-5 mars 1904) (Paris: Ligue française pour la défense des droits de l'Homme et du citoyen, 1904).

La Révision du Procès Rennes, Enquête de la chambre criminelle (5 mars-19 novembre 1904) (Paris: Ligues des droits de l'Homme, 1908-09), 3 vols.

La Révision du procès de Rennes. Réquisitoire écrit de M. le procureur général Baudouin (de 1905) (Paris: Ligue française des droits de l'homme, 1907).

La Révision du procès de Rennes. Mémoire de Maître Henri Mornard pour M. Alfred Dreyfus (de 1905) (Paris: Ligue française des droits de l'homme, 1907).

La Révision du Procès Rennes, La révision du procès Dreyfus. Débats de la cour de cassation. Chambres réunies. (15 juin-12 juillet 1906) (Paris: Ligue des droits de l'Homme, 1906), 2 vols.

Connected proceedings and investigations

L'affaire Henry-Reinach, Revue des Grands Procès contemporains, (juin-octobre 1902 & novembre 1903-février 1904).

L'affaire Picquart devant le Cour de Cassation (8 décembre 1898, 2 et 3 mars 1899) (Paris: Stock, 1899).

Charles Maurras et Maurice Pujo devant la Cour de justice du Rhône: les 24, 25, 26 et 27 janvier 1945 (Lyon: Vérités françaises, 1945) reprint, ed Paris: Ed. du Trident, 1994).

L'instruction Fabre et les décisions judiciairies ultérieures. [Le procès du colonel Picquart et de Me Leblois] (Paris: Siècle, 1901).

L'instruction Fabre et les décisions judiciairies ultérieures. Supplément (Paris: Stock, 1909).

Le procès Dautriche (25 octobre-7 novembre 1904) (Paris: Société Nouvelle de Librairie et d'Edition, 1905).

Le procès du Panthéon. Grégori, Dreyfus et Zola devant le jury (4 juin-10 & 11 Septembre 1908) (Bureaux de *La Libre Parole,* 1908).

Le procès Zola devant la Cour d'Assises de la Seine et la cour de Cassation (7-23 février et 31 mars-2 avril 1898) compte rendu sténographique *in extenso* et documents annex (Paris: Stock, 1898), 2 vols.

Le procès Zola devant la Cour d'Assises de la Seine et la cour (7-23 février 1898) compte rendu sténographique *in extenso* (Paris: Stock, 1998).

Le Procès Zola (7-23 février 1898): selected extracts, chosen and annotated by Marcel Thomas (Geneva: Idegraf, 1980).

Other   *Le procès de la Patrie française* (Paris: Perin et Cie, 1899).

              Le procès de la Ligue antisémite, Revue des Grands Procès contemporains (Paris 1900).

              Le procès de la Ligue française pour la défense des Droits de l'Homme et du Citoyen. Réquisitoire de M. Boulloche (Paris: Stock, 1899).

              Le procès des Assomptionnistes (Paris: G. Bellais, 1900).

Works by Alfred, Mathieu and Pierre Dreyfus

ENGLISH   Dreyfus, A., *Dreyfus: his life and letters by Pierre Dreyfus*, trans. B. Morgan (London: Hutchinson, 1937).

              Dreyfus, A. and Dreyfus P., *The Dreyfus Case, The Man Alfred Dreyfus and his son Pierre Dreyfus,* trans. D.C. McKay (New Haven: Yale University Press, 1937).

              Dreyfus, A., *Five Years of my Life*, trans. J. Mortimer (London: George Newnes Ltd, 1901) reprinted (Freeport, NY, Books for Libraries Press, 1971).

              Dreyfus, A., *Five Years of my Life. The Diary of Captain Alfred Dreyfus,* intro. by N. Halasz (New York/London: Peebles Press, 1977).

              Dreyfus, A., *Lettres d'un innocent: the Letters of Captain Dryfus to His Wife*, trans. L.G. Moreau (New York, London: Harper & Brothers, 1899).

FRENCH   Dreyfus, A., *Carnets (1899-1907)*, *Après le procès de Rennes*, ed. P. Oriol, preface by J.D. Bredin (Paris: Calman-Lévy, 1998).

              Dreyfus, A., *Cinq années de ma vie 1894-1899* (Paris: Charpentier 1901); reprinted with preface by F. Mauriac, (Paris: Fasquelle, 1962); reprinted with preface by P. Vidal-Naquet and epilogue by J.L. Lévy (Paris: Maspero, 1982; reprinted La Découverte, 1994).

              Dreyfus, A., *Lettres d'un Innocent* (Paris: Stock, 1898).

              Dreyfus, A., Capitaine, *Souvenirs et Correspondance publiés par son fils* (Paris: Grasset, 1936).

              Dreyfus, M., *L'Affaire telle que je l'ai vécue* (Paris: Grasset, 1978).

              Dreyfus, M., *Dreyfusards! Souvenirs de Mathieu Dreyfus et autres inédits,* ed. R. Gauthier (Paris: Gallimard/Julliard, 1978).

GERMAN   Dreyfus, A., *Fünf Jahre Meines Lebens 1894-1899* (Berlin: Dr. John Edelheim, 1901; reprinted Berlin: Globus, 1930).

Works by the principal characters involved in the Dreyfus Affair

ENGLISH   Guyot, Y. *La Révision du procès Dreyfus, faits et documents juridiques* (Paris: Stock, 1898).

              Lazare, B., *Antisemitism: Its History and Causes,* trans. (London: Britons Publishing Co., 1967).

              Lazare, B., *Antisemitism: Its History and Causes,* trans. ed. R. S Wistrich,. (Lincoln: University of Nebraska Press, 1995).

              Paléologue, M., *My Secret Diary of the Dreyfus Case 1894-1899,* trans. E. Mosbacher (London: Secker & Warburg, 1957).

              Péguy, C., *Temporal and Eternal (Notre Jeunesse)*, trans. A. Dru (London: Harvill Press/ New York: Viking, 1958).

              Schwartzkoppen, M. von *The Truth About Dreyfus from the Schwartzkoppen Papers,* ed. *B.* Schwertfeger, trans. E.W. Dickes (London: Putnam, 1931).

              Zola, E., *The Dreyfus Case. Four Letters to France* (London and New York: John Lane, 1898).

              Zola, E., *The Dreyfus Affair: 'J'Accuse' and Other Writings*, ed. A. Pagès, trans. E. Levieux (New Haven and London: Yale University Press, 1994).

              Zola, E., *Truth* (Guernsey: Alan Sutton, 1994).

FRENCH   Blum, L., *Souvenirs sur l'Affaire* (Paris: Gallimard, [1935] 1981).

              Brisson, H., *Souvenirs: Affaire Dreyfus, avec documents* (Paris: Cornély, 1908).

              Clemenceau, G., *Contre la Justice* (Paris: Stock, 1900).

Clemenceau, G., *Des Juges* (Paris: P.-V. Stock, 1901).

Clemenceau, G., *Justice militaire* (Paris: Stock, 1901).

Clemenceau, G., *Injustice militaire* (Paris: Stock, 1902).

Clemenceau, G., *L'Inquité* (Paris: Stock, 1899).

Clemenceau, G., *La Honte* (Paris: Stock, 1903).

Clemenceau, G., *Vers la Réparation* (Paris: Stock, 1899).

Cuignet, L., *Souvenirs de l'Affaire Dreyfus Le dossier Trarieux-Tornielli-Reinach* (Paris: Société Anonyme d'Edition Belleville, 1911).

Esterhazy, F.W., *Les dessous de l'Affaire Dreyfus* (Paris: Fayard, 1898).

Esterhazy, F.W., *Ma déposition devant le Consul de France, à Londres* (Paris: Le Siècle, 1901; Paris: Société générale d'impression, 1908).

France, A. *Discours pronouncés aux obsèques d'Emile Zola* (Paris: Fasquelle, 1904).

Freycinet, C. de, *Souvenirs, 1878-1893* (Paris: Delagrave, 1913).

Guyot, Y., *L'Innocent et la traître* (Paris: Le Siècle and Stock 1898).

Guyot, Y., *Les Raisons de Basile: L'Affaire Dreyfus* (Paris: Stock, 1899).

Jaurès, J., *Les Preuves* (Paris: *La Petite République,* 1898).

Jaurès, J., *Le Faux impérial: discours prononcé à la Chambre des députés, séances des 6 et 7 avril 1903* (Paris: Société nouvelle de librairie et d'édition, 1903).

Journal Officiel der débats parlementaires (Chambre des députés et Sénat) 1894–1906.

Labori, M.F., *Labori. Ses notes manuscrites. Sa vie* (Paris: Victor Attinger, 1947).

Lazare, B., *L'Antisémitisme, son histoire et ses causes* (Paris: Chailley, 1894; reprinted Paris: Editions de la Différence, 1900).

Lazare, B., *Comment on condamne un innocent: l'acte d'accusation contre le Capitaine Dreyfus* (Paris: Stock, 1898).

Lazare, B., *Contre l'antisémitisme (Histoire d'une polémique)* (Paris: Stock, 1896).

Lazare, B., *Une erreur judiciaire: La vérité sur l'affaire Dreyfus* (Brussels: Imprimerie Veuve Monnom, 1896).

Lazare, B., *Une erreur judiciaire: l'Affaire Dreyfus (Deuxième mémoire avec des expetises d'écritures)* (Paris: Stock, 1897).

Lazare, B., *Une erreur judiciaire: L'Affaire Dreyfus,* ed. P. Oriol (Paris: Allia, 1993).

Leblois, L., *L'Affaire Dreyfus: L'Inigquité. La Réparation. Les principaux faits et les principaux documents* (Paris: Aristide Quillet, 1929).

Loew, L., *La loi de dessaisissement par un Dessaisi* (Paris: Editions Fischbacher, 1910).

Mirbeau, O., *L'Affaire Dreyfus,* ed. P. Michel and J.F. Nivet (Paris: Librairie Séguier, 1991).

Mirbeau, O., *Combats politiques,* ed. P. Michel and J.F. Nivet (Paris: Librairie Séguier, 1990).

Paléologue, M., *Journal de l'Affaire Dreyfus 1894-1899. L'affaire Dreyfus et le Quai d'Orsay* (Paris: Librairie Plon, 1955).

Péguy, C., *Notre jeunesse. Nouvelle Revue Française* (Paris: Gallimard, 1910).

Pressensé, F. de, *L'Affaire Dreyfus. Un Héros. Le Colonel Picquart* (Paris: Stock, 1898).

Scheurer-Kestner, A., *Mémoires d'un sénateur Dreyfusard,* ed. A. Roumieux, Intro. A. Plantey (Strasbourg: Bueb & Reumaux, 1988).

Schwartzkoppen, *Les Carnets de Schwartzkoppen (la Vérité sur Dreyfus),* ed. B. Schwertfeger, trans. A. Koyré, intro. L. Lévy-Bruhl (Paris: Rieder, 1930).

Stock, P.-V., *Mémorandum d'un éditeur: l'Affaire Dreyfus anecdotique* (Paris: Stock, [1938] 1993).

Vaughan, E., *Souvenirs sans regrets* (Paris: F. Juven, 1902).

Zola, E., *L'Affaire Dreyfus. Lettre a la jeunesse* (Paris: Fasquelle, 1897).

Zola, E., *L'Affaire Dreyfus. Lettre a la France* (Paris: Fasquelle, 1898).

Zola, E., *L'Affaire Dreyfus. Lettre a M. Félix Faure, Président de la République* (Paris: Fasquelle, 1898).

Zola, E., *L'Affaire Dreyfus: Lettres et entretiens inédits,* ed. A. Pagès, (Paris: CNRS Editions, 1994).

Zola, E., *La Vérité en marche* (Paris: Fasquelle, 1901; reprinted Paris: Garnier-Flammarion, 1969).

Zola, E., *Correspondance. Lettres à Maître Labori (1898-1902)*. Collection des Oeuvres Complètes (Paris: Françoise Bernouard, 1929).

Zola, E., *Vérité* (Paris: [Fasquelle, 1903] Claude Tchou, 1968).

GERMAN   Paléologue, M. *Tagebuch der Affäre Dreyfus,* trans. Ins Dt. H. Lindemann (Stuttgart: Dt. Verl.-Anst, 1957).

Schwartzkoppen, M. von, *Die Wahrheit über Dreyfus* (Berlin: Verlag für Kulturpolitik, 1930).

Steinthal, W., *Dreyfus* (Berlin: Osterheld & Co., 1930).

Zola, E., *An die Jugend! Offener Brief z. Prozess Dreyfus* (Berlin: H. Steinitz, 1898).

Zola, E., *Mein Kampf um Wahrheit und Recht* (Dresden: C. Reibner, 1928).

Publications by P.-V. Stock on the Dreyfus Affair

Georges Clemenceau: 1. *Contre la Justice* 2. *Des Juges!* 3. *La Honte!* 4. *L'Iniquité!* 5. *Injustice militaire!* 6. *Justice militaire!* 7. *Vers la réparation.*

Joseph Reinach: 8. *À l'Ile du Diable* (booklet) 9. *Les Blés d'hiver* 10. *Une Conscience, Le Lieutenant Colonel Picquart* 11. *Le Crépuscule des traîtres* 12. *Le Curé de Fréjus* (booklet). 13. *Les Enseignements de l'histoire* (booklet). 14. *Essais de politique et d'histoire* 15. *Les Faits nouveaux* (booklet). 16. *Les Faussaires* 17. *Tout le Crime* 18. *Vers la Justice par la Vérité* 19. *La Voix de l'Ile* (booklet).

Yves Guyot: 20. *Analyse de l'enquête* 21. *L'Innocent et le Traître, Dreyfus et Esterhazy* (booklet). 22. *Les Raisons de Basile.* 23. *La Révision du procès Dreyfus.*

Bernard Lazare: 24. *Comment on condamne un innocent* 25. *La Vérité sur l'Affaire Dreyfus* (booklet). 26. *L'Affaire Dreyfus.*

Capitaine Paul Marin: 27. *Esterhazy* 28. *Le Lieutenant Colonel Picquart* 29. *Le Capitaine Lebrun Renault* 30. *Le Lieutenant Colonel du Paty de Clam* 31. *Le Lieutenant Colonel Henry* 32. *Rochefort* 33. *Drumont* 34. *Quesnay de Beaurepaire* 35. *Félix Faure* 36. *Déroulède* 37. *Le Général de la Girennerie et Colonel Allaire* (booklet). 38. *Histoire populaire de l'Affaire Dreyfus* 39. *Menteur immonde.*

H.-G. Ibels: 40. *Allons-y.*

J. Ajalbert: 41. *Quelques Dessous du procès de Rennes.*

Paul Brulat: 42. *Violence et Raison.*

Philippe Dubois: 43. *Les Machinations contre le Colonel Picquart* (pamphlet).

René Dubreuil: 44. *L'Affaire Dreyfus devant la Cour de Cassation.*

E. Duclaux: 45. *Avant le Procès* 46. *- Propos d'un solitaire.*

F. de Pressensé: 47. *Un Héros, Le Lieutenant-Colonel Picquart.*

A. Reville: 48. *Les Etapes d'un intellectuel.*

Séverine: 49. *Vers la Lumière.*

Michel Colline (Paul Stapffer): 50. *Les Billets de la province. Un Ancien Officier d'Artillerie* (Albert Hans): 51. *Le bordereau est-il d'un artilleur ? Un Intellectuel.* 52. *Gonse Pilate et Autres Histoires.*

Partie documentaire

53. *Révision du procès Dreyfus à la Cour de Cassation.* 54. *Le Procès Zola,* 2 vols. 55. *La Plainte en escroquerie contre le Commandant Esterhazy.* 56. *Instruction Fabre, avec supplément,* 2 vols. 57. *L'Affaire Picquart devant la cour de cassation.* 58. *Enquête de la cour de cassation 1898-1899,* 2 vols. 59. *Débats de la Cour de Cassation,* mai-juin 1899. 60. *La Révision du procès de Rennes,* juin-juillet 1906, *Débats de la Cour de Cassation,* 2 vols. 61. *Conseil de guerre de Rennes,* 3 vols. 62. *Le Procès de Rennes,* index alphabétique (booklet). 63. *Esterhazy, Ma déposition devant le consul de France à Londres.* 64. *Lettres de Monsieur Scheurer-Kestner et de Maître Leblois* (booklet). 65. *Maître Leblois et les arrêtés du Conseil de l'Ordre* (booklet). 66. *Les Faits et les Preuves* (booklet).

R. Allier: 67. *Voltaire et Calas.*

Un Ancien Officier d'Artillerie (Albert Hans) : 68. *Dreyfus était-il joueur?* (booklet). 69. *Le Témoignage du Lieutenant-Colonel Jeannel* (booklet).

L'Archiviste: 70. *Drumont et Dreyfus* (booklet).

AzbeL: 71. *L'Esthétique dans l'Affaire Dreyfus et sa Philosophie* (pamphlet).

Jacques Bahar: 72. *Esterhazy contre lui-même* (booklet). 73. *Etrennes à Dreyfus* (booklet). 74. *Le Traître* (booklet).

Bergougnan: 75. *L'Affaire Fabus et l'Affaire El-Chourfi* (booklet).

Saint-Georges de Bouhelier: 76. *La Révolution en marche* (booklet).

Un Catholique (Quincampoix): 77. *Les Victimes d'une iniquité* (booklet).

Julien Cordier: 78. *Une Bataille pour une idée.* 79. *Pour la Paix, par la Vérité, par la Justice* (booklet).

Dagan: 80. *Enquête sur l'antisémitisme* (pamphlet).

Demnise: 81. *Dreyfus, l'officier traître* (booklet).

P. Desachy: 82. *Bibliographie de l'Affaire Dreyfus* (booklet).

Dulucq: 83. *Le Procès Zola-Dreyfus-Esterhazy et l'Etat-Major* (booklet).

A. Dreyfus: 84. *Lettres d'un innocent.*

L. Franck: 85. *Le bordereau est d'Esterhazy* (pamphlet).

Paschal Grousset: 86. *Le Mot de l'énigme* (pamphlet).

Léon Guérin: 87. *Les Anti-Dreyfusards sur la sellette* (booklet). 88. *Gare la famine* (booklet).

Louis Guétant: 89. *Dites-nous vos raisons* (booklet).

E. de Haime (E. de Morsier): 90. *Les Faits acquis à l'histoire.*

Louis Havet: 91. *L'Amnistie* (booklet). 92. *Le Devoir du citoyen français* (booklet). 93. *Dépositions de Monsieur Cavaignac et du Général Roget.*

Dr Herzl et Max Nordau: 94. *Discours prononcés au Deuxième Congrès sioniste de Baie* (booklet).

Lieutenant-Colonel Humbert: 95. *Lettre Ou Commandant Marchand* (booklet).

Boudin: 96. *Lettre ouverte aux RR. PP. Jésuites* (booklet).

Juin: 97. *Le Triomphe de la Vérité* (booklet).

Karl: 98. *Karl et Quesnay de Beaurepaire* (booklet).

Leblois: 99. *Discours prononcés à l'inauguration du monument de Scheurer-Kestner* (booklet).

Pierre Ledroit: 100. *À la France* (pamphlet).

Lemazurier: 101. *Catéchisme dreyfusard* (booklet)

H. Leyret: 102. *Lettres d'un coupable*

L. F.: 103. *Les Défenseurs de la Justice, album panorama.*

Pierre Marie: 104. *Le Général Roget et Dreyfus.* 105. *Le Petit Bleu.*

P. Mole: 106. *Exposé impartial de l'Affaire Dreyfus* (pamphlet).

Palle de la Barrière: 107. *Coup d'œil sur l'histoire de l'Affaire Dreyfus* (booklet).

H. Rialèse: 108. *Vingt-Quatre heures à Rennes* (booklet).

H. de Saint-Andiol: 109. *Résumé historique de l'Affaire Dreyfus* (booklet).

Scheurer-Kestner: 110. *Biographie et discours prononcés à l'inauguration du monument (pamphlet).* 111. *Le Sifflet, pamphlet in-4. illustré.*

Testis: 112. *Esterhazy et Schwartzkoppen* (booklet).

L. Trarieux: 113. *Lettre à Godefroy Cavaignac* (pamphlet).

Unus: 114. *Le Syndicat de trahison* (pamphlet).

Justin Vanex: 115. *Coupable ou Non* (pamphlet).

Varennes et May: 116. *Les Etapes de la Vérité* (booklet)

Maurice Vauthier: 117. *La France et l'Affaire Dreyfus* (pamphlet).

Verax (Dr Oyon): 118. *La Conscience militaire et l'Affaire Dreyfus* (booklet). 119. *Essai sur la mentalité militaire à propos de l'Affaire Dreyfus* (pamphlet).

E. Villane: 120. *L'Opinion publique et l'Affaire Dreyfus* (booklet)

Villemar: 121. *Dreyfus intime.* 122. *Essai sur le Colonel Picquart.* 123. *La Clé de l'Affaire Dreyfus,* poster. 124. *Histoire d'un innocent, image d'Epinal.* 125. *Affaire Esterhazy, placard reproduisant le bordereau.* 126. *Fac-Similé du diagramme de Monsieur*

Bertillon'. 127. *Album comparatif des écritures d'Esterhazy.* 128. *Album comparatif des écritures d'Esterhazy.* 129. *Affiches et Placards divers, photographies et brochures sur l'Affaire Dreyfus.*

Source: P.-V. Stock, *L'Affaire Dreyfus, Mémorandum d'un éditeur* (Paris: Stock, [1938] 1994), pp. 15-20.

Press

FRENCH		
L'Action française	*Le Gaulois*	*Le Petit journal*
L'Antijuif	*La Gazette de France*	*La Petite République*
L'Antijuif d'Alger	*Gil Blas*	*Psst!*
L'Aurore	*L'Illustration*	*Le Radical*
L'Autorité	*L'Intransigeant*	*Le Rappel*
La Croix,	*Le Jour*	*La République française*
Les Droits de l'homme	*Le Journal*	*Le Siècle*
L'Echo de Paris	*La Lanterne*	*Le Soir*
L'Eclair	*La Libre Parole*	*Le Temps*
Le Figaro	*Le Matin*	*La Vérité*
La Fronde	*La Patrie*	*Le Voltaire*

AMERICAN		
New York Evening Journal	*New York Herald*	*New York Times*
New York Evening Telegram	*New York Sun*	*New York Tribune*

ENGLISH		
Daily Chronicle	*Jewish Chronicle*	*The Times*
Observer	*Standard*	

GERMAN		
Berline Neueste Nachrichten	*National Zeitung*	*North-German Gazette*
Berliner Tageblatt	*Neue Freie Presse*	*Voissiche Zeitung*
	Neues Wiener Tagblatt	

Bibliographical works

L'affaire Dreyfus: ouvrages, sources et documents des bibliothèques rennaises (recensement bibliographique F. Vallet (Rennes: Musée de Bretagne, 1995).

Autour de l'affaire Dreyfus: une bibliographie commentée, catalogue de l'exposition de la bibliothèque municipale de Mulhouse (1981).

Blum, A. and Dreyfus, C., 'Bibliographie du centenaire de "J'accuse!" II. Presse étrangère (ordre chronologique)', *Bulletin de la Société Internationale d'histoire de l'affaire Dreyfus*, 5 (été 1998).

Busi, F., 'Bibliographical overview of the Dreyfus affair', *Jewish Social Studies,* 40, 1 (1978).

Desachy, P., *Bibliographie de l'Affaire Dreyfus* (Paris: Cornély, 1905).

Drouin, M., Cahm, E. and Blum, A., 'Bibliographie', *Bulletin de la Société internationale d'histoire de l'affaire Dreyfus,* 3 (automne 1997).

Drouin, M., 'Bibliographie générale', in M. Drouin, *L'Affaire Dreyfus de A à Z* (Paris: Flammarion, 1994), 627-285.

Duclert, V., 'Bibliographie internationale du centenaire de l'affaire Dreyfus en 1993-1995', *Jean Jaurès, Cahiers trimestriels,* 138 (septembre-dècembre 1995), 130-81.

Guieu, J.M., *The Dreyfus Affair: Its Time and Legacy. A Comprehensive Digital Bibliography of the Dreyfus Affair* (San Diego, Calif.: Société littéraire des amis d'Emile Zola/Centre d'études sur Zola et le Naturalisme/Georgetown University, 2000), CD-ROM.

Lispschutz, L., *Une Bibliothèque Dreyfusienne Essai de bibliographie thématique et analytique de l'Affaire Dreyfus* (Paris: Editions Fasquelle, 1970).

Oriol, P., and Pagès, A., 'Bibliographie du centenaire', *Les Cahiers Naturalistes,* 72 (1998), 435-42.

Oriol, P., 'Contribution à une bibliographie de l'affaire Dreyfus. Recension des éphémères', *Bulletin de la Société internationale d'histoire de l'affaire Dreyfus*, 2 (automne 1996).

Oriol, P., 'Inventaire des sources de l'affaire Dreyfus. I. le Fond Dreyfus du Musée d'Art et d'Histoire du Judaïsme', *Bulletin de la Société internationale d'histoire de l'affaire Dreyfus*, 4 (hiver 1997-98), 28-32.

SECONDARY SOURCES

Dates are those of editions used and not necessarily of first editions

ENGLISH   *Anti-Semitism and Human Rights*. Proceedings of a Seminar in Melbourne Australia (Melbourne: Australian Institute of Jewish Affairs, 1985).

Arendt, H., *The Origins of Totalitarianism* (New York: Schocken Books, 2004).

Barlow, G., *A History of the Dreyfus Case. From the Arrest of Captain Dreyfus in October 1894 up to the Flight of Esterhazy in September 1898* (London: Simpkin, Marshall, Hamilton Kent & Co. Ltd, 1899).

Barnes, J., *The Beginning of the Cinema in England 1894-1901*, vol. 4, *1899* (Exeter: University of Exeter Press, 1996).

Benda, J., *The Treason of the Intellectuals (La rahison des clercs)*, trans. R. Aldington (New York: Norton, 1969).

Berkovitz, J.R., *The Shaping of Jewish Identity in Nineteenth-Century France* (Detroit: Wayne State University Press, 1989).

Bottomore, S., 'Dreyfus and documentary', *Sight and Sound*, 53, 4 (1984), 290-3.

Brée, G., 'Proust et l'affaire Dreyfus à la lumière de *Jean Santeuil'*, in P. Larkin (ed.),*Marcel Proust: A Critical Panorama* (Urbana: University of Illinois Press, 1993).

Bredin, J.-D., *The Affair. The Case of Alfred Dreyfus*, trans. J. Mehlman (New York: George Braziller, 1986).

Brennan, J., *The Reflection of the Dreyfus Affair in the European Press, 1897-1899* (New York: Peter Lang Publishing, 1998).

Burns, M., *Dreyfus, A Family Affair 1789-1945* (New York: HarperCollins, 1991).

Burns, M., *France and the Dreyfus Affair. A Documentary History* (Boston/New York: Bedford/ St. Martin's, 1999).

Burns, M., *Rural Society and French Politics: Boulangism and the Dreyfus Affair, 1886-1900* (Princeton: Princeton University Press, 1984).

Busi, F., *The Pope of Antisemitism. The Career and Legacy of Edouard-Adolphe Drumont* (Lanham/New York/London: University Press of America, 1986).

Byrnes, R.F., *Antisemitism in Modern France. vol. 1, The Prologue to the Dreyfus Affair* (New Brunswick, NJ: Rutgers University Press, 1950).

Cahm, E., *The Dreyfus Affair in French Society and Politics* (revised edition of the French, 1994) (London/New York: Longman, 1996).

Caron, V., *Between France and Germany: The Jews of Alsace-Lorraine 1871-1918* (Stanford: Stanford University Press, 1988).

Chapman, G., *The Dreyfus Case* (London: Rupert Hart and Davies, 1955) reprinted as *The Dreyfus Trials* (London: B.T. Batsford Ltd, 1972).

Chapman, G., *The Dreyfus Case: A Reassessment* (Westport, CT: Greenwood Press, 1979).

Charpentier, A., *The Dreyfus Case*, trans. J. Lewis May (London: Geoffrey Bles., 1935).

Clary, N.J., 'French Antisemitism During the Years of Drumont and Dreyfus, 1886-1906'. PhD dissertation, Ohio State University, 1970.

Cohn, N., *Warrant for Genocide: The Myth of the Jewish World-Conspiracy and the Protocols of the Elders of Zion* (London: Eyre & Spottiswoode, 1967).

Conybeare, F.-C., *The Dreyfus Case* (London: George Allen, 1898).

Coulon, E. De J., *Realistic Descriptions of American Life and Institutions: Prophetic Letters on the Dreyfus Affair* (New York: D.V. Wiem, 1905).

Coward, D., *The Dreyfus Affair* (Leeds University Press, 1983).

Curtis, M., *Three against the Third Republic: Sorel, Barrès and Maurras* (Princeton: Princeton University Press, 1959).

Curtis, M. *Verdict on Vichy, Power and Prejudice in the Vichy France Regime* (London: Weidenfeld & Nicolson, 2002).

Datta, V., *'La Revue blanche' (1889-1903), Intellectuals and Politics in Fin-de-Siècle France* (New York: université de New York, 1989).

Dejohn, W.A., *The Dreyfus Affair and the Chamber of Deputies 1897 to 1899: An Analytical and Interpretive Study* (Wisconsin: University of Wisconsin Press, 1975).

Derfler, L. (ed.) *The Dreyfus Affair, Tragedy of Errors? Problems in European Civilization* (Boston: D.C. Heath & Co., 1963).

Derfler, L., *The Dreyfus Affair* (Westport, CT: Greenwood Press, 2002).

Dudley, E.S., *Military Law and the Procedure of Courts-Martial* (New York: John Wiley & Sons, 1907).

The Dreyfus Centenary Bulletin (London, 1994).

The Dreyfus Affair. Voices of Honor, ed. L. Beitler Catalog of the Exhibition, 17 September–30 October, (United States Military Academy, West Point, 1999).

Ellmann, R., *Oscar Wilde* (London: Hamish Hamilton, 1987).

Elon, A., *Herzl* (New York: Schocken Books, 1986).

Erens, P., *The Jew in American Cinema* (Indiana: Indiana University Press, 1984).

Ezra, E., *Georges Méliès. The Birth of the Author* (Manchester: Manchester University Press, 2000).

Feldman, E., *The Dreyfus Affair and the American Conscience 1895-1906* (Detroit: Wayne State University Press, 1981).

Finkelstein, N., *Captain of Innocence: France and the Dreyfus Affair* (New York: Putnam, 1991).

Forth, C.E., *The Dreyfus Affair and the Crisis of French Manhood* (Baltimore/London: Johns Hopkins University Press, 2004).

France, A., *Penguin Island*, trans. A.W. Evans (New York: G. Wells, 1924).

Frank, H. and Pankiw, M., *The Dreyfus Affair: The Clique of Saint-Dominique Street* (Sherbrook, Canada: Naaman, 1986).

Friedman, L.E., *Zola and the Dreyfus Case: His Defense of Liberty and its Enduring Significance* (Boston: Beacon Press, 1937).

Fulcher, J.F., *French Cultural Politics & Music: From the Dreyfus Affair to the First World War* (New York: Oxford University Press, 1999).

Gagnon, P.A., *France Since 1789* (New York and London: Harper-Row, Pubs, 1964).

Goldberg, H., *The Life of Jean Jaurès* (Madison Milwaukee, and London: University of Wisconsin Press, 1962).

Greenhalgh, D., *'The Times' and the Dreyfus Case: Reportorial, Editorial and Popular Opinion, 1898-1899* (Providence, Rhode Island, 1978).

Griffiths, R., *The Use of Abuse. The Polemics of the Dreyfus Affair and its Aftermath* (New York/Oxford: Berg, 1991).

Grosser, P.E. and Malperin, E.G., *Anti-Semitism: Causes and Effects* (New York: Philosophical Library, 1983).

Guieu J.-M. and Sarde M. (eds.), *Memories for the 21st Century. Cultural Experiments in 20th Century France* (Washington DC: Georgetown University Faculty of Languages & Linguistics Publications, 2002).

Haas, J. de, *Theodore Herzl: A Biographical Study* (New York: The Leonard Co., 1927).

Halasz, N., *Captain Dreyfus. History of a Mass Hysteria* (New York: Simon and Schuster, 1955).

Hale, R.W., *The Dreyfus Story* (Boston: Small and Maynard & Co., 1899).

Halpern, R.A., 'The American Reaction to the Dreyfus Case'. Unpublished MA. thesis, Columbia University, 1941.

Harding, W., *Dreyfus: The Prisoner of Devil's Island*. (New York: Associated Publishing Company, 1899).

Harwick, M., *Prisoner of the Devil: The Dreyfus Affair* (London/New York: Proteus, 1980).

Healy, C., *Confessions of a Journalist* (London: Chatto & Windus, 1904).

Hertzberg, A., *The French Enlightenment and the Jews* (New York: 1968).

Herzl, T., *The Complete Diaries of Theodor Herzl*, ed. R. Patai, trans. H. Zohn (New York:

Herzl Press & Thomas Toseloff, 1960). 5 vols.

Herzog, W., *From Dreyfus to Pétain: 'The Struggle of a Republic'*, trans. from German by W. Sorell (New York: Creative Age Press, 1947).

Hoffman, R.L., *More Than a Trial. The Struggle over Captain Dreyfus* (London: Collier Macmillan Publishers, 1980).

Horne, A., *The French Army and Politics, 1870-1970* (London: Macmillan, 1984).

Howard, M., *The Franco-Prussian War: The German Invasion of France, 1870-1871* (London: R. Hart-Davis, 1961).

Hubert, R.R., *The Dreyfus Affair and the French Novel* (Boston: Eagle Enterprises, 1951).

Hyde, H.M., *Oscar Wilde: A Biography* (London: Eyre Methuen, 1976).

Hyman, P., *From Dreyfus to Vichy. The Remaking of French Jewry, 1906-1939* (New York: Columbia University Press, 1979).

Iiams, T., *Dreyfus, Diplomatists and the Dual Alliance, Gabriel Hanotaux at the Quai d'Orsay* (Genève: Droz, Minard, 1962).

Irvine, W.D., *The Boulanger Affair Reconsidered. Royalism, Boulangism and the Origins of the Radical Right in France* (New York: Oxford University Press, 1989).

Jankowski, P. F., *Stavisky: A Confidence Man in the Republic of Virtue* (Ithica: Cornell University Press, 2002).

The Jesuits and the French Army: The Dreyfus Business Examined (Melbourne: *c.* 1894–1900, 'Victorian Standard' Print).

Johnson, D., *France and the Dreyfus Affair* (London: Blandford Press, 1966).

Johnson, H.H., *The Moral of the Dreyfus Case* (Birmingham: Imprimerie Charles J. Buller & Co., 1899).

Johnson, M. P., *The Dreyfus Affair: Honour and Politics in the Belle Epoque* (New York: St. Martin's Press, 1999).

Joly, B., 'The Jeunesse antisémite et nationaliste 1899–1904', in R. Tomas (ed.) *Nationhood and Nationalism in France from Boulangism to the Great War 1899–1918* (London: HarperCollins, 1991).

Jussem-Wilson, N., *Charles Péguy* (New York: Hillary House, 1965).

Kafka, F., *The Trial*. Epilogue by Max Brod, Introduction by George Steiner, trans by Willa and E. Muir (London: Minerva, 1992).

Kalman, J. A., *'Evolutions in Hatred: Anti-Jewish Sentiment in Restoration and July Monarchy France'*. Ph.D Thesis, University of Melbourne, Department of History, 2004.

Kayser, J., *The Dreyfus Affair*, trans. from French by N. Bickley (London: William Heinemann Ltd, 1931).

Kedward, R.H., *The Dreyfus Affair. Catalyst for Tensions in French Society* (London: Longman, Green & Co. Ltd, 1965).

Kleeblatt, N.L. (ed.), *The Dreyfus Affair. Art, Truth and Justice* (Los Angeles/London: University of California Press, 1987).

Kohler, M.J., *Some New Light on the Dreyfus Case* (Vienna: reprinted from the Freidus Memorial Volume, [1929], 1937).

Laqueur, W., *A History of Zionism* (New York: Holt, 1972).

Larkin, M., *Church and State after the Dreyfus Affair: The Separation Issue in France* (London: Macmillan, 1974).

Latour, A., *The Jewish Resistance in France, 1940-1944*, trans. I.R. Ilton (New York: Holocaust Library; Distributed by Schocken Books, 1981).

Lerner, L.S., *The Dreyfus Affair in the Making of Modern France* (Woodbridge, CT: Research Publications, 1996).

Lewis, D.L., *Prisoners of Honor: the Dreyfus Affair* (New York: Morrow, 1973).

Lewisohn, L. (ed.), *Theodor Herzl, a Portrait for this Age* (Cleveland: World, 1955).

Lindemann, A.S., *The Jew Accused. Three Anti-Semitic Affairs (Dreyfus, Beilis, Frank) 1894-1915* (New York: Cambridge University Press, 1991).

Malino, F. and Wasserstein, B. (eds.), *The Jews in Modern France* (Hanover: University Press of New England, 1985).

Mandelle, R., 'The Affair and the Fair: Some Observations on the Closing Stages of the

Dreyfus Case', *Journal of Modern History*, 37 (1967), 253–65.

Marrus, M.R., *The Politics of Assimilation*. (Oxford: Clarendon Press, 1971).

Marrus, M.R. and Paxton, R.O., *Vichy France and the Jews* (New York: Basic books, 1981).

Martin, B., 'The Dreyfus Affair and the Corruption of the French Legal System', in N.L. Kleeblatt (ed.) *The Dreyfus Affair: Art, Truth and Justice* (Berkeley and Los Angeles: University of California Press, 1987).

Martin du Gard, R., *Jean Barois,* trans. S. Gilbert (New York: Viking, 1949).

Mitchell A., 'The Xenophobic Style: French Counter-Espionage and the Emergence of the Dreyfus Affair', *Journal of Modern History* (September 1980), 414-25.

Mitchell, A., *Victors and Vanquished: The German Influence on Army and Church in France after 1870* (Chapel Hill: University of North Carolina Press, 1984).

Nilus, S., *The Protocols of the Elders of Zion* (1902).

Nolte, E., *Three Faces of Fascism. Action Francaise. Italian Fascism. National Socialism,* trans. L. Vennewitz (London: Weidenfeld and Nicolson, 1965).

Nordau, M., *Max Nordau to His People: A Collection of Addresses to Zionist Congresses together with a Tribute to Theodor Herzl* (New York: Scopus, 1941).

Partin, M.O., *Waldeck-Rousseau, Combes and the Church, 1899-1905* (Durham, NC: Duke University Press, 1969).

Pawel, E., *The Labyrinth of Exile. A Life of Theodor Herzl* (New York: Farrar, Straus & Giroux, 1989).

Paxton, R.O., *Vichy France: Old Guard and New Order, 1940-1944* (New York [1972]: Columbia University Press, 2001).

Proust, M., *Jean Santeuil,* trans by G. Hopkins (New York: Simon & Schuster, 1955).

Proust, M., *The Past Recaptured*, trans. F.A. Blossom (New York: Random House, 1959).

Ralston, D.B., *The Army of the Republic – The Place of the Military in the Political Evolution of France, 1871-1914* (Cambridge: Cambridge University Press, 1967).

Rudorff, R., *The Belle Epoque: Paris in the Nineties* (New York: Saturday Review Press, 1973).

Rutkoff, P.M., 'The Ligue des patriotes': The nature of the radical right and the Dreyfus affair', *French History Studies*, 8, 4 (Autumn 1974), 584-603.

Sand, S., 'Dreyfus in Hollywood', in *L'Histoire* 173. *L'Affaire Dreyfus, vérités et mensonges* (January 1994), 120-3.

Sanderson, E., *Historic Parallels and L'Affaire Dreyfus* (London: Hutchinson & Co., 1900).

Sartre, J.-P., *Anti-Semite and Jew*, trans. G.J. Becker (New York: Schocken Books, 1976).

Shahn, B., *The Dreyfus Affair: The Ben Shahn Prints*. (Cincinnati: Crossroads Books, 1984).

Shane, A.L., *The Dreyfus Affair and the Literature: An Exhibition* (London: JHSE, 1988).

Schechter, B., *The Dreyfus Case: A National Scandal* (Boston: Houghton Mifflin, 1965).

Schwarzfuchs, S., *Napoleon, the Jews and the Sanhedrin* (London/Boston/Henley: Routledge and Kagan Paul, 1979)

Schwarzschild, S.S., 'The Marquis de Morès, the story of a failure', *Jewish Social Studies,* 22, 1 (January 1960), 3-26.

Sherrod, R.L., *Images and Reflections: The Response of the British Press to the Dreyfus Affair* ((Michigan: Michigan State University, Department of History, 1980).

Silvera, A., *Daniel Halévy and His Times: A Gentleman-Commoner in the Third Republic* (Ithaca, NY: Cornell University Press, 1966).

Silverman, D.P., *Reluctant Union: Alsace-Lorraine and Imperial Germany, 1871-1918* (University Park, Pennsylvania State University Press, 1972).

Simon, M.J. *The Panama Affair* (New York: Charles Scribner's Sons, 1971).

Snyder, L.L., *The Dreyfus Case. A Documentary History* (New Jersey: Rutgers University Press, 1973).

Soucy, R., *French Fascism: The Case of Maurice Barrès* (Berkeley, Los Angeles, London: University of California Press, 1972).

Steed, H.W., *Through Thirty Years 1892-1922. A Personal Narrative* (London: Heinemann Ltd, 1924).

Steed, H.W., *The Press* (London, Penguin Books Ltd, 1938).

Steevens, G.W., *The Tragedy of Dreyfus* (London and New York: Harper and Brothers, 1899).

Steinthal, W., *Dreyfus,* trans from German by Captain R. Johnes (London: George Allen & Unwin Ltd., 1930).

Sternhell Z., 'Paul Déroulède and the origins of modern French nationalism', *Journal of Contemporary History*, 6, 4 (October 1971), 46-70.

Sternhell, Z., *Neither Right nor Left. Fascist Ideology in France*, trans. (Princeton: Princeton University Press, 1996).

Swart, K.W., *The Sense of Decadence in Nineteenth Century France* (The Hague: Martinus Nijhoff, 1964).

Thomson, D., *Democracy in France since 1870* (London/Oxford: Oxford University Press, 1969).

Urquhart, R., 'The American Reaction to the Dreyfus Affair: A Study of Anti-Semitism in the 1890s'. PhD dissertation, Columbia University, 1972.

Vatican Council II, Constitutions, Decrees, Declarations. The basic sixteen documents. A Completely Revised Translation in Inclusive Language, ed. A. Fannery, (New York: Costello Publishing Company/Dublin: Dominican Publications, 1996).

Verneuil, L. *The Fabulous Life of Sarah Bernhardt* (New York: Harper & Bross, 1942).

Vidal-Naquet, P., *The Jew. History, Memory and the Present* (New York: Columbia University Press, 1996).

Vizetelly, E.A., *With Zola in England. A Story of Exile* (London: Chatto & Windus, 1899).

Watson, D.R., *Georges Clemenceau: A Political Biography* (London: E. Methuen, 1974).

Weber, E., *Action Française: Royalism and Reaction in Twentieth-Century France* (Stanford: Stanford University Press, 1962).

Webster, P., *Pétain's Crime. The full story of French collaboration in the Holocaust* (London: Macmillan, 1990).

Werstein, I., *J'accuse: The Story of the Dreyfus Case* (New York: Messner, 1967).

Whyte, G.R., *The Accused: The Dreyfus Trilogy* (Bonn: Inter Nationes, 1996).

Wilson, N., *Bernard-Lazare: Antisemitism and the Problem of Jewish Identity in Late 19th Century France* (Cambridge: Cambridge University Press, 1978).

Wilson, S., *Ideology and Experience: Antisemitism in France at the time of the Dreyfus Affair* (London/Toronto: Association University Press, The Littman Library of Jewish Civilization, 1982).

Wilson, S., 'The Ligue Antisémitique Française', *Wiener Library Bulletin* 25 (London, 1972), 33-9.

Wilson, S., 'The Anti-Semitic Riots of 1898 in France', *Historical Journal*, 16, 4 (1973), 789–806.

Wistrich, R., 'French Socialism and the Dreyfus affair', in R. Wistrich, *Between Redemption and Perdition: Modern Antisemitism and Jewish Identity* (London and New York: Routledge, 1990), 133–49.

Wistrich, R., *Anti-Semitism: The Longest Hatred* (London: Thames Methuen, 1991).

Wright, G., *France in Modern Times: 1760 to the Present* (Chicago: Rand McNally & Co., 1968).

Zeldin, T., *France 1848-1945. Intellect & Pride* (Oxford University Press, 1979).

Zweig, S., *The World of Yesterday* (London: Cassell, 1943)

FRENCH *Affaire Dreyfus* grav. et portraits (Bruxelles: Alliance typographique, 1897).

L'Affaire Dreyfus et le tournant du siècle (1894-1910). Catalogue d'exposition, ed. L. Gervereau and C. Prochasson, (Nanterre: BDIC, 1994).

L'Affaire Dreyfus. Juifs en France. Actes du 6ème Symposium Humaniste Internationale de Mulhouse, 28-30 janvier 1994 (Mulhouse: Cêtre, 1994).

L'affaire Dreyfus: les voix de l'honneur: exposition des oeuvres et des documents de la Fondation Beitler. Catalogue d'exposition, 11 février-11 mars 2000, ed. L. Beitler (Bruxelles: Bibliothèque royale de Belgique; Edgewater, NJ: The Beitler Family Foundation, 2000).

L'Affaire Dreyfus. Cinq semaines à Rennes, 200 photographies de Gerschel. Texte Louis Pagès (Paris: E. Juven, n.d. [1899]).

Une Affaire toujours actuelle. Catalogue, Musée de Bretagne (Rennes: Musée de Rennes, 1973).

Afoumado, D., *La Propagande Antisémite en France sous l'Occupation par l'Affiche et l'Exposition, (Septembre-Octobre)* (Nanterre: Universite Paris X, 1990).

Ajalbert, J., *Quelques dessous du procès de Rennes* (Paris: Stock, 1901).

Allier, R., *Le Bordereau Annoté : Etude de critique historique* (Paris: Société Nouvelle de Librairie et d'Edition, 1903).

Almanach des Patriotes et du Drapeau (Paris: Bureaux du Journal *Le Drapeau*, 1899).

Arnoulin, S., *M. Edouard Drumont et les Jésuites* (Paris: Librairie des Deux-Mondes, 1902).

Anspach, L., *Le péril clérical et l'affaire Dreyfus* (Bruxelles: P. Weissenbruch, 1899).

Badinter R., *'Libres et égaux …': L'émancipation des juifs sous la Révolution française 1789-1791* (Paris: Fayard, 1989).

Bancquart, M.-C., *Les Ecrivains et l'histoire d'après Maurice Barrès, Léon Bloy, Anatole France, Charles Péguy* (Paris: A.G. Nizet, 1966).

Barrès, M., *Scènes et Doctrines du nationalisme* (Paris: [Félix Guven, 1902] Editions du Trident, 1987).

Barrès, M., *Les Déracinés* (Paris: Fasquelles, 1897).

Basch, F., *Victor Basch ou la passion de la justice: de l'Affaire Dreyfus au crime de la milice* (Paris: Plon, 1994).

Basch, F. and Hélard, A. (eds), *Le deuxième procès Dreyfus, Rennes dans la tourmente - Correspondances de Victor Basch* (Paris: Berg International, 2003).

Basch, F., Crips, L. and Gruson, P. (eds), *Victor Basch 1863-1944: un intellectuel cosmopolite* (Paris: Berg International, 2000)

Basch, V., *A Jean Jaurès* (Paris: Librairie de l'Humanité, 1916).

Basch, V., *Le Fascisme ne passera pas* (Paris: Ligue des Droits de l'Homme, 6 février, 1935).

Baubérot, J., *Histoire de la laïcité française* (Paris: PUF 'Que sais-je', 2000).

Baubérot, J., *Vers un nouveau pacte laïque* (Paris: Seuil, 1990).

Baumont, M., *Aux sources de l'affaire. L'Affaire Dreyfus d'après les Archives Diplomatiques* (Paris: Les Productions de Paris, 1959).

Bedel, J., *Zola assassiné*, Intro. H. Mitterand (Paris: Flammarion, 2002).

Benda, J., *La Jeunesse d'un clerk* (Paris: Gallimard, 1936).

Bensimon, D., *Les Grandes Rafles: Juifs en France, 1940-1944* (Toulouse: Privat 1987).

Bernard, M., *Le Bordereau. Explication et réfutation du système de M.A. Bertillon et de ses commentateurs* (Paris: Le Siècle, 1904).

Bernier, G., *La Revue Blanche ses amis, ses artistes* (Paris: Hazan, 1991).

Birnbaum, P., *Un mythe politique: La 'République juive' de Léon Blum à Pierre Mendès France* (Paris: Fayard, 1988).

Birnbaum, P., *L'Affaire Dreyfus – La République en péril* (Paris: Découvertes Gallimard, 1994).

Birnbaum, P., *Le moment antisémite: un tour de la France en 1898* (Paris: Fayard, 1998).

Blum, A., 'Romain Rolland, *Les Loups* et l'Affaire Dreyfus', PhD dissertation, Yale University, 1977.

Blumenkranz, B. (ed.), *Juifs en France au XVIIIème siècle* (Paris: Commission française des archives juives, 1994)

Blumenkranz, B. and Soboul, A. (eds), *Les Juifs et la Révolution française* [Actes du Colloque sur les Juifs et la Révolution française, Paris, 24 novembre 1974] (Paris: les Belles lettres, 1989).

Boisandré A. de, *Petit catéchisme antijuif* (Paris: Librairie Antisémite 1899).

Boll, G., and Ingold, D., 'Les ancêtres du capitaine Alfred Dreyfus', *Bulletin de la Société d'histoire de Rixheim*, No. 16 (2000), 15-20.

Bonnamour, G., *Le Procès Zola. Impressions d'Audience* (Paris: A. Pierret, 1898).

Bonnamour, G., *La déposition Bertillon devant la Cour de cassation* (Paris: Lepue, 1899).

Bourgin, H., *De Jaurès à Léon Blum. L'Ecole normale et la politique* (Paris: Fayard, 1970).

Boussel, P., *L'Affaire Dreyfus et la Presse* (Paris: Armand Colin, 1960).

Bouvier J., *Les deux scandales de Panama* (Paris: Julliard, 1964).

Bouvier J., *Le Krach de l'Union Générale* (Paris: PUF, 1960).

Bredin, J.-D., *L'Affaire* (Paris: Julliard, 1983).

Bredin, J.-D., *Bernard Lazare: de l'anarchiste au prophète* (Paris: Ed. de Fallois, 1992).

Bülow, B. von, *Mémoires du chancelier prince de Bülow*, trans. H. Bloch and P. Roques (Paris: Plon, 1930-31) vol. 1, *Le Secrétariat d'Etat des Affaires étrangères et les premières années de chancellerie, 1897-1902*).

Cahm, E., *L'Affaire Dreyfus, histoire, politique et société* (Paris: LGF, 1994).

Cahm, E., and Citte, P. (ed.), *Les représentations de l'affaire Dreyfus dans la presse en France et à l'étranger* (Tours: Université de Tours, François-Rabelais, 1997).

Calef, N. (Nissim), *Drancy 1941. Camp de représailles. Drancy la Faim* (Paris: FFDJF, 1991).

Calvaire d'un Innocent, 912 chapters, Livraison 647 x Fascicules.

Caperan, L., *L'Anticléricalisme et l'Affaire Dreyfus 1897-1899* (Toulouse: Imprimerie régionale, 1948).

Capitan-Peter, C., *Charles Maurras et l'idéologie d'Action française* (Paris: Seuil, 1972).

Charensol, G., *L'Affaire Dreyfus et la Troisième République* (Paris: Editions Kra, 1930).

Charle, C., 'Champ littéraire et champ du pouvoir ; les écrivains et l'Affaire Dreyfus', *Annales ESC,* 2, March-April, 1977.

Charle, C. *Naissance des 'intellectuels' (1890-1900)* (Paris: Ed. de Minuit, 1992).

Charles Maurras et Maurice Pujo devant la Cour de justice du Rhône: les 24, 25, 26 et 27 janvier 1945 (Lyon: Vérités françaises, 1945; reprinted Paris: Trident, 1994).

Charlot, J. and Charlot, M., 'Un rassemblement d'intellectuels: la ligue des droits de l'homme', *Revue Française de science politique*, 9, 3, (septembre 1959), 995-1028.

Charpentier, A., *Historique de l'Affaire Dreyfus* (Paris: Rieder, 1930).

Charpentier, A., *Le Côtés mystérieux de l'Affaire Dreyfus.* (Paris: Les Editions Rieder, 1937).

Chêne, J. and Aberdam D. (ed.), *Comment devient-on Dreyfusard?* Actes du Colloque de l'Université de Grenoble II- Pierre Mendès-France, décembre 1994 (Paris: L'Harmattan, 1997).

Chéradame, A., *L'affaire Dreyfus à l'étranger* (Paris: Imp. F. Levé, 1899).

Chérasse, J.-A. and Boussel, P., *Dreyfus ou l'Intolérable vérité (déclarations et documents recueillis et présentés)* (Paris: Pygmalion, 1975).

Christen, F., *L'Affaire Dreyfus et la presse d'opinion Genevoise. Le Journal de Genève et le Courrier de Genève face à une Affaire qui divisa la France* (Genève: Histoire Nationale et Régionale, 1988).

Clébert, J.-P., *Fort Chabrol 1899. Roman vrai* (Paris: Denoël, 1981).

Cointet-Labrousse, M., *Vichy et le fascisme* (Paris: Complexe, 1987).

Cornély, J., *Notes sur l'Affaire Dreyfus* (Paris: H. May, 1899).

Cosnier, C., *Rennes pendant le procès Dreyfus* (Rennes: Ouest France, 1984).

Courian, R., *Les pots-aux-roses dans l'histoire de l'Europe: essai* (Genève: Hofcour, 1995).

Crémieu-Foa, E., *La Campagne antisémitique. Les duels. Les responsables* (Paris: Alcan-Lévy, 1892).

Dansette, A., *Le Boulangisme 1886-1890* (Paris: Perrin, 1946).

Dardenne-Cavaignac, H., *Lumières sur l'Affaire Dreyfus* (Paris: Nouvelles Editions latines, 1964).

Daudet, L., *Au Temps de Judas: Souvenirs des milieux politiques, littéraires, artistiques et médicaux* (Paris: Nouvelle Librairie Nationale, 1920).

Dayen D. 'Un prêtre creusois dreyfusard: l'abbé Pichot' in M. Cassan, J. Boutier, N. Lemaître (eds) *Croyances, pouvoirs et société. Des Limousins aux Français* (Treignac: Ed. les Monédières, 1988).

Delhorbe, C., *L'Affaire Dreyfus et les écrivains français* (Paris: Attinger, 1933).

Delmaire, D., *Antisemitisme et Catholiques: Dans le Nord pendant l'Affaire Dreyfuss* (Lille: Presses Universitaires de Lille, 1991).

Delporte C., 'La guerre des caricatures', *Histoire* 173, *L'Affaire Dreyfus, vérités et mensonges* (janvier 1994), 86-9.

Deniau, J.F., *Le bureau des secrets perdus* (Paris: Odile Jacob, 1998).

Denis, M., Laurée, M. and Veillard, J.-Y. (eds), *L'Affaire Dreyfus et l'opinion publique en France et à l'etranger* (Rennes: Presses Universitaires de Rennes, 1995).

Desachy, P., *Louis Leblois. Une Grande figure de l'Affaire Dreyfus* (Paris: Rieder, 1934).

Desachy, P., *Répertoire de l'Affaire Dreyfus 1894-1899* (s.l.n.d. [1905]).

Dieckhoff, A., 'Le jour où Théodor Herzl devint sioniste,' *Histoire* 173, numéro spéciale, 'L'Affaire Dreyfus: vérités ou mensonges' (janvier 1994), 106-11.

Doise, J., *Un secret bien gardé. L'histoire militaire de l'affaire Dreyfus* (Paris: Seuil, 1994).

Dreyfus avant Dreyfus. Une Famille juive de Mulhouse. Catalogue de l'exposition tenue du 1er au 23 Octobre 1994 à la Filature, 20 allée Nothan Katz, Moulouse, ed. O. Jurbert, and M.-C. Waill, (Mulhouse. 1994).

Dreyfus, G., and Mars, H.C., 'La Famille du capitaine Dreyfus', *Revue du Cercle de Généalogie Juive,* 36 (Paris, winter 1993), 18-24.

Drouin, M., *L'Affaire Dreyfus de A à Z* (Paris: Flammarion, 1994).

Drumont, E., *La France juive.* essai d'histoire contemporaine. (Paris: Flammarion, 1886).

Drumont, E., *La Fin d'un monde. Etude psychologique et sociale* (Paris: Albert Savine, 1889).

Drumont, E., *Le Testament d'un antisémite* (Paris: E. Dentu, 1891).

Drumont, E., *Les Juifs contre la France. Une nouvelle Pologne* (Paris: Librairie antisémite, 1899).

Dubois, P.H., *L'Affaire Dreyfus. Les machinations contre le Colonel Picquart* (Paris: Stock, 1898).

Dubreuil, R., *L'Affaire Dreyfus. Devant la Cour de cassation* (Paris: Stock, 1899).

Duclert, V., *L'Affaire Dreyfus* (Paris: La Découverte, 1994).

Dumont, H., *William Dieterle. Antifascismo y compromise romantico* (Filmoteca Espanola, 1994),

Durin, J., *Drancy 1941-1944* (Le Bourget: GM Impremerie, 1988).

Durin, J, *Emile Zola et la question juive 1890-1902* (Bourget: GM, 1989).

Duroselle, J.-B., *Clemenceau* (Paris: Fayard, 1988).

Durury, G., *Pour la justice et pour l'armée* (Paris: P. Ollendorff, 1901).

Dutrait-Crozon, H., *Précis de l'Affaire Dreyfus avec un répertoire analytique* (Paris: Nouvelle Librairie Nationale, 1924).

Ehrhardt, A., *A Travers l'Affaire Dreyfus. I. Henry et Valcarlos* (Paris: Klincksieck, 1977); *II. Le silence de Val'Carlos* (Strasbourg: Librarie Becker, 1979).

Elbaz, A.E., 'Edmond Fleg et l'Affaire Dreyfus', *Revue de l'Université d'Ottawa* (septembre 1974), 384-9.

Elbaz, A.E., *Correspondance d'Edmond Fleg pendant l'Affaire Dreyfus* (Paris: Librairie A.-G. Nizet, 1976).

Epstein, S., *L'Antisémitisme francais aujourd'hui et demain* (Paris: Belfond, 1984).

Epstein, S., *Les dreyfusards sous l'Occupation* (Paris: Albin Michel, 2001).

Eydoux, E., *Capitaine Alfred Dreyfus. Théâtre* (Basel: Jüdische Rundschau Maccabi, 1967).

La France et la question juive 1940-1944. Actes du Colloque du Centre de Doccumentation Juive (Paris: Sylvie Messinger, 1979).

Faure, S., *Les Anarchistes et l'Affaire Dreyfus* (Paris: Le Libertaire, 1898).

Finkielkraut, A., *L'Avenir d'une négation* (Paris: Seuil, 1982).

Figueras, A., *Ce Canaille de Dreyfus* (Paris: Publications André Figueras, 1982).

Fleg, E., *Anthologie juive* (Paris: Flammarion, 1956).

Fleg, E., *Ecoute Israël* (Paris: Flammarion, 1954).

Fleg, E., *L'Enfant prophète* (Paris: Gallimard, 1926).

Fleg, E., *Pourquoi je suis juif* (Paris: Les Belles Lettres, 1995).

Foucault, A., *Un Nouvel aspect de l'Affaire Dreyfus* (Paris: Les Œuvres Libres, 1938).

France, A., *L'île des Pingouins* (Paris: Calmann-Lévy, 1903).

France, J., *Autour de l'Affaire Dreyfus. Souvenirs de la Sûreté Générale* (Paris: Rieder, 1936).

Frank, L., *Le bordereau est d'Esterhazy* (Bruxelles: H. Lamertin, 1898).

Frédéric, R., *Zola en chansons, en poésies et en musique* (Sprimont: Mardaga, 2001).

Garrigues, J., 'Mourir pour Dreyfus', *Histoire* 173, Numéro spéciale *L'Affaire Dreyfus, vérités et mensonges* (janvier 1994), 52-3.

Garros, L., *Alfred Dreyfus 'L'Affaire'. Les Dossies Ressuscités* (Paris: Mame, 1970).

Gaulle, C. de, *La France et son armée* (Paris: Plon, 1971).

Georges, R., *L'affaire Dreyfus* (Paris: Librairie Perrin, 1970).

Giolitto, P., *Histoire de la milice* (Paris: Perrin, 1997).

Girard, P., *La Révolution française et les Juifs* (Paris: R. Laffont, 1989)

Girardet, R., *Le Nationalisme français* (Paris: A. Colin, 1966).

Giscard d'Estaing, H., *D'Esterhazy à Dreyfus* (Paris: Plon, 1960).

Gohier, U., *L'Armée contre la Nation* (Paris: Revue blanche, 1898).

Grand-Carteret, J., *L'Affaire Dreyfus et l'image 266 caricatures françaises et étrangères* (Paris: Flammarion, 1898).

Granoux, X. and Fontane, C., *L'Histoire par la cartophilie, 'L'Affaire Dreyfus'* (Paris: Daragon, 1903).

Grousset, P., *L'Affaire Dreyfus et ses ressorts secrets* (Paris: Société d'éditions illustrées, 1898; A. Godet, 1899).

Grumberg, J.C., *Dreyfus.* (Paris: Stock, 1974).

Guérin, J., *Les Trafiquants de l'antisémitisme: La maison Drumont et Cie* (Paris, F. Juven, 1905).

Guieu, J.-M. (ed.), *Intolérance et indignation: L'affaire Dreyfus* (Paris: Editions Fischbacher, 2000).

Guieu, J.-M., 'L'Iconothèque électronique à l'Université de Georgetown,' *Cahiers de l'Affaire Dreyfus*, No. 1 (Société Internationale de l'Affaire Dreyfus, 2004).

Guillemin, H., *L'Enigme Esterhazy* (Paris: Gallimard, 1962).

Guiral, P., *Clemenceau en son temps* (Paris: Grasset, 1994).

Halévy, D., *Apologie pour notre passé* (Paris: Cahiers de la Quinzaine, 1910).

Halévy, D., *Regards sur l'affaire Dreyfus.*, ed. J.-P. Halévy (Paris: Ed. de Fallois, 1994).

Hebey, P., *Alger 1898, La grande vague antijuive* (Paris: Nil, 1996).

Hélard, A., *L'Honneur d'une ville, la naissance de la section rennaise de la Ligue des droits de l'homme* (Paris: Apogée, 2001).

Hermann-Paul, *Deux cents dessins (1897-1899)* (Paris: Revue blanche, 1900).

Herzl, T., *L'Affaire Dreyfus. Reportages et réflexions, traduits par Léon Vogel* (Paris: Fédération sioniste de France, 1958).

Herzl, T., *L'Etat de juifs (suivi de) Essai sur le sionisme: de 'l'Etat des Juifs' a l'Etat d'Israël,* Commenté et traduit Claude Klein (Paris: La Découverte, 1990).

Herzl, T., *Journal, 1895-1904: le fondateur du sionisme,* morceaux choisis et présentés par Paul Kessler, pref. Cathérine Nicault (Paris: Calmann-Lévy, 1990).

Hess, J., *A l'Ile du Diable: Enquête d'un Reporter aux Iles du Salut et à Cayenne.* Orné de nombreuses illustrations d'après les photographies de l'auteur (Paris: Librairie Nilson, n.d. [1898]).

Hirt F., *Du délit d'espionnage: étude de droit français et de législation comparée,* (Paris: Librairie du Recueil Sirey, 1937).

Hommage des artistes à Picquart. Album de 12 lithographies. Préf: O. Mirbeau (Paris: Société libre d'édition des gens de lettres, 1899).

Hyman, P., *De Dreyfus à Vichy. L'évolution de la communauté juive en France 1906-1939* (Paris: Fayard, 1985).

Ibels, H.G., *Allons-y ! Histoire contemporaine racontée et dessinée par H.G. Ibels* (Paris: Stock, 1898).

Isaac, J., *Expériences de ma vie. Péguy* (Paris: Calmann-Levy, 1959).

Isaac, J., *Genèse de l'Antisémitisme: essai historique* (Paris: Calmann-Levy, 1985).

Israël, A., *Les vérités cachées de l'Affaire Dreyfus* (Paris: Albin. Michel, 1999).

Ivan-Villard, S., *L'affaire Dreyfus.* trans. Georges Hubeau & Carlo Remy (Bruxelles: Walter Beckers, 1970).

Jackson, A.B., *La Revue Blanche, 1899-1903* (Paris: Minard, 1960).

Jean-Bernard (Passerieu, J.-B.), *Le procès de Rennes 1899. Impressions d'un spectateur* (Paris: Lemerre, 1900).

Jean Jaurès. Cahiers trimestriels, 136, *Le centenaire de l'affaire* (Paris: Société d'études jaurésiennes, 1994-1995).

Joly, B., *Déroulède, l'inventeur du nationalisme français* (Paris: Perrin, 1998).

Joly, B., *Dictionnaire biographique et géographique du nationalisme français (1880-1900). Boulangisme, ligue des patriotes, mouvement antidreyfusards, comités antisémites* (Paris: Champion, 1998).

Joly, L., *Xavier Vallat. Du nationalisme chrétien à l'antisémitisme d'Etat (1891-1972)* (Paris: Grasset, 2001).

Joly, L., *Darquier de Pellepoix et l'antisémitisme français* (Paris: Berg International, 2002).

Jurt, J., 'L'Affaire Dreyfus: le rôle de l'opinion', *Bulletin de l'Amitié judéo-chrétienne,* 4 (1981).

Katz, P., 'La recherche généologique juive en Alsace', *Revue du Cercle de Généalogic Juive,* 36 (Paris, hiver 1998), 8–12.

Klarsfeld, S., *La Shoah en France* (Paris: Fayard, 2001), 4 vols. 1. *Vichy-Auschwitz: la solution finale de la question juive en France*; 2. *Le calendrier de la persécution des juifs de France, 1940-1944: 1er juillet 1940-31 août 1942*; 3. *Le calendrier de la persécution des juifs de France, 1940-1944: 1er septembre 1942-31 août 1944*; 4. *Le mémorial des enfants juifs déportés de France.*

Knobel, M. 'Des incidents au théâtre de l'Ambigu', *Revue d'Histoire du théâtre* (1989), 264-70.

Knobel, M., 'Chronique dreyfusienne: En cette année 1994 … L'Affaire Dreyfus', *Cahiers naturalistes* 69 (1995), 302-10.

Koren R., and Michman D. (eds), *Les intellectuels face à l'Affaire Dreyfus alors et aujourd'hui: perception et impact de l'Affaire en France et à l'étrange.* Actes du colloque de l'Université Bar-Ilan, Israël, 13-15 décembre 1994 (Paris/Montréal: L'Harmattan, 1998).

Lacouture, J., *Léon Blum* (Paris: Seuil, 1977).

Landau, P.E., *L'opinion juive et l'Affaire Dreyfus* (Paris: Albin Michel, 1995).

Le Blond-Zola, D., *Emile Zola. Raconté par sa fille* (Paris: Grasset, [1931] 1986).

Le Blond-Zola, M., 'L'Exposition '1898, l'année de *J'accuse ...!*' du Musée de Médan (4 octobre 1998-30 septembre 1999),' *Les Cahiers Naturalistes,* 73, 1999, 416-19.

Lecanuet, R.P., *L'Eglise de France sous la Troisième République* (Paris: Alcan, 1930).

Legrand-Girarde, F., *Au Service de la France* (Paris: Presses Littéraires de France, 1954).

Lenepveu, V., *Le Musée des horeurs,* cinquante et une planches lithographiques en couleurs (Paris: Imprimerie Lenepveu, 1899-1901).

Leroy, G., *les Ecrivains et l'Affaire Dreyfus.* Actes du colloque organisé par le Centre Charles Péguy et l'université d'Orléans, octobre. 1981 (Paris: PUF, 1983).

Lethève, J., *La Caricature et la presse sous la IIIe République* (Paris, 1961).

Leuilliot, P., *L'Alsace au début du XIXème siècle* (Paris: S.E.V.P.E.N., 1959), 3 vols.

Levaillant, I., 'La genèse de l'antisémitisme sous la Troisième République', *Revue des Etudes Juives,* 53 (1907), lxxvi–c.

Lévy, L., *Jaurès: Anthologie,* preface by M. Rebérioux (Paris: Calmann-Lévy, 1982).

Leymarie, M. (ed.), *La postérité de l'affaire Dreyfus: dix études* (Villeneuve d'Ascq: Presses Universitaires du Septentrion, 1998).

Livet, G. and Oberle, R., *Histoire de Mulhouse des origins à nos jours* (Strasbourg: Editions des 'Dernières nouvelles d'Alsace', Istra: W. Fischer, 1977).

Locard, E., *L'Affaire Dreyfus et l'expertise des documents écrits* (Lyon: Desvigne, 1937).

Lombarès, M. de, *L'Affaire Dreyfus. La clef du mystère* (Paris: Robert Laffont, 1972).

Lonlay, D. de, *Francais & Allemands. Histoire anecdotique de la guerre de 1870-1871* (Paris: Garnier Frères, 1887-91), 6 vols.

Martin du Gard, R., *Jean Barois* (Paris: Gallimard, 1913).

Massis, H., *Maurras et notre temps* (Paris/Genève: La Palatine, 1951).

Maur, J., *Le juif sur l'Ile du Diable ou critique de la raison impure* (Berne: Steiger & Cie, 1898).

Maurras, C., *Au Signe de Flore: Souvenirs de vie politique, Affaire Dreyfus, la fondation de l'Action Française, 1898-1900* (Paris: Les Oeuvres Représentatives, 1931).

Mayeur, J.-M., *Les Débuts de la IIIe République, 1871-1898* (Paris: Seuil, 1973).

Mazel, H., *Considérations psychologiques autour de l'affaire Dreyfus* (Bruxelles: P. Weissenbruch, 1898).

Mazel, H., *Histoire et psychologie de l'Affaire Dreyfus* (Paris: Boivin & Cie, 1934).

Mazel, H., *La Psychologie du kaiser* (Paris: La Renaissance du livre, 1919).

Menier, M.-A., 'La Détention du Capitaine Dreyfus à l'Ile du Diable, d'après les archives de l'administration péniteniaire', *Revue française d'histoire d'Outre-Mer* 44 (1977), 456-75.

Merle G., *Emile Combes* (Paris: Fayard, 1995).

Miquel, P., *L'Affaire Dreyfus* (Paris: PUF, [1959] 2003).

Miquel, P., *Albert de Monaco, Prince des mers* (Paris: Glénat, 1995).

Miquel, P., *Une énigme? L'Affaire Dreyfus* (Paris: PUF, 1972).

Mitterand, H., *Zola journaliste. De l'Affaire Manet à l'Affaire Dreyfus* (Paris: A. Colin, 1962).

Mollier, J.-Y., 'Chronique Dreyfusienne, L'Affaire Dreyfus un siècle après', *Cahiers naturalistes* 69 (1995), 280-91.

Mollier, J.-Y., *Le Scandale de Panama* (Paris: Fayard, 1991).

Oriol, P. (ed), *Bernard Lazare, anarchiste et nationaliste juif* (Paris: Campion, 1999)

Oriol, P., *Bernard Lazare* (Paris: Stock, 2003).

Ory, P. and Sirinelli, J.-F., *Les Intellectuels en France, de l'Affaire Dreyfus à nos jours* (Paris: Armand Colin Editeur, 1986).

Oyon, Docteur, *Précis de l'Affaire Dreyfus* (Paris: 'Pages Libres', 1903).

Pagès, A., *Emile Zola. Un Intellectuel dans l'Affaire Dreyfus Histoire de J'Accuse* (Paris: Librairie Seguier, 1991).

Palmade, G., *Le Capitalisme français au XIXème siècle* (Paris: A. Colin, 1961).

Paraf, P., *La France de l'Affaire Dreyfus* (Paris: Editions Droit et Liberté, 1978).

Le Parlement et l'Affaire Dreyfus (1894-1906), douze années pour la vérité (Paris: Assemblée nationale, 1998).

Pflimlin, P., *L'Alsace. Destin et Volonté* (Paris: Calmann-Levy, 1963).

Pichot, A.L., *La conscience chrétienne et la question juive* (Paris: Société d'éditions littéraires, 1899).

Pierrard, P., *Juifs et Catholique français (1886-1945)* (Paris: Fayard, 1970).

Pierrard, P., *Les chrétiens et l'affaire Dreyfus* (Paris: Ed. de L'Atelier, 1998).

Pisani-Ferry, F., *Le Général Boulanger* (Paris: Flammarion, 1969).

Poliakov, L., *Histoire de l'antisémitisme* (Paris: Calmann-Lévy, 1973).

Prajs, L., *Péguy et les juifs* (Paris: Nizet, 1967).

Proust, M., *Jean Santeuil* (Paris: Gallimard, 1952).

Quesemand, A. and Berman, L., *Le Tournage ensorcelé* (Paris: Théâtre à Bretelles, 1995).

Quillard, P., *Le Monument Henry : Listes des souscripteurs classés méthodiquement et selon l'ordre alphabétique* (Paris: Stock, 1899).

Rabaut, J., *Jean Jaurès* (Paris: Librairie Académique Perrin, 1981).

Raphaël, F. and Weyl, R., *Les Juifs en Alsace: Culture, société, histoire* (Toulouse: Privat, 1977).

Rebérioux, M., 'Aux origines, la justice', *Jean Jaurès cahiers trimestriels*, 137, (juillet-septembre, 1995).

Rehfisch, H. and Herzog, W., *L'Affaire Dreyfus*. French version of the play by Jacques Richepin (Paris: A. Michel, 1931).

Reinach, J., *Histoire de l'Affaire Dreyfus*. (Paris: Editions de la Revue Blanche et Fasquelle, 1901-11), 7 vols.

Reinach, T., *Histoire Sommaire de l'Affaire Dreyfus* (Paris: Ligue des Droits de l'Homme, 1924).

Réville, A., *Les Etapes d'un intellectuel. À propos de l'affaire Dreyfus* (Paris: Stock, 1898).

Remond, R., 'Les catholiques choisissent leur camp' *Histoire* 173, *L'Affaire Dreyfus, vérités et mensonges* (January 1994), 70-3.

Remond, R. *Les Droites en France* (Paris: Aubier-Montaigne, 1982)

Reynaud, P., *Waldeck-Rousseau* (Paris: Grasset, 1913).

Rioux, J.-P., *Nationalisme et Conservatisme: la Ligue de la patrie française 1899-1914* (Paris: Beauchesne, 1977).

Roget, J., *L'affaire Dreyfus. Ce que tout Français doit connaître* (Paris: Librairie d'Action française, 1925).

Rolland, R., *Les Loups* (Morituri: G. Bellais, 1898).

Rolland, R., *Péguy* (Paris: A. Michel, 1944).

Roth, F., *Raymond Poincaré* (Paris: Fayard, 2000)

Roux, G., *L'Affaire Dreyfus* (Paris: Librairie Académique Perrin, 1972).

Salmon, A., *L'Affaire Dreyfus* (Paris: Emile-Paul Frères, 1934).

Sartre, J.-P., *Réflexions sur la question juive* (Paris: P. Morihien, 1946).

Sée, H., *Histoire de la Ligue des Droits de l'Homme* (Paris: Ligue des Droits de l'Homme, 1927).

Singer, C., *Vichy l'université et les juifs. Les silences et la mémoire* (Paris: Belles lettres 'Pluriel', 1992)

Solet, B., *Il était un Capitaine* (Paris: Robert Lafont, 1986).

Sorel, G., *La Révolution dreyfusienne* (Paris: M. Rivière, 1909).

Sorlin, P., *Waldeck-Rousseau* (Paris: A. Colin, 1966).

Sorlin, P., *'La Croix' et les juifs (1880-1899): Contribution à l'histoire de l'antisémitisme contemporain* (Paris: Grasset, 1967).

Spiard, C., *Les Coulisses du Fort Chabrol* (Paris: E. Spiard, 1902).

Spire, A., *Quelques juifs et demi-juifs* (Paris: Grasset, 1928).

Spire, A., *Souvenirs à bâtons rompus* (Paris: A. Michel, 1962).

Sternhell, Z., *Maurice Barrès et le Nationalisme français* (Paris: A. Colin et Fondation nationale des sciences politiques, 1972).

Sternhell Z., *La droite révolutionnaire, les origines françaises du fascisme 1885–1914* (Paris: Seuil, 1984).

Sternhell, Z., *Ni droite, ni gauche, l'idéologie fasciste en France* (Paris: Seuil, 1983).

Strauss, H., *La cage du capitaine Dreyfus* (Zurich: Caesar Schmidt, 1897).

Strauss, H., *L'Epilogue de l'Affaire du Capitaine Dreyfus. Le Faussaire Esterhazy et ses complices* (Zurich: Caesar Schmidt, 1897).

La Suisse face à l'Affaire Dreyfus: exposition du 12 mai au 10 juillet 1995, Petit Palais, Musée d'art moderne, Genève. Catalogue réalisé sous la direction de Viviane Benhamou, avec le concours d'Alain Clavien, Dominique Ferrero, George Whyte (Genève: Petit Palais, 1995).

Tavernier, D., *L'Opinion belge et l'affaire Dreyfus* (Université libre de Bruxelles, 1979-80).

Texier, R., *Le fol été du Fort Chabrol* (Paris: France-Empire, 1990).

Thomas, M., *L'Affaire sans Dreyfus* (Paris: Fayard, 1961).

Thomas, M., *Esterhazy. l'envers de l'Affaire Dreyfus* (Paris: Vernal/Lebaud, 1989).

Une tragédie de la belle époque. L'Affaire Dreyfus. Catalogue d'exposition, hôtel de ville Paris, 11ème, 15 October-30 November, ed. B. Philippe (Paris: Comité du centenaire de l'Affaire Dreyfus, 1994).

Van Itterbeek, E., *Socialisme et poésie chez Péguy: de 'Jeanne d'Arc' à l'affaire Dreyfus* (Leuven: Druk. der HH. Harten, 1966).

Viau, R., *Vingt ans d'antisémitisme 1889-1909* (Paris: Fasquelle, 1910).

Vidal-Naquet, P., *Les Juifs, la mémoire et le présent* (Paris: La Découverte, 1991).

Weil, B., *L'Affaire Dreyfus,* trans. (Paris: Gallimard, 1930).

Wellers, G., *De Drancy à Auschwitz* (Paris: Editions du Centre, 1946).

Willard, C. And Botticielli, E., *Le Parti ouvrier français, l'Affaire Dreyfus et l'entente sociale : les guesdistes* (Paris: Editions Sociales, 1981).

Wilson, S., 'Le monument Henry; la structure de l'antisémitisme en France, 1898-1899' *Annales ESC* (March-April, 1977), 265-91.

Winock, M., *Edouard Drumont et Cie. Antisémitisme et fascisme en France* (Paris: Seuil, 1982).

Winock, M., *Nationalisme, antisémitisme et frascisme en France* (Paris: Seuil, 1982).

Winock, M. (ed.), *Histoire de l'extrême droite en France* (Paris: Seuil, 1993).

Winock, M., *La France et les juifs, de 1789 à nos jours* (Paris: Seuil, 2004).

Zangwill, I., *Chad Gadya!*, trans. M. Salomon, intro. de Charles Péguy (Paris: Cahiers de la quinzaine, 1904).

Zévaès, A., *Le Cinquantenaire de 'J'Accuse'* (Paris: Fasquelles, 1948).

Zieger, K., (ed.), *Emile Zola, 'J'accuse ...!'. Réactions nationales et internationales* (Valenciennes: Presses Universitaires de Valenciennes, 1999).

GERMAN

Brand, A., *Ein fall Dreyfus in Deutschland* (Berlin: A. Brand, 1899).

Czempiel, E.-O., *Das deutsche Dreyfus-Geheimnis. Eine Studie über den Einfluss des monarchischen Regierungssystems auf die Frankreichpolitik des Wilhelminischen Reiches* (Munich-Berne-Vienne: Scherz, 1966).

Ducler, V., *Die Dreyfus-Affäre* (Berlin: Wagenbach, 1994).

Duscher, G.G., *Feinstrukturelle und neuroanatomische Untersuchung der Rezeptoren auf der Labialspitze und der Stechborsteinspitze bei Dreyfusia nordmannianae Eckstein 1890* (Wien: Univ., Dipl.-Arb, 2001).

Frank, W., *Affäre Dreyfus. Soldatentum u. Judentum im Frankreich* (Hamburg: Hanseat, 1939).

Fuchs, E. and Fuchs, G., *'J'accuse!': Zur Affäre Dreyfuss* (Mainz: Decaton-Verl, 1994).

Die Große Politik der Europäischen Kabinette 1871-1914. Sammlung der Diplomatischen Akten des Auswärtigen Amtes. Im Auftrag des Auswärtigen Amtes herausgegeben von Johannes Lepsius, Albrecht Mendelssohn Bartholdy und Friedrich Thimme, 9 & 13. Band: Der nahe und der ferne Osten, 2. Auflage (Berlin, 1924).

Hermann, F., *Die Dreyfus Affäre im Spiegel und Karikatur* (Zürich: Jedlicka, 1974).

Herzl, T., *Der Judenstaat. Versach einer modernen Lüsung der Judenfrage* (Leipzig: Verlag, 1896).

Herzog, W., *Der Kampf einer Republik. Die Affäre Dreyfus.* Dokumente und Tatsachen (Zürich/Wien/Prag: Büchergilde Gutenberg, 1933).

Hofer, J., *Auswirkungender Affäre Dreyfus auf die Beziehungen des Deutschen Kaiserreiches zu Frankreich* (Graz, Univ., Dipl.-Arb, 1994).

Hohenlohe, *Denkwürdigkeiten der Reichskanzlerzeit* (Stuttgart: Deutsche Verlagsanstalt, 1931).

Leusser, C., *Die Affäre Dreyfus* (München: Verlag Kurt Desch, 1948).

Liebknecht, W., *Nachträgliches zur 'Affair'. In der Zeitschrift ,Die Fackel',* Herausgeber: Karl Kraus. No. 18, 19 und 20. Ende September 1899, Anfang Oktober 1899, Ende Oktober 1899.

Los von Teufelsinsel!: Dreyfus-Bilderbuchs. II. Theil imit 132 Karikaturen (Berlin: Eysler & Co., 1899).

Lüdemann H.-U., Alfred Jude Dreyfus: der nicht vollendete Justizmord (Schwedt: Kiro, 1995).

Mann, H., 'Zola', in René Schickeles Zeitschrift: *Die weißen Blätter'* (Leipzig: Verlag der Weißen Bücher, 1915).

Martin du Gard, R., *Jean Barois* (Berlin: Wein-Verlag, 1930).

Matray, M., *Dreyfus. Ein Französisches Trauma* (München: Langen Müller, 1986).

Michaelis, R., *Der prozeß Dreyfus* (Hamburg: Kriminalistik Verl., 1963).

Michaelis, R., *Rechtespfelge und Politik in der Affäre Dreyfus* (Karlsruhe: C.F. Müller, 1964).

Michaud, E., *Rom und die Lüge. Die Affaire Dreyfus und der Klerikalismus* (Bern: Stämpfi & Cie, 1899).

Mittelstädt, O., *Die Affaire Dreyfus. Eine kriminalpolitische Studie* (Berlin: J.Guttentag, 1899).

Moser, B., *Zolas Kampf um Wahrheit und Gerechtigkeit in der Dreyfus-Affäre* (Salzburg: Univ., Dipl.-Arb, 1994).

Rehfisch, H. and Herzog, W., *Die Affäre Dreyfus* (München: V.K. Desch, 1929).

Reinach, J., *Geschichte der Affaire Dreyfus 'Der Prozess von 1894'* (Berlin and Leipzig: Verlag von Friedrich Luckhardt, 1901).

Schoeps, J.H., *Theodor Herzl und die Dreyfus-Affaire* (Wien: Picus-Verl, 1995).

Schoeps, J.H., *Dreyfus und die Folgen* (Berlin: Druckhaus Heinrich, 1995).

Steinthal, W., *Dreyfus*. Die erste vollständige deutsche Darstellung der klassischen Kriminal-Affäre aus hoher Politik (Berlin: Oesterheld und Co., 1930).

Stenogramm der Verhandlungen im Prozeß gegen den Kapitän Dreyfus vor dem Kriegsgericht zu Rennes. In *acht Lieferungen* (Dresden: Kaden & Comp, 1899).

Strauss, H., *Der Käfig des Kapitäns Dreyfus* (Zürich: Schmidt, 1987).

Stuhlmeier, A., *Emile Zola unf die Affäre Dreyfus* (Wien: Univ., Dipl.-Arb 1994).

Thalheimer, S., *Die Affäre Dreyfus* (München: Deutscher Taschenbuch Verlag Dokumente, 1963).

Thalheimer, S., *Macht und Gerechtigkeit. Ein Beitrag zur Geschichte des Falles Dreyfus* (München: C.H. Beck'sche 1958).

Vizetelly, E.A., *Emile Zola, sein Leben und seine Werke* (Berlin: Egon Fleischel & Co., 1905).

Weil, B., *Der Prozeß des Hauptmanns Dreyfus* (Berlin: Grunewald: Dr. W. Rothschild, 1930).

OTHER LANGUAGES

CHINESE   法国与德雷福事件 [海外中文图书]   / (美) 麦可·本恩斯 (Michael Burns) 著   郑约宜译 —台北: 麦田出版, 2003—344页: 图, 照片; 21.cm. —(纯智历史名著译丛; 11). —986-7691-62-8

十九世纪末法国的一起大冤案 [专著] : 德雷福斯案件/周剑卿编著. — 北京 : 商务印书馆, 1981. —41页 : 照片 : 19cm. — : ¥0.16—11071.508

CZECH   VACHEK Emil. Aféra. Naše vojsko Praha 1958.

SOLET Bertrand. Byl jeden kapitán. Mladá fronta Praha 1961. Překladatel Tamara Sýkorová

DREYFUS Mathieu. Dreyfusova aféra, jak jsem ji zažil. Odeon Praha 1984. Překladatel Eva Musilová

VOSS Tage. Kanóny: zrádce Dreyfus. Naše vojsko Praha 1990. Překladatel František Fröhlich

REHFISH Hans. Žluji. Dilla Praha 1965. Překladatel Jan Tomek

ZOLA Emile. Žaluji. Průlom. Praha 1931. Překladatel Věra Petříková

DANISH   *Bilag til Johannes Marers Foredrag om Dreyfusbeviserne den 5. Oktober 1898 i Industriforeningen i Kjøbenhavn.* ['Handout at Johannes Marer's Lecture on the Dreyfus evidence, held 5th October 1898 at the Industrial Club in Copenhagen'] (Kbh, 1898).

Jaurès, J., *Dreyfus – Beviserne* ['Dreyfus – The Evidence', trans. *Les Preuves* by E. Stensgaard and H. Koch'] (Kbh, 1900).

Langgaard, C., *Alfred Dreyfus. Et Blad af Frankrigs Historie* ['Alfred Dreyfus. A Page of France's History'] (Aarhus, 1906).

Munch, P., *Dreyfusaffæren og dens Følger* ['The Dreyfus Affair and its consequences'] (Kbh, Universitetsudvalget, 1908).

Rasmussen, W. F., *Ret for Dreyfus: Døm den skyldige* ['Justice for Dreyfus: Sentence the Guilty'] (Kbh, 1899).

Thorsteinsson, Th., *To franske retssager: Sagen mod Jeanne d'Arc og Dreyfus-affæren* ['Two French Court Cases: The trial of Jeanne d'Arc and the Dreyfus Affair'] (Kbh: Gyldendal, 1970).

Trier, S., *Gengældelsen. Judas. Nogle Strejflys over en berømt 'Affære'* ['The Retribution. Judas. Some Lights on a Famous 'Affair'] (Kbh, 1906).

Yaari, Uri, *Uretten er sat: Dreyfus-affæren* ['Injustice in Session: The Dreyfus affair'] (Kbh: Munksgaard, 1982).

Stender Clausen, J., *Georg Brandes og Dreyfusaffæren* ['Georg Brandes and the Dreyfus Affair'] (Kbh: C.A. Reitzel, 1994).

DUTCH

Een Meester in de rechten, *Kan eene zaak als die van Dreyfus bij onze militaire rechtspleging voorkomen?* (Haarlem, 1898).

Pinto, A.A., *Het proces Dreyfus getoetst aan wet en recht* ('s-Gravenhage: Belinfante, 1898).

Weil, B., *De zaak Dreyfus*. Geautoriseerde vert. [uit het Duits] van P. Roosenburg (Amsterdam: Maatschappij voor geode en goedkoope lectuur, 1991).

Zola, E., *De waarheid rukt op: alle teksten over de Dreyfus-affire*. Ingel., vert. [uit het Frans] en van comment voorz door Henny van Schaik ('s-Hertogenbosch: Voltaire, 2001).

HEBREW

אופיר, ע. "פרשת דרייפוס ובתי-ספר פוליטיים אחרים", **תיאוריה וביקורת** 6, 1995, 176-161.

ביין, א. "הרצל ומשפט דרייפוס", בתוך: **עם הרצל ובעקבותיו**, מאמרים ותעודות, מסדה, תל-אביב, תשי"ד 1954.

בינדר, ע. "מאה שנים לפרשת דרייפוס", **בעיות בינלאומיות: חברה ומדינה** ל"ג, 1994, 20-12.

ברדן ז.ד. **פרשת דרייפוס**, עברית: מ. שניאורסון, עם עובד, תל-אביב, תשנ"ב 1992.

גרימברג ז.ק. **דרייפוס** (מחזה), עברית: י. סובול, בית צבי, רמת-גן, תשמ"ד 1984.

דורי, נ. **פרשת דרייפוס ורישומה בספרות הלאדינו**, (M.A) אונ' בר-אילן, רמת גן, תש"ס 2000.

דורי, נ. "פרשת דרייפוס והשתקפותה בשני רומנים בלאדינו", בתוך: **לאדינאר** ג', תשס"ד 2004, 113-125.

דרייפוס, א. **אגרות האסיר מאי השדים**, תרגם א.ש. פריעדבערג, ורשה, תרנ"ט 1898.

האלאס נ. **דרייפוס**, עברית: ד. סיון, ל. רוקח, מעריב לעם, תל-אביב, 1959.

האלאס נ. **היסטריה המונית: פרשת דרייפוס**, עברית: ד. סיון ל. רוקח, קרני, ירושלים, תשט"ז 1956.

הרצל, ת. **בפני עם ועולם**, נאומים ומאמרים ציוניים, עורכים: ד"ר א. ביין, מ. שרף ו. ונקרט, הספריה הציונית, ירושלים, תשל"ו (1976) [הערך דרייפוס: ע' 403].

הרצל, ת. **מבולאנז'א עד דרייפוס**, כתבות מפריס 1895 – 1891, עברית: ש. מלצר, עורכים: א. ביין ומ. שרף, הספריה הציונית, ירושלים, תשי"ד 1954 [הערך דרייפוס: ע' 1177, 1178, 1224-1222].

ויסטוריך ר.ס. "אמת וצדק בפרשת דרייפוס: לאזאר, זולא וקלימנסו", בתוך: **משפט והסטוריה** עורך: ד. גוטוויין, מרכז זלמן שז"ר,ירושלים, תשנ"ט 1999.

ויסטוריך ר.ס. "מקס נורדאו ופרשת דרייפוס", **נתיב** 3 (50), תשנ"ו 1996, 30-24.

ויסטוריך, ר.ס. "על עלילות ומשפטי ראווה נגד יהודים", מחניים, תשכ"ז, ק"י- קי"א.

חיימוביץ מ. "הצבא הצרפתי מצדיע לדרייפוס", מעריב, 14.9.1995, 6.

טברסקי, י. **אלפרד דרייפוס**: רומן הסטורי, הקיבוץ הארצי השומה"צ, מרחביה, תש"ד 1944.

יארבלום, מ. "שני יובלות" (100 שנה להולדתו של ב. לאזאר, 60 שנה לרהביליטציה של קפיטאן דרייפוס), **הפועל הצעיר** ל"ח, 1967, 17-11.

כהן, י. "משפט דרייפוס והיהודים", בתוך: **שנאת ישראל לדורותיה**, עורך: ש. אלמוג, מרכז זלמן שז"ר, ירושלים, תש"ם 1980.

כהן, ה. "חובת הכבוד שלנו כלפי דרייפוס", **משא**, תשל"ו 1976, 171-159.

מנצ'ר, א. "פרשת דרייפוס בלבוש עברי מקורי", **כיוונים** 17, תשמ"א 1983, 139-135.

מיקאל פ. **פרשת דרייפוס**, עברית: א. אמיר, מזרחי, תל-אביב, תשכ"ה 1965.

סחיק, ש. "פרשת דרייפוס בעתונות הערבית", **מיכאל**, י"ד תשנ"ז 1997, קפ"ז-רי"ד .

פורמאנוב, י. "חליפת מכתבים בין פ. אקסלרוד וג. פלכאנוב מסביב לפרשת דרייפוס", **מאסף** ז' תשל"ה 1975, 171-159.

קאר, מ. "פרשת דרייפוס", **דבר**, י"א אלול תשכ"ו 1966.

קובובי, ש. "גריג ודרייפוס" (על סרובו של גריג להופיע בפאריס בעת פרשת דרייפוס) **הארץ**, תרבות וספרות, 12.4.2002, ה, 4 .

קוטיק מ. "אלפרד דרייפוס אנטי-גיבור", **דבר השבוע**, 2.8.1985, 12.

קוטיק מ. "דרייפוס – 100 שנה", **עת-מול** כ' 4, 1995, 6-8.

קוטיק, מ. **פרשת דרייפוס**, מלוא, תל-אביב, תשמ"ב 1982.

קופרשטיין ל. "דרייפוס, המשפט והפרשה", **דבר**, 16.4.1982.

קוץ, ג. "דרייפוס – הגילוי, המשפט, המבוכה, מה כתבה העתונות העברית בראשית הפרשה?" **קשר** 16, 1994, 4-17.

קוץ, ג. "הוא זכאי! או לא? העיתונות היהודית והעברית באירופה ובארץ-ישראל בראשית פרשת דרייפוס; מאבק בעלילה אנטישמית, או נסיון לצמצם נזקים?" **קשר** 33, 2003, 41-53.

קליבלאט, נ., עורך, **פרשת דרייפוס והשתקפותה בספרות, באמנות ובתקשורת**, עברית: נ. כרמל, משרד הבטחון, תל-אביב תשנ"ב 1992.

שורצפוקס, ל. "שיר דני על הקפטן דרייפוס", **קרית ספר** ס"ג, תש"ן – תשנ"א 1990/91, 683-685.

שטראוס, ז. "תגובות ראשונות למשפט דרייפוס בעתונות העברית", ברית עברית עולמית, כנס 11, תשנ"ד, 175-181.

שטיק, נ. "אור חדש על משפט דרייפוס", **הצופה**, 16.12.1955, 4.

שמיר, ח. "צילינדרים, מדים ועלילת בגידה", הרקע הדיפלומטי והצבאי של פרשת דרייפוס, **בעיות בינלאומיות** ל"ג, 1994, 27-39.

שפירא, ד. **דרייפוס בתודעה הקולקטיבית היהודית בצרפת בין השנים 1894-1994**, (M.A), האוניברסיטה העברית, ירושלים, 2001.

YIDDISH

ברנארד ט. **די מלחמה פון אמת מיט דעם שקר: אדער דרייפוס אויף דעם טייפעל אינזעל**, ווארשא, תרנ"ח (1898).

גרודזנסקי מ. **דיא אמת ארויס**: געניוע, ריכטיגע בערשרייבונג פון די דריי פראצעססען דרייפוס, עסטערהאזי און עמיל זאלא, ווארשא, דרוק האלטער, תרנ"ח 1898.

דרייפוס א. **פינף יאר מיינס לעבענס**, עורך ל.א. גראסבערג, בודאפעסט, [תרנ"ט?].

זקהיים, מ.צ. **קאפיטאן דרייפוס, אדער, לעבעדיג בעגראבען**, לונדון, 1898.

זיפערט, מ. **מגילת דרייפוס, אדער, דיא געשיכטע פון איין אונשולדיגען**, ניו-יורק, תרנ"ט 1898.

פריד מ. **דרייפוס' בריוו**, איבערגעזעצט דורך מ.י. פריד, ווארשא, תרנ"ט 1898.

פרלמוטר, א. **דאס משפט פון קפיטאן דרייפוס: אין פיר לידער**, ווארשא, תרנ"ח 1898.

דער פראצעס פון דעם יודישען הויפטמאן דרייפוס אין פריז, לעמבערג, 1898.

שלום עליכם, **קיינאירע ניט: דרייפוס אין קאסרילעווקא**, מאסקווע, עמעס, 1938.

LADINO

ארדיטי, א.ש. **דרייפו'ס, או איל רומנסו די און אינג'נטי**, שלוניקי, תרס"א 1901.

דרייפו'ס, א. **סינקו** אניוס די מי ב'ידה, תרגם א. גבאי, קונסטאנטינופלה, תרס"א 1901.

לורייה, ז'. **דרייפו'ס**, דראמה אין סינקו אקטוס, סופ'ייה, 1903.

פילו .ס.ס. **איל איג'ו דראייפוס**, פוליישון די לה טרומפיה, שלוניקי, 1922.

HUNGARIAN

Blum, L., *Emlékek az "Ügy"-ről* (Budapest: Európa, 1985).

Csernyak, J., *Szent Johannától Dreyfus kapitányig évszázadok politikai perei* (Budapest: Kossuth Kaidó, Uzsgorod, Kárpáti Kiadó, 1974).

Dreyfus, A., *Öt év az életemből [Cinq années de ma vie, 1894-1899]* (Budapest: Orsz. Közp. Községi, 1901).

Dreyfus Alfred kapitány tragédiája. Hiteles források alapján ismerteti egy Párisban élő hazánkfia (Vas, Márkus, 1899).

Dreyfus, A (Alfred)-pör. Az uj tárgyalás teljes története gyorsírói jegyzetek alapján (Kiad. Magyar Hirlap, 1899).

Halasz, N., *Dreyfus kapitány: Egy tömeghisztéria története* (Budapest: Gondolat, 1967).

János, Szász, *Vihar Franciaországban egy régi ügy időszerűsége* (Bukarest: Kriterion, 1996).

Labori, C., *Dreyfus kapitány, vagy Ártatlanul elítélve [Regény]* (Budapest: Székely, 1899).

Sass, I., *Dreyfus kapitány tragédiája* (Budapest: Remény, 1931).

Tolnai, A., *Dreyfus* (Bratislava: Slovenská Grafia, 1930).

ITALIAN

L'Affaire Dreyfus in Italia (Pisa: ETS, 1991).

Assante, A., *Alfredo Dreyfus: Confessioni, Lettere e documenti* (Napoli: Libr. Edit. Anacreonte Chiurazzi, 1899).

Baumont, M., *L' affaire Dreyfus et l'opinion italienne d'après les archives diplomatiques* (Roma: Istituto poligrafico dello Stato 1964).

Bizzoni, A., *Il dramma di Alfredo Dreyfus, narrato da Fortunio* (Milano: Casa editrice Sonzogno, 1899).

La Caricatura nell'Affare Dreyfus: 150 caricature tratte dai più celebri giornali umoristici, riflettenti il pensiero di tutti i popoli (Milano: Tipografia Editrice Verri, 1899).

Il caso Dreyfus; a cura di Gianni Rizzoni (Milano: A. Mondadori, 1973).

Ciccotti, E., *Il caso Dreyfus innanzi alla storia* (Torino: Germinal Edit., 1899).

Cittadini Cipri, A.M., *Proust e la Francia dell'Affaire Dreyfus* (Palermo: Palumbo, 1977).

Coen, F., *Dreyfus* (Milano: Mondadori, 1994).

Di Fant, A., *L'affaire Dreyfus nella stampa cattolica italiana* (Trieste: Edizioni Università di Trieste, 2002).

Doria, G., *Terzo uomo dell'affare Dreyfus* (Napoli: [s.n.], 1957).

Dreyfus: l'affaire e la Parigi fin de siècle nelle carte di un diplomatico italiano/a cura di Pierre Milza (Roma, 1994).

Dreyfus, il deportato innocente: La tragedia di una vittima dello spionaggio (Milano: Casa Edit. Vecchi Edit. Tip., 1932).

Dreyfus, A., *Cinque anni della mia vita; otto disegni autografi di Dreyfus; i ritratti di famiglia dell'autore e della sua famiglia* (Milano: Sonzogno, 1901).

Dreyfus, M. *Dreyfus mio fratello* (Roma: Editori Riuniti, 1980).

Dubois, C., *Dreyfus: il prigioniero dell'isola del diavolo:* narrazione storica documentata, traduzione dal francese di Ch. Dubois (Roma: Voghera 1898).

Favi, D., *Bernanos e Dreyfus* (Bologna: Storia contemporanea, 1995).

Il fondo Paulucci di Calboli sull'affaire Dreyfus; a cura di Marco Grispigni (Bologna: Patron, 1996).

Halasz, N., *Il capitano Dreyfus: una storia d'isterismo di massa* (Milano: Club degli editori, 1974).

Halasz, N., *Io accuso L'affaire Dreyfus: Romanzo* (Milano: Baldini e Castoldi, 1959).

Kleeblat, N.L., *L'Affaire Dreyfus: la storia, l'opinione, l'immagine* (Torino: Bollati-Boringhieri, 1990).

Lazare, B., *L'affaire Dreyfus: un errore giudiziario* (Faenza: Mobydick, 2001).

Locatelli, A., *L'affaire Dreyfus (la più grande infamia del secolo scorso)* (Milano: Corbaccio, 1930).

Luzzatto Voghera, G., *Antisemitismo e nazione: Italia e Francia alla vigilia dell'affare Dreyfus* (Tesi datt [S.l.: s.e]).

Michal, B., *I grandi enigmi della 'belle époque', presentati da Bernard Michal;* con la collaborazione di Edmond Bergheaud ... (Ginevra, Cremille, 1969).

Niboyet, P., *Il dramma Alfredo Dreyfus* (Milano: Società editrice Sonzogno, 1899).

Parente, L., *Zola, l'affare Dreyfus e Napoli* (Napoli: Istituto universitario orientale, 1990).

Peguy, C., *La nostra giovinezza; a cura di Giaime Rodano* (Roma: [stampa 1947] Editori Riuniti, 1993).

Peguy, C., *La nostra gioventù; Il denaro; a cura di Dona bienaime Rigo* (Torino: stampa, 1972).

Pelli, F., *Di un duplice falso nel campo dell'arte letteraria romantica, ovvero pro e Contro Zola e pro Dreyfus alla gemina Luce della verità e della carità: Conferenza tenuta la sera del Giorno 28 febbraio all'Accademia olimpica di Vicenza e alla Sala Dante in Roma il 19 Marzo 1898* (Roma: Tip. Forzani e C., 1898).

Processo Dreyfus: bollettino telegrafico straordinario (Milano: Tip. G. Rossi, 1899-No.1).

Processi razziali: Sacco e Vanzetti, Rosenberg, Alfred Dreyfus, Banca romana / [a cura di Guido Guidi e Giuseppe Rosselli] (Palermo: Edizioni ER.GA, 1984).

Processo Zola: resoconto stenografico delle 15 sedute, preceduto da un sunto del processo Dreyfus, e del processo Esterhazy, da tutte le lettere e gli articoli relativi (Milano: Fratelli Treves tip. edit., 1898).

La Puma, L., *Zola Dreyfus: la stampa italiana tra ideologia e politica* (Parigi: Istituto universitario di studi euroafricani, 1996).

Paulucci di Calboli, R., *Parigi 1898: con Zola per Dreyfus: diario di un diplomatico;* a cura di Giovanni Tassani (Bologna: CLUEB, 1998).

Revel, B., *L'affare Dreyfus, 1894-1906* (Milano: Mondadori, [1936], 1967).

Rizzoni, G., *Dreyfus: cronaca illustrata del caso che ha sconvolto la Francia,* prefazione di Indro Montanelli (Milano: Gianni Rizzoni, 1994).

Rizzoni, G., *Il Caso Dreyfus* (Milano: Mondadori, [1973], 1993).

Rocco Garibaldi, G., *Dreyfus o il romanzo d'un innocente* (Napoli: Mario Nobile, 1899).

Tassani, G., *Dreyfus cent'anni dopo: galleria dell'affaire: obiettivo sulla storia* ([S.l : s.n.], 1998).

Tutino, S., *La revoca della rivoluzione francese: Note giuridico-sociali sulla questione Dreyfus* (Roma: Tip. Partenopea Fratelli Amoroso, 1898).

Valletta, A., *Le famigerate perizie calligrafiche del processo Dreyfus* (Bologna: Grafiche Liguori, 1982).

Venturino, N., *L'affaire Dreyfus e la stampa milanese* (Milano: Università degli Studi, 1992).

Zola, E., *Io accuso; Storia del processo Dreyfus;* saggio introduttivo di Vincenzo Vitale (Acireale: Bonanno, 1988).

Zola, E., *Il caso Dreyfus/Emile Zola.* Presentazione di Giuliano Ferrara; postfazione di Tiziana Goruppi (Milano: A. Mondadori 1988).

Zola, E., *J'accuse: il caso Dreyfus e la verità in cammino (*Roma: Atlanti de stampa, 1996).

Zola, E., *Le sue lettere ed articoli e il suo processo per l'affaire Dreyfus* (Milano: f.lli Treves, 1898).

Zola, E., *Io accuso, con la storia del processo Dreyfus (J'Accuse)* (Napoli: Società Editrice Partenopea, 1898).

Zola, E., *Il caso Dreyfus,* introduzione e traduzione di Manuela Raccanello (Pasian di Prato: Campanotto, 1999).

Zuccarelli, A., *L'antropologia nell'avvenimento Dreyfus-Zola* (Roma: f.lli Capaccini, 1899).

JAPANESE   『ドレーフュス事件』ピエール・ミケル著 渡辺一民訳 白水社 1960（文庫クセジュ）

『ドレイフュス事件研究』黒田礼二著 半座書店, 1936

『ドレフェス事件』大仏次郎著 創元社 1951（創元文庫；A 第50）

『大仏次郎記念館所蔵「ドレフュス事件関連資料」目録』大仏次郎記念会編 大仏 次郎記念会 1994.10

『ドレフュス事件』大仏次郎著 朝日新聞社, 1974. --（朝日選書；19）

『われらの青春』シャルル・ペギー著 磯見辰典訳 中央出版社 1976

『ドレフュス事件とゾラ』稲葉三千男著 青木書店, 1979.2

『もう一つのドレフュス事件』シャルル・ペギー著 大野一道訳 新評論, 1981.9

『事件』マチュー・ドレーフュス著 小宮正弘訳 時事通信社, 1982.11

『ドレーフュス事件』渡辺一民著 筑摩書房, 1972

『国家主義とドレフュス事件』モーリス・バレス著 稲葉三千男訳 創風社, 1994.6

『ドレフュス革命』ジョルジュ・ソレル著 稲葉三千男訳 創風社, 1995.8

『ソレルのドレフュス事件』川上源太郎著 中央公論社, 1996.5. --（中公新書）

『ドレフュス事件とエミール・ゾラ：告発』稲葉三千男著 創風社, 1999.11

『ドレフュス事件とエミール・ゾラ：1897年』稲葉三千男著 創風社, 1996.11

『ドレフュス家の一世紀』平野新介著 朝日新聞社, 1997.8. --（朝日選書；582）

『ドレフュス事件の思い出』レオン・ブルム著 稲葉三千男訳 創風社, 1998.4

『ドレフュス事件のなかの科学』菅野賢治著 青土社, 2002.11

『ドレフュス獄中記』アルフレッド・ドレフュス著 竹村猛訳 中央大学出版部, 1979.11

NORWEGIAN   Bruland, M., *Dreyfus-saken i norsk presse: tre hovedstadsavisers omtale av Dreyfus-saken* (Oslo: M. Bruland , 2002 - 157 s.). Lang: nor Thesis: University of Oslo, Faculty of History.

Christiansen, T, *Charles Maurras, neoroyalismen og de politiske brytninger innen fransk katolisisme: fra Dreyfus-krisen (1899) til konflikten mellom Action Francaise og Vatikanet (1926-27)* (Oslo, 1952). Lang: nor Thesis: University of Oslo, Faculty of History.

Dreyfus, A., *Fem Aar af mit Liv.* Autoriseret Oversættelse for 'Verdens Gang' (Verdens Gangs Trykkeri).

Dreyfus-billedbog, Karikaturer fra alle lande om Dreyfus-Affæren 'Dreyfus' Picture Book. Cartoons from All Countries on the Dreyfus Affair' (Kristiania: Tyrihans 1899).

Hagtvet, B., *Hvor gjerne vilde jeg have vært i Deres sted-: Bjørnstjerne Bjørnson, de intellektuelle og Dreyfus-saken* (Oslo: Forum, Aschehoug, 1998).

Halasz, N., *Kaptein Dreyfus.* Oversatt av Einar Th. Schøning (Oslo: Dreyer, 1958).

Hammer, S.C., *Hjem fra Djævleøen: kort fremstilling af Dreyfus-sagen fra revisionens indledning til Dreyfus' hjemkomst* (Kristiania: Cammermeyer, 1899), 32.

Stenholt, L.A., *Fangen paa Djävleöen: Dreyfus* (Minneapolis: Waldm. Kriedt, 1900).

Wiers-Jensen, H., *Dreyfus og Djævleøen. Efter franske og tyske kilder* 'Dreyfus and Devil's Island. After French and German Sources' (Kristiania: Cammermeyer, 1898).

Zola, E., *Brev til Frankrig*; autoriseret oversættelse ved Fr. J. Holst (Kristiania: P.T. Mallings Boghandel, 1898).

PORTUGUESE   Barbosa, R., *O Processo do capitão Dreyfuss.* Apresentação Alberto Dines; escorço histórico-crítico José Alexandre Tavares Guerreiro (São Paulo: Giordano, 1994).

Bredin, J.-D., *O caso Dreyfus.* Tradução: Maria Alice Araripe de Sampaio Dória, Renata Maria Parreira Cordeiro (São Paulo: Scritta 1995).

Calheiros, P., 'L'impact de l'affaire Dreyfus au Brésil et au Portugal' in *Actes du colloque: Portugal, Brésil, France: histoire et culture*, Paris, 25-27 May 1987 (Paris: Fondation Calouste Gulbenkian, 1988), pp. 89-133.

Dreyfus, A., *Diários completos do Capitão Dreyfus.* Organização e apresentação Alberto

Chagas, João, 'Emílio Zola e a questão Dreyfus' in *Homens e factos 1902-1904* (Coimbra, F. França Amado, 1905), 29-37.

Dines; tradução: Bernardo Ajzenberg (Rio de Janeiro: Imago 1995).

Lazare, B., *Como se condemna um innocente* : questão Zola-Dreyfus (Porto: Empreza Lit. e Typ. Ed., 1899).

Medina, J., 'O Caso Dreyfus em Portugal', *Revista da Faculdade de Letras* 16/17, 5 (Lisboa, 1994), 115-231.

Reinach, J., *Na Ilha do Diabo*, (Porto, Bibliotheca da elite social, série 'questão Zola-Dreyfus', Empreza litteraria e tipographica, 1898).

Senna H., *Uma voz contra a injustiça: Rui Barbosa e o caso Dreyfus* (Rio de Janeiro: Fundação casa de Rui arbosa, 1987).

Zola, E., *Acuso ...* Trad., pref. e anot, (Jaime, Brasil, Lisboa: Guimarães, imp. 1998).

Zola, E., *Carta à mocidade*: questão Zola-Dreyfus/Emilio Zola (Porto: Empreza Lit. e Typ. Ed., 1898).

Zola, E., *Carta á França*, (Porto, Bibliotheca da elite social, série 'questão Zola-Dreyfus', Empreza litteraria e typographica, 1898).

Zola, E., *Carta á Mocidade*, (Porto, Bibliotheca da elite social, série 'questão Zola-Dreyfus', Empreza litteraria e typographica, 1898).

Zola, E., *O 5. Acto* (Porto, Bibliotheca da elite social, série 'questão Zola-Dreyfus', Empreza litteraria e typographica, 1899).

ROMANIAN   Dreyfus, A., Din Insula Dracului. Glasul unui nevinovat. Scrisori. Precedate de un autograf original al doamnei Lucie Dreyfus cărte traducotirul M. Lupesco (Bucuresci, 1898).

Dreyfus, A., Scrisorile unui inocent (Bucuresci: Editura Sălei de Depeși a ziarului 'Adevărul', 1898).

Dreyfus, A., Cinci ani din viața mea (București: Editura Tipografieie 'Universul', 1901).

Reinach, T., Afacerea Dreyfus. O expunere documentară (București: Editura Societății Anonime 'Adeverul', 1929).

Baumont, M., In miezul afacerii Dreyfus (București: Editura Politic C, 1980).

Bianu, G., Din dosarele marilor procese politice (Bucureşti: Editura Politică, 1972).

Laser, C., 'Afacerea Dreyfus' (traducere după Le Figaro) în Egalitatea 48 (9.12.1894), 380-1.

Lindemann, A.S., Evreul acuzat. Trei procese celebre. Dreyfus, Beilis, Frank (1894-1915) (Bucureşti: Editura Hasefer, 2002).

M.S. (Moses Schwatzfeld), 'Condamnarea Căpit. Dreyfus', în Egalitatea 50, 23.12.1894, 396.

'Vocea presei în cazul Dreyfus', în Egalitatea 50, 23.12.1894, 396-97.

Maidanek, J.D., Edvard Grieg şi 'Afacerea Dreyfus', în Realitatea Evreiască 138 (938) 1-16.4.2001, 13.

Schwartz, G., Procesul, O Drama Evreiasca (Timisoara: Editura Helicon, 1996).

Wigoder, G., Evrei în lume. Dicţionar biografic ('Alfred Dreyfus') (Bucureşti: Editura Hasefer, 2001), 133-35.

RUSSIAN

Еврейская энциклопедия. С.-Петербург, 1913.

Черняк Е.Б. Приговор веков. Москва, 1971.

Фиш Д. В измене обвиняется Альфред Дрейфус. Сборник "Исторические этюды". Москва, 1980.

Закревский И. По делу Дрейфуса. С.-Петербург, 1900.

В пучине измены. Новейшее и единственно достоверное описание процесса Дрейфуса. Варшава, 1898.

Процесс Золя, 15 заседаний Парижского суда. С.-Петербург.

Дрейфус А. Письма невинно осужденного. Варшава, 1898.

Дрейфус А. Пять лет моей жизни. 1894—1899гг. С.-Петербург, 1901.

Ревилль А. Как я поверил в невиновность Дрейфуса. Одесса, 1898.

Брусиловский А. Дело Дрейфуса и процесс Золя. Журнал "Советская юстиция", No. 1, 1938.

Молчанов Н. Жорес. Москва, 1969.

Витте С.Ю. Воспоминания, Москва, 1960.

Короленко В.Г. Знаменитость конца века. Москва, 1959.

Переписка Плеханова Г.В. и Аксельрода П.Б. Москва, 1925.

Прайсман Л. Дело Дрейфуса. Иерусалим, 1987.

SERBO-CROATIAN

Kocijančić J., *Kao nekada Alfred Drajfus*, Polja: list za kulturu i umetnost, Novi Sad, september, god XIII str. 12.

Nedeljković D., *Besede pod zatvorenim nebom* (Banja Luka, Beograd: Zadužbina 'Petar Kočić', Novi Sad: Skolska knjiga, 2000).

Pages, A., and Rizzoni, G., *Posljednja noc Emilea Zole.*, trans from Italien by L. Avirovic and D. Celebrini (Zagreb: Durieux, 2003).

SPANISH

Aguilar, M., *El proceso Dreyfus* (Santiago de Chile: Zig-Zag, c.1900).

Alvarez N.M., y L de Olive y Lafuente, *El ultimo recurso: comedia en dos actos y cuatro cuadros: escrita sobre el pensamiento de una obra de A. Dreyfus* y (Madrid: R. Velasco, 1907).

Coll i Amargós, J., *El catalanisme conservador davant l,affair Dreyfus (1894-1906)*, pròleg de J. Casassas (Barcelona: Curial, 1994).

Dreyfus, A., *Cinco años de mi vida: 1894-1899*, traducción del francés por Ramón Orts Ramos (Barcelona: Casa Editorial Maucci, 1901).

Eduardo P. de Bray y Sempau R., *El Capitán Dreyfus: (un proceso célebre)* (Barcelona: Casa Editorial Maucci, 1899).

Fola Igurbide J., *Emilio Zola o El poder del genio: drama en 6 actos ... inspirado en el famoso proceso del capitán Dreyfus* (Castellón: Santiago S. Soler, 1904).

Guereña, J.-L., *Aunque fuera inocente: el 'Affaire' Dreyfus y el antisemitismo en la crisis española de fin de siglo* (Tübingen: Niemeyer, 2003).

Halasz, N., *El Capitan Dreyfus, relato de una histeria colectiva*. Traduccion de Enrique Pezzoni (Buenos Aires: Editorial Sudamericana, 1957).

Inman, F.E., 'El año de 1898 y el origen de los *Intelectuales*' in *La Crisis de fin de siglo: Ideologia y Literature* (Barcelona: Ediciones Ariel), 1975, 17-24.

Jareno Lopez, J., *El Affaire Dreyfus en España: 1894-1906* (Murcie: Godoy, 1981).

Miquel, P., *El caso Dreyfus*. Traduccion. de F. Blanco Sasueta (Mexico: Fondo de Cultura Economica, 1988).

Muñoz-Alonso A., *La influencia de los intelectuales en el '98. francés: el asunto Dreyfus* (Madrid: Fundación para el Análisis y los Estudios Sociales, 1999)

Florentino J., and Perez, Javier de (ed.),*El 'Caso' Dreyfus* (Madrid: Ediciones Urbión. Buenos Aires: Hyspamérica, Biblioteca histórica: Enigmas y misterios, 1984).

Weil, B., *El proceso Dreyfus* trad. de la edición francesa y revisado sobre la alemana por Luis Villa (Madrid: Cénit [1931])

Weil, B., *El proceso Dreyfus* [braille] (Mexico: Comite Internacional Pro-Ciegos, 1968).

Weil, B., *El proceso Dreyfus,* trad. del aleman por Luis Vila (Mexico: Cia. Gral. de Eds., 1961).

Zola, E., *La verdad en marcha, Yo acuso,* trad. de José Elías (Barcelona: Tusquets, 1969).

Zola, E., *Yo acuso ...!: declaracion de Zola ante el jurado, carta a la juventud.* Discurso pronunciado en los funerales de Emilio Zola, por Anatole France (Buenos Aires, c.1900).

Zola, E., *Yo acuso o la verdad en marcha: (el caso Dreyfus)*, prólogo de Maurice Blanchot; trad. de Josep Torrell (Barcelona: El Viejo Topo, 1998).

Zola, E., *Yo acuso ... seguido de otros textos relacionados con el 'affaire' Dreyfus* (San Juan de Puerto Rico: Cultural Puertorriqueña, 1979).

Zola y Dreyfus: el poder de la palabra. Concha Sanz Miguel (Barcelona: Bellaterra, 2001).

Zola y el caso Dreyfus: cartas desde España (1898-1899). Edición de Encanación. Medina Arjona Cadiz: servico de Publicaciones, universidad de Cadiz, 1999.

SWEDISH

Brandell, S., *Striden om Dreyfus: hvad är bevisadt?: efter ,Le procès Zola comopte rendu sténographique' samt framställningar i franska pressen* (Stockholm: Gernandt, 1898).

Busse, H., *Grafologiens grunder: En kort redogörelse, med särskildt af eende på Dreyfus-Esterhazy fallet: Med 57 skriftprof* (Stockholm: Geber, 1898).

Den svenska Dreyfusprocessen: Historik och document (Stockholm: Fram, 1916-19).

Dreyfus, A., *Fem år af mitt lif (Cinq années de ma vie)* (Stockholm, 1901).

Dreyfus, A., *Fem år af mitt lif (1894-1899)* (Stockholm: Hey'l, 1901).

Dreyfus, A., *Dreyfus-affären/skildrad av Alfred, Lucie och Pierre Dreyfus; tll svenska av Hans Langlet* (Stockholm: Hokerberg, 1938).

Dreyfusaffären i bilder: med 19 potr. Och 17 illustr (Stockholm, 1899).

Dreyfusprocessen i Rennes: fullständigt stenografiskt referat (Stockholm: Ad. Bonier, 1899).

Franzén, N.-O., *Dreyfus affären* (Stockholm: Ordfront, 1983).

Laurin, C.G., *Dreyfus-affären* (Stockholm: Wahlström & Widstrand, 1899).

Zola, E., *Jag anklagar ...! oppet bref till Felix Faure, Franska republikens prsident/från Emile Zola* (Stockholm: Bonier, 1898).

TURKISH

Bayir, M., *Bir Savunma Bir Inanç Oykūsū (Emile Zola ve Dreyfus* (Ankara: Hatay Barosu Dergisi, 1990).

Dūlger, B., *Dreyfus meselesi: itham ediyorum* (Istanbul: Rek-Tur Kitap Servisi, 1966).

Gūngor, N., *Caglar Boyunca Unlū Davalar ve Savunmalardan Seçmeler: Dreyfus Davasi* (Istanbul: Yeni Dūşūn, 1987).

Dreyfus meselesi (Istanbul: Alem Matbaasi, 1315).

Kadioglu, A., *Tūrkiye'de Yaşanan Hiziplęşme ve Dreyfus Meselesi* (Istanbul: Birikim, 1994).

Reşat, A. and Hakko, I., *Dreyfus meselesi ve esbab-hafryesi* (Istanbul: Sirketi, Mūrettibiye Matbaasi, 1315).

Teber, S., *1789 Fransiz Devrimi, Re-Aksiyon' (Dreyfus Davasi) Aktion Franses* (Instanbul: Felsefe Dergisi, 1989).

Zola, E., *Gerçek yürüyor: Dreyfus olayi* (Istanbul: Yelken Matbaasi, 1976).

Zola, E., *Dreyfus olayi: Adalet için bir savaşm oyküsü* (Istanbul: Yalçm Yaymlan, 1984).

Zola, E., *Dreyfus olayi: Adalet için bir savaşm oyküsü* (Istanbul: Yalçm Yaymlan, 1986).

Zola, E., *Dreyfus olayi (Adalet için bir savaşm oyküsü)* (Istanbul: Yalçm Yaymlan, 1995).

Zola, E., *Dreyfus olayi: Adalet için bir savaşm oyküsü* (Istanbul: Yalçm, 2002).

INDEX